The Light of Days

ALSO BY JUDY BATALION

White Walls: A Memoir About Motherhood,
Daughterhood, and the Mess in Between

The Light of Days

The Untold Story of Women Resistance Fighters in Hitler's Ghettos

Judy Batalion

HARPER LARGE PRINT

An Imprint of HarperCollinsPublishers

HarperCollins books may be purchased for educational, business, or sales promotional use. For information, please e-mail the Special Markets Department at SPsales@harpercollins.com.

FIRST HARPER LARGE PRINT EDITION

ISBN: 978-0-06-299987-0

Library of Congress Cataloging-in-Publication Data is available upon request.

20 21 22 23 24 LSC 10 9 8 7 6 5 4 3 2 1

In memory of my Bubbe Zelda,
and for my daughters, Zelda and Billie.
L'dor v'dor . . . Chazak V'Amatz.

In honor of all the Jewish women of Poland
who resisted the Nazi regime.

Warsaw with a weeping face,
With graves on street corners,
Will outlive her enemies,
Will still see the light of days.

—*From "A Chapter of Prayer," a song dedicated
to the Warsaw ghetto uprising that won first
prize in a ghetto song contest. Written by a
young Jewish girl before her death, published in
Women in the Ghettos, 1946.*

Contents

Part 3: "No Border Will Stand in Their Way"

Part 4: The Emotional Legacy

Cast of Characters

Tosia Altman: a leader of The Young Guard and one of its most active couriers, based in Warsaw.

Vladka Meed (nee Feigele Peltel): a Bundist courier in Warsaw.

Chajka Klinger (pronounced in English as *Hay*-ka): a leader of The Young Guard and the fighting organization in Będzin.

Gusta Davidson: a courier and leader of Akiva, based in Kraków.

Hela Schüpper: a courier for Akiva, based in Kraków.

Bela Hazan: a Freedom courier, based in Grodno, Vilna, Białystok. Worked with **Lonka Kozibrodska** and **Tema Schneiderman**.

Chasia Bielicka (pronounced in English as *Has*-ia) and **Chaika Grossman** (pronounced *Hay*-ka): two Young Guard couriers who are part of a ring of anti-Fascist operatives in Białystok.

Ruzka Korczak (pronounced in English as *Rush*-ka): a leader of The Young Guard in Vilna's fighting organization (FPO) and a partisan leader in the forests.

Vitka Kempner: a leader of The Young Guard in Vilna's fighting organization (FPO) and a partisan leader in the forests.

Zelda Treger: a Young Guard courier based in Vilna and the forests.

Faye Schulman: a photographer who becomes a
partisan nurse and fighter.

Anna Heilman: an assimilated Warsaw Young
Guard member who takes part in the resistance at
Auschwitz.

The Light of Days

Introduction: Battle-Axes

The British Library reading room smelled like old pages. I stared at the stack of women's history books I had ordered—not *too* many, I reassured myself, not *too* overwhelming. The one on the bottom was the most unusual: hard-backed and bound in a worn, blue fabric, with yellowing, deckled edges. I opened it first and found virtually two hundred sheets of tiny script—in Yiddish. It was a language I knew but hadn't used in more than fifteen years.

I nearly returned it to the stacks unread. But some urge pushed me to read on, so, I glanced at a few pages. And then a few more. I'd expected to find dull, hagiographic mourning and vague, Talmudic discussions of female strength and valor. But instead—women, sabotage, rifles, disguise, dynamite. I'd discovered a thriller.

Could this be true?

I was stunned.

I had been searching for strong Jewish women.

In my twenties, in the early 2000s, I lived in London, working as an art historian by day and a comedian by night. In both spheres, my Jewish identity became an issue. Underhanded, jokey remarks about my semitic appearance and mannerisms were common from academics, gallerists, audiences, fellow performers, and producers alike. Gradually, I began to understand that it was jarring to the Brits that I wore my Jewishness so openly, so casually. I grew up in a tight-knit Jewish community in Canada and then attended college in the northeast United States. In neither place was my background unusual; I didn't have separate private and public personas. But in England, to be so "out" with my otherness, well, this seemed brash and caused discomfort. Shocked once I figured this out, I felt paralyzed by self-consciousness. I was not sure how to handle it: Ignore? Joke back? Be cautious? Overreact? Underreact? Go undercover and assume a dual identity? Flee?

I turned to art and research to help resolve this question and penned a performance piece about Jewish female identity and the emotional legacy of trauma as it passed over generations. My role model for Jewish female bravado was Hannah Senesh, one of the few female resisters in World War II not lost to history. As a child, I attended a secular Jewish school—its philosophies rooted in Polish Jewish movements—where we studied Hebrew poetry and Yiddish novels. In my fifth-grade Yiddish class, we read about Hannah and how, as a twenty-two-year-old in Palestine, she joined the British paratroopers fighting the Nazis and returned to Europe to help the resistance. She didn't succeed at her mission but did succeed in inspiring courage. At her execution, she refused a blindfold, insisting on staring at the bullet straight on. Hannah faced the truth, lived and died for her convictions, and took pride in openly being just who she was.

That spring of 2007, I was at London's British Library, looking for information on Senesh, seeking nuanced discussions about her character. It turned out there weren't many books about her, so I ordered any that mentioned her name. One of them happened to be in Yiddish. I almost put it back.

Instead, I picked up *Freuen in di Ghettos* (*Women in the Ghettos*), published in New York in 1946, and flipped through the pages. In this 185-page anthology, Hannah was mentioned only in the last chapter. Before that, 170 pages were filled with stories of other women—dozens of unknown young Jews who fought in the resistance against the Nazis, mainly from inside the Polish ghettos. These "ghetto girls" paid off Gestapo guards, hid revolvers in loaves of bread, and helped build systems of underground bunkers. They flirted with Nazis, bought them off with wine, whiskey, and pastry, and, with stealth, shot and killed them. They carried out espionage missions for Moscow, distributed fake IDs and underground flyers, and were bearers of the truth about what was happening to the Jews. They helped the sick and taught the children; they bombed German train lines and blew up Vilna's electric supply. They dressed up as non-Jews, worked as maids on the Aryan side of town, and helped Jews escape the ghettos through canals and chimneys, by digging holes in walls and crawling across rooftops. They bribed executioners, wrote underground radio bulletins, upheld group morale, negotiated with Polish landowners, tricked the Gestapo into carrying their luggage filled with weapons, initiated a group of anti-Nazi Nazis, and, of course, took care of most of the underground's admin.

Despite years of Jewish education, I'd never read accounts like these, astonishing in their details of the quotidian and extraordinary work of woman's combat. I had no idea how many Jewish women were involved in the resistance effort, nor to what degree.

These writings didn't just amaze me, they touched me personally, upending my understanding of my own history. I come from a family of Polish Jewish Holocaust survivors. My *bubbe* Zelda (namesake to my eldest daughter) did not fight in the resistance; her successful but tragic escape story shaped my understanding of survival. She—who did not look Jewish, with her high cheekbones and pinched nose—fled occupied Warsaw, swam across rivers, hid in a convent, flirted with a Nazi who turned a blind eye, and was transported in a truck carrying oranges eastward, finally stealing across the Russian border, where her life was saved, ironically, by being forced into Siberian work camps. My *bubbe* was strong as an ox, but she'd lost her parents and three of her four sisters, all of whom had remained in Warsaw. She'd relay this dreadful story to me every single afternoon as she babysat me after school, tears and fury in her eyes. My Montreal Jewish community was composed largely of Holocaust survivor families; both my family and neighbors' families were full of similar stories of pain and suffering. My genes were stamped—even altered, as neuroscientists now suggest—by trauma. I grew up in an aura of victimization and fear.

But here, in *Freuen in di Ghettos*, was a different version of the women-in-war story. I was jolted by these tales of agency. These were women who acted with ferocity and fortitude—even violently—smuggling, gathering intelligence, committing sabotage, and engaging in combat; they were proud of their fire. The writers were not asking for pity but were celebrating active valor and intrepidness. Women, often starving and tortured, were brave and brazen. Several of them had the chance to escape yet did not; some even chose to return and battle. My *bubbe* was my hero, but what if she'd decided to risk her life by staying and fighting? I was haunted by the question: What would I do in a similar situation? Fight or flight?

At first, I imagined that the several dozen resistance operatives mentioned in *Freuen* comprised the total amount. But as soon as I touched on the topic, extraordinary tales of female fighters crawled out from every corner: archives, catalogues, strangers who emailed me their family stories. I found dozens of women's memoirs published by small presses, and hundreds of testimonies in Polish, Russian, Hebrew, Yiddish, German, French, Dutch, Danish, Greek, Italian, and English, from the 1940s to today.

Holocaust scholars have debated what "counts" as an act of Jewish resistance. Many take it at its most broad definition: any action that affirmed the humanity of a Jew; any solitary or collaborative deed that even unintentionally defied Nazi policy or ideology, including simply staying alive. Others feel that too general a definition diminishes those who risked their lives to actively defy a regime, and that there is a distinction between resistance and resilience.

The rebellious acts that I discovered among Jewish women in Poland, my country of focus, spanned the gamut, from those involving complex planning and elaborate forethought, like setting off large quantities of TNT, to those that were spontaneous and simple, even slapstick-like, involving costumes, dress-up, biting and scratching, wiggling out of Nazis' arms. For many, the goal was to rescue Jews; for others, to die with and leave a legacy of dignity. *Freuen* highlights the activity of female "ghetto fighters": underground operatives who emerged from the Jewish youth group movements and worked in the ghettos. These young women were combatants, editors of underground bulletins, and social activists. In particular, women made up the vast majority of "couriers," a specific role at the heart of operations. They disguised themselves as non-Jews and traveled between locked ghettos and towns, smuggling people, cash, documents, information, and weapons, many of which they had obtained themselves.

In addition to ghetto fighters, Jewish women fled to

the forests and enlisted in partisan units, carrying out sabotage and intelligence missions. Some acts of resistance occurred as "unorganized" one-offs. Several Polish Jewish women joined foreign resistance units, while others worked with the Polish underground. Women established rescue networks to help fellow Jews hide or escape. Finally, they resisted morally, spiritually, and culturally by concealing their identities, distributing Jewish books, telling jokes during transports to relieve fear, hugging barrack-mates to keep them warm, and setting up soup kitchens for orphans. At times this last activity was organized, public, and illegal; at others, it was personal and intimate.

Months into my research, I was faced with a writer's treasure and challenge: I had collected more incredible resistance stories than I ever could have imagined. How would I possibly narrow it down and select my main characters?

Ultimately, I decided to follow my inspiration, *Freuen*, with its focus on female ghetto fighters from the youth movements Freedom (Dror) and The Young Guard (Hashomer Hatzair). *Freuen*'s centerpiece and longest contribution was written by a female courier who signed her name "Renia K." I was intimately drawn to Renia—not for being the most well-known, militant, or charismatic leader, but for the opposite reason. Renia was neither an idealist nor a revolutionary but a savvy, middle-class girl who happened to find herself in a sudden and unrelenting nightmare. She rose to the occasion, fueled by an inner sense of justice and by anger. I was enthralled by her formidable tales of stealing across borders and smuggling grenades, and by the detailed descriptions of her undercover missions. At age twenty, Renia recorded her experience of the preceding five years with even-keeled and reflective prose, vivid with quick characterizations, frank impressions, and even wit.

Later, I found out that Renia's writings in *Freuen* were excerpted from a long memoir that had been penned in Polish and published in Hebrew in Palestine in 1945. Her book was one of the first (some say *the* first) full-length personal accounts of the Holocaust. In 1947 a Jewish press in downtown New York released its English version with an introduction by an eminent translator. But soon after, the book and its world fell into obscurity. I have come across Renia only in passing mentions or scholarly annotations. Here I lift her story from the footnotes to the text, unveiling this anonymous Jewish woman who displayed acts of astonishing bravery. I have interwoven into Renia's story tales of Polish Jewish resisters from different underground movements and with diverse missions, all to show the breadth and scope of female courage.

Jewish lore is filled with tales of underdog victory: David and Goliath, the Israelite slaves who tantalized Pharaoh, the Maccabee brothers who defeated the Greek Empire.

This is not that story.

The Polish Jewish resistance achieved relatively miniscule victories in terms of military success, Nazi casualties, and the number of Jews saved.

But their resistance *effort* was larger and more organized than I ever could have imagined, and colossal compared with the Holocaust narrative I'd grown up with. Jewish armed underground groups operated in more than ninety eastern European ghettos. "Small acts" and uprisings took place in Warsaw as well as in Będzin, Vilna, Białystok, Kraków, Lvov, Częstochowa, Sosnowiec, and Tarnów. Armed Jewish resistance broke out in at least five major concentration camps and death camps—including Auschwitz, Treblinka, and Sobibor—as well as in eighteen forced-labor camps. Thirty thousand Jews joined forest partisan detachments. Jewish networks financially supported twelve thousand fellow Jews-in-hiding in Warsaw. All this alongside endless examples of daily acts of defiance.

Why, I kept asking myself, had I never heard these stories? Why had I not heard about the hundreds, even thousands, of Jewish women who were involved in every aspect of this rebellion, often at its helm? Why was *Freuen* an obscure title instead of a classic on Holocaust reading lists?

As I came to learn, many factors, both personal and political, have guided the development of the narrative of the Holocaust. Our collective memory has been shaped by an overarching resistance to resistance. Silence is a means of swaying perceptions and shifting power, and has functioned in different ways in Poland, Israel, and North America over the decades. Silence is also a technique for coping and living.

Even when storytellers have gone against the grain and presented resistance stories, there has been little focus on women. In the odd cases where writers have included women in their tales, they are often portrayed within stereotypical narrative tropes. In the compelling 2001 TV movie *Uprising*, about the Warsaw ghetto, female fighters are present but classically misrepresented. Women leaders were made minor characters; "girlfriends of" the protagonists. The sole female lead is Tosia Altman, and though the film does show her fearlessly smuggling weapons, she is depicted as a beautiful, shy girl who took care of her sick father and passively got swept up into a resistance role, all wide eyed and meek. In reality, Tosia was a leader of The Young Guard youth movement well before the war; her biographer emphasizes her reputation for being a feisty "glam girl" and "hussy." By rewriting her backstory, the film not only distorts her character but also erases the whole world of Jewish female education, training, and work that created her.

Needless to say, Jewish resistance to the Nazis in Poland was not a radical woman-only feminist mission. Men were fighters, leaders, and battle commanders. But because of their gender and their ability to camouflage their Jewishness, women were uniquely suited to some crucial and life-threatening tasks; in particular, as couriers. As described by fighter Chaika Grossman, "The Jewish girls were the nerve-centers of the movement."

The eminent Warsaw ghetto chronicler Emanuel Ringelblum wrote about the courier girls at the time: "Without a murmur, without a second's hesitation, they accept and carry out the most dangerous missions. . . . How many times have they looked death in the eyes? . . .

The story of the Jewish woman will be a glorious page in the history of Jewry during the present war."

Back in 1946, the whole purpose of *Freuen* was to inform American Jews about the incredible efforts of Jewish women in the ghettos. Several contributors simply assumed that these women would become household names, suggesting that future historians would map this incredible terrain. Fighter Ruzka Korczak wrote that these female resistance stories are "our nation's great treasures" and would become an essential part of Jewish folklore.

Seventy-five years later, these heroes are still largely unknown, their pages in the book of eternal memory unwritten. Until now.

Prologue: Flash Forward—
Defense or Rescue?

From above, one might mistake the small town, with its glistening castle and pastel buildings, its streetscapes of candy colors, as a magical kingdom. A settlement since the ninth century, Będzin was first erected as a fortress city, guarding the ancient trade route between Kiev and the West. Like many of Poland's medieval cities, especially those in this forest-filled area in the south of the country, Będzin's landscape is glorious. The verdant vistas don't suggest division and death, endless battles and decrees. Viewed at a distance, one would never guess that this royal town topped with a golden turret was an emblem of the near destruction of the Jewish people.

Będzin, located in the Polish region of Zaglembie, had been home to Jews for hundreds of years. Jews worked and flourished in the district since the 1200s AD. In the late sixteenth century, the king granted Będzin Jews the rights to own prayer houses, buy real estate, engage in unlimited trade, slaughter animals, and distribute alcohol. For more than two hundred years, as long as they paid taxes, Jews were protected and established strong trade relationships. In the eighteen hundreds, the town flipped to stringent Prussian and then Russian rule, but local groups opposed these foreign colonists and advocated Polish Jewish brotherhood. In the twentieth century, the economy boomed, modern schools were established, and Będzin became a center for novel philosophies, especially socialism. New waves of practice led to passionate and productive internal conflict: Jewish political parties, professorships, and press abounded. As in many towns across the country, Jews comprised a growing percentage of the population, intricately woven into the fabric of everyday life. The Yiddish-speaking residents formed an essential part of the area; in turn, Zaglembie became an integral part of their identity.

In 1921, when Będzin was referred to as "the Jerusalem of Zaglembie," Jews owned 672 local factories and workshops. Nearly half of all Będziners were Jewish, and a good number were well-to-do: doctors, lawyers, merchants, and the owners of manufacturing plants. They were a liberal, secular, moderately socialist group who visited coffee shops, had summerhouses in the mountains, enjoyed tango nights, jazz and skiing, and felt European. The working class and religious Jews also thrived, with dozens of prayer houses and a wide selection of parties to vote for in the Jewish council. In the 1928 municipal election, twenty-two parties were represented, seventeen of them Jewish organizations. Będzin's deputy mayor was a Jew. Of course, these Jews did not know that the dynamic world they had built would soon be utterly destroyed—or that they would have to fight for their legacy and their lives.

In September 1939 the invading German army over-ran Będzin. The Nazis burnt down the town's grand, Romanesque synagogue—a centerpiece proudly built just downhill from the castle—then murdered dozens of Jews. Three years later, twenty thousand Jews wear-ing Star of David armbands were forced into a small neighborhood outside the town, with several families pushed together into shacks and single rooms. People who had enjoyed centuries of relative peace, prosper-ity, and social integration, centuries of culture, were squashed into a few disheveled blocks. The Będzin community had a new pocket. A dark and dank pocket. The ghetto.

The ghettos in Zaglembie were some of the last in Poland to be "liquidated," Hitler's army arriving there at a later stage to complete their "Final Solution." Many of the ghetto inhabitants had work permits and were sent to forced labor in German weapons factories and workshops rather than immediately being hauled off to death camps. In Będzin, postal communication was still possible. These ghettos had contact with Russia, Slovakia, Turkey, Switzerland, and other non-Aryan lands. Even in these dark pockets, then, emerged cells of Jewish resistance.

Among the crammed houses, amidst an atmosphere of panic, restlessness, and terror, was a special building. An edifice that held strong, not just by its firm foundation (indeed, it would soon rest upon underground bunkers) but thanks to its inhabitants, their brains, their hearts, and their muscles. Here was a Będzin headquarters of the local Jewish resistance. A resistance born out of the philosophy of the Labor Zionist movement that cherished Jewish agency, the work of the land, socialism, and equality. The "comrades" were raised on a unique diet of physical work and female empowerment. This was a center for the Freedom youth movement.

In February 1943 the ghetto was gripped by cold, the air heavy as lead. The bustling commune building was unusually quiet. The old buzz of Freedom's cultural programs—language courses, musical performances, seminars on the connection between the heart and the land—had vanished. No voices, no songs.

Renia Kukielka, an eighteen-year-old Jewish woman and an emerging warrior of the underground resistance movement, came up from the laundry room. She made her way to the meeting being held around the large table on the ground floor of the headquarters where their most important planning took place. It was a familiar spot.

"We've obtained a few papers," Hershel announced.

Everyone gasped. These were golden tickets—out of Poland, to survival.

Today was decision day.

Frumka Płotnicka with her dark eyes and furrowed brow, stood at one end of the table. From a poor, religious family in Pinsk, Frumka had joined the movement as an introverted teenager and, given her inborn seriousness and analytic thinking, rose in its ranks. With the onset of war, she quickly became a leader in the underground.

Hershel Springer, her coleader of the Będzin "troop,"

was at the other end of the table. Beloved by all, Hershel had "so much Jewish folk character in him" that he made frank conversation with anyone with shared roots, from a wagon driver to a butcher, dwelling in their most trivial matters. As always, his warm, goofy smile was a soothing force countering the destruction outside; the filthy ghetto that grew emptier each day, the echo of nothing.

Renia took her spot in between them at the table, along with the rest of the young Jews.

She often caught herself staggered in disbelief, jolted by her reality. In only a few years, she'd gone from being a fifteen-year-old girl with six siblings and loving parents, to an orphan, not even aware of how many of her brothers and sisters were still alive or where they might be. With her family, Renia had run though fields covered in corpses. Later, she'd fled through fields completely on her own. Just months earlier, she'd bolted from a moving train and disguised herself as a Polish peasant girl, taking up the post of housemaid for a part-German family. She'd insisted on going to church with them as a cover, but the first time, she shook with every movement, fearful she wouldn't know when to stand, how to sit, what to cross. The teenager had become an actress, constantly performing. The head of the household liked her and commended her for being clean, industrious, even educated. *"Of course,"* Renia had semi-lied. *"I'm from a cultured family. We were rich. Only when my parents died did I have to take on manual work."*

She was treated well, but as soon as she was able to secretly contact her sister Sarah, Renia knew she had to be with her, with what was left of her family. Sarah had arranged for Renia to be smuggled to Będzin, to this center for the Freedom youth group to which she'd belonged.

Renia was now an educated girl who did laundry, hidden in the back. She was an illegal here, an interloper among the interlopers. The Nazis had divided conquered Poland into distinct territories. Renia had papers only for the General Government, the area that was to serve as a "racial dumping ground," with an endless supply of slave labor—and ultimately, as a site for the mass extermination of European Jewry. She did not have papers to be in Zaglembie, an area annexed by the Third Reich.

Now, to Renia's right, sat Frumka's sister and polar opposite, Hantze, her exuberant spirit and relentless optimism lighting the dark room. Hantze loved to tell the comrades how she tricked the Nazis by dressing as a Catholic woman, parading right in front of them, fooling them time and again. Sarah, her face chiseled with sharp cheekbones and dark, penetrating eyes, was present, along with Hershel's girlfriend, Aliza Zitenfeld, who with Sarah cared for the ghetto's orphaned children. Fresh-faced Chajka Klinger, an outspoken, feisty leader of a sister group, may also have been at the table, ready to fight for her ideals: truth, action, dignity.

"We've obtained a few papers," Hershel repeated. Each one allowed a person entry into an internment camp; allowed one person to live. They were fake passports from allied countries where Germans were being held captive. The holders of these allied passports were to be kept by the Nazis in special camps and were intended to be exchanged for Germans in those countries—one of numerous passport schemes that they'd heard of in the past years. Perhaps, they hoped, this one was legit. It took months to organize and obtain these documents, a hugely expensive and dangerous process that involved sending secretly coded letters with photos to specialist counterfeiters. Who would get one?

Or should no one take them?

Defense or rescue? Fight or flight?

This was a debate they'd been waging since earlier in the war. A few Jews with even fewer guns were not going to topple the Nazis, so what was the point of resistance? Were they fighting to die with dignity, for revenge, for a legacy of honor for future generations? Or were they fighting to inflict damage, to rescue and save—and if so, whom? Individuals or the movement? Children or adults? Artists or leaders? Should Jews fight in ghettos or forests? As Jews or with Poles?

Now a real decision had to be made.

"Frumka!" Hershel called from across the table, staring right into her dark eyes.

She looked back at him, just as firmly, though keeping quiet.

Hershel explained that a directive had come in from their revered leader in Warsaw, Zivia Lubetkin. Frumka was to use a passport to leave Poland for The Hague, home to the UN's International Court of Justice. She was to represent the Jewish people, tell the world what was happening. She would then travel to Palestine and serve as an official witness of Nazi atrocities.

"Leave?" Frumka replied.

Renia looked at Frumka, her heart racing. She could sense Frumka reeling too, almost see her sharp mind at work beneath her quiet face. Frumka was their leader, the rock supporting them all, both the men and the women. Who would be asked to go with her? What they would be without her?

"No," Frumka declared in her firm but gentle way. "If we must die, let us all die together. But"—and here she paused—"let us strive for a heroic death."

Hearing her words, her assurance, the whole room sighed audibly. As if the entire building had been resuscitated, the members began tapping feet, some actually smiling. Frumka placed her fist on the table, as simple and quick as a gavel. "It's time. It's time to get energized."

And that's how they had their unanimous answer: defense.

Renia, always ready, sprang from her seat.

PART 1

Ghetto Girls

Heroic girls. . . . Boldly they travel back and forth through the cities and towns of Poland. . . . They are in mortal danger every day. They rely entirely on their "Aryan" faces and on the peasant kerchiefs that cover their heads. Without a murmur, without a second's hesitation, they accept and carry out the most dangerous missions. Is someone needed to travel to Vilna, Białystok, Lemberg, Kovel, Lublin, Częstochowa, or Radom to smuggle in contraband such as illegal publications, goods, money? The girls volunteer as though it were the most natural thing in the world. Are there comrades who have to be rescued from Vilna, Lublin, or some other city? — They undertake the mission. Nothing stands in their way. Nothing deters them. . . . How many times have they looked death in the eyes? How many times have they been arrested and searched? . . .

The story of the Jewish woman will be a glorious page in the history of Jewry during the present war. And the Chajkes and Frumkes will be the leading figures in this story. For these girls are indefatigable.

—*Emanuel Ringelblum, diary entry, May 1942*

Chapter 1
Po-Lin

Renia
October 1924

On Friday, October 10, 1924, as the Jews of Jędrzejów were settling in for their Sabbath eve, shutting shops, closing tills, boiling, chopping, frying, Moshe Kukielka rushed from his store. His family home at 16 Klasztorna (Monastery) Street was a small stone structure on a verdant main road, just around the bend from a magnificent medieval abbey known for its turquoise and gilded interior. Tonight the house was particularly abuzz. As sunset approached, the orange autumn light bleeding red into the lush valleys and rolling hills of the Kielce region, the Kukielkas' oven heated, their spoons clanged, their stove hissed, and the church bells formed their usual backdrop to the family's Yiddish and Polish clatter. And then, a new sound: a baby's first wail.

Moshe and Leah were both modern and observant, as were their three older children. They engaged in Polish culture and celebrated Jewish traditions. Moshe was used to hurrying home or to a *shtiebel* (prayer house) for the Shabbat meal and prayers, walking briskly through the open town square, with its rows of pastel-colored buildings, passing Jewish merchants and Christian farmers who lived and worked side by side. This week, he rushed even more hastily through the cool fall air. Traditionally, candles were lit and Shabbat itself was welcomed as a bride into the home, but that day Moshe had a new guest to greet. An even better one.

And then he arrived to find her: his third daughter, who immediately became the shiny apple of his discerning eye. Rivka in Hebrew, a name whose roots have various meanings, including *connection*, *union*, and even *captivating*. In the Bible, Rivka was one of the four matriarchs of the Jewish people. Of course, in this partly assimilated family, the baby also had a Polish name: Renia. The name Kukielka resembles the Polish Kukielo—the surname of family who for generations had run the local funeral home. Jews often constructed last names by adding winsome endings such as -ka to Polish names. Kukielka means "marionette."

It was 1924, just a year after the new Poland was finally recognized by the international community and had its boundaries set, following years of occupation, partitioning, and constantly fluctuating borders. (As the old Jewish joke went, a man asks whether his town is now in Polish or Soviet territory. He's told, "This year, we're in Poland." "Thank goodness!," the man exclaims. "I simply could not take another Russian winter.") The economy was afloat, and though most Jews in Jędrzejów lived below the poverty line, Moshe succeeded as a small businessman, running a *gallenteria* shop that sold buttons, clothing, and sewing supplies. He raised a middle-class family and exposed them to music and literature. Their Shabbat table, set that week by the Kukielkas' older two daughters and relatives while Leah was otherwise occupied, served up the delicacies of the day, which Moshe was able to afford: sweet liquor, ginger cake, chopped liver with onions, *cholent* (a slow-cooked beans and meat potage), potato and sweet noodle kugel pudding, compote of plums and apples, and tea. Leah's gefilte fish, offered most Fridays, would become Renia's favorite. No doubt, the meal was extra festive this week.

Sometimes traits of personality are visible, even unmistakable, in the earliest hours of existence; psychologies stamped on the soul. It's possible that Moshe knew when he first held her—infusing her with his gentleness, intelligence, and incisiveness—that his spirit would carry her forward on journeys a person in 1924 could scarcely imagine. It's possible he knew then that his little Renia, with the big green eyes, light-brown hair, and delicate face—his little, captivating marionette—was born to perform.

Jędrzejów was a *shtetl,* Yiddish for "small city," and a word that referred to Polish market towns with significant Jewish populations. Renia's birth added one to the 4,500 Jews in the village, who composed almost 45 percent of the population. (Her younger siblings, Aaron, Esther, and Yaacov, or little Yankel, would soon add three more.) The Jewish community, established in the 1860s when Jews were finally allowed to settle in the region, was largely poor. Most Jews worked as traveling salesmen, peddlers, and small business owners with shops on or around the breezy market square. The rest were mainly artisans: shoemakers, bakers, carpenters. Jędrzejów was not as modern as Będzin, which bordered on Germany and the West, but even here a small number of elite locals were doctors, emergency medical workers, and teachers; one Jew was a judge. About 10 percent of the town's Jews were wealthy and owned timber mills, flour mills, and mechanical workshops, as well as property on the main square.

As in the rest of Poland, modern Jewish culture flourished as Renia grew into a child of the 1930s. At that time, Warsaw alone had a staggering 180 Jewish newspapers: 130 in Yiddish, 25 in Hebrew, and 25 in Polish. Accordingly, dozens of magazine subscriptions passed through the Jędrzejów post office. The local Jewish population grew. Different prayer houses were established to suit various flavors of Judaism. Even in that small town, three Jewish bookstores, a publishing house, and Jewish libraries opened; drama groups and literary readings proliferated; political parties boomed.

Renia's father was engaged in Jewish learning and charitable endeavors, feeding the poor, tending to the dead with the *chevra kadisha* burial society, and serving as a local cantor. He voted Zionist. The religious Zionists honored writer Theodor Herzl's nineteenth-century ideals, believing that a true and open Jewish existence could be achieved only in a homeland where Jews were first-class citizens, in Palestine. Poland may have been their home for centuries, but it was temporary. Moshe dreamt of one day moving his family to "the promised land."

The parties organized lectures and political rallies. One can imagine Renia accompanying her beloved, bearded father to one of the large and increasingly popular Zionist town meetings, like a talk on "The Struggle for a Jewish Palestine," on May 18 1937. Clad in her Polish schoolgirl white-and-navy-blue "sailor" suit, pleated skirt, and knee-high socks, forever a lover of promenades, Renia clasped Moshe's hand as they marched past the two new Zionist libraries to the lively gathering where hundreds of Jews debated and discussed—riled by questions of belonging. As Poles negotiated their new identities in their newly stabilized homeland, so did Jews. How did they fit into this novel country, a place where they had lived continually for more than a thousand years, yet were never truly considered Polish? Were they Polish first or Jewish first? The modern question of Diaspora identity was at a fever pitch, especially due to rapidly rising antisemitism.

Moshe and Leah Kukielka prized education. The country saw a mass influx of Jewish schools: secular Hebrew schools, Yiddish prep schools, single-sex religious schools. Of Jędrzejów's four hundred Jewish children, one hundred studied at a charity Talmud Torah, a Jewish nursery, or the local branch of

the Beit Yaakov girls' elementary school, where students wore long sleeves and stockings. For reasons
of proximity—and because religious education was
costly and often reserved for sons only—Renia, like
many Jewish girls, attended Polish public school.

No matter. She was at the top of her class of thirty-
five. Renia had mainly Catholic friends and spoke
fluent Polish in the schoolyard. Unbeknownst to her
at time, this cultural immersion, including her capacity to banter in the national tongue without a Jewish-
sounding accent, would be her most critical training
for the underground. But while Renia excelled and assimilated, she was not entirely included. At a ceremony
when she was called up to receive an academic award, a
classmate threw a pencil case at her forehead, leaving a
lasting impression—literally. So, was she in or was she
out? She personally straddled the centuries-old hurdle:
the "Polish Jewish identity" question.

Since its foundation, Poland was evolving. With
ever-changing geographical boundaries, its ethnic
composition varied as new communities folded into its
borders. Medieval Jews migrated to Poland because
it was a safe haven from western Europe, where they
were persecuted and expelled. Jews were relieved to
arrive in this tolerant land with economic opportunity.
"Polin," the Hebrew name for the country, comprises

"Po" and "Lin," and means "Here, we stay." Polin offered relative freedom and safety. A future.

A coin from the early twelve hundreds, on display at the POLIN Museum of the History of Polish Jews in Warsaw, shows Hebrew letters. Already, Yiddish-speaking Jews were a large minority, integral to Poland's economy, working as bankers, bakers, and bailiffs. Early Poland was a republic, its constitution ratified around the same time as America's. Royal power was curtailed by a parliament elected by the small noble class. Jewish communities and nobles had mutual arrangements: the gentry protected the Jews who settled in their towns and gave them autonomy and religious freedom; in turn, Jews paid high taxes and carried out economic activities forbidden for Christian Poles, such as loaning and borrowing capital at interest.

The 1573 Warsaw Confederation was the first document in Europe to legally mandate religious tolerance. But as much as Jews were officially integrated into Polish culture and shared philosophies, folklore, and styles of dress, food, and music, they also felt different, threatened. Many Poles resented Jews' economic freedom. Jews subleased whole towns from nobles, and Polish serfs begrudged the rule of their Jewish landlords. The Catholic Church disseminated the hateful and absurd falsehood that Jews murdered Christians—especially babies—in order to use their blood for religious rituals. This led to attacks on Jews, with occasional periods of wide-scale riots and murder. The Jewish community became close-knit, seeking strength in its customs. A "push-pull" relationship existed between Jews and Poles, their cultures developing in relation to the other. Take, for instance, the braided challah: the soft, egg-rich bread and holy symbol of the Jewish Sabbath. This loaf is also a Polish *chalka* and a Ukrainian *kalach*—it's impossible to know which version came first. The traditions developed simultaneously, societies tangled, joined under a (bitter)sweet gloss.

In the late seventeen hundreds, however, Poland broke down. Its government was unstable, and the country was simultaneously invaded by Germany, Austria, and Russia, then divided into three parts—each one ruled by a captor that imposed its own customs. Poles remained united by a nationalist longing, and maintained their language and literature. Polish Jews changed under their occupiers: the German ones learned the Saxon language and developed into an educated middle class, while the Austrian-ruled (Galician) Jews suffered from terrible poverty. The majority of Jews came to be governed by Russia, an empire that forced economic and religious decrees on the largely working-class population. The borders shifted, too. For example, Jędrzejów first belonged to Galicia; then Russia took it over. Jews felt on edge—in particular, financially, as changing laws affected their livelihoods.

During World War I, Poland's three occupiers battled each other on home ground. Despite hundreds of thousands of lost lives and a decimated economy, Poland was victorious: the Second Republic was established. United Poland needed to rebuild both its cities and its identity. The political landscape was bifurcated, the long-honed nationalist longing expressed in contradictory ways. On the one side were nostalgic monarchists who called for reestablishing the pluralistic Poland of old: Poland as a state of nations. (Four in ten citizens of the new country were minorities.) The other side, however, envisioned Poland as a nation-state—an ethnic nation. A nationalistic movement that advocated for purebred Polishness grew quickly. This party's entire platform was concerned with slandering Polish Jews, who were blamed for the country's poverty and political problems. Poland had never recovered from World War I or its subsequent conflicts with its neighbors; Jews were accused of siding with the enemy. This right-wing party promoted a new Polish identity that was specifically defined as "not the Jew." Generations of residency, not to mention formal equal rights, made no difference. As espoused by Nazi racial theory, which this party adopted giddily, a Jew could never be a Pole.

The central government instituted a Sunday-Rest law and discriminated against Jews in public employment policies, but its leadership was unstable. Just a few years later, in a 1926 coup d'état, Poland was taken over by Józef Piłsudski, an unusual mix of monarchist and socialist. The former general and statesman championed a multiethnic land, and although he did not particularly help the Jews, they felt safer under his semiauthoritarian rule than under representative government.

Piłsudski, however, had many opponents, and when he died in 1935, as Renia turned eleven, the right-wing nationalists easily assumed control. Their government opposed direct violence and pogroms (which occured anyway), but boycotts of Jewish businesses were encouraged. The Church condemned Nazi racism but promoted anti-Jewish sentiment. At universities, Polish students championed Hitler's racial ideology. Ethnic quotas were enforced, and Jewish students were corralled into "bench ghettos" at the back of the lecture hall. Ironically, Jews had the most traditionally Polish education of any group, many speaking Polish (some exclusively) and reading Jewish newspapers in Polish.

Even the small town of Jędrzejów saw increasing antisemitism through the 1930s, from racial slurs to boycotting businesses, smashing storefronts, and instigating brawls. Renia spent many evenings staring out her window, on guard, fearing that anti-Jewish hooligans might burn down their house and harm her parents, for whom she always felt responsible.

The famous Yiddish comedy duo Dzigan and Schumacher, who had their own cabaret company in Warsaw, began to probe antisemitism on stage. In their eerily prescient humor sketch "The Last Jew in Poland," they portrayed a country suddenly missing its Jews, panicking about its decimated economy and culture. Despite growing intolerance, or perhaps inspired by their discomfort and hope, Jews experienced a golden era of creativity in literature, poetry, theater, philosophy, social action, religious study, and education—all of it enjoyed by the Kukielka family.

Poland's Jewish community was represented by a multitude of political opinions; each had its own response to this xenophobic crisis. The Zionists had lost patience feeling like second-class citizens and Renia frequently heard her father speak of the need to move to a Jewish homeland where Jews could develop as a people, not bound by class or religion. Led by charismatic intellectuals who championed the Hebrew language, the

Zionists disagreed fundamentally with the other parties. The religious party, devoted to Poland, advocated
for less discrimination and that Jews be treated like any
other citizen. Many Communists supported assimila-
tion, as did many in the upper classes. With time, the
largest party was the Bund, a working-class, socialist
group that promoted Jewish culture. Bundists were
the most optimistic, hoping that Poles would sober up
and see that antisemitism wouldn't solve the country's
problems. The diasporic Bund insisted that Poland was
the Jews' home, and they should stay exactly where
they were, continue to speak Yiddish, and demand
their rightful place. The Bund organized self-defense
units, intent on staying put. "Where we live, that's our
country." *Po-lin.*

Fight or flight. Always the question.

As Renia matured into early adolescence, it's likely that
she accompanied her older sister, Sarah, to youth group
activities. Born in 1915, Sarah was nine years older than
Renia, and one of her heroes. Sarah, with her piercing
eyes and delicate lips that always hinted at a smile, was
the omniscient intellectual, the savvy do-gooder whose
authority Renia simply felt. One can imagine the sisters, walking side by side at a clipped pace, all duty
and energy, both donning the modern fashion of the

day: berets, fitted blazers, shin-length pleated skirts, and short cut hair pulled back in neat clips. Renia, a fashionista, would have been put together from head to toe, a standard she upheld her entire life. The interwar style in Poland, influenced by women's emancipation and by Paris fashions, saw the replacement of jewels, lace, and feathers with a focus on simple cuts and comfort. Makeup was bold, with dark eye shadow and bright-red lipstick, and hairdos and skirts were shortened. ("One could see the entire shoe!" wrote a satirist at the time.) A photo of Sarah in the 1930s shows her wearing low, thick-heeled pumps that allowed her to march—a necessity because women in this era were constant walkers, traveling long distances to work and school by foot. No doubt heads turned when the sisters entered the meeting room.

In the decades between world wars, growing anti-semitism and poverty brought about a collective depression among Polish Jewish youths. They felt alienated from their country, their futures uncertain compared with those of their forbears. Jews were not allowed to join the Polish Scouts, and so a hundred thousand joined Jewish youth groups affiliated with the different political parties. These groups provided existential paths and hope for the future. Jędrzejów's young Jews participated in a thriving youth group scene. In some photos, members wear dark colors and pose as sober intellectuals, arms crossed; in others, they stand outdoors in open land, gripping rakes, muscles flexed, tanned, and flushed with life.

Like her father, Sarah was a Zionist, but unlike Moshe, she belonged to Freedom, a group of secular, socialist Labor Zionists. Mainly middle class and worldly, Labor Zionists hoped for a homeland where they would live in collectives, speak Hebrew, and feel a sense of belonging. While they encouraged reading and debate, physicality was also prized as a way to denounce the myth of the slothful, intellectual Jew and to promote personal agency. Engaging in manual labor and contributing to the group's resources was paramount. They idealized the working of the land; agricultural self-sufficiency went hand in hand with communal and personal independence.

There were several Labor Zionist youth groups—some more intellectual or secular; others devoted to charity, advocacy, or pluralism—but all took traditional Polish values of nationalism, heroism, and individual sacrifice and gave them a Jewish context. Freedom focused on social action and, uniquely, drew members from the Yiddish-speaking working class. The group established summer camps, training camps (*hachshara*), and communal farms (kibbutzim) as preparation for emigration, teaching hard labor and cooperative living—often to a parent's dismay. Not only did Moshe bemoan Freedom for being overly liberated and insufficiently elite, but also "comrades" were prioritized over the birth family, with leaders treated as role models—almost like surrogate parents. Unlike the Scouts or sports organizations, these youth movements touched every part of their members' lives; they were physical, emotional and spiritual training grounds. Young people defined themselves based on their group.

Sarah championed social equality and justice, and was especially keen on counseling young children. The Ghetto Fighters' House Museum holds several photos of her at a training camp in the city of Poznán, two hundred miles from Jędrzejów, in 1937. In one, she stands tall in front of a statue, wearing a tailored suit with a high collar, her hat tilted modishly to the side; she holds a book, serious, determined. The modern world was hers for the taking.

Women in Poland held both traditional and progressive roles, spurred on by a positivist education philosophy and by World War I, which had pushed them into employment. In the new republic, elementary school was mandatory, including for girls. Universities were opened to female students. Polish women received the vote in 1918, before most Western countries.

In western Europe, Jewish families were largely middle class and constrained by broader bourgeois mores, with women relegated to the domestic realm. But in the East, most Jews were poor, and out of necessity, women worked outside the home—especially in religious circles, where it was acceptable for men to study rather than toil. Jewish women were enmeshed in the public sphere: in 1931, 44.5 percent of Jewish wage earners were female, though they earned less than men. The average marriage age was pushed back to the late twenties, even thirties, largely due to poverty. This resulted in declining fertility and, in turn, women in the workplace. In fact, to some degree, their work-life balance resembled modern gender norms.

Centuries earlier, Jewish women were accorded "the right to know." The invention of the printing press led to a proliferation of Yiddish and Hebrew books for female readers; religious rulings allowed women to attend services; new synagogue architecture included a female annex. Now Jewish women were poets, novelists, journalists, traders, lawyers, doctors, and dentists. In universities, Jews made up a large percentage of the female students, enrolled in mainly humanities and science programs.

While the Zionist parties were certainly not "feminist"—women did not hold public office, for example—young women experienced a degree of parity in the socialist youth realm. One youth group, The Young Guard, to which Renia's older brother, Zvi, belonged, founded the idea of the "intimate group," with a dual leadership structure. Each section was led by a man and a woman. "Father" was the learning leader, and "Mother," the emotional leader; equally powerful, they complemented one another. In this family model, "their children" were like siblings.

These groups studied Karl Marx and Sigmund Freud, as well as female revolutionaries like Rosa Luxemburg and Emma Goldman. They explicitly advocated emotional discussion and analyses of interpersonal relationships. Members were primarily in their late teens, an age where many women were more mature than the men and, consequently, became organizers. Women led self-defense training; they were taught to be socially conscious, self-possessed, and strong. The Pioneer (Hechalutz) Union, the umbrella organization that included several Zionist youth groups and promoted agricultural training for pioneer life in Palestine, had an emergency plan B in case of conscription to the Polish army, which put exclusively women in charge. Countless photos of 1930s youth show women standing alongside men, dressed in similar dark coats and belts, or work clothes and pants; they too hold up scythes like trophies and grasp sickles like swords, preparing for lives of hard manual labor.

Sarah was a devoted Labor Zionist. Bela, the sister between her and Renia, joined Freedom too, and Zvi was fluent in Hebrew. Renia, too young to join, spent her early teens absorbing her siblings' passions, and one can picture her dropping in on meetings, sports games, and festivities—the little sister tagging along, taking it in, wide eyed.

In 1938 fourteen-year-old Renia was completing elementary school. A small group of Jewish students received general secondary education at the Coeducational District Secondary School in Jędrzejów, but she was not able to attend high school. In some accounts, Renia blamed this on antisemitism; in others, she explained that she needed to earn money instead of continuing her studies. Many young women's memoirs of the time speak of their ambitions to be nurses and even doctors, but perhaps Jędrzejów's more traditional setting, or Renia's urgent financial needs, made her seek out a secretarial career. She enrolled in a stenography course, hoping to set off on a life of office work. Little did she know that the work she was soon to take on would be of a rather different nature.

The youth groups all organized summer activities. In August 1939, young Labor Zionists gathered at camps and symposia where they danced and sang, studied and read, played sports, slept outdoors, and led countless seminars. They discussed the recent British white paper that had limited Jewish immigration to Palestine, and considered ways to relocate, desperate to carry on the work of their collective ideals, to save the world. The summer programs ended, and on September 1, the members were just settling back at home, undergoing the transition between the chosen family and the birth one, summer and school, green and ocher, warm breeze and chill, the country and the city.

Also, that was the day Hitler invaded Poland.

Chapter 2
From the Fire, to the Fire

Renia
September 1939

Rumors flew like shots. The Nazis were burning, looting, gouging eyes, cutting tongues, murdering babies, slicing off women's breasts. Renia didn't know what to think, but like everyone in town, she knew that the Germans were coming to Jędrzejów. She knew they were after the Jews. Dust clouded over families, tornados of panic. No one knew where to go. Houses were shuttered. Bags were packed. Walking en masse town to town, civilians and their children stepped alongside retreating columns of Polish soldiers. There were no trains.

Along with many of their neighbors, the Kukielkas decided to head east to Chmielnik, a similarly small town on the other side of the Nida River, where they hoped they would be beyond the Germans' reach, and where they believed the Polish army still held strong. The Kukielkas had relatives in Chmielnik. They took nothing with them. Joining the throngs, they set off by foot.

The twenty-one-mile road was littered with the corpses of people and cattle—all casualties of the Nazis' relentless air attacks. German planes dropped explosives on all sides. Renia, suffocated by the rancid smell, often found herself knocked off her feet, limbs splayed wide, to a backdrop of burning villages. It was safer, she learned quickly, to stay put as the bombs fell; stillness was a shield. Another blast, then a plane flew low and peppered the air with machine-gun bullets. Their whistle was all she could hear—that and the babies. Mothers clutched children into their bodies but were killed, going limp, leaving surviving infants and toddlers shrieking "to the skies," she later described. A day and night of hell to reach Chmielnik.

But Renia could tell right away, Chmielnik was no safe haven. The town was a collection of rubble from which scorched, half-alive people were being dragged. And those were the lucky ones. People from here, it turned out, had fled to Jędrzejów, hoping for safety there. "Everyone was trying to escape from the frying pan into the fire."

Chmielnik sizzled with anticipated violence. Rumors from back home were nightmarishly vivid: Nazis had taken over Jędrzejów, were firing indiscriminately, and had rounded up and shot ten Jewish men in the town square, the brightly colored, bustling center of their lives. This act was meant as a warning to the local Jews, demonstrating what would happen if anyone disobeyed them. Chmielniks knew that they were next.

At that point, it was believed that, as in all past wars, only the men were in danger, not women and children. Many Jewish males, including Renia's father, Moshe, fled town toward the Bug River, where the Soviets had advanced, and they hoped to find protection hiding in the countryside. Renia later wrote that the women's screams during the separation from their men were simply unbearable. One can only imagine the terror she felt, letting go of her beloved Dad, for who knows how long, to where, to what.

Chmielnik's wealthy, Renia heard, had rented horses and fled to Russia. Houses stood empty.

Not surprising, but still horrifying, their time came. One night Renia was able to see the German tanks from afar. She recorded with pride that from the whole town, only one Jewish boy was brave enough to confront them. He ran out firing a gun, but Nazi bullets sliced him to shards. Within ten minutes, Renia wrote, the Nazis were strolling through town, entering houses and restaurants, looting food, grabbing rags for washing their horses. They took whatever they wanted.

Renia peeped through a crack from the attic where she was hiding with her family. She saw the local streets illuminated by burning houses. People were crouched in garrets and basements, doors shuttered, windows locked. Renia heard the nonstop cackling of machine-gun fire, walls being demolished, moans, cries. She craned her neck to try to make out anything else: a whole part of town was engulfed in flames.

And then. A knock at their gate. It was an iron gate, sealed with iron rods, but the German soldiers were not deterred. They smashed the windows. Renia heard their footsteps as they entered the house. Her family quickly, quietly, pulled up the ladder to the attic. Renia sat holding her breath as she heard Germans below, rummaging through the home.

Then, silence. The Nazis had left.

Unlike many of their neighbors, whose homes were looted, and whose men and boys were taken outside to be shot in a courtyard, the Kukielkas were safe. Unlike the town's wealthiest Jews, who were locked inside the grand synagogue which was doused in gasoline and set aflame, unlike locals who jumped out of burning buildings only to be shot in midair, Renia's family was not found out. Not this time.

At nine o'clock the next morning, doors began opening. Renia carefully stepped out to digest the damage. One quarter of the population of Chmielnik, a town that had been 80 percent Jewish, had been burnt alive or shot.

That was night number one.

For ten days, as Renia's shock began to thaw, a picture of her new life came into focus. Thirsty Jews were forbidden to go out on the streets to search for water. The roads stank of rotting cadavers. But after that, the Germans promised normalcy, promised no killing as long as people obeyed. Life and work resumed, but starvation had already entered their lives. Bread—now a gray, hard, and bitter substance—was rationed, and even though most bakers were Jewish, the Nazis pushed the Jews to the back of the lines. To think, Renia used to dread this time of year for its solemnity. A lover of the joyous springtime festivities of Passover and Shavuot, she'd recoiled at the sadness of the autumnal high holidays, the pleas, confessions, fasting. What she would give for a Rosh Hashanah challah now.

As soon as her father had returned, mercifully—with other men, he'd reached another town only to realize it was as dangerous as Chmielnik—the Kukielka clan decided to go back to Jędrzejów. On the daylong walk home, "just as we saw on our way the Polish army running away from the fighting, hungry and ragged, now we see an arrogant German army, full of pride."

Renia wrote, "It didn't take long, and we learned to know the German." The Nazi occupiers drove out and murdered the Jewish intelligentsia and shot groups of men accused of owning weapons. They planted a gun in a large apartment building occupied almost exclusively by Jews, and then—as a punishment for this pistol—took one man from each flat. They ordered that every single Jew in town gather for the execution. The Nazis left the innocent bodies hanging all day, swaying back and forth from the trees all along Main Street, the town's peaceful artery slashed forever.

Chapter 3
Founding the Female Fight

Zivia and Frumka
December 1939

It was New Year's Eve, and Zivia Lubetkin was in the northeast of Poland, just outside Czyzew, a town already devastated by fighting. Cold air cuffed her cheeks. *One foot in front of another.* In darkness, she clambered up winding paths, snow up to her neck, her chin frozen. Every corner, each turn, was a potential end. Zivia was the only woman here, the only Jew. The Polish students who were being transported across the Soviet-Saxon border by the same smuggler hoped that if they were caught, it would be by the Germans rather than the Russian Bolsheviks, whom they loathed. But

Zivia was "trembling with fear at the prospect of being caught by Nazis." As dawn approached, they reached German territory without incident. Zivia was back in her old Poland.

The dream for most Jews was to flee Nazi occupation; Zivia came back.

While Renia began to experience the horrors of German occupation in Jędrzejów, a new community with avant-garde ideas—one that would ultimately transform her life—was developing in other parts of Poland. Despite the war, the Jewish youth movements kept on. When the comrades returned from their summer retreats in September 1939, they did not disband but actually strengthened, constantly redeploying and reforming their missions under the leadership of a few ardent, courageous, and young leaders—many of whom could have easily fled but didn't. They stayed, or even returned, and arguably, shaped the rest of Polish Jewry.

One of those leaders was Zivia, a shy and serious young woman, born in 1914 into a lower-middle-class and religious family in the small town of Byten, where the only road was lit by kerosene lamps. Lubetkin's parents wanted her to function comfortably in Polish society, so they sent her to Polish state elementary school; she was also her after-school Hebrew teacher's star pupil and became fluent in the language. Zivia was clever, had an excellent memory, and, of her six siblings, was the one her father trusted most. Instead of attending high school, she worked in his grocery. But she was taken by the idealism of Freedom, living for its egalitarian philosophy and muscular cause. Soon she was donning baggy clothes and a leather jacket (the sartorial sign of a socialist), nearly unrecognizable to her parents on her visits home from the kibbutz that she attended against their wishes.

Thanks to her Zionist and socialist passions, her self-control, and work ethic, Zivia (meaning "gazelle" in Hebrew) made quick strides in the movement, and, despite her timidity and awkwardness, was promoted to leadership roles. (Her family used to urge her to loosen up; when guests came over, they forced her to practice giving speeches standing on a chair in the kitchen. She blushed and could barely utter a word.) At twenty-one, she was sent on a mission to lead the failing kibbutz in Kielce, a community that was crowded with "imposters" who wanted to go to Israel but did not subscribe to Freedom's principles. Her success was hard-won and evident to all; she also had romantic success and met her first boyfriend, Shmuel.

Zivia, strict with others and with herself, was unafraid to offend, always speaking her truth. Her own emotions, including self-doubt, almost never poked through her tough facade. She became known for the ease with which she settled others' disputes, and commanded respect, even from those rattled by her honesty. Each night, after completing her administrative duties, Zivia joined her female comrades for manual labor in the laundry or at the oven baking bread, and she insisted on trying men's labor too, like constructing rail lines. She once single-handedly fought off a group of hooligans who'd been taunting the comrades. A stick in her hand, she threatened them until they ran. Zivia was "the Big Sister," responsible for the whole family.

Promoted to coordinator of The Pioneer's training programs for all of Poland, Zivia moved to Warsaw, accompanied by Shmuel. The British white paper, which severely restricted Jewish immigration to Palestine, made Zivia's work even more challenging. Youth hoping to emigrate lost morale while lingering in preparation kibbutzim, but she managed to sustain educational programs and push for additional visas. Her leadership role took her to Switzerland in August 1939 as a delegate at the twenty-first Zionist Congress, a meeting of Zionist delegates from around the world. She enjoyed Geneva, liked strolling along the elegant streets, taking in the manicured lawns, the shop windows, the smartly dressed women. "If I, Zivia, ever decide to write a novel," she said, "I shall call it *From Byten to Geneva*." But despite the city's dazzle, twenty-four-year-old Zivia was eager to rejoin her pupils, poor children, and teach them the path to personal fulfillment. The delegates sensed the difficult political future ahead; many leaders found ways to flee Europe from Switzerland. Zivia was given a special certificate allowing her to travel immediately to Palestine and completely bypass the impending war.

She did not use it.

France had closed its borders, roads were blocked, trains rerouted. It was not easy for Zivia to return to Poland, but she arrived in Warsaw on August 30, right in time for the first day of Hitler's campaign. In the early days of the war's chaos, Zivia traveled to shut down movement farms and seminar sites. The Pioneer's plan B went into effect, placing her and fellow female movement leaders at the helm.

But with the immediate retreat of the Polish army, this plan, like so many that responded to the constantly shifting political reality, was revoked. Instead, Zivia and her comrades were told to head east, past the Bug River, to Russian territory, the same direction in which

Renia's family fled. For several months, the movements were based in towns that were under Soviet control, where the youth had relative freedom. During this period of upheaval, the groups solidified as strong and organized units. Zivia ensured that Freedom stayed committed to its ideals while learning how to handle new situations, like the increasingly forceful Soviet ban on religion and Jewish activity. Her new skill: quickly shifting to a new modus operandi when circumstances flipped.

As early as November 1939, dozens of branches of Freedom were active in the Soviet area, continuing to promote their Zionist, socialist, and pioneer values. Of the four main leaders, two were women: Zivia, who managed communications and intelligence, and Sheindel Schwartz, who coordinated educational activity. Sheindel was romantically involved with a third leader, Yitzhak Zuckerman, who became known by his nom de guerre, Antek.

Zivia, based in Kovel, toured the area, connecting comrades. "We raced about like madmen in the face of constant and mortal danger in an attempt to contact lost and remote members of the movement" she later wrote. She helped comrades find sustenance and comfort, but also focused on identifying escape points, trying to get people illegally to Palestine via Romania.

Even though her superiors would not let her start an underground movement to fulfill her socialist Zionist aims, Zivia persisted. "It was impossible for us not to establish the pioneer-youth underground."

She sent her boyfriend Shmuel on one of the escape routes that she'd organized, but he was caught, imprisoned, and disappeared. Devastated, Zivia kept her feelings private, and threw herself even more fiercely into work.

Zivia was in demand. Serious Frumka, who had already returned to Warsaw to lead the youth there, wrote to the Freedom leadership to request that her dear friend Zivia return too, claiming that she'd be the best person to deal with the new Nazi government. Everyone senior had fled Warsaw, leaving that vital city with only second-tier captains who were ill-prepared to liaise with German authorities or with Poles.

Because of the growing Soviet threat, Zivia was supposed to relocate to Vilna, a city newly controlled by Lithuania, which she felt was Freedom's way of protecting her. She resisted this coddling, insisting that she go to Warsaw to help guide her movement, to comfort the youth whose lives had been thrown into chaos, and to promote pioneer education and Labor Zionist goals. As usual, she made her own decisions and plunged headfirst into the fire.

On New Year's Eve 1939, Freedom held an all-night conference, which was part fete, part first official underground meeting. "We ate, drunk, and made merry," Zivia wrote later, "and between drinks discussed the Movement and its future course." In a member's apartment in Lvov, Zivia feasted on chocolate, sausage, and black bread with butter, and listened as leaders reiterated the importance of keeping the Zionist flame alive, of "upholding Jewish humanity" in the Soviet area and in German-occupied Poland.

That night, despite pleas from Antek, the tall, blond, and handsome coleader with whom Zivia had become increasingly close, she left in the direction of Nazi-occupied Poland, afraid of what she'd encounter and doubting whether she would be able to withstand life in the new regime. She was saddened to leave friends with whom she'd spent stormy months engaged in dangerous work, whom she'd come to rely on to greet her at the end of difficult missions. But Zivia was also determined. "While I was still preoccupied with these grim thoughts," she later testified, "the train thundered to the platform, and people pushed their way into the cars." She felt warm hands, warms tears, and then she too was off, lurching away from her comrades.

Zivia was smuggled back into Nazi territory in a plan arranged by Frumka. She endured a long journey of train rides and that all-night, snow-drenched hike alongside a group of male Polish students who were trying to get home. Once the group reached the border town, their courteous attitude toward Zivia changed. In Soviet land, a Jewish mate was an asset, but in Nazi territory, Zivia became an inferior being. At the station, they watched as a German slapped a group of Jews and told them they could not wait in the same waiting room as Poles and Aryans. Zivia's group complained that she too should be removed, but she didn't react. "I clenched my teeth and didn't move an inch." Zivia had to develop a new type of inner strength; the ability to hold her head high in the fog of degradation. The train car was nearly pitch black—there was no lighting— and everyone hid from the Germans. A man heaved a sigh, and Zivia watched as he was brutally attacked by a group of Poles who accused him of giving "a Jewish sigh." He was thrown out of the carriage.

It was now 1940. A brand-new year. A brand-new experience of being a Jew—from pride to humiliation. And, she thought, as her train rolled into Central Station, past the grand boulevards and open squares of pecking pigeons, a brand-new Warsaw.

Jews had arrived relatively late to Warsaw. Antisemitic laws banned them from the Middle Ages until French emperor Napoléon I's conquest in the early eighteen hundreds. Jews financed his wars, initiating the city's Jewish banking culture. In the mid-nineteenth century, by then under Russian occupation, the Jewish population increased, and a small class of assimilated, "progressive" Jews developed in this verdant metropolis that spread along both banks of the Vistula River, bustling with vendors and trams, and crowned by a striking medieval castle.

After 1860, when the Jews from the Pale of Settlement—the Russian territory where they had been allowed to settle—were permitted access to the city, the population exploded. By 1914, Jews were a dominating force in Warsaw's industry, and finally authorized to settle wherever they wanted. Jewish culture— theater, education, newspapers, publications, political parties—proliferated; the population comprised both the urban impoverished and the wealthy cosmopolitan. The thriving community was symbolized by its Great Synagogue, a grandiose building consecrated in 1878. The largest synagogue in the world, it was designed by Warsaw's leading architect, with elements of imperial

Russian style. Not a traditional prayer house, it hosted an elite congregation, with an organ, a choir, and sermons delivered in Polish. The spectacular edifice was a marker of Jews' prosperity and acculturation—and of Poland's tolerance.

The Warsaw that Zivia knew was the epicenter of all prewar Jewish life. When the Nazis invaded, 375,000 Jews of all backgrounds called it home, about a third of the capital's population. (For contrast, in 2020, Jews make up roughly 13 percent of New York City's population.)

Zivia had been gone barely four months, but came back to a dramatically divided landscape: non-Jewish Warsaw and Jewish Warsaw were now two different territories. She immediately noticed that the streets were crowded—with Poles only. Antisemitic legislation had been put into place right after the occupation, with new discriminatory regulations passing each day. Jews were no longer allowed to work in Christian factories or take trains without special permission. Only a few Jews were visible on the avenues, with the white armbands they were forced to wear—their "badges of shame"— stepping quickly, their eyes darting to ensure they weren't being followed. Zivia froze, horrified. How would she ever get used to this? But then she wondered whether the Jews wore their bands defiantly, in secret contempt for their oppressors. She held this thought and let it reassure her.

The roads were filled with elegant cars, carriages, red trams. But Zivia preferred to walk rather than take the streetcar. She wanted to see up close the dynamic city she'd left behind; the city she recalled for its café terraces, balconies adorned with flowers, and lush parks lined with mothers, nannies, and their ornate prams. She'd heard rumors of the city's ruin, but now, with her first steps into town, aside from a few bombed buildings, things looked quite as they had been. Poles filled the streets, business as usual. "There was a pleasant feeling in the air," she recalled, "as if nothing had happened." The only change came with the appearance of German convoys down the streets, scattering the terrorized population.

And then there was the old Jewish neighborhood. Zivia headed straight for The Pioneer headquarters. She found a pile of rubble. Here it was clear that times had changed. Zivia was reentering a new world, with Jews hiding in the shadows, fearing open air, clinging to buildings to avoid contact with a German and whatever humiliation might be inflicted.

Searching for Jews of "a different mettle," Zivia headed to the Freedom headquarters at 34 Dzielna

Street, where many movement members had lived before the war. Dzielna, four three-storey buildings set around a courtyard, had always been a lively locale, but Zivia was stunned by the thick crowd, which included hundreds of comrades who'd made it to Warsaw from small towns. They, in turn, were shocked, and elated, to see her. The man in charge of food threw a spontaneous party in her honor, declaring it "an official holiday," serving extra rations of bread and jam. Zivia and Frumka huddled affectionately, reviewing everything that had happened since the Nazis attacked, what had been done, and, most important, what had to be done next.

One can imagine Frumka's joy at seeing her old friend and trusted comrade Zivia walk into their headquarters. For several months, she had been a main leader of the Freedom movement in Warsaw, helping to reestablish Dzielna as a site of family, of warmth, hope, and passion, despite all the new horrors.

Born near the overwhelmingly Jewish and intellectual eastern city of Pinsk, Frumka Plotnicka was the same age as Zivia, twenty-five, which suddenly made them among the eldest members of the group. Frumka, with her pronounced features, her high forehead and straight hair, was the middle of three daughters in a poor Hasidic family that followed the Karliner rabbi, whose values included straightforwardness and the pursuit of perfection. Frumka's father had trained to be a rabbi but, on his rabbi's advice, instead became a merchant in order to support his family. The family business was the steer trade. Unfortunately, he was not a natural steer trader. Frumka's parents could not afford to educate her, so she was taught by her older sister, Zlatka, a sharp thinker who excelled at a *gymnasium* (Polish prep school). Zlatka was a Communist who, like their father, held her emotions close.

Frumka, on the other hand, was like their mother: industrious, devoted, and humble. An ardent socialist Zionist, she joined Freedom at age seventeen and was fully committed—an extra sacrifice for a poor girl whose family needed her help. Though she was a deeply analytic thinker, she was awkward, with a serious and somber demeanor. She had trouble connecting with people and sustaining friendships, and remained on the sidelines of the movement for some time. Through activity, however, Frumka channeled her turbulent emotions and her natural compassion. She cared for comrades and insisted that a sick member stay at the training camp rather than go home; she managed retreats, organizing everything from curricula to catering, and disciplined the youths, getting lazy ones to work, and refusing handouts from local farmers. She shone in a crisis, where her moral compass was unwavering.

"In gray times, she hid in a corner," a senior emissary wrote about her, "but in critical moments, she held herself at its head. Suddenly she revealed greater merit and virtue than anyone; her moral vigor, the intensity of her analysis always led to action." Frumka, he continued, had the unique ability to "unite her capabilities at analyzing life experience with gentleness, love, and motherly worry." Another friend explained, "Her heart never beat to the rhythm of minutia. She seemed to be waiting for the big moments where she could unload the love inside her."

Frumka could usually be found wrapped in her wool coat, in a dark crook of the room, listening. Really listening. She remembered every detail. On other occasions, she would suddenly address the whole room in her "magical accent"—a folksy, literary Yiddish. One comrade recalled a spontaneous speech she gave "about the fears of a Jewish girl who found her way but still hasn't found peace in her heart." She gripped everyone's attention with her simplicity and sincerity: "the blush in her face turned into fire." A friend wrote a story about their time together in the Białystok public garden, noting how Frumka skipped through the flowers, entranced by their beauty.

Frumka's soft chin rounded out her stark features, revealing her warmth. Comrades appreciated her composure and passion, and she was constantly being asked for advice. Like shy Zivia, Frumka had been an obedient introvert, and she, too, surprised family with her leadership role. If dedicated, no-nonsense Zivia was the group's big sister, then empathetic, gentle Frumka became "Die Mameh" (the mother, in Yiddish).

After slowly ascending the ranks, one rung at a time, and traveling around the country teaching seminars, Frumka moved to Warsaw to work for The Pioneer headquarters with Zivia. In the summer of 1939, activity proliferated, but emissaries from Palestine began postponing their visits, and Frumka took on senior responsibilities. Moving to Eretz Israel, the "land that's all sun," was her dream. She was supposed to make "aliyah" (emigrate to Palestine) that summer, but the leadership asked her to wait until the fall. She dutifully accepted, even though her yearnings overwhelmed her, and she was terrified of never making it. Indeed, it was not a good fall.

Once war broke out, Frumka went east as instructed. But fleeing a crisis did not suit her, and she immediately asked the Freedom leaders to let her leave the area where her family lived and return to Nazi-occupied Warsaw. Her comrades were stunned. Frumka was the first one to go back.

Now Zivia was here too.

Frumka and Zivia found themselves a secluded corner in a quiet room, and Frumka filled Zivia in on all that she'd achieved at Dzielna over the past three months. The commune provided refuge for youth fleeing their towns; most of its residents were women. Frumka led them in establishing aid initiatives and became known around town for providing food, employment, and comfort in these times of hunger, confusion, and scattered families. The ethos of Freedom had shifted: it no longer focused solely on its movement and pioneering goals but on helping the suffering Jewish masses. Zivia, who'd always championed social equality, was immediately on board.

With support from "the Joint"—the American Joint Distribution Committee, or JDC, founded in 1914 to aid Jews across the world—Frumka established a public soup kitchen that fed six hundred Jews. She set up study groups, spearheaded collaborations with other movements, and housed nonmovement people in any available room. Just across from the infamously brutal Pawiak Prison, in an area filled with police, spies, and lethal gunshots, this buzzing nest of revolutionaries inspired new thoughts and action. According to a female Freedom youth group counselor, "The Pioneers longed to live, to act, to realize dreams. . . . Here one did not run away from the truth, but also, didn't make peace with it. . . . The work broke bodies and ruined spirits, but in the evening, when everyone assembled in our house on Dzielna, we felt no anger." Zivia sensed the warm camaraderie and positive spirit that infused the space, thanks to Frumka and the young women around her.

Frumka had also been working outside Dzielna, even outside Warsaw, prescient about the need to forge long-distance connections. She'd dressed up as a non-Jew, covering her face with a kerchief, and traveled to Łódź and Będzin to glean information. The Freedom kibbutz in Będzin ran a laundry and served as a hub, helping local refugees. In Łódź, the commune was led almost entirely by women who had refused to flee, including Frumka's sister Hanzte, as well as Rivka Glanz and Leah Pearlstein. The women sewed for the Germans who, on many occasions, threatened to confiscate their equipment. Each time, feisty and responsible Leah stood up to the Nazis. She always won.

That first evening, together with other Freedom leaders, Zivia and Frumka decided to focus on finding escape routes to Palestine as per their Zionist goals, and also on community aid. To do both, they needed to uphold the movement's values, while keeping its regional kibbutzim strong.

Not to be outdone by Frumka's activity, Zivia barely took a moment to rest at Dzielna before she was off. First, to make connections and begin lobbying at the Judenrat.

Early on, the Nazis decided to pit Jew against Jew. The ghettos, they decreed, would be managed and whipped into shape by Jews themselves—not the elected *kahals*, that had governed Jewish communities for centuries, but by Nazi-controlled councils, or Judenrats. Each Judenrat registered all Jewish citizens, issued birth certificates and business permits, collected taxes, distributed ration cards, organized labor forces and social services, and oversaw its own Jewish police or militia. In Warsaw, these militiamen—who wore caps and boots and wielded rubber clubs—were mainly educated middle-class men, often young lawyers and university graduates. To many, including Renia, the militias enlisted "only the worst type of people," who dutifully fulfilled Gestapo orders, searching, regulating, and surveilling Jews. Some Jews claimed that they were forced into the Judenrat at the risk of being killed; some hoped that by volunteering to participate, they would save their families (they didn't) or even help the larger community. The Judenrats as an institution were a tool to suppress Jews, but the subjective will of their many individual members varied, and their tone varied by ghetto. These were heterogeneous groups, with players ranging from heroic helpers to Nazi collaborators.

Unlike others who feared the Judenrat, seeing them as Gestapo puppets, Zivia badgered them for additional food ration permits. Hair unbrushed, a cigarette dangling permanently from her lips, as if her "vexations dissolved in the rings of smoke that she blew," she became an enduring fixture in the halls of the main Jewish community organizations. She spent entire days at 5 Tlomackie, the Jewish Self-Help organization, with its white, marble pillars and grand, open hallways. Built adjacent to the Great Synagogue in the 1920s, the building had been Warsaw's Judaic Library and the first Jewish research center in Europe that focused on both theological and secular studies. In wartime, it became the center of Jewish mutual aid.

There, Zivia spent afternoons haggling with the heads of the JDC and welfare organizations, exchanging information with youth group leaders, trading underground publications, and convincing rich Jews to loan her significant sums. She was in charge of the money sent to Warsaw for the Zionist youth groups, and the recipient of secret correspondence from foreign units. At night, Zivia toiled with her female comrades in the laundry. Eating little herself, and growing so thin she worried others, she was constantly giving members pep talks, listening to their woes, and, of course, jolting them with her straight talk. The young comrades adored her lack of pretension, quick decision-making, and frank advice.

In a climate of hunger and humiliation, Zivia felt responsible for feeding and housing the youth and tried her best to protect them from being abducted and sent to work camps. In Warsaw, all Jews aged twelve to sixty were subject to forced labor, a violent and abusive situation they all feared constantly. To obtain workers, the Germans would cordon off a street and snatch all the Jews who happened to be there—even those running home with a slice of bread for their children. People were herded into trucks and driven away to do hard labor while being beaten and starved. Zivia intervened on several occasions, freeing captured comrades, a string of cigarette smoke tracing each of her movements.

A main project of hers was negotiating the reestab-
lishment and maintenance of communal training farms,
which, so far, had been spared by the Nazis. During
the war, the farms in Grochów and Czerniaków became important sites for labor, employing in the fields,
flower gardens, and dairy farms youths who might
otherwise have been abducted. They also served as
centers for education, with singing and dancing. Zivia
used to travel extensively in her attempts to coordinate
educational activities in the regions, but she particularly enjoyed visiting these leafy landscapes, where at
night she could expose her Jewish features and revel in
the relative freedom, and which served as escapes from
hunger, lice, and the rampant epidemics of Warsaw, not
to mention random shootings and daily torture.

Later in the war, Zivia used to bribe a Jewish policeman, scale the ghetto wall, and leave via the cemetery. Then she'd fume at the waste of time it took
to get out. This is also how Zivia would accompany
émigrés out of the ghetto: slip cash at the right instant and then cross the gate, carrying a briefcase, appearing like an assured schoolgirl striding down the
street, ready for a day's work.

But for now, there was no walled ghetto in Warsaw. Despite despair, confusion, and the odd violent
episode, there was not even the premonition of the

imprisonment and murder that was to come; the youths' worst fear was that pogroms would erupt among Poles when the Nazis inevitably lost and retreated. For now, these young Jews were simply busy social activists, passing on pioneer values by teaching history and social theory. For now, they were busy strengthening units that would soon come to serve a wholly, and holy, different purpose.

One day in spring 1940, Zivia returned to Dzielna to find the usual hum of activity. Also, Antek.

He too had returned to Nazi-occupied territory. Some suspected he'd followed Zivia. Guarding her emotions, Zivia wrote nothing about their personal relations; Antek, on the other hand, reminisced about their earliest interactions. Once, back in Kovel, when Zivia was sick, he trekked out in the mud to bring her fish and cake. Instead of a warm thanks, she scolded him for looking so messy. "I was amazed at her nerve," he said. "She was talking like a wife." Months later, he saw her deliver an impassioned lecture, pounding her fist with verve—and fell in love.

Antek joined Zivia and Frumka as leaders, and they built up Freedom in Warsaw and the provinces. Despite her "Jewish nose" and "halting" Polish, Frumka maintained connections between Warsaw headquarters and the Polish towns, offering support and recruiting new members. She traveled more and more, to lead seminars and maintain cross-country connections among the movement, but also, some guessed, to avoid Antek and Zivia. She was rather fond of Antek, but it was increasingly clear that his romantic interest was directed entirely at her best friend.

At Dzielna, Zivia (and Frumka, when she was there, and Antek) enhanced the mood in the evenings by sharing an anecdote from the day, a quiet song, a short play—all behind draped windows. The community drew courage from stories of bravery in Jewish history. They read books, learned Hebrew, and engaged in stormy discussions. They maintained their beliefs in compassion and social action in a world of terror, murder, and every man for himself. They hoped to build strong Jews who would survive the war (most of them, they still thought). They were preparing for a future they still believed in. A light mood existed among the members—a "spirit of freedom," as was once articulated by the famed poet Yitzhak Katzenelson, who lived and taught at Dzielna for several months.

"Zivia" became the secret code name for the entire movement in Poland.

Chapter 4

To See Another Morning—
Terror in the Ghetto

Renia
April 1940

While it's true that the horrors of the Holocaust evolved as a series of small steps, each one a mild escalation compared with the last, building toward mass genocide, for Renia, the terror of the early war cleaved her life irreparably into "before" and "after." The job she'd successfully found as a court secretary disappeared, her hopes for a future vanished. Renia's life was turned inside out.

In 1940 decree upon decree was passed in communities throughout Poland, including the tiny town of Jędrzejów. These rulings were intended to single out, humiliate, and weaken the Jews. Also, to identify them. The Germans could not differentiate between a Pole and a Jew, so Renia and all Jews older than ten were forced to wear a white ribbon with a blue Star of David at the elbow. If the ribbon was dirty, or its width incorrect, they could be punished by death. Jews had to take off their hats when they passed Nazis; they could not walk on the sidewalk. Renia watched, sickened, as Jewish property was seized and gifted over to *folksdeutsch*: Poles of part-German heritage who applied for this elevated status. Suddenly, she wrote, the poorest Poles became millionaires, and Jews became servants in their own homes, forced to pay rent and teach the *folksdeutsch* to manage their former mansions. Then the Jewish families were thrown out altogether, becoming panhandlers on the streets. Their shops were taken over. Their belongings, especially gold, fur, jewels, and valuables that they hadn't managed to hide in their gardens or tuck under loose kitchen tiles, were confiscated. Leah passed her Singer sewing machine and fine candlesticks to a Polish neighbor for safekeeping. Renia overheard Poles window-shopping as they walked through town, fantasizing about what might become theirs next.

In April a forced "Jewish neighborhood" was established, an initiative that many Jews hoped would help protect them. Renia's family—except for Sarah, who had already joined a Freedom kibbutz; and Zvi, who had escaped to Russia—were told that they had two days to relocate their entire lives to an area a few blocks off the town's main square: a squalid locale of small low-rise buildings and narrow alleys that had previously housed the town's riffraff. They had to abandon furniture, property—almost everything, except a small satchel and some linen. Accounts tell of mothers who did not sleep all night as they frantically packed, their children running to and fro, moving all they could carry on their backs or in baskets: clothing, food, pots, pets, soap, coats, shoehorns, sewing materials, and other means of livelihood. Hidden jewels were plastered to bodies. A gold bracelet was sewn into the sleeve of a sweater. Money was baked into cookies.

The crowding was impossible. Every apartment housed several families, sleeping on floors or improvised bunkbeds—Renia slept on a sack of flour. Fifty people could be crammed into a small home. Rare photos of ghetto dwellings show multiple families sharing a former synagogue sanctuary, rows of siblings sleeping on the bimah and under pews. A person barely had room to stretch his or her arms. Personal space did not exist. Sometimes Jews were lucky to know someone who lived in the ghetto area and moved in with them;

most, though, had to live with strangers, often with differing habits. Jews from surrounding villages and from varying classes were forced together, increasing tension, disrupting the normal social order.

Even if people brought furniture, there was no room for it. Makeshift beds were dismantled during the days to make space for washing and eating; clothes hung from single nails attached to walls; small tubs were used to wash body parts and the laundry, which dried on neighbors' roofs. Tables and chairs sat in piles outside. As the weeks dragged on, Renia's family used the staples of their old life as firewood. Fundamentals up in flames.

All told, the Germans established more than four hundred ghettos in Poland, with the objective of decimating the Jewish population through disease and starvation and concentrating the Jews so they could easily be rounded up and transported to labor and death camps. This was a massive operation, and each ghetto had slightly different rules and qualities, depending on local Jewish culture, local Nazi rule, its natural landscape, and its internal leadership. Still, many elements of ghetto policy were standard across the country, from remote town to even more remote village, including imprisonment.

At first, the Kukielkas were allowed to leave the ghetto in order to work and buy food; likewise, Poles could enter the gate and bring bread to trade for valuables. But soon, as in all ghettos, access was shut down. Jews could leave only with a passage certificate issued by the Judenrat. From 1941 on, no movement across the ghetto boundary—for Jew or Pole—was permitted. A physical fence sealed off part of the area, a river another. Eventually, stepping out meant nothing less than execution.

And yet . . .

Renia put on layer after layer: stockings, another pair, a dress on top, thick as a Polish peasant would wear. Esther wore two coats and a kerchief. Fumbling in the dark, Bela helped fasten her sisters' outfits before folding several shirts into to her waistband, feigning a pregnant belly. They all stuffed small articles into their pockets, fabric inside fabric; a palimpsest of merchandise and disguise, everything on the body. This, Renia reminded herself, was how she could help her mother, her little brother, the family.

For a second, the teenager flashed to a land far away, which was really just a few miles over and a few months past—before her middle-class life disintegrated. She daydreamed of how her mother, a force of nature, had taken care of everything: cooked, cleaned, managed the money. Their Polish neighbors used to approach Leah in disbelief. "How can you clothe seven children on your wages and make them look so rich?" In Yiddish, Leah was a *balabasta:* a virtuoso homemaker who always had a house filled with educated, well-behaved kids and their friends yet kept it miraculously tidy and ordered. She had her answers ready: *"Buy expensive clothing because it keeps. Then pass it on. And get each child a pair of handmade shoes—a size too big. Room to grow."*

What you wore, how you wore it. Now the girls were wearing it all as both costume and livelihood. It was almost nine o'clock at night—time to go. They waved a quick good-bye and together made their way down the street, out of the ghetto. Renia never revealed how she exited this ghetto, but she may have bribed a guard, squeezed through a loose slat or grate, climbed over a wall, through a cellar, or across a roof. These were all ways that smugglers—mostly women—came in and out of Poland's Jewish confines.

Because Jewish men were often kidnapped, they stayed home. Women, from impoverished to high society, became the foragers, selling cigarettes, bras, objets d'art, even their bodies. It was also easier for children to creep out of the ghetto and seek food. The ghettos created a whole cascade of role reversals.

The Kukielka sisters made it to the village and began walking up and down the streets. Stepping quickly, Renia thought of how she used to go with her mother to the bakery every Friday, picking out cookies, all colors and shapes. Now, bread ration cards: ten decagrams a day, or a quarter of a small loaf. Selling bread beyond the allowed quantity or price meant execution.

Renia approached a house. Every step was a risk. Who knew who could see her standing there? Poles? Germans? Militiamen? Whoever answered the door could report her. Or shoot her. Or the person might pretend to buy, then simply not pay and threaten to turn her in to the Gestapo for a reward. Then what could she do? To think that Renia used to work in the courthouse with lawyers, justice, laws that made sense. No longer. Night after night, women went out like this, mothers, too, trying to feed their families.

Other girls helped their families by performing forced labor for municipalities or private enterprise. All Jews aged fourteen to seventy-five were supposed to work, but sometimes younger girls wore high heels to look older because they wanted food. Some Jews were forced to be tailors, seamstresses, and carpenters;

others were put to work dismantling houses, repairing roads, cleaning streets, and unloading bombs from trains (which sometimes went off and killed them). Even though Jewish women walked miles to work to break rocks, often in knee-deep snow and bone-chilling slush, starving, their clothes torn, they would be beaten mercilessly if they asked for a rest. People hid their injuries, dying later of infection. Body parts froze. Bones were broken in beatings.

"No one says a word," described one young female laborer about her four-o'-clock-in-the-morning marches to work, surrounded by Nazi guards. "I take care not to step on the heels of the person in front of me, trying in darkness to estimate his pace and the length of his strides. I pass through the vapor of his exhalation, the odor of unwashed clothing, and the stench of the overcrowded nighttime homes." Then there were the late arrivals home covered in bruises, stiff, disappointed that they hadn't been able to sneak even a carrot for their families because of ghetto gate searches. Despite their terror of being beaten, the workers went back to their job sites the next day, including mothers, leaving their children to take care of themselves. What else could they do?

Caring for families in the ghettos, keeping Jewish children alive—physically and spiritually nurturing the next generation—was a mother's form of resistance. Men were wrested away or ran away, but women stayed to look after their children and often their parents. Like Leah, many were familiar with budgeting money and apportioning food, only now they had to work with extreme deprivation. A day's stamps—which procured dishes like bitter cornbread made from grains, stems, and leaves; a few groats; pinches of salt; a handful of potatoes—did not provide adequate nourishment even for breakfast alone.

The poor suffered the most, Renia noted, as they could not afford goods sold on the black market. A mother would do just about anything to avoid having to watch her children starve—"the worst kind of death," Renia reflected later. Unable to provide basic existential needs, they foraged for nutrients, hid their children from violence and, later, deportations (silencing them in hiding spots, and sometimes forced to smother their own crying babies), and treated illness as best they could without medication. The women in the ghetto, always vulnerable to sexual assault, went out to work or smuggle, risking being caught and leaving their children alone in the world. Others handed over their babies to Polish caregivers, often with hefty sums of money, and sometimes had to watch from a distance as their children were abused or told lies about them. In the end, countless mothers who could have been spared for work ultimately went to the gas chambers with their children, refusing to let them die alone—comforting and holding them to the last second.

When husbands remained, marital conflicts often erupted. Men, who arguably had less tolerance for hunger, tended to eat whatever food they found. Women had to hide rations. Sex in cramped quarters and between starving bodies was usually not a possibility, also adding to the tension. According to the Łódź ghetto records, many couples filed for divorce, despite the fact that being single made one more susceptible to deportation and death. In many cases, they were the first generation to enjoy love matches rather than arranged unions, but romantic bonds disintegrated with chronic hunger, torture, and terror.

Women, who had been trained in domestic skills, also took great care to delouse, clean, and stay primped—skills that helped them survive emotionally and physically. Women, some said, suffered more from the lack of hygiene than even from starvation.

Despite best efforts to cope, the insufficient food, crowding, and lack of running water and sanitation had led to a typhus epidemic in the Jędrzejów ghetto. Each infected house was shuttered, and the sick were taken to a Jewish hospital set up especially for this disease, which spread through lice. Most patients died from lack of treatment. Special bathhouses disinfected bodies and clothes, often rendering the garments unwearable. Renia heard rumors that the Germans prohibited treating typhus patients and ordered the sick to be poisoned. (The Nazis were notoriously germophobic. In Kraków, noninfected Jews mingled at the contagious hospital to save their lives.)

Hunger, infestation, the stench of unwashed bodies, the lack of work and of any daily schedule, and the constant fear of being snatched for forced labor and beaten was the everyday reality. Children played Nazi-versus-Jew in the streets. A little girl yelled at her kitten not to leave the ghetto without its papers. There was no money for Hanukkah candles or Shabbat challahs. Even affluent Jews ran out of the money they'd brought into the ghetto or the money they received selling goods. While their items sold to Poles for next to nothing, the black market was exorbitant. A loaf of bread in the Warsaw ghetto cost a Jew the equivalent of $60 today.

Now, at the door, was Renia's chance; she was desperate for funds. Like so many Jewish women across the country, she did not think of herself as a political person. She was not part of any organization, yet here she was, risking her life in action. She reached out her fist, each knock a potential bullet.

A woman answered, ready to bargain. *They buy happily*, Renia thought. *They have nothing else to spend money on.* Hastily, she offered a small amount of coal. Renia asked for a few coins, so much less than the heirloom lace placemats were worth. "Okay." Then she walked away quickly, heart thumping. She fingered the change in her pocket. Measly, but at least she had done something.

One morning, the dreaded knock. The militia. An order. The Jewish community was directed to select 220 strong, healthy men to be taken to a forced-labor camp outside of town. Renia's younger brother Aaron was on the list.

The Kukielkas pleaded with him not to go, but he feared the threat of noncompliance: that his whole family would be executed. Renia's insides burnt as she watched his tall, blond figure disappear out the door. The group was gathered in the firehouse, where they were examined by doctors and tortured by the Gestapo, forced to sing Jewish songs, dance Jewish dances, and beat one another up until they bled, while the Gestapo laughed. When the bus arrived to take them away, the Gestapo—armed with dogs and machine guns—hit any lingerers with such force that the other boys had to carry them onto the bus.

Renia's brother told her later that he'd been sure he was being taken to his execution, but to his surprise, he was delivered to a forced-labor camp near Lvov. This may have been the Janowska camp, a transit camp that also had a factory where Jews were made to toil for free in carpentry and metalwork. The Nazis established more than forty thousand camps to facilitate the murder of "undesirable races," including transit camps, concentration camps, extermination camps, labor camps, and combinations. The SS leased some of the labor camps to private companies, which paid it per slave. Women cost less, and so companies were drawn to "leasing" them and putting them to work at arduous hard labor. At state-owned and private labor camps across Poland, conditions were atrocious, and people died from starvation, constant beatings, illness from the unsanitary surrounds, and exhaustion from overwork. In the early years of war, labor camp prisoners were demoralized by being forced to carry out humiliating and often pointless tasks, like stone breaking; with time, the need for workers to help meet the demands of the German army intensified as did the tasks. The daily menu at one camp consisted of a slice of bread and a bowl of black soup made with vetch, a crop that fed animals and tasted like boiled pepper. The prospect of being enslaved in a forced labor camp terrified the Jewish youth.

Despite the country's utter social collapse, postal networks still functioned, and one day a letter arrived. Shaking, Renia unfolded the pages to find that Aaron was alive. But the horrors of his life shocked her: the boys slept in animal stables on straw that was never changed; they worked from dawn to dusk, and were starving and freezing, eating wild berries and weeds picked from the ground. They were beaten daily, carried home on their friends' shoulders. At night, they were forced to do calisthenics, and if they couldn't keep up—death. Lice chewed through their flesh. There was no sink. No toilet. The stench was deadly. Then came dysentery. Realizing their days were numbered, many boys escaped; because of their conspicuous clothing in the winter cold they had to avoid towns and cut through forests and fields. The Gestapo started chasing after the escapees, while torturing the boys who remained.

Renia immediately sent her brother care packages. She included clothes with money sewn into the pockets so that he could buy a ticket home if he managed to run away. She watched out daily for any retuning escapees. The sight of them was sickening: skin and bones, bodies covered with ulcers and rashes, clothes full of insects, limbs swollen. Boys suddenly looked like frail old men. Where was Aaron?

So many Jews were sent to the unknown. "A father, brother, sister, or mother," Renia wrote. "Every family had one person missing."

But everything can become relative. Renia would soon come to know that only "one person missing" was good. Even "one person alive" meant you were lucky.

Renia knew that she had to make her own luck.

One night, dusk weighing down on the ghetto's ramshackle roofs, a notice arrived. Each message, every thin note, had the potential to change your life forever; to smash whatever fragile comfort you had managed to construct in order to cope. Now the Kukielkas, along with the other 399 wealthiest families in the ghetto, were being forced to leave town. By midnight.

Renia had seen how the rich tried to pay their way out of decrees, bribing the Judenrat to put workers in their place, or hiring laborers to work instead of them. People dealt with hardship in the ways they knew, playing systems the way they always had—only now the games had no rules. The rich were respected only by other Jews; Germans didn't care. The wealthiest families tried to pay their way out of this forced departure too, but the Judenrat's coffers were filled from previous bribes—in fact, they gave each wealthy family fifty złotys toward relocation costs.

The Kukielkas frantically packed their possessions onto a sled and were off into the middle of the night. It was freezing in Wodzisław, where they were dumped. This was part of the Germans' plan, Renia deduced: shuttling Jews from town to town for no reason other than to shame and depress them. Renia shivered, pulled her coat tighter around her (lucky to still have one), and observed, helpless, as hysterical mothers watched their babies' flesh turn blue from the cold. The Jews of Wodzisław let the mothers and their half-dead babies into the sheep pens in their yards, which at least protected them somewhat from the howling winds.

Eventually all the Jews were herded into the freezing synagogue, icicles hanging from the walls, and fed soup from a communal kitchen. Once the most affluent and influential people in their community, they now accepted that the only important thing was to stay alive. "The result was that the Germans hardened the hearts of the Jews," Renia wrote, sensing the toughening of her own core. "Now each person cared only for themselves, willing to steal food out of the mouth of their brethren." As a survivor remarked about the callousing of the soul that took place over time in the Warsaw ghetto: "If you saw a dead body on the street, you took its shoes."

As in all the ghettos, the decrees only became more barbaric.

"One day the Germans invented a new way to kill Jews," Renia wrote. Was it possible to feel more terrorized? Somehow, despite it all, the shock had not yet faded. With each sadistic innovation, Renia felt a sick haunting, a deeper sense of the boundless malice, the myriad ways that her murderers might inflict violence. "At night, a bus full of Gestapo would arrive, drunk out of their minds." They came with a list of thirty names, grabbed these men, women, and children from their houses, and beat and shot them. Renia heard yelling and firing, and, in the morning, saw bodies strewn in the alleys, black and blue from flogging. The families' unbearable wails broke Renia's heart. Each time, she imagined that one of her own might be next. It took days for the community to calm down after these incidents: Who had made up this list of names? Who did one have to be careful around? Whose bad side were you on? People were afraid to even speak.

This is how Jews in the ghetto came to feel fully occupied. Their territory, their skin, even their thoughts were threatened. Anything they did or said—the smallest movement or motion—could result in their execution and their entire families'. Every element of their physical and spiritual existence was under surveillance. "No one could breathe, cough, or cry without having an audience," described a young female ghetto dweller. Who could be trusted? Who was listening? To have a candid conversation with an old friend required prearranging a meeting spot, then walking together as if on a household chore. Polish Jews feared that even their dreams would somehow betray them.

Sometimes the Gestapo arrived in the ghetto at night and simply shot people to death. One night the whole Judenrat and all their families were executed. On another memorable evening, several buses of Gestapo forced Jews, half naked, barefoot in nightclothes, to go outside and run around the snow-filled market while the Gestapo chased them with rubber clubs, or told them to lie in the snow for thirty minutes, or forced them to flog their fellow Jews with whips, or to lie on the ground and have a military vehicle run over them. The Nazis poured water over freezing people and made them stand at attention. "You never knew if you'd wake up alive the next morning" was Renia's new reality. Why did she?

Daytime nightmares began. Machine guns echoed in the forest. Nazis had Jews dig their own graves and made them sing and dance in the pits until they shot them. They forced other Jews to bury the victims—or, sometimes, bury them alive. Elderly Jews were also made to sing and dance, the Nazis plucking out their beard hairs one by one and slapping them until they spat out their teeth.

The ghetto was a closed-off society—no radios allowed—but Renia sleuthed for information. Hundreds of women were taken to unknown locations, never to be heard from again. A candid soldier revealed to her that these women were sent to the front to serve as prostitutes. They contracted sexually transmitted diseases and were burnt alive or shot to death. She listened raptly as he told her that one time, he saw hundreds of young women revolt. They attacked the Nazis, stealing their bayonets, wounding them, gouging out their eyes, and then killing themselves, screaming that they would never be made into prostitutes. The girls who remained alive were eventually subdued and raped.

What was a fifteen-year-old to do? Renia remained vigilant, knowing instinctively that she had to gather information and face the truth. She listened to rumors streaming in from other towns. People were starving to death en masse, begging for potato peels, food trash.

Jews were taking their own lives and killing their own children so they wouldn't fall into German hands. Whole transports—sometimes ten thousand Jews—were forced to walk from the ghetto to the train station; they left cities to unknown locations. People were sorted and allegedly taken to work. Jewish communities heard from a select few who, it was thought, were intentionally left alive by the Germans to misinform them. Most people simply disappeared. "They leave as if into an abyss," Renia wrote. Where were they all going?

Collective punishment was the Nazi way. The SS decreed that any Pole who helped a Jew would be killed. Ghetto Jews feared that if they escaped, their entire families would be murdered in retaliation. Stay and protect your community? Or run? *Fight, flight.*

The slaughtering was constant. Extermination committees made up of *folksdeutsch*, "Ukrainian savages," as Renia wrote, and "young, healthy Germans for whom human life meant nothing" set to work. "They were always bloodthirsty," Renia explained about the Nazis and their collaborators. "It was their nature. Just like an addiction to alcohol or opium." These "black dogs" wore black uniforms and hats decorated with skulls. When they showed up with their hardened faces, bulging eyes, and large teeth—wild animals ready to pounce—everyone knew that half the population would be executed that day. The second they entered the ghetto, people scurried to hide.

"For them," Renia wrote, "killing a person was easier than smoking a cigarette."

Chapter 5
The Warsaw Ghetto—
Education and the Word

Hantze and Zivia
October 1940

On Yom Kippur 1940, the dining room at 34 Dzielna Street was filled with comrades who'd traveled to Warsaw from the farms for a conference. Yet it was completely quiet, captivated by a lecture being given by Frumka's younger sister, Hantze, who delivered it with her characteristic allure and sweet voice. The sermon was about Jewish pride; about the importance of staying human.

Four years her junior, Hanzte was in many ways Frumka's opposite. Blonde to Frumka's brunette. Bubbly to Frumka's intensity. Gregarious to Frumka's solemnity. Imaginative to Frumka's analytic nature. "I've never had a more exciting, stirring meeting with anyone else," the famous Israeli political figure Rachel Katzenelson wrote later of Hantze. "There was something magical about her laughter, the way she moved. There was something in her that exceeded mere beauty—openness, willingness to take whatever life throws at her, and optimism—that was captivating."

An ebullient charmer to whom things came easily, from making friends to learning languages, Hantze had grown up leading the local kids, skipping and climbing trees, always at the head, usually laughing. Pampered by her father, Hantze diffused the family tensions as they argued politics after Shabbat dinners: the religious dad, Communist Zlatka (also Hantze's teacher), and her Zionist brother, Elyahu. Frumka kept her thoughts to herself, but Hantze threw in jokes. The sisters were usually referred to as "Hantze and Frumka," with Hantze's name first. That's how it was whenever they walked into a room together, the younger sister's energy stealing the attention.

When Hantze was just fourteen, Elyahu found her to be so preternaturally mature that he introduced her to Freedom just before he left for Palestine. Despite her childish gaiety, the girl exhibited intellectual depth and a desire to be challenged; she surprised comrades with her refined aesthetic taste and love of poetry. She became an active member and, with money sent by her brother, participated in seminars and events, although not always happily. In one letter written from a training camp, Hantze expressed feeling lonely and upset about how the girls talked about her when they thought she was asleep. ("She's crazy . . . but pretty.") She felt ambivalent about being the object of boys' attention and was unsure about her potential romance with one Yitzhak: "He promised to edit my book of poems, and I'm butchering his short stories." The sisters' relationship was filled with both affection and conflict. They adored each other, but Hantze sometimes felt suffocated by Frumka's worrying over her. Living together could be difficult: Frumka loved solitude; Hantze loved "movement, people, life."

During the first weeks of the war, Freedom sent Hantze east to Lvov, to bolster movement activity. She inspired everyone with her energy, reminding them of their good fortune to be on the Soviet side, and generally boosting morale. In Pinsk, she visited her parents with her radical news. A friend wrote: "I will always remember the moment when Hantze told her parents that she had decided to go back to the Nazi part of Poland. Suddenly it was quiet in the house. A world was broken and turned to stone. One could not see even the smallest movements on the faces of her parents while she made the difficult announcement. After a moment of dreadful silence, her father became fully alert and said, '*Nu*, little daughter, if you feel that you must go, then go, with the help of God.'" Of course she needed to go. When her first attempt to steal across the border failed—Hantze froze up when she entered the cold river she was supposed to swim across—she insisted on trying again.

Now, on the holiest day of the Jewish year, in the Freedom dining room in Warsaw, far away from her hometown, Hantze, wearing her usual swinging braids, a kerchief over her head, and a floral blouse with puffy, short sleeves, was giving a speech about dignity—when her sister Frumka burst through the doors.

Frumka delivered the news: the Jewish Quarter was going to be sealed off. They would lose ties to the outside world, to work, to the other groups, to food, to everything. The members were familiar with ghettos in the provinces but hadn't imagined that this would happen in Warsaw, a European capital city. Zivia and Frumka knew that the movement was going to have to redeploy its resources, reorganize, and retrain. Once again, another twist.

When the ghetto gates were locked, confining more than four hundred thousand Jews to a tiny area surrounded by tall, thick walls topped with broken glass, Freedom's focus on aid, education, and cultural activity did not wane, but waxed. This, Zivia believed, was how they would maintain their spirits and weather German occupation.

Freedom was not alone. Many organizations hosted cultural and aid activities. Thousands of ghetto Jews risked their lives to perform in shows: amateur and professional, Yiddish and Polish, rehearsed spectacles and competitions. Jews staged satirical performances in coffeehouses and educational performances in theaters. Actors participated in secret shows in basements to earn extra money. There was a "Broadway" in the Warsaw ghetto consisting of thirty performance venues on one street alone. The Bund also hosted concerts. They opened seven soup kitchens and two tearooms, and founded a large-scale school system, day camps, sports organizations, an underground medical school, literary events, and the Socialist Red Cross. Given that political meetings were illegal, communal kitchens served as clandestine sites for many rendezvous.

For Freedom, education was a priority. Dzielna hosted three large seminars in 1940–41, despite Judenrat opposition. The first was attended by fifty people, from twenty-three branches across Poland, as well as luminaries including poet Yitzhak Katzenelson, historian and social activist Emanuel Ringelblum, and educators Janusz Korczak and Stefa Wilczynska, all of them friends of Zivia's from the Judenrat corridors. For six weeks, attendees studied and pondered the future. Dzielna's ongoing cultural program offered Bible classes, literary readings, science speakers, and a drama group.

With all Jewish schools having been forcibly closed, Zivia worried that ghetto children were becoming idle and boorish. In response, Freedom established underground elementary and high schools, serving 120 students, including Hantze, who was the most senior. Thirteen teachers worked with no supplies, permanent classrooms, or guaranteed salaries, teaching secular and Jewish subjects. They roved from apartment to apartment, crowded into tiny rooms where whole families were forced to live. The instructors were starving, their legs swollen from the winter cold, yet they'd lecture on Bible studies, biology, mathematics, world literature, Polish language, and psychology. They taught students who were shivering and bloated from starvation "how to think." The poet Katzenelson inspired his students to love their heritage; the whole household would break into song. This "flying gymnasia," which even administered exams, existed for two years. It was a hotbed for future underground fighters.

Young children were also a priority. Dzielna offered a training course on caring for youngsters; nursery and kindergarten specialists ran a day care center. Orphanages, previously overseen by the Polish government, fell into disrepair, so Freedom girls gathered clothes and writing kits, taught the children plays, stories, and folk songs, and arranged holiday festivities. Many ghetto children lived on the streets, trading goods or begging for bread. Zivia, Antek, and people from other groups organized a "children's kitchen" to feed and teach boys and girls reading, writing, Hebrew, and Yiddish.

"With all our strength, we tried to give them back a bit of their sweet childhood, a bit of laughter and joking," one female comrade wrote. "When German inspectors came, they . . . ate and did nothing more. Children of eleven, twelve years old learned to hide like adults, behaving in a way that did not accord to their age." The Freedom children's choir and dramatic groups attracted thousands of Jews seeking emotional sustenance.

Dzielna's address was well known on the Jewish streets. The Freedom community, run largely by women, claimed more than a thousand members. The comrades spent hours singing with the children, taking them out for walks and to play in fields—that is, among the destruction that was left standing between the walls. Older Jews would stand and watch the children having fun, a spark of hope.

For all this teaching, Freedom needed books.

An integral part of the early resistance was literary. The occupying Germans banned and burnt Yiddish and Hebrew volumes, as well as titles by Jewish writers and political opponents. Needless to say, anti-Nazi publications were forbidden, and even carrying one brought imprisonment or death. To keep a diary and "compile evidence" against the Nazis was equally punishable. Jews, long known as people of the book, resisted by writing—to distribute information, to document, and for personal expression. Readers, they rebelled by saving stories.

As no new books were being published, and most old books were no longer accessible, Freedom formed its own imprint. Their first book, published on a mimeograph, was a historical literary anthology full of stories of Jewish suffering and heroism; they wanted to present young people with powerful examples of Jewish courage. Several hundred copies were smuggled to branches across the country. They published educational handbooks, as well as Katzenelson's biblical play, *Job,* which their drama group produced. While Antek made copies, the movement kids sang in their loudest voices, to cover up the noise of the machine.

Communication in the face of the Nazi-imposed information blackout was crucial. Jews from all factions printed underground publications to distribute across the country, offering information about the ghettos and camps. Freedom published an underground newspaper in Polish and Yiddish that discussed the questions of the day; later, its members put out a Yiddish weekly with news they heard over their secret radio. According to historian Emanuel Ringelblum, "Political publications sprouted like mushrooms after the rain. If you publish your paper once a month, I'll publish mine twice a month." Overall, some 70 periodicals containing political debate, literary works, and news from outside the ghetto were secretly printed in Polish, Hebrew and Yiddish on Gestetner cyclostyle copiers using whatever paper they could muster. Print runs were small, but each copy was read by multiple people.

Reading was a form of escape and a source of critical knowledge; saving books was an act of cultural and personal salvation. Libraries were forbidden, so one woman member explained the movement's idea for creating its own form of a catalogued library in Warsaw: "If we're not allowed to concentrate the books in one room, then we will make lists of all the books found in each house and make them available for all inhabitants."

Many others across Poland developed secret home libraries. Henia Reinhartz, a young Bundist in the Łódź ghetto, explained that a group of Bundists rescued piles of books from the city's Yiddish library and brought them to her family's apartment. Along with her sister and a few friends, she sorted the volumes and then built shelves to hold them. "Our kitchen thus became the ghetto library," she explained later. "This was an underground library, which means that it was kept secret so that neither the ghetto administration nor the Germans were to know about it." Henia traced her love of reading to the ghetto. "Reading meant escaping into another world," she wrote, "living the lives of the heroes and heroines, sharing their joys and sorrows, the joys and sorrows of a normal life in a normal world unlike ours, full of fear and hunger." She read *Gone with the Wind* in Polish while hiding from a deportation.

With many out of work and out of school, stuck in small spaces, hungry and listless, isolated and bored, writing became a convenient and common pastime. Jews wrote personal accounts to maintain their humanity and a sense of agency over their lives. Autobiographical writing records inner development; introspection validates identity and strengthens individuality. As in the famous example of Anne Frank, or the less famous diary of Rutka Laskier, a Będzin-based teen, Jewish women explored their shifting perceptions and sexuality, their fears and social analyses, their frustrations with their suitors and their mothers. Anne and Rutka, like many other women, were well educated; they believed in a liberal humanism that was destroyed. Writing provided a sense of control over their destinies, an attempt to refute terrifying social decay and preserve faith and order. In writing, they searched for meaning among senseless brutality, for a way to repair their collapsed world.

A few blocks over from Dzielna, every Saturday Emanuel Ringelblum met with the Oneg Shabbat group: a collective of intellectuals, rabbis, and social workers who, feeling a responsibility to the Jewish people, were driven by a need to bear witness and chronicle the war from a Jewish perspective. The Nazis relentlessly documented Polish Jews through photography and film. The Oneg Shabbat was determined that the Germans' biased version of events not be the only history. Its members compiled a large archive of materials for future generations, with objects and writings about life in the Warsaw ghetto, all of which they later buried in milk cans. Among the items that survived is a crayon sketch of a dozing toddler, *Sleeping Girl*, drawn by her mother, painter Gela Seksztajn. The intimate depiction of a dark-haired girl lying on her side, curled over her arm, shows a rare moment of calm. "I do not ask for praise," the artist's testimony read, "only for me and my daughter to be remembered. This talented little girl is named Margolit Lichtensztajn."

Conditions in the Warsaw ghetto deteriorated rapidly. "The great crowding, the loneliness, the tormented worries about making a living," a female comrade wrote. "Jews dragged all this out onto the streets. Jews walked around in groups, speaking their hearts." Most buildings extended back from the street into mazes of units (richer folks lived in the front apartments with good light). Inner courtyards served as meeting spots and even hosted communal organizations. Despite the loud social thrum, hunger, illness, and terror prevailed. Disease was rampant, and corpses lined the streets. Jewish businesses were shuttered, and work was hard to come by. Bloated bellies and desperate pleas for food were a constant backdrop. Zivia found the children's cries for bread, audible all night, tormenting.

Zivia and Frumka placed even more emphasis on bolstering the Jews' spirits and continued to run their soup kitchen. The comrades divided their meager portions of soup with each new member, setting out a long row of dishes with their lunch leftovers. But after a while, their own hunger grew too intense, and they stopped this custom.

Countless Jewish women rose to lead and help their people in Warsaw. Nearly two thousand "House Committees" provided medical care and cultural activities—almost all were organized by female volunteers. The Oneg Shabbat member Rachel Auerbach, an eminent journalist, fiction writer, and philosophy graduate, ran a soup kitchen. Paula Alster, who with her "Greek appearance and grand poise" had been arrested for political work while still in middle school, led a kitchen that became a center of underground activity. Basia Berman, an impassioned educator, founded a children's library from scratch. Bundists Manya Wasser and underground leader Sonya Novogrodsky ran a workshop where they turned discarded clothes into garments for street children, for whom they also provided food and medical attention. Shayndl Hechtkop, an honors graduate from Warsaw University's law faculty and an active Freedom member, ran the Peretz library, led a people's kitchen, and organized academic conferences. When she was captured by Nazis, the movement arranged to free her, but she refused to leave her mother's side.

As circumstances in Warsaw worsened over the year, Freedom's work continued outside the city. Movements collaborated and established countrywide programs for youth living in fear and inactivity. Zivia frequently left Warsaw to coordinate groups of pupils, meeting with local activists at train stations to save time. It was important to her to set up lines of communication that could function across ghetto walls—a visionary priority that would soon pay off.

To accomplish this, Zivia sent comrades from Warsaw to the towns; the type of daring work Frumka had been doing all along. These messengers—young women, usually with Aryan appearances—connected with designated locals and instructed them to create a "five": a group of five people who would carry out pioneer work. Chana Gelbard was an early courier. For her initial mission, Zivia gave Chana fake Polish documents. She pretended to be a traveling merchant, when she was really distributing movement literature. At the time, train travel was difficult even for Poles, and Chana went by wagon, hypercautious, suspicious of everyone, including her fellow Jews. Whenever the young woman received an address from central command, she took pains to make sure that she was speaking to the right person, that he would not lead her into a trap, and that he would not think she was a Gestapo plant. She interrogated him before handing out any pages.

Visits from the girls were welcome, especially when they brought hopeful words about movement activity. On her second mission outside Warsaw, Chana traveled with a valise full of underground literature: book chapters about Jewish history, workers' literature, and national holidays. "It was dangerous to travel with such 'stories,'" she recounted, but she was determined to disseminate the material. On one trip, Chana wrote, a five did not assemble, but two fives did. They all sat in a wooden house, in the dark, and she told the ten comrades about Freedom's activity, stressing that not everything had been destroyed and that they should draw strength from their history. The youths listened with bated breath; later, they spread out, each to his or her own corner and to his or her own worries, but glowing with renewed courage. Chana's golden words had brought knowledge and reprieve, helping young Jews feel "strong against the clouds in these stormy times."

These girls, known as "Zivia's girls," were developing a role that would soon become one of, if not the, most important of the resistance.

Chapter 6
From Spirit to Blood—
Becoming the ZOB

Tosia, Zivia, and Vladka
December 1941

Vilna, 1941. A December snow, light and fluffy, swirled in the wind. Six months earlier, the Nazi war machine had rumbled east, taking control of the region. The towns to which Zivia and the youth had fled in 1939, where they carried out Zionist and Bundist activity under Soviet and Lithuanian rule, were no longer safe. Before 1941, Jews still had jobs, relative freedom of movement, and education. (In fact, many women spoke gratefully of the superior instruction they received under the Russians.) But all that came to an abrupt halt. Ghettoizing, anti-Jewish laws, and torture were imposed immediately, the Jews' lives descending into darkness, the abyss.

A little Nazi occupation, however, would not deter Tosia Altman. If anything, this mission was one of her most critical.

The twenty-three-year old Young Guard leader arrived in Vilna, her thick, golden locks catching snowflakes and bouncing along with her springy steps. To get to the tiny ghetto, set in the old Jewish area, she passed the formidable Neris River, snow-filled parks, medieval buildings built along cobblestone streets, and the Jewish libraries, synagogues, yeshivas, and archives that had blossomed in this town, a centuries-old Polish center of Yiddish poetry, rabbinic scholarship, and intellect. Tosia had also fled to Vilna at the start of the war, so she knew the city. She'd spent the better part of the past two years traveling nonstop throughout Nazi-ruled Poland, her itinerary appearing like a mad scribble, indiscernible with her number of trips. Dealing with the Germans of Vilna was just another day's work.

Tosia had been a Young Guard leader well before the war, and, like Zivia and Frumka, was a key figure in the group's plan B. Born to a well-to-do, cultured, and loving family, boisterous Tosia grew up in Włocławek, a small town in central Poland where the astronomer Nicolaus Copernicus was schooled, and where, centuries later, her father owned a watch and jewelry shop. A Zionist, he was very involved in the community. Tosia, too, became active in the movement, and with her curiosity, social ease, and desire to be at the heart of the action, she rose quickly through the ranks. Her own aliyah to Palestine was curtailed as she was made head of youth education for The Young Guard in Warsaw. She envied her friends now residing in the promised land, where they no doubt led action-packed lives, and regarded her somewhat older Polish coleaders as a bit too serious. With time, however, she connected with them.

Tosia was considered a fashionable Polish type. She was a "glam girl"—a well-educated, well-spoken young woman who wore sporty outfits—and a "hussy" with many boyfriends. In particular, she was obsessed with the inventive and intellectual Yurek Horn (whose aloofness her father did not like). She was a romantic, and a bookworm—constantly sitting in the corner cross-legged with her nose in a tome. Tosia was afraid of dogs and darkness, so she forced herself to walk out at night during a pogrom to overcome her anxieties. She hummed tunes and was always laughing, displaying large, pearly teeth. A joker who made friends easily, she scrupulously avoided social arguments and was perturbed by misunderstandings.

While Frumka had been the initial Freedom member to return to Warsaw to care for the comrades left behind, Tosia was selected by The Young Guard to be one of that organization's first. She was not an authoritative ideologue but was chosen for her passion, energy, and ability to connect with people of all ages; also because of her glowing blue eyes and wealthy, non-Jewish looks. She agreed to the mission immediately, intellectually accepting that movement life took priority over individual life. Privately, however, this caused her great emotional turbulence. She cried only to her closest friends, sad that she would have to leave Vilna and forego Palestine, which had been her dream. Regardless, she went forth with gusto, and though it took her three tries to cross the border, she finally made it to Warsaw. With her blonde charm and fluent Polish, her "iron softness," in the words of her Hebrew biographer, she quickly became The Young Guard's main messenger, constantly traveling through the county to connect chapters, bring information, organize seminars, and encourage clandestine educational activity, her wide smile and whippy hair a treat for every host. Tosia often dressed like a country girl, donning layers of skirts, hiding contraband in their folds. Her work had its share of setbacks, but the young woman's sassiness, bravado, and keen instinct usually led her to emerge relatively unscathed. In one account, she was caught in Częstochowa by a Nazi border guard, but she twisted out of his arms and ran fifteen miles by foot to a farm in Żarki.

Countless comrade memoirs recount "the day that Tosia arrived" in their ghettos. Her appearance was like an injection of sunshine into their dark lives—"a jolt of electric energy." People did not sense her ambivalent interior; they rejoiced, cried, and hugged her close. She brought warmth, "inexhaustible optimism," a sense of connectedness, the relief at not being forgotten, the feeling that things might somehow be okay. Even in wartime, Tosia taught comrades "the art of living" and how not to be so serious all the time.

Now in wintery Vilna, it was similar. The journey had been particularly brutal: long, dangerous, replete with checkpoints. Tosia had spent sleepless nights in freezing filth clutching a stash of fake IDs. When she arrived, she needed a moment to defrost, but then thawed into her old cheerful self. "If you were not there under those ghetto walls with us, you simply cannot understand what it meant that this 'phenomenon' crossed the borders of the ghetto," wrote Vilna-based Young Guard leader Ruzka Korczak. "Tosia came!

Like a happy spring, the information spread among the people: Tosia is visiting from Warsaw, as if there was no ghetto, Germans and death around us, as if there wasn't danger in every corner. . . . Tosia is here! A well of love and light."

Tosia entered The Young Guard headquarters, where comrades slept on tables and unhinged doors. Filled with inexplicable happiness and youthful passion, she told them stories about Warsaw—the terror and hunger, but also how the comrades continued to work. "She opened up for us a new, almost unbelievable world," Ruzka later reflected. "We heard how in the darkness of Warsaw ghetto life, there emerged a new song that was filled with vigor." Even after two full years of Nazi occupation and inhuman conditions, they were not broken and still believed in a higher purpose.

As with all the ghettos she visited, Tosia brought news. Tonight, in Vilna, she was also to confirm news. She had been sent at the same time as a couple of Freedom couriers. Back in Warsaw, they'd heard rumors of mass executions. But were they true? And what could she do to help? She was prepared to aid the Vilna group in relocating to Warsaw, which the comrades assumed was safer.

The next night, Abba Kovner, the local Young Guard leader, called a meeting of 150 ghetto youths from several movements, The youth's first mass gathering took place in a damp, candlelit room in the Judenrat building under the guise of a New Year's party. Once everyone had arrived, Abba read a pamphlet in Yiddish. Then he immediately gestured to Tosia and asked her to deliver it in Hebrew, to show that a leader from Warsaw was committed to his radical ideas. She was stunned by what she heard; what she had to relay.

One young Vilna girl, Sara, was taken to Ponary, at one time a popular vacation site. Now it was a mass killing ground where, over the course of the next three years, seventy-five thousand Jews were stripped and shot next to massive twenty-foot-deep pits that collected their bodies. Shot but not killed, Sara awoke in the ditch of frozen cadavers, naked, staring into the eyes of her dead mother. She waited until dark and climbed her way out, then hid for two days in the forest before running back to Vilna, arriving unclothed and hysterical, relaying the massacre that she'd witnessed. The head of the Judenrat did not believe her, or at least claimed not to, and warned her not to tell people, so that they didn't panic.

Sara was hospitalized. There, Abba Kovner met her. Kovner did believe her; to him, the Nazi plan to kill all Jews was very clear. At the New Year's eve meeting, Tosia read his conclusions: "Don't believe those who are deluding you. . . . Hitler plotted to exterminate all the Jews of Europe." She ended with what became his famous resistance mantra: "Let us not go like sheep to the slaughter!" Abba insisted that all Jews must be warned and must fight back. The only answer: self-defense.

Tosia, a woman of plans, never sat in one place for long. Now she needed to travel to ghettos to deliver not comforting words of the movement but this horrific, urgent message. The Nazis planned to kill all Jews. All.

It was time to resist.

How do you react to news that you are going to be killed? Do you try to stay optimistic, to harbor delusions in order to maintain your sanity? Or do you face the darkness straight on and look the bullet in the eye? When Zivia heard the news from Tosia and the Freedom couriers—the same news also brought back by religious Jews and Polish activists—she didn't doubt it for a second. Vilna was simply a confirmation. Other Jews had escaped from death camps such as Chelmno and shared their shocking stories back in the ghettos. Hitler's threats, which she'd dismissed—they'd all dismissed—as "the hollow phrases of an arrogant madman," suddenly, piercingly, rang true.

If anything, Zivia was hit by a torrent of guilt. *Of*

course, this was happening. Why hadn't she seen it all more clearly? Why hadn't she grasped that the Nazis had developed a sickening systematic plan to annihilate the Jewish people? Why had she shied away from community leadership, concentrating only on the youth, assuming those more senior would step up to the task? Why hadn't she focused on self-defense and procuring weapons? Why hadn't she done something sooner? Precious time had been wasted.

Zivia tried to explain away these regrets. How could anyone have known what atrocities were being planned, especially when the Nazis took great pains to keep them secret specifically to avoid retaliation and global censure? How could a suffering minority fight an army that was conquering entire countries? How could people who were starving and ill make tactical plans for military action? Had they not focused intensely on promoting self-respect, education, and camaraderie during those early years, there may not have been the spirit, trust, and ethos that enabled a fighting force. But still, she was consumed by regret.

Numerous courier girls, including Frumka, spread the news of the mass execution at Ponary and the underground's understanding of the Final Solution. Runaway witnesses also testified in front of large gatherings of community leaders. But they were often not believed. Many Jewish communities were reluctant to accept stories that simply seemed too monstrous to process. They refused to believe that similar atrocities would be carried out in western Poland, where, despite torturous living conditions, there been no inklings of mass murder. Their communities supplied the Reich with indispensable slave labor; it made no sense economically for the Nazis to execute them all.

Many Jews harbored the illusion that it was still possible to survive. They wanted to believe the best, wanted desperately to live. No one wanted to think that their mothers, their siblings, their children had been dispatched against their will to be slaughtered—or that their own impeding deportation almost certainly meant death. And Warsaw, of all places, was in the heart of Europe. How could they deport a whole capital city? Polish Jews had previously lived in segregation for centuries—they never imagined that Hitler's ghettos were part of a murder machine. Jews had prepared psychologically for what they knew: World War I. Unfortunately, this was not that war.

In Tosia's final letter to Palestine, dated April 7, 1942, she wrote of the torment of seeing such destruction yet being unable to stop it: "Jews are dying before my eyes and I am powerless to help. Did you ever try to shatter a wall with your head?"

In one account, a young Jewish woman tells of embarking a train to Auschwitz. Suddenly she saw a note card being pushed through the boards of the train, between the wooden slats. She read: "[T]his train is taking you to the worst death camps. . . . Do not enter this train."

But the woman ignored the warning. It simply sounded too crazy to be true.

Zivia however, knew: "This is wholesale planned murder." In the days after the couriers' return, she walked around the bustling, anxious ghetto, already imagining everyone dead. The only thing that kept her from suicide was the sense that she had a purpose: maybe not to save lives, but to salvage honor, to not go quietly. Pushing aside her feelings, Zivia knew to act. Her Freedom comrades also knew the truth; the movement had to pivot once again and now make defense its primary goal. But setting up a resistance battalion to fight Hitler was cosmically daunting, for reasons of resources and experience, as well as internal conflict—with the Judenrat, with Jewish leaders, between youth movements, and within the movement as well.

As a youth group, Freedom had no contact with the growing Polish underground, and Zivia was concerned that they wouldn't be all that keen to help Jews—the comrades needed the "adults'" help. The leaders of several youth movements convened and met with the community heads, hoping for them to acknowledge the threat and take charge. But the adult leaders' faces blanched from fear and anger. "They reproached us for irresponsibly sowing the seeds of despair and confusion among the people," Zivia later wrote. She and Antek were cautioned by the head of the Joint Distribution Committee to act with restraint. Though the man understood the significance of the murders, she explained, he warned them that hasty actions would result in a grave situation and that the Jewish nation would never forgive them. The Warsaw Judenrat supervisors, on the other hand, either did not believe the rumors or would not react at all, worried that any action would provoke the Nazis to greater violence. They were hopeful that lying low and playing by the rules would spare the Jewish community—and perhaps themselves. Middle-aged, with families and children, they did not want to endanger the entire population because of some youngsters' idealistic vision of guerilla warfare for which they had no training.

Freedom members grew wildly agitated as these meetings dragged on. Feeling "frustration and helpless rage," Zivia and her comrades knew they had to work on their own. First, they needed the support of the masses. They would have to expose the horrifying reality to their fellow Jews themselves. "It is our duty to look at the truth as it is," Zivia believed. To her, "Our greatest enemy was false hope." The public would never resist, even hide, until they accepted the fact that death was imminent.

Freedom comrades knew how to publish an underground bulletin to get out the message, but were generally at a loss about how to form an army. As Zivia remarked, "None of us knew what had to be done when the Germans were armed and powerful—whereas we had only two revolvers." Before the war, the Bund and the Revisionist Zionists—the right-wing faction who championed private enterprise and Jewish military units—had established self-defense leagues. But the Labor Zionist youths were trained primarily to debate social theory. They studied self-defense but were not organized to fight. Freedom needed allies with connections or military training.

Zivia persisted. Drawing on years of honed negotiation skills and resilience, she continued to work on the community leaders but was met with partisan politics again and again. In March 1942 she helped initiate a meeting of Jews from a variety of parties in the

Bund's kitchen. Antek, representing Freedom, pleaded with leaders to understand the urgency of preparing a response, and proposed a program for establishing a collective Jewish defense movement. The meeting ended with no practical outcomes. The Zionists wanted to work with the Bund, which had connections with the Polish parties; the Bund, however, didn't trust the bourgeois, Palestine-obsessed Zionist groups and preferred to fight with the Polish underground, which actually had a few weapons. The main party leaders rebuked the youth movements, accusing them of being naïve and hasty alarmists with zero soldierly experience. Agreement with the well-armed Revisionist Zionist youth group, Betar, was impossible.

Feeling sickeningly helpless, the Zionist youth tried to contact the Polish resistance themselves. Then they participated in the Anti-Fascist Bloc initiated by the Jewish Communists. The Communists wanted to collaborate with the Soviet Red Army outside the ghetto, but Zivia, who was in a leadership role, argued for internal defense. Before they could agree on a way forward, the Communist leaders were arrested, and the alliance fell apart. Now Freedom's members had no idea where they'd get weapons. Even Zivia was stumped.

And then she knew: *We are too late.*

To say the clock was ticking down is a grotesque understatement. This was the summer of 1942, when the main *Aktion*, a Nazi euphemism for mass deportation and murder of Jews, occurred in the Warsaw ghetto. It had started in April, on "Bloody Sabbath," when SS units invaded the ghetto at night and, following preprepared lists of names, gathered and murdered the intelligentsia. From that moment on, the entire ghetto became a killing field, and terror reigned. In June Frumka arrived with news about the existence of Sobibor, yet another death camp, 150 miles to the east.

Vladka Meed (nee Feigele Peltel), a twenty-one-year-old Bundist who helped print the underground Bund newspaper and run illegal youth groups, later wrote about July 1942 in the ghetto. The rumors of impending doom, stories of roundups, constant shootings. A little boy, a smuggler, told them that the other side of the wall was lined with German and Ukrainian soldiers. Fear. Confusion.

And then the poster appeared.

The Jews crowded into the otherwise deserted streets to read for themselves: anyone who did not work for the Germans would be deported. Vladka spent days scurrying around the ghetto, frantic, wild, looking for work papers, for "life papers" for her and her family.

Hundreds of anguished Jews cued up in the scorching heat, pushing, waiting in front of factories and workshops, desperate for any job, any papers. Some lucky ones clutched their own sewing machines, which they hoped would get them hired more easily. Scalpers forged work documents, bribes were rampant, family heirlooms were offered in return for official employment. Mothers wandered in a daze, deciding what to do with their children. Those who had jobs—who'd temporarily secured life—avoided any conversation, out of guilt. Wagons filled with weeping children taken from their parents passed by.

"Fear of what awaited us there," Vladka wrote later, "dulled our ability to think about anything except saving ourselves."

Sensing the futility of standing in endless lines, Vladka was elated to receive a message from an underground friend. She was to appear with photos of herself and her family, and would receive work cards. She ran to the address. Inside, thick cigarette smoke and pandemonium. Vladka spotted Bund leaders and historian Ringelblum, and heard about how they'd obtained false work cards and were trying to set up new workshops—all to help save youth. But the leaders felt that hiding was still the best bet, even though being found by the Nazis meant certain death. "What to do?" they mumbled.

And then, panic: the building was surrounded. Vladka ran to grab the falsified work papers and managed to stick with a group who bribed a Jewish police guard—a common sight as more and more Jews were snatched, and were always resisting, Vladka noticed, albeit unsuccessfully. Women physically fought the policemen who pushed them up onto trucks; they jumped from trains, usually in vain. But why hadn't Vladka done anything to help?

The deportations went on and on, with Germans and Ukrainians joining the Jewish police in conducting roundups. The Jewish police had quotas for how many Jews they had to apprehend each day—if not, they and their families would be taken. After grabbing the young and the elderly, nonworkers, and the names on the list, the deportations were carried out by street. People waited in terror for their street to be blockaded; then many tried to go into hiding, crawling onto rooftops or locking themselves in cellars and attics. Vladka's fictitious papers were no longer valid. She had no secure hiding place. Jews were urged to appear voluntarily at the *umschlagplatz*—the departure point from which Jews were deported to death camps—to receive three kilos of bread and one kilo of marmalade. Again, people hoped and believed it was for the best. Many, starving and desolate, keen to stick with family members, went there—and were taken away. "That's how the life of a Jew became worth a slice of bread," wrote one underground leader.

And then, her street. Vladka ran to hide, but a fellow hider decided to open the locked door when the soldiers pounded on it. Resigned to her fate, searching the crowd for her family, who had been hiding a few houses over, Vladka was herded to the "selection," and handed over a friend's scribbled work paper. For some reason, it was accepted. She was sent to the right, to live. Her family, to the left.

Numb, she went to work in one of the workshops that remained open—constant exhaustion, constant waiting, worrying, beatings, bloating, and sick from hunger. The limited work was threatened, there were inspections and roundups, anyone caught idle or hiding or seeming too old or too young—death. People collapsed at their sewing machines. Selection after selection. Vladka tried to procure an official ID card when the building was surrounded. She hid in a cupboard for hours.

The ghetto was emptying, dwindling each day.

Liquidations and street closures were quotidian affairs. Janusz Korczak and Stefa Wilczynska were gone, killed along with their orphans; Vladka saw them being taken from a window in her hiding place during a night raid at a Bund leader's home. The streets were empty except for broken furniture, old kitchen utensils, a "snow" of down, the "disemboweled intestines of Jewish bedclothes"—and dead Jews. Smuggling was no longer possible. Total starvation set in. Piercing the silence were the shrieks of children being torn from their mothers who had work cards. Vladka's heart was most shattered by hearing eight-year-olds try to convince their mothers to go on without them, reassuring them that they would find a way to hide themselves. "Don't worry," went the refrain. "Don't worry, Mama."

Fifty-two thousand Jews were deported in the first Aktion in the Warsaw ghetto.

The next day, Freedom members met with community leaders to discuss a response. They proposed attacking the Jewish police—who weren't armed—with clubs. They also wanted to incite mass demonstrations. Again, the leaders warned them not to react hastily or upset the Germans, cautioning that the murders of thousands of Jews would be on *the young comrades'* heads.

Now, in the face of such mass killing, the youth

movements felt that the adults were being outrageous in their overcautiousness. Who cared if they rocked the boat? They were shipwrecked and sinking fast.

On July 28 Zivia and her fellow youth group leaders all met at Dzielna.

There was no more discussion.

Without the adults or the Polish resistance, they established their own force: the Jewish Fighting Organization. In Yiddish: Yiddishe Kamf Organizatsye. In Hebrew: EYAL. In Polish: Zydowska Organizacja Bojowa, or, the ZOB. The ZOB was no powerhouse. It had no money, no weapons besides those two pistols, and, for the Freedom contingent, not even a local hiding place. (The group hid 140 members at a farm.) Regardless, they had a vision: to stage a Jewish protest. They were Jews fighting as and for Jews. Theirs would be a countrywide operation carried out by the connections that Zivia had already meticulously put in place. Now she would send her young female couriers on life-risking missions, not to distribute educational material or news, but to organize preparations for defense. (Though Zivia had a false ID as "Celina," she had to stop traveling because of her conspicuously Jewish looks.) Establishing the fighting force assuaged some guilt and anxiety—Zivia felt they could finally move forward on the right path. But with no arsenal or military training, much internal squabbling ensued over how to proceed; the tension mounting as more Jews were taken away to be slaughtered.

Zivia was the only elected woman leader in the ZOB. She was part of a fighting group. She learned to use a firearm. She trained to be on guard duty. She also cooked, laundered, and was responsible for maintaining the young fighters' optimism and spirit. Other women leaders—Tosia, Frumka, Leah—were sent to the Aryan side to forge ties and procure weapons.

While they waited for arms, the ZOB decided to mark its territory. One night, from its headquarters opposite Pawiak Prison, members headed into the ghetto silence on their first missions, divided into three groups. One group was going to inform the ghetto inhabitants about this new force that would fight on their behalf. They were to put up posters on billboards and buildings explaining that—as they had learned from messengers who had followed the trains—Treblinka meant certain death, that Jews must hide, and the youth must defend themselves. "It is better to be shot in the ghetto than to die in Treblinka!" the slogan read.

The second group was to set fire to abandoned homes and warehouses of looted goods. The Nazis had specialists assess the deported Jews' possessions, then forced the living to rigorously organize the valuable ones.

The third group was going to commit murder. One of their double agents, a young man named Israel Kanal who was in the resistance and also working undercover in the militia, was to gun down the chief of the Jewish police. The ZOB wanted vengeance, but also to spread fear among the militiamen who were enforcing the Nazis' edicts.

Zivia was part of the second group. Her heart beat wildly in the dark. Her sweaty palms gripped the ladder as she climbed up rung by rung, the brick of the building brushing her side. A few more steps, and she had scaled the wall, reached her destination.

She and her comrades laid down the incendiary material. But something went wrong. The house didn't catch fire. They decided quickly to pile up all the flammable contents and set those on fire instead. "Success!" she later noted. "The flames swept into a great blaze and crackled in the night, dancing and twisting in the air. We rejoiced as we saw the reflection of the revenge that was burning inside us, the symbol of the Jewish armed resistance that we had yearned for, for so long."

Everyone met up at 34 Dzielna Street a few hours later, all three missions having been accomplished; even the Jewish police had been afraid to take down Kanal after he shot the chief of police but failed to kill him. Then, that night, the Russians, bombed Warsaw for the first time. For Zivia, it was a night of pure elation.

And then, a wonder. By late summer 1942, one leader snuck five guns and eight hand grenades from the Aryan side into the ghetto. Tosia used ZOB money to purchase several hand grenades and guns, transported in boxes of nails. Frumka, some say, was the first to bring in weapons; she blended in with a returning labor group carrying a large sack filled with potatoes—and underneath, guns. Vladka, who was approached by a fellow Bundist and asked to work on the Aryan side, became a major weapons source, eventually transporting dynamite into the ghetto's makeshift weapons lab. The smugglers climbed over the ghetto wall themselves or paid off a Polish guard to whisper a password to a fighter on the inside who would climb up and grab the package. They also brought in weapons through the windows of the houses that lined the ghetto border. Each addition to the arsenal brought ecstasy. Next, plans began for an ambush on the Germans. They would hide in building entrances, attack the Nazis by throwing grenades and then, in the confusion, steal their guns.

The joy of success, however, was curtailed by a new series of setbacks. Instead of jumping on board with the ZOB's accomplishments, Jewish Warsaw was frightened by its actions. So pervasive was the community's fear and paranoia that many assumed the recent acts of rebellion were merely German ploys, and that they were being set up to be punished. Jews were pleased to learn that someone had tried to assassinate the Jewish police chief; but they attributed the attempt to the Polish resistance, not believing that their fellow Jews had the strength or courage. Zivia was horrified to see anxious Jews tearing down ZOB posters and beating up comrades who tried to put up more.

Many fighters had been sent out of the ghetto to partisan groups in the forest, where they would be better armed, but most were killed on the way. Then a Young Guard leader, Josef Kaplan, was captured at a weapons storage site and killed. Another beloved leader went to rescue him; he, too, was caught and shot to death. Despondent, the group decided to move its cache to Dzielna. Regina Schneiderman, a young female member, put their weapons in a basket and set out, only to be stopped in the street by German soldiers, who found the arms. (As Antek later reflected: "You can imagine the size of our 'armory' if a girl could carry it in a basket.") This trilogy of tragedies was "a stunning blow,"

Zivia said. The group lost morale, commanders, and its plans.

The ZOB continued to debate: Should they fight immediately or strategize carefully? The talk was ceaseless. Meantime, in three Aktions carried out over three months, three hundred thousand Jews were transported from Warsaw to the gas chambers at the Treblinka death camp, and 99 percent of the children from the Warsaw ghetto were killed. It appeared that there would be no Jewish future. The sixty thousand people left within the ghetto walls were unable to look one another in the eye because they had remained alive, Zivia later wrote.

On the last night of the Aktion, September 13, a few dozen comrades sat together at 63 Mila Street. The ones who were riled up, hungering for a hotheaded response, were sent to a different room. The older members, those in their midtwenties, stayed to discuss what to do next. Conversation was despondent. "We came together and sat," Zivia wrote, "mourning and bleeding." Consensus was that it was too much, too late; they were too traumatized. It was time for a group suicide mission. They would take the petrol, kerosene, and single gun that they had left, and set fire to German warehouses, shoot some Nazis, and be killed, but with honor.

Zivia, a pessimist, was outspoken: it was time to die.

It was Antek who spoke up against his colleagues, and his love. First in a whisper, then loudly: "I reject the proposal. . . . The crisis is great, and the shame is great. But the proposed act is an act of despair. It will die with no echo. . . . It is an act that is good for each of us on a personal level, because under such circumstances, death can appear as salvation. But the strength that has held us until now and motivated our activity— was it only in order to allow us to choose a beautiful death? Both in our fight and in our death, we wished to save the honor of the Jewish people. . . . We have a legacy of countless failures, and we shall have a legacy of defeats. We have to start all over."

His words clashed with the fighters' moods, arousing incredible anger—he was stalling their only chance. But eventually those who craved a drastic-heroic act couldn't refute Antek's logic, and the mass suicide plan was abandoned. The comrades had to stand tall with weapons in their hands and go fight, Zivia knew. Their movement, above all, believed in the collective over the individual. From now on, resistance was the raison d'etre. Even if it killed them.

Zivia got to work gluing the movement back together for its next phase: a militia.

Chapter 7
The Days of Wandering— Homeless to Housekeeper

Renia
August 1942

On a warm August morning in 1942, during the period of mass murders in the Warsaw ghetto, the sun in Wodzisław was blazing orange, the air fresh. Seventeen-year-old Renia woke from sleep. Her nightmares had rattled her: dreams of turmoil where she was "fighting, but then falling like a fly," leaving her weak. But the glorious morning soothed and reinvigorated her. "My head bursts out of its place, and I want to devour life . . . my face is shining. I am alive. I am invincible!"

But one glance at her parents changed her mood.

Their faces sank into their hands. They looked crazed. That night, there'd been a deportation in nearby Kielce. People who tried to escape were shot or buried alive, regardless of age or sex. The Nazis had promised no more deportations, promised to return all deportees after England had demanded that the Jews were not to be harmed.

All lies.

"Your father and I are still young, but we've had joy in life," Renia's mother told her, as always, to the point. "But these poor babies, what wrong did they do? I would gladly die right here, right now, to spare the babies' lives." Leah, in her midforties, was frantically concerned with hiding her youngest, saving them from death.

In the past weeks, stories of atrocities abounded. Escapees from nearby villages who'd evaded being shot by Germans or turned in by Poles had come to Wodzisław, where they'd heard Jews still lived. They were barely able to stand, carrying with them nothing but worn satchels and horrific tales—often of the children. One man told the story of his wife, who'd pulled their two babies out of the deportation line. A German, foaming at the mouth, lunged at her and killed the infants by kicking them with his spiked boots. The mother was ordered to watch, then dig them graves. The German crushed her skull with the butt of his rifle. For a long time, the man recounted, his wife convulsed in pain until she finally died.

On another day, Renia saw a group of half-insane women, raggedy, pale, blue-lipped, and shaking like willows. Through hysterical sobs, these starving women told her that their town had been surrounded. Gunshots flew in every direction. Their children had been playing outside and ran to their houses. But a Nazi caught them and beat the kids to death, one by one. The women, half naked in nightgowns, barefoot, fled to the fields and forests, begging for food from kind farmers' wives, wandering aimlessly.

Another group of 17 showed up. Of 180 who had run together, only they had survived. They'd been attacked by Poles, robbed of everything, and threatened with exposure. The men wore only underwear or covered themselves with handkerchiefs; the children were naked. They were sickeningly thirsty, not having drunk or eaten in days, and all seemed half dead. Yet they were happy—they'd sidestepped death. The others had perished, or sliced their own veins so as not to fall into German hands, or just disappeared. Young people's hair went gray overnight.

Renia, shocked at the sight of them, gave out clothes and food. She had to do something, anything, to help.

One of the most difficult experiences Renia faced was when she met five young siblings who explained that when their mother realized that the Germans were rounding up Jews, she hid them in closets, under beds, inside blankets. Minutes later, they heard the rumble of German boots. They fell into a frozen silence. A Nazi entered their room with a rifle and started searching. He found them all.

But instead of killing them, he quietly gave them each a slice of bread. "Hide still until nightfall," he urged them. He promised that their mother would return and escape with them. The children exploded with gratitude, and the Nazi laughed, then began to cry, patting them on their heads, saying that he was a father; that his heart would not allow him to kill children. At night, the city quiet as death, the youngsters emerged to find that their two-month-old baby sister had suffocated under the blanket where she was hidden, her body cold. The eldest girl, aged eleven, picked up little Rosa, heavy in death, and took her to the basement out of fear of being caught outside. She dressed her siblings and waited for their mother. Had she forgotten them?

Their mother never returned. At dawn, the sister held the others' hands and led them out through the window, looking for neighbors, all the time feeling that their mother was walking behind them. She led her siblings out of the town, asking peasants for bread, sleeping on the ground, avoiding farm boys who threw stones at them. The girl told the peasants that their mother had died, but nothing else. They had heard that there were still Jews alive in Wodzisław, so they came there, their bare feet cut from walking, their faces and bodies swollen, their clothes torn and dirty. They were afraid to talk to anyone, in case he or she might be a German in disguise. "Mother is surely looking for us and crying. What happens if we don't find her? The poor babies can't stop crying 'Where is Mother? Where is Mother?'" The children were taken in by wealthy families, but, Renia asked, where would they go now? Anyone who escaped the hand of the hangman would be subject to this kind of wandering, barefoot and naked, crazed, begging for a slice of bread.

Panic, pure panic. It felt to Renia like the situation was unraveling by the minute. Every moment was the most crucial of their lives. Every day she survived was pure luck. No one slept at night, which was probably best, since that's when the Nazis usually operated. "The wise have suddenly lost their wisdom. The rabbis have no advice. They shaved off their moustaches and beards, but still they look like Jews," Renia later wrote. "Where can they go?"

Everyone was trying to leave. But to where? What was safe? How would they hide? All day, groups huddled in the streets, questioning obsessively. Did any towns still have Jews? What if they fell into German hands? They had no weapons, nothing. People traded furniture for bread. Despite the ghetto crowding, Renia found her home eerily empty. Everything had been sold to the Poles for pennies, and she feared that the little that was left would be stolen by them soon.

A large number of ghetto Jews escaped one night, running to the forests and the fields. The rich bribed the townspeople to hide them in attics, cellars, and sheds, but most Jews set off wandering with no guide or destination. Most, in the end, were killed.

Renia knew that while scaling the ghetto walls was risky, surviving on the outside was wildly perilous. One way to get by in Aryan territory was to physically hide. Jews with semitic features often paid hefty fees to Poles who were willing to conceal and feed them. Some Poles acted benevolently, risking their own lives to help, but others extorted Jews financially (and even sexually), threatening to turn them in to the police. Hiding places were frequently discovered, so that at any moment, Jewish exiles might have to hasten off into the night and relocate.

A second way was to hide one's soul and assume a new identity. These Jews performed as non-Jews, an act that many assimilated Jews had rehearsed, playing down their differences. Now Jews had to take advantage of the false construct of what constituted a "Jewish appearance" by deemphasizing those traits and accentuating their non-Jewish characteristics to whatever extent that they could.

Renia had the great fortune—greater than actual fortune—of looking Polish. Jews who did not appear Jewish had the potential to "pass" and be reborn, so to speak, as Christians. Those with money and connections purchased counterfeit travel documents or expensive originals if they knew Polish officials. They'd move to new cities, where they were unrecognizable. If they were lucky, they registered under a new name, found work, and started fresh, nobody imaging their true identity. It was easier for girls, who landed jobs in offices or stores and as actresses and housemaids. Educated women who'd never done a day's physical labor eagerly took on housekeeping jobs. Some joined nunneries. It was harder for men: if the Germans suspected that a man was Jewish, they ordered him to pull down his pants. An entire family could be caught because of a circumcised baby boy. Plastic surgeons developed an operation to reverse a circumcision—

according to Renia, the surgery cost 10,000 złotys (roughly equivalent to US $33,000 today) and was rarely successful; others reported better outcomes. In children, the technique to restore foreskin required surgical intervention, special massage, and bearing weights. Some men obtained fake medical certificates claiming that they'd been circumcised at birth due to genital problems. The tiny Association of Tartar-Muslims in Warsaw also provided false papers to a few Jews, explaining away their circumcisions.

Even for those "imposters" who made it to the Aryan side, life was difficult. "*Schmaltzovniks*," or blackmailers (literally, "greasers"), approached disguised Jews on the streets, threatening to turn them in if they didn't pay up. The Poles had a better sense of who was Jewish than the Germans did. If a Jew was leaving the ghetto for a short trip, she had to carry a pile of cash just to hand out to the *schmaltzovniks* on her way. Gangs of Poles extorted Jews, stole from them, beat and threatened them, and sent them anonymous notes demanding payments be left at random locations. Sometimes they extorted the same Jew over a period of time, living off of her. Or they'd take the money and still hand her over to the Gestapo, which offered small rewards for each Jew caught alive, like a bit of cash, two pounds of sugar or a bottle of whiskey. Some greasers worked directly for the Gestapo, splitting the loot with them.

Several Jews ran to the forests instead of to the cities, pretended to be Polish, and tried to join partisan troops or spent months, even years, simply wandering. Children were placed in orphanages, usually for a bribe. Kids worked on the Aryan streets, selling newspapers, cigarettes, and shoe polish, hiding from Polish children who might recognize them, flog them, and then hand them in.

Regardless of the difficulties, Renia had no choice. It was rumored that the Aktion would take place any day. No one's name could be taken off the list this time. The only people who'd be allowed to stay were the ones selected to dismantle the ghetto and sort the Jews' possessions. A man who escaped from the deportation camp in nearby Kielce ran with a warning: he'd witnessed the Nazis torture young men and force them to write fake letters to their families telling them that they were fine, that it was not a deportation to death. Those who refused to comply were shot on the spot. This man was sure that the trains he'd seen stuffed with people were heading to certain death.

The Kukielkas needed to flee. They gathered all the cash they'd received from selling furniture and divided it equally among the children. Renia's parents and her little brother Yankel would leave for the forests. Her two sisters would travel to Warsaw disguised as Aryans, stay with relatives, and then attempt to bring over Leah and Moshe. "No matter what happens," Moshe told his children, "promise me you will always stay Jewish."

Renia was to set off alone. This would be her last night in her family's home.

Saturday, August 22. Renia made it to a Nazi-run Jewish labor camp on the outskirts of Sędziszów, thanks to her brother. Aaron had escaped from the first work camp, returned to the family by pretending to be a Pole wandering the woods, and then came here to build train tracks. He was particularly well liked among the guards and had arranged for Renia to join him. The camp was composed of five hundred talented Jewish boys who paid thousands of złotys in order to work, believing they'd be safe from deportation. Alongside them were twenty Jewish women doing light labor, like counting bricks.

Renia was relieved to arrive, which she did with a friend, Yochimovitz, from the ghetto, but she obsessed over her parents and their farewell. Leah and Moshe had been beside themselves when saying goodbye. Renia could not stop thinking about her father's tears, her mother's wails, the parting of their arms, hands, fingers. And Yankeleh, his little eyes flooded over, his warm grip on her back, the little fingers. No, she could not let that be the last time she saw them, never, never.

And so, soon after beginning her work on railway bridges, Renia convinced her supervisor to admit her father and sisters to the camp.

But it was too late.

A few days later, a sharp, sunny morning, Renia woke up ready for work, when a message hit her like lightning. Just a few hours earlier, at four o'clock, an Aktion had begun in Wodzisław. Renia would no longer be able to communicate with her family. Had they managed to leave in time?

But there was more. The Nazi camp commander approached the girls. He called Renia over and softly told her that women were no longer allowed to work at the camp. The Gestapo had asked him to add them to the upcoming transport list. "Escape," he urged Renia quietly. "Go wherever you can."

Go? Away? Again?

No, no, no, the despair was too great.

But he tried hard to convince her. "You are still young," the German said. "Run away, and maybe you will make it out alive."

What about Yochimovitz? Renia refused to leave without her.

If it was up to him, the German said, he'd want them to stay there. If it wasn't for the great danger, he'd take them all in himself. "Good luck," he said, honestly, gently. "Now go."

August 27, 1942, the first day of the next phase of her life—Renia's days of wandering. She was now one of those Jews meandering without a guide, sans destination. Aaron and his friend Herman had helped her and Yochimovitz, fetching water for the girls to wash with and a pack of food from the German. Then they brought the two of them to the forest, near where they worked, and left.

Now Renia and Yochimovitz were alone. Where to?

Suddenly they heard screaming, gunshots, barking in all directions.

Then a command to a dog, in German: "Stop the damn Jews, Rex! Bite!"

The girls ran, trying to flee. Within minutes, they were being chased by two policeman who accused Yochimovitz of being a Jew. They were taken to a cabin for train conductors where other Jews who had been caught were being held. From outside, Renia heard screams emerging from the basement.

Renia resolved right there that she would absolutely not go into that basement.

"Do you have children?" she asked the policeman.

"Yes, four."

"I am also the daughter of a mother and father. I too have sisters and brothers," Renia pleaded as the other officers urged him to take the girls downstairs. "Do you really think I'm a Jew?"

"No," he said, tearing up. "You look and speak Polish. You are one of us. Walk away, quickly. Take your friend."

The girls began to move, fast. This was not good. Yochimovitz had the wrong look. Was her friend a liability or a life support? Would Renia have to leave her?

Sometimes questions answer themselves.

She heard shots. Renia turned around.

On the ground in front of her.

Yochimovitz was dead.

In 1942 eighteen-year-old girls in New York City explored their new adulthood by ogling Humphrey Bogart, or singing along to Bing Crosby's hit "White Christmas" while sipping milkshakes at the corner drug store. In London, Renia's peers were jiving across the polished floors of the dance hall boom. Even in

Aryan Warsaw, young people sought distraction from the war, promenading at the park, flirting as they rode on musical carousels. But weeks before her eighteenth birthday, in the forest, Renia's coming of age played out differently.

"From that moment on," she later wrote. "I was on my own."

September 12, 1942
It's a beautiful night. The moon shines in all its glory. I am lying in a field between potatoes, shivering from cold, recounting my recent experiences to myself. Why? Why should I bother to suffer so much?
And still, I don't want to die.

Renia awoke to the dawn. Days and nights in the field, nothingness but the odd barking dog, and suddenly she knew could not just stay there, nibbling on grains she'd collected from the ground. She needed to move, to find a place where Jews still existed. Where the idea of herself existed. Her legs dragging like lead, Renia was lost and filled with sorrow for her friend. It was too much to go through this hardship alone. But after hours of wandering, she finally came across a small village.

Renia tried desperately to fix her appearance—which meant everything now—before finding the nearest train station and boarding a train to a town where she knew a railway worker: a client at her parents' shop. After disembarking, she moved quickly, despite her thick exhaustion. All Renia could think about was how badly she wanted to shower and resemble the people around her.

Suddenly a miracle. On the ground was a woman's purse. Renia rummaged through it and found a bit of money. But much more important: the owner's passport. Renia clutched it, knowing this was her ticket to travel, to make her way.

Renia scurried through town, finally knocking on her acquaintance's door, her hands shaking with fatigue and fear. He opened up to reveal a warm, clean, comfortable abode—a sight from another life. He and his wife were elated to see her, but shocked by her courage and appearance. "Rivchu, you look terrible," was their greeting.

"My face is flabby," Renia wrote, "but who cares?" The couple fed her tomato soup with noodles and gave her clean clothes and underwear. They all sat in the kitchen, crying over the incredible Leah, her mother, their friend.

That's when, through the window, they overheard

the young son tell the neighbor that Rivchu, a girl from whom the family used to buy clothes and socks, was visiting.

"That's a strange name," the burly neighbor asserted.

"Well," the boy said, "she's a Jew."

Renia's hosts bolted from their seats and pushed her into a cupboard, covering her in piles of clothes. Renia could hear the knock on the door, the muffled accusations.

"No, no, no." The couple mocked their child's imagination. "We had a guest, not a Jew."

That night, her hosts handed Renia money and a train ticket. After a brief respite of semisecurity, one she had not allowed herself to sink into too deeply, she was off again. Only now, she was off with new clothes and a new name: Wanda Widuchowska. This may have been the name on the ID in the pocketbook she'd found; in another account, Renia relayed that her family friends sought help from their priest, who gave them the papers of the recently deceased Wanda Widuchowska, a local woman in her twenties. The husband used a marker to blur the original fingerprint and put Renia's on top.

Fake documents for Polish Jews included identity cards (*Kennkartes*, which everyone was required to carry), birth certificates, travel permits, work, residence and food cards, and baptismal certificates. Most Jews held a mix, especially as different IDs were required in different regions. The best type of fake ID was a real one from a deceased or even living person. (The Gestapo sometimes called to see if a person was verified in town books.) Like Renia, Jews would supplant their photographs and/or fingerprints on top of the originals; sometimes they needed to replicate the stamp or part thereof, as it might have overlapped with the original photo. The second-best type of ID was real papers with false names. To obtain these, someone had to steal or procure blank forms, stamps, and seals, and then submit an application to the town hall. Some forgers carved out seals from rubber erasers, or requested municipal documents by post—the return envelopes had seals that they would save and use.

Most Jews' fake IDs were complete fabrications. The forger received a photo and had to invent an identity. It was best if first and last names were related to that person's actual class (they often used similar-sounding or similar-meaning names from the Jewish ones); if their profession related to their appearance and, if possible, to their real profession; and if their place of birth was somewhere familiar to them—say, for Varsovians, Łódź was a good choice. If someone had a pronounced Polish accent, the ID maker might indicate he or she was from Belorussia, in the East. The fabricated documents were least reliable, as a bad forgery would arouse suspicion that the holder was a Jew—worse than having no papers at all.

The best way to get fake ID was through friends (women tended to be better at asking for favors) or via the black market. But in the latter case, the quality was less reliable, and despite the expense, the creator could not always be trusted; for example, the young educated man whose new forged ID identified him as a middle-aged shoemaker. How could he act the part? The black market also left one open to blackmail, since you'd have to reveal your true identity to a total stranger. And, as Renia was learning, that was something to avoid at all costs.

Another day, another small village. A totally unknown place. Renia was offered a job as housekeeper in a mansion. She considered it momentarily, but how could she? She felt so weary, so weak. And so afraid of being found out. Her papers were good only for a small municipal area. Registering her identity here meant death.

Another long, hard walk, another train station. That night felt especially dark, the moon hiding, the stars as tired as she was.

Renia, in her fine Polish, bought a ticket to the town of Kazimierza Wielka, where she'd heard Jews still lived. She needed to find a base, to figure out if her family was still alive.

The train jerked into motion, and suddenly Renia's blood ran cold.

A man was staring into her eyes. She knew right away he was from Jędrzejów. He recognized her.

Much to her relief, he walked off, but for a while, people kept passing her seat. "Yes, that's her," she overheard in the darkness. "She has it easy. She doesn't resemble a Jew."

Renia froze. Everything went blurry. She was sure she was going to faint. Everywhere she looked, she saw her persecutors. She was surrounded, drowning.

Renia got up and moved to the end of the train, to a little platform that jutted outside. The cold air slapped her cheeks. Sparks from the smokestack snapped at her mercilessly. She took a breath. But just one. The car door opened, and the conductor appeared. "Good evening."

She immediately knew he was trying to assess her accent, to see if she was a Jew.

"It's so cold out, and the sparks are dangerous," he said. "Why don't you come inside?"

"Thank you for your kindness," Renia replied, "but the cars are so crowded and stuffy. I'd rather get some air."

He looked at her ticket, checked her destination, and then ducked back inside. There was no doubt. At the next station, he was going to hand her in to the gendarmes, the German military police, probably for a reward of a few złotys.

The train slowed down as it began to ascend a hill. There was no time to think, to feel. Now or never.

Renia threw her tiny suitcase off, then jumped right after it.

For a few minutes, she lay on the ground unconscious, but a wallop of cold jolted her awake. She checked in with her body, making sure all her limbs were accounted for. Her legs hurt, but who cared? She had saved her life, and that was most important.

Using all her energy, she propelled forward into the thick, dark strangeness. The dew on the grass caressed her feet, relieving her pain slightly.

A light in the distance; a small house. The dog barked, the landlord arrived. "What do you want?"

"I'm on the way to see my relatives," Renia lied. "I don't have a certificate proving my Aryan origin, and I know the Nazis are searching. I need to wait out the night somewhere safe. If Germans see me during the day, they'd know right away I wasn't a Jew."

The man cocked his head sympathetically and gestured her inside. She breathed. He gave Renia a warm drink and showed her to a bushel of hay where she could sleep. "You must leave in the morning," he warned. "I'm not allowed to accept guests without registering them."

The next morning, Renia set off again by foot, but at least she was rested, invigorated. She kept on going, prompted by the hope that her family was still alive; that she had something to live for.

The Jews of Kazimierza Wielka, knowing that the nearby villages had already been "exterminated," were gripped by tension. Few had escape plans, few had money. Even the best-hearted Christians were not helping Jews hide at this point, fearing for their own lives.

The Nazis had decreed that the Jews in town could not take in Jewish refugees, and the Jews obeyed, hoping that doing so might save them from deportation. Renia knew this was delusional, but what could she do? She felt completely naked, with no roof over her head, no money. She needed work. But how? How did one get a job in the middle of an annihilation?

She wandered this town of strangers, helpless, nauseous, consoled only by the sight of the Star of David armbands, which reassured her that a few Jews still lived. One evening she spotted a Jewish militia member and declared desperately that she was a "*yiddishe kind.*" A Jewish child. "Where can I spend the night?" she asked.

Warning her not to meander through the streets, he let her stay in the corridor of his house until morning. Renia got to know the family, the only Jewish home she knew. And they, in turn, were the only people who knew she was Jewish. Who knew who she was.

Renia's charm took over. It wasn't long before she met a Polish girl who became fond of her, and, thinking she was Polish, got her a job as a housekeeper in the home of a half-German family. Renia had already defied the Nazi regime by smuggling, hiding, scheming, and running; now began her chapter of disguise.

Life at the Hollanders was a calm reprieve. A day of work, she felt, was the best medicine for the wounds and insults she'd incurred along the way. Sure, she still had to disguise herself, constantly pretending to be a simple, happy-go-lucky girl, each evening muffling her all-night sobbing and insomnia, perpetually disguising her agitation with a smile. But at least she had a temporary home. She could focus on her goal: tracking down her family.

Renia's boss adored her. Occasionally she called the young woman over and overflowed with praise. "I'm so lucky," Mrs. Hollander gushed, "to have found such a clean, hardworking, God-fearing, experienced, knowledgeable, and educated girl."

To which Renia, of course, smiled. "I'm from a wealthy, educated family," she semi-lied. "But after my parents died, I needed to find household work."

The Hollanders gave Renia gifts, never treating her like a servant. Mrs. Hollander did not register her new housekeeper with the police; she must have sensed that Renia was a Jew. In order not to further arouse suspicions, Renia took an aggressive strategy, complaining that she did not have the right clothes for church. How could she, a religious Catholic, not pray and observe? The Hollanders eventually gifted her a set of fancy clothes. Only now, a new problem: she would have to attend church.

On that first Sunday, she rushed to get dressed, trembling. Though Renia grew up around Polish children at school and in the schoolyard, she had never been to Mass and had little clue about Catholic traditions; she certainly didn't know the hymns and prayers. Would her behavior betray her as a fraud? Nauseous as she entered the building, she was scared that everyone would be looking at her; that they would see through her act. "Everywhere I go," she wrote, "I must play a part."

With a wildly beating heart, she joined the throngs in the pews, wondering what her parents would think if they saw her now. Renia glued her eyes on her neighbors, imitating every motion. When they crossed themselves, she crossed herself. When they kneeled, she kneeled. When they prayed to the heavens with great devotion, so did Renia. "I hadn't even known that I was such a good actor," Renia later reflected, "able to impersonate and imitate."

At last, the service was over, and everyone headed for the door. Renia observed each microgesture. They kissed the statue of Jesus, she kissed the statue of Jesus.

Outside, in the cool, clear air, she was overwhelmed by relief. The Hollanders and all the neighbors had seen her at church, and witnessed her sincere prayers. It was a grand performance, and she'd passed.

And then, another miracle. Bliss, sheer bliss.

Renia had written a letter to her sister Sarah, who, the last she'd known, had been at a Freedom kibbutz in Będzin. Even in the horror of 1942, a fairly reliable Judenrat-run postal service still functioned; the militiaman had posted it for her.

Now, a few days later, she received a reply—from Sarah!—containing the most wonderful news in the universe: Renia's parents, brothers, and sisters were all alive. They'd found shelter in the forest west of Wodzisław, close to the town of Miechów. Aaron, meanwhile, was still at the labor camp.

By the time Renia finished reading, her tears soaked the page.

Although overjoyed her loved ones were alive, Renia found it unbearable to imagine them living in the forest, in the cold of late autumn. How could she enjoy a clean, warm bed in a part-German home while they suffered from hunger and frost? Renia imagined little Yankeleh, such a smart kid, destined to become a great adult, shivering and starving. Her longing to be with him overwhelmed her.

Renia lived day by day, hour by hour, waiting, worrying. And then arrived a letter from her parents.

Again, the thrill of receiving their note was accompanied by great pain at their suffering. Moshe and Leah were living in destitution, no roof over their heads, starving. Yankeleh, they wrote, tried to cheer them up, to give them a reason to live. There'd been no word from the two sisters who'd fled to Warsaw. Renia felt sick with helplessness.

She wrote immediately to Sarah and Aaron, asking

them to help their parents. The two siblings managed to convince nearby farmers to deliver a few supplies, which cost them enormous amounts of money.

More letters came from Sarah. Leah and Moshe had been elated to learn that Renia was alive and well. But they feared that it was too dangerous for her to stay where she was without the proper documents—the passport that she'd found at the station was not valid in this area. Renia knew that her family was probably right: if and when Mrs. Hollander eventually decided to register her with the police, she would be exposed.

And so, Renia decided, it was time to go see Sarah. To go to Będzin, to the Freedom kibbutz.

Chapter 8
To Turn to Stone

Renia
October 1942

S arah had arranged everything.

It was a bright autumn day, and Renia was returning from church, like a regular Catholic girl. She arrived at the Hollanders to find the sister of the militiaman who had taken her in. "A smuggler from Będzin is here," she whispered.

"Already?" Renia's heart leapt into her throat. This was it.

Sarah had hired a woman to help Renia cross the border from the General Government to the Third Reich annex. En route, she would be passing Miechów, the town where Jews—including her family, who had recently been caught—were being temporarily trapped. Her heart ached, longing for them. She was determined to stop there on the way. Today, at last, she would see her parents and her beautiful, sweet Yankeleh.

Renia served the Hollanders dinner in a state of exhilaration, her limbs light, cheeks flushed, heart bounding with energy. Mrs. Hollander noted how happy she seemed—so unusual for her.

That evening, after scheming with the militiaman's family, Renia approached her boss. "My aunt fell ill," she claimed. "They called for me to come quickly, to care for her for a few days."

Mrs. Hollander, of course, understood. Why wouldn't she trust her best employee?

The bright sun turned to clouds and rain, then the night's darkness set in. Total quiet. Renia, posing as "Wanda" from the found documents, waited for the train, her heart beating wildly. Even once she and the other passengers were speeding along, every moment felt like an hour. Over and over, she played through her mind the upcoming scene of glee: how her parents' faces would glow when they saw her.

And yet, why did her stomach ache ominously?

They arrived at a small station. "Is this Miechów?" Renia quietly asked her non-Jewish smuggler.

"Not yet. Soon, soon."

And then it was soon. "This one?"

"We cannot get off at Miechów."

"What? Why?" Renia froze.

"It will make your journey too difficult," the smuggler whispered. Renia was about to protest, when the woman added, "I don't have time to take you."

Renia pleaded. No was not an option.

"I promise," the smuggler told her, quieting her, "that as soon as I get you to Będzin, I will turn back and go to Miechów. I will get your parents and your brother. I will bring them to you in Będzin."

"No." Renia put her foot down. "I must go see them now."

"Listen," the smuggler said, leaning into her. "Sarah said you absolutely cannot go to Miechów. I cannot take you there."

As the locomotive chugged past fields and forests, Renia's mind whirred. She did not have long to decide. Should she ditch the smuggler, get off, stay here, and try to cross the border later somehow? But Sarah was older, wiser, more competent. And it made sense that Renia cross the border quickly; that she get the most dangerous part of the journey over with.

Renia passed the Miechów station glued to her seat, her heart leaden, her brain in a fog.

She spent a few days at the smuggler's house in Częstochowa, snacking, sleeping, longing, waking up jolted by frantic thoughts. It had been several years since she'd seen her sister—a lifetime. What did Sarah look like now? Would they recognize each other? Would she make it across the border? Renia felt weirdly comfortable in this alien part of Poland, where she was a stranger. Her foreignness was an asset: no one would recognize her. Her Jewishness was buried that much deeper.

The border crossing went without incident, and once in Będzin, Renia set out along the streets that sloped uphill to the castle, passing the town's colorful and ornate facades, its Art Deco–rounded balconies and Beaux Arts gargoyles and balustrades that marked the area's prewar glory. To the Freedom kibbutz! Feeling optimistic, the eighteen-year-old leapt up the stairs and threw open the door. She saw a hallway that glistened in the sunlight, and a room with young men and women, all dressed in clean clothes, sitting around tables, reading. It seemed so normal.

But where was Sarah? Why didn't she see her sister?

A young man, Baruch, introduced himself. He, like everyone here, knew who she was. Renia took one moment for a deep breath. What a treat—to be herself.

Baruch struck Renia as kind, resourceful, and full of life. He led her up two more flights of stairs to the sleeping quarters. The room was quiet, dark. She stepped in gingerly. Then she made out a muffled moaning.

It was Sarah, lying in bed. Sarah!

Baruch took Renia's arm, led her over. "Sarah," he said, gently, "would you like it if Renia came to see you?"

Sarah jumped out of bed. "Renia!" she cried. "You are all I have left in the world. I was sick worrying for you."

Sarah's kisses and embraces were warm on Renia's skin. Tears pooled on the mattress. Despite the older girl's weakness, she led Renia straight to the kitchen to feed her. In the kitchen light, Renia could see how skinny her sister's face had become, all bone and edge. She tried not to think about how, years earlier, Sarah had obtained papers to immigrate to Palestine. The owner of the shoe store where she worked had even offered financial help, but their father had been too proud to ask his relatives for the additional funds she'd need. So, she had stayed. *She looks so much older*, Renia noted, disturbed. Sarah's face was not the countenance of a twenty-seven-year-old. But watching her sister assemble a meal for her, full of gusto, Renia thought, *She's still young in spirit.*

The sisters, needing a plan to save their parents, spent days rolling through ideas, but there were no good ones. The smuggler's promise of bringing them back, it turned out, had been a lie—a betrayal that Renia refused to dwell on for fear her anger would consume her. Sarah and Renia faced a multitude of problems. To begin with, the kibbutz didn't have room for the Kukielkas. And besides, the fee for smuggling them over was extraordinary. Impossible.

Then a letter from Renia's parents arrived, the contents horrifying.

Moshe and Leah had spent the past days in a small, dirty neighborhood in Sandomierz, a town east of Miechów, living like animals. The Jews huddled in tiny, moldy rooms, where they slept on the floor or on a thin mattress of hay. They had no food and no fuel for heating. Their days were filled with fear: deportation, extermination, execution, the whole ghetto could be set on fire. Any of these atrocities, at any moment.

Yankeleh, too, composed a letter, begging his siblings for help and to bring him to Będzin, even just temporarily. All he wanted was to be with his sisters, the only people he could count on. Despite the inhuman horrors he'd witnessed, he clung to life. "Our parents may do the unthinkable and commit suicide," he wrote. "But as long as I am with them, I keep them sane." He escaped from the ghetto each day, trying to earn some money. Every grosz he received went to the 120 złotys per night they had to pay to sleep on exposed board, crammed together like fish in a barrel. Mother, father, and son warmed one another, "as worms ate our flesh," Yankeleh described. They hadn't changed clothes or underwear in months. There was no detergent, no running water.

As Renia's eyes galloped over the words, she felt sick. What could she do? She lay awake for several nights, terrified that the end was coming for them all.

And then, the last letter, the final farewell: "If we don't survive," her mother and father wrote, "then please fight for your lives. So you can bear witness. So you can recount how your loved ones, your people, were murdered by sheer evil. May God save you. We are about to die, knowing that you are going to stay alive. Our greatest pain is the fate of Yankel, our youngest. But there's no anger toward you. We know that you would do everything possible to save us. This is our fate. If this is God's will, we must accept it."

As if that wasn't enough, the letter also told of the fate of Renia's sisters Esther and Bela. They had stopped in Wodzisław, and, sensing a roundup of Jews, hid in an outhouse. The landlady's seventeen-year-old son came out to use the facilities, discovered them, and alerted the Gestapo.

They were sent to Treblinka.

Lost. All was lost.

But Renia shed no tears. "My heart," she later wrote, "turned to stone."

These were horrible days for Renia. "I am an orphan," she repeated to herself, the sick reality sinking in. Renia felt disoriented, as if she were lacking her memory, her sense of place, of self. She had to realign her being, remind herself that now she lived for her sister, for her comrades. This was her new family. Without them to ground her, to provide her with a sense of reality and personhood, she would have gone mad.

Then the girls lost contact with Aaron. Rumor had it he was transferred to the arms factory at Skarżysko-Kamienna, where Jews were forced to perform brutal labor, barefoot, clothes torn, for a mere slice of bread and cold water. More than twenty-five thousand Jewish men and women were brought to this labor camp; the vast majority did not survive the unsanitary conditions and exposure to toxins that turned hair green and skin red. Aaron, Renia heard, contracted typhus. His superiors liked him, which saved him from immediate execution, but his health was fragile. As an "unproductive," he was barely fed.

And yet.

Renia and Sarah were alive. They were shadows of selves, empty shades, but still, alive. As with so many of the Jewish youth who lost their parents, their new-found freedom accompanied grief and guilt but also energy. The ties binding them to normal life had been severed; they were no longer responsible to others. To live, to retain any sense of human spirit, they needed to stay active, to blur their intense and overwhelming pain by plunging into demanding work that would curb introspection.

"If I'm destined to go down," Renia said, personally uttering Abba Kovner's mantra of resistance. "I will not die like a clueless sheep sent to the slaughter."

Her zeal fanned a hot fire that was already burning among the Będzin youth.

Chapter 9
The Black Ravens

Chajka and Renia
October 1942

Chajka Klinger sprinted through the streets and alleyways of Będzin. Her first mission. In her bag, hidden flyers. Her curly, short, brown hair was tucked behind her ears, her eyes surveilled, her heart pounded. Each step was sheer danger but also contained careful joy. She was heading out to distribute news about guerillas, mass deportations, and politics. The truth. Hands shaking, she taped one notice to a door, then handed another to a pedestrian. She even ventured outside the Jewish area.

At last, she was *doing* something!

The Będzin that Renia came to was already sizzling with the spirit of resistance. One of its most vocal proponents: twenty-five-year-old Chajka Klinger.

Born in 1917 to a poor Hassidic family in Będzin, Chajka was brainy and fiery, clever and passionate. Her family was barely supported by her mother's grocery store; her father studied Torah and Talmud all day. She received a rare scholarship to attend the secular Jewish Furstenberg Gymnazium, a top-tier prep school, where she became fluent in numerous languages and dreamed of becoming an intellectual. Będzin, with its sizable Jewish middle-class population, was an early host of many Zionist movements. Relatively free from antisemitism in the 1930s, the town served as a passionate hub of twelve youth groups. Chajka's school, a beacon of Będzin's well-to-do, liberal community, supported socialist Zionism, and outside of school, Chajka was entirely taken by the intellectual rigor and philosophies of The Young Guard—a rare choice of groups among her peers because of its strictness.

The Young Guard, which invented the "intimate group" model, blended the striving for a Jewish homeland with Marxism, heavy romanticism, and beliefs in the superior state of youth and life in the wild for a sound body and mind. They read a profusion of European revolutionaries, promoted a culture of conversation and self-actualization, and aimed to create a new type of Jew. Committed to truth, the group had its own ten commandments, including laws of purity: no smoking, alcohol, or sex allowed. The psychoanalytic study of sexuality was encouraged, but the act was considered too distracting to the collective cause.

Chajka, in her collared shirts and wire-rimmed glasses, adopted these radical views zealously, seeing The Young Guard as an avant-garde movement that would eventually lead the Jewish nation to a complete social and national revolution. Rebelling against her own background, she felt connected to its mantra of intergenerational conflict. Also, her first boyfriend was a dedicated member. Chajka was extroverted, sensitive, and always falling in love.

Devoted, she was critical of others but also of herself when she did not live up to The Young Guard's high standards. She quickly became a counselor, then an editor, and then a regional movement leader.

Her boyfriend had been drafted into the Polish army. While he was serving, she became aware of tall, slim David Kozlowski, a comrade who had pockets stuffed with newspapers, and a terrible stutter. They met at the library when the librarian refused to give Chajka a book because David wanted it, and he was their top reader. He smiled at her. Upset, she pretended not to know him. (He never forgave her.) Then he submitted a poem to the newspaper Chajka edited, and she was overwhelmed by its lyricism and yearning. Suddenly she noticed how velvety brown his deep-set eyes were, how much pain they held, "the eyes of a dreamer."

In the late 1930s, the couple joined a kibbutz to prepare for aliyah; this was a significant decision for David, whose elite parents forbade it, and for Chajka, who knew that she'd be giving up her intellectual ambitions for a life of austerity on the land. Sensitive, shabby David, a rabid leftist in theory, endured a difficult proletarianization: he could wax poetic about China's Chen, the Soviet Union and the Spanish Revolution, but could not bear the monotony of sitting behind a sewing machine. Chajka, an incurable romantic, felt it her duty to help this "delicate savior," this "young tree" blossom, and she supported him until he became a spiritual leader of the group. They were supposed to move to Palestine on September 5, 1939.

Four days before that, when the Nazis attacked Poland, she attempted to escape the country, not with her family but with David. They took to the crowded roads, jumped off an air-bombed train, and dodged bullet after bomb after falling tree. But they couldn't get out. They were preparing to flee east, when a message came from The Young Guard HQ instructing them to stay put in Będzin and revive the movement. If the Jewish community remained in Poland, The Young Guard community would too, to "live, grow, and die with it." As local leaders, Chajka and David heeded the order. They were, however, shocked by the Nazis' brutality; to Chajka, Germany was an enlightened culture, and she'd even anticipated a progressive rule.

Because the Zaglembie region had been annexed by the Third Reich rather than form part of the General Government, the environment was more conducive to learning. The Jews in this area were forced to work in German factories. Zaglembie, which means "from the depth" and refers to its mining reserve, was a rich industrial region, and dozens of textile factories producing clothing, uniforms, and shoes were set up. Work in these "shops" was not easy. "Outside the windows, apple trees and lilacs are blooming," one teenager wrote of her days, "and you have to sit in this suffocating and stinking room and sew." Jews worked for meager salaries and scraps of food, but conditions were much better than at labor camps, and several owners protected their cheap labor from deportation.

One notable example was Alfred Rossner, a German industrialist who never joined the Nazi Party.

After the occupation, he moved to Będzin to take over one of the Jewish factories and employed thousands of Jews. Rossner's workshop, which manufactured Nazi uniforms, was considered indispensable. Every worker had a yellow *Zonder* pass that spared him or her and two relatives from deportations. Similar to the now famous Oskar Schindler, Rossner was protective of and kind toward his Jewish workers; later in the war, he warned Jews of deportations and rescued them directly from trains.

Chajka reinstituted and led the local Young Guard, along with her boyfriend David and several other women—among them two sisters, Leah and Idzia Pejsachson, whose Bundist father had taken part in the Russian Revolution. The group of dear friends met clandestinely in private homes. Since aliyah was impossible, their main objective was to teach the youth language and literacy, culture, ethics, and history. Despite Chajka's private disappointment, she went straight to work, focusing on nurseries, orphanages, and those aged ten to sixteen, who she feared were suffering from neglect and poverty, with no guardians. Dirty and unsupervised, the kids were smuggling pretzels, rolls, sweets, shoelaces, and corsets, and selling them on the streets. Chajka had no plan (for which she was typically self-critical) but a lot of zeal, and she began with the poorest children, finding them shoes and clothes, cleaning them and serving them lunch. She proposed to the Judenrat that they set up day care centers to help laboring parents. The Young Guard did all the planning but the Judenrat took over. Regardless, she was happy that the kids were looked after. These young orphans and refugees, she hoped, would one day implement their movement's ideals.

In the first winter of occupation, Będzin's Young Guard organized a Purim festival. Traditionally, Purim was a merry holiday during which Jews dressed in costume, put on satirical sketches (Purim *shpiels*), read the holiday scroll, and spun noisemakers known as *graggers* to drown out every mention of Haman, the evil Persian minister who planned to kill all the Jews in the land. Jews celebrated their savior Queen Esther, a Jewish woman who disguised herself as a non-Jewish queen and, using her intelligence and wiles, convinced King Ahasuerus to cancel Haman's plans.

The Będzin Jewish orphanage was packed, dozens of children in their best clothes, laughing. Chajka stood at the back of the room, flicking from rapture to keeping watch like a jail guard. Her dark eyes twinkled with pride as Irka, the third and youngest Pejsachson sister, conducted the group in a holiday ceremony. The children walked in singing loudly. They wrote and put on their own plays about Israel and about their hard life on the streets, a Purim miracle. Then the space was quickly transformed, and a meeting of 120 Young Guard members began, everyone wearing a gray or white shirt. The comrades chanted their mantra in unison: "We shall not let ourselves be blindly led by fate. We shall go our own way." Chajka couldn't believe how many people had shown up, especially with the war raging around them.

Będzin's Freedom kibbutz, which had hosted sixty members before the war, became a social center for all the movements. Freedom organized sing-alongs, Hebrew classes, and a library, as well as children's programs. Sarah, Renia's sister, was a dedicated worker on this front, playing out a family passion inherited from her mother. She cared avidly for children and helped run the kibbutz's orphanage, called Atid, the Hebrew word for "future." The town of Będzin's relatively porous boundaries—there was no closed ghetto, and its postal service reached Switzerland and other countries—made it a center for education and training. Frumka frequently traveled here two hundred miles from Warsaw, organizing seminars; The Young Guard leaders did too.

At their peak, these underground activities involved two thousand Jewish youth and many took place at a nearby farm. The Judenrat had given the Zionists thirty fields and gardens as well as horses and goats, to plow, sow, and tend. Photographs show youths from various groups donning caps and kerchiefs—and no yellow stars—smiling while snipping crops and dancing the hora. Images of Sarah Kukielka depict her at an outdoor celebration among dozens of comrades seated at long, white-bedecked tables, honoring the birthday of the late Hebrew poet Chaim Nachman Bialik.

The youth organized memorial evenings, when they sat in the fields, sang about freedom, shared memories, and spoke out against Fascism. "Hundreds joined us for Shabbat," Chajka wrote, "looking to breathe, looking for a patch of green grass." The farm, where "the pots on the wall sparkled as if in a festive way," was their rejuvenation, reflection, and renewal point.

By the fall of 1941, Będzin's Young Guard was in its prime, and Chajka was its mother.

Then, one night, a roundup. The evenings leading up to it had been terrifying. No one slept, including Chajka. They waited for the marching and whistles of military men coming to kidnap and take them to labor camps with horrific, backbreaking, disease-ridden conditions. That night, it actually happened. She hoped they'd missed her building, but alas. They were pounding on the gate, ready to tear the superintendent to shreds for taking so long to open up. She hoped they'd skip her apartment, but then they were inside, searching every corner.

"Get dressed," they ordered Chajka. Her mother was crying, begging the Nazis to leave her alone.

"Be quiet!" Chajka shouted. "Don't you dare beg them or humiliate yourself in front of them! I'm going. Be well."

Outside it was pitch dark, and hard for Chajka to make out the convoys, all the girls. She could hear only the opening of gates. The Germans arranged the girls into rows, then escorted them into the enormous municipal school building. So many girls: two thousand of them.

Chajka immediately began to look around for her friends. Leah, Nacia, Dora, Hela—the comrades were all there. As they were on the second floor, she considered jumping out the window, but she glanced out and saw guards all over the courtyard.

There would be a selection and deportation in the morning. For now, Chajka and her comrades wanted to deal with their current chaos. It was loud, like a market square. The Będzin girls were pressed together tightly, their faces nearly touching. An ocean of heads, crying, screaming, hysterical laughter, frightening suffocation.

Leah Pejsachson took action. Chajka's strong and shapely Young Guard coleader always woke up first, at five in the morning, ready to sift, plow, and drive the tractor, nudging the others: "Get up, lazies!" Now Leah ran from one room to the next. She looked for people she knew, and on the way, opened windows so the women wouldn't asphyxiate. She heard children crying wildly. With Nacia, she collected them all into one corner, combed their hair, and gave out bread. "Don't cry," Leah reassured the girls. "They are not worth your tears. This is a humiliation! They won't send you away; you are too young." Nacia made sure that the Nazis checked their ages and had them all released.

In the morning, the classification began. Each woman presented the German commissioner with her work certificate. The girls who worked for the weapons factory were freed.

Though Leah was one of the first to be set loose, she did not run off. Instead, she waited nearby for other girls who were coming out and took their work papers. Then she sent the papers back into the building for those who didn't have valid documents. She stayed outside the entire time, "bustling around," Chajka desribed, and enabled a large number of girls to get out.

When the Germans finished their selection, they'd fallen shy of their quota and roamed the streets, capturing any women who remained in the area. Leah was among them. Now she couldn't help herself with work papers. Straight into the wagon!

Leah was deported to a labor camp, the first one of their group. "We missed her terribly," Chajka wrote. "How strongly we had connected with her."

Leah wrote letters from the camp, telling of hunger and beatings, even for women. "I long for you, but I'm alright here," she assured them. Half the day, she worked in the kitchen, the other half in the sick ward. Even under the Nazis' watchful eyes, she managed to sneak in bread for prisoners who had ashen, dying faces. She knew that those with broad shoulders and strong bodies would not be harmed by the small portions, but the pale men who came straight from a yeshiva and refused to eat unkosher meat needed to be helped. *Where did she get the food?* Chajka wondered. *How did she divide it all up without the Germans seeing?* "Even the fields and winds did not know," Chajka wrote. Working as a nurse was difficult, but Leah knew she had to stay, as she was useful to many, even though she imagined she would end up in prison.

The kitchen was no better. The female cooks took bribes and gifts, stole, and gave the best rations to their friends. Leah tried to appeal to their consciences, preaching and moralizing: "It can't go on like this."

"Leah," Chajka wrote to her, "you are not alone in your fight. The same battle is being conducted by Rachel in Gutan-Bricke, Sarah in Markshdadt, and Guteh in Klatandorf." The Jewish women of Będzin were everywhere, smuggling, stealing, saving.

Despite its special status, the situation in Zaglembie deteriorated significantly. Work was no longer the ultimate savior. Following a smaller deportation Aktion in May 1942, the Nazis arrived en masse in August, at the same time as the Aktions in Warsaw. The Jews of Będzin were called to the soccer stadium the next day for a document check. The youth movements were wary and warned Jews not to attend; the Nazis knew of this, and so they staged a pretend check of documents in a neighboring town to convince everyone that it would be safe. After that, the ZOB debated whether it was safer to attend or not. In the end, its members decided to go. Chajka too.

Thousands walked over at five thirty in the morning. They sat on bleachers, even in a good mood, dressed festively—as the Judenrat had encouraged them—until they noticed that they were surrounded by soldiers with machine guns. People fainted, children wailed. There was not a drop of water to combat people's extreme thirst, until a lengthy rain shower drenched them all. At three o'clock, the selection started: Return home. Go to forced labor. Further inspection. Or deportation and death. The Judenrat, not wanting to rile the Nazis, had lied to their fellow Jews.

As people began to realize what the three lines meant, and families were torn apart, chaos erupted. Many tried switching sections. The Germans then started "having fun," wrote Chajka, cruelly separating parents and their children—one to life, one to death— bashing people with their rifle butts, dragging frantic mothers by their hair.

Twenty thousand Jews had gathered. Eight to ten thousand of them were now locked into the public kitchen, the orphanage, and another Judenrat building, awaiting deportation to who knows where. SS guards prevented any food or medical supplies from reaching them. People began to kill themselves.

But as always, the youth leaders of Będzin did not simply accept their fate. They knew that thousands of Jews outnumbered the Jewish police and the SS. That night, the movements decided to act. Without a plan, they improvised. Freedom members gathered children who had been slated for deportation, and at their signal, the children broke into a sprint and ran. Others got hold of Jewish police hats and made their way into the crowd, pushing and kicking people into the "safe" lines. When the Judenrat convinced the SS to allow in food, comrades donned makeshift police hats and entered one of the buildings, bringing people out in the containers used to deliver bread or in giant soup pots. Still others tried to dig escape tunnels.

The women of The Young Guard knew they had to break into the locked buildings at any cost. They quickly convinced the Judenrat that they needed to set up an infirmary inside the orphanage. Jewish girls in white aprons entered and spread to all corners. These "nurses" comforted and bandaged the sick, but their main job was to help as many women as possible escape. Each girl took off her white uniform and handed it to one of the captives, instructing, "Get dressed quickly, take the certificate, and without showing any fear, walk straight out of here through the main entrance. No one will stop you. Then send the uniform back in."

Each time a "nurse" left the building, she had to be careful about which gendarme was guarding the gate. One of them had been promised a gold watch by the girls. But if it was the lieutenant, she had to smile beautifully and put on an innocent face.

While this was going on, Irka Pejsachson discovered a pathway from the attic through a block of unguarded civilian houses, and to the outside. The girls stationed someone as a lookout at the attic door, and busted a hole in the wall. Though shaking with fear, they managed to send Jews out, one by one. According to one account, two thousand people were freed.

Suddenly German officials barged into the building, demanding documents. One helper was missing a uniform, another had no papers. They were taken away. As Chajka knew, "There were always sacrifices."

Będzin's youth movements, including The Young Guard and Freedom, began working together, propelled by these brutal deportations; by stories of mass executions in Vilna and at Chelmno; by energizing visits from Tosia, who in particular urged the movement girls to go on missions and take action; as well as by inspiring tales of Warsaw's resistance activity and partisan pursuits. They'd seen firsthand that with just a bit of organization, they could save lives.

In the summer of 1942, Chajka hosted Mordechai Anilevitz, one of The Young Guard leaders who had come from Warsaw. She held Anilevitz in the highest esteem, calling him the "pride of the movement" with his "unusual, rare abilities" of being both a man of theory and a practical leader. "Mordechai was brave," she went on. "Not because he wanted to be brave, but because he truly was brave."

In late summer, while the Warsaw ghetto was being liquidated, leaders from various Zionist groups assembled in the Będzin youth farm kitchen to listen to a two-hour keynote given by Anilevitz, entitled "A Farewell to Life." He stood tall, with his open-collar shirt, and told them what he knew. Chajka attended with her boyfriend David and the Pejsachson sisters; her hair stood on end as she heard about gas chambers and mass deaths by suffocation at Treblinka. But he also told them about resistance efforts that were underway in Vilna, Białystok, and Warsaw. Anilevitz called for action, for honorable deaths, a romantic vision that appealed to Chajka.

The Zaglembie ZOB was then officially founded, a satellite of the resistance cell in Warsaw, comprising two hundred comrades from various movements. Będzin had already established a strong connection to Warsaw, and couriers were dispatched to collect information, plans, and arms. Będzin was also connected by post to Geneva, where The Pioneers coordinating committee was based. Secret coded postcards were sent from Będzin to Switzerland telling of the activities of the ZOB in Warsaw as well.

Surviving postcards written by Frumka, Tosia, and Zivia to Jews outside Poland are filled with secret codes. They often turned events into people. For instance, to indicate that they were holding a seminar, Tosia wrote that "Seminarsky is visiting us at the moment . . . and will stay for a month." Frumka wrote: "I am waiting for visits from guests: Machanot and Avodah should be coming here." *Machanot* and *Avodah* are the Hebrew words for *camps* and *work*, respectively; she was referring to Nazi labor camps. "E.C. is in hospital in Lemberg," meant that he'd been arrested. "Pruetnitsky and Schitah lived with me"—Hebrew words for *pogroms* and *destruction*. In heartbreaking letters, Zivia begged American Jews to send money "for doctors to help V.K.'s illness"—that is, for weapons to save the Jewish people.

Anilevitz's call for self-defense transformed Chajka. She became more radical than him, and one of the ZOB's fiercest proponents. "No revolutionary movement, let alone [one of] the young, had ever faced problems similar to ours—the single, naked fact of annihilation, of death. We stood face-to-face with it and found an answer. We found a path . . . *hagana* [defense]." The Young Guard could no longer propose a philosophy of radical optimism, she understood, but of violence. Armed defense—to fight as Jews, alongside

Jews, leaving a Jewish legacy—was the only way forward. She rejected all plans for escape or rescue. "The avant-garde," she later wrote, "must die where its people are dying."

Like Zivia, Chajka felt compelled to share the truth, furious at leaders who tried to hide it. "We had to open [the nation's] eyes, prevent it from sedating itself on opium, and show it the naked reality," she insisted. "Because we wanted to trigger a reaction." In her diary, she wrote, "Only we, the black ravens, say that if there is a campaign, they will no longer handle us with kid gloves. They will finish us off once and for all."

But as in Warsaw, it was not easy to form a military corps. Będzin also lacked weapons, training, contact with Polish underground groups, and support from the Judenrat and community. The youth had little money and felt deeply embittered toward foreign Jews who were not helping. When The Young Guard leaders were killed in Warsaw and the weapons lost, Anilevitz had to return there, leaving the Będzin ZOB branch in limbo, without a leader who could engage in top-level affairs, waiting for cash and instructions. Comrades pined for any words from Warsaw or the Polish resistance and felt idle, restless. Many dreamed of joining the partisans, preferring to die in the forest than in camps. At last, at the end of September, Zvi Brandes, a leader whom Chajka knew well from *hachshara*, and respected for his "thick, sinewy, muscular arms," rocklike build, and confident stride, arrived to help run the underground—and to harvest potatoes, when manpower was needed.

Zvi shifted focus from the failure to contact partisans to defense and propaganda. Action began right away. They formed groups of fives: as in their long-established education model, these were secret five-member fighting units, each with its own commander. The fighters planned for ways to defy and attack the Judenrat. They published underground bulletins, letters, and a daily newspaper. Comrades who worked in uniform factories printed German flyers imploring soldiers to throw down their weapons; they stuffed them in the new shoes being sent to the front.

This is when Chajka first went out on her missions, sprinting through streets and alleyways, distributing underground flyers, telling people the truth, telling them to rebel.

How quickly one gets used to a new normal. Despite forced labor and deportations to murder, life in Będzin was "heaven" for Renia. The communal abode felt so calm. They made soup from vegetable scraps and baked bread. Thirty-seven comrades worked. Many had the

Zonder permits that enabled them to move around, protected from forced labor and execution. Due to a shortage of workers, comrades went out for daily work, then labored in the kibbutz laundry or farmed in the evenings. As soon as Renia, the youngest of them, arrived, she was assigned to work in the laundry, which became property of the Judenrat; it appears the comrades were paid a small sum to clean Nazi uniforms. The torment that Renia had witnessed in the General Government section of Poland was not felt yet in Zaglembie.

"Sometimes I look at the comrades living here, and I can't believe my eyes," she wrote later. "Can there really be Jews here, living as humans, visionaries who can see a future?" She was amazed at their focus on Eretz Israel, talking and singing as if they were in a dream, as if they had no awareness of the unspeakable atrocities that were happening all around them.

And then Hantze Płotnicka arrived, bringing with her even more positive spirit. Hantze had been staying at Grochów outside Warsaw. The farm had become a center of the resistance and a way station for couriers: a place they could spend the night before entering the ghetto the following day and where they could hide underground materials. When the farm was closed down, Hantze was sent to Będzin. Her journey was filled with danger, but once she arrived, Renia felt that the whole group began a new life. Renia was impressed by how Hantze upheld a good mood. She knew all the kibbutz members and noted their unique strengths. She refused to halt cultural work. After a hard day's labor, she gathered the members for a philosophical *siche*, or conversation, and when she spoke of the kibbutzes in Palestine, her face lit up. She helped comrades in their preparations for resistance. She maintained connections with members in the surrounding areas and in Warsaw, especially with her sister Frumka.

Hantze liked to tell them about the terrible conditions at Grochów, the hunger and persecution, the meals of cooked fat, rotting cabbage leaves, and potato skins. Laughing, she recounted how she used to fool the Germans by walking the long way to Warsaw, disguised as a Gentile. When the Będziners used to complain about the difficulties in their lives, Renia wrote, Hantze teased them. "In Grochów, the conditions were much worse," she'd say with a smile, "and even *they* stayed alive . . ."

One day, Renia relayed, the comrades met up with a Polish train conductor who told them what he knew, adding firm details to the vague accounts they'd heard. He'd been on a train to the village of Treblinka, northeast of Warsaw, where trains arrived from all of Europe. A few stations before Treblinka, he was suddenly told to disembark and was replaced by a German conductor—all meant to keep the mass-murder site a secret. At Treblinka, Nazis beat the Jews and made them move quickly, so that they wouldn't notice their surrounds. The Germans promptly took the sick to a tent and shot them.

The other new arrivals assumed they were going to be put to work. Men and women were separated. Children were given bread and milk. Everyone had to strip; their clothes added to a growing pile. The Germans gave out soap and towels, and told them to hurry so the water wouldn't get cold. The Nazis followed them—wearing gas masks. Then people started wailing and praying. Gendarmes pressed the gas button. The Jews closed their eyes, their muscles tensed like taut strings, and they suffocated, sticking to each other in a giant, petrified lump. The lump was cut into smaller parts, the conductor said, then lifted with cranes into train cars and unloaded into pits.

"The ground takes everything in," Renia later wrote, her inner resolve strengthening, "except for the secret of what had happened." The stories, she knew, would find their way out.

More stories arrived with Frumka. Like her sister, she'd been sent from Warsaw to Będzin, originally to look for a route to Palestine via Slovakia, on Poland's south border; she was to escape there and serve as the messenger of the nation. Disguised as a Christian, Frumka had "gone through hell" in the preceding months, as she'd traveled among Białystok, Vilna, Lvov, and Warsaw. She arrived in Będzin tired and broken— though Renia recalled the day as one of the happiest in the two sisters' lives: "I remember how they both sat for a full hour talking about everything that they'd been through." Sisters meant everything.

Frumka spent her evenings telling the kibbutz about the atrocities being carried out across the country, of the extermination committees made up of hundreds of Ukrainians and Gestapo men—and assisted by the Jewish militia, who were later executed themselves. Pools of blood stained the streets of Vilna's Jewish neighborhood. Murderers strutted around with a maniacal glee. Streets, alleys, and apartment buildings were carpeted by dead bodies. Everywhere, screaming and moaning like wild animals. "There's no help coming from anywhere!" Frumka cried. "The world has forsaken us." Her tales were so horrid and vivid, Renia couldn't get them out of her head for days. She attended every one of the frequent assemblies, during which Frumka asked for one thing from each member: defense!

Renia, taken by Frumka's dedication, watched "the mother" carry the weight of the kibbutz on her shoulders while also embarking on larger community missions. As in Warsaw, everyone in Będzin knew and appreciated Frumka. She eased their suffering with words of consolation and heartfelt advice. She didn't let the Judenrat rest. She had several decrees rescinded and saved more than one person from "the nail of death." She said little about her activities, but everyone knew that Frumka aided the imprisoned and tried to contact Jews in other countries. Each time she achieved a goal, she was giddy; her passion touched them all.

Frumka's tales, Hantze's vigor, the train conductor's story, and all they'd heard from Anilevitz spurred on the fledgling Zaglembie ZOB. Chajka watched proudly as members brought in watches, clothes, and food packages they'd received from outside the country— anything of value they could sell in order to buy supplies that would make them attractive to the partisans, even shoes. They dreamed of buying guns. They asked for contributions from rich Jews, although Chajka was firm that they never take one groshen more than necessary, even when the donor had millions. They ended up collecting roughly 2,500 reichsmarks, enough for more than ten people to "apply to" a partisan detachment. The comrades established their first workshop, where members fabricated knives and experimented with homemade explosives, hoping to master grenades and bombs.

Chajka Klinger could not wait to set one off.

Indeed, a spirit of rebellion was in the air. That autumn of 1942, the nearby town of Lubliniec was the site of an impromptu revolt. One afternoon, Nazis ordered all the Jews to gather in the market and undress. Men, women, the elderly, and children were forced to peel off their clothing, even their underwear, on the pretext that the garments were needed for the German army. Nazis stood over them, brandishing whips and sticks. They tore clothes off women's bodies.

Suddenly a dozen naked Jewish women attacked the officers, scratching them with their nails. Encouraged by non-Jewish bystanders, they bit them with their teeth, picked up stones, and hurled them with their trembling hands.

The Nazis were shocked. Panicking, they ran away, leaving behind the confiscated clothing.

"Jewish Resistance in Poland: Women Trample Nazi

Soldiers" was the headline in the Jewish Telegraphic Agency's report of this incident, filed from Russia and published in New York City.

After that, many Jews from Lubliniec, including the women, decided to join the partisans. It was right around this time that the first armed Jewish resistance erupted—right in the capital of the General Government.

Chapter 10
Three Lines in History— A Krakówian Christmas Surprise

Gusta

THE AKIVA PLEDGE

I pledge to engage in active resistance within the framework of the Jewish Fighting Organization of the Halutz Youth Movement.

I swear by everything most dear to me, and above all by the memory and honor of dying Polish Jewry, that I will fight with all the weapons available to me until the last moment of my life to resist the Germans, the National Socialists, and those in league with them, the mighty enemies of the Jewish people and of all humanity.

I pledge to avenge the innocent deaths of millions of children, mothers, fathers, and aged Jewish people, to uphold Jewish spirit, and to raise the flag of freedom proudly. I pledge to shed my own blood fighting to achieve a bright and independent future for the Jewish nation.

I pledge to fight for justice, freedom, and the right of all human beings to live in dignity. I will fight side by side with those who share my desire for a free and equitable social order. I will serve humanity faithfully, dedicating myself without hesitation to achieving human rights for all, subordinating my personal desires and ambitions to that noble cause.

I pledge to accept as a brother anyone willing to join me in this struggle against the enemy. I pledge to set the seal of death on anyone who betrays our shared ideals. I pledge to hold out to the end, not to retreat in the face of overwhelming adversity or even death.

October 1942

Gusta Davidson arrived in Kraków, the capital of the General Government, exhausted. She had been on the move for days, waking at dawn, walking for miles, constant nervous tension, constant danger. First, she'd helped her family members, who were trapped in a town surrounded by police. Then, the sleepless trip back to Kraków involved endless logistical quagmires: connections, horse and buggy, droshky carriage, motorcycle, and hours of waiting in train stations.

Gusta's swollen legs now dragged her into her city and to the Jewish Quarter, a small area of low-rise buildings on the south bank of the river, far from the city's red-roofed, grandiose castle and colorful, winding medieval center. Before the war, sixty thousand Jews lived in Kraków, or a quarter of the city's population; the old Kazimierz area hosted seven historic synagogues with magnificent architecture dating back to 1407.

She approached the ghetto, her normally glossy lips and high cheekbones unusually pale. Black bags lingered under her eyes. She was overcome by fatigue. But as Gusta neared the barbed wire and heard the purr of the busy streets, of crowds "wafting the hum and buzz of their existence into the surrounding buildings," as she recognized faces she knew and noted those she didn't, she felt energized, ready to hug them all. The ghetto had been formed more than a year earlier but was constantly changing. Jews fled, then refugees came, as if it was a safe haven. Like Gusta, everyone had been on the run, from one besieged city to the next, fleeing in circles until they ran out of money or strength, or an Aktion caught them by surprise. She felt secure, even belonging, in her very homelessness. She was tempted to ask each Jew she passed, "Where did you escape from?"

Many of them, she sensed on that warm Sunday afternoon, had lost the will to live, knowing they were nearing their end. Still, they hoped for death to catch them by surprise; they refused to surrender. *Make them chase us down.* Gusta also understood how "older folks lacked the fighting spirit"—how years of degradation and baiting affected their "bruised, despairing souls." The youth, on the other hand, had such a lust for life that, ironically, they pushed themselves to resistance and certain death.

At the narrow gate, an opening in the ghetto walls, which were shaped purposefully to resemble tombstones, Gusta was met by several comrades who helped drag her along. Their voices and faces, their concern over her delayed return, all merged into one warm blur. One of the few Jewish communities left, Kraków was now a center of the resistance movement, despite being a city swarming in top-level Nazis. Gusta, who'd grown up in an extremely religious family, was a leading member of Akiva, a local Zionist group. A friend had introduced her to it, and she was taken by the idealism and self-sacrifice. She served on the central committee, as writer and editor for their publication, and as record keeper for the whole organization. Unlike the secular leftist Zionist groups, Akiva emphasized Jewish tradition, celebrating Oneg Shabbat, a Sabbath ceremony, each Friday.

Just that past summer, the group was based on a farm in the nearby village of Kopaliny, a peaceful oasis amid the brutality and violence. "The stillness exhaled by the deep woods floated down from the sky to be inhaled by the earth," Gusta described. "Not so much as a single leaf quivered." They lived communally among pear trees, orchards, ridges, and ravines, under a sun that "rolled slowly through the azure sky." But Gusta's husband, Shimshon, an Akiva leader, knew that the movement would die—that most of them would die. He called a meeting. The war was not a momentary tremor: the savagery would be worse than they'd imagined; the diabolical mass killings a success. Gusta and her comrades believed Shimshon, but they also felt committed to their Akiva ideals: "to move the youth into the vanguard . . . to counteract the spreading cynicism," to maintain decency and humanity and "cling to life."

At the outbreak of war, Shimshon had been arrested for anti-Fascist writings. The couple, who married in 1940, made a pact that if one of them was caught, the other would turn themselves in. So Gusta went to jail too. They got out by paying an enormous bribe, and kept working. "You can't try to preserve fighters by shielding them in a shelter," they believed. During the summer of 1942, however, like their comrades in Warsaw and Będzin, they realized that the movement had to change.

"We want to survive as a generation of avengers," Shimshon declared at a meeting. "If we survive, it has got to be as a group, and with weapons in our hands." They debated: Would the Nazis' retaliation be too great? Should they rescue only themselves? But no, they had to fight. Even Gusta—violence wholly alien to her bookish nature—felt the deep desire for revenge; to kill the enemy who had killed her father and sister. "Hands, now caked with fertile loam," she wrote, "would soon be soaked in blood." Akiva's creation would be destruction. By August, they had merged with The Young

Guard, Freedom, and other groups to form Kraków's Fighting Pioneers.

Now, just inside the gates, she heard the comrades murmuring about Shimshon's temper; how worried he'd been by her delayed arrival. She blushed, laughed loudly to conceal her embarrassment that she was the subject of gossip. Her husband even tore himself away from his work to greet her. She felt the pressure of his hard, narrow palm on her back and stared at his steely-blue eyes as they stood face-to-face. Gusta suddenly understood: he was now a full-time combatant, his fight was his "femme fatale." She, alone, would take care of everything else. He no longer saw her—with those piercing, dark eyes, that movie-star bob—but the future.

"I only have a moment to spare," he whispered, and she knew that was forever. He had to go to a meeting. Gusta had been to many of the weightiest leader sessions, but here she was not invited. She sensed it: they were planning their own action.

Kraków was a strategic city for the Nazis, and so they claimed it was a Saxon town, with Prussian roots. It was made the capital of the General Government in place of Warsaw and was thus heavily protected. The

Jews who lived here, then, did so in close proximity to many high-ranking SS officers. The youth resistance worked in this particularly charged environment.

So, weeks later, when Shimshon did not return home for days, Gusta was beside herself. Catastrophe could strike in a second; if someone merely thought he or she recognized Shimshon, he was finished. But her husband was savvy, she consoled herself, and considered that if the resistance had put as much effort into actually fighting the enemy as it had into proclaiming its readiness to fight, it would have won many battles by now! When Shimshon finally returned, he did so only for a moment before heading back out. She was overcome with sadness. Was it better to be separated physically and imagine their reunion, or to have him close yet emotionally distant?

From Shimshon's return, everyone knew that a momentous battle was being planned, inside the ghetto and in the forest. Everyone wanted to be involved despite cold autumn conditions. As per the underground blueprint, the Kraków group split into fives, each self-sufficient unit having its own leader, communications expert, administrator, and supply officer. Each group had its own weapons, provisions, operating area, and independent plan of action. Only members in a group knew who the other members were and knew of its plans, and even within a group, members did not know the others' whereabouts.

All this military secrecy was anathema to their youth group culture of openness and nonviolence. But the devotion among members, who'd each lost home and family, was formidable. "The group had become the last refuge on their mortal journey," Gusta explained, "the last port of their innermost feelings." Though comrades were not supposed to congregate—their laughter and camaraderie were simply too conspicuous to others—they couldn't resist. "Their displays of exuberance provided a desperate outlet for their prematurely scarred psyches," Gusta intuited. "If someone were to ask whether they might be too immature to be effective movement fighters, then what answer could one give, since they had never had the chance to experience youth at all and never would?" The leaders forgot their movements' ideological differences and congregated in the heart of the ghetto, even though these gatherings were exposed and risky.

Shimshon, an amateur typesetter experienced in etching and engraving, was in charge of the "technical bureau." It was an age of "papers, clutter, stamps, passes, certifications," Gusta observed, and Shimshon forged fictitious papers to ensure the fighters' freedom of movement. At first, Shimshon carried the whole office "in his coat pockets," searching furiously for a room whenever he needed to make a document and unfolding his equipment onto a tablecloth. But he needed more space and started carrying a briefcase to work out of; he would roam the ghetto, from empty room to room, with his "floating office." Alas one briefcase didn't suffice, so he needed two. Then more. A team of assistants trailed behind him, carrying his collection of valises, boxes, a typewriter, packages—this became a serious security issue for the entire workshop brigade. The bureau needed a permanent home.

In Rabka, a small town outside Kraków, Gusta set up an apartment in a beautiful villa. In addition to a large room with two windows, it had a kitchen and a veranda, and was "furnished modestly but tastefully and glowed with domestic tranquility." She placed flowers on the table, hung curtains on the windows, and put up pictures on the wall—all to give the space a homey feel, like a "cozy nest," she wrote.

Here Gusta was to "play the role of an ailing wife spending the golden autumn" in a resort region. Her six-year-old nephew Witek was with her; during the days, they would frolic in the garden, go for walks, or rent a boat on the calm river. Shimshon took the bus to Kraków each morning, becoming friendly with the other commuters. He was mysterious, wore a firm expression, and "cut an intimidating figure," Gusta wrote. People thought he held a government job, so they gave up their seats for him. Everyone assumed the family was wealthy and that he brought work home in his briefcase to spend more time with his young wife and son. No one suspected that their villa housed the Jewish resistance's forgery factory.

In one corner, away from the window, Gusta set up a full office: desk, typewriter, equipment. If her days were spent reveling in domestic tranquility, her nights, after Shimshon's late arrival, were all work. When lights went out in the village, Gusta covered the windows and bolted the door. Until three in the morning, she forged documents and wrote and published their underground newspaper. Issued every Friday, the *Fighting Pioneer* consisted of ten typed pages, which included a list of Jewish collaborators. Gusta and Shimshon printed 250 copies that were distributed by pairs of fighters throughout the Kraków region. Then they grabbed a few hours of sleep before Shimshon had to make the seven o'clock bus back to the city—on which he had to appear refreshed.

Hanka Blas, an Akiva comrade and Shimshon's courier, lived twenty minutes away. She and Gusta shared a "sisterly love," according to Gusta, and though it would have been safer for them to cut all contact, they simply couldn't stay apart, comforted in the company of friends who knew their true identities and understood their despair. The neighbors assumed that Hanka was Witek's nanny. Hanka smuggled underground bulletins, and some mornings, loaded her basket with eggs, mushrooms, apples and the material from the night before, put on a kerchief, and got on the bus as if she were going to market. Sometimes Hanka sat right next to Shimshon, pretending she didn't know him.

One beautiful day, Gusta relayed, Hela Schüpper arrived in the Kraków ghetto, having returned from Warsaw. A "voluptuous beauty," with a fair complexion and full, rosy cheeks, Hela used her charm, eloquence, and deep savvy to become Akiva's main courier. Hela grew up in a Chasidic family and attended a Polish public school. When organizers from a women's nationalist organization came to recruit students and no one volunteered, Hela joined, ashamed by her Jewish peers' lack of patriotism. Their meetings exposed the girl to culture, sports, and riflery and pistol practice, but she eventually quit, repulsed by what she perceived to be an antisemitic motion proposed by an affiliated leader. Shimshon convinced her to join Akiva, promising that it was not an atheist group. The Schüppers were more upset about this than about her participation in the Polish organization. Hela ran away from her family—the movement became her home.

Possessing confidence and impeccable self-control, as well as a commerce degree, she had represented Akiva that past summer at the Warsaw meeting when the youth groups decided to form a fighting force; she'd been carrying information and documents between the cities. But this morning in the fall of 1942, Hela arrived with something new: a stash of weapons. Two Browning rifles hung inside her loose sports coat, and she had three hand weapons and several clips of cartridges in her fashionable bag.

"No one had ever been greeted with the outpouring of affection that was showered on Hela," Gusta later wrote. "It is impossible to describe the ecstasy inspired by those weapons." People stopped into the room where she was resting just to glimpse the bag hanging on the wall, and Shimshon, she recalled, was "happy as a child." The leaders began to fantasize: with these weapons they could garner exponentially more. This was the start of a new era.

However, they didn't have any military training, or even the faintest military ethos. They felt uncomfortable leading their members to their deaths, to say the least. They knew they needed to collaborate with the PPR, the underground Polish Communist Party. Their main link was Gola Mire, a feisty Jewish poet who had been thrown out of The Young Guard years earlier because of her radical left-wing views. An active Communist, she'd been sentenced to twelve years in prison for organizing strikes. (Her trial defense was so moving, the prosecutor bought her roses.) In the chaos of the Nazi invasion, Gola led an escape from the women's jail and searched the country for her boyfriend. They married in Soviet territory, and he joined the Red Army. Eventually, to avoid a Nazi manhunt, she went into hiding and delivered her first baby alone, cutting the umbilical cord herself.

After several months, though, Gola needed help and made it to the ghetto, where her infant died in her arms. She worked in a German factory, secretly puncturing holes in the food tins until the sabotage became too dangerous. Gola maintained connections with the PPR, and though the party was reluctant to collaborate with Jews, she convinced its members to help find them forest guides and hiding places. Akiva saw her as "a fierce fighter with a genuinely female heart." The PPR, however, could not always be counted on. One time, party members were supposed to guide a Jewish five to a rebel group in the forest; instead, they misled and betrayed them. In other instances, they promised weapons and money that never arrived.

The Jewish party decided to become an independent force. The youth ate dry crusts, wore boots with holes, and slept in cellars, but they were proud. They raised money for weapons. The technical bureau sold false documents, and other monies were received, likely through robbery. One group of fighters scoured for złotys, another scouted the forests for potential bases. Hela and two other women sleuthed for safe houses around the forest. Other women were dispatched to nearby towns to warn of impending Aktions. Gusta found hiding places, accompanied groups to the forest, consulted with leaders, and connected communities. She maintained contact with Kielce, where the comrades debated whether to focus on rescuing young Jewish artists or their own families. The group had developed various proposals and sought money, but Gusta felt that they were deluding themselves. She wasn't the right person to sell their ideas to the leadership.

Gusta was frustrated that women were not only barred from attending high-level resistance meetings but also were admonished for merely disturbing the men. Women were seemingly equal—the group had many active leading females—yet they remained outside the select circle of major decision makers. She worried that the four male leaders could be hotheaded and stubborn, but she consoled herself by hoping that at least one of the men would remember: every life counted.

A balmy October day, the sun's autumnal rays still strong, no sense of anything unusual. But this was the morning of a massive Nazi Aktion in Kraków. Taking place a day earlier than the movement expected, they were caught off guard. Gusta and her comrades were unable to save their parents, barely making it out of the ghetto alive themselves. They hid in a warehouse, then moved from basement to basement. The worst part, Gusta felt, was the absolute silence. If in other towns the Aktions were grotesque, bloody affairs, with whole families being mowed down by machine guns, this was a "capital city" event: quiet and orderly. Most of the Jews were too weak from hunger to even scream. This silence, the loss of their families, the horror—all spurred on the youth. For distraction and revenge, they launched into action.

It was an exceptionally beautiful fall. "The leaves held on to their green freshness well into the season," Gusta wrote. "The sun turned the earth to gold, warming it with benevolent rays." But the movement knew that each day was a gift. When the cold, wet autumn arrived, it would be too difficult for them to navigate the forest. And so, they changed tack. The fighters decided to commit their acts right there in the city, targeting high-ranking Nazis so that "even a minor attack here would strike at the heart of authority and could damage an important cog in the machine," Gusta wrote, eager to raise havoc and stir anxiety among the authorities. "Rational voices" told the youth to wait it out and not arouse the Nazis with small acts, but the fighters simply didn't think they'd be alive much longer.

This was an incredibly busy time, with all the comrades working dusk to dawn. They quickly set up bases inside and outside the ghetto, as well as contact points and safe apartments in surrounding cities. The comrades went in groups of two or three to make inquiries, work as couriers, spy on the secret police, continue technical work, distribute flyers on busy streets, and confront enemies. Fighters would jump from a dark alley, deliver a blow, confiscate a weapon, and disappear. They prioritized killing traitors and collaborators. Because they looked Jewish, it was hard for many of them to work on the Aryan side without disguises; one leader donned a Polish police uniform and then "promoted himself" to a Nazi.

New and intense bonds formed among the group, and the members created a novel kind of family life to help heal from the ones that had been destroyed. For comrades across the country, the movement was their whole world, and their decisions were life-or-death, their mutual reliance paramount. The youth were college age, a time in life when partnerships are central to self-concept and identity. Some became lovers, their development rushed, rerouted. Sexual relations were often passionate, urgent, and life-affirming. Others became surrogate parents, siblings, and cousins to one another.

In Kraków, the ghetto base at 13 Jozefinska Street, a first-floor, two-room apartment, accessible off a long, narrow corridor, became their home—one that they all knew would probably be their last. Because most youth were the only living members of their families, they brought their "inheritances" (underwear, clothes, boots) to the hideout and would "arrange a liquidation": redistributing belongings to those who needed them. Or they'd sell them for common funds. They deeply wanted to love and be loved, and created a commune where they shared all, with a common cash box and kitchen. Elsa, an intense but good-humored comrade, took the reins at the stove, and "dedicated her life and soul to kitchen management." The kitchen was tiny, with pots and pans stacked on the floor. One had to move them to open the door. The apartment served as the base of operations, where they'd check in and then be dispatched to their posts. A minute before curfew, they all ran back, reporting success or failure, telling tales of dodging bullets—literally.

The group ate meals together at Jozefinska. Every evening was extraordinary, with conversation and laughter. Anka, who was so strong that when she was arrested, it looked like she was walking the police; Mirka, charming and radiant; Tosca, Marta, Giza, Tova. Seven people slept per bed, others on chairs or the floor. It was neither sophisticated nor particularly clean, but it was their cherished abode and the final place where they could live their true identities.

All this time, the group kept up the Akiva tradition of Oneg Shabbat. On Friday, November 20 they met for festivities from dusk to dawn. They'd spent two days preparing the meal, and came together in white blouses and shirts, at a table set with a white tablecloth. After a moment of silence, they bellowed the same songs they'd been singing for years in a deluge of harmonies. But tonight they greeted the Sabbath bride together for the final time. Someone called out, "This is the last supper!" *Yes, that's right*, they all knew. At the head of the table, a leader spoke at length about how death was near. It was time "to fight for three lines in history."

Activity ramped up. The group had to leave the ghetto because of deteriorating conditions. One night the leaders hid in a park and shot a Nazi sergeant as he walked by. They sauntered out of the bushes, mixed into the scared crowds, and zigzagged back to Jozefinska; no one even followed them. But this bold act was more than authorities would tolerate. The Nazis, determined to crush this humiliating rebellion, lied to the public about what had happened, beefed up security, moved up curfew, took hostages, made a list. They were after the leaders, who were themselves planning for their climax: an open-air fight.

After a few more successful Nazi killings in town, the movement decided to escalate activity and combined forces with Jewish members of the PPR for their crescendo. On December 22, 1942, when many Nazis were in town shopping for Christmas gifts and attending holiday parties, forty Jewish men and women fighters headed into the Kraków streets. Women distributed anti-Nazi posters throughout the city, while men carried flags of Polish partisans and left a wreath of flowers on the statue of a Polish poet—all so that Jews wouldn't be blamed for what was about to happen. Then, the fighters attacked military garages and set off fire alarms across town, causing confusion. At seven o'clock in the evening, they descended upon three coffeehouses where Germans gathered and bombed a Nazi Christmas party. Fighters threw grenades into the Cyganeria, a café in the magnificent old town that was an exclusive meeting spot for eminent German soldiers. This effort killed at least seven Nazis and wounded many more.

Though resistance leaders were arrested and killed afterward, Jews continued to bomb targets outside the city, including the main station in Kraków, coffeehouses in Kielce, and a movie house in Radom—all with Gola Mire's help.

A few weeks after the December attacks, Hela was on a train, panicking about where to sleep and what to eat, when she struck up a conversation with a young Polish academic. He reassured her, "The war will soon be over."

"How do you know?" she asked.

He explained that Polish forces had started to move. He was so proud of the Polish underground—they had blown up the café!

Hela could not control herself. What if she was the last Jew? She needed him to know the truth. She had no one left to betray. "You ought to be aware, kind sir," she said, "that the attack to which you referred, on the Kraków cafés, was the work of young Jewish fighters. If you live to see the end of the war, please, tell the world about it. And by the way, I too am a Jew."

The man was stunned. The train approached Kraków.

"Come with me," he said firmly when they arrived. Was this Hela's end? Did it even matter?

Then he brought her to a warm apartment to safely spend the night.

Chapter 11
1943, a New Year—
Warsaw's Minirebellion

Zivia and Renia
January 1943

At six in the morning, a few weeks after the inspiring uprising in Kraków, Zivia was awoken with news: Nazis had infiltrated the Warsaw ghetto. A surprise Aktion.

The ZOB had assumed the Nazis were distracted with a large-scale manhunt on the Aryan side, where they'd been arresting thousands of Poles. In fact, the organization had asked all its couriers to come back *to* the ghetto, which seemed to be safer. Even the Polish underground had hidden in the ghetto.

But Himmler had new quotas.

It had been a late night of planning and meetings, but Zivia rushed to get dressed, then went downstairs to examine the scene. The streets were surrounded. A German sentry was posted in front of every house. There was no way to get out, no way to contact the other units. All of yesterday's scheming was worthless; their battle plans could not be carried out. Would the Germans destroy the ghetto altogether?

Zivia panicked. How could they be so unprepared?

Over the past months, despite the massive death toll of the summer Aktions, the ZOB's progress had stirred hope. As in Kraków, the youth groups were composed of people who already trusted one another and were primed to become secret fighting units. The ZOB recruited new members to add to the several hundred comrades still alive in the ghetto, careful to scour for informers. They reattempted alliances with other movements. Again, they were not able to agree on terms with the better-armed Revisionist group Betar, which formed its own militia, the ZZW (Jewish Military Union). The Bund, however, finally acceded to collaborate. Along with the "adult" Zionist parties, they joined the ZOB and formed a new alliance.

With this fresh credibility, the ZOB was able at last to connect with the Polish underground, made up of two rival factions. The Home Army (known in Poland as the Armia Krajowa or AK) was affiliated with the predominantly right-wing government in exile in London. The Home Army had an antisemitic leadership, even though many individual members were liberals who helped Jews. (Jan Żabiński, the now famous zoo-keeper of Warsaw, was an AK member.) The People's Army, on the other hand, was affiliated with the Communist group (PPR), and, at the time, was the weaker of the two factions. The leadership of the People's Army (Armia Ludowa, or AL) cooperated with the Soviets, and was more willing to collaborate with Jewish ghetto and forest fighters—frankly, with anyone who wanted to topple the Nazis. But they lacked resources.

The Home Army had been reluctant to help the ZOB for various reasons. Its leaders felt that the Jews didn't fight back; what's more, they feared that a ghetto uprising would spread, and they did not have enough weapons to sustain a citywide rebellion. They worried that a premature revolt would be detrimental and were hoping to let the Germans and Russians bleed each other before they jumped in. The Home Army had refused to enter into serious discussion with measly youth groups; however, it *was* willing to meet with the new alliance.

The meeting was a success. The Home Army sent

ten mostly functional shotguns as well as instructions for how to make explosives. One Jewish woman discovered a formula for firebombs: take electric lightbulbs collected from abandoned houses and fill them with sulfuric acid.

Hot with fervor, the ZOB began to act broadly. Just as Frumka was sent to Będzin, members were dispatched across Poland to lead resistance units and maintain foreign connections. (Zivia later mocked herself for being so naïve as to think that they were not receiving outside help because the world didn't know.) Rivka Glanz went to Częstochowa. Leah Pearlstein and Tosia sought weapons in Aryan Warsaw.

The Bundists strengthened their fighting units. Vladka Meed was approached by the Bund leader, Abrasha Blum, and invited to a resistance meeting. Because of her straight, light-brown hair, small nose, and gray-green eyes, Vladka was asked to move to the Aryan side. The thought of leaving the ghetto, where most Jews toiled in horrific conditions as slave labor, filled her with elation.

One night in early December 1942, Vladka received word that she was to exit with a work brigade the following morning and to bring with her the latest Bund underground bulletin, which featured a detailed map of Treblinka. She hid the pages in her shoe, then found a brigade leader who accepted her 500 złoty bribe and slotted her in with the group as they awaited inspection at the ghetto wall in the freezing cold. All was well until the Nazi inspecting Vladka decided he didn't like her face. Or, perhaps, liked it too much. She was pulled out of the formation and directed to a small room lined with splatters of blood and photographs of half-naked women. The guard searched her and made her undress. She just had to keep her shoe on . . .

"Shoes off!" he barked. But just then, a Nazi rushed in to inform her tormentor that a Jew had escaped, and both jetted off. Vladka dressed quickly and slipped out, telling the guard at the door that she had passed inspection. She went on to meet comrades on the Aryan side and began her work establishing contact with non-Jews, finding places for Jews to live and hide, and procuring arms.

Most important, the ZOB was determined to eliminate collaborators, who they felt made the Nazis' job so much easier. Throughout the ghetto, they hung posters declaring that the organization would avenge any crime committed against the Jews—then promptly made good on the threat by killing two leaders of the Jewish militia and council. To Zivia's amazement, the assassinations left an impression on the ghetto Jews, who began to respect the ZOB's power.

A new authority ruled the ghetto.

The fighting group was a few weeks away from launching a full-scale uprising. According to one of the Bund's leaders, Marek Edelman, they had set the big date: January 22.

When the Nazi Aktion began on January 18, Zivia was shocked. The comrades had no time to convene and decide upon a response. Several members weren't sure where they were supposed to be stationed. Most units had no access to arms except for sticks, knives, and iron bars. Each group was on its own, unable to connect.

But there was no time to lose. Two groups improvised and launched straight into action. If anything, the lack of time for committee discussion pushed them to mobilize.

Zivia didn't know it at the time, but Mordechai Anilevitz quickly commanded a group of male and female Young Guard fighters to go out into the streets, let themselves be caught, and then slip in among the rows of Jews being led to the *umschlagplatz*. As Anilevitz approached the corner of Niska and Zamenhofa Streets, he gave the command. The fighters whipped out their concealed weapons and opened fire on Germans who were marching nearby. They threw grenades at them while screaming at their fellow Jews to escape. A few did. According to Vladka Meed's account, "The mass of deportees fell upon the German troopers tooth and nail, using hands, feet, teeth, and elbows."

The Germans were stunned. "The Jews are firing at us!" In the confusion, the Jewish youth kept shooting.

But the Nazis regained their composure and retaliated quickly. Needless to say, the rebels' handful of pistols was no match for the Germans' superior firepower. Reich soldiers chased down the few ZOB fighters who'd managed to run off. When Anilevitz ran out of bullets, he snatched a gun from a German, retreated into a building, and continued to fire. A Jew in a nearby bunker pulled him in. Only Anilevitz and one female fighter survived. The results were tragic, but the influence of these actions was tremendous: Jews had killed Germans.

The second group was Zivia's. Commanded by Antek and two other men, this unit took a different tactic. Most of the remaining Jews were in hiding, which meant that the Germans had to enter buildings to find them. Instead of an open-air battle, which they were sure they'd lose, they decided to wait for the Nazis to approach and shoot from inside. Zivia figured that ambushing the Germans would inflict the most casualties.

She stood on the alert at one of the Freedom bases in an apartment building on 56-58 Zamenhofa Street.

Forty men and women took up positions. They had four hand grenades and four shotguns among them. Most were armed with nothing more than iron pipes, sticks, and the makeshift acid-filled lightbulb fire-bombs.

Zivia and her comrades knew that they were fighting to their deaths, but waited eagerly for the Nazis to arrive so they could do their damage and go down with honor. For six months, the Germans had been systematically murdering Warsaw's Jews, and not a shot had been fired at them.

Absolute silence, except for a few piercing cries of people being forced to the *umschlagplatz*. As Zivia stood waiting for the confrontation, anxiously gripping her weapon, she felt terrifically adrenalized—and yet, at the same time, deeply sad. Later, reflecting on that moment, she described her inner turmoil as "a kind of emotional stock-taking at the final moments of my life." The friends she would never see. The aliyah she would never make.

Yitzhak Katzenelson, the poet, broke the silence with a short speech: "Our armed struggle will be an inspiration to future generations. . . . Our deeds will be remembered forever. . . ."

And then: sharp boots beating against the stairs.

The front door flung open. A gang of German soldiers burst in.

One comrade pretended to be reading a book by Sholem Aleichem. The Germans rushed right past him and entered the room where Zivia was sitting with others. Miserable Jews, they appeared to be, awaiting their executions. Just then, the young man who was feigning reading sprang up and shot two of the Germans in the back. The other Nazis retreated to the stairwell. All the fighters sprang out from of closets and hiding places and began to brawl using whatever arms they had. A few focused on stripping the dead soldiers of rifles, pistols, and grenades.

The Germans who survived beat a hasty retreat.

Barely equipped Jews had slayed Nazis!

And now they were also rich in weapons.

After a few moments of elation, there was shock. They were confused, truly bewildered. Zivia couldn't believe that they'd felled Germans and *survived*. Overwhelmed with emotion, the fighters knew they had to stay focused. The Nazis would be back. What next? "We were totally unprepared," Zivia later wrote. "We hadn't expected to remain alive."

They needed to flee. They helped their one injured comrade, hid him, and then withdrew out of the building's skylights and crept single file along the sloped roofs covered in snow and ice, five storeys high, to finally make it inside the attic of an unknown building, shaken, hoping for time to rest, to redeploy.

But Germans entered this building as well, boots stomping up the stairs. The Freedom comrades began to open fire. Two members tossed a German down a stairwell shaft. Another threw a hand grenade at the entrance, blocking the Nazis' escape. The Germans dragged off their dead and wounded; they did not return that night.

The next day, the Nazis attacked the empty apartments and this new "base." Again, the comrades came out alive. Only one injury. No losses.

As soon as it was dark, Zivia's troop headed to the Freedom post at Mila 34 to meet comrades who'd arrived from the farm, only to find that "the silence of death permeated the air." Furniture was broken. Pillow feathers covered the floor. Zivia found out later that they'd been taken to Treblinka. A few, including several brave women, had jumped from the train.

The group settled into the most strategic apartments in the building. Each unit was briefed and assumed position. Lookouts were posted to warn of any surprise attacks. For the first time, they outlined a plan of retreat and an alternate meeting spot. Finally, sleep.

At dawn, the ghetto was still. Zivia figured that the Nazis were now sneaking into buildings quietly. They sent the Jewish police to assess the safety of an area first. The house searches became less thorough. The Nazis were scared "of a Jewish bullet."

Zivia felt reinvigorated, a new reason to live.

"At the same time as thousands of Jews were cowering in their hiding places, shaking at the sound of a falling leaf," Zivia wrote, "we who had been baptized in the fire and blood of battle, sat back confidently with almost all traces of our former fear having disappeared." One comrade went out to the courtyard to find a match and sticks to light the stove. He even came back with vodka. They sat by the fire and drank. They reminisced about their battles, joked, and teased one fighter who had been so depressed, he was about to kill them all with a grenade until their commander stopped him.

They were still joking when the lookout entered. "There's a large company of SS men in the courtyard," he warned.

Zivia glanced out the window and saw them yelling for Jews to leave the building. No one budged.

Once again, the Germans entered, and were momentarily tricked by a fighter who pretended to surrender. The others then fired, and "a shower of bullets greeted them on all sides." The Nazis retreated, only to be ambushed by comrades waiting outside. Zivia saw several wounded and dead Germans strewn on the steps.

Again, she was amazed that she and her comrades were alive. No casualties, even. The fighters collected the dead soldiers' weapons and left through the attics, where they stumbled upon a camouflaged hideout. The Jews hiding there welcomed them in, and a rabbi sang his praises for their work. "If we still have you left," he said, "young Jews fighting and taking revenge, from now on, it shall be easier for us to die."

Zivia blinked back tears.

The Germans returned to the original building. But there were no Jews left for them to kill.

The January Aktion lasted only four days. Eventually the ZOB ran out of ammunition, the Nazis were sleuthing for their hiding spots, and many comrades fell. Thousands of Jews were snatched from the streets. Even Tosia was caught and driven to the *umshlagplatz*, but a double-agent militiaman who was helping The Young Guard rescued her.

Overall, however, it was a grand success. The Nazis' intention to clear the ghetto was foiled by Zivia's and other fighting groups. A Bundist fired at an SS commander during a selection at the Schultz workshop, killing him. Masked ZOB fighters threw acid at a Nazi at Hallman's furniture shop; they bound the guards at gunpoint and destroyed their records. One comrade leapt on a Nazi, threw a sack over his head, and tossed him out a window. Another poured boiling liquid on Germans' heads below. What should have been a two-hour operation took the Nazis days, and they apprehended only half their quota. The Jews had almost no food, but they had new hope. This small uprising helped foster unity, respect, morale—and status. Both the Jewish masses and the Poles considered the German retreat to be a ZOB victory.

The fighters were elated by their success, but also regretful. Why had it taken them so long to act when it hadn't even been *that* hard? Regardless, they had no choice but to keep fighting for honorable deaths. The masses, on the other hand, now believed that hiding might keep them alive. The ghetto was becoming a united fighting post. It was the "golden age" of the Warsaw ghetto.

Despite the excitement and growing hope in Warsaw, and its reverberations across other towns, Będzin was "a literal shambles," Renia wrote. After Renia's initial burst of heaven, winter was "torture," physically, existentially, emotionally. "Hunger was a constant guest in our house. Sicknesses multiplied, there were no medications, and death carved its graves." Each day, convoys of Jews over age forty, apparently too old to work, were sent away. Any minor infraction was reason for execution: crossing the street diagonally, walking on the wrong side of the sidewalk, breaking curfew, smoking a cigarette, selling anything, even owning eggs, onion, garlic, meat, dairy, baked goods, or lard. Police entered Jewish homes to inspect what they were cooking. The Judenrat and militia aided them, following every German order. They were ruthless in their white hats, Renia wrote, and if they heard that a Jew was hiding something, they'd demand hush money. They fined people for the slightest of infractions and pocketed the cash.

Hantze became ill. Nightmares tortured her day and night. Gripped by the horror she'd witnessed in Grochów and on the way from Warsaw to Będzin, she burnt up with fever. Still, she had no choice but to stand on shaky legs and work in the laundry. The kibbutz barely had provisions. Renia, too, began to feel the effects of hunger: fatigue, confusion, a relentless obsession with food.

Through all this, manhunts ensued, and Renia was a target. She had to be doubly careful, as she was a "nonkosher." At night, the gendarmes and Jewish militia hunted for her and other refugees from the General Government. Just taking in nonkoshers would lead to immediate deportation for her comrades. Renia, Hanzte, Frumka, Zvi, and another boy spent their nights in hiding places, tortured by night terrors. Without sleep, in the mornings, the group went to work in the laundry, so that the kosher members could do more public-facing chores. "But we took it all with love," Renia wrote later. "Our desire to live was stronger than all the torture."

Then, one morning, Renia sat in the main room, overhearing group members discuss how they needed a small piece of metal for their oven. A seventeen-year-old boy, Pinchas, decided to search at work. "Little Pink" saw one, picked it up, looked at it. That was enough. His German employer noticed. He was deported. Killed.

Of all things, this murder jerked the comrades' resolve, and their sense of purpose began to slip. Why read, learn, work? Live? Why bother anymore?

It got worse. Rumors began. The Jews would be "resettled" to a locked ghetto, in the neighborhood of Kamionka, on the other side of the train station.

Twenty-five thousand Jews were to be housed in living quarters meant for ten thousand. Those like Renia, who had already lived in a ghetto, were all too aware of the nightmare that awaited them. Even those who hadn't lived in ghettos were dismayed. "In the summer, it will be unbearable," a Będzin teenager wrote in her diary when she heard the news, "to sit in a gray locked cage, without being able to see fields and flowers." Frumka and her fellow Freedom leader Hershel Springer walked around as if poisoned, pale and sick. What to do? To move to the ghetto or to flee? *Fight or flight*.

Heated discussion ensued. Ultimately it was decided that struggle would be futile, even leading to unwanted consequences. The time for fighting had not yet arrived.

Instead, Frumka and Hershel spent entire days at the Judenrat trying to arrange housing for the Freedom kibbutz as well as for the Atid group, now comprising nineteen teenagers from the shuttered orphanage who lived with them. The Judenrat office was packed. Yelling, screaming. The rich, Renia wrote, had an easier time because they could offer bribes. "Without money, you're like a soldier without a gun."

The Jews were shoved into the ghetto. Though Kamionka is now a hilly and leafy suburb, during the war, it resembled a crowded refugee camp: poor, neglected, unhygienic. Small stoves were everywhere, exuding noxious smoke. People sat on the ground, eating what they could. Furniture and packages piled up in front of every house. Next to the piles, babies. Those who couldn't afford apartments built huts in the square, like chicken coops, for protection from the rain. Stables, attics, and outhouses all became homes. Ten people lived in a converted cowshed, and they were lucky. Many slept with no roof at all. There was no room for furniture inside any abode except for necessary tables and beds. Each day Renia saw Jews hauling mattresses outside so that more people could move inside, calling up her horrid memories of living in ghettos with her family. Jews moved around like shadows, Renia wrote, like raggedy living corpses. At the same time, she felt that many Poles were pleased, robbing Jewish homes of possessions and commenting callously, "It's a pity that Hitler didn't come earlier." Some Jews burnt their belongings or chopped their furniture into firewood just to prevent Poles from eventually taking them.

The Freedom members left for the ghetto, packing their bare necessities into a car. Frumka and Hershel had managed to secure an entire two-storey house, half for them, half for the Atid orphans. Though this was much better than most living quarters ("a pal-ace," Renia called it, happy it was clean), it was small. There was no room to walk between the beds. Their closets and tables stood out in the yard, to be used as kindling.

The ghetto was closed, guarded by the militia. Po-lice walked the Jews to and from work as tailors, cob-blers, and metal workers in German workshops. Then workers stopped going to work, saying they needed child care. (Renia proudly noticed the Jews' sense of rebellion.) The Judenrat created communal day cares where kids were fed while their parents labored. Later, they built shacks in front of the workshops, so that the babies could sleep there at night. Each workshop had its own shack; desperate people moved into them before they were even completed. As Renia recalled, Kamionka was a "disgraceful site."

Any infraction brought death. The night was so silent, it was dangerous to go outside after eight o'clock. Complete blackout was mandatory. A militiaman stood on each corner, enforcing the curfew, his flashlight flickering in the stale air. Suddenly a gunshot. In the morning, a funeral. A man had been trying to walk to another building.

Every week, Renia watched as groups were sent to Auschwitz to be killed: the elderly, parents who'd hid their children, toddlers torn from mothers' breasts, young people accused of being politically active, people who didn't show up for a couple days' of work. They were brought to the station, beaten, and thrown into cattle cars. A man who took something by accident was flogged, strangled, trampled, and, if necessary, shot. But it was never necessary—he had already died.

Suddenly a sickening scream. A German grabbed a baby from his mother's arms, held him by his feet, and bashed his head against a brick wall, breaking the baby's skull in two. Blood was splattered all over the building, the sidewalk. He threw the baby's corpse to the ground. The sight haunted Renia for the rest of her life.

Renia watched this inhumanity in abject horror. Children witnessed these atrocities and wailed uncontrollably. The ghetto was becoming less crowded as residents were being taken each day, someone from every household. "All the hearts are broken," she wrote. "It's a wonder people maintain their sanity."

It was in this context that all the cultural activities in the kibbutz had ceased. This is when the fake passports came in and when Freedom held its meeting, with Hershel at one end of the table and Frumka at the other. This is when the youth groups had to decide: fight or flight. This is when Frumka said no, she would not go. This is when they all decided to join the armed struggle that had begun in Kraków and Warsaw. This is when they decided on defense, revenge, self-respect.

This is when Renia sprang up, ready for action.

PART 2

Devils or Goddesses

They were not human, perhaps devils or
goddesses. Calm. As nimble as circus performers.
They often fired simultaneously with pistols in
both hands. Fierce in combat, right to the end.
Approaching them was dangerous. One captured
Haluzzenmädeln looked timid. Completely resigned.
And then suddenly, when a group of our men got
within a few steps of her, she pulls a hand grenade
out from under her skirt or her breeches and
slaughters the SS while showering them with curses
to the tenth generation—your hair stands on end!
We suffered losses in those situations, and so I gave
orders not to take girls prisoner, not to let them get
too close, but to finish them off with submachine
guns from a distance.

—*Nazi commander Jürgen Stroop*

Chapter 12
In Preparation

Renia and Chajka
February 1943

Będzin was buzzing. From daybreak to the eight o'clock nighttime curfew, the kibbutz and its yard were full of comrades. Neighbors noticed. "We gained the reputation of being people of action," Renia wrote, proud of their newfound respect, "of people who have taken control over their future and who will know what to do when the time comes."

Zvi Brandes and Baruch Gaftek, the sole comrade who had military experience, instructed the leaders of the fives, meeting with them and scheming each day. Everyone was taught to use firearms, as well as axes, hammers, sickles, scythes, grenades, and flammable liquids—and to use nothing but their fists. They were trained to fight to the bitter end, to never be taken alive. Renia and the crew collected sharp tools, flashlights, knives—anything that could be employed in battle.

When the first weapons arrived from Warsaw, they were treated as almost holy. Chajka gingerly picked up a gun, energized yet hesitant. Like most youth for whom firearms were so foreign to their upbringing, she worried that it was hot or would go off accidentally. In time, however, she developed confidence. Clinging to her pistol, she saw herself as a true revolutionary, fulfilling a human mission, part of a great historical event.

The PPR smuggled weapons into the ghetto and worked on housing Jews outside Kamionka so that they could fight from the other side. The ZOB trained members to smuggle from the Aryan side; some people went out three times a week. They developed their workshops, and comrades now produced brass knuckles and daggers, studied chemistry, and created bombs, grenades, and bottles filled with explosive materials. They used pipes, coal powder, and sugar. As their skills grew, their homemade bombs became better than the ones they bought.

After working hard all day at forced labor, the comrades spent the nights building bunkers. The Judenrat had no idea: the young, hungry Jews received no external help and were exhausted. "It's horrifying to see the dwindling, weary faces," Renia lamented, noting that they also built bunkers for Jews in private apartments, for no fee. The Young Guard members, including David Kozlowski, sketched out the plans, debating for days, "smart like engineers with diplomas." Where is the best place to build them? How can the entrances and exits be camouflaged?

Building plans arrived via couriers from Warsaw, where the bunkers were feats of engineering: underground corridors ran several kilometers long, spanning the length of the ghetto and terminating on the Aryan side. Main tunnels led to tributary tunnels with lighting, water, radios, food, and stashes of ammunition and explosives; each knew the password to their squadron's bunker. "Such ingenuity," Renia recorded. In Będzin, dugout entrances were to be carved out in ovens, walls, closets, sofas, chimneys, and attics. Walls were built around entire rooms to camouflage them. The comrades dug tunnels with their bare hands. Hiding places were set up in staircases, stables, firewood storehouses. Jews considered how to stage rooms so that it looked like the inhabitants had left in a hurry. Electric lighting, water, radios, benches, small ovens, toast for those with stomach ailments—everything was planned for.

When the time came, all they would have to do was enter their well-stocked bunker. They were ready.

All this zeal led to an episode of resistance—within the Jewish community. In February 1943 the Jewish militia needed more men. Renia knew that this meant the deportation was imminent. The militia would be the ones herding their fellow Jews to the trains, and it wanted six male Freedom comrades to join its forces. Laundry work, which the comrades had continued to do in Kamionka, was now suspended. The Judenrat sent the kibbutz a summons saying that the men were to appear and collect their white hats. If not, their *Zonder* permits would be confiscated, and they would be deported to a camp in Germany.

The Judenrat had already sent a few boys from the ghetto to Germany; none had returned. Regardless, the comrades absolutely refused to be part of what they called the Jewish Gestapo. They were willing to lose their work papers; they would never help Nazis take Jews to death camps. When the boys did not show up at their assigned time, a militiaman arrived at the kibbutz with an order from the Judenrat president to confiscate their *Zonders*. They duly handed them over, even though getting caught walking around without papers meant being sent to forced labor or death. De-

spite this forfeiture, the next day, the Jewish police surrounded the kibbutz armed with clubs and an order to
deport the summoned boys to Germany. The policemen blocked the door and checked identity papers.

That's when two Freedom boys jumped out the
window. Militiamen ran after them; the boys punched
them and continued to flee. The remaining comrades
hollered, "Damn the militia!" They would never let the
police snatch their members! The deputy commander
ordered the militiamen to beat them all and take the remaining boys hostage until the escapees turned themselves in. Renia stared at the clash, stunned.

Frumka worried that someone was going to get
killed in the scrimmage, or worse, that the Germans
would arrive and kill everybody. "No one will be taken
hostage," she declared. She ordered those on the list to
go to the office. The young men obeyed, and the entire
kibbutz followed them along the packed street to the
bus. Then one of the boys, "strong as an ox," escaped
from the police's grasp and started running. A brawl of
clubbing and punching ensued between the militia and
the kibbutz, with a female member, Tzipora Bozian,
severely injuring several militiamen. The beaten commander ordered his men to board the bus. "We'll drive
to the gendarmes' office," he commanded. "They'll
tear into these people." The ghetto residents watched,

and when they realized that not all Jews were afraid of the police, the crowd broke into applause. Renia was flushed with pride.

Frumka, however, feared that if the German gendarmes found out about this, they'd all be finished. She began to calm the militia's commander and his troop, negotiating with them to keep silent. They respected her, and so acquiesced, but on the condition that they take hostages in exchange for the escapees. The summoned men boarded the bus with three hostages: Hershel Springer, his brother Yoel, and, Frumka. She had volunteered herself. Renia watched, impressed and frightened, as the vehicle drove off.

The higher commander heard about this skirmish and, that night, ordered that the kibbutz be locked and the members confined to the courtyard. Frumka and Hershel returned, thankfully, but told them that because they'd humiliated the militia and its commander, all the men would be sent to Germany. That night, Renia and her comrades sat outside under the stars. Sympathetic neighbors came by to invite them in, but Frumka forbade it. She wanted to show the militia that they could handle spending a night outdoors, despite the danger of being outside after curfew, despite the roaming Nazi guards. Throughout the night, militia came by, but only to check that the lead seals on the doors were still fastened.

The group was not caught and stayed outside all of the next day, too, hungry and cold. Frumka and Hershel returned to the Judenrat to plea for the men. That evening, Renia and her comrades ate a meager dinner at the Atid orphanage. Then the militia came and unlocked the doors. The punishment was over. But where were Frumka and Hershel? Renia was afraid to even think about it.

Late that night, they all returned. No one was sent away, drafted to the police, or put in forced labor. The whole ghetto gossiped about Freedom's bravery.

As they'd been learning, it was possible to say no.

News trickled in from Warsaw: the Aktion there was imminent. Zivia and Antek informed the Będziners that they were preparing for defense, that the Jews no longer cared about party politics or ideological differences but were ready to fight. Comrades refused to escape to the Aryan side even when they could, so eager were they to die facing their enemies.

In February Zivia wrote to the Będzin underground, once again demanding that Frumka travel abroad. She needed to stay alive and recount to the outside world the "barbarian butchering of the Jews." Then another letter in March: Hantze needed to come to Warsaw to be smuggled out of the country. "No excuse, no argument." This was her commanding order.

Like Frumka, Hantze refused. She didn't want to hear about saving her life. How would she leave her sister for such uncertainty? "Those two sisters would go to hell and back for one another," Renia wrote. Frumka also couldn't fathom a separation, but she begged Hantze to go. Hantze couldn't refuse her sister; she didn't want her to worry.

A smuggler was called to come over as soon as possible.

Hantze was depressed preparing for her journey, packing a satchel of fashionable, Aryan-looking clothes. Would she ever see her comrades again? She begged Frumka to join her, but Frumka refused. "Hantze, with her semitic features, looked ridiculous dressed as a Gentile peasant girl," Renia wrote, worried she'd never make it.

Two days later, a telegram arrived from Częstochowa. Trembling, Renia read: Hantze crossed the border into the General Government and would soon be moving on. Then, another telegram. She'd arrived in Warsaw! In a few days, she'd journey out of Poland. Everything had been arranged. Renia exhaled in relief.

Renia noticed that one Polish woman, who risked her life time and time again for the ZOB, was mentioned in almost all correspondence. Renia referred to her as A.I.R., hiding her identity, but she was speaking of Irena Adamowicz, by now a good friend of Zivia, Frumka, and Tosia. A devoutly Catholic woman from an aristocratic family, and a former Scout then in her early thirties, Irena was one of the ZOB's main contacts with the Polish resistance movement. After graduating from the University of Warsaw with a degree in pedagogy, Irena worked with The Young Guard, visiting its kibbutzim, sympathetic to the Jewish nationalist cause. During the war, she became close with Freedom and Young Guard members—she even learned Yiddish.

Irena held a job with the Warsaw municipality inspecting children's homes and had a permit that allowed her to visit the ghetto on "official business." In 1942 she traveled to Vilna to tell The Young Guard leaders about the liquidation of the Warsaw ghetto; disguised as a German nun, she visited numerous ghettos, exchanging information and offering encouragement. She approached her friends, leaders in the Home Army, about helping Warsaw's Jews. She distributed letters and publications between the Jewish and Polish undergrounds. She sheltered Jews in her apartment and helped groups cross the border.

Though Irena hid her activity from her own house-mates, she was a legend among the Jewish youth, even in Będzin. "We were all amazed by her personality," Renia wrote, "even though we had no idea what she looked like."

On the other hand, the letters from Warsaw contained stories of tragic failures, mentioning couriers who ended up at Pawiak Prison and Auschwitz. In her diaries, Chajka also recorded tales of Będzin couriers who were caught and murdered. Her coleader, Idzia Pejsachson, was the epitome of tough, curt, and stony, the kind of person Chajka would follow blindly through fire and water. "You can't be occupied with feelings of love now," Idzia would say. "The time has passed when sentimentality was the most important concern."

Idzia insisted that the Będzin group unite as Warsaw did. She wanted to travel to the former Polish capital—at any price. "I must see their work with my own eyes," she said. "Then I'll return and plant the seeds of uprising here. I'll also bring a gift: the first transport of weapons." The comrades tried to convince her not to go: she didn't have the right appearance and was shortsighted, which Chajka believed made her chronically nervous. But they couldn't stop her. Idzia wanted to embolden other girls to follow in her steps. In February 1943 she left—but never returned.

She managed to tell Warsaw of the Będziners' desire to fight, and to obtain three pistols and grenades, but then fell into Nazi hands in Częstochowa.

There were various hypotheses about her demise. According to one rumor, Idzia caught the attention of a secret agent, who followed her. She sensed his presence and meandered from street to street to lose him, but, unfamiliar with the Aryan side, she headed to the ghetto. The agent saw this and chased her. She ran, and a revolver fell from the loaf of bread that she was carrying. She was shot on the spot. In another version, when she realized that the secret agent was following her, she decided to flirt. He invited her back to his house—she had no choice but to go. Her contact in Częstochowa saw who she was with and left their meeting spot. The secret agent tried to attack her. She took out her revolver and shot at him, but he ran away and brought the police. Whatever the circumstances of Idzia's death, the whole group felt deep sorrow and regret over her loss; they shouldn't have sent their best.

Astrid took Idzia's place. Also known as A, Estherit, Astrit, and Zosia Miller, Astrid was not "typical intelligence" but knew many contacts as well as all the trains, roads, and highways that connected Warsaw to the province. Each time she went out, she assumed a new identity—a peasant boy, for instance, or a teacher from the city, wearing a large hat. She carried weapons, money, letters, information, false documents, and detailed defense plans sewn into her clothes. She hid pistols in a large teddy bear (and looked very sweet clutching her stuffed animal), a marmalade tin with a secret compartment, loaves of bread, or simply a coat pocket; she complained about feeling empty once she handed them over. Despite that, whenever Astrid arrived in Będzin, they threw a party with vodka, as, after all, "Warsaw customs had to be introduced." She also smuggled people.

Chajka noted that Astrid was attractive, with a shapely figure, but was also flighty and vain, going on about clothes, buying new outfits for every journey because, ostensibly, it was important to look neat and fashionable on the Aryan side. She possessed both a fine Aryan appearance and extraordinary courage. A real "daredevil," according to Chajka, she'd look straight into the eyes of the secret agents with chutzpah and a naughty smile and ask if they wanted to check her documents. She was very lucky for a long time, but, like most of these courier girls, Astrid eventually ended up in prison. Tortured. Tragic. Dead.

Then, a flurry of communication. A letter about Hantze: her leaving the country was delayed, and, for now, she would remain in Warsaw. Another letter. The situation was dire. The general deportation might occur at any moment. "If you don't hear from us again, it means the Aktion has begun," wrote a Warsaw ZOB member. "But this time it will be much more difficult. The Germans are not prepared for what we have in store." A courier arrived in Będzin to report that there was great fear in the ghetto, but that the comrades were ready. Then she rushed back to Warsaw to make sure she could contact the ghetto from her base on the Aryan side.

A few weeks later, the courier returned. There had been a terrible slaughter in Warsaw, was all she knew. The battle raged on, but so many had fallen. A telegram came from the Aryan zone: **"Zivia and Tosia are dead."**

Then, total silence from Warsaw. Nothing. No telegrams, no letters, no messengers. No information. No news. Was every single person dead? Had they all been murdered?

Someone had to go to Warsaw, with money, to obtain information. But so many women had been killed on the road already. The group needed a courier who didn't look Jewish and who could pull off a fact-finding mission in these particularly dark moments. Frumka and all the leaders decided: Renia.

Little Renia, a teenager from Jędrzejów.

She didn't think about the girls who'd gone missing, the disappearances, the endless deaths. By this time, she was a woman of action, with clear goals, decisive. She felt her anger, her rage, her need for justice.

"Of course," Renia said. "I'll go."

Chapter 13
The Courier Girls

Renia
May 1943

Renia's new world, the world of the couriers, was a world of disguises, where human worth was calculated by physical appearance. To live as a Jew on the Aryan side was a constant performance; a life-or-death acting job that required incessant high-level calculation and reassessment, alongside an animal instinct for danger, a basal sense for knowing whom to trust. As Renia knew, it was hard to scale a ghetto wall; but it was much harder to *be* on the other side, to work and commune, not to mention plot and smuggle, en plein air.

That very same day, the Będzin ZOB leaders contacted the smuggler from Częstochowa, who'd by now figured out the best way to sneak out of the ghetto. Hours later, he arrived at the kibbutz and came straight to Renia, ready to take her out on her first formal mission.

Renia set off, no different from a usual day of ghetto occupation—except for the money. She had sewn several hundred złotys into her garter belt; the group thought that the cash might be useful to the Warsaw fighters. She got all the way to Strzebin by train using the same ID that she'd miraculously found in the street months earlier. They disembarked one station before the border of the General Government.

Before them: a seven-and-a-half-mile trek through fields and forests until they'd reach a small border crossing where the smuggler knew the guard. They would have to cross by foot, and quickly, trying to avoid any police. Renia's heart stopped when they immediately were confronted by a soldier. The smuggler handed him a flask of whiskey. "He let us go through without saying a word," Renia later wrote. "He even showed us the way."

She recalled, "Quietly and carefully, we stole our way between trees and bumps." Any sound scared her: the leaves, the light swaying of branches.

Suddenly, a rustling noise. Something, somebody, a silhouette—and it was close by. Renia and the smuggler dropped to the ground and crawled under the small trees nearby, squeezing themselves under a bush. Careful steps approached them. Heart throbbing, sweating, she looked out from her hiding spot.

A person, shaking with fear, approached them. He'd been traveling from the other side of the border and was sure that Renia and her smuggler were gendarmes lying in wait, ready to pounce on him.

An alternate world existed in the Polish forests.

"From here, it's quiet," the stranger reassured Renia, as he too began breathing freely again.

Minutes later, she was out of the woods, in what was now another country.

Warsaw. Renia strode with purpose—but not too much purpose. Her train had deposited her right in the center of the city, and she paused a moment to take in the novel surrounds, the gray and cream-colored buildings, the slouching cupolas, the slanted roofs. It was not how she'd imagined her first trip to the big city, for Warsaw was as disguised as she was—even more so. The early-spring sunshine, the stretching miles of low-rise buildings, the grand squares and buzzing street vendors were now obscured by a miasma of smoke and ash. Daily traffic was barely audible among the explosions and cries that, she wrote, sounded "like the wails of jackals." The avenues were full of death, thick with the smell of burning buildings and burning hair. Drunken Germans drove riotously through town. There were police checkpoints at almost every intersection, inspecting each package.

Renia could barely take a step forward without a guard searching through her purse. She'd memorized every detail of the new ID she'd obtained the day before from her smuggler, mentally rehearsing yet another identity, trying, as always, to become the person on the card; to inhabit the hazy portrait. This ID was not one of those custom-designed cards with a Polish version of her Yiddish name and a birthplace that accorded with her accent. This identity was by happenstance—it belonged to the smuggler's sister. The papers were more suitable than the ID Renia had found on the street, but still, they had no photo, no fingerprints.

Looking down the street to see more Nazi checkpoints, Renia feared that even though these false documents may have worked in the countryside, they were not good enough for the city. The side of her hand brushed her torso, and she felt the thick lump of currency. Still there.

"Papers!" another policeman barked. Renia handed over the ID, looked him in the eyes. He rummaged through her purse, then let her pass and board the tramway.

Arriving at her stop, Renia got off and walked some more. The police stopped each passerby; even the smallest streets were crawling with gendarmes and secret agents clothed as civilians looking for Jewish runaways who'd escaped the ghetto. They shot any suspect on sight. "My head was dizzy," Renia later wrote, "seeing this terrifying image."

Renia pulled herself together, then moved swiftly toward her target.

At last, she came to the address. "I'm here to see Zosia," Renia said to the rotund landlady who stared at her from the open crack of the door. This was the Catholic Irena Adamowicz's code name.

"She's not here."

"I'll wait for her."

"You have to leave. Guests are not permitted. We can be killed for letting in a stranger."

Renia's heart stopped. Where would she go? She knew no one, not a single person, in Warsaw.

She may have passed all the checkpoints so far, but it didn't mean she wouldn't be caught the next time.

"Besides," the woman hissed. "I think Zosia might be a Jew." She paused, then whispered. "The neighbors are suspicious."

"Oh no, I don't think so," Renia replied. Her voice was calm, childlike, but she was sweating. "I once met her on a train, and she told me to stop by if I was ever in town. She looks Catholic, not like a Jew." Could this landlady somehow see through the layers of her skirt, to the secrets sewn into its fabrics? Renia had been sent on this fact-finding mission because of her Polish looks, but was it enough? She barely wore any disguise; certainly nothing sophisticated.

"If she was Jew," Renia continued, on the offense, not sure what game they were even playing, "we'd sense it right away."

The woman looked at Renia, pleased with her answer. Then she coughed loudly and retreated inside. Renia turned around.

There stood Zosia.

Now it hit Renia. She wasn't just a Jew in disguise, but an underground operative, privy to secrets and codes, tests and twists. She was one in this war's lineage of couriers, or in Hebrew, *kashariyot*—a more nuanced term that better describes the job: connector. *Kashariyot* were usually unmarried women, aged fifteen to the early twenties, who had been leaders in or highly dedicated to their youth movements. They were energetic, skilled, and brave, willing to risk their lives repeatedly.

Connectors had many roles, and they shifted as the war progressed; Renia joined in a later stage. The courier practice began at the start of the war with Frumka, Tosia, and Chana Gelbard, who traveled between ghettos, connecting with comrades in the provinces to lead seminars, pass on publications, educate local leaders, and sustain spiritual growth. These women formed networks, using them to smuggle food and medical supplies. To prevent the Jews from obtaining information and help, the German occupiers saw to it that the ghettos were cut off completely from the world, becoming "carved-out kingdoms," as Zivia described. Radios and newspapers were prohibited, and mail was often confiscated. Travel was not easy: trains had no schedules, women had to spend hours waiting in stations, and it was suspicious to appear to be lost in a new city. "One did not ask directions to a ghetto," Białystok courier Chasia Bielicka wrote. When a *kasharit* arrived with news about families and politics, it was a sign that they hadn't been forgotten, that life went on outside their confined torture, that not everyone was depressed. These women were lifelines, "human radios," trusted contacts, supply dispatchers, and sources of inspiration. Thanks to them, news "blitzed like meteors" across the country. Like Tosia, they were often greeted with hugs and kisses.

But with time, alongside hope, the *kashariyot* also had to pass along the painful news of mass killings and of the Final Solution. They witnessed deportations and murders firsthand and had to carefully relay their stories, as well as others' accounts, persuading Jews of the truth and convincing them to resist.

As the killings broadened, and as youth movements evolved into militias, the couriers' paths and techniques, the knowledge they'd gained to date (such as the guards' routines, the spots where it was easier to sneak out, the most effective outfits and cover stories), and their confidence at outwitting the Nazis were all adapted to suit their new functions. Now they began smuggling fake IDs, money, information, underground publications, and Jews themselves in and out of the ghettos. They found safe rooms for meetings; they worked as fixers for male resistance leaders who went undercover, using their street smarts to navigate cities, help plan their missions, and obtain their work papers. They posed as the men's official "escorts," promenading next to them to make them seem like a nice couple out on a stroll or even necking all night in train stations while waiting to enter the ghetto in the morning. Because she spoke better Polish than her male comrades, the *kasharit* bought them their train tickets and rented their flats. A courier had to be constantly aware of the male comrade's whereabouts in case he was captured. The poise and composure required for this kind of work was superhuman. Did Renia have it in her?

Most connectors had to be female. Jewish women did not have the obvious bodily marker that circumcised men did, nor did they lose confidence fearing the "pants-drop test." It was also less suspicious for women to travel during the days. While Polish men were expected to be at work, women could roam—perhaps on their way to lunch or shopping—without being immediately stopped or snatched for forced labor. Nazi culture was classically sexist, and women were not expected to be illicit operatives; why would that nice, young peasant girl have bulletins sewn into her skirt or a pistol inside her teddy bear? Plus, a flirtatious smile never hurt. Often courier girls appealed to Nazis with their displays of womanly elegance or "little girl" looks and faux naïveté, even asking them for help carrying their bags—the very bags filled with contraband. It was normal for women to carry handbags, purses, and baskets on the street; these chic accessories became weapons caches. At the time, Polish women were also smugglers and peddlers, their handbags loaded with illegal imports of all kinds. Some couriers, like Tosia and Vladka, accessed ghettos and camps by pretending to be non-Jewish smugglers. Tosia once arrived at a ghetto dressed in sports clothes, as though she were a Pole there to buy Jewish goods for cheap.

Usually only women who did not look semitic were selected to go on missions. Like Renia, these women had light hair and blue, green, or gray eyes; they looked "good." Rosy cheeks were important, since they showed health. Those who were trying to "pass" dyed their hair and wrapped it in pieces of paper to create Polish styles. Women (and men) made efforts to dress in Polish clothes, especially fancier, more middle-class and upper-class styles. (The joke at the time was that if you saw a handsomely dressed Polish gentleman, he was probably Jewish.) Both Frumka and Hantze donned headscarves to partly obscure their faces, and although Frumka had to be convinced to make time for cosmetics, she put on makeup to appear more Aryan.

The girls also had to appear Polish in their gestures and demeanor. Something as simple as wearing a fur muff helped curtail the Jewish-seeming habit of gesticulating while talking. Renia had a Polish countenance as well as deportment, able to walk with confidence and react without hesitating—and she spoke the language flawlessly. Polish Jewish women were more likely to be linguistically proficient. For financial reasons, sons more typically went to Jewish schools, daughters to public schools. Girls like Zivia and Renia learned to speak like natives, without the characteristic Jewish accent. They studied Polish literature; they spent their days with Poles, absorbing their mannerisms and idiosyncrasies.

Polish Jewish women were at an advantage, counterintuitively, because of their poverty. Before the war, they'd had to work, and through employment, got to know non-Jews, socializing with them and forming friendships. Women knew their Polish neighbors, had smelled their cooking, saw them raise kids, and were familiar with Polish customs, both religious and mundane. For example, they knew that while Jews brushed their teeth every day and many wore eyeglasses, most Poles did neither.

Specialists in Warsaw, such as the Institut de Beauté salon, helped disguise Jews. They provided nose (and penile) surgeries, makeup consultations, and hair bleaching and styling. Bangs, curls, and frizz were all suspicious, so they ensured that hair was neatly swept up off the forehead in Aryan coifs. But they also offered manners classes, teaching Jewish women to cook pork and order moonshine, to gesticulate less, and say the

Lord's Prayer more. When Tosia visited Będzin, she encouraged the female comrades to learn how to recite Catholic prayers in case they were stopped and tested.

Jews learned catechisms and to celebrate their and their friends' patron saint days. Jewish expressions (for example, "What street are you from?") had to be replaced with their Polish counterparts ("What district are you from?"). The nuances were endless.

Perhaps because they were more comfortable in the Polish milieu, or because women were taught to be empathetic, adaptable, and attuned to people's nonverbal cues, these Jewish women tended to have strong intuition. Their feminine skills, along with good memories, helped them understand others' motives. *Is he a true contact or a Nazi collaborator? Will this Pole give me up? Is a search imminent? Will this guard need to be bribed? Is she staring at me a little too intensely?*

Thanks to their youth movement training, women had the expertise for this work. They had absorbed messages about self-awareness, independence, collective consciousness, and transcending temptations. They knew how to stay straight and not give in to the normal impulses of someone in her late teens or early twenties. Once, on a train, when Tosia was disguised as a village girl, she noticed an attractive man and suddenly craved his attention. She flirted, and he invited her back to his home, a mansion. Tosia was so tempted to risk it all for one day of normalcy and pleasure; it took all her strength to turn away.

Kashariyot had fake IDs, fake backstories, fake purposes, fake hair, and fake names. Equally important, they had fake smiles. One could not walk around with sad eyes—an instant giveaway. Courier girls were trained to laugh, laugh loud, laugh a lot. They had to look up, drink in the world, pretend that they had no cares, that their parents and siblings hadn't just been tortured and murdered, that they weren't starving, and that they weren't carrying a sachet of bullets in their jam jar. They even had to joyfully join antisemitic discussions with their fellow passengers on trains. It wasn't easy, as Gusta Davidson articulated, "to feign lightheartedness while steeped in such sad thoughts . . . [it] tired her to the limits of her endurance." Chasia Bielicka described the constant repression: "We couldn't cry for real, ache for real, or connect with our feelings for real. We were actors in a play that had no intermission, even for a moment, a stage performance with no stages. Nonstop actresses."

And because they went in and out of ghettos, the *kashariyot* were also prime targets for the *schmaltzovniks*. They carried cash intended specifically for the extortionists. In one instance, when Chaika Grossman was followed by a greaser as she left the Warsaw ghetto concealing documents and money, she yelled, cursed, and threatened to report him to the Gestapo. Vladka Meed also used an offensive strategy: she asked the blackmailers to follow her (to avoid a scene), threatened to report them, and walked calmly toward a Nazi guard until they grew alarmed and ran off.

To Gusta, every moment outside the ghetto was one of terror, "every step outside the barbed wire was like passing through a hail of bullets . . . every street a dense jungle that had to be cleared with a machete."

And yet, out went the courier girls before her.

Out went Renia.

Chapter 14
Inside the Gestapo

Bela
May 1943

Renia knew that one of the most successful and daring couriers was Freedom comrade Bela Hazan, who worked primarily in the East. Bela and her whip-smart, Aryan-pretty "colleagues" were legends, assigned the most dangerous missions.

Like her first name, Bela was a blonde beauty. Like her surname, Bela's father was a *hazzan* (cantor) in a tiny and almost exclusively Jewish town in southeastern Poland; the family lived in a dark basement room under the synagogue. He died when Bela was six, and her mother single-handedly raised six children, teaching them not to accept handouts or pity but to be proud and self-reliant. A respected figure in the community, Bela's mother was uneducated but had keen street smarts. She insisted on giving her children the schooling she'd never had and sent them to Hebrew school, refusing financial assistance and attending every school event even if it meant closing her shop. She washed their clothes each night so that they'd look as neat as the rich children. When Bela graduated, her mother sent her out to be a private Hebrew teacher and supported her with food packages and letters filled with "motherly warmth and love."

Bela's mother was a religious Zionist who allowed her to attend movement activities—just not on the Sabbath. In 1939 Bela was selected by local leadership to participate in a special self-defense course, preparation for life in Palestine. Bela learned to use weapons, as well as sticks and rocks; she attended lectures and was especially moved by Frumka's and Zivia's talks. Excelling at her exams, she was chosen to be a defense instructor at the Freedom kibbutz in Będzin. She went straight to Zaglembie, scared that if she returned home first, her mother wouldn't let her go. Her mother was indeed angry and did not reply to her letters for three months before ultimately asking Bela's forgiveness. By that point, late summer, she was trying to find papers for the whole family to make aliyah.

Bela was practicing defense training when Hitler invaded. The comrades sat in the kitchen listening to the radio, aware that Nazis would arrive in their border town within minutes. The leadership decided to relocate members deeper into Poland—that is, except for a few men and Bela, who would stay back to care for the Będzin kibbutz. The German bombardment, however, was so violent that Bela and her comrades fled for their lives. The roads were crowded with panicked, shoving people; as were the platforms of cargo trains. Bombs exploded all around them. After wild days of running, Bela returned to Będzin, where at least she had a roof. She cried with belonging—*this* was her home.

Soon after, however, she was urged by Freedom to go to Vilna, from where aliyah might still be possible. Her chaotic journey included a nighttime boat ride across a river and three weeks in a Russian prison, where she was forced to stand for the entire time. After days of pleading, she went to the head prison guard's house, cried, and insisted—successfully—that they release her fellow comrades. Back en route to Vilna, Bela went to see her mother, who thought she'd been killed. The joyful reunion lasted only two hours, though: Bela had to leave by car and foot to head east in her attempt to reach Palestine. She promised her family she would bring them over. It was the last time she saw them.

In Vilna, Bela participated in the thriving yet hungry youth movement scene, where agricultural and cultural work continued, even under the Russians (just more quietly). Germany's invasion in 1941 brought horror. One image that stood out to her from the first days of occupation was finding a Jewish man glued to a tree with his penis cut off. Soon after, all the usual anti-Jewish laws were put in place. Stars of David, shootings, ghettoization.

But Bela never caved. From the get-go, she would leave the ghetto with a work group or through small passageways or via the houses on the ghetto border; then she'd tear off her Jewish patch (which she'd pinned on instead of sewed—a criminal offense), head to the market, and buy food and medicine for her friends. She was a stranger in Vilna—and a blonde one. She didn't worry about being identified as a Jew by sight, but her Polish accent was very Jewish, and so she spoke as little as possible. In the ghetto, she lived in a three-room apartment with thirteen families— they always welcomed refugee Jews. She slept on a Ping-Pong table. Though she had no medical background, Bela found a job in a hospital as a "nurse" in the operating room. She mopped up blood and once had to hand tools to the surgeon as he operated with just candlelight.

After hearing of the mass slaughter at Ponary, in the forest outside Vilna, the comrades began to organize the resistance. Abba Kovner of The Young Guard initiated a rebel group. Freedom leaders sought non-Jewish-looking girls to work as couriers between the ghettos. Bela already had experience going out as an Aryan, and she volunteered. Still, she needed papers to be able to move freely. She approached a non-Jewish acquaintance at the hospital who was just a few years older than her, claiming that she wanted to go see her family. Her colleague didn't ask questions and gave Bela her own passport, though she warned the girl never to come to her house because her husband hated Jews. And so, at age nineteen, Bela Hazan became Bronislawa Limanowska, or Bronia for short. The Freedom leaders replaced the photo and stamp; though clearly a forgery, it lasted for years.

Bela's job was to connect Vilna, Grodno, and Białystok, smuggling bulletins, money, and weapons. She was instructed to find a safe house for couriers in Grodno and to set up a base. She left the ghetto in the morning with a work group and, for ten gold coins, bought a cross to wear around her neck and a Christian prayer book. The wild wind screeching in her ears, she journeyed by military vehicle, wagon, and carriage, sleeping in demolished houses, until she made it to the colorful medieval Grodno, with its bold sloped roofs and cobblestone streets. She knocked on the door of an older Polish woman's house, and, as the woman did laundry by an oil lamp in the kitchen, Bela told her that her house had been bombed, her family killed, and she needed shelter—terrified the whole time that a Hebrew or Yiddish word would accidentally emerge from her mouth, or that she would say "God" instead of "Joseph Mary." The woman consoled her and put her up. But Bela didn't sleep that night, afraid she might shout in Hebrew in her sleep.

Bela, needing to find a job in Grodno, went to the employment office.

"Can you speak German?" the clerk asked her.

"Sure." Yiddish was, after all, so close.

The clerk quizzed her. She turned her *vus* into *vas* (what).

"You speak very well," he complimented. Her bad Yiddish had come out as decent German. "I have a job for you," he offered. "You can be a translator—at the Gestapo office."

A job with the Gestapo? An insane risk, Bela knew, but also a position that could help her in extraordinary ways.

The next day, she began working at the Grodno Gestapo, mainly an administrative office. The boss liked her immediately, as did most of the primarily German staff. Bela was in charge of translating Polish, Russian, and Ukrainian into German. "Suddenly," she recalled, "I was multilingual!" She also cleaned and served tea.

To find a flat, Bela evaded the intellectual neighborhood where her accent would be recognized. She rented a room on the outskirts of town from a Belorussian widow who, Bela hoped, wouldn't notice her linguistic errors. She tried to make herself comfortable in the tiny surrounds, where Jesus icons lined the walls. But when she came home from her ten-hour shifts, those Jesus images filled her with fear, as did her Sundays at church—more so than her days surrounded by Nazis. Bela was always careful to go to church with a colleague and stand behind her, so that she could imitate every movement.

A week into her job, Bela asked her boss for official papers stating that she worked for the Gestapo. He signed on the spot. With these, she went to Grodno city hall, explained that all her ID had been destroyed, and asked for a full new set. The clerk was so afraid to mess with a Gestapo worker that he rushed her to the front of the line. They drew up an ID with false details. Bela had won the lottery: free movement.

With her papers, she was able to stay out past curfew, even near the ghetto, where she went to help. She had to report to Vilna and offer the comrades her new papers as samples for forgeries. But it was nearly impossible to obtain train travel permits—these were reserved for the military. So, one morning, Bela went to work in tears. She explained that her brother had died in Vilna, and she needed to bury him; the Polish tradition said he'd have to be buried in three days. Then she would need to take care of errands—it would take a week. Her Gestapo boss consoled her and personally accompanied her to get the train passes.

Overjoyed, Bela arrived in Vilna and, dressed as a Christian woman, planned for the right moment to enter the ghetto and pin on her star, which she'd buried in her wallet. Near the ghetto gate, a woman with long blonde braids approached her. "Don't we know each other?"

Bela's heart raced. Who was this? "What's your name?"

"Christina Kosovska."

The woman took out a photo from her wallet. It was

a group of comrades. Bela was among them! "My real name," she whispered, "is Lonka Kozibrodska."

Lonka. Bela had heard plenty about her. A master courier with impeccable Polish and a very pretty, Christian look, Lonka had the wisdom and charm of "a high priest, with her long blond braids arranged like a halo around her head." Comrades often wondered if she was sent by the Gestapo as a plant. In her late twenties, and from a cultured family just outside Warsaw, tall and slender Lonka had studied at university and was fluent in eight languages. While Bela, almost a decade younger, was a street-smart working-class girl, burly and quick, a crafty commoner, Lonka had the confidence of an educated, worldly woman. Lonka did not use her bold looks to intimidate comrades, but she did to impress Nazis. "More than once," her comrade wrote, "a 'Gestaponik' helped her carry her valise with forbidden materials because he thought she was a Christian girl." Lonka, who had quickly risen up the ranks in Freedom with her joyful but diligent demeanor, traveled through the country, transporting weapons, documents, and once, an archive. Now she was here on a mission from Warsaw. Together they blended into a workers' group and entered the ghetto—the first of many collaborations.

Bela had a joyful reunion with her comrades (who

were worried about her high-risk employment) and gave them her papers, which they spent all night copying in their "fake document office." After a few days, Bela returned to Grodno with instructions to inform the Judenrat about Ponary and request financial help for smuggling Jews out of Vilna. She was also to meet with Freedom members and share plans for an underground revolt.

Just before leaving Vilna, Bela replaced her Jewish armband with a black ribbon of mourning. On the train, she burst into tears, crying for the destruction of the Jews. Passengers consoled her about her brother. That is, when they weren't blaming the Jews for all the country's problems. Back in her flat, her landlady and neighbor helped calm her down. When she returned to work, she found a sympathy card from her Nazi office mates saying how saddened they were by the loss of her brother. This, at last, made her laugh.

Bela petitioned for a special permit to enter the ghetto. She explained that she needed to be seen by a very good Jewish dentist—she got a two-week pass. At the Judenrat, she presented her information and requests. Could they spare some money for the poorest in Vilna? Would they take in refugees? But the men on the council didn't believe her. Besides, they said, where would they put more people? And they couldn't just give money to anybody. In the hall, Bela sobbed. One Judenrat member approached her and quietly offered to help the refugees, handing her money and fake IDs. In the basement library, she met the Freedom group. There were eighty of them— many familiar—who assembled for lectures and Hebrew lessons. She told them about Ponary and the need for the youth to rise up.

Just before Christmas 1941, Bela decorated her first tree and told her landlady that a friend would visit for the holidays. Tema Schneiderman arrived in Grodno, wearing her favored elegant but casual clothes, including fashionable black winter boots. She was known to always bring a gift—even when entering a ghetto—like wild flowers that she'd picked on the way, smuggled lemons, or an article of her own clothing.

Warsaw-native Tema (also known as Wanda Majewska) was a tall, restrained, Christian-looking courier whose gently smiling face was crowned with two auburn braids. Tema lost her mother at a young age and was independent and practical; she'd spoken Polish at home and attended public school before becoming a nurse. She joined Freedom through her fiancé, Mordechai Tenenbaum, and learned Yiddish. Earlier in the war, the two of them forged emigration documents and sent comrades to Palestine. Mordechai took her name for his fake ID; he adored Tema and sent her on the most dangerous missions. Her reports were published in underground bulletins, and she wrote an essay for a Polish underground paper meant for Germans, telling them of the war's horrors. Tema had been working in the area as a courier and people smuggler.

Bela took Tema to her office—the condolence card was still hanging on the bulletin board. Tema also had a good laugh.

A Nazi who was enamored of Bela invited her to the office Christmas party. She couldn't refuse. That night, Tema and Lonka were both staying in her apartment, so she brought them along. The three of them got dressed up and attended the Gestapo holiday festivities, posing for a photograph that has since become the iconic image of courier girls. Each one got a copy.

Soon after, the underground summoned Bela to Vilna. She told her boss she needed to be in the hospital for two weeks and took a train there. The passenger car was packed with Nazi soldiers, with whom she chatted—money stashed in her bra, Jewish star in her coat pocket. She entered the Vilna ghetto with a group of women workers, offering to help carry their sacks of potatoes. A few blocks felt like miles.

Soon after, Bela found herself in the Białystok ghetto. There she and Lonka collaborated to smuggle in a package that concealed an infant who had been born in Grodno. Bela was so happy to be among friends, and open as a Jew, that she decided to stay. Frumka arrived in Białystok to lead a three-week seminar, intent that the comrades continue to learn and think. Lonka and Bela spent days trawling the region, finding Jews to smuggle to the seminar, in disguise, and by car, train, and foot. The seminar made them feel like they were living a normal life.

Vilna, Białystok, Volhynia, Kovel—Bela spent the next months traveling nonstop, evading liquidations—once by hiding in cement barrels—and finally arriving home to find her family's house inhabited by Ukrainians, her mother's living room decorated with images of Jesus. Bela threw out a few antisemitic remarks, then asked what happened to the local Jews.

"Gone."

Bela ran, managing to get out of earshot before she began wailing. She knew then that if she wanted to go on living, living for revenge was her only option.

In the spring, Lonka was sent on a mission to Warsaw, carrying four revolvers.

She disappeared.

The leaders in Białystok decided that someone had to find her. Bela volunteered. "Go bring back your bones," they told her, everyone nervous.

Bela's boyfriend, Hanoch, walked her to the station. Strong, muscular, a man who'd stolen weapons from Nazis, he inspired her bravery. They planned to get married after the war and move to Palestine.

He gave her two guns, which Bela hid in her oversized pockets. She wove a Hebrew underground bulletin printed on thin paper inside her braids. She felt confident on her way to Warsaw and passed all inspections with her fake papers.

Until she reached the village of Malkinia Gorna.

An officer got on the train and approached her.

"Yes?"

"Come with me," he said. "We've been waiting for you for a long time."

Without a word, Bela got up and followed him off the train.

The train left.

The officer took her to a small room in the station, searched her body and suitcase, found the weapons. There was nothing she could do. Bela stared at them holding her guns and knew: she was going to be executed. The teenager decided to act as if nothing unusual was occurring. Men came to escort her to the forest, yelling at her to run, beating her on the back. She didn't want them to shoot her from behind. She hummed a melody to calm herself.

They arrived at a small prison in the middle of nowhere. Bela panicked: What about the Hebrew material on her? They knew she was an arms smuggler, but they could not—must not—know that she was a Jew. She asked for a bathroom. They brought her to an open hut with a dug out. Somehow she managed to pull the paper bulletin from her braids and throw it down the hole.

In a small room, everything was taken from her. This was the end. No one would ever know what happened to her. Bela began to bawl. The officer hollered, "Stop crying or I'll kill you!" The interrogation began. She lied incessantly, speaking Polish only, desperately playing with her accent.

"Yes, my father was the first cousin of the famous Polish politican Limanowski."

"I bought my travel papers from a man on the train for twenty marks."

"The weapons are mine."

They beat her mercilessly. Then they asked about Polish officers, and Bela realized they thought she was part of the Home Army.

Suddenly one of them asked, "Do you know Christina Kosovaska?" Lonka.

"No."

"Tell the truth, or I'll kill you." The man took out a photograph and thrust it in her face—the photo of Lonka, Tema, and Bela from the Gestapo Christmas party. Lonka had been so confident, she'd carried it with her on her missions. They'd found it.

"Do you recognize yourself?"

She said she'd met Lonka for the first time at the party. They didn't believe her and beat her again, breaking a tooth.

After six hours of interrogation, Bela was exhausted and thrown on the cold dirt floor. All night, the guards tried to enter the room. She scared them off by screaming loudly. At five in the morning, she was handcuffed and put on a train with an escort. Passersby shot her pitying looks, but Bela held her head high.

She was brought to Warsaw's Gestapo headquarters on Szucha Street. "Szucha"—as this Nazi head office came to be known—was in a stately Polish government building, that had been taken over by the Nazis. Set in a posh neighborhood with rolling boulevards and upscale Art Deco apartments—including the first Polish domicile to have an elevator—one might not have imagined that the white-columned structure had a torture dungeon in its basement. Arrestees waited for their interrogations in dark "tramway" cells, where the seats were arranged tram style, linked closely and all facing the same direction. A radio blasted music to cover the sounds of whips and screams, of clubs and bats and cries. All over, desperate messages were scratched into the concrete walls.

Bela was put in another tiny room, and noted a German slogan on the wall: "Look only forward, you can never look back." For three hours, she heard muffled shrieking and wailing. Then she was taken to the third floor. Another interrogation by an officer with shifty eyes; more fake answers. "If you do not tell us immediately where you got the weapons, we will make you tell."

She was pushed back to the basement, beaten brutally the whole way. The Gestapo officer forced her to take off her clothes and lie on a wooden plank in the middle of the floor. He took out a club and beat Bela on one part of her body at a time. He gagged her mouth with his hands until she passed out. She woke up covered in blood. Unable to move, her body black and bloated, she lay there for three days. Then the officer came back, told her to get dressed, and they took her to Pawiak, the political prison that happened to be inside the ghetto, right across from Dzielna Street. A special car paraded prisoners between the two torture locations several times a day; outsiders watched with dread.

Pawiak was known as hell, but Bela was actually happy.

She'd found out: Lonka was there.

"**Lonka threw** a note from Pawiak when she was arrested," Irena Adamowicz explained to Renia as they strode purposefully through Warsaw. "The comrades found it and learned of her whereabouts."

Despite the dangers at every step, Irena and Renia had gone out into the city. Loyally bound to the women fighters, Irena took Renia in with open arms. Irena was tall, slender, with delicate features. Her fair hair, speckled with gray, was gathered around her neck. She wore a long, dark skirt, a white blouse, and heavy shoes. As they walked, Renia begged her for help answering all the desperate questions they'd had in Będzin.

"Was it true that Zivia was murdered?"

Irena, self-assured and discreet, had spent years exchanging addresses, maintaining connections, and organizing youth actions across Aryan Warsaw, but times were particularly difficult. It had been several days since she'd had any contact with the ghetto. However, she explained, as far as she knew, Będzin had indeed heard false news.

"Zivia is alive," she said. "At this very moment, she's fighting in the ghetto."

Renia exhaled deeply. This, she decided, she needed to see for herself.

Chapter 15
The Warsaw Ghetto Uprising

Zivia
April 1943

A few weeks earlier, the night before Passover, April 18, 1943, Zivia was sitting with her comrades, enjoying themselves at a *kumsitz* (Yiddish for "come, sit," and a term for a movement get-together). It was already two in the morning, but they were debating their plans for the future. That's when a comrade walked in, serious. "We received a phone call from the Aryan side," he announced. They all froze. "The ghetto is surrounded. The Germans will begin their attack at six." They had not known that April 20 was Hitler's birthday, and Himmler wanted to offer him the ghetto's destruction as a little gift.

Zivia felt a tremor of joy, then a shudder of terror. They'd been preparing for months, praying for this very hour, yet it was hard to face the beginning of the end. Then she suppressed her emotions and reached for her gun. It was time.

Ever since the January "mini uprising," the Warsaw ghetto had been planning its grand revolt. Jews saw they could kill Germans, halt an Aktion, and live, and Zivia sensed that the ghetto psychology had shifted. There were no more illusions about the safety of work; everyone knew that deportation and death were imminent. Jews who had money bought Aryan papers and tried to flee. Others found building material in the rubble and constructed sophisticated, well-camouflaged hideouts, filled with stashes of food. They made first aid kits, connected to electricity grids, created ventilation systems, linked to the city sewers, and dug tunnels to the Aryan side. Vladka, too, noticed this swing in mood: during a spring visit to the ghetto, she saw ZOB posters hanging on walls telling Jews not to listen to German orders but to resist; Jews read them carefully. An acquaintance asked her where to buy a gun. Jews purchased their own weapons. The ZOB's revolt was no longer perceived to be a bunch of kids with homemade bombs, but a respected national struggle.

The Home Army, also impressed by January's uprising, finally decided to provide more significant help. They sent fifty pistols, fifty hand grenades, and several kilograms of explosives into the ghetto. Antek put on a suit that was only slightly too small for him and disguised himself as a Pole; he moved to the Aryan side to lead activity and make connections. The ZOB bought weapons from Poles, ghetto Jews, and German soldiers, and stole them off Polish and German police. Their new arsenal was such a hodgepodge, though, that the different caliber bullets made in various labor camps didn't always match their weaponry.

The resistance HQ expanded, and they added workshops and a lab. Vladka described the dark "munitions factory," with its long table and chairs, its pungent smell, as a space of quiet sanctity. It was hushed for a reason: one miscalculation, and they'd blow up the building. The ZOB made primitive bombs out of the larger water pipes from empty houses. They sawed off footlong pieces, soldered one side, and inserted a thin metal pipe loaded with explosives, as well as metal and nails. Wind, short wicks—there were many operational hazards.

A Bund engineer learned from his PPR friends how to make Molotov cocktails. The youth collected thin-glass bottles. (Thicker glass didn't work.) They obtained gasoline and kerosene from a Jew whose family had owned a fuel storage plant, as well as from a large truck that came to the Judenrat each day—they arranged that the driver fill the tank before entering and let them siphon off some. Cyanide potassium and sugar were smuggled in from the Aryan side. The cocktails were wrapped in heavy, brown paper and lit while being thrown. They learned to aim them at tanks and soldiers' helmets. They also made electric-catalyzed mines and placed them under ghetto entrance points using reinforced cement and beams.

The ZOB took official control of the ghetto in place of the Judenrat and, as Zivia wrote, was now effectively "the government." She joked about how they once received a request from a Jew who wanted to open a ghetto casino. Bakers helped. Cobblers offered to make holsters to replace the ropes fighters had been using to hold their guns. The organization cleared the ghetto of collaborators and informants, and collected money. As Zivia noted, it took millions of złotys to arm hundreds of fighters. Despite earlier warnings to act prudently, the American Joint Distribution Committee contributed significant funds. In addition to being charged with finding new recruits, Zivia was appointed to colead the Finance Committee, set up to solicit donations. When this proved inadequate, they imposed taxes, first on the Judenrat and then on the ghetto bank, which was being guarded by Polish police. "One fine day," she wrote, "we went in with pistols and took all the money from the bank." The ZOB levied taxes on rich Jews, particularly those who maintained ties with the Germans. They wrote notes demanding payment, negotiated, kidnapped family members, and sent armed fighters (disguised as Poles, who were seen to be more threatening than fellow Jews) to search their homes, but nothing was as effective as setting up their own jails. Here they would detain wealthy Jews whose money came from corrupt sources until they (or usually their families) agreed to pay.

The ZOB never killed other Jews for money, however. It was important for Zivia to maintain a high moral sense among the "rampant demoralization" and gluttony that surrounded them. They amassed millions, but the fighters ate only modest portions of dried bread. Zivia stressed that they must never spend the money on themselves.

Zivia was among the central command of ZOB leadership, along with energetic Varsovian Young Guard leader Miriam Heinsdorf, who had been romantically

involved with Josef Kaplan, the leader who'd been captured at the weapons storage site. But it appears that
both women were officially demoted in the broader
umbrella organization that included the Bund and adult
parties. No women had official top-tier capacity here,
but Zivia still participated in all daily ZOB meetings,
and her opinion carried weight. Tosia also took part in
high-level discussions.

According to Zivia's reflections, they used their
time wisely for people who had been educators with
zero army experience, developing military strategy
and combat methods for face-to-face warfare, nighttime guerilla attacks, and bunker fighting. The ZOB
studied the labyrinthine ghetto streets, considered the
results of the January battle, and was alert for sur-
prises. Its members stuck with the less dramatic and
more methodical fighting tactic of Zivia's January
group: attacking from hidden locations from which
they could withdraw through attics and rooftops. Surprising the Nazis was their best bet. Strategic posts
that overlooked street corners were meticulously selected. Twenty-two fighting groups, totaling five
hundred fighters (aged twenty to twenty-five), were
organized according to youth movement. One third
were women. Each group had a commander, a specific fighting post, knowledge about its particular

area, and plans in place in case it lost connection with central command. The fighters took preparatory first aid classes. Every night, until late, they trained in patrolled alleyways, without using bullets and marking up cardboard targets. They learned to strip and assemble their guns within seconds.

Zivia, certain that the Warsaw ghetto fighters would not survive, focused on finding people who could tell the world how the Jews fought back. She entertained no thoughts of leaving Poland herself but had selected Frumka and Hantze to be emissaries and had written to them in Będzin, insisting that they leave. No one engaged in rescue plans, no one prepared escape routes or bunkers. The ZOB prepared only a "medical bunker" to treat casualties of the fight—which they knew was imminent.

Still, it was always a surprise when their fantasies materialized.

Weapon in hand, Zivia knew this "morning marked the beginning of the end." The ZOB messengers ran through the ghetto spreading the news; people took up arms or went into hiding. Panic. From her top-floor position, Zivia watched a mother who was holding a screaming baby and dragging a bag of belongings run from bunker to bunker, trying to find room. Knowing they would not see the light of day for some time, others tried to quickly dry out bread—a true Passover story. Inside the bunkers, people crushed together on makeshift wooden shelves, quieting children whose sobs were too loud. Then, Zivia saw the ghetto become ghostly empty, silent, except for the distant shadow of a woman who'd dangerously run to get something she'd forgotten and stopped to glance lovingly at the fighters, stationed in position.

Zivia was one of thirty fighters posted on the highest floors of a building at the intersection of Nalewski and Gensia Streets—the first unit to encounter the Germans. The anxiety, the excitement, was nearly overwhelming. While they were no army, they were so much more organized than they'd been in January, hundreds of them in strategic locations armed with pistols, rifles, automatic weapons, grenades, bombs, and thousands of Molotov cocktails, or, as the Germans came to call them, "the Jews' secret weapon." Many women clutched bombs and explosives. Each fighter had his or her personal kit (assembled by female comrades) containing a change of underwear, food, a bandage, and a weapon.

As the sun rose, Zivia saw the German forces advancing toward the ghetto, as if it were a real battlefront. Two thousand Nazis, panzer tanks, machine guns. Polished, lighthearted soldiers marched in, singing tunes, ready for an easy final coup.

The ZOB fighters let the Germans pass the main entrance. Then they pressed the switch.

A thundering blast. The mines they had planted under the main street went off. Severed arms and legs went flying into the air.

A new group of Nazis marched in. Now Zivia and her comrades threw hand grenades and bombs, a rain of explosives. The Germans scattered; the Jewish fighters chased them down with guns. Pools of German blood covered the streets along with a "pulverized, bloody hulk of dismembered bodies." One fighter, Tamar, was so moved, she joined the chorus of joy and yelled, "This time they shall pay!" in a voice she didn't recognize.

Zivia's unit fought the Germans for hours, their commander running, fortifying, urging. Suddenly a weak spot, and the Nazis entered the building. More Molotov cocktails. Germans "rolling in their own blood."

No Jewish fighter was injured.

The intoxicating joy of revenge. The Jews were stunned, breathless, shocked to be alive. The fighters embraced, kissed.

They headed to find bread and a place to rest, but they heard a whistle, then the sound of motors. They ran back to their positions, threw cocktails and grenades at the Nazi tanks. A direct hit! They'd blocked the advance. "This time we were bewildered," Zivia later reflected. "We ourselves couldn't understand how it had happened."

That night, makeshift Passover seders were held in the bunkers of the German-free ghetto. The Jews sang about liberation and salvation, asked why this night was different from all other nights, and belted out *"Dayenu."* Even just this would have been enough. The Judenrat food stores were opened, and people stocked up.

The following days of fighting, however, were difficult. Most bunkers were cut off from the electricity grid, water, and gas—almost all militia units were cut off from one another. German artillery stationed on the Aryan side bombarded the ghetto nonstop. It was hard to move. Zivia maintained her authority and, as always, acted on her own initiative, conducting recon missions and night tours of the fighters' posts and bunkers, reassuring them, calculating plans, trying to determine the Germans' position. These nocturnal explorations were wildly dangerous. Once, she was spotted by a German soldier and opened fire. Several times, she climbed on top of a ruined building to bask in the nighttime calm. "For hours," she recalled, "I would lounge there, in a preoccupied silence, the skies galloping over in their early springtime, and it was sometimes so good to lie like that, to feel in my hand the pleasant stroke of my gun."

One night, she and two comrades went out to make contact with the primary Freedom fighting groups on Mila, the main street in the ghetto, "stealthily maneuvering through rubble," cutting across streets and alleyways, weaving their way close to the houses. Her heart pounded as she approached the address—there was no sign of life. Devastated, she could barely utter the code word.

And then, the camouflaged door opened. All of a sudden, comrades, old friends, were hugging her, kissing her. In their unit, which had attacked Germans entering the ghetto from behind, only one life had been lost. This bunker had a radio that blared joyful music. Then the tune stopped. "The Jews of the ghetto," a secret Polish broadcast announced, "are fighting with unparalleled courage."

Zivia was exhausted and needed to visit others. But the comrades wouldn't let her go. This bunker had been prepared as the medical unit, with a doctor, nurses, equipment, first aid, medicine, and hot water. They insisted that Zivia take a hot bath; they roasted a chicken and opened a bottle of wine in her honor. They couldn't stop talking, feeling, emotions flooding, acknowledging what they'd done. One had thrown a Molotov cocktail that struck a Nazi in the head, turning him into a shaft of fire; another hit a tank, leaving a pillar of smoke; others stripped guns from German corpses.

Additional units had similar stories of success: mines at entrances, hours of battle, getting cornered in attic passageways but bombing their way out. A detachment of three hundred Germans was "ripped to bits" by an electric mine, and "shreds of uniform and human flesh flew in all directions." As another fighter described after his unit's bomb detonated: "crushed bodies, limbs flying, cobblestones, and fences crumbling, complete chaos." In one group's battle, Nazi soldiers reentered the building waving a white flag, but the ZOB wasn't fooled. Zippora Lerer leaned out the window and threw bottles of acid onto the Germans below. She heard them scream in disbelief: *"Eine frau kampft!"* "A woman is fighting!" They began to fire back at her, but she did not retreat.

Bundist Masha Futermilch climbed onto the roof of a building. She shook in excitement, so much so that it took extra time to light the match to ignite the wick of her explosive. At last, her partner flung the grenade at the Germans. A thundering explosion, falling Nazis, and then she heard one scream. "Look, a woman! A woman fighter!" Masha was awestruck. A sense of relief washed over her: she had done her part.

She grabbed a pistol and shot, down to the very last bullet.

Hantze prepared to leave Warsaw, as had been the plan. But woman plans, and God laughs. Days before her departure: the Warsaw ghetto uprising. Now, it was determined, Hantze was not to go abroad but to return to Będzin and help with defense in Zaglembie. If it was meant for her to die in battle, she wanted to die alongside her sister and comrades there. On the second day of the uprising, during a break in the fighting, Hantze snuck though the ghetto's small, winding streets toward the train station, accompanied by two armed comrades. Every second was precious. They reached the open space between the ghetto and the Aryan aside. Behind Hantze was the rebellious battlefield, the difficulty to her back. One more step.

Suddenly a savage voice: "Halt!"

The armed comrades tore out their revolvers and shot. A swarm of police reinforcements arrived. Hantze ran with all her strength. But the Nazis chased her into the yard "and caught our girl," Renia later wrote about her dear, luminous friend. "They dragged her to a wall by her hair and pointed their machine guns. She stood motionless and stared death in the face. The bullet ripped through her heart."

After the first five days of fighting, of street skirmishes and attic attacks, the ZOB was left with a shocking result: most everyone was alive. This was, of course, good news, but it also presented a challenge. Because they had been prepared to die, they hadn't planned any escape routes or short-term survival plans, and they had no hideout and barely any food. They grew tired, hungry, weak. Now Zivia was involved in a new, wholly unexpected, discussion: How would they *keep going*?

Renia stayed at a hotel on the Aryan side. The next morning, "a friendly woman," as Renia described her, likely a contact of Irena's, took her to see the ghetto battle close up. Every street that led to the ghetto was filled with German soldiers and tanks, buses, and motorcycles. Nazis wore armored helmets and held weapons, ready to pounce. The clouds had turned red, reflecting the flames of burning houses. Even at a distance, the air was choked with screams. The closer Renia got to the Jewish quarter, the more shocking the shrieks. Nazi soldiers and gendarmes lay under barricades. Special SS troops, in full battle array, stood opposite the ghetto wall. Machine-gun muzzles protruded from the balconies, windows, and roofs of the adjacent Aryan homes. The ghetto was completely surrounded, with armored tanks firing shells from all sides.

But Renia saw it for herself: Nazi tanks were being destroyed—by Jews. By her people, resistance fighters who were scrawny, disheveled, and starving, lobbing hand grenades, pointing machine guns.

Up high, German planes, gleaming in the sun, swooped low and swirled above the ghetto, hurling blazing bombs, setting the streets on fire. Buildings crumbled into rubble, floors collapsed, pillars of rising dust. This clash was so tremendous, it resembled a civil war. "It seemed not merely that some Jews were fighting the Germans," Renia wrote, "but that two entire countries were at battle."

Renia was watching up close, planted near the ghetto wall. It was her mission, her responsibility, to witness and report. As she watched the ghetto burn, she snuck along its perimeter, trying to view the battle from as many vantage points as possible. She saw young Jewish mothers throw their children from the top storeys of burning buildings. Men threw their families, or threw themselves, jumping to their deaths, trying to soften the falls of their wives and elderly parents.

Not everyone was able to commit suicide. Renia saw ghetto residents trapped on the upper floors of an apartment as a fire rose higher and higher. Suddenly a burst of flame made one of the walls crack. Everyone fell, sliding into the rubble. From under the destruction emerged a horrid cry. A few mothers who had miraculously survived the flames with children in their arms wailed for help, begging for the lives of their babies.

A Nazi soldier ripped the children out of their mothers' clutches. He proceeded to hurl them to the ground, stomping their tiny bodies with his feet and pummeling them with his bayonet. Renia watched, transfixed, as he threw the squirming, broken bodies into the fire. The soldier beat one of mothers with his stick. A tank approached and rolled over her dying body. Renia witnessed grown men with gouged-out eyes convulse in anguish, begging the Germans to shoot them. The Nazis simply laughed and let the flames do the work.

Even amid this depravity, this sickening chaos, Renia willed herself to view the battle for the hope it offered, the promise it could deliver to the fighters in Będzin. Through the smoke, she could hazily make out young Jewish men with machine guns standing on the roofs of the houses that were not in flames. Jewish girls— Jewish girls!—shot pistols and hurled bottles of explosives. Small Jewish children, boys and girls, ambushed the Germans with stones and iron rods. Seeing the fight flare, Jews who were not part of any organization, who had no clue about a resistance movement, grabbed anything they could find and joined the fighters. Because otherwise, there was only one way out: death. The ghetto was full of the dead. Mostly Jews, but as Renia saw, Germans too.

Renia stood by the ghetto walls and witnessed the fighting unfold over the course of the day, surrounded by non-Jews who were also watching. A photograph shows a large group of Poles, adults and children, standing, chatting, wearing caps and coats, hands in their pockets, looking on, whorls of black smoke in front of them. Vladka, who was also on the Aryan side, saw thousands of Poles, from all over Warsaw, gather to watch. Renia noted how the bystanders of these horrific scenes reacted, often in tellingly different ways. Some Germans spat at the sight and stepped to the side, no longer able to witness the horror. In the window of a nearby apartment building, Renia saw a Polish woman tear the clothes from her breast. The woman wailed, "There is no God in the world if he could watch such scenes from above and stay silent."

Renia felt like her feet were breaking under her. The things she'd seen, the graphic images, all felt as if they were pulling her to the ground. But at the same time, she sensed a lightness in her heart, "something of a happiness that there were still Jews here, living people who were fighting against the Germans."

Shaken, still actively posing as a Polish girl, Renia eventually returned to her hotel as the battle raged on. She tried to rest but was tortured by the visions, by the very information she'd come to obtain. "I couldn't believe that I'd seen this with my own eyes. Could my senses have been fooling me?" she kept asking herself. Were those tormented Jews, broken and decimated by hunger, really able to conduct such a heroic battle? But yes, yes, she had seen it: "The Jews picked themselves up, wanting to die like people."

For the rest of the day, news from the ghetto spread throughout the city: the number of Germans killed, the number of weapons that the Jews took from them, the number of tanks destroyed. The Jews would fight until their last breaths, was the rumor. All night, as she tried to sleep, Renia's bed shook from the bomb blasts.

She left for the train station in the early morning, walking through the city more calmly than she had the day before. Renia, a young Jewish woman from a tiny town on the outskirts of Kielce, was becoming an expert at navigating the death traps of Warsaw's wild, war-ravaged streets. She spent the entire day traveling in train wagons with Gentiles who could not stop talking about their awe over the heroism and courage of the Jews.

Like the long line of female couriers before her, Renia benefited from being underestimated and misjudged, and she was able to slip through Warsaw without anyone guessing that she was a resistance operative. Appearing to be an innocuous, young Polish girl who happened to be taking a stroll through town or a train ride to the country, Renia was afforded a front-row seat to the war's greatest rebellion and even the candid discussion of its aftermath. "Poles must be fighting alongside the Jews," she heard many of them guess. "There's simply no way that the Jews are capable of conducting such a heroic battle." This was the grandest compliment, really.

The train whizzed on, approaching the border. Renia could barely contain her good news. It was time for uprisings everywhere. Next, Będzin!

Chapter 16
Bandits in Braids

Zivia
May 1943

Zivia was blinded by the glare. The middle of the night resembled the middle of the day. Roaring flames, every direction.

After the initial fighting, the Nazis restrategized. Instead of marching into courtyards—from which Jews no longer emerged—they slipped quietly into the ghetto in small groups, aiming for addresses where they suspected Jews were hiding. The ZOB attacked them inside. Then, faced with the prospect of drawn-out skirmishes, the Germans changed tactics again. In early May the commander ordered for the systematic destruction of the ghetto's mainly wood-framed buildings—by fire.

Within hours, Zivia wrote, the whole ghetto was ablaze. The Nazis destroyed one building at a time, shooting any Jews who ran from their smoking hide-outs. Even in metal bunkers, people died of heat and smoke inhalation. Families, groups, children ran fran-tically through the crumbling streets, searching for shelter that wasn't flammable. Zivia watched in horror. "The Warsaw ghetto was burnt at the stake," she de-scribed. "Pillars of flames rose, and sparks crackled in the air. The sky glowed with a terrifying red light. . . . The pitiful remains of the largest Jewish community of Europe fluttered in the last throes of death." This ter-ror, she wrote, took place while, just outside the ghetto walls, Poles visited a carousel, enjoying the spring day.

The ZOB fighters were no longer able to fight from inside buildings, nor could they cross over the roof-tops. All attics and passages had been destroyed. They put wet cloths over their faces and rags on their feet to deflect the heat and reverted to bunker warfare, using civilians' bunkers, having not prepared any of their own. Most Jews were happy to share their space, and listened to the ZOB's orders not to go outside and thus end up alerting the Germans. But in the end, the burn-ing beat the steadfast rebellion. Smoke, heat, whole streets were engulfed in fire. Zivia continued to tour the ghetto each night, into the "rampage of flames, the tumult of collapsing debris, the crash of broken glass, pillars of smoke reaching the sky." She wrote: "We were burning alive."

Groups of people ran from fire into the open ghetto, flames scorching their faces and eyes. Hundreds of fighters and thousands of civilians gathered in a remaining courtyard on Mila Street, begging the ZOB for direction: "*Tayerinke, wohin?*" "Dear one, where shall we go?" Zivia felt responsible but had no answer—what now? The ZOB's plans had shattered at last; the final face-to-face combat they'd dreamed of was impossible. They'd been ready to wait it out, to shed Nazi blood one small ambush at a time. They had simply not imagined that they would be destroyed this way, with their killers at a safe distance. As Zivia stressed later, "It was not the Germans we had to fight, but the fire."

Zivia moved into Mila 18. A few weeks earlier, Mordechai Anilevitz had relocated the HQ of the ZOB to this enormous underground bunker that had been prepared by notorious thieves of the Jewish underworld. Dug under three collapsed buildings, the bunker had a long corridor with bedrooms, a kitchen, a living room—even a "salon," with a hairdresser chair in the middle, and a hairdresser who helped people prepare to go to the Aryan side. They nicknamed each room after a concentration camp. (At the Yad Mordechai Museum in Israel, named for Anilevitz, visitors can explore a reproduction of the bunker. The brick-lined space is full of wooden bunks, clothes draped over long ropes, basic pots and pans, a radio, tables, chairs, woolen blankets, a telephone, a toilet, and basins.)

At first, the bunker had a well and water taps, fresh bread, and vodka smuggled in by the thieves' cronies. The heavyset gang leader, who respected Anilevitz, was in charge of all arrangements and rations—and he was fair. He sent his men to help the ZOB fighters, showing them German positions, back alleys and side streets, even when most of the area was destroyed. "Our hands have a knack for locks," he told Zivia. The group's central command lived there, as did 120 fighters who'd been forced out of their burning shelters, and civilians, too. Intended for a few dozen criminals, by the time Zivia arrived, Mila 18 housed more than 300 people, crammed in every nook. Now the stowaways really began to suffer from overcrowding, insufficient oxygen, and dwindling food supplies. In a letter to Antek, Anilevitz wrote that it was impossible to light a candle for lack of air.

During the day, Mila 18 was crowded, and fighters tossed and turned, yearning, hungry. (No cooking was allowed during the day, as the smoke would be visible.) Zivia lay next to Hela Schüpper, smoking rolled tobacco. At night, however, when the Nazis clocked off work? Vitality. Couriers connected with other bunkers; reconnaissance missions went out to find weapons, contacts, and any telephone that still functioned. (Until the fire, Tosia spoke with outside comrades each night; for months, the fighters had been using the workshop phones to update comrades on the Aryan side.) Others ransacked empty bunkers, looking for anything useful, even cigarette butts. More than a hundred fighters were desperate for weapons and knew the Germans were aware of their location, yet they still spent evenings talking about their dreams of Palestine. They ventured outside, stretched aching muscles, walked freely, breathed deeply, "even if it was the air of the ghetto where the crackling and whispering of the embers still pierced the darkness," Zivia wrote. Ghetto Jews who spent their days inside sewage canals also came up after dark. The ghetto was nocturnally alive, "even in the midst of burning desolation."

Zivia continued: "Then, with the rising of the sun, the Germans guards came sniffing around like hungry dogs in search of prey. Where are those blasted Jews, *those last Jews?*" Reprieves were short, to say the least.

Roughly ten days into the fighting, the ZOB decided to leave for the Aryan side via a limited number of tunnels and sewers. Several fighters had already tried this, to no avail: they were either shot or got lost underground and died of thirst and despair. But now there was no choice. The ghetto was nearly demolished, the streets were blocked by large chunks of concrete, and it was almost impossible to breathe from the smoke, not to mention the smell of scorched bodies. Zivia was afraid of tripping on whole families of corpses when she went out on missions.

The Nazis hunted to find every bunker, hiding and eavesdropping on Jews' conversations, even taking tormented, starving Jews hostage. Every night, fewer people came out for air. The ZOB debated whether they should rescue civilians or themselves. They sent messengers, including a seventeen-year-old boy named Kazik, out through the ZZW tunnels to see if any hideouts had been secured for them on the Aryan side. (The ZZW had waged a great ghetto battle, waved its flag, and used its preemptively made escape routes to reach the Aryan side, where its fighters planned to join the partisans. Most were killed.) Despite Antek's many secret meetings on the Aryan side, efforts were not progressing well—the fighters had no shelters to run to.

Inside the ghetto, Anilevitz had tasted his dream of revenge, but, still, he became depressed. What now? He met with Zivia, Tosia, his girlfriend Mira Fuchrer (another brave leader who was supposed to have escaped with Hantze), and other commanders to review the situation. There was no help from outside, and tenuous links with the PPR. Their campaign was over.

"There is hardly anything left to fight with or anyone against whom to have a war," Zivia wrote. They felt the peace of fulfillment, but were hungry, awaiting a slow death. None had ever imagined that they would still be alive, clutching weapons, waiting for who-knows-what. The comrades turned to Zivia for encouragement, reassurance, and instructions. For all her pessimism, she was able to snap from her mood and spring into action. Warsaw's extensive sewer system was her only answer.

Zivia accompanied the first group—fighters with Aryan looks, including Hela—as they left for a sewage escape mission, to set off from the "garbage collectors" bunker which was connected to underground cellars. She was going to convince the leader of the bunker and a guide to go through with the plan and escort the Jews out.

First, to cross the ghetto. The group was calm on the surface, joking, but comrades clutched their pistols and said, perhaps, their last good-byes. They wriggled out of Mila 18 on their bellies like snakes, yearning for a drop of daylight in the pitch black—would they ever see sun again? They breathed sooty, smoky air, listening to the guards direct them away from active shooting, their feet wrapped in rags to muffle any sound, walking through side streets, fingers on triggers, surrounded by the "scorched skeletons of houses" and by total silence but for a window banging in the wind. They stepped on broken glass and charred corpses, they sunk into tar molten from the heat. Zivia led them to the bunker at last, where she successfully negotiated with the leader and guide, who apparently knew fourteen routes in the canals.

The group was given a few crumbs of food, a chunk of sugar, and instructions. They left that very night. Zivia used all her strength to control her emotions; she heard water splash as each one jumped in, then fading steps. Two hours later, the guide returned to report that the group had made it to the Aryan side and climbed out of the manhole in the middle of the street. As instructed, they then hid in nearby rubble while Hela and another "good"-looking comrade went to find a courier girl. (Only later did Zivia find out that they were attacked by Germans. The guide took them to the wrong exit; Hela, who'd cleaned herself up, changed her stockings, and splashed water on her face, ran. She was the sole survivor.)

It was nearly dawn when Zivia, exhausted, was ready to set off for Mila 18 to report her good news to Anilevitz. But the comrades, in particular the fighter whom Anilevitz had placed in charge of Zivia's safety, refused to let her walk outside in daylight. Zivia, always active, didn't want to be seen as a coward, but after a long fight with Bund commander Marek Edelman, she capitulated.

That night, Zivia, her guard, and Marek left for Mila 18. Marek disobeyed rules and lit a candle, but it blew out immediately. They bumped into buildings and corpses. Suddenly, Zivia fell into a hole that had opened up between two buildings because of a collapsed roof. She could not call out for help, could not utter a sound. She immediately checked for her gun to make sure she hadn't lost it. But now what? Somehow the men found her and pulled her out. "Limping and bruised, I continue to walk," she recalled. She charged forward with her escape plan, excited by the prospect of seeing her comrades at Mila 18. She was even thinking of funny ways to tease them. So when she approached the building and saw that the camouflaged entrances had been opened and the guards nowhere in sight, she thought they'd hit the wrong address. Then it dawned on her that this must be part of a plan for more intense camouflage. She checked all six entrances. Uttered the password. Heart in her throat.

Nothing.

Then.

*"**Tosia and** Zivia, heads of the Pioneer underground in Poland, fell in Warsaw in defense of the Jewish people's dignity,"* read *Davar.*

News hit the Aryan side. A telegram reached Frumka in Będzin. She sent coded word to Palestine. "Zivia is always near Mavetsky [death] Tosia is with Zivia." Their deaths made front-page headlines in the Hebrew press.

The youth movements, the entire country, mourned. Zivia and Tosia had become mythical symbols of the Jewish fighting woman—the "Jeanne d'Arcs of the underground." Comrades were referred to as "friends of Tosia." Movement instructors were called "Zivia A" and "Zivia B." The name Zivia was known to Jews in Poland, Palestine, the United Kingdom, and Iraq. "Zivia" was all of Poland, and a whole country collapsed with her killing. "Their names," the obituaries read, "will shape a new generation. . . . Their fighting and camaraderie that rose in the flames of sacrifice, has the potential to crush rocks and uproot mountains."

The obituaries, however, were dead wrong.

That night, after the nothingness, Zivia noticed several comrades in the yard nearby. She ran up to them in relief, assuming it was the regular nightly patrol. It wasn't. She recoiled as she saw fighters drenched in blood and refuse, writhing in pain, shivering, fainting, gasping for air—the "human remains" of what had been a slaughter in the bunker. Tosia was there, head and leg badly wounded.

Sick with horror, Zivia heard the story. When the Nazis arrived at Mila 18, the fighters couldn't decide whether to escape through a back exit and attack, or to stay put, assuming the Germans would be too fearful to enter. They knew the Germans used gas but had been told that holding wet cloths over their mouths and noses would be sufficient. It wasn't. The Nazis infused the gas in slowly, suffocating them gradually. One fighter called for suicide, several followed. Others choked. In all, 120 fighters died, with only a handful escaping through a hidden exit.

Zivia was stunned, destroyed. "We raced about like madmen," she recalled, "and tried to break into the rock-sealed bunker with our bare hands and nails to reach the bodies of our comrades and retrieve their weapons."

But there was no time for madness, no time to mourn their closest friends, their everything. The remaining ZOB had to heal the wounded, find shelter, and decide what to do next. Zivia, Tosia, and Marek took command. Walking, "a convoy of lifeless bodies among the shadows, like ghosts," they headed to a bunker where they believed there was still activity, and Zivia announced that the HQ address had changed. She was always doing, always moving forward, never falling into passivity, which would have meant giving in to despair. "Responsibility for others brings you back to your feet," Zivia wrote, "despite everything."

They arrived at the new HQ carrying the wounded fighters only to find out that Germans knew of that location, too. Despite the danger, Zivia decided to stay put—the wounded members were too injured to be moved. All the fighters, sick and exhausted, were ready to collapse and die together. But Zivia insisted that they go on. She sent another group off on a sewer escape mission. She kept others busy tending to the wounded to stop them from collapsing into hysterics—the same turmoil she felt all night but kept deeply hidden. *I should have been there* . . . Hidden in the burning ghetto, her own life hanging from an unspooling thread, she was already consumed by survivor's guilt.

But again, she didn't have long to worry. The group of fighters who'd set off through the canals to find a way out came back to report that they'd miraculously met Kazik, with a Polish guide, in the tunnels.

Kazik, who had been sent out through the ZZW tunnels, had made it to the Aryan side and tried to find help. The Home Army refused to provide the ZOB with a map of the sewage canals or a guide, but the group secured the help of the PPR, as well as a *schmaltzovnik* ringleader—naturally, for a steep fee—and several other allies. Kazik then went back into the tunnels with a guide, on the pretense that they were rescuing Poles and gold. But the guide kept stopping; Kazik had to cajole him, offer him alcohol, and, finally, threaten him at gunpoint. At last, creeping on their bellies through the narrowest holes, stinking like skunks, they reached the ghetto at two in the morning. But Kazik had been horrified to find nothing at Mila 18 except corpses and the cries of the dying. On the brink of insanity, he turned around to exit the ghetto empty-handed. In the sewers, he called out the ZOB code word—"Yan"—a desperate last plea.

Suddenly he heard a female voice respond, "Yan!"

"Who are you?" Guns cocked.

"We're Jews." Emerging from around a bend: the surviving fighters. They hugged and kissed. Kazik told them that there was more help outside than they'd assumed. He followed them back to Zivia and the others.

On May 9 a group of sixty fighters and civilians gathered in the new HQ bunker, on the threshold of flight. Zivia was still devastated that the 120 fighters who had just been killed were not with them. She worried that there were additional fighters still in the ghetto who could not be reached in daylight. Some comrades were badly injured and could not move, while others could barely breathe from gas and smoke inhalation. People refused to leave, people were confounded.

Ultimately, "the big sister" had to make a snap decision to save whomever she could. She leapt down into the sewer. "I now felt the full meaning of the plunge," Zivia wrote later. "It seemed as if you were leaping into the darkness of the depths, with the filthy water splashing and spraying about you. You are overcome by a terrible feeling of nausea. Your legs are drenched with the foul-smelling cold slime of the sewer. But you keep on walking!"

In the sewers, Kazik and the guide took the lead, and Zivia was the rear guard for dozens of fighters, single file, hunching through the slime, unable to see even one another's faces. She held a candle in one hand (it kept blowing out) and her precious gun in the other. The canals were dark, her head was lowered. At some crossings, the water and excrement flowed neck high, and they had to hold their guns over their heads. Some parts were so narrow, it was hard for even one person to fit. They were starving and carrying their injured comrades; hours with no drinking water, an eternity. The whole time that Zivia's body was immersed in sewage, her brain was immersed in thoughts of the friends she'd left behind. Tosia, meanwhile, felt demoralized. She was injured and occasionally begged to be left behind, but she ultimately managed.

Miraculously, the entire group arrived before dawn to the sewer under Prosta Street on the Aryan side, in central Warsaw. Kazik explained that the truck that was supposed to transport them out of the city wasn't there; that it wasn't safe for them to exit. He climbed out to find help. Zivia, at the back of the line, did not know what was happening. She knew no details of this rescue plan and could not communicate with the outside, which made her anxious. She did not dwell on her own precarious future, however; her worry for the comrades still in the ghetto "gnawed cruelly at my heart."

For an entire day, the group sat below the manhole on Prosta listening to the sounds of the street above—carriages, streetcars, Polish children playing. Finally, Zivia couldn't take it anymore. She and Marek, who had also been at the back, pushed their way to the crowded area at the front. No one had any information. Suddenly, in the middle of the afternoon, the manhole cover was opened, and a note was thrown in. It said that the rescue would take place that night. Most sighed in desperation, but Zivia exclaimed, full of vigor, "Let's go back and bring the others!"

Two fighters volunteered to return and bring the rest of the ZOB to the canal entrance. Then they all waited.

At midnight, the manhole cover was raised; soup and bread were lowered in for the fighters, or at least those who could get some, though Zivia claimed they were all so violently thirsty they could barely eat. They were told that the local streets were patrolled by Germans and that they would have to continue to wait. A group of fighters went off to a secondary location, a thirty-minute walk away, to alleviate the overcrowding in the feces-filled water. Dangerous methane gas was accumulating in the air around them. One member collapsed and drank sewage water in desperation.

Zivia waited and worried for the two volunteers who went to retrieve the others. She took position near the manhole to make sure no one made any hasty moves. She could see a single ray of new sunlight piercing through the opening, a reminder of fresh air. The sounds of life cascaded right above her but were a world away.

Early morning, May 10. The couriers who'd gone back to the ghetto returned safely. But they were alone. They reported that the Germans had sealed off all the canal openings and raised the water level through the entire sewage system; they'd had to turn back. With the hope of saving more members dashed, Zivia became immensely depressed. (She did not know about the ongoing drama above ground, as every attempt to find a truck to collect the fighters was fruitless.) Then, German voices.

Was this the end? Zivia felt so dejected, she secretly wished it was.

At ten in the morning, the manhole was raised. Sun poured in, and people recoiled and panicked with the light—had they been discovered? "Hurry! Hurry!" No, it was Kazik, who urged them to get out immediately. They had to clamber up the metal shaft, and were pulled from above and pushed up from below.

With stiff limbs and damp, filthy clothes, they were not quick. The exit lasted forever—one account says over thirty minutes—during which time forty people emerged from the ground and got into a truck. There was almost no security, perhaps two armed helpers. Polish people watched from nearby sidewalks.

On the truck, Zivia finally saw what they looked like: "We were filthy, covered in dirty, bloodstained rags, our faces emaciated and despairing, our knees caving in from weakness. . . . We had almost lost all semblance of humanity. Our burning eyes were the only evidence that we were alive." They stretched out, clutching their guns. The trucker had been told he was transporting shoes, not Jews. He was directed, at gunpoint, to listen to instructions.

Suddenly word came that there were Germans nearby. The twenty fighters who had gone to the secondary location and the one who went to fetch them had not yet returned to the manhole. Here there was a "famous fight" between Zivia and Kazik, though Zivia never wrote about it. According to Kazik, Zivia insisted that the truck wait for the fighters to arrive. Kazik insisted he'd instructed everyone to stay near the manhole and that now it was too risky and they had to leave immediately. Kazik promised to send another truck and ordered the driver to drive. Zivia, furious, threatened to shoot him. (Many years later, the translator of Kazik's memoir questioned him: "I understand that you fought with Nazis . . . but with Zivia?!")

Then, they were moving through morning traffic. As Zivia put it, "The truck, loaded with forty armed Jewish fighters, set off on its way in the heart of Nazi-occupied Warsaw."

It was a new day.

The second rescue attempt—of the twenty remaining fighters—failed. The Germans had found out about the morning's very public operation in the middle of the street and waited for the fighters to emerge. The ZOB simply could not wait anymore in the excrement. Unaware that the area was filled with Germans, they climbed out—and were ambushed. They fought the Nazis hand to hand, shocking the Polish bystanders. When Kazik returned to the manhole, he saw the street strewn with their bodies, shot to death.

Several Jews ran back to the ghetto. Later, Zivia learned that they fought for another full week.

Both Zivia and Kazik were haunted by the knowledge they had deserted friends. She had promised that she would wait for them, and hadn't. This guilt plagued Zivia constantly until her death.

Overall, more than a hundred Jewish women fought with their movement units in the Warsaw ghetto uprising. In a Nazi inner circle meeting, it was reported that the battle was surprisingly tough and that devilish, armed Jewish girls, in particular, fought up to the bitter end. Several women committed suicide at Mila 18 and other locations; many died "with weapons in their hands." Lea Koren of the Gordonia youth movement escaped through the canals but was killed after she returned to the ghetto to nurse the wounded ZOB fighters. Regina (Lilith) Fuden, who connected the units during the revolt, returned through the sewers to save fighters several times. "Up to her throat in water," read her obituary, "she did not give up and dragged members through the canals." She was killed on one attempt, age twenty-one. Courier Frania Beatus held her post in the uprising, then committed suicide on the Aryan side at age seventeen. Dvora Baran, a girl who "dreamed of forests and the fragrance of flowers," fought in the central ghetto area. When her bunker was discovered, her commander ordered her to emerge first, and she successfully distracted the Nazis with her incredible beauty, stopping them in their tracks. Then she hurled hand grenades, "scattering them to the wind," while her colleagues took up new positions. She was murdered the next day, age twenty-three. Rivka Passamonic, of Akiva, shot one of her friends in the forehead and then killed herself. Rachel Kirshnboym fought with a Freedom group and joined the partisans; she was killed, age twenty-two. Bundist Masha Futermilch, who had lobbed explosives with trembling fingers, escaped via the canals.

Niuta Teitelbaum, from the Communist group Spartacus, had been notorious in the Warsaw ghetto. In her midtwenties, she wore her flaxen hair in braids, appearing like a naïve sixteen-year-old—an innocent disguise that hid her role as an assassin. She walked straight into the office of a high-ranking Gestapo officer, found him at his desk, and shot him in cold blood. She pulled the trigger on another officer in his own home, while he was in bed. In yet another operation, she killed two Gestapo agents and wounded a third who was taken to the hospital. Niuta, disguising herself as a doctor, entered his room, and mowed down both him and his guard.

Another time, she walked into a German command post dressed like a Polish farm girl with a kerchief in her hair. An SS soldier was taken by her bright blue eyes and blonde hair, asking if there were other Loreleis among the Jews? Little Niuta smiled, then whipped out her pistol. In another instance, she strolled up to the guards outside Szucha, feigned shame, and whispered that she needed to speak to a certain officer about a "personal matter." Assuming that this "peasant girl" was pregnant, the guards showed her the way. In her "boyfriend's office," she pulled out a concealed pistol with a silencer and shot him in the head. On the way out, she smiled meekly at the guards who'd let her in.

This "self-appointed executioner," as described by a fellow fighter, had studied history at Warsaw University, and now worked for the ZOB and the People's Army, smuggling explosives and people. Niuta organized a woman's unit in the Warsaw ghetto, teaching them how to use weapons. During the uprising, she helped raid a Nazi machine-gun position located on top of the ghetto wall.

"Little Wanda with the Braids," her Gestapo nickname, was on all of its most-wanted lists. She survived the uprising, but was eventually hunted down, tortured, and executed a few months later, aged twenty-five.

The Nazis' grand finale was blowing up the Great Synagogue on Tlomackie Street, the edifice constructed at the high point of Warsaw Jewish enlightenment; a symbol of Polish Jewish prominence and belonging. The entire gigantic structure roared in flames, as if calling out the end of the Jewish people.

Burn marks from the fire still scorch the floors of the neighboring building, which hosted the Jewish self-help organization where Vladka and Zivia had spent her time. This smaller white brick building became the first Holocaust museum and is now home to the Emanuel Ringelblum Jewish Historical Institute. One of the world's most historic Jewish buildings, it is still thriving and growing, despite its scars.

The truck ride out of Warsaw was not easy. Zivia lay on the cramped floor, silent, shocked, exhausted, filthy, and horrified about having left comrades behind. Everyone on board stank. Their weapons were wet and useless. And she had no idea where she was being taken. For an hour, no one uttered a sound. Then they were outside the city and in the Lomianki Forest, a sparsely wooded area with low, thick pine saplings, near many villages and German military units, good only for temporary shelter. Comrades who'd escaped the ghetto earlier met them, shocked that they were alive, shocked by the new group's "pale and starving faces. Their hair had been stuck to the sewage canals, their clothes soiled. . . . [T]he battles they had fought, followed finally by two torturous days in the sewage canals had changed their appearance irrevocably."

The settled comrades offered the new group hot

milk, and Zivia drank it, head spinning, "heart over-flowing." It was a pleasant May day, the leafy sur-rounds fragrant and floral, a pastoral scene. It had been so long since Zivia had smelled the spring. Suddenly, for the first time in years, she began to weep. Before it had been forbidden, disgraceful to cry. But now she let go.

The fighters, still in shock from it all, sat down under the trees. They peeled off their rotting clothes and scratched the dirt from their faces until they bled. They ate and drank and, after many hours of silence, gathered around a bonfire, sure they were the last Jews on earth. Zivia could not sleep, her head spinning, pondering. "Was there anything left to do that we had not done?"

In the forest, where eighty fighters reunited, a temporary command was established. Zivia, Tosia, and fellow leaders set up a "sukkah," a hut made of branches, and deliberated what to do next. They created a register of all their weapons, money, and jewelry that one fighter had taken from the ghetto. They split into groups and collected sticks to construct shelters. As hours passed, they realized that no more ghetto survivors would be joining them. After two days, Antek arrived, having heard that Zivia had survived and was there.

Antek, despite his endless meetings, had not been able to set up safe houses in Aryan Warsaw; the Home Army did not provide its promised help. Vladka's attempts were also fruitless. The ZOB accepted the People's Army's offer to transfer most of them to partisan camps in the Wyszków Forest, while a few sick and wounded were placed in hiding in Warsaw. Antek moved the leaders to his apartment, with its hiding place behind a double wall. He also moved Zivia, even though she wasn't an official commander. "[I]f anyone blames me for taking care of my wife, so be it," he later said. He wanted them all nearby.

Antek had paid a large sum of money to the owner of a celluloid factory in Warsaw to cease production; several comrades who'd escaped the sewers were housed inside, in a loft accessed by a ladder that was removed when it wasn't in use. The attic was lit by small skylights, and the fighters slept on large sacks filled with celluloid. A Polish watchman guarded the site and brought the comrades food. The factory was a good place to consult; a leaders' plenary was scheduled to take place there on May 24, two weeks after their exit from the canals.

On May 24 Tosia, who now lived in a safe house, was in the loft waiting for the meeting. One comrade lit a match for a cigarette, and the piles of celluloid caught the flame, causing a blazing fire. In another version: Tosia lived in the loft, injured and immobile, and was heating up ointment to treat her wounds when the fire erupted.

The flames spread quickly, and because the ladder was put away and the skylights too high up, it was almost impossible to escape. A few fighters broke out of the flaring ceiling, jumped and lived. Tosia, whose clothes were on fire, made it, but she was badly burnt and tumbled off the roof. Poles found her and handed her over to the Nazis. They tortured her to death. In another version: she jumped to kill herself, determined to not be taken alive.

Chapter 17
Arms, Arms, Arms

Arms—for those who had never once before thought about these tools of destruction.

Arms—for those who were trained for a life of work and peaceful trade.

Arms—for all those who saw in the gun, above all, a hateful thing. . . .

For these very people, arms became a thing of holiness. . . .

We used arms in holy battle, in order to become free people.

—*Ruzka Korczak*

Renia
May 1943

"It's not your fault, Frumka," Renia repeated for the umpteenth time, watching her friend, her leader, scream and spin. Renia had successfully returned from her mission with news—but not all of it was good. "Please, Frumka, calm down."

Frumka's tumultuous interior, her passions and self-analysis, were spiraling out of control. When she'd found out that Zivia was still alive, she'd flushed with excitement, a new wave of motivation. But all that crashed when she heard about Hantze's death in the Warsaw ghetto.

"I'm responsible," Frumka shrieked. She pounded her first into her breast with such ferocity that Renia jumped. "I'm the one who sent her to Warsaw." Frumka hyperventilated. Renia didn't know whether to hold her or flee. The comrades had kept the news of her sister's death from Frumka for as long as possible, fearing just this sort of breakdown. In her diaries, Chajka pegged Frumka as a leader who was not really fit for the overwhelming realities of wartime.

Other comrades joined in. "It's not your fault."

"I'm responsible!" Frumka shrieked again and

again. "Responsible for the death of my own little sister!" Then she wept, torrents of tears and pain.

"But man is made of iron," Renia later wrote, "callous to suffering. Frumka returned to herself, even after this terrible blow." If anything, one thought rang through Frumka's mind with even greater focus and fury: revenge!

Renia watched as Frumka's grief expressed itself in action, in anger and passionate cries for both rescue and suicide missions. She had felt the same when she learned of the death of her parents. It was fuel to the fire. Frumka became obsessed: anyone who is capable of fighting should not wait to be saved! Self-defense is the only means of redemption! Die a heroic death!

But it wasn't just Frumka: the fervor for *hagana* grew within Renia, too—in fact, within the whole Będzin group. The six-week battle in Warsaw was the first urban uprising against the Nazis of any underground, anywhere. Fighters in every ghetto wanted to follow the example set in the Polish capital. Chajka wanted the Zaglembie effort to not only mirror but also surpass Warsaw. The Będzin group developed plans to burn down the entire ghetto and offered classes on how to use the weapons that trickled in. After Idzia Pejsachson's mysterious capture in Częstochowa, the underground's policy changed: all couriers who were transporting weapons had to travel in groups of two.

Renia would now become one of those *kashariyot*.

She was paired with twenty-two-year-old Ina Gelbart of The Young Guard, whom Renia described as "a lively girl. Tall, agile, sweet. A typical daughter of Silesia. Never for a moment feared death."

Renia and Ina both had fake papers enabling them to cross the border into the General Government. Obtained from an expert counterfeiter in Warsaw, the papers had cost a fortune, but as Renia reflected later, it was hardly the time to negotiate a bargain. When the girls arrived at the border, they assuredly handed over the mandatory documents: a government-issued transit permit with photo ID, and an identity card, also inlaid with a portrait. At that time, the road to Warsaw was more lax, so if they passed document control peacefully, they knew their trip would likely be successful.

The guard nodded.

Renia was now more confident operating in Warsaw; she felt seasoned, like she knew the city. The two girls had to find their contact, Tarlow, a Jew who lived in the Aryan quarter and was connected to forgers and weapons dealers. "He took care of us," Renia wrote, "and got paid dearly."

The revolvers and grenades that Renia smuggled came primarily from the Germans' weapons store-houses. "One of the soldiers used to steal and sell them," Renia explained, "then another sold them; we got them from perhaps the fifth hand." Other women's accounts speak of weapons coming from German army bases, weapons repair shops, and factories where Jews were used as forced labor, as well as from farmers, the black market, dozing guards, the Polish resistance, and even Germans who sold guns they'd stolen from Russians. After losing Stalingrad in 1943, morale in the German military fell, and soldiers began selling their own guns. Though rifles were the easiest to come by, they were hard to carry and hide; pistols were more efficient and more expensive.

Sometimes, Renia explained, a weapon was smuggled and brought all the way to the ghetto only for them to find that it was too rusty to fire or did not come with compatible bullets. There was no way to try before you buy. "In Warsaw, there was no time or place to try out the weapons. We had to quickly pack any defective one up in a concealed corner and get back on the train to Warsaw to exchange it for a good one. Again, people risked their lives."

The girls found Tarlow without a problem, and he directed Renia and Ina to a cemetery. That's where they would buy the cherished merchandise: explosives, grenades, and guns, guns, guns.

To Renia, each weapon smuggled in was "a treasure."

In all the major ghettos, the Jewish resistance was established with barely any arms. At first, the Białystok underground had one rifle that had to be carried between units of fighters so that each could train with a real weapon; in Vilna, they shared one revolver and shot against a basement wall of mud so they could reuse the bullets. Kraków began without a single gun. Warsaw had those two pistols to start.

The Polish underground promised arms, but these shipments were often canceled, or stolen en route, or delayed indefinitely. The *kashariyot* were sent out to find and smuggle weapons and ammunition to ghettos and camps, often with little guidance, and always at tremendous risk.

The courier girls' psychological skills were especially important in this most dangerous task. Their connections and expertise in hiding, bribing, and deflecting suspicion were critical. Frumka was the first courier to smuggle weapons into the Warsaw ghetto: she placed them at the bottom of a sack of potatoes. Adina Blady Szwajger did the same with ammunition, and one time, when a patrol ordered her to open her bag, her smile and the cocky way in which she opened it saved her. Bronka Klibanski, a Freedom courier in Białystok, was smuggling a revolver and two hand grenades inside a loaf of country bread in her suitcase. At the train station, a German policeman asked her what she was carrying. By "confessing" that she was smuggling food, she managed to avoid having to open her bag. Her "honest confession" evoked a protective response from the policeman, who instructed the train conductor to take care of her and make sure no one bothered her or her suitcase.

Renia knew she wasn't the first courier to bring in booty for a rebellion: *kashariyot* had obtained and transported weapons into the ghettos for both the Kraków and Warsaw revolts. When Hela Schüpper, Akiva's master courier in Kraków, was sent to Warsaw to buy guns, she knew she'd be spending twenty hours undercover on trains. She scraped her face with special soap to hide her scabies, dyed her hair bright blonde (using a potent blue capsule of bleach), tied her hair in a turban-like scarf, borrowed a stylish outfit from a non-Jewish friend's mother, and purchased an expensive jute handbag with a floral print, fashionable in wartime. She looked like she was on her way to an afternoon of theater. Instead, she met a People's Army contact, Mr. X, at the gate of a clinic. She was told he'd be reading a newspaper. As per instructions, she asked him for the time and to see his newspaper. He walked away, and Hela followed at a distance, embarking a different train car and landing at a shoemaker's apartment.

Hela waited several days for the goods: five weapons, four pounds of explosives, and clips of cartridges. She taped the handguns to her skin and hid the ammo in her chic purse. She did not go to the theater; she *was* the theater. A photo of her in Aryan Warsaw shows her smiling, content, wearing a tailored skirt suit that ends just above the knee, loafers, an updo, and a lapel pin; she clutches a small, stylish tote. As Gusta described Hela: "Anyone who observed the way she flirted shamelessly on the train . . . flashing her provocative smile, would have assumed she was on her way to visit her fiancée or to go on vacation." (Even Hela got caught on occasion. Once, she broke out of a jail bathroom and bolted. She never wore long coats on missions, making sure to keep her legs unencumbered.)

In Warsaw, ZOB members on the Aryan side spent months trying to obtain weapons. Posing as Poles, they used basements or convent restaurants for quiet meetings, changing subjects whenever the waitress approached. Vladka Meed began by smuggling metal files into the ghetto—these were for Jews to carry so that if they were shoved onto a train to Treblinka, they could cut through the window bars and jump. She dressed like a peasant, headed to a Gentile smuggling area, and jumped over the wall. Some couriers paid Polish guards to whisper a password at the wall; a ZOB member waiting inside would climb up and grab the package. Vladka procured her first gun from her landlord's nephew for 2,000 złoty. She paid her landlord 75 złoty to put the box through a hole, or *meta*, in the wall, in an area where guards were easily bribed. People bearing "gifts" also passed to and from the Aryan side by joining labor groups and jumping off trains that ran through the ghetto. Items were smuggled in garbage trucks and ambulances, and sent through drain pipes. In Warsaw, many couriers used the courthouse, which had entrances on both the Jewish and Aryan sides.

Once, Vladka had to repack three cartons of dynamite into smaller packages and pass them through the grate of a factory window in the subcellar of a building that bordered the ghetto. As she and the Gentile watchman, who had been bribed with 300 złotys and a flask of vodka, worked frantically in the dark, "the watchman trembled like a leaf," she recalled. "I'll never take such a chance again," he mumbled when they finished, drenched in sweat. When Vladka left, he asked her what was in the packages. "Powdered paint," she replied, careful to gather up some spilled dynamite from the floor.

Havka Folman and Tema Schneiderman smuggled grenades into the Warsaw ghetto in menstrual pads, and in their underwear. As they rode through the city in a crowded streetcar, a seat became available and a Pole chivalrously insisted Tema take it. If she sat down, however, they all might explode. The girls savvily chatted their way out of it, their loud laughter covering their tremendous fear.

In Białystok, courier Chasia Bielicka did not work alone. Eighteen Jewish girls collaborated to arm the local resistance, while leasing rooms from Polish peasants, and holding day jobs in Nazi homes, hotels, and restaurants. Chasia was a maid for an SS man who had an armoire filled with handguns to shoot birds. Chasia periodically grabbed a few bullets and dropped them into her coat pocket. Once, he called her over to the cupboard in a rage; she was sure she'd been caught, but he was upset only because the weaponry wasn't adequately organized. The courier girls stashed ammo under their rooms' floorboards, and passed machine-gun bullets to the ghetto through the window of a latrine that bordered the ghetto wall.

After the Białystok ghetto's liquidation and the youth's revolt, the courier ring continued to supply intelligence and arms to all sorts of partisans, enabling them to break into a Gestapo arsenal. To get a large gun to the forest, the girls transported each steel piece on a separate journey. Chasia carried a long rifle in broad daylight in a metal tube that resembled a chimney. Suddenly two gendarmes appeared in front of her. Chasia knew if she didn't speak first, they would. So she asked them for the time.

"What, it's already so late?" she exclaimed. "Thank you, they'll be worried about us at home." As Chasia put it, "feigning extreme confidence," was her undercover style. In offices, she'd complain to the Gestapo if she had to wait long for her (fake) ID. On one occasion, a Nazi saw her trying to enter the ghetto, and, without thinking, she pulled down her pants and urinated, throwing him off. Similarly, if a Polish woman was suspicious of a Jewish man, he was wise to immediately offer to drop his pants and prove his lack of circumcision—this was usually enough to startle and repel her.

Chasia got a new day job; her new boss was a German civilian who worked for the German army as a building director. She knew he'd helped feed his Jewish workers, and one night she told him she was a Jew herself. Her roommate, Chaika Grossman, who'd led the Białystok uprising and fled the deportation, also worked for an anti-Nazi German. The five courier girls who were still alive initiated a cell of rebellious Germans. When the Soviets arrived in the area, they introduced them too and chaired the Białystok Anti-Fascist Committee, composed of all local resistance organizations. The girls passed guns from the friendly Germans to the Soviets, provided all the intelligence for the Red Army's occupation of Białystok, and collected weapons for them from fleeing Axis soldiers.

In Warsaw, too, after the ghetto uprising, fighters needed weapons for defense, as well as for revolts in other camps and ghettos, like Renia's. Leah Hammerstein worked on the Aryan side as a kitchen helper in a rehab hospital. Her Young Guard comrade once stunned her by asking if she might be willing to steal a gun. He never mentioned it again, but Leah became obsessed with the idea. One day, she passed an empty German soldiers' room. Without thinking, she approached the closet, and a pistol was right there, waiting for her. She slipped it under her dress, then walked to the bathroom and locked the door. What now? She stood on the toilet and noticed a small window that opened onto the roof. She wrapped the gun in her underwear and slipped it out. Later, when it was her turn to throw out potato peelings, she went up to the roof, retrieved it, and threw it into the hospital garden. A hospitalwide search ensued, but she wasn't worried—no one would suspect her. At the end of her shift, she picked the wrapped gun out of the weeds, put it in her purse, and went home.

In the Warsaw cemetery, Renia pulled out cash that she'd stashed in her shoe. She and Ina purchased the weapons, and she strapped the guns to her tiny body with belts made of sturdy fabric. The rest of the contraband—grenades, Molotov cocktails—she placed in a bag that had a double bottom, a secret compartment.

The trip back from Warsaw to Będzin, however, was more difficult than the way there. On the train ride south, as they whizzed past tree after tree, they were faced with surprise searches, more frequent and more thorough. Renia tried desperately not to tremble as one officer pawed through every single small valise. Another officer grabbed all the food parcels. A third looked for weapons. "It cost an ocean of money, strength, and nerves—for both couriers and those who awaited them," Renia recalled. "If a messenger did not come back at the designated time, the comrades went crazy. Who knew what had happened during the delay?"

When the officers reached her, she used the same tactic as Bronia and pretended she was a food smuggler. "Just a few potatoes, sir."

He took a few for himself and let her go.

During the entire trip, Renia and Ina were ready for anything to happen at any second. They were ready to be shot and, if necessary, to jump from the moving train. They had to know exactly what to do during a thorough search. They had to know what to do if they were captured. They had to know how to never be caught as a Jew; to never look unhappy or respond to a Nazi stare with anything but a smile. They had to know that even under torture, they could not say anything, could not disclose one iota of information. Some couriers carried cyanide powder with them in case they were taken to interrogation. If they pulled a thread, the powder, wrapped in a paper bag and partly sewn into a pocket of their coat lining, would be in hand.

Renia, however, had no such escape. "You had to be strong in your comportment, firm," she explained. "You had to have an iron will." This is what she repeated to herself, on the train, speeding through forests, past inspections, guns taped to her torso, a smile pasted on her lips. A lesson she came to know well.

Not quite the life of a stenographer that she'd envisioned.

Chapter 18
Gallows

Renia
June 1943

Back in Będzin. In the early morning hours, Renia heard faraway shots. She looked through the window to discover the sky lit bright as day. Searchlights illuminated the turmoil. Police, Gestapo, and soldiers surrounded the ghetto. People ran through the streets wearing only shirts or stark naked, "like bees who'd been driven out of their hive."

Renia jumped out of bed: the deportation! Just days after her return from Warsaw, after the comrades' glee at her weapons stash, after Sarah nearly fainted in relief at her safe return. And now this.

But, at last, they were prepared.

It was four o'clock. Frumka and Hershel ordered everyone to go down into the bunker. Almost everyone. To stave off suspicion, a few were to remain in their rooms—those with *Zonder* passes. If the Nazis found the building empty, they would search. If they found the bunkers, everyone would be dead. Better to seem as if they were going about their business as usual.

No time to think. No time to implement any ambitious plans. Nine people stayed in their rooms. The rest, including Renia, crawled through the top of the stove, which was lifted off. One by one, they entered their prepared safe room. One of the comrades who stayed above fastened the cover back on the stove.

Renia sat.

An hour later, the stomp of boots. Then, German voices, cursing, opening closets, turning over furniture. Tearing rooms apart. They were searching—for them.

Renia and her comrades did not move, did not twitch, barely breathed.

Stillness.

At last, the Nazis were gone.

But the members stayed seated, immobile, for many more hours. Nearly thirty people were stuffed inside their tiny bunker. Air flowed in from a tiny crack in the wall. Absolute stillness but for the quiet buzzing of a fly. An unbearable heat set in. Then the stench. People flapped their hands, sending air to each other, trying to keep friends from fainting. Suddenly Tziporah Marder collapsed. Fortunately, the group had stashed some water and smelling salts and tried to revive her, but the young woman remained completely soaked and still. What were they supposed to do? They themselves could barely breathe. They pinched her all over until, at last, she stirred, weak. The lack of oxygen was nauseating. "Our mouths were thirsty, so thirsty," Renia remembered.

Eleven in the morning. No one had returned. Seven hours in the bunker; how much longer could they go on? They sat for thirty more minutes. Then from afar, a single voice. A sound that seemed to emerge from a grave. A chorus of horrific cries and screams. Renia could hear thrashing, convulsing bodies above them.

The group waited for a comrade to lift the stove top. "Who knows if they are still there?" asked Frumka, her hope deflating. No one came.

At last, footsteps. The door was opened.

Comrades Max Fischer, who'd cared for the Atid orphans, and the young Ilza Hansdorf were back. Thanks to a mishap, they alone were not deported. A howl rose from Renia's throat: seven of their best people. Gone.

It took great effort for Renia to even hear what the comrades were relaying. Everyone had been driven into an empty lot cordoned off by a rope that was held by the Jewish militia. The Jews were put into a long line. The Germans did not look at work certificates, did not differentiate between young and old. A Gestapo walked around with a stick, dividing the people: some he sent to the right, others to the left. Which group would be driven to their murders and which would stay and live? Finally, the right wing was taken to the train station to be shipped off; the others, sent home. With a small wave of a small baton, left or right, a Jew was sentenced to life or death.

Many bolted and were shot while trying to run away.

Renia and her comrades went outside and stood in front of their little house. All was futile. It was impossible to remove people from the group destined for the trains. Around them, people ran to and from the police station, wailing. One was missing his mother, another her father, husband, son, daughter, brother, sister. From everyone who remained, "they had torn one away." People fainted in the streets. A mother who'd gone half crazy wanted to join the deportation group—the Nazis had grabbed her two grown sons. Five children returned with a cry: they had taken their father and mother. They had nowhere to go. The eldest was fifteen. The daughter of the Judenrat's vice chair fell to the ground, tore off her clothes. They had deported her father, mother, and brother; she was alone. Why should she live? Cries, despair. All, useless. Those taken would never return.

Including Hershel Springer. Hershel, who spent his days and nights helping and saving people, loved by all the Jews, respected by the community. People cried over him like they would over their own fathers, including Renia.

The street was lined with the unconscious, with people who wriggled in agony, their bodies disfigured by poisonous dumdum bullets. Their relatives had brought them outside and helpless to relieve their agony, left them there to flail. Passersby stepped over their bodies. No one tried to resuscitate them. There was no help. Each person had her own torments, thought her own pain was the worst. Bullet-riddled corpses were placed on wagons. The grains in the field were trampled upon by people who'd hidden between stalks of corn; the rotting dead were strewn all over. All around her, Renia could hear the sighs of the dying.

It was too difficult for Renia, for anyone, to witness this. The group returned to the house. The beds were turned over; in each corner, a person lay on the ground and wailed. The children from Atid were inconsolable. Renia could not quiet their sobs.

Frumka tore the hair from her scalp, then banged her head on the wall. "I am guilty!" she screamed. "Why did I tell them to stay in their rooms? I murdered them, I sent them to their deaths," Once again, Renia tried to calm her.

Minutes later, the comrades found her in the next room with a knife aimed at herself. They wrestled it from her hand as she screamed, "I am their killer!"

The shooting did not stop. The group to be deported stood at the station, guarded by armed soldiers. A few attempted to run and jump over the metal barrier that separated them from the road. On the other side of the barrier, Poles and Germans watched, seemingly content. "It's a shame that a few are left, but their end will come soon," Renia heard one say. "They couldn't send everyone at once." Others replied, "Whomever Hitler will not kill now, we will murder after the war."

The train arrived. The Nazis shoved people into overpacked cattle cars. There was not enough space. The leftover Jews were pushed into a large building that had once served as an orphanage and senior home.

Renia watched as the wagons left for Auschwitz.

All aboard would be dead by the end of the day.

The remaining locked-up Jews peered out the

fourth-floor windows, searching madly for a savior. The building was surrounded by Gestapo. Militiamen mulled around, anxiously considering whether they could help a family member or friend. In the end, Rossner's specialized workforce was freed. As long as he lived, Rossner said, he would not let his workers be dragged away. But the Gestapo knew it didn't make a difference. Sooner or later, all the Jews would be killed.

The leftover Jews were to be sent out the following morning. The Nazis needed another few hundred people to make up a whole thousand—the full contingent of a transport. "We couldn't understand what's so special about that round number," Renia later wrote. "We used to joke that that's the minimum number of people they can kill." Even in this barbarism, gallows humor helped Jews diffuse fear, deny the importance of death, and feel some control over their lives.

A few hours later, the Gestapo tore into one of the workshops and grabbed the remaining number. And so, in two days, the Nazis took eight thousand people out of Będzin to be murdered, not counting those who were shot or perished from grief and fear.

With Hershel gone, Frumka was no longer capable of running the kibbutz. She could not bear all the worry or plan for the future. Freedom began to fall apart. No one had any desire to go out. "What taste was there for work when an expulsion hung over our heads?" Renia posed. The comrades knew that it was only a matter of time—short time—until they'd all be killed. They began to think about leaving the ghetto and dispersing, each fleeing to his or her own destination.

The Judenrat leaders addressed the community with "positive speak": work and only work will save the lives of the remaining Jews. Some sought normalcy and returned to labor. A heavy mood in each step.

Then, several days after the Będzin expulsion: a minimiracle. A militiaman delivered a note. Renia couldn't believe her eyes: Hershel's handwriting. Was it for real?

Renia, Aliza Zitenfeld, and Max Fischer followed the police back to the workshop, a route speckled with Gestapo men stopping each passerby. They passed a militiaman who was bleeding heavily, his ear torn apart, his cheek smashed. His white suit was red, his face pale. A Gestapo had shot him for amusement.

Their militiaman escort brought them to the top floor, into a cluttered small hall. He moved piles of merchandise. In between, as if in a nest, Hershel.

Renia ran over to him. He was badly beaten, nearly unrecognizable. His face was scratched, his feet wounded. But he chuckled and hugged them like a father, tears trickling down his sunken cheeks. He reassured them, saying that nothing too dangerous had happened. His legs may have been smashed, but "the most important thing is that I'm still alive, and I got to see you all. Nothing was lost." He showed them the contents of his pockets, then told them his story:

"They shoved us into the train car. . . . We were all beaten. . . . I looked for a way to escape. I had a pocketknife and a chisel with me. It wasn't easy, but I managed to pry the window open. It was very crowded, so no one noticed, but when I was about to jump, people held down my arms and legs, screaming, 'What are you doing? Because of you they'll kill us like cattle!'

"The train kept moving. Yoel and Gutek took out razor blades to kill themselves. I wouldn't let them. I told them to wait until everyone was distracted, and we would jump. Suddenly the opportunity arrived. I didn't think and leapt. Another person jumped out behind me. . . . I preferred to die this way than to end my life in Auschwitz. Behind me I heard gunshots, coming from the Germans who were guarding the road. I threw myself into a pit. The train moved on. In the distance, I saw people lying on the road—probably jumpers shot dead. Not far from me, a Polish woman worked in the field. She pulled me into the field, away from the tracks.

My feet were bruised. I could no longer walk. She told me that Auschwitz was nearby, that I was smart to jump, that all the Jews were being taken to their deaths. She brought me food from her home, tore off my jacket, and used it to bandage my foot. Then she told me to leave, because if the village peasants saw me, they'd hand me over to the Germans. By now, it was night. I got up on all fours. I crawled in the direction she showed me. During the days, I lay in the field and ate carrots, beets, plants. After a week of crawling, I arrived here."

That night, with the help of a militiaman who was kind (some were, Renia recognized), Renia brought Hershel to the kibbutz. He would have to move into the bunker permanently to avoid the Gestapo. People were incredulous. Their father had returned from the dead. Life would somehow turn out okay.

They knew, however, that their joy was temporary. The Judenrat had begun to notice the kibbutz's activities and became suspicious. The Kamionka ghetto was by now filled with the empty apartments of the murdered, so the Freedom group split into three. Each ten-member unit took up residence in a different part of the ghetto. They still, however, maintained communal life. "We are all one family"—the mantra that guided them, always.

Chapter 19

Freedom in the Forests—
The Partisans

Renia, Faye, Vitka, Ruzka, and Zelda
June 1943

It was late spring 1943 when blond-haired, blue-eyed Marek Folman returned to Będzin from Warsaw, energized by the recent uprising and his own success. A few months earlier, Marek and his brother, disguised as Poles, had joined a partisan group in central Poland. They attacked German barracks, planted mines under military trains, and burnt down government buildings. Tragically, Marek's brother had been killed in an altercation; but he was killed as a fighter. Renia listened to his stories, each word a miracle.

Now Marek had a plan. His group refused to accept any Jews, but he'd been in touch with a Polish officer named Socha who was willing to help Zaglembie's Jews connect with local units that would include them. Socha lived with his family in Będzin.

The entire kibbutz was excited. At first, their philosophy had been to fight as Jews in the ghetto. But as the liquidations raged on and the chances of an effective uprising decreased, the comrades had few choices. Joining the partisans was a way to action, a golden opportunity. They'd tried to contact detachments, but never with success.

Who was this Polish man willing to help Jews? Marek and Zvi Brandes needed to assess the situation. They went to Socha's simple apartment. Babies crying for food, a typical peasant wife, a working-class family. Socha left a positive impression on the boys.

Yes, they said. We will go with you.

The ZOB decided to send a few members from each movement. All were boys; several got pistols. They were to escape the ghetto, remove their Jewish stars, meet Socha at an agreed-upon spot, then follow him into the forest. They were asked to write home when they arrived.

A long week later, the comrades heard that Socha had returned to town. The kibbutz hadn't wanted to give him their address, so Marek went anxiously to his apartment.

Socha had good news: the comrades had arrived safely and were accepted with open arms. They went out to fight the Germans that very day. Socha apologized—they were so excited, they forgot to write.

At last, revenge! Elated, the ZOB prepared to send out a second group. With the general expulsion imminent, everyone begged to be included. Renia pleaded, itching to *do*, to take action, to fight.

They read the list. From The Young Guard: Chajka Klinger's boyfriend, leader David Kozlowski as well as Hela Kacengold, whom Chajka described as a symbol of the new wartime girl: "In high boots and jodhpurs, with a gun, it was difficult to tell that she was a woman." From Freedom: Tziporah Marder, five men, and one Atid orphan boy. Again, those leaving were asked to write home and tell them how to prepare the next group. The remaining comrades, envious but hopeful, watched as the new group packed matchboxes with bullets; they all drank vodka in celebration.

Renia, however, was devastated when her name wasn't called. Frumka and Hershel explained that the ZOB needed her to make several trips to Warsaw for guns, especially now that the fighters going to the forest had taken all the weapons with them. Only when those trips were completed would Renia be allowed to join the partisans.

Renia sighed. She understood. But, oh, how she had wished, how she had hoped, to join the fight!

It was extremely difficult to join a partisan brigade, especially for a Jewish woman. Though there were many types of partisan groups, each with its own allegiances and philosophies, they generally agreed on two things. One, they did not accept Jews, out of nationalism, or antisemitism, or they simply didn't believe that Jews could fight. Most Jews arrived in the forest without weapons or military training and in severe physical and mental distress—they were seen as a burden. Two, women were not considered to be combat material, and were thought to be useful only for cooking, cleaning, and nursing.

Despite this, about thirty thousand Jews did enroll in partisan detachments, often hiding their identities, or having to prove themselves and work twice as hard. Of these, 10 percent were women. Most Jewish women joined units that operated in the East; their escapes were usually planned in advance. Joining the partisans was often their only chance for survival, so they took risks.

Just reaching a partisan camp was life threatening. She could be recognized as a Jew and reported to the police, or killed en route by non-Jewish civilians because of growing antisemitism spurred by Nazi policy. Partisans often shot any unaffiliated stragglers, including refugee Jews. Some partisan units suspected women of being Nazi spies. One partisan commander was told that the Gestapo had sent a group of women to poison their food, so his unit shot dead an entire group of Jewish women who approached them. The forests were full of bandits, spies, Nazi collaborators, and hostile peasants who feared the Germans. Partisans themselves could be violent. Many women were raped.

The great majority of Poland's prewar Jews were urban. The forest, with its animals and insects, waterways and swamps, icy winters and scalding summers, was another universe—one full of constant physical and psychological discomfort. Women faced loneliness and lack of protection. Generally referred to by partisans as "whores," they were often turned away unless they had a particular medical or cooking skill, or were attractive. Most Jewish women were dependent on men, trading sex for clothing, shoes, shelter. Some felt compelled to have "gratitude sex" with the guide who brought them. Camps were sometimes raided at night, and women needed to sleep near a defender. As one partisan complained, "In order to obtain some relative peace during the day, I had to agree to a 'lack of peace' during the night." A sexual/defense economy developed: he protected her, she was his girl. One Jewish woman recalled immediately being told to "select an officer." A female partisan described how a Soviet unit "took women to have sex with." She added, "I cannot call this rape, but it was close." Once, a Soviet partisan commander entered as she was showering with the girls; one threw a bucket of water on him. He started shooting. More than one woman paired up with a man just so that *other* men would stop harassing her.

Intimate relations were complex on many levels. For one, these traumatized, grieving women and girls had just lost their entire families and did not feel particularly romantic. Second, the social-class differences were significant. In prewar life, the urban Jewish women were educated, with middle-class aspirations. The non-Jewish partisans, however, were largely rural, illiterate peasants. Elite city men became "useless" in the forest; only the strong man with a gun had real status. Women not only had to hide their Jewishness, but also they had to shift their more cosmopolitan ways of thinking, talking, being.

Regardless, many women became commanders' "wartime wives." Sometimes a real romance ensued; often it did not. Abortions, performed without anesthetic in a dugout, were common. Captain Fanny Solomian Lutz, a Jewish physical therapist, became the chief doctor of a brigade near Pinsk, specializing in using herbal medicines she extracted from the forest. She performed several successful abortions with quinine, though many times the procedure resulted in death on the operating table.

For the most part, Jewish partisan women submerged their identities and relied on men. Any guns they had were confiscated, and they were forced to make leather boots for the male fighters, cook and wash, their skin peeling off with the clothes. Cooking, incidentally, was no easy task in the forest: women had to gather firewood, transport water, and be highly inventive with the limited supplies. In unit headquarters, women were clerks, stenographers, and translators, and a few were doctors and nurses.

Some Jewish women, however, were exceptions, serving as intelligence agents, reconnaissance scouts, supply capturers, weapons transporters, saboteurs, locators of escaped POWs, and full-fledged forest combatants. Local peasants would be shocked when they showed up armed, their backs strapped with guns and sometimes children.

Faye Schulman was a modern-orthodox photographer from the eastern border town of Lenin. She had been spared from a mass shooting in which 1,850 Jews, including her family, were killed, because of her "useful skill"—she was forced to develop pictures of Nazis tormenting Jews. Sensing her end was near, Faye fled to the woods and, shaking wildly, begged a partisan commander to let her join. He'd known she was related to a doctor and ordered her to become a nurse. She knew nothing of medicine, but quickly got over her squeamishness and managed her psychological distress. The blood of the patient became the blood of her mother, leading her to imagine the murder scenes of every person in her family. Trained by a veterinarian, she performed open-air surgeries on an operating table made of branches, used vodka to numb a partisan before snipping off his finger bone with her teeth, and once lanced her own infected flesh before anyone noticed her fever and killed her for being a burden. Faye was her own whole world, constantly having to make life-or-death decisions at the age of nineteen.

Faye insisted on participating in combat and on raiding her own town for vengeance. "The Nazis had covered the graves with dirt and sand, but days later, the grounds still continued to shift as the bodies settled; the top layer cracked and blood continued to seep out . . . like a giant bleeding wound," she later wrote. "It became impossible for me to remain behind while my own family's blood still flowed from the trenches." She retrieved her camera, which she then kept buried in the forest during her more frequent guerilla missions. Along with her lens, her gun became her best friend, and she embraced it at night instead of a lover, conscious of how the war had thwarted her sexual development. "I had lost my youth in a painful way," she reflected. She had loved dancing, but dancing was over. "My family was killed, having been tortured and brutalized. I could not allow myself to have fun or be happy." True, she once woke from sleep to find a gun pointed at her head by a man whose advances she'd refused (a friend had unloaded the weapon), but generally she felt like "one of the boys," eating with them from a communal pot (each pulled a spoon from his or her boot), sharing their dessert of tobacco rolled in newspaper, trekking through landmine-filled forests, and, honored as a top warrior, being invited to stab a group of captured spies. (Faye arrived late on purpose in order to avoid committing these murders; she was iron brave but never hardened.)

All the while, she kept her Jewishness secret from most, making up stories when she ate by herself during Passover. Only forty years later did she discover that a man she'd wanted to befriend ignored her because he was a secret Jew and feared it would be suspicious to be seen with her. Even among rebels, the hiding was constant.

Unless, that is, you were enrolled in a partisan unit made up entirely of Jews. These unique detachments were usually established by Jewish leaders in the dense forests of the East. They were primarily family camps that sheltered Jewish refugees (the famed Bielskis, a 1200-strong Jewish unit, welcomed all Jews); they also committed acts of sabotage. Many more women were included, with some going out on missions and others serving as armed guards. One group of Jews arrived in the Rudniki Forest en masse, ready for partisan action. These were the Vilna comrades.

After Abba Kovner's initial underground meeting during which he coined "We shall not go like sheep to the slaughter," Vilna's various Jewish groups came together quickly and eagerly. They formed the FPO—the Yiddish acronym for the United Partisan Organization. A large number of women were involved as couriers, organizers, and saboteurs, including Young Guard comrades Ruzka Korczak and Vitka Kempner.

Back when Hitler invaded Poland in 1939, tiny Ruzka Korczak traveled three hundred miles along an underground railroad set up by fleeing Jews and made it to Vilna. There she moved into a former poorhouse that suddenly housed a thousand teenagers, Zionist refugees awaiting aliyah, which was still possible from there (the city was suddenly ruled by Lithuania). Family, school, struggles, dreams—nothing from Ruzka's old life was relevant. Her excellent listening and conflict resolution skills quickly made her a leader.

One morning, as Ruzka was engrossed in a tome about socialist Zionism, she was approached by a bouncy girl with long eyelashes and perfect Polish.

"Why such a serious book?" the girl carped.

"The world is a serious place," Ruzka told her. Ruzka's hometown had few Jews, and when her public school teacher made an antisemitic remark, she moved her desk into the hall, permanently. She was a shy outsider who spent her free time in the library.

"I think the world is not so serious," the young girl, Vitka, replied. Then she explained that even if it is, "all the more reason not to read a serious book." Her favorite was *The Count of Monte Cristo*.

Vitka had come to Vilna after fleeing her own small town by climbing out the bathroom window of the synagogue where the Nazis had locked all the Jews. A top student at Jewish school, Vitka was the first woman to join Betar and receive its "semi-military" training. She considered herself a Polish patriot; she tried various youth groups before settling in at The Young Guard but was never one for dogma.

Ruzka and Vitka became fast friends. Ruzka had integrity and humility; Vitka had a determined silliness, despite all that had been lost. One day, they noticed an awkward Young Guard leader observing the youth. A hat was pulled all the way down to his eyes. Everyone thought he was attractive; Vitka thought he was strange. No one dared approach him. "I asked myself why no one was talking to him," Vitka said later. "What, is he so scary?" She went to say hi. This was Abba Kovner.

When Vilna was occupied by the Russians, Vitka fled, but she returned when the Nazis took over. If Germans were everywhere, she figured, she may as well be with Ruzka. She hitched a ride with a Nazi, but when she told him she was a Jew, he panicked and ran. She took a freight train, and, once in Vilna, paraded boldly down the sidewalk, wearing no yellow star. Ruzka was shocked to see her. "Are you crazy? Are you trying to get killed?"

Together they moved to the ghetto, shared a bed, and managed to evade wildly violent actions, once pretending to be officers' wives. The Young Guard sent Vitka to the Aryan side. Ruzka dyed her hair for her, but it came out red, so they paid a Jewish barber to do it with peroxide. According to Ruzka, "Even the color of her hair could not hide her slightly long Jewish nose, her eyes that held a particularly Jewish expression." Regardless, with endless confidence, Vitka was ready to fool the Poles. Fooling Germans, she observed, was easy: "Germans believe what they are told." Once, when she forgot her star, she stuck on a yellow leaf instead.

In December 1941 Vitka's mission was to retrieve Abba, who was hiding in a convent and dressed in a nun's habit. She brought him to the ghetto to meet with Sara, the girl who'd survived the Ponary massacre. He heard her story, understood that the only way out was armed revolt, called the famous New Year's meeting, initiated the FPO, and moved in with the girls. He shared their bed. "I sleep in the middle," he told a fighter. The three of them walked down the ghetto streets arm in arm in arm, stirring rumors about a ménage a trois. (Legend has it that when one student asked Vitka why she joined the resistance, she immediately replied, "For the sex!")

With Vitka and Ruzka's deep engagement, the FPO amassed guns, stones, and bottles of sulfuric acid. The group lined its headquarters with a thick wall of "bulletproof" volumes of Talmud, typed out notices calling for resistance, and planned a revolt.

Then Abba sent Vitka on a ground-breaking mission, his declaration of love. Her assignment: to blow up a German train carrying soldiers and supplies. For two weeks, she left the ghetto each night, exploring the tracks to find the best location for a bomb, somewhere far enough from any Jews so that they would not be hurt or blamed and punished, but also close to the forest, where the saboteurs could hide, and not too far from the ghetto, so that she could exit and enter at the right times. She studied the tracks up close, taking note of all the details, since the act would have to be carried out in the pitch black of night. The train lines were policed by Germans and closed to civilians. More than once, Vitka was stopped. "I'm just looking for my way home," she lied. "I had no idea it was forbidden to walk here." She strolled away from the gullible Nazi and got close to the line farther along the track.

Once, unable to return to the ghetto on her usual route because dogs were barking and curfew had passed, Vitka stumbled into a German shooting range. She was nearly gunned down. She pretended to be lost and approached a Nazi in tears. The soldier pitied her and ordered two others to walk her out. She claimed later that whenever she was in a dangerous situation, she was overcome by an "icy calm," a sense that she was viewing the situation from a distance, and, as such, was able to assess it and proceed in a way that would extricate her safely.

On a warm July night, she exited the ghetto with two boys and a girl. Slender Vitka usually slipped in and out of cracks in the ghetto wall, but this time she led them over chimneys and rooftops. Under their jackets, pistols, grenades, and a detonator. Under her jacket, a bomb built by Abba, made from a pipe. (Ruzka was part of the Paper Brigade, a group that smuggled Jewish books for safekeeping. In Vilna's Yiddish Scientific Institute, or YIVO, library, she came across a Finnish pamphlet, written when the Nordic country was preparing for a Russian invasion. The pamphlet provided a course in guerilla warfare and building bombs, including diagrams. This became their recipe book.)

Vitka led the group to the perfect spot that she'd found and, in darkness, affixed the contraption to the tracks, looking up intermittently to check for the approaching train. Then she hid with her fighters in the woods. Suddenly the rushing locomotive—a wild orange blazed through the sky. Vitka ran by the train as it sped, lobbing additional grenades. Then the train derailed, cars lay smoking, the engine sunk in the gorge. Germans shot madly into the forest, killing the girl she'd brought with her. Vitka buried her in the forest, then ran back to the ghetto before dawn. Though in the coming seasons, wrecking Nazi trains would become common subversion among partisans, at the time, Vitka's was the first such act of sabotage in all of occupied Europe.

A few days later an underground newspaper reported that Polish partisans had blown up a train transport, killing more than two hundred German soldiers. The SS killed sixty peasants in the nearest town as retribution. "This is not something I felt guilty about," Vitka said later. "I knew that it was not me killing these people—it was the Germans. In war, it is easy to forget who is who."

After that, Vitka constantly crept in and out of the ghetto, helping two hundred comrades escape to the forest. She spent days wandering through Vilna, walking dozens of miles, searching for areas where groups of Jews could pass without being noticed. Vitka used to see them off. First, though, she'd take them to a cemetery where guns and grenades had been buried in a fresh grave. ("The Germans did not allow one living person through the [ghetto] gate," Ruzka once wrote, "but the dead were allowed to leave.") Vitka distributed the weapons to her comrades, explained the route she'd scouted for them and kissed each one good-bye. She herself was one of the one hundred FPO fighters to stay in the ghetto to fight. Her battalion was immediately ambushed. One of the only survivors: Vitka. "She had just walked off, her strides carefree and confident, like she had somewhere else to be," a chronicler later described. "No one stopped her."

Without the Jewish public's support, the FPO's dream of a grand ghetto battle was a shattering disappointment, with only a few shots fired. Arranged and led by Vitka, the fighters escaped the ghetto through Vilna's sewers and reached the forest, raring to fight, energized to shift gears from defense to offense. Abba became the commander of the Jewish brigade, which was split into four divisions. He led the "Avenger" unit, while Vitka commanded her own scouting corps.

In the forest, the Soviet officers with whom their brigade was affiliated told Abba to build a family camp to house the girls, who would do cooking and sewing. Kovner, recognizing no difference between men and women, refused. Everyone who could fight would fight, he said. Everyone would borrow a weapon from the communal arsenal and get a chance to restore their self-respect. Plus, he'd witnessed the remarkable courage of these women. According to Vitka, Abba insisted that at least one girl go on every mission, even though the boys were not pleased—the explosives could weigh up to ten kilos, the treks thirty miles, and most girls did not share in the carrying.

Ruzka was selected to go on the initial Jewish-led sabotage operation, along with four men; they were to hike forty miles and blow up a munitions train. Back in the ghetto, Ruzka, whose trusting, calm demeanor earned her the moniker "Little Sister," not only smuggled books but also recruited fighters, maintained fervor, and was second in command in the ghetto fighting unit. Abba knew her toughness would prove the worth of Jewish women in combat.

Ruzka and the men set out early evening in the freezing cold, each one carrying a gun and two grenades. Tiny Ruzka insisted on taking her turn carrying the mine, which weighed more than fifty pounds. They crossed frozen paths to a river, where water flowed just under the surface. The unit had to traverse with all their ammunition by inching along a log. Ruzka fell in. She caught the log and hauled herself up, even though her legs were numb and heavy. The commander saw her soaking wet and ordered her back to camp so she wouldn't freeze to death. But she insisted on staying: "You will have to put a bullet in my head to keep me from this mission." So, a few miles later, the group broke into a peasant home and stole dry clothes for Ruzka—men's clothes, which she had to roll up and stuff with socks. Then they held a peasant at gunpoint, and he directed them to their site. Fifty Nazi soldiers were killed as a result of the mission, and a storehouse of German weapons destroyed.

"I remember our first ambush on the Germans as if it happened today," Ruzka wrote later. "The greatest happiness for me since the war first broke out was that moment when I saw, lying in front of me, a destroyed car with eight smashed Germans. We carried it out. I, who thought I was no longer capable of feeling happiness, celebrated." Ruzka became the patrol unit commander.

Alongside her daring combat duties, Ruzka was also the quartermaster. Life in the forest could be surprisingly developed. Partisan camps differed based on location and how long they were staying put, but some encompassed a whole village of underground huts, with a clubhouse, printing press, infirmary, transmission radios, cemetery, and "shvitz bath" made by heating stones in water. Food, boots, clothes, coats, and supplies were mainly stolen from peasants, often at gunpoint. Partisans cooked only at night to avoid the smoke revealing their location. They filled containers pilfered from villagers with water from springs and rivers that were sometimes located hours away from camp. In the winter, they melted snow and ice for drinking water, and slept dozens in a row in underground, camouflaged *ziemlankas:* dugouts made of branches and logs, covered with grass and leaves, and sloping so that snow would not collect. From aerial and side views, the *ziemlankas* resembled brushy ground, little hills. These well-built hideouts were crowded, the air "putrid and nauseating."

In the Avengers, Ruzka ran camp health. Flu, scurvy, lice, pneumonia, scabies, rickets, gum disease, and skin sores from lack of vitamins proliferated. (Vitka once lent her coat out, and it came back full of lice. She threw her coat over a horse and let all the insects transfer to the animal.) Ruzka established laundry: twice a week, partisans brought their clothes to a pit where they were boiled in water and ashes. She assessed their frostbite. She divided bread rations—a treasure among the exclusively meat-and-potatoes diet—and gave it to the sick.

Medications, like weapons, were hard to come by, and both were retrieved by couriers who trekked to Vilna. Tiny, golden-haired, blue-eyed Zelda Treger was a major *kasharit*. In her quiet but determined way, she completed eighteen trips from the forest to the city, traveling solo on pathless routes through swamps and lakes. Zelda was raised by her dentist mother who died when Zelda was fourteen. She studied to be a kindergarten teacher. When war broke out, she escaped the ghetto and found work on a Polish farm where the farmer registered her as a family member, giving her an official Christian identity. Months later, Zelda developed an infection from a hand injury and returned to the ghetto, seeking Young Guard comrades and joining the FPO.

Thanks to her looks, Zelda immediately became a *kasharit*, transporting weapons in coffins and wrapped as peasant parcels. She found routes for fighters escaping to two different forests (one, some 125 miles away) and chaperoned groups out of the ghetto. She fought in the small revolt, then helped Vitka run the sewer escape. She aided in the rescues of hundreds of Jews from labor camps and ghettos, bringing them to the forest. She was caught on several occasions, but always escaped, often playing a naïve countrywoman, acting like a devout Christian peasant who was visiting her sick grandmother, or stammering and pretending to be mentally ill, or simply grabbing her papers and fleeing.

On one cold winter Saturday, on a mission to obtain weapons, Zelda put on her peasant fur jacket and lowered her headscarf over her eyes. In her basket were coded letters for the underground in the city. She walked directly on the road to town, passing guards with her head held high. By the time she arrived, it was late, and she had to spend the night with a Christian woman she knew. One of the neighbors tried to blackmail her, but Zelda pushed her away. While Zelda and the Christian friend were talking—a knock on the door. Her heart pounded.

In walked a Lithuanian police officer and a German soldier. They demanded her ID; she showed them her fake documents. But still they were suspicious and began to search Zelda's clothes. They found a note from the ghetto. "You're a Jew!" the Nazi yelled, slapping her. "We're taking you to the Gestapo."

Zelda bolted into the next room, jumped out the window, tumbled down a hill, and started to run in the dark. She bumped into a fence, dogs began barking, gunshots were fired from behind her. The Nazi caught her arms, held her down. "Why did you escape?"

"Please, just kill me," Zelda insisted. "Don't take me for torture."

The Lithuanian officer whispered, "You can stay alive for gold."

Zelda saw her chance. She invited them back to her host's apartment for a drink. "I'll give you something now and get the rest from the Jews later," she promised. The officers held her arms and walked her back. Her friend and her children were hysterical. "Is this your payment?" the friend asked Zelda angrily. "Look at these children who will now become orphans."

Zelda concealed her terror and consoled her friend, told her to set the table, and offer the men a drink. The Nazi drank, tried to calm down the children himself, and told Zelda of his deep love for a Jewish woman. "I don't want the Jews to die," he slurred, drunk. "But an order is an order, and I need to take you in." His duty time was nearing, and his temper was short. He called Zelda outside. "Give me your money and run away."

"I don't have a penny," Zelda pleaded. "Tomorrow, I promise, I'll get it."

The Lithuanian seemed to believe her—he told the Nazi that he'd deliver it to him tomorrow. The Nazi left. The Lithuanian guard grabbed Zelda by the arm and took her home with him. What else could she do but go along?

As they entered his house, however, the landlord began yelling, telling him not to bring girls home. He picked up an ax and directed it at the cop's head. Chaos. A riot. And so Zelda slipped out, hiding in the pitch-black garden while the officer searched for her, waiting for him to finally give up.

Then she went on with her mission.

The Soviet partisans aimed to destroy a German stronghold city, and though they had the weapons, they did not have the intelligence. They approached Abba Kovner and asked "to borrow a few Jewish girls." Abba turned the tables, saying this should be a Jewish mission, and the Russians should give them the weapons. On Erev Yom Kippur, two boys and two girls left the Jewish camp dressed as peasants. One of the girls—Vitka—carried a battered farmer's suitcase. Inside: magnetic mines and time bombs that could stick to any metal surface.

The group headed into the hills around Vilna and reached the fur factory at the Kailis forced-labor camp, where some Jews still worked, intending to spend the night with them. They spoke to Sonia Madejsker, a blonde Jewish Communist who lived in a factory house, their only remaining link to the underground in Vilna. Sonia said that the factory was soon going to be shut down, and the Jews would be sent to their execution. They wanted to flee with Vitka to the forest.

The partisan commander had already been upset by the number of Jews living in their camps as refugees and had asked them to cut back on new arrivals. Most of the Jews had no combat experience, could not use weapons, and weren't that keen to learn. They wanted to wait out the war, but still needed food and clothes. Vitka explained this to Sonia and told her she had come to town as a soldier, not a humanitarian. Sonia retorted that if Vitka didn't take the people, they would die.

First, though, Vitka had to carry out her mission. That morning, amid the workers and who went about their day as if all were normal, she seethed with hatred and found her targets. The boys would blow up the waterworks (the city's sewers and taps); the girls, the electrical transformers (the city's lights). At dusk, the boys climbed down a manhole and planted the bomb. The girls entered Vilna's factory area along the river. The humming electrical transformer grids were completely open. But Vitka's mines—covered in paint—would not stick. They kept slipping, the clock ticking. Vitka furiously scratched away the paint with her nails until her fingers bled. The girls hid in the shadows, holding their breath each time German patrols passed. It took twenty minutes, but they managed it. Both boys and girls had set their timers for four hours.

The boys were tired and wanted to rest that night at the fur factory, but Vitka insisted that after the bombs went off, security would be tightened, and it would be dangerous to travel. The boys would endanger the lives of everyone in the factory. The boys scoffed: the Germans would never suspect the Jews of such a massive attack! The argument went back and forth. Eventually Vitka knew she was running out of time. She told Sonia to bring her all the people who were ready to leave— she was taking them to the forest immediately. The boys stayed.

Within an hour, Vitka was leading a group of sixty Jews down dark roads, out of the city. They heard the bombs explode and saw Vilna go black.

The next day, the boys were caught. "We made it, and the boys did not," Vitka said, "because they were tired and we were tired, too, but the women were stronger than the men." The women, Vitka felt, were guided by a moral code. Not only were they as capable fighters as the men, but also they did not relent, took risks, and rarely made excuses to get out of things. "Women had more stamina," she reflected.

Years later, explaining why she smuggled those factory Jews into the forest against the commander's orders, Vitka was nonplussed. "What can he do?" she had asked herself at the time. "If the sixty Jews come in . . . they'll remain. And I will have disobeyed an order. No great tragedy!"

"She didn't know what fear was, her heart did not know to be afraid," Ruzka said of Vitka. "She was always sweet, full of energy and initiative."

Ruzka, Vitka, Zelda, and the Jewish partisans continued to work through the difficult winter of 1943–44. They learned to walk without leaving footmarks in the snow; sometimes they walked backward to make it seem like they were going in the opposite direction. They blew up vehicles and structures, and invented safer types of bombs to do so. In 1944, Jewish partisans alone destroyed fifty-one trains, hundreds of trucks, dozens of bridges. They used their bare hands to rip down telephone poles, telegraph wires, and train tracks. Abba broke into a chemical factory and set barrels on fire, burning down a bridge. The Germans couldn't cross the frozen lake. The Nazis and Jews just stood and stared at one another, the roaring flames reflected in the ice between them.

One April morning, the sun out, the girls were laughing and joking, and Abba approached with a sad smile. "Where am I going?" Vitka asked, sensing his mood.

She left for Vilna with a manifesto for the Communist rebels of the city to revolt, as well as a list of necessary medicines. En route, an old peasant saw Vitka
and asked if she could join her for the journey. They
crossed a bridge, and suddenly the peasant whispered
to a Lithuanian soldier, standing with a Nazi. A partisan and a Jew, Vitka was worth a hefty reward.

Vitka was asked to hand over her papers. The Lithuanian deemed them phony. The German said she had
blonde hair. The Lithuanian said, "But the roots are
black." Her clothes, he argued, were singed from partisan bonfires. Her eyelash tips, white.

Vitka ripped the manifesto and threw it in the air,
but the peasant grabbed the pieces and handed them to
the soldiers. They searched her and found the medicine
list. "For people in my village," she tried. They sent
her to the Gestapo.

Vitka sat in the back of their horse cart, talking
about her Catholic girlhood, not believing that this,
here, now, was her end. Torture, then murder. Should
she jump and have them shoot her in the forest? She
watched their every twitch, noted each bump in the
road, waiting for her moment.

Suddenly Vitka changed tack. "You're right. I am a
Jew and a partisan. That is why you should let me go."
She explained that the Nazis were losing, and whoever

killed her would soon be killed himself. Plus, many policemen worked for the partisans. At Gestapo head-quarters, one of the police took her to the side entrance. He shoved her papers in her hand, told her never to cross that bridge again, and added that he hoped one day to meet her commander.

When Vitka came back to camp, after a black-market purchase of medication and an episode of hiding in a haystack that was searched with a pitchfork, inches from her head, she declared that she'd completed her last mission. "It is a miracle that I made it back," she said. "How often can a person depend on miracles?"

It turns out, not that often. Some miracles are little more than mirages.

A few days after the second group left Będzin to join the partisans, one of the participants, Isaac from The Young Guard, returned. His face was barely recogniz-able, his clothes were torn, he shook with terror, hardly able to walk. Renia was stunned.

He told them what had happened on that hot June day:

"We left the ghetto, removed our Jewish patches, and once we saw the first trees, became excited, took out our weapons, our dreams of killing Germans about to come true. . . . After six hours of walking, as it turned to night, Socha told us we were no longer in danger of being caught by the Germans and that we could safely sit down and eat supper. He gave us water as we rejoiced, elated that we'd escaped the horrid ghetto. He told us to rest for a moment before we continued on our hike, and went to check on our location.

"Suddenly we were surrounded. Military men on horses. They started shooting wildly. I'd been sitting under a bush, so I fell but wasn't injured. I managed to stay alive. But the Nazis killed everyone else. Everyone. Then they took out their flashlights and searched the corpses, robbing them of whatever they had in their pockets. I hid under the shrubbery, lying motionless. One German lifted my leg, satisfied I'd been murdered. After they left, I crawled out of my spot and ran."

The Będzin resistance could not believe his words.

It had all been a ruse. They'd been sold out by Socha, whom they'd trusted. Even the man's apartment with the crying babies was fake. For all their own efforts at disguise, the ZOB hadn't recognized their enemy's charade.

Their best people, dead. Some during the liquidation, and now this, twenty-five souls lost in the two groups. There were hardly enough people left to fight.

"The news stunned us," Renia later wrote. "We are failing in everything we do."

Marek wanted to kill himself. Mad with remorse, he slipped out of the ghetto. No one saw him leave.

Adding to the pain of this betrayal was Chajka's loss. The comrades did not know that, a while earlier, Chajka and David had been secretly married by a rabbi. David had been offered papers to leave Poland but would not go. Promoted to commander, he'd insisted on fighting alongside the boys he trained and had taken some with him into the forest with Socha. "He did not sleep, but forged and created," Chajka described. "Omnipresent, he dreamed of action." At least, she consoled herself, he'd had no time to suffer, no time to think.

Now Chajka was a widow, in despair, boiling with anger. More vengeful than ever.

Chapter 20
Melinas, Money, and Rescue

Renia and Vladka
July 1943

Weeks after the deadly partisan fiasco, the head of the Będzin Judenrat was arrested. Renia knew what that meant: the final expulsion was coming. The end of the ghetto. The end of them.

The kibbutz had to prepare.

But there was discord. Most of the group no longer dreamed of a grand battle. So many potential fighters had died already. It was time to run. Chajka and comrade Rivka Moscovitch, however, refused to leave, still insisting on revolt. *Fight or flight.*

Frumka and Herschl decided to send out the children; the strong would go last. Aliza Zitenfeld, the Atid teacher, disguised the orphans as Aryans in order to ship them to German farms. Renia and her comrades transformed documents, covering up old data with false information and fingerprints. At dawn, Ilza Hansdorf snuck the children out and accompanied them to the town council of a rural village. The children explained that they had no parents and sought work. Many farmers agreed—the cheap labor was welcome. In a matter of days, Ilza found places for eight children. As per plan, the orphans wrote letters, directing them to a Polish address, reporting that all was well. Then two girls stopped writing. Renia figured they'd been recognized, "and who only knows what happened to them."

The children who looked the most Jewish remained in the ghetto.

Zivia wrote to the Będzin group from her hiding spot in Warsaw. One missive urged them to give up their dreams of rebellion. Having seen the results of her own uprisings, she no longer promoted fighting— the death toll was not worth it. If they wanted to stay alive, she told them, come to Warsaw.

Chajka was livid and called this message "a slap in the face that stunned us." She guessed that the Warsaw fighters were "spiritually exhausted" and "afraid of what they had started with their own hands, and the responsibility that had fallen on their shoulders was too great." Why should the Będziners live in the shadow of *their* glory and rest peacefully on *their* laurels?

Zivia suggested that those with Aryan appearances could manage in the big city with false papers. Those with mixed appearances would live in bunkers. "The Poles would let them sit in their hiding places," Renia explained, "naturally, for great sums of money." The hidden business of hiding.

Later in the war, especially after ghettos were destroyed, a main role of the courier girls was the rescue and sustenance of Jews in concealment—either as Aryans or in physical hiding. The *kashariyot* relocated ghetto Jews, including many children, in the Aryan side of town; found them apartments and hiding places (*melinas*) inside homes, barns, and commercial spaces; supplied them with false papers; and paid the Poles who hid them, taking care of room and board. In the East, they placed many Jews in partisan camps. In Warsaw and western towns, the *kashariyot* visited their charges—but not too often—bringing them news and moral support. They constantly had to stave off *schmaltzovniks* who threatened to "burn" the hideouts, and frequently had to relocate Jews when their landlords gave them up or because they were on the verge of being found out. They did this all while maintaining a disguised life themselves.

Vladka Meed began rescuing children while the ghetto was still intact. The Nazis were particularly brutal with children, who represented the Jewish future. Boys and girls who were not useful for slave labor were some of the first Jews to be killed. Along with two other Bundist couriers—Marysia (Bronka Feinmesser), a telephone operator at the Jewish children's hospital, and Inka (Adina Blady Szwajger), a pediatrician, she tried to place Warsaw's few remaining Jewish children with Polish families. These women took children from crying mothers' arms—mothers who had already saved their sons and daughters time and time again; mothers who knew this might be their final farewell but also knew their kids' chances of survival were likely better on the Aryan side.

Jewish children had to cross the wall, keep their identities a secret, take on new names, and not slip up or mention the ghetto. They could not ask questions or engage in childlike babble. They had to speak proper Polish. They could not give away information if captured. *And* the host families had to commit and not pull out at the last minute. One hostess was upset that the ten-year-old twins delivered to her door had brown eyes and dark hair. In the end, she accepted them, but they were miserable away from their mother and stopped eating. Vladka visited them frequently, bringing letters. When the host family moved to an apartment facing the ghetto, the girls realized they could see their mother through the window. The children begged the husband—who worked in the ghetto—to bring food to their mother and tell her about the window. The mother passed by many times a day; the girls were overjoyed to see her but had to sneak their peeks. If a guard saw them, he'd point his carbine directly at the window. Vladka had to harden her heart and warn them that what they were doing could endanger everyone's lives.

In another family, Vladka brought a Jewish toddler dresses, toys, and food, but the host gave them all to her own children. Vladka kept moving a six-year-old boy because his hiders either could not deal with his depression or became fearful of German raids—despite the fact that they were being paid 2,500 złotys a month. (Currency values fluctuated a great deal during the war, but according to rates for 1940–41, that would have been the equivalent of about $8,000 today.) In a testimony given at the Holocaust Survivors' Centre in London in 2008, "hidden child" Wlodka Robertson recalled being shipped from family to family. Each month, she worried that no one would come pay her "rent," but each month, Vladka Meed arrived, courageous and flirtatious, gaining access wherever needed.

Once the ghetto was razed, the resistance workers on the Aryan side were at a loss—the uprising had been their raison d'etre. The stench of burning still lingered, the Germans were everywhere, searching and arresting Poles, killing those who helped any Jews. Local Polish defense forces were established: they provided security for their neighborhoods but reported all outsiders, which made Vladka's job even harder. Now the ZOB's efforts went toward helping the surviving fighters as well as other surviving Jews. Several Jewish relief organizations, based on party affiliations, were established. Żegota (the Council for Aid to the Jews), a Catholic Polish organization founded in 1942, was also hard at work. Żegota's leader—an outspoken antisemite before the war—claimed that they would do everything to help Jews, and risked their lives to do so (though, apparently, with the hope that after the war, the Jews would leave Poland for good).

These organizations, which found Jews hiding places, supported them, helped children, and kept up contact with the Polish underground, labor camps, and partisans, had many overlaps. They all received foreign money, some via the Polish government in exile in London. Funds came from the US Jewish Labor Committee (supporting the Bund) and the American JDC, the same body that financed the ghetto soup kitchens and the uprising. Before 1941, the JDC was able to send money—donated mainly by American Jews—directly to Poland. After 1941, borders were closed, and funds were borrowed from wealthy Jews within Poland (who were not allowed to possess more than 2,000 złotys), and from those who were fleeing and could not take their savings with them. Most of the capital came from prewar wealth, though some Jews continued to earn money in the Warsaw ghetto, as smugglers, from selling off the goods stored in warehouses in the ghetto area, and in manufacturing for the German army and the private Polish market. Other money was smuggled into Poland illegally. Memoirs tell of cash that arrived from London and was converted from dollars to pounds to złotys on the black market—and, how groups accused one another of skimming off exchange rates. Overall, the JDC provided more than $78 million in US dollars to Europe during the war, or roughly equivalent to $1.1 billion today, with $300,000 donated to Poland's Jewish underground in 1943–44.

Rescue groups used the funds to smuggle crucifixes and New Testaments into camps for Jews who wanted to escape, and to support penis and nose surgeries as well as abortions. Żegota had a "factory" to forge fake documents, including birth, baptismal, marriage, and work certificates, as well as a medical department with trusted Jewish and Polish doctors who were willing to visit *melinas* and treat sick Jews. Vladka found a photographer who could be trusted to come to Jewish hiding places to take pictures for fake documents. She became a main courier for rescue; her organization helped twelve thousand Jews in the Warsaw area. And the young woman did all this without keeping written records of Polish names or current addresses, which was too risky. Some couriers used fudged receipts that they hid under their watchbands; many used code names. Vladka remembered everything.

Most of the Jews who survived until late 1943, Vladka found, were adults, and of the professional class. They'd been able to pay smugglers, they'd had Gentile contacts, they spoke a more refined Polish. Some of them had stored valuables with Gentile friends, but most were left with nothing. An estimated twenty thousand to thirty thousand Jews remained in hiding in the Warsaw area, and Vladka's work spread by word of mouth. Jews found her through mutual friends, approaching her at random on the streets. To receive aid, Jews had to submit a written application detailing their position and their "budgets." Vladka read through these scribbled appeals.

Most applicants were the sole survivors of their families, having run from camps or jumped off trains. An oral surgeon requested dental instruments so that he could work; another man requested money to support his orphaned niece and nephew. A young newspaper delivery boy had outlived his family and found shelter with a Polish family that cared for him as long as he brought in wages. He refused to enter a hiding spot and coveted his freedom, but he was desperate for a winter coat so he could continue to work during the cold months. The organization had only enough to offer 500 to 1,000 złotys per person per month, when the cost of living was about 2,000. But it did all it could. Young, Aryan-looking Jewish women went out to deliver the monthly funds, visit their charges, and help when plans backfired—as they often did.

Some ads for rooms were traps, some neighbors were nosy, and, in some cases, the landlord would raise his price once the Jew arrived. *Kashariyot* often had to imply that the Polish resistance was involved, to make the hosts feel proud. In one *melina*, a woman started hallucinating in Yiddish. The son of the Pole hiding them poisoned her out of fear and hid her body under the floorboards of the bunker. The other Jews, includ-

ing this woman's daughter, were traumatized. Vladka
arranged for a new apartment to house the Jews and
the landlady.

Similarly, Vladka found a young Jewish woman
named Marie a housekeeping job—these were the
best situations because they provided food and lodging and one rarely had to go outside. One day the little
girl of the house asked Marie what life was like in the
ghetto. Marie panicked. It turned out the girl's mother
was Jewish, and the father had banished his wife to the
ghetto. The Gestapo came over to search their home
for the missing mother. Marie felt unsafe, so Vladka
found her a new shelter.

One Jewish couple lived with their former maid in
her miniscule bedroom inside an SS residence—Vladka
had to move them. Another woman and her son lived
under a pile of debris, in the dark, crouching there for
months on end; they had not washed the whole time.
The landlady had sold all their clothes. Again, Vladka
had to carefully relocate them and provide medical
treatment.

As the Germans began to lose on the eastern front,
the reign of terror in Warsaw peaked. Poles were kidnapped for slave labor or sent to Pawiak Prison. Hiding
places had to be even more creative. In one apartment,
a wall was built next to a toilet so that a Jew could hide

in the remaining space in the bathroom. The wall was painted and hung with decorative brushes. Another Jew hid in a hollow tiled stove.

Some people hid in more "liveable" *melinas*, where—despite the anxiety and depression caused by being confined—they could still function. Vladka brought composition paper to a hidden musician who'd been playing on a tuning fork; she gave two women books to tutor the household children. Vladka's fellow underground operative, Benjamin, hid with his family in the kitchen of a shed inside a Catholic cemetery on the outskirts of town. They had little food but were able to light Sabbath candles.

Thirty Jews—including the historian Emanuel Ringelblum—lived in a secure suburban hideout under a garden; the admission fee was 20,000 złotys per person. These Jews collected research and wrote essays and reports. To hide his large food shipments, the host opened a grocery store. Tragically, the man had a fight with his mistress, the only person outside his family who knew about the bunker. She reported it—everyone was killed.

Vladka made connections with Hungarian smugglers, with partisans, and with Jews outside Warsaw. She traveled without papers to help a group of Jewish fighters who'd escaped from the Częstochowa ghetto and were hiding with peasants in the countryside. On the train, she pretended to be a smuggler, carrying fake merchandise—money for the Jews was hidden under her belt. At a major inspection, a "fellow smuggler" directed her to a freight train where all the smugglers hid. She learned that Polish smugglers had good tactics for avoiding Nazis and often followed them. She arrived in the village and found the house that Antek had described, but the landlady denied all knowledge. Vladka persisted, and finally the woman led her to a shed. The comrades—already in debt—were ecstatic, and from then on, she brought them cash, clothes, and medication on a regular basis. Once, funds from the US and London were delayed, and she visited later than expected to find that the landlady had evicted them. Several had been killed, others joined partisan groups, a few hid in the forests, skeletal. Vladka arranged for new Poles to take them in.

Vladka also helped Jews in forced-labor camps, most of whom were in horrific physical and spiritual condition. She had great difficulty accessing the Jews in a brutal labor camp in Radom. She asked locals where she could go to buy cheap goods from Jews. They explained that the Jews had nothing good left to sell but informed her about the Jewish bathing time, when one could approach the fence. Vladka found it crowded with smugglers selling scraps of food. They didn't want competition and tried to kick her out, but she convinced them she was a buyer. Eventually she managed to speak to a Jew, but he didn't trust her—even when she used Yiddish. Another contact kept the money she handed him for himself.

Finally, she spoke with a Jewish woman who was responsive. The woman was overjoyed that they hadn't been forgotten and asked Vladka for news, mainly curious about hidden children. While she was conversing, local kids threw stones at Vladka and yelled "Jew!" Vladka ran, found a horse and carriage, and sped to the train station, where she waited all night. Soon after, she returned to the camp with 50,000 złotys. She asked a Ukrainian guard for permission to enter to buy shoes from the Jews and successfully delivered the cash. The guard expected to take her out on a date that evening, but by dinnertime, she was gone.

Through all this harrowing work, each courier had to maintain her own life fiction, dealing with extortionists and informants. Marysia was once recognized on the street by a Pole from her childhood neighborhood who offered her a choice: come with me to the Gestapo or to a hotel room. She ran into a candy shop, and the owners walked her "home" to a nearby house. To avoid being found out again, she spent the night in the forest.

Vladka moved flats several times. She had hidden the head of the Bund youth movement at her place, and her apartment was "burnt," or ratted out, by an informant. The Poles locked them in. She set fire to all her papers, and she and the Bundist tried to escape from the window by climbing down bedsheets, but the leader was badly wounded. They were both arrested, but comrades bribed the prison guards, and she was released for 10,000 złotys. The Bund leader, however, died. The movement sent Vladka to the countryside for a while so that she'd be forgotten by authorities. Though she felt free in the forest, where she didn't have to pretend in front of the trees, she found the constant pretense—in particular, spending Sundays at a village church—to be particularly oppressive.

When back in Warsaw, Vladka continued to search for good ID papers for herself, and to move around, pretending to be a smuggler to explain why she was out all night. She rented a tiny, dreary apartment passed on by another Jewish courier. Benjamin, the operative who was living in the cemetery shed, helped her create hiding places like a valise with a double bottom and a ladle with a hollow handle. The neighbors found out that the former tenant was Jewish and began to suspect Vladka. But if she left, it would reinforce their suspicion and detract from the Christian identity she'd spent so long cultivating. She stayed and acted ultra Polish: she arranged for a Polish friend, her "mother," to visit her frequently; she obtained a phonograph and played cheerful music; she invited her neighbors over for tea. In order to prove themselves, Jews in hiding mailed themselves letters from nearby towns to make it seem that they had local friends and family; Chasia had a "suitor" visit her. Vladka's "mother" hosted her patron saint day party, to which Vladka invited her surviving Bundist friends. They sang only in Polish, with Yiddish whispers. A party was a difficult thing for the young Jews—the more joy they pretended, the more sadness they felt.

Like Vladka, roughly thirty thousand Jews survived by "passing," their lives a constant act. Most were young, single, middle-class and upper-middle-class women with "good" Polish accents, documents, and looks. Half were—or had fathers who were—in trade or worked as lawyers, doctors, and professors. More women than men tried to pass because of the relative ease of disguise. Women also asked for help and were generally treated more courteously. Many Jews were galvanized into saving themselves once their parents (in particular, mothers) were killed, and they finally felt alone and free. Men usually made this decision alone, spontaneously, while women were often encouraged by friends or relatives. Some parents urged their children to flee to the Aryan side, giving them the mission, and permission, to "live for their family." Most passers had previously been mistaken as non-Jews, so they felt confident they could pull off the role. They usually had to share rooms, giving them no privacy or reprieve.

Those who had a Jewish social circle where they could be "out" lived a double identity but ultimately fared better psychologically because they had a "backstage"—a rest from their constant performance and time to recharge. Friends who appreciated their strength fed their confidence at playing a "front stage" role. Most passers were not affiliated with any organization, but some were recruited by the Polish underground, which assumed they were non-Jews. These women lived in a "city within a city, the most underground of all underground communities," wrote Basia Berman, a leader of rescue efforts. "Every name was false, every word that was uttered carried a double meaning, and every telephone conversation was more encrypted than the secret diplomatic documents of embassies."

In this constant pageant of deception, Vladka and the Jewish rescue committee had become a family.

Many Poles helped them, not for money but out of Christian morals, anti-Nazi sentiment, and sympathy, offering Jews jobs, hiding places, meeting spots, bank accounts, food, and testimony to their non-Jewishness. The resistance members had to avoid landlords who became suspicious of visitors; they aimed for places where they could hide documents under floorboards and install concealed safes for money. In one such flat, two nails protruding near the front door were actually a clandestine doorbell—comrades placed a coin between them, setting off a current and a bell. Inka and Marysia rented an apartment that became a main meeting spot. Each floorboard and nook contained hidden documents and cash. A record player muffled sound, vodka was consumed, and the neighbors assumed they were prostitutes, hosting endless streams of men.

Another hub of activity was Zivia's *melina*. She looked too semitic to go out on the street. After years of relentless, life-or-death activity, Zivia now had a lot of time on her hands. To be in hiding was to be cooped up with people who you didn't necessarily choose to live with, or even like. The world outside "was filtered through others" and every knock on the door sent you panicking to a shelter. Antek brought back detective novels to help her pass the time, but her guilt and depression ballooned. She busied herself with obsessive housekeeping and letter writing, especially as she desperately wanted to share her advice. Having seen the death toll in Warsaw, Zivia pleaded with the Będzin group to flee instead of fight; she begged Rivka Glanz to run to the partisans. But she also refused to leave her people, and so she stayed put in Warsaw.

Zivia began to work for Żegota, becoming a main administrator in charge of distributing money and fake documents. She corresponded, managed budgets, and once again dispatched "Zivia's girls" on around-the-clock missions to connect, inform, and protect Jews. She also sent out girls to look for fighters who were in trouble and, once in a while, to locate couriers who'd mysteriously gone missing.

Chapter 21
Blood Flower

Renia
July 1943

The Będzin ZOB heard Zivia's pleas and made a plan. People who looked Aryan would travel to Warsaw by train. The others would be smuggled to Warsaw on a bus, to be arranged by Antek. Forged documents for the travelers came in via couriers from Warsaw—but only a few. The remaining visas would be ready to collect when Renia and Ina Gelbart came to town. By now, Renia and Ina had pulled off several trips together, carrying money, weapons, and instructions in their bras, bags, belts.

Ina left one evening, armed with addresses, money,

and items for the counterfeiter. Renia left the next morning, with the same items as well as Rivka Moscovitch. The twenty-two-year-old Rivka, the last survivor of her Będziner working-class family and a committed Freedom girl, had fallen ill and needed to be sheltered while she recovered. Rivka had a Christian face, as well as a visa and a document for crossing the border. She'd wanted badly to stay and fight. But the group insisted that she heal and then help them find hiding spots in Warsaw. Finally, they convinced her that she was too sick to handle the coming days, and Rivka packed a valise of personal items.

Renia had told Ina to meet her at an assigned place in the city. She and Rivka traveled by train disguised as Wanda and Zosia, two Polish girls taking a trip to the big city. On the inside, two Jews on the brink of murder, risking their lives to help save others. The entire time, Renia kept chanting prayers in her head, in her heart, pleading that they would be able to cross the border peacefully.

They arrived at the border. "Document inspection!"

Renia had to brace herself, to stop herself from shaking, shivering, up and down her body. Could Rivka do it? Could she keep up the lies, the story, not tremble for an instant?

"*Gut!*"

Breathe.

There was no chance, however, for even a full exhalation, no moment of relief. The train car was packed, with hardly an inch of free space; there was no air. Rivka, already ill, felt sick rammed up against others. She looked like she was going to faint, which would cause a commotion. Renia glanced around furtively and spotted an empty seat in the middle wagon, a military carriage. Rivka felt better sitting down, but Renia, inside, felt absolutely sick. She had to smile and hold her head high, calm every single nerve, harness steel resolve, and pretend to be the opposite of every single thing she was feeling, while listening to soldiers talk about killing Jews with sick "bestial joy."

"I was there," said one. "I saw them take the Jews of Zaglembie to their deaths."

The others laughed. "Nonsense! They're not actually killing the Jews."

Renia gleaned that they were traveling from the front, where people still did not know of the murder machine that was churning in Poland.

"A happy image!" she overheard the first one continue. "A feast for the eyes to see the Jews heading to their deaths like true sheep."

Renia did not think about her murdered family,

did not think about her dead friends, her little baby brother. Did not think.

Renia smiled. Watched Rivka. Smiled more.

A whole day's journey. Trees, towns, stops, whistles. At last, exhausted from the trip, from the performance with no intermission, the girls arrived in Warsaw. They walked alone through quiet evening streets, determined to meet Ina at the agreed-upon time and location. There was no room for a mistake, not an inch. Renia noticed that down the street, two corners up ahead, police were checking all passersbys' documents. She calculated quickly that though their fake passes had been adequate for the journey, the Warsaw gendarmes would recognize that the stamps were forgeries. Gesturing to Rivka, Renia began to walk quickly, turning corners, sliding into the crowd. The girls never looked back— not once—just forward, forward, part of the throng.

At last, they reached the meeting spot. Breathe.

But Ina was not there.

How long could they just stand there? How long should they wait?

It looked suspicious. Sometimes meeting spots were adjacent to storefronts; one could pretend to window-shop, skimming books on offer, fiction, romance, spy novels. But here, nothing.

Had Ina been arrested on the way?

Where was she? Nearby? Who could see them?

Renia had no other addresses. No operative ever carried too much information at once, in case she was caught, tortured.

She had enough money for only one more day.

And no backup plan.

A minute was a lifetime. Thoughts crashed through Renia's mind as she tried to figure out the next steps. She had to take Rivka somewhere, had to find someone from the underground, someone she knew. But where? What to do if they didn't connect with anyone? Take Rivka back to Będzin? She was too sick.

Renia decided to drop off Rivka at the inn where she had planned to stay. She'd venture out herself, try to find answers.

Then she had an idea. The sister of an acquaintance from Będzin lived in the Aryan quarter. Renia thought of Marek Folman—maybe he'd made it back here after the tragic partisan fiasco?

"Would you happen to know Marek's address?" Renia asked as soon as she arrived.

The woman perused her little notebook for a long time as Renia waited, knots inside, and then finally: the address of Marek's mother.

Every morsel of information was gold.

Still no Ina.

Renia returned to the inn and spent most of their money on their rooms.

The next morning, she took an ailing Rivka to the address. Marek's mother, Rosalie, was there, as was his sister-in-law—now a widow after her husband had been killed in partisan battle. Marek's sister, Havka, had been the Freedom courier who carried dynamite in her underwear; Renia had heard that she was in Auschwitz. Marek's mother also helped the ZOB—a true fighter family. To Renia's dismay, however, she knew nothing about Marek's whereabouts; the last she'd heard, he was in Będzin with Renia. "I'm so sorry," Rosalie said, shaking her head, "but I can't keep Rivka in my home." Sergeants and collaborators had been knocking on her door daily. In fact, she was planning on moving apartments as soon as possible.

But she had an idea. They brought Rivka to a Polish neighbor.

Renia bid the girl farewell, hoping she would be safe hidden there; another Jew stashed in the bowels of the city.

Now, alone, Renia walked through Warsaw, business as usual, crowded squares, shops open, despite the former ghetto's devastation. Despite it all. She had just enough cash for one more night in the inn. The next morning, Marek's mother put Renia in touch with Kazik, the ZOB fighter who'd led the sewage escape.

Renia went to meet him on a street corner, but before she could utter a sentence, they heard a gunshot. A policeman was after Kazik, and he fled, disappearing into traffic. Renia quickly headed off in the opposite direction, never running, never looking back.

Fortunately, Kazik arranged a rendezvous with Antek—*the* Antek whom Renia knew from letters and stories, the busy commandant of the Jews in the Aryan quarter who took meetings with the Polish underground, ran financial affairs, sent people to the partisans, smuggled weapons, and was connected with document forgers. A whole staff helped him, she'd heard.

Renia and Antek were supposed to meet on yet another street corner, this time in front a vocational school, or *technikum*. Renia wore a dress and new shoes that had been arranged for her. A bright red flower was fastened in her braided hair so that he would recognize her. Renia walked to the assigned spot, praying that all would go well, that she would find him there, that she would get what she needed and rush back to Będzin, to her friends, her sister Sarah. From afar, Renia spotted a man. He held a newspaper, folded under his arm—his sign.

She could not believe it. "He was a true Antek," she wrote, referring to his Polish moniker. She tried not to stare too obviously at this tall, blond young man, "with a fine moustache like that of a rich lord." He was dressed head to toe in a green outfit.

She passed by, making sure to slow down and show her flower.

But he didn't budge.

What now?

She took a risk, turned around and paced back down the street.

Still nothing.

Why wasn't he approaching? Was it the wrong man? A plant? Or did he know they were being watched? Being framed?

Her gut told her to take a chance. "Hello," Renia offered in Polish. "Are you Antek?"

"Are you Wanda?" he asked.

"Yes."

"You claim you're Jewish?" he whispered, looking surprised. Then he genuflected. Her performance had been *too* good.

"You claim *you're* Jewish?" Renia answered back in relief.

Antek walked next to Renia with assured steps, strong and propulsive on the Aryan concrete that

somehow held them up, together. She could not believe that this "seeming nobleman with a confident
gait" was really a Jew. She described him as being cun-
ning and sure like a squirrel, alert as a rabbit, taking in
everything around him. His eyes, she felt, looked at
you, and he knew who you were.

When she began talking to him, however, she noticed his creaky Polish accent. She could hear it: a Jew
from Vilna.

Antek and Renia spoke with sorrow about Ina's sudden disappearance. "She must have stumbled at the
border's document control," Renia said.

"We don't know for sure," Antek replied, trying
to console her. "Maybe a mishap caused her to return
home." Later, Renia reflected that he treated her caringly, gently, like a daughter. In this world of premature orphans, his nine years on her felt like ninety.

Antek promised Renia that he would prepare the
visas for the remainder of the group, as well as a bus for
those who looked semitic, as quickly as possible. None
of this was easy; it would take days to arrange. They
parted, for now.

Until the comrades found a permanent apartment
for Rivka, they decided to place her in hiding. Antek
gave Renia the address and the 200 złotys per night,
plus extra for food.

Renia waited in Warsaw for several days, sleeping in the entrance to a cellar. A Jewish boy who looked Polish lived in this basement corridor; Renia pretended to be his sister. They told the head of the household that Renia had escaped from Germany illegally to see her brother, which was why she didn't want to register her pass. Renia promised she'd stay only for a few days. She spent her time trying to avoid the landlady; she could not stumble in front of her or the neighbors. Most "passing" Jews concocted stories about daytime activity (work, family), then left for eight hours, roaming town, acting as if they were on their way to something, anything.

Really, all Renia did was wait for the visas, for concrete information about the bus, her impatience growing exponentially. Each day, she met Antek, urging him to hurry. She simply couldn't delay returning to Będzin. The general expulsion could come at any time. *Is it better to leave with the documents that are ready and not wait any longer?* she mulled over and over. In Renia's heart, she felt—she knew—that each passing day was critical. The clock was ticking, the hands circling faster and faster toward murder.

The waiting dragged on, postponement after postponement. Finally, after a few days, the bus was prepared, and Renia arranged for a telegram to be sent to her informing her of when it would approach the Kamionka ghetto. Several of the visas were ready. She had not been able to obtain any more weapons. But she took what she could get. Renia told Antek that she simply could not stay in Warsaw any longer.

Renia traveled home with twenty-two false visas pasted onto her body and sewn into her skirt, as well as photographs and travel papers for each visa. From the moment she stepped onto the street, her heart pounded wildly. At each instant, she feared she'd stumble. *What had happened to Ina?*

On the train, regular inspections, but now an additional personal search. The gendarmes approached her.

Even just glancing at them, she later wrote, could make her become confused. But she dared not lose her straight spirit.

She looked sweetly into their eyes. She bravely opened her packs. "They searched inside them like chickens pecking in sand," she recalled. Holding herself assuredly, smiling confidently, Renia kept chatting with them, maintaining eye contact, so they wouldn't want to search her body. No sign of fear.

They left, without any suspicion.

Still, the act had to go on.

Renia decided to stop briefly in Częstochowa to see operative Rivka Glanz and share updates. Temperamental, sensitive, full of life, Rivka was well known in the underground as a leader, smuggler, and organizer. When the Nazis first invaded, she had been on a mission in the port city of Gdynia; she'd watched comrades flee, some by ship right out to sea. She stayed—until the Nazis expelled her. Rivka quickly packed a small suitcase, then suddenly noticed the kibbutz's harmonica. She was overwhelmed by a feeling of attachment to the little mouth organ that had brought so much happiness to the comrades. She dropped her valise and grabbed the musical instrument. But she arrived in Łódź ashamed: here she was with no clothes, with nothing practical. She hid the harmonica next to the door of the kibbutz, entering empty-handed. "I couldn't bring anything with me," she announced. Later, she learned, the comrades had found the instrument. They understood her desire to save this object of joy. The harmonica became a movement legend.

Renia thought of the harmonica and wanted terribly to see Rivka, to connect with her kindness, her courage. But—this was no longer possible. To Renia's absolute horror, she arrived in the border town to see that the entire ghetto had been razed, burnt down to the ground. Not one trace of her people anywhere. Extinguished.

"What happened?" She managed to find her words.

Local Poles related that a few weeks earlier, there had been a battle in the ghetto. Young Jews, poorly armed with few guns and a few hundred Molotov cocktails, resisted by hiding and firing. Some managed to steal weapons from Nazis. Others had used vats from the ghetto kitchen to smuggle in aluminum, lead, carbide, mercury, dynamite and chemicals for explosives from ammunition factories. They'd dug several tunnels. They were easily outmanned and outgunned yet managed to sustain fighting for five full days. Many Jews ran into the forest; now they were living there like animals. The Germans, afraid of partisan activity in the woods, sent the local police to search for hidden Jews. They rooted them out one at a time—but not everyone.

All Renia could find out about Rivka Glanz was that she'd been killed in battle, commanding a unit, weapons in her hands. "How my heart cried over her!" Renia wrote. "She was like the mother of every Jew in Częstochowa." She thought about how, when Rivka had wanted to leave, the remaining Jews in the town hadn't allowed it. As long as Rivka was with them, they said, they felt secure.

Renia swiftly headed back to the train station, blinking back any emotion. She needed to get home, now. The train rumbled through the forested countryside the whole night. Her stinging eyes begged to shut, but no, no, no, she could not fall asleep. Renia had to maintain clear thinking the whole time. Awake and aware. Who knew when an inspection, a check of documents, anything would come? Who knew what would be?

Only later did Renia find out that Ina had been caught by a female Nazi guard at a checkpoint near the border. While the Gestapo drove her to Auschwitz, Ina jumped out of the car and ran. Exhausted, depressed, and beaten, she took refuge with a friend in a local ghetto. But the Nazis put a high price on her head (Ina or twenty Jews killed), and the Jewish militia handed her over. This time the Gestapo supervisor personally transported her to Auschwitz, commanding a dog to attack and bite her in the car. She spat in the officer's face and died in transit.

Chapter 22
Zaglembie's Jerusalem
Is Burning

Renia
August 1943

August 1, 1943.

At last, Renia arrived in Będzin, dirty, broken, tired from the road. But as soon as she got off the train, everything—the platform, the recognizable large square Deco clock—turned black before her eyes. Nazis were chasing the passengers away from the station.

From afar, Renia could hear piercing screams, turmoil.

"What's happening?" Renia asked some Poles who were gathered nearby, trying to make out what they could.

"They've been taking Jews out of the city since Friday. One group after another."

It was Monday, the fourth day. And it was not the end.

"Will they expel all the Jews?" Renia asked in a voice that was nothing like her own, pretending that not only did she not care but also that she was glad. Pretending to be one of the world's bystanders. Pretending this wasn't the moment she had both anticipated and dreaded for months.

All this, she later wrote, while "my heart was ripped into pieces of pain." They were expelling all of Renia's friends, her sister, everyone in her universe. She had no idea what would happen to them or if she would ever see them again.

The ghetto was completely surrounded by SS squads. There was no way to enter. Renia eavesdropped, heard rumors, tried to see as much as she could. Inside, Germans were exposing bunkers and murdering people on the spot. For fours days without stop, they had been pushing Jews into cattle cars, shooting into the ghetto from all directions. The Jewish militia brought out stretchers of the wounded and dead, covered in rags. In the streets, Germans led rows of youth, chained with shackles like criminals, to the trains. They kicked at their feet. These boys and girls had tried to run away, but Poles had caught them and handed them over.

Civilian-clothed Gestapo dashed through the city like wild dogs, checking documents, peering into each person's face, looking for more victims.

Then Renia spotted an open area next to the station, on the other side of the barrier. There stood a mass of people. Among them, her friends. The Poles stared at them, at these "guilty criminals," as if they were animals in a zoo. Her comrades, her loves, were surrounded by hooligans with rifles, whips, and revolvers.

She didn't see Sarah anywhere.

Renia could barely remain on her feet. She was going to faint. She knew she needed to flee as fast as possible. If they checked her documents, she'd be finished.

"But," Renia later wrote, "I saw in that moment that my own heart had turned to stone, for how could I leave without knowing anything about the fate of those nearest to me?" She was watching the only family left to her being driven to their deaths. She turned around—but it was futile. She could not get into the ghetto. "In my heart, I thought: My life has lost all meaning. Why live, now that they have taken everything from me—my family, my relatives, and now my beloved friends?" She had reestablished her life, was willing to risk everything for these comrades. Her sister.

"An inner demon told me to put an end to my own life," Renia recalled. "And then I felt shame for this

The Great Synagogue (right) and the Judaic Library (left), Warsaw. Photograph by K. Wojutynski, 1936–39. The Judaic Library housed the Jewish Self-Help Organization during the war and is now the Emanuel Ringelblum Jewish Historical Institute. *(Courtesy of the Emanuel Ringelblum Jewish Historical Institute in Warsaw, Poland)*

Members of a pioneer training commune (kibbutz hachshara) in Jędrzejów, 1935. Zivia Lubetkin is standing third from the right. *(Courtesy of Ghetto Fighters' House Museum, Photo Archive)*

The Young Guard
members in Włocławek,
Poland, during Lag
b'Omer, 1937. Tosia
Altman is at the bottom.
*(Yad Vashem Photo
Archive, Jerusalem)*

Tosia Altman. *(Courtesy of
Moreshet, Hashomer Hatzair
Archives)*

Hantze Plotnicki during her stay at a pioneer training commune (kibbutz hachshara) in Baranowice, 1938. *(Courtesy of Ghetto Fighters' House Museum, Photo Archive)*

Comrades from the pioneer training commune (kibbutz hachshara) in Białystok, 1938. Frumka Plotnicki is standing second from the right. *(Courtesy of Ghetto Fighters' House Museum, Photo Archive)*

Gusta Davidson (left) and Minka Liebeskind at an Akiva summer camp, 1938. They both became members of the Kraków ghetto underground. *(Courtesy of Ghetto Fighters' House Museum, Photo Archive)*

Left to right: Tema Schneiderman, Bela Hazan, and Lanka Kozebradska. Photograph taken at a Gestapo Christmas party, 1941. *(Yad Vashem Photo Archive, Jerusalem. 3308/91)*

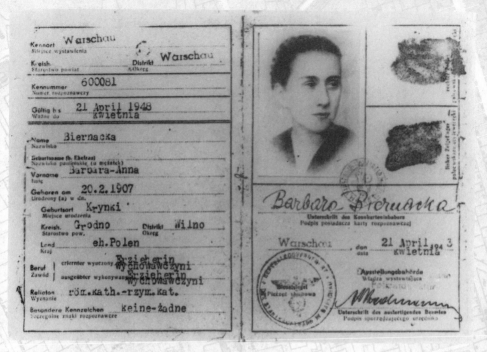

Lanka Kozebradska's forged Aryan identity card, 1943. *(Courtesy of Ghetto Fighters' House Museum, Photo Archive)*

Margolit Lichtensztejn. *Sleeping Girl*, chalk on paper, by Gela Seksztajn. *(Courtesy of the Emanuel Ringelblum Jewish Historical Institute in Warsaw, Poland)*

Sarah Kukiełka, 1943.
(Courtesy of Ghetto Fighters' House Museum, Photo Archive)

Chajka Klinger. *(Courtesy of Ghetto Fighters' House Museum, Photo Archive)*

Youth movement members of the agricultural training farm in Będzin, dancing the hora at a party celebrating the birthday of poet Hayim Nahman Bialik, 1943. *(Courtsey of Ghetto Fighters' House)*

A meeting of Zionist youth at the agricultural training farm in Będzin during the war. Chaika Klinger is in the center. *(Courtesy of Ghetto Fighters' House)*

The Funfair in Krasinki Square, next to the Warsaw ghetto. Photograph by Jan Lissowki, 1943. *(Courtesy of the Emmanuel Ringelblum Jewish Historical Institute in Warsaw, Poland)*

A Nazi photograph of sleeping quarters inside a bunker prepared for the Warsaw ghetto uprising, 1943. The original German caption reads: "Pictures of a so-called residential bunker." *(United States Holocaust Museum, courtesy of National Archives and Records Administration, College Park)*

Niuta Teitelbaum as a schoolgirl in Łódź, 1936. During the war, she became known as "Little Wanda with the Braids." *(Courtesy of Ghetto Fighters' House Museum, Photo Archive)*

Hela Schupper (left) and Shoshana Langer disguised as Christians on the Aryan side of Warsaw, June 26, 1943. *(Courtesy of Ghetto Fighters' House Museum, Photo Archive)*

Vladka Meed on the Aryan side of Warsaw, posing in Theater Square, 1944. (The United States *Holocaust Museum, courtesy of Benjamin [Międzyzecki] Meed)*

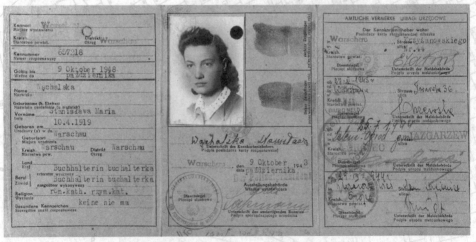

Vladka Meed's false indentification card, issued in the name of Stanisława Wąchalska, 1943. *(Courtesy of Ghetto Fighters' House Museum, Photo Archive)*

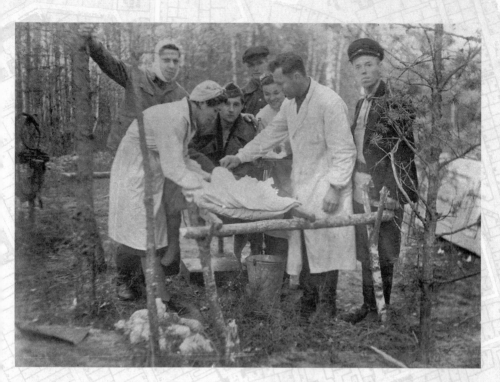

Faye Schulman assisting at an operation for a wounded partisan. *(United States Holocaust Memorial Museum, courtesy of Belarusian State Museum of the History of the Great Patriotic War)*

Left to right: Vitka Kempner, Zelda Treger, Ruzka Korzak. *(Yad Vashem Photo Archive, Jerusalem.)*

העלדישע מיידלעך : זעלדע טרעגער (לינקס),
רייזל קארטשאק, איטקע קעמפנער

A partisan dugout in the Rudniki forest, photograph taken in 1993. (*Courtesy of Rivka Aygenfeld.*)

Portrait of Ala Gertner in Będzin, 1930–39. (*United States Holocaust Memorial Museum, courtesy of Anna and Joshua Heilman*)

No. 41 or No. 43 Promyka Street, on the Aryan side of Warsaw. Zivia Lubetkin and her comrades hid in the cellar after the Warsaw uprising of 1944. *(Courtesy of Ghetto Fighters' House Museum, Photo Archive)*

Freedom comrades in Budapest, 1944, including Renia Kukiełka (bottom right), Chawka Lenczer (bottom left), Max Fischer (top left), Yitzhak Fiszman (top row, second from the right, and "little Muniosh" (Moniek Hopgenberg, bottom center). *(Courtesy of Ghetto Fighters' House Museum, Photo Archive)*

Renia Kukiełka in Budapest, 1944. *(Courtesy of Merav Waldman)*

Antek (Yitzhak) Zuckerman, Warsaw, 1946. *(Courtesy of Ghetto Fighters' House Museum, Photo Archive)*

Zivia Lubetkin and Antek (Yitzhak) Zuckerman, after the war. *(Courtesy of Ghetto Fighters' House Museum, Photo Archive)*

Zivia Lubetkin speaking at Kibbutz Yagur, 1946. *(Courtesy of Ghetto Fighters' House Museum, Photo Archive)*

Former Warsaw ghetto fighters and their families at the Ghetto Fighters' House in 1973. Figures include: Zivia Lubetkin (bottom row, left), Vladka Meed (top row, second from the left), Pnina Grinshpan Frimer (top row, third from left), Benjamin Meed (top row, fifth from the right), Yitzhak (Antek) Zuckerman (top row, six from the right), Masha Futermilch (top row, second from the right). *(Courtesy of Ghetto Fighters' House Museum, Photo Archive)*

Renia Kukiełka and her eldest granddaughter, Merav Waldman, at Merav's sister's wedding, Israel. *(Courtesy of Merav Waldman)*

weakness. No! I will not ease the Germans' work with my own hands!" Instead, her thoughts turned to vengeance.

Renia walked aimlessly. She had no home now, no home at all.

There was only path available to her: back to Warsaw. But how? The next train didn't leave until five o'clock the next morning.

Renia Kukielka was the last remaining Freedom courier.

By three in the afternoon, Renia had been on the road all night, all day. She was tired, broken, and hadn't eaten for as long as she could remember. All she could think about was bread. But a loaf was obtainable only with a ration card. She couldn't go into a store without one, or they'd suspect her of being a Jew. Suddenly she remembered someone she knew: a non-Jewish Russian woman, a dentist, Dr. Weiss, in Sosnowiec, a town about four miles west of Będzin.

Renia took the tramway. At the other end of the car, they were checking documents. She rode as far as she could, then hopped off and got on a second train. She meandered from wagon to wagon, switching trains often, until her destination.

In Sosnowiec, the ghetto was surrounded.

The expulsion was happening here too. Nazis everywhere, the screaming, the shots.

Renia flew to the dentist's home. *Only a few more streets*, she repeated to herself. Small streets.

Dr. Weiss opened her door and stared at Renia in shock. "How did you get here?"

She offered Renia a chair, afraid the girl would collapse. Then she went to the kitchen to make tea.

Only then, once Renia sat down, did she realize how close she had been to losing consciousness. She pulled herself together. She wanted to tell Dr. Weiss everything.

But she couldn't.

A pressure in her throat.

Suddenly she began to cry. Wild, convulsive sobs.

Renia felt ashamed. But her suffering overflowed, and she could not stop. If she didn't cry, she feared her heart would explode in anguish.

Dr. Weiss patted her head. "Don't cry," she said. "You have always been brave. I hold you up as a hero. Your courage is an example for me. You must be strong, my child. Maybe some of your people are still alive."

Renia felt a sharp hunger, but could not eat. She was at her limit. This was it. "My heart wanted to die," she wrote.

But slowly she began to relax, eager for a few hours to rest, regroup. To stay alive.

"I would love for you to spend the night in my home," Dr. Weiss said, and Renia exhaled. "But," she continued, "the Germans often break into houses out of nowhere, searching for hidden Jews. If they're in the area, they'll surely come here. I'm Russian. They already suspect me of maintaining connections with Jews." She sighed. "Forgive me, but I cannot risk my life."

Renia could barely believe her ears. She was despondent. And terrified. Where could she go right now, at this very moment, to spend her night? At the train station, they would inspect her documents. The streets were endlessly dangerous. She knew no one else in town.

Dr. Weiss gave her some food for the road. She blessed her, tears in her eyes, and again, asked for Renia's pardon. "I'm so sorry."

Renia left her haven, clueless. "I just walked where my feet carried me," she recalled.

She left the damned city and neared a sparse forest. Daylight faded to dusk once again; it was a luminous summer night. The moon sent its glow straight to her, the stars sparkled for her eyes. Renia had visions of her parents, her brothers, the comrades. She saw them as if they were right next to her, all their faces sad, distorted, altered. Suffering had left traces all over their bodies. She desperately wanted to embrace them, to turn to them and hold them to her heart, clutching with love. But the images began to dissolve, the apparitions disappeared like pictures fading on cinema screens. She could hold on to nothing.

Renia took stock of her life. "On whom did I place so many burdens? How great were my sins? How many people have I murdered? Why has all this suffering come to me?"

Suddenly she saw the image of a man between the trees. Who could it be, so late in the evening? The figure approached her. A frost ran through her bones. The man was drunk. He sat down near her. She moved away. He moved closer. His beady eyes were enlarged in their sockets like a predatory animal. He began to yell at her; the words blended together into a ball of anger, hostility, rage. Renia could not scream, nor could she run. She was nowhere, with no one to hear her. And he would just follow her, follow her and do whatever he wanted.

Sexual violation against Jewish women, ranging from humiliation to rape, was extant, even widespread, during the Holocaust. Though some of the earliest postwar memoirs mention sexual abuse and violence, these stories were largely silenced after the war. Interviewers for research rarely pressed the question, and information was rarely volunteered. Most victims did not know their tormentors' names. Many women were killed after being raped; others were too ashamed to speak of it, fearing they would no longer be marriage material. Those who did raise the issue were often actively discouraged and many times not believed. They were shunned instead of comforted.

In concentration and work camps, the Nazis set up official brothels. Laws prohibited SS guards from having sexual relations with inmates, especially Jews, yet at least five hundred brothels operated in which Jewish women were "sex slaves." Some Nazis kept personal sex slaves, particularly in the East. German camp commanders and Polish superiors molested and impregnated Jewish women; in one case, pretty Jewish women were chosen to be naked servants at a Nazi's private feast, after which they were raped by the guests. Most were killed. One Nazi in Warsaw used to arrive at the ghetto homes of beautiful girls with a hearse—he'd rape and kill them on the spot. (A pretty teenager rubbed a paste of flour on her face to make herself less attractive.) Nazis raped women who were about to be murdered in killing fields. In the village of Ejszyszki, local Poles supplied Nazis with a list of all the pretty, unmarried Jewish women. The women were led to nearby bushes and gang-raped by Germans before being slaughtered. At a labor camp in Lublin, Jewish women of all ages were beaten, tormented, starved, and forced to work endless hours. When a work mistake was discovered, all the women from that unit were told to take off their underwear, and a Nazi lashed between their legs with a rod twenty-five times.

Sexual hierarchies existed among Jews too. In the Skarzysko-Kamienna labor camp, barefoot girls brought in from Majdanek were "objects to be purchased"; some women became "cousins" of the male camp elite and moved into barracks with them. As with the partisans, romances between middle-class Jewish girls and Jewish "cobblers" from the shtetl ensued for protection, and some even lasted after the war. In the ghettos, sex was a commodity to be traded for bread.

Chasia Bielicka related that at a camp near Grodno, Jewish girls and women whom the commandant deemed beautiful were given evening gowns and delivered to German parties. Each woman, in turn, was asked to dance with one of the men in front of all the guests. Then, at some unexpected moment, the commandant approached, pulled out his handgun and shot the woman in the head. "I only try to imagine the terror and the deathly chill that prevailed inside the ballroom dresses that clung to the women's bodies when they were worn," Chasia reflected decades later. "I try to understand how the women's legs did not tremble or their knees fail as they were led to the dance floor. How their dread did not turn into a cascade of sounds that surged into the circle around the couple in motion."

The procedure for entering concentration camps was itself sexually violating: women were pushed into shower rooms and forced to take off their clothes in front of male strangers and Nazi guards. In states of confusion and pandemonium, ripped from their children and families, smelling burning flesh, the new women prisoners were violated by SS men who made lewd remarks, commented on their shapes, poked their breasts with their crops, and let their dogs loose on them. Women's heads were shaved and their bodily cavities were examined—including forced gynecological exams in which Germans searched naked Jewish women to make sure they hadn't hidden jewels in their vaginas. Women were subjected to "medical" experiments ostensibly related to fertility and pregnancy. Some female SS guards engaged in sexual behavior with their boyfriends specifically in front of Jewish women while they were being forced to watch horrific beatings, tormenting those who had lost their loved ones—cruelty and debauchery linked.

Several Jewish ghetto leaders were complicit in sexual violence by providing Nazis with Jewish women in their attempts to stave off a deportation, and several women accused the ghetto heads of sexually abusing them. In one account, Rivka Glanz left work at the Łódź Judenrat because the leader sexually harassed her; others have claimed that this megalomaniac attempted to harass them too.

Several Gentiles who protected and hid Jews sexually abused the women in hiding or required sex as payment. *Schmaltzovniks* could demand sex along with money, or instead of it. Anka Fischer, of the Kraków resistance, found an apartment and job on the Aryan side but was blackmailed: the greaser threatened to report that she was a Jewess if she didn't perform sexual favors. She refused and, soon after, was arrested. Teenage girls in hiding complied with sexual orders to shield their younger sisters. Sex was the only currency they had, their only protection against murder, temporary as it was.

Finally, there was the sexual violence experienced by Jewish women on the run. Fifteen-year-old Mina

Fischer decided one day she'd had enough of the ghetto. She fled from her forced-labor assignment and found herself wandering in the forest. After escaping from two farmers who had set her up to expose her, she ran farther into the woods. At night, she had nowhere to hide. Suddenly three men were upon her, gang-raping her. "I had no idea what they were doing to me, as I knew little about sex," she recalled, "but during the terrifying assault, they actually started biting me like wild animals; they bit at my arms, bit off one of my nipples." Mina passed out. They must have thought she was dead. But she awoke, shocked, pained, bleeding, unable to stand. Only years later, when she became pregnant and nearly died, did Mina understand the damage they'd done to her organs.

Despite Renia's despair and exhaustion, despite the blackness of the forest, the young woman made sure she kept a clear head. The man inched closer and began barraging her with questions. Renia instinctively gave him foolish answers, acting like a dunce.

The whole time, she kept thinking that she could not wait. It was already one in the morning; every minute counted. She slowly began to distance herself from him, and then suddenly she launched into a sprint.

He ran after her.

With whatever energy she had left, she darted until she reached a house. She found an open door, clambered inside the building and into a dark corridor. She held her breath and crouched under the stairwell, waiting, "sitting like a chased dog."

In the morning, Renia, tortured and weary, left for Warsaw.

PART 3

"No Border Will Stand in Their Way"

They are ready for anything and no border will stand in their way.

—*Chaika Grossman, on the movement's women, in* Women in the Ghettos

Chapter 23
The Bunker and Beyond

Renia and Chajka
August 1943

To have no home. No physical abode, no spiritual shelter. No makeshift lodging, let alone bread. No family. No friends. No job, no money, no recorded identity. No country, despite your family's thousand-year legacy. To have nothing expected of you, no one to wonder where you are. No one to know if you are even alive.

But survivors had to go on, to keep on surviving.

At last, in Warsaw, sheltered by Antek's contacts, Renia was distraught. As she would describe, "One merely had to glance at me to see what had happened and what information I'd brought with me from Będzin." No one could calm her down. Even Renia felt that at any moment she might lose her mind.

Day in, day out, she awaited any news, any letter from Będzin.

What happened to her friends, her loves, her sister?

And now that there would be no Zaglembie uprising, what would happen to her? Renia needed to know where things stood so she could plan her own next steps.

It took three weeks, but, at last, a postcard arrived from Ilza Hansdorf. "Come to Będzin immediately." Renia guzzled each word. "I'll explain everything once you get here."

Within hours, Renia contacted Antek and was packing for her trip. The underground provided her with a wildly expensive false travel permit, as well as two extras in case anyone else was still alive in Będzin. Renia was also given several thousand marks for unexpected needs: *schmaltzovniks*, police bribes, shelter, food, equipment, who knew?

Back on the train. She arrived at the address from Ilza's postcard: the home of a Polish mechanic who worked for the kibbutz's laundry. He'd stayed in touch with the Freedom members throughout the war, always trying to help. They all knew his address.

Renia could hear Frau Novak, the head of the household, fumble with a key. She could barely contain herself.

The door opened. Silence. Two lone figures sat at a table, emaciated and haggard. But they were happy to see Renia.

The couple was Meir Schulman and his wife, Nacha. Meir was not a member of the movement but a dedicated friend. He'd been a kibbutz neighbor. He was a very capable person—a perfectionist, according to Renia. Knowledgeable about technology, he'd helped build the bunkers and install secret radios. He cleaned and fixed their broken and worn weapons. When they'd received instructions from Warsaw for making explosives, it was Meir who'd brought them the necessary materials. He fabricated fake rubber stamps and attempted to print counterfeit money.

Now, here he sat with, she hoped, the answer to her burning questions: Where was everyone? What had happened during the deportation? What had happened to the fighters? To Sarah?

Chajka had her own version of the story.

A few weeks earlier, at three o'clock on a Sunday morning: shots.

Even Chajka was surprised. She couldn't believe the

Nazis would ruin their holiday. Everyone woke up. Zvi Brandes opened the bunker slat and withdrew a handful of weapons. "Why so few?" Chajka asked.

It turned out they hadn't been prepared. Most of the weapons were in a different location; the Freedom shelter at Hershel's had none. Chajka became furious. "Have we been cultivating the thought of *hagana* in our heads only to be empty-handed now? . . . We won't let them deport us. We'll do something stupid—maybe only one shot will be fired, but something will happen, something must happen." One of the Warsaw ghetto fighters who was with them grabbed a weapon, angry that it was so dirty. He began cleaning it.

They all went downstairs. They snatched two loaves of bread and a pot of water. Then, through the oven, twenty of them entered The Young Guard bunker.

It was small, unfinished. The squeeze was unbearable.

They locked the oven door behind them. A thin stream of air entered from a hole in the appliance. There was no bucket. Chajka was indignant with humiliation. To be forced to urinate where they slept seemed worse than the most brutal tortures.

Their hideout was located under the intersection of two streets. Nazis repeatedly entered the building, searching above. They hacked at the floor with pick-axes, they tried to open the oven. They began to tear apart the ground right over their heads. Zvi looked for his gun and ordered the Warsaw fighter to get ready. "Run away," he told everyone. "If you succeed, good; if not, too bad."

Breathless. At any second their existence could be blown apart. A relentless soundtrack of shooting.

This went on for three full days. Ten times a day.

No word from the outside. No ability to communicate with the other ZOB hideouts. They feared they were the last Jews. Zvi decided to go check on the Freedom kibbutz. Chajka and the comrades were terrified for him, their beloved, respected leader, brother, and father.

He left. Another horrible day of hammering, pick-axes, "bated breaths, mortal fear, and nervous tension." Nazis worked near their bunker for three hours, tore up half the floor, calling at them to come out. Panic. Chajka used all her willpower to calm everyone. A quiet hiss: "On the floor." They obeyed. "I have instinctively taken command," she wrote later. "I hoped for one thing: their laziness. And I was not disappointed." The Germans left.

Zvi returned, a tremendous relief. But there simply were not enough supplies. The group ran out of water. They opened the hatch. Heard shots. Someone in the hall. They could not move. But they would die without water. They lifted the oven door, creating "a hell of a noise." Everyone was terrified. Zvi, always first, went out with another man. They returned with water. Thank God.

But what now? "How long can we endure staying in this dungeon?" It was too stuffy. People were getting weaker by the day. By any definition, said Chajka, this was hell, "no matter if you heard about it or saw it in a painting."

They were a mass of thirsty figures, individual faces unrecognizable in the dark. "You can see young bodies, stripped, half naked, lying on rags. Lots of legs, one next to another. . . . Arms, so many of them. . . . Palms so wet and sticky, pressing on you," Chajka wrote. "It's disgusting. And the people make love here. These might be their final moments. Let them at least bid their farewells." Chajka couldn't resist reproaching Zvi and his girlfriend Dora about their lack of dedication, the time they'd all wasted.

The next day, no water again. This time nothing above ground. The Nazis had cut the water supply. Pesa, Zvi's sister, spiraled into a hysterical episode, screaming at the top of her lungs that she wanted the Nazis to kill her already. Everyone tried to quiet her. Nothing worked.

Zvi decided they needed to move to the Freedom kibbutz bunker. Dora and a woman named Kasia went. Zvi and his sister. Chajka left with a comrade, Srulek, creeping out of the oven and into the world. At first, the road was clear. Then—suddenly—rockets lighting up the entire street. Shots fired, lights blared, shrapnel and stones, from all directions. They hit the dirt. Chajka's heart pounded. Why did she have to die this way, not having *done* anything, alone in a field, fleeing instead of fighting? The misery, the loneliness, it was all too achingly unbearable. But she'd also had some good in her life, she consoled herself as she lay on the ground. She'd had companions, deep intimacy, wonderful moments with David. Now she too would be shot, destined to die like he did. "Tough luck," she told herself.

Somehow Chajka managed to crawl to a nearby building and entered a flat. She felt her body: Could she still be alive? She and Srulek kissed in celebration, they drank water. They made it to the Freedom kibbutz. It was three o'clock. Everyone was there. Twenty people, more.

Zvi's sister was placed in a flat above ground; they hoped that open space would calm her, but she was still hysterical. A Nazi found her.

Zvi shot him down from behind.

"The first shot," Chajka wrote. "I am so proud. I am so happy."

Her delight was short-lived. One German down, but before Chajka could even catch her breath, she found out that so many comrades had been killed. "We were supposed to all go together and not like that, like pieces of living, healthy flesh being torn off piece by piece. Why, we were to do something, something great," she later wrote. "[It] makes me furious, screams inside me, and rips my intestines apart."

This new hiding place, where Meir and Nacha had taken refuge, was worse than the one she'd left. There were no guns except the two they'd brought with them. It was stuffy, sweaty. Everyone's skin glistened. They walked around half naked in pajamas or shirts. Mostly they lay on the floor, like corpses. Chajka could barely breathe and was grateful for the electric fan, its blades turning nonstop—*chop-chop-chop*—a small relief. Plus, they had an actual kitchen with an electric cooker. Everyone was supine, but Chawka Lenczner, the Freedom medic, cooked semolina for Aliza Zitenfeld. The group, including Renia's sister Sarah, ate warm lunches together instead of slices of bread. Chajka liked Chawka, who stood by the hot stove and looked after the comrades, bandaging wounds, handing over talcum powder for skin, ordering people to wash so that they didn't become infested with lice. "It's so nice to look at her," Chajka reflected fondly, "so clean and kind." At first, Chajka had been mad at Hershel for keeping her in the bunker when she had such a fine Aryan appearance, but he'd said that without her, they'd all be finished.

Chajka looked around: the living dead. She couldn't take it.

"I want to breathe my last on the surface, look up at the sky once more, and swallow my fill of water and air," she contemplated. The suffocation, the thirst, the ceaseless darkness were overwhelming. *I will not go into a wagon alive.*

At night, they opened the hatch. Chajka left with the boys, elated by the air, "live, healthy, fresh air." She breathed as deep as she could, hoping to take in as much as possible, to bank it for later.

Suddenly shots.

Rockets lit the building. She retreated. Then, angry with herself for being scared, Chajka forced herself to walk outside. She saw the bright light of the barracks, the deportation center where the Germans put the Jews on trains. Searchlights. Observation posts. There was no escape. More rockets. Chajka laughed out loud: this was the front. The Nazis were launching a full-fledged war against thirsty, unarmed Jews in bunkers. A war they would, of course, win.

The boys returned with water. They'd risked their lives for it, and Chajka decided that next time, she'd go with them. They all went back into the cellar. She'd thought it would be better to get fresh air, but it had just made everything worse, because now her lungs had to readjust to breathing nothing. Plus, there was a fuss in the bunker: women were arguing about rags, with the hatch open no less. How ridiculous. Chajka was so furious that she burst into tears. Why did she have to sit here with these people? Where were the loves who had been so dear to her? David? The Pejsachson sisters? Perhaps it was better, she reasoned, that they weren't there to see their dreams shattered. But then she thought it would have been different with them—of course it would have been—and her heart grieved more than she knew it could.

They sat underground. What was the point? They would suffocate. Surely it was *Judenrein*—"cleansed" of Jews—outside. The water supply was unreliable, the lack of air. They'd be found out. They were going to die in here. Each day, the group drew lots to see which couple would try to make it to the Aryan side. No one wanted to go; no one wanted to detach from the group.

They had no addresses, no safe destination. They complained that they weren't prepared to run off into the unknown. "We thought that we'd go together," they all said. Chajka's sadness was overwhelming. As was her anger. They were all such cowards. They did nothing. They heard from no one. Was anyone else alive?

One comrade went out seeking information. Hours later, he returned, panting. He reported that a few Jews remained and were working in a liquidation camp that had been set up to clear the ghetto of any remaining Jewish possessions.

Then one day it was Chajka's turn. The group was dwindling. No more procrastinating. She wanted to leave with Zvi or Hershel, but Aliza Zitenfeld kept putting it off. She could go with Zvi's brother and sister. Should she do it? Now?

Out of nowhere, a shout. Germans nearby. They were scraping at the coal. Opening the hatch.

They'd been discovered.

A comrade who escaped had arranged a plan with Wolf Bohm, who ran the liquidation camp. Bohm sent a Jew to get them out of the bunker and bring them to the camp, but he was accompanied by two Nazis.

Chajka, having not known about the deal, couldn't understand how they had been found.

Commotion. People grabbed briefcases and bundles. They decided: girls and children out first. Chajka slipped a dress over her naked body, she had no shoes, nothing. Meir and Nacha opened a second exit, and Chajka was about to follow them out when—*bang!*—they slammed it shut. Too many guards.

Finally, Chawka went out. She quickly returned, flustered, stuttering. The Nazis had asked if Hershel was there and told her that if they all came out at once, they would be sent to a street near Rossner's factory. Chajka guessed correctly that Bohm was behind this. *A ray of hope*, she thought. But what about the guns? Zvi shouted for Meir to grab his gun and leave, but he refused and hid under the cots. People were exiting, hurrying. Hershel and Zvi were confused. Hershel distributed a large stash of cash among them. "I have never seen so much money," Chajka later wrote.

She walked out. Three Nazis stood at the entrance. They frisked each Jew and took all currency. Aliza, pale, asked quietly about moving them to the street near Rossner's. Chajka watched from the coal cubbyhole, wondering what to do with her portion of the money, worried the Germans were taking all their savings. Where could she hide it—in her knickers?

Pesa, next to her, whispered, "What should I do with my gun? They gave it to me, thinking that they wouldn't frisk the girls." Chajka went cold with terror. Whose idiotic idea was that? That gun should have either been used or been hidden deep underground.

Chajka told her to put the gun in the coal. Thinking about the gun, she lost focus; the Nazis immediately took all her money.

Then the Germans walked over to the coal, reached in, and pulled out a bag covered in red blood.

The gun.

A Nazi yelled, "So, you have something to attack us with!"

The girls started crying, pleading, "It's not ours. Somebody's planted it."

"Disgusting," another Nazi muttered. "We were going to help you, and you were going to kill us."

They were doomed. Chajka snuck back to the bunker. Zvi was panicking. He'd lost the other gun. He thought he put it in a briefcase. Everyone searched, frantic.

The Warsaw fighter came back down. "They've arranged everyone on the ground, and [they] threaten to execute everybody unless you come out."

Silence.

"I'll be the sacrifice," said Zvi. "I'll go." He left the bunker.

Meir and Nacha refused to budge. Chajka decided, *Okay, I'll go.*

Twelve people lay on the ground, arms outstretched. Chajka joined them.

"Is there anybody else in there?"

They sent Hershel to check. "Nobody's there." He would not give away Meir and Nacha.

The Nazi descended one stair, picked up a briefcase, reached inside. The gun. He took it out and burst out laughing. "Not yours, right?!" He fumbled inside the briefcase and retrieved a photo of Aliza Zitenfeld. "How dumb to have left the photograph!" they guffawed.

Aliza began to plead. "It's not mine."

Chajka was boiling in anger: Aliza could have at least tried to be brave.

Then he pointed right at Chajka. "And this is yours."

Fate has passed its sentence, Chajka thought. Done deal. "What, mine?"

He said nothing, but kicked her twice and then struck her with a wooden pole. She only squealed at the end, when she saw how furious he was becoming.

From the ground, she looked up, absorbed everything, convinced it was the last time she would see the sky.

The Germans ordered them all to stand. Chajka was forbidden to put on shoes or take the briefcase. Her dress was dirty from lying on the ground.

They ordered Chajka to walk last, hitting her with a rifle butt from behind. "I will finish her off now," one of them said.

The other Nazi said, "Let her be. Don't do anything on our own initiative."

Single file. They arrived at the square opposite the barracks. Soldiers, officers. Everyone was pointing at them.

Aliza was crying, pleading.

"You idiot, *calm down*," Chajka hissed. "Have some dignity."

The ghetto was deserted. The Aktion had been going on for a week. Soldiers who were specially trained in liquidating Jews were called in to drag them out of bunkers. Everyone was herded into covered cattle cars, except the Judenrat, who rode in hansom cabs. People tried to escape. Rossner hid five hundred people, but they were all caught. A few Jews were sent to work camps; a small number were kept in Kamionka to clear the ghetto apartments. The deportees were being held in a barrack where they could move about freely, but the resistance group was forced to sit on the ground outside, not allowed to budge, inspected by guards as if they were "in a menagerie."

Chajka watched people "dash for the water buckets

like wild animals." The thirst was unbearable. They hadn't had proper water in weeks, drinking rainwater or even urine. Chajka pitied the elderly and the children, so scared, so dirty.

Jews tried to bribe Germans to get work. But they had nothing left to bribe them with. Chajka's group volunteered—they were ignored. Chajka wanted to live, but how? She did not believe in miracles.

The Nazis called her and Aliza.

This was it. Chajka's execution.

"Farewell," she said, and strutted boldly, head up.

They marched her to the building of the former militia—a closed building, no witnesses. Aliza went in. Chajka was told to wait outside. A Judenrat clerk walked by, looking frightened. "What are you doing here?"

"Nothing really," Chajka said. "They want to execute me."

"How come? What for?"

"They found something in our bunker."

He was carrying a tray with apples. Chajka leisurely stretched out her arm, took one, and bit into it. He looked at her as if she were out of her mind. Was she? While still chewing, she was called into the building. She threw the apple core to the ground and rehearsed the line she planned to say in her final moment: "Murderers, your day of reckoning will come. Our blood will be avenged. Your end is already near."

As Chajka walked to her execution site, she wanted to scream—but it was desolate, no one would hear her. She controlled herself for the sake of the others. Though not under orders to do so, she remained silent. And self-critical.

Aliza was in the corner of the room. Bloody. Severely beaten. Broken.

Now Chajka realized that she would be tortured.

They ordered her to lie down. The command came: beat her to death. The blows began. Her whole body. Relentless, fierce. Then, they started on her head. She wanted to refrain from shouting and show them "what a lousy Jewess was capable of." But she was disclaiming them, so she had to scream out her innocence.

"Say whose gun this is, and we'll leave you alone!" they shouted.

"I don't know," Chajka answered. "I'm innocent. Mama! Mama!"

Finally, they stopped and moved back to Aliza. "I must be a vile animal," Chajka later wrote, "because I didn't react." How could she have covered her face and not gone over and slapped them for beating her friend? But she was in too much pain, and also, felt a perversely fierce joy—she was sure she could endure.

Then they started on her again. A Nazi approached. "A tall, skinny greyhound," she wrote. "[The] familiar eyes of a snoop." Chajka gave him a derisive look. It seemed to her that that's why he beat her.

Cheek, face, eyes. Blood gushed out. "One more centimeter, and I would have lost my eye." He put his sinewy arms right around her thin neck, strangling her. She began to wheeze. He released his hold. "I was about to find out at what point one can die," she reflected. "I'd always been curious when the process of agony began." But he stopped choking her, and they were escorted out. She overheard the mention of Auschwitz.

Chajka could barely drag herself back to the group. When the comrades saw her and Aliza, they all burst into tears.

People with towels or shirts offered them to Chajka to sit on. Her body was "hard as stone, hard as rubber. And so black. Not blue, but black," she described. "Instead of sitting, I curled up like a cat and was lying on Pesa." No coat, shoes, stockings. It was dark, cold. The soldiers were cutting up old furniture for a bonfire.

Suddenly Zvi sprang to his feet.

He rushed ahead so fast that Chajka's eyes could not even follow him.

He was fleeing!

Commotion among the soldiers. Shooting, running. The commander was incensed. "Chase him and bring him back dead or alive."

Minutes went by. Chajka's heart pounded. The soldiers returned. It was too dark to see their faces, but she heard one say, "Already done! I got him!"

Chajka told herself it might not be true; he might just be bragging. Deep in her heart, however, she knew, Zvi was dead. They'd lost the best one of all: a companion, a true leader. Her dear, dear friend.

His sister and brother sat next to her. "What were they saying?"

"I don't know," Chajka lied. She sat, her insides hollow. "If you knocked on me," she wrote, "there might be an echo."

In the dark, Chajka's thoughts turned to the soldiers' lives, to a potential escape, to curiosity about what went on at Auschwitz. She promised herself that she would never go, she would run, jump, shoot herself first. In the toilet, later, she considered crawling to the laundry, sneaking out. But the guard was too close. She didn't have the courage. She thought of Zvi. Tomorrow might be too late.

Morning, and the torment resumed. No food. They begged for water. The Jews who passed could have slipped them a few drops, but instead they kept their distance and averted their eyes. This is the nation she wanted to die for? Then again, she understood. The Nazis had made them this way.

At last, the German guard took pity on them, and ordered them to get up. He gave them water and a bit of food for the Atid children.

In the afternoon, Nazis came over. They took a group of four men. Chajka reasoned they would be executing them four at a time.

But no. The men returned carrying something.

Zvi's body.

To show what they are capable of.

His sister was moaning. Chajka wanted her to stop; for her to look proudly into their faces.

But something howled inside her. "All the skin on my head has gone numb. . . . I think that my hair's about to turn gray." The boys carrying him looked like their legs would give out. Zvi's face looked horrible, "his body so mutilated and as full of holes as a sieve." Their beloved, righteous friend. Hershel sobbed.

The boys were sent to dig pits—their own graves, they assumed. Ten times a day, they thought the Germans were coming to kill them. "The waiting was worse than death," Chajka wrote. In the evening, an order came. Chajka was to go into the barrack. She would mix with the other Jews. And then tomorrow she'd be transported to Auschwitz.

She was gripped with fear. Would she go back on her promise and go to Auschwitz? Why had she waited? At least outside there was a chance of escape. Could she blend in with the crowd and run off? Hershel consoled her: the transport wouldn't happen so soon.

In the morning, Jews grabbed their towels and washed their faces, as if this were a normal day. Chajka was incensed. *For God's sake, revolt! Jump out of a window . . .* Why was everyone so calm? Rumor was, the train would come at ten o'clock.

Or was she just criticizing herself? *She* should have run.

Among the deportees, Chajka noted a young, resourceful boy, Berek. Chajka trusted him—he had honest eyes. He usually went out on work detail and was going out that day too. He wanted to help and offered to escort the girls to the kitchen. Chajka's wounded face made her too recognizable to go. The boys left for work, and Chajka pushed Hershel to go with them. But he stayed.

Almost ten. Berek was standing with horses next to the barrack.

She had to go.

Waiting, waiting, waiting for the right moment. Suddenly a flurry of people. Berek winked at her.

Flight.

She did it; she walked over to him.

"Go to the kitchen building," he whispered.

"Come with me."

"No," he insisted. "Go alone."

Chajka went.

A soldier stood in front of the door.

He let her in.

Aliza, Pesa, Chawka, the Warsaw fighter, and Sarah—Renia's sister—joined Chajka in the kitchen. They told the militia to go get Hershel. Then the commander arrived. Chajka knew she'd be sent back because of her face. Aliza went to hide. But Chajka didn't. She couldn't take it anymore.

The commander looked at Chajka for a long time, then shook his head. "New faces," he said. "But [okay], they should stay."

At ten o'clock, the transports left for Auschwitz. Hershel left with them. "How odd," Chajka reflected later. "A two-minute walk from the barrack to the kitchen has saved me for now from Auschwitz, from death. How strange this whole life of ours is!"

Meir told Renia that after the others were taken out-side the bunker, he and Nacha hid under the cots for several days before escaping to this Polish mechanic's house. "We have a little bit of money," he said. "But what will happen when it runs out?" They knew that a couple of Young Guard girls were still in Będzin, dis-guised as Gentiles. The Schulmans didn't know any-thing else and did not know about those who'd crossed to the kitchen.

Renia's written accounts from the 1940s do not men-tion her sister Sarah here—perhaps for security rea-sons, perhaps because Renia was so distraught that it was difficult to write about her, perhaps out of respect for the movement, where one was not supposed to favor birth siblings over comrades. But what had happened to Sarah? Was she dead? Was any other Kukielka alive? Or was Renia completely alone?

She was indeed going to lose her mind.

Fortunately, Ilza arrived at the mechanic's apart-ment just then. Crying, she grabbed Renia, hugged her, words rushing forth, too much for her to contain. "Frumka died, our comrades died."

Ilza sat with Renia and recounted the tale of a dif-ferent bunker, "the fighters' bunker," under a small building on a slope, a modest, ugly edifice on a grassy surround. Frumka and six other Freedom comrades were staying in a well-camouflaged cellar under this house. It was the team's finest construction, with an entrance superbly concealed in the wall, as well as electricity, water, and a heater.

The whole time, these seven heard every noise from outside. Freedom leader Baruch Gaftek stood by a small crack and guarded the bunker. Suddenly, German voices—they were standing right above, booming loud. Had they seen light emanating through a crack? Without thinking, filled with rage, Baruch called out, "Let's retaliate before we fall!" Then he cocked his gun and shot right through the opening. Two Germans fell to the ground, their sturdy bodies shaking the earth.

His girlfriend hugged him from behind so intensely that the others heard their bones crack.

The shot's echo drew attention. A mob of panting Germans besieged the house, but did not get too close. They carried away the two Nazi corpses, crazy with rage, astonished that there were still Jews willing to fight.

Frumka, chain-smoking despite the ban in the bunker, stood taller than anyone. She held her weapon, tough and cold, an unusual sparkle shimmering in her long-depressed eyes. "Practice caution," she called out, "but kill a few and die an honorable death!" The comrades cocked their guns and fired.

The Nazis, dozens of them, ambushed the house with grenades and smoke bombs. It became dark in the bunker. The haze from the bombs and the burning house above them made the fighters' eyes smart. They began to suffocate. They grabbed their throats, cried that they wouldn't be able to use their weapons. "Barbarians!" they screamed, and skillfully lobbed a grenade, but the Nazis jumped out of the way. The Germans used a special pump brought in from Auschwitz to fill the bunker with water, to drown them all.

"The house stood on fire," Ilza described. "The dark smoke bellowed to the skies and with it, the stench of burning bodies and hair. One could hear shots, sighs, cries, moans, curses, German voices— deafening. The feathers from cushions wafted through the air. An ocean of flames."

The Gestapo ordered the Jewish militia to extinguish the blaze; a German put the barrel of his revolver to militiaman Abram Potasz, a member of the corpse unit, and told him to bring out the bodies. Abram climbed into the bunker through the hole made by a thirty-minute hail of machine-gun bullets. On the ground, black, charred bodies, some half alive, twitching and wriggling, barely human. Abram saw smashed skulls, brains pouring out. "An inhuman moan resembling a hum of a whole aircraft squadron was coming from the mouths of the prostrate *chalutzim* [pioneers]," he later described. The pillows and eiderdowns had caught fire from the fusillade, giving off a column of thick smoke. Teeth clenched, Abram pulled each deformed body, one after the other, out to the garden. Frumka, half burnt, was still clutching a six-shot revolver.

Seven blistered skeletons, broken heads, exposed skulls, frozen eyes. Abram was ordered to lay the bodies face up and strip the women naked.

Frumka lifted the upper part of her body—the lower part was entirely scorched. Proud, she wanted to speak, but her expression was horrible, she seemed blind. She murmured something, looked around, and then her head drooped. One of the Gestapo men leaned in to hear her in case she was offering useful information. But a second one quickly jumped in, laughing, and kicked her in the face with his heavy boot. He trampled over her body "with perfect stoic, sadistic calm." They shot her in the head and heart, attacking her dead body over and over again.

The Gestapo fired at all seven corpses from seven machine guns. But bodies as "full of holes as sieves" wasn't enough. Chajka described how they stamped on the half-dead cadavers. Kicking, shooting at corpses, they "pounced on them like hyenas on carrion," until their faces were a "sticky, red pulp of blood and flesh" and their bodies "blue, bloodied, smashed pieces of humans."

The next day, what remained of Frumka's body was shipped to Auschwitz to be burnt.

Around the time of Renia's return to Będzin, as she sat in the mechanic's apartment, Chajka was alive and working in the liquidation camp kitchen, preparing food for the people who were clearing out objects from the now-vacant Jewish apartments. She was the last leader of The Young Guard, of the Będzin resistance. The other Jews pitied Chajka's wounds. Yet they taunted her and wanted her to run away—they were afraid they'd all be killed if the Gestapo remembered who she was. Whenever the man who had beat her entered the quarters, Chajka hid under the bathtub.

She witnessed the barracks where the murdered Jews' possessions were collected. She was left "speechless" by "the German pace and organization." She saw a whole series of huts, each one dedicated to a specific type of object, curated like a gallery. Chajka later described the meticulousness: "One barrack contains carefully arranged blue kitchen utensils. They have been beautifully sorted according to quality." There were barracks for pots, glassware, silk, silverware, everything. When ordered to do organizing work herself, she wanted to smash the porcelain sets into a million bits. German women wearing stolen Jewish two-piece suits and fox furs came into the camp to select objects for their families, showing off to one another, trying to prove their superior taste.

Chajka was no more fond of "the chosen" Jewish girls: the pretty ones who worked in the kitchens and were given goose and layer cakes to eat, dresses, their own rooms, and three pillows. They shared nothing with anyone else. "Oh, you Jewish whores!" she later wrote. "I would strangle you."

In an environment of constant selections, each Jew was balancing on the thinnest edge of life, a fingernail from death. Camp life was particularly untamed and morally corrupt: beatings, stealing, looting Jewish homes, black-market sales. Not to mention Jews gorging on food and sex, predeath hedonists seizing the day. Vodka, wine. Men harassed Chajka constantly. "No, I don't want to be with you!" she wanted to scream at them all. "I somehow don't want to indulge myself before death. It makes me want to vomit."

The soldiers who had been stationed in Będzin were ordered to the front, presumably to defend against Russian advances. New, older German soldiers arrived. Chajka befriended them. They too suffered. They didn't believe the stories of mass murder, and as the movement had asked, she took responsibility to spread the word, to enlighten the Germans, to tell them exactly what they were doing.

Chapter 24
The Gestapo Net

Renia
August 1943

*B*ut how to get them out?

Desperate, wired, Renia could think of nothing else but how to help her comrades in the liquidation camp. Aside from Chajka, she'd heard that Aliza was there, Chawka Lenczner, children from Atid—even her sister Sarah. Each day, more Jews were deported to death. Renia did not know the guards or the layout of the entrance; she couldn't get in by herself.

She frantically inquired and found out about Bolk Kojak, a member of The Zionist Youth (Hanoar Hatzioni), a less political Zionist youth group that focused on Jewish pluralism and rescue. Bolk knew several guards, and went in and out of the camp each day. He lived in Aryan Będzin, disguised as a Catholic. He'd been friends with several Freedom members, and Renia prayed that he'd help her—at least give her advice. Taking Ilza with her, Renia "stood in the street like a dog" waiting for two days to meet him. Suddenly Kojak appeared from afar, and Renia jumped up and ran toward him, inflated with hope.

They walked together, as if strolling on a promenade, then sat down on a bench in the market. They acted natural, but whispered, noting that two older Polish women sat nearby. Renia begged. "Please help me."

"My priority is to rescue members of the Zionist Youth," he told her, crushing her heart. She was so close, too close.

But Renia did not let up. As always, she did everything she could to get what she wanted. In her hushed tone, she begged, negotiated. Finally, she offered him several thousand marks if she saved even one Freedom kibbutznik.

"Meet me again the day after tomorrow," he said. "Six in the morning."

They parted, Bolk going one way, and Renia and

Ilza walking in the other direction. They hurried to catch the tram to the nearby town of Katowice, where they were going to spend the night. Suddenly the two women who'd been sitting near them on the bench appeared. "You're Jewish, aren't you?"

They started chasing the girls, followed by a group of children yelling "Jews! Jews!"

"Let's run," Ilza whispered.

"No." Renia didn't want to raise suspicion. They strode quickly to an empty building that had been previously occupied by Jews. By then, however, a herd of people were after them, led by the two older women, who yelled, "You're disguised as Poles. You met with a Jewish man!" A mob gathered around them. "We should kill you Hebrews, all of you!" One lady yelled, "If Hitler doesn't get the job done, we will."

Without thinking, without a moment of hesitation, Renia slapped the woman across the face. Then slapped her again. And again. "If I'm actually a Jew," Renia said between whacks, "you should know what a Jew is capable of."

"Call me a Jew again," she threatened, "and you'll get more of the same."

Two undercover Gestapo agents arrived at the scene, which actually came as a relief. "What's going on?" they asked.

Renia told them the story in Polish; a boy from the street translated. "The woman is not in her right mind if she suspects that I am a Jew," Renia said, calm, then whipped out their fingerprinted papers. "Check our documents."

The Gestapo asked her full name, age, birthplace. Of course, she'd memorized everything, as had Ilza. Like all those in disguise, they spent hours rehearsing each detail of their faux lives; you could wake them in the middle of the night, and they would recite entire fictional lineages. Another gendarme approached. "If they don't speak German," he said, "then they must be Polish. All Jews know German."

The crowd agreed, saying that the girls did not actually look Jewish.

The older lady now felt ashamed. Renia slapped her again, this time in front of the Gestapo detectives and gendarmes. "Find her name and address," Renia told the Gestapo. "Maybe one day I can get back at her."

The Gestapo men laughed. "You're both Polish pigs," one said. "What in the world could you do to her?"

The girls turned away. Behind them, children goaded, "You should have broken her teeth for suspecting you were Jewish!"

"She has gray hair, she's elderly," Renia answered them. "I wouldn't want to disrespect her."

That night, the girls stayed with a German woman, a sympathetic acquaintance of Sarah's. If only she could, she told them, she would help save the comrades. She tried to calm Renia, consoling her after the day's drama. Renia was gearing up to meet Bolk the next day and tell him about the trouble he'd caused them.

At five in the morning, with the town still asleep, Renia boarded the tram and headed to the meeting place with money from Warsaw. She waited for an hour. No Bolk.

At first, Renia was surprised. Then she grew angry, so bloody angry. He should have known how dangerous it was for her to stand in one place, to make her wait. After two full hours, Renia felt it was just too unsafe. She left. But now what? She needed to find someone else who could sneak into the camp, who knew his way around it.

Several days passed, the question constantly occupying Renia, who knew only too well, too tragically, that in this sick world, every minute counted.

And then suddenly, at the German woman's house, an apparition seemingly from a dream.

Sarah.

Renia's joy was enormous, staggering.

Right away, her sister told the story of her escape: she dressed up as a Gentile, a militiaman bribed the guards, and she snuck out into the Aryan zone. Now that she had a system for escape, she had to find a place where she could hide a few people. Sarah had promised she would do everything to help their comrades get out.

Sarah returned to the camp that very day. There was never a second to spare.

Meanwhile, Renia needed to take Ilza to Warsaw and settle her on the Aryan side. After that, she would have to figure out where to settle herself.

Katowice to Warsaw. The tickets were purchased. Ilza and Renia held passports and travel papers for crossing the border, two hours away. As they both had fake documents from the same dealer in Warsaw, the girls sat in different cars. Renia kept reminding herself of her success crossing the border when she'd brought over Rivka Moscovitch, praying it would be simple this time too.

A quarter past midnight, and they reached the border crossing. She could see guards walking outside, preparing to enter the cars. Ilza was at the front of the train—they would check her first. Renia waited, cautiously optimistic. It had worked so many times before, she told herself.

But then she kept waiting. Why was it taking so long? Were those heavy footsteps? Usually, inspecting tickets and passports took less time. Or was it her imagination acting up? Finally, the door to her car opened. Renia handed over her passport and papers, just as she'd done countless times before.

They examined her documents.

"This is the same one as in the previous car," one of them said.

Renia's heart skipped a beat, then began to race. She said nothing, pretended as always that she didn't speak German.

They did not give her back her papers.

Firmly, in German, they told Renia to take all her belongings and follow them.

She pretended not to understand.

A polite man translated for her.

She looked right into the guards' eyes, bravely. But at that moment, a new thought passed through her mind: this is the end.

Renia stayed focused. It was nighttime. Gendarmes everywhere. As inconspicuously as possible, Renia opened her bag, fished out the addresses, and shoved bits of paper into her mouth, swallowing them whole. She threw aside her stash of money. Her Reich finger-printed documents and a few more Warsaw addresses were sewn into her garter belt—but there was no way for her to get at them in public.

They took her to the customshouse. She saw Ilza, surrounded by gendarmes.

The gendarmes asked Renia if she knew this woman. "No."

Ilza's face flushed. Renia could tell her eyes were saying, "We've fallen into the hands of our hangmen."

They took Renia to a small examination room. "A fat German policewoman who wheezed from her nose like a witch," was there to investigate. She searched Renia's clothes—jacket, shirt, skirt—using a knife to slit open seams. Renia tried to remain still while she slashed so close to her skin. Too close.

And there she found it, in Renia's garter belt: the fingerprinted document and the addresses.

Renia tried right away to appeal to her conscience. "Please."

Nothing.

Renia removed her watch and offered it on condition that the policewoman destroyed the papers.

"No."

The guard escorted Renia to a large hall. Not only did she present the papers and the addresses, but also she reported Renia's attempts to bribe her.

Gendarmes gathered around. They started to laugh. Who are these girls? What should be done to them?

Renia was barefoot. Her shoes had been cut open, her jacket unraveled, her bag cut to pieces. She saw that they'd pierced her tube of toothpaste looking for hidden materials. They'd shattered her small mirror, dismantled her watch. Examined everything.

First, they questioned Ilza, then turned to Renia. Where did she get the papers? How much did she pay for them? How did she get her photo into the passport? Which ghetto did she escape from, and was she Jewish? Where was she going? Why?

"I'm Catholic. The papers are authentic. I got them from the company where I work as a clerk." Renia stuck to her story. "I intended to visit a relative who works in Germany, but I met a woman who told me that my relative had moved, so I'm returning to Warsaw. I stayed in the country with people I didn't know. I paid them for my stay."

"So, let's go back," an officer said. "Show us where you stayed."

Renia didn't miss a beat. "It was my first time in the area. I don't know the people. My memory isn't good enough to remember the name of the town and the exact house. If I knew, I'd write the address down for you right now."

Renia's answers angered the gendarmes. One of them hit and kicked her. He grabbed her hair and dragged her across the floor. He ordered her to stop lying and tell the truth. But the more they yelled and hit, the more hardened Renia felt.

"More than ten Jews with these exact papers were shot to death like dogs just this week," said one gendarme.

Renia chuckled. "Well, that would be proof that all the passports issued in Warsaw are fake and that all their holders are Jews. But obviously that's not true, since I'm Catholic, and my papers are real."

They told her she'd be better off if she was honest, threatening, "We never fail to get the truth when we want it."

Renia held firm.

So, they went through the protocol. They compared her face to the photo. They made her sign her name over and over again, comparing her signature with the one in the passport. All her papers were in order except for the stamp, which was slightly different from the genuine.

Renia's head was throbbing. On the floor, a pile of

hair that had been yanked from her scalp. The interrogation had been going on for three hours. It was four
in the morning.

They made her scrub the floors.

Renia looked around for a way to escape, any opening. But the doors and windows were covered in metal
lattices. She was guarded by an armed gendarme.

At seven, the gendarmes began their workday. Renia
was thrown into a narrow cell. She'd never been locked
up before. Would she be shot? What inhumane torture
awaited her? Her thoughts began to spiral downward.
She envied those who had fallen, wishing they'd just
shoot her now, end her suffering.

In her exhaustion, Renia nodded off for a second
while sitting on the floor. She was awoken by the turn
of a key. Two gendarmes, one old, one young, entered
the cell, then took her to the main hall for further investigation. The young one smiled at her. Wait a minute: she knew him! He used to check her passport at
the border. Whenever she carried contraband items
from Warsaw to Będzin, she'd ask him to hold her bag
during the inspection, explaining that it contained food
and she didn't want the border patrol to confiscate it.

Now it was his shift at the jail. What wonderful luck!
He patted her head and told her not to worry. "No

harm will be done to you. Chin up, you'll be out in no time." He took Renia back to her cell, locked her in.

If he had any idea I was a Jew, Renia thought, *he wouldn't be so nice.*

She could hear the guards arguing in the main hall. The young gendarme kept his word. "No, we can't assume she's Jewish," he said. "She crossed the border with me many times. Just last week, I inspected her papers en route from Warsaw to Będzin. We should release her right away."

But the older, stricter officer—the one who'd beaten her the night before—was not having it. "You didn't know that her papers are fake," he said. "Now we know that Warsaw papers with this stamp are frauds." Wild laughter. "This is her last ride. In a few hours, she'll sing like a canary and tell us everything. We've had plenty of songbirds like her."

Every few minutes, the gendarmes opened her cell door to see what she was doing. They laughed mockingly. Renia wanted so badly to retaliate, to taunt them for their smugness. She did not stay silent. "Does this make you happy?" she jabbed. "To hurt an innocent woman?" Silently, they shut the door.

At ten o'clock, the door opened wide. Ilza was there. The gendarmes led them both to the main hall, handcuffed them, and told them to take all their belongings. Renia's watch, jewelry and other valuables were put into the bag of a Gestapo officer who now accompanied them back to the train station.

As they left, the young gendarme looked at Renia sympathetically, as if to let her know he'd tried to help but was unsuccessful because her crime was too severe.

The train arrived. The passengers stared as the Gestapo man shoved them into a special car and locked it. A prisoners car. Through the small window, a ray of light tried to comfort them, provide a momentary reprieve from the bleak thoughts about the hours to come.

The Gestapo man kept warning them of the terrible things that lay ahead. "We'll find out everything at the Gestapo office in Katowice," he said. He slapped their faces and didn't allow them to sit the entire way.

When they disembarked, a crowd of passengers followed them, wondering why these two young women had been arrested.

The girls were tied together. The handcuffs were tight, cutting Renia's skin. Ilza was pale, shaking. Renia felt sorry for her. She was so young, just seventeen. Renia whispered to her, "Do not to confess that you are Jewish, ever. And do not say a word about me."

The Gestapo man kicked her. "Move faster."

After thirty minutes of walking, bound, they reached a narrow street and a large, four-storey building decorated with German flags and swastikas. The Gestapo office took up the entire edifice.

Renia and Ilza climbed up the green carpeted stairs, shoved from behind by the Gestapo man. Wailing and moaning emerged from a row of rooms. Someone was being tortured.

The Gestapo agent opened the door to one of the rooms. Renia saw a man, about thirty-five, tall and sturdy. Glasses rested on his wide-nostrilled eagle nose. His bulging eyes were evil.

The man who led them in ordered them to stand facing the wall. He told his chief the story. After every few words, he hit Renia so hard she saw nothing but streaks of white light. Then he took out the false papers. A younger Gestapo man entered and removed their handcuffs. A few more blows.

"This is the Katowice prison!" the man that brought them shouted. Katowice was a Nazi jail and detention center for political prisoners, known as one of the most brutal. "Here they'll cut you into pieces if you don't tell the truth."

Their belongings stayed in the room upstairs. The girls were taken to the damp basement and locked in different cells.

It was a hot summer day, but Renia shivered. Her eyes adjusted slowly to the pitch blackness. She saw two cots, and sat down on one, only to find that it was covered with congealed blood. Disgusted, she leapt up. The window was reinforced with two metal lattices. She successfully pulled out the first one—but the window was too small, even for her head. She put back the screen so that no one would notice.

How could she feel healthy and strong, yet so helpless, waiting for torture? She felt colder with every passing moment. "Water is dripping from the wall," she would write, "as if it is crying." She sat at the edge of the cot and curled herself into a ball, trying to warm up. *Whatever will be, will be,* she repeated, self-soothing.

Church music wafted in through the little window. It was Sunday: for Poles, the day of the Lord.

Renia's mind whirred as she replayed the recent days. Was this life of suffering even worth living? She felt guilty that there were people waiting for her help, waiting for her to return from Warsaw with more money. At least she'd left Meir and Sarah the address for their ally Irena Abramowicz; they'd call her if needed. Then Renia forced herself to stop thinking, especially about her comrades. Who knew, someone may have been reading her mind through a hole in the wall. Anything was possible.

Late afternoon. The girls were removed from the cellar. They were ordered to collect their belongings—a sign they weren't to be shot just yet. The Gestapo walked them down the street, "like dogs on a leash," holding a chain connected to their handcuffs. Renia recalled once seeing a young man who'd murdered an entire family being led this way. Passersby stared. German children threw stones. The Gestapo man grinned.

They approached a tall building. The main prison. The small windows were covered in thick metal bars. The iron gate opened with a loud screech. The guards saluted the Gestapo. The gate closed behind them. The Gestapo man removed the handcuffs and handed them over to his supervisor. He whispered a few words in her ear, then left. Renia felt better. As long as he was around, her fear was overwhelming.

A clerk took down their formal details: appearance, age, place of birth, place of arrest. They were locked in another cell together.

At eight o'clock, the supervisor opened the door. Two young, gaunt girls handed them small slices of dark bread and coffee served in military pitchers. Renia and Ilza took the food; the door was bolted again. They hadn't eaten for an entire day, but they couldn't touch the meal. The pitcher was disgusting, the bread inedible.

Escape was impossible. The girls huddled together and discussed options for suicide. Ilza was sure that she would break under torture; that under the blows she would tell them everything: who she was, who she'd stayed with. "They'll shoot me, and that will be the end of it."

Renia wasn't surprised; Ilza was young, inexperienced. Would the girl have the will to stay silent? She explained to Ilza that if she spoke, it would result in many more casualties. "Yes, we failed," she said firmly. "But there's no point bringing suffering to others."

Weary, they lay down on the dirty straw mattresses. But they couldn't lie for long: fleas started biting them, painfully. They scratched uncontrollably. In the dark, they hunted for bugs, crushing them on their skin. The stench was suffocating. Eventually they lay down on the bare ground.

At midnight, a dozen women were placed into their cell. These were "tenured" prisoners, en route to Germany, just there for the night. Young and old, each had her own story. One German woman had been sentenced to five years in jail for having a French fiancé; three years in, she was being transferred to hard labor. Two young girls cried nonstop. They'd been in Germany working for peasants who overworked and starved them, so they'd escaped. They spent nine months in Warsaw until a neighbor turned them in; they too were going to hard labor. Two elderly women had been caught on a train transporting liquor and pork fat. They didn't even know their sentence; they'd been jailed for a year and a half, and this was their sixth prison. Another frail, older woman had been jailed for months because her son had evaded the draft to the German army. Her gentle, pained gestures stirred Renia's heart.

Despite their hardships, Renia envied these women. Hard labor was a dream compared with the torture she was about to face.

"What are you in for?" the women asked Renia and Ilza. "You're so young."

"We tried to steal across the border and were caught."

"Oh, for that you'll only get six months," the women comforted them. "They'll take you to work in Germany."

They all lay on the ground like sardines, covered by blankets damp with strangers' sweat. Some of the women were filthy from weeks of prison transfers. Renia scratched—she'd already caught lice. The women kept the light on to protect from the fleas, who felt freer in the dark. Still, they kept biting. Renia could not sleep.

By dawn, the women were gone. Renia and Ilza were covered in red dots left by the insects, which were now crawling all over their clothes. "At least we have something to occupy ourselves with," Renia, darkly optimistic, later wrote, "hunting the fleas."

Eight o'clock. Bread, coffee, bathroom. Renia met the young wife of a Polish officer who was suspected of anti-German activities. She resembled a skeleton, hardly able to drag her feet. She was to be hanged in a few weeks. Her only hope: that the war ended first. Her husband was dead. What would become of her three young children?

Another Polish woman in the bathroom told Renia that her sister had been decapitated a few days ago, in this very prison, for illegally slaughtering a pig. She left behind seven children. There had been another in her belly.

As they were talking, the evil key keeper approached, like the angel of death. She was known to smash prisoners on the head with her bundle of keys. They became quiet.

Through the meshed windows, the women could make out the men's jail nearby and the gaunt male faces. They bent over when the supervisors passed to make it seem like they hadn't been looking, curious, desperate. Near the prison, they knew, was the area where the hangmen carried out the death sentence—usually by decapitation. Not a day passed without several executions. Farewells from family and friends were not allowed; neither was a confession. The jail prided itself on its medieval techniques.

After lunch, Renia and her fellow captives washed and were clothed in prison uniforms. Ilza seemed happy, hoping that the Gestapo had forgotten about them. Perhaps they'd just stay in jail for a few months, wait it out until the war was over. The girls sat in their cell all day long, looking at one another with disbelief. They were actual prisoners, wearing long burlap dresses, underwear, and blouses made of patches upon patches. Every piece of clothing displayed the Katowice prison stamp.

Night arrived, and with it, the day's tensions slackened. The Gestapo didn't work after hours. But then there were the fleas. Renia dozed off. Suddenly she awoke and couldn't believe her eyes. Ilza was trying to hang herself. She'd used the belt from her dress. But the belt tore under her weight. She fell.

Renia burst into uncontrollable laughter, as if she'd gone mad. Then she contained herself. She went over to Ilza, but the girl pushed her away, angry at her own suicide failure. This was why resistance operatives carried cyanide capsules, why partisans held extra grenades for self-destruction.

At dawn, the supervisors drove them out, screaming and cursing. They were moved to separate cells. Renia's new cell, which held eight women, was an improvement. The beds were covered with mats; bowls and spoons were stored on shelves; there was a clean bench to sit on.

"What are you in for?" asked a woman with delicate features.

"I was arrested for trying to cross the border."

"I was arrested for reading cards," the woman said, beginning to cry. She was a midwife with two adult sons, one an engineer and the other a clerk. One of her neighbors, out of malice, told the Gestapo that she was a fortune-teller. The woman had been at Katowice for seven months without having even been sentenced yet. "Be careful what you say to the other women," she whispered to Renia. "There are spies among them."

Renia nodded. This woman seemed pleasant. Motherly.

Do not think of your family, she told herself. *Do not feel.*

After breakfast, they were moved to the main corridor. The key keeper hit Renia hard for no reason. "You probably want to sit idle and do nothing. That would be unthinkable for us Germans. Get to work! I won't tolerate spoiled ladies!"

The corridor was lined with long tables of ladies "plucking feathers," or, rather, removing the hard quills from the down. Renia joined them. As she worked, she looked around cautiously for Ilza. She spotted her nearby, but they could not talk. Supervisors with whips stood next to them—chatting was verboten. Sitting across from Renia was the woman with the delicate features. Renia stared at her sad, pretty eyes, noting that they emanated a twinkle, radiating empathy. The woman's face spoke of the tortures she'd endured and the pity she felt for Renia, and she began tearing up. Renia, pained by this, had to turn away. Time flew, as Renia focused on the future. Would she be there for long? Executed? That would be better than the beatings.

They returned to their cell for lunch: burnt broth with vegetable leaves. When Renia rejected the meal in disgust, the other prisoners grabbed her bowl and devoured her food. "After some time here," they said, "you'll beg for this kind of soup."

"She's a lady," one of the peasant women mumbled resentfully. "She feels that this soup is beneath her, but she'll miss it."

After lunch, back to work: four more hours of plucking feathers. At first, Renia was restless. But then, every fifteen minutes, a prisoner was called and taken outside for interrogation.

Shivers ran down her body whenever the door opened, sweat when a different name was announced. Until.

"Wanda Widuchowska!"

Renia froze. A whip hit her on the back.

"Come with me."

Chapter 25
The Cuckoo

Bela and Renia
August 1943

Renia was not the first courier to be imprisoned, interrogated, and tortured as a Christian Pole. Bela Hazan maintained her non-Jewish disguise long after she'd ever imagined she could. It was a terrible burden of secrecy, yet it had obvious advantages.

After arriving at Pawiak Prison from Szucha, Bela had hoped to find Lonka Kozibrodska, the only soul on earth who understood her, but was instead placed in an isolation chamber: a pitch-black dungeon. She felt around for the narrow bed, but it was too painful for her to lie down, so she spent most of her time pacing her tiny, dank space, nibbling on bread crusts, sipping water and fake coffee, listening to other prisoners' screams. She was terrified that she would die and no one would know what had happened to her. And yet Lonka was so close.

After six weeks of recovery from her beatings, Bela was moved to the sick ward. Nearly blind from so much time in darkness, she was given sunglasses so she could get used to the light gradually. Then she was moved to a cell.

There was Lonka. Skeletal, no meat on her body, pallid face. Of course, they could not run to each other, so for a few minutes they just stared, embarrassed, tears filling their eyes. Bela could not stand it any longer. She went over. "I think I know you from somewhere," she said in Polish.

Lonka nodded.

Soon, when everyone else was distracted, they had a moment. "Were you caught as a Jew or a Pole?" Lonka whispered.

"A Pole."

Lonka sighed in relief. "How did you end up here?"

"I came looking for you."

"Is it not enough that I'm suffering? Why should you suffer too?" Lonka stopped Bela from speaking further, lay down on her mattress, and cried.

"Why are you crying?" the Polish cell mates asked.

"My teeth hurt," Lonka replied.

Bela found that her time in solitary had earned her the admiration of her cell mates. She got down on her knees and prayed with the Poles; she befriended them, including older women from the Polish intelligentsia. She grew close to a painter who had been ordered to make images for the Germans; the woman drew a portrait of Bela in front of the window overlooking the ghetto. This painter was religious, and Bela trusted her keen eyes. One night as bombs fell on Warsaw like snow, one blowing up the men's jail next door, she confessed to the painter that she was Jewish. The painter hugged her and promised to help. After she was released, she sent Bela food packages through the Red Cross. The guards confiscated the meat, but Bela appreciated her notes. Knowing that someone on the outside was thinking about her made her own life feel real.

On the other hand, Bela was rarely able to speak to Lonka. She was constantly aware that collaborators circulated in their midst. The couriers tried to work near one another in the yard, and chatted mostly on the way to and from the bathroom, exchanging info about friends and family. Lonka was beloved in the cell for her upbeat demeanor. Still, Bela hated noticing how

Lonka, who had come from a wealthy, pampered life, was not able to endure the physical hardships of prison reality. Diarrhea, bouts of stomach pain—her body was deteriorating.

Bela's window faced the ghetto; they were across from Freedom. "I feel like they're watching us," Lonka used to say, and they'd imagine that Zivia and Antek could see them. Lonka dropped notes outside the window; she once saw someone pick one up, and prayed the others knew where she was. From the window, Bela could see Jewish children playing in the orphanage, but she also saw police terrorizing Jews. Bela had to pretend to be happy about this. Once, she heard wild screaming and pulled over a chair to stand on to get a better view. She witnessed Nazis beating Jewish children to death, then bludgeoning an older man who'd pleaded with them to stop. After they shot him, his son said, "Kill me too, I have no reason to live." The Gestapo agreed happily, but first made him bury his father. The son bawled, kissing his dead dad on the forehead. The Nazi shot him and ordered all the nearby Jews to wash away the blood. Bela was frozen, overcome with desire for revenge, unable to tell her inquiring cell mates what she'd seen, too afraid she would break down and cry.

The conditions in the nearby cell for Jewish political prisoners were even worse. The Jews lay half-naked on the floor, barely ate, and were forced to clean toilets. Twice a day they were taken outside to do calisthenics while being beaten. Lonka recognized one of the prisoners as sixteen-year-old Shoshana Gjedna, the only daughter of a Warsaw working-class family. She had joined Freedom at a young age and participated in underground activities in the ghetto. Shoshana had been caught while carrying a movement newspaper. She tried to catch Bela's and Lonka's eyes from the courtyard, elated if she met them in the bathroom, telling them they needed to be witnesses after she was killed.

One night Bela heard screams spiral to the sky. She could not sleep, terrified for Shoshana. First thing in the morning, she requested permission to go to the bathroom. Pale, crying, Shoshana told Bela that the Jews were taken out during the night in their nightgowns, and dogs were released on them. She lifted her dress: a whole piece of flesh had been ripped off her right leg. She was in debilitating pain but kept cleaning the toilets. Bela went straight to the female doctor and had her secretly bandage Shoshana's wounds in the bathroom. Bela covered the bandage with a scarf.

Female prisoners—Polish too—were constantly being taken to their executions. After any kind of incident against the Germans, several would be hung in the city squares as a warning to the Polish people.

One night the girls were forced out of bed to run to another building in lines of ten. Bela was seventh in line; Lonka, ninth. Every tenth was told to move sideways. Bela found out later that they were hanged from lampposts throughout Warsaw.

The prisoners received very little news from outside, but sometimes Polish secretaries brought in bits of newspaper. When they heard Russian planes fly overhead, they were thrilled.

On Sundays, an entire entourage inspected them. One week, Bela begged the Polish commander for a job, saying she'd go crazy without work. The next day, she got a position in the laundromat. She told the commander that her friend "Chrisa" also wanted work, and so Lonka was sent to the kitchen to peel potatoes. The work distracted them from hunger and weakness and sped up the day. Lonka stole a few potatoes and cooked them on the hearth in the kitchen. She gave several to Shoshana for the Jewish women.

Bela continued to be interrogated over four months. Once, she was told that if she didn't confess who'd given her weapons, she would be killed immediately. As always, she insisted they were hers. She was kicked and beaten, then dragged through the streets to a forest and told she had one more hour to live. After a while, though, the guards relented and brought her back to the cell. Lonka was waiting at the window. "When I saw her face," Bela wrote later, "I forgot about my pain."

In November 1942 fifty names were read aloud: deportation. Bela and Lonka were on the list. Bela was actually excited: finally, maybe, a chance to escape. The girls were given bread and jam, forced into covered vehicles filled with guards, commanded to silence, and then pushed into a pitch-black prisoner train with no openings. Bela and Lonka sat in a corner in their summer dresses, hugging each other, warming each other, staying alert the whole time.

Many hours later, they arrived and disembarked. A band played German march tunes. They read the name of the station: Auschwitz. The ironwork above the gate read, "*Arbeit macht frei.*" Bela didn't know what this meant, but right away she noticed that while the entrance was huge, there were no exits.

Auschwitz-Birkenau was established originally as a prison and slave labor camp for Polish leaders and intellectuals. Now Bela and Lonka were separated from the Jews, ordered to march past barbed wire, past hundreds of women in stripes watching them, yelling, sick, beaten. The Slovakian Jewish women who worked in the showers were happy that Poles had been brought in. Bela was tormented by having to hide her true identity from her own people.

They took Bela's boots and leather jacket. Standing naked, she was inspected by male inmates for infections. She wanted to die. She tried to bribe the haircutter to leave more on her head instead of just "stairs" (layers). "If *I* don't have hair," the cutter said, "*you* won't either." Bela reminded herself, *As long as I have a head on my shoulders, my hair will grow again.* Then she received clothing: striped dress, jacket with a shoelace, and water canteen. No bra, no underwear. Clogs that didn't fit. After hours of standing, her right arm was tattooed with digits. Electric pen. Awful pain. But no one around her cried as they became numbers. The rain poured. On a mat on the muddy ground, Lonka and Bela huddled in the corner and fell asleep.

At three in the morning, roll call. Bare feet sinking into mud, tens of thousands of women, half asleep, pounding one another on the back to stay warm. Hours of standing. Armed guards and dogs on leashes. No water to drink. Then marching, marching, forced into rhythm with a rubber club. Weaker women who fell were beaten. The guards were agitated with the women for not understanding German. Rain poured. Bela was soaked. They were taken to be photographed so they could be tracked if they escaped—once with a kerchief, once without. Bela's "mug shot" showed her smiling, even looking healthy.

An entire day of waiting, marching, starving. Bela slept on the top bunk—farthest from the rats—at the feet of six other women, smelling burning flesh from the crematoria in the distance. She lay in her wet clothes without blankets, unable to move an inch all night. At least the other women's body heat kept her warm. During the night, she was jabbed by sharp objects in the mattress. Later, she found out these were the bones of previous prisoners. That was her first day at Auschwitz.

Bela and Lonka were assigned to work in the fields. They had hoped it would be promising to be out of the camp, but even there they were under heavy guard. The women guards, she found, were more vicious: the more they tortured the prisoners, the quicker their promotions. Each murder earned them stripes. Burman, a fifty-year-old woman who held on to her dog Trolli's leash, was Bela's guard. Trolli attacked anyone who couldn't march to a beat. Bela received a pickax and was to work straight through from seven in the morning until four in the afternoon; if not, twenty-five lashes. Her arms ached, but she kept going—at least it kept her warm.

At the end of the day, the women helped position the weaker ones in the center of the formation, to help prevent Burman from beating them. The *kommandos*, or work units, returned to camp together, ordered to sing. A marching band met them at the gate, along with a thorough inspection. (The band was composed of prisoners forced to play for the Nazis' enjoyment, as well as to deceive new arrivals.) Once, Bela was caught with four potatoes. She was forced to kneel on her knees all night without moving her face to the right or left, or she'd be shot. "I must have been very strong," she later reflected. "My mother gave me the tools to withstand this kind of torture."

Bela and Lonka brainstormed all night, figuring out how they could get different jobs. One morning after roll call, the girls hid in the bathroom, which the female prisoners referred to sardonically as the "community center" or "coffeehouse." Dozens of women, of all languages and nationalities, were there avoiding work. After the *kommandos* left, the two girls approached their commander, speaking in German and stunning her. Lonka argued that she spoke many languages and could work in the office, while Bela explained she was a trained nurse. It worked. Lonka was sent to the office as a translator, Bela to the *revier*, the hospital ward.

The women's hospital was split into Polish, German, and Jewish sections. Bela was sent to the German division. Though she was not pleased about helping Germans, she was happy to be working under a roof. Then again, there were three patients per bed, most with typhus, dysentery, or diarrhea. They were incontinent and howled in agony. There was no medicine.

As the only Pole, she was treated badly by the German patients, who threw their soiled sheets at her head. She was assigned the most difficult tasks, like carrying carts loaded with some thirteen gallons of water from the kitchen. Once, she was told to bring lunch for the entire staff. She lifted the tray, but was simply too weak and dropped it. For that, she was kicked repeatedly in the stomach, then beaten while lying on the floor. Bela cried inconsolably and asked to go back to work outside, where at least the trees and the wind were not cruel.

Bela returned to the fields, overhearing the Poles' antisemitic conversations, blaming the dirty Jews for all this torture. She was terrified that her identity would be revealed, terrified she might mumble in Yiddish in her sleep. In the field, she thought of her friends, of Hebrew songs, and looked for ways to escape, but it was impossible. When she returned, Lonka, who spent her days trying to help Jewish women in the SS office, waited for her with bits of bread.

The barracks became more crowded. Typhus, carried by lice, was rampant, and after a month of fieldwork, Bela caught it. She lay in her barrack for four days. When she asked her supervisor if she could stay in bed during roll call, the woman knocked her to the ground. Her fever rose above 104 degrees, which meant she was allowed to go to the infirmary. The ward, now mixed because of overcrowding, held six girls to a bed, tucked into each other, all but stuck together from weeks of sweat. There was no water for showers, no compresses, no room to lie down. Bela had to sit up. She couldn't find her own legs. Drafts came from every which way, and everyone pulled the sheet in her own direction. German patients hit Bela and stole her food. Constant noise, yelling, pleas for help. Bela was sure she'd die of thirst, yet she could not sip the rainwater brought to her. She clung to her neighbors, not noticing when they were already dead.

Polish friends prayed for her; some thought she was dead too. Some hoped to take her food. But a miracle: she recovered. One day Bela opened her eyes and recalled nothing, worried she'd given away her secret in fevered hallucinations. She added extra "Jesus and Mary"'s (instead of "God") to all her conversations.

When Lonka came to visit, Bela could see that she too was sick, and becoming weaker. Physically and emotionally, Lonka was losing the will to live. Bela watched her friend gather her strength to encourage her. But as Bela's condition improved, Lonka's worsened, and she was brought into the same hospital block, nearly unrecognizable. Bela pleaded with the doctor to put them in the same bed. They held each other all day and night.

After six weeks, Bela felt better. She wrapped her swollen feet in rags and was able to walk. She ate, even appreciating the taste of the soup. She knew she needed to get out and work, or else she'd be gassed. But she also needed to stay close to Lonka and nurse her back to health. Bela decided to start working again at the hospital. She was an "illegal," and so she was assigned the hardest jobs, like removing mud from the stones between the beds with a knife and emptying the urine and feces buckets.

Meanwhile, Lonka was burning up with typhus. Then she contracted the mumps. And dysentery. Bela was beside herself, doing whatever she could, washing her friend with snow, risking her own life by stealing drinking water, and sneaking medicine from the male camp via the sewage cleaners—one of whom was the brother of a friend.

Then Bela heard that Mengele, the SS physician who conducted inhumane medical experiments on prisoners and was known as the Angel of Death, was coming for a selection. She knew that Lonka, being so ill, would be sent to the gas chambers. Bela carried Lonka out of the *revier* to her own block, telling people that her friend was merely worn out from all the grueling work. But it was too difficult to hide her typhus and to stand her up for long hours of roll call, so Bela brought Lonka back to the hospital. She deteriorated; her eyes lost their color and sank into her face. She was all bones.

Lonka called Bela over to her bed. "I'm worried I'll leave you alone, and you will not be able to keep your secret," she whispered. "You must not reveal that you are Jewish." Lonka kept Bela by her bed for four hours, talking, crying, mentioning Freedom comrades, her own brother. She hated being so detached, so lonely. She grabbed Bela's hand. "I have pulled the thread of life until its end, but you must go on and tell our story. See it through. Stay sweet. Look everyone in the eye. Do not lose yourself, and you will survive."

Lonka whispered good-bye. Her last breath.

Bela could not move. She refused to let go of Lonka's hand. How would she continue to live in this hell without her dearest friend? Who would she rely on? Talk to?

The only person in the universe who knew where she was, who she was—gone.

Polish women came over, praying, placing holy cards and icons of Jesus between Lonka's fingers. Bela hated seeing her best friend die as a Christian. All her energy went to biting her tongue.

The *kommando* that collected dead bodies approached; they usually grabbed corpses abruptly, tossed them onto wooden planks, stomach down, head and feet dangling off the ends. Bela would not let Lonka be taken this way. She asked the doctor for special permission to borrow a stretcher, claiming that Lonka was her relative, and she wanted to take her to the "cemetery"— where they piled corpses before cremation. At first, he refused to "discriminate among the dead" but eventually he relented.

All the Poles who knew Lonka from Pawiak gathered. Bela, shivering, transferred the body from the cot and discreetly lifted the blanket to remove the Jesus cards and icons. Four women carried the stretcher; others sang mournful tunes. In the corpse area, Bela raised the cloth that covered Lonka's face one more time. She couldn't stop looking; she couldn't move. She said a silent Kaddish, the Jewish mourner's prayer.

Then she remembered Lonka telling her to go on.

"In all of the years to come," Bela would write, "Lonka's character accompanied me everywhere."

But in this life, Bela was alone.

Now, plucking feathers at Katowice prison, Renia looked at Ilza one last time. "Come with me," echoed in their ears. She was being summoned. Ilza returned her look, embarrassed, sympathetic.

Renia walked up several flights to the top of the building and entered the supervisor's office. Her vision was hazy, she felt weak. A Gestapo man awaited her with a strict gaze and bulging eyes. He was the one who'd been sitting at the desk when she and Ilza had first been brought in. "Go get dressed," he ordered. Where were they taking her?

Renia put on her skirt and sweater. She took nothing with her. The supervisor and the Gestapo man discussed her arrest. The Gestapo agent whispered, then said out loud, "For now, her name is Widuchowska, but in the interrogation, she'll sing, and we'll find out her real name." (Ironically, the other meaning of Kukielka is "cuckoo"—a songbird who is solitary and secretive.)

The supervisor asked if Renia would be returning to the prison. The Gestapo man said he didn't know.

Again Renia found herself walking in the street, chained, led by a Gestapo guard. "Take a good look at the dress you're wearing," he said to her in German, which she pretended not to understand. "After the beating, it will be torn to shreds."

Renia was amazed at herself. She did not feel fear. His words did not shake her. It was as if he were talking about someone else. She was distancing herself from her bodily experience, preparing to endure.

Back at the Gestapo building. Renia was asked if she understood German. She said no. In return, two thunderous slaps. Renia stood calmly, as if nothing had happened.

Four more Gestapo entered, along with a female interpreter. Chief Gehringer, the deputy head of the Gestapo in Katowice and the one who'd brought her here, was the lead interrogator.

The cross-examination began. Renia was drowned in questions. The men kept outsmarting one another, trying to confuse her.

But she toughened in response, sticking to her story: The papers were authentic. Her father was a Polish officer taken prisoner by the Russians. Her mother was dead. She made a meager living working at an office and selling family valuables, until they'd run out. One of the Gestapo men withdrew a bundle of papers from a drawer, saying that all the people with these papers were caught at the border. The documents were identical to Renia's, with the same forged stamp.

Renia's blood froze. Luckily, her cheeks were still flushed from the slaps, or they would have seen her turn pale.

They awaited her response. Of course she knew that the counterfeiter had sold these papers to anyone who paid. But she didn't blink. "Those people's documents may be fake, but it doesn't prove that mine are. The company I work for is real. I've been working there for three years. My passage document was written by a clerk from the firm. The stamp is from the mayor of Warsaw. My documents aren't forged."

Agitated, the Gestapo plowed on: "Everyone who was caught said the same thing and were later found to be Jews. They were all shot the next day. If you admit your crime, we'll ensure that you stay alive."

Renia smiled ironically. "I have many talents, but lying is not one of them. My papers are authentic, so I can't say they're fake. I'm Catholic, so I can't say I'm Jewish."

Her words angered them, and they hit her viciously. The interpreter, purely of her own volition, vouched for

Renia not being Jewish—her features were Aryan, she stressed, her Polish perfect.

"Then you're a spy," the Gestapo head said. Everyone agreed.

A new line of questioning. For which organization did she serve as a courier? The socialists or that of Władysław Sikorski, the late prime minister of the Polish government in exile? What did they pay her for her services? What did she transport? Where are the partisan outposts?

One of them played good cop. "Don't be naïve," he told her. "Stop protecting your superiors. When they hear that you failed, they won't help you. Tell us the truth, and we'll set you free."

Renia fully understood these "kind" words. "Okay," she said slowly, "I will tell you the truth."

They all listened intently.

"I don't know what a courier is," she said. "Is that a newspaper delivery person?" She put on her best naïve expression. "I don't know the PPR or the Sikorskis; I've only heard them mentioned in conversation. All I know about the partisans is that they live in the forests and attack unarmed people. If I knew where they were, I would gladly tell you. If I wanted to lie, I'd come up with names already."

Now the Gestapo men were furious. The interrogation had gone on for three hours, and still, nothing.

Asked about her education, Renia replied that she'd attended elementary school up to the seventh grade.

"No wonder she won't talk." They laughed. "She's too stupid to understand that her life is more precious than others'."

One of them interjected, "Just as she lied about everything else, she's lying about her education. A simple girl who didn't attend high school couldn't cheat this way." They all agreed with him.

Realizing that his efforts were futile, the chief ordered that Renia be moved to a different room, large and vacant. She was followed by several Gestapo men holding thick whips. "After this lesson, you'll sing like a bird. You'll tell us everything."

They kicked her to the ground. One of them held her feet, the other, her head, and the rest started lashing her. Renia felt pain everywhere. After ten lashes she yelled out, "Mama!" Even though they were holding her, she began convulsing like a fish caught in a net. One of the murderers wrapped her hair around his hand and dragged her across the floor. Now the lashes struck not just her back but her entire body—face, neck, legs. She became weaker and weaker, but still Renia didn't speak. She would not show frailty. She would not. Then everything went dark, and the pain faded away. Renia fainted.

She woke up feeling like she was inside a pool, swimming in water. She was wearing nothing but a skirt. Around her were buckets they'd used to pour water on her and revive her.

Two Gestapo men helped her stand up. She fumbled for her sweater, and put it on, embarrassed.

They resumed the interrogation.

They checked if her testimonies matched. Why wouldn't she confess?

A pistol in his hand, one Gestapo man said, "If you don't want to talk, come with me. I'll shoot you like a dog."

Renia followed him down the stairs. The gun glistened. Renia felt happy. Finally, an end to this torment.

She turned to the sunset for the last time. She drank it in, tasting each color, each shade of the ombré. So perfectly beautiful nature was, demarcating each transition and transformation with accuracy and grace.

Outside, on the street, the Gestapo man asked her with genuine wonder, "Don't you feel it's a waste to die so young? How can you be so stupid? Why won't you just tell the truth?"

Without thinking, Renia responded. "As long as there are people like you in the world, I don't want to live. I told you the truth, and you're trying to force a lie out of me. I will not lie! I'm content with being shot."

He kicked her a few times, then took her back inside and handed her over to the others. "He was probably sick and tired of dealing with me," Renia later recalled.

One of the Gestapo men pulled out a chair for her. Renia figured he was trying to get at her with kindness. He promised that if she told the truth, they'd send her to Warsaw to work for the Gestapo as a spy. She agreed, but she did not change her testimony.

The commander told them to stop playing with her. "Administer twenty-five more lashes until she begs to tell the truth."

Two Gestapo men started beating her with fury, merciless. Blood poured from her head and nose. The interpreter couldn't take seeing the torture and walked out of the room. The pain made Renia jump from one side of the room to the other. The commander told the men to continue, and he too joined in with a few kicks.

Renia blacked out. No memory, no feeling. After some time, she sensed someone open her mouth and pour in water. Her eyes remained shut. Someone was speaking, close to her face. "She's already dead. She's cold and foaming at the mouth." More buckets of water were poured on her. She was half naked and freezing and pretended to be unconscious. Two Gestapo men checked her pulse, slapped her a few times. "We still have her—she has a heartbeat." They leaned in closer, to hear if she was saying anything. They looked into her bulging, crazed eyes. "She's completely lost it." They laid her on a bench. Blood and water oozed off of her. In that moment, she regretted having been brought back to life. She would be beaten again, and she would not be able to take it next time. Her heart was hardly beating. She took comfort in the thought that now that they'd realized they wouldn't get anything from her, they would just shoot her.

Renia was unable to stand up on her own. One Gestapo man bandaged her head with a soiled rag, put her sweater over her, held her by the arm, and led her to the desk. He handed her the report and said, "Sign your name on these insolent lies." As he spoke, his wife entered. She winced when she saw Renia's face, and turned away. Then she noticed Renia's watch on the table and told her husband that since Renia was going to die anyway, she wanted it. He explained that she'd get the watch, but not yet. This angered her, and she left in a huff.

The Gestapo helped Renia hold the pen, and she signed.

Next, they called a taxi.

The driver invited the Gestapo guard to sit next to him, since she was so "unpleasant."

But the guard refused. "Even though she looks like a corpse," he said, "she's capable of tearing the door down and escaping."

Nighttime. Darkness. From the men's conversation, she realized she was not returning to Katowice but being taken to the prison at Mysłowice.

The taxi driver chuckled. "I suppose it's the only remedy for her insolence."

Chapter 26
Sisters, Revenge!

Renia and Anna
September 1943

Mysłowice. They entered a large courtyard in the darkness. Giant dogs leapt at them from all sides. Armed guards roamed the yard, ready for action. The Gestapo man went inside to hand her testimony to the office, then returned to the cab and was driven off. A new Gestaponik, about twenty-two years old, looked at Renia. "They really plowed your skin good, didn't they?"

Renia didn't answer.

With his fist, he gestured for her to follow him.

He locked her in a cellar. She squinted to see in the dark. One bed. She couldn't sit, couldn't lie down because of the pain. Unbearable pain. Finally, she managed to stretch out on her stomach. Her bones, ribs, and spine felt like they'd been broken to pieces. Her whole body was swollen. She could not move her arms or legs.

How she envied those who'd died. "I never would have thought any human being could endure such beatings," she later wrote. "A tree would have broken like a matchstick if it had been struck like I was, and still I'm alive, breathing and thinking."

Renia's memory was off, though; things were confused in her mind. She was lucid enough to tell that her thoughts were not lucid. This, of course, was not ideal.

Her condition worsened. She lay on that bed in bandages for days. For lunch, she was given diluted soup and a glass of water, which she used to wash her mouth and face. She hadn't showered. There was nowhere to relieve herself. The stench was suffocating. So was the darkness. She'd been buried alive. "I await my death, but at no avail" is how she later described her state of mind. "You can't order death."

A week in, a young woman arrived at her cell. She brought Renia to an office. A Gestapo agent questioned her and took down details. Renia was surprised. Why had she not been executed? Would they lock her in another cell? The woman took her to a bath and, seeing her pain, helped her undress.

Now Renia saw the results of the beatings. There was no white flesh left on her body, only yellow, blue, and red skin, with bruises black as soot. The bath attendant sobbed, speaking in Polish, caressing and kissing her, full of pity. Her concern brought Renia to tears. *Could someone still care about me? Are there Germans left who are capable of compassion? Who is this woman?*

"I've been imprisoned for two and a half years," the woman told her. "I've spent the last twelve months here. This is an interrogation camp, where they hold people until they're done with questioning. There are two thousand prisoners at Mysłowice."

She went on. "Before the war I was a teacher," "But when the war began, all those suspected of political activity in my town of Cieszyn were arrested. My friends were all imprisoned. I hid for a while but was caught. I too suffered." She showed Renia the marks on her body, scars from being beaten with chains and having red-hot metal pins shoved under her fingernails. "My two brothers are also here. They're half dead. They've been chained to their beds for six months, constantly guarded, beaten for any little movement. They are suspected of belonging to a covert organization. Terrible things are happening here, unimaginable. Not a day goes by that fewer than ten people are whipped to death. There's no distinction here between men and women. This camp is for political prisoners. Most will be executed."

Renia soaked in her bath, all this new information sinking in.

The woman offered to be Renia's friend. She would get her whatever she needed. "Up to now, I was locked up in a cell, but now I manage the bath," she told Renia. "I'm still treated like a prisoner, but at least I can walk around the grounds freely."

Renia was brought into a long room with two metal-mesh-covered windows. Bunk beds lined one wall. Next to the door stood a table for the room monitor, one of the nicer prisoners, who was responsible for cleaning the room. In the corner, a pile of slop bowls, the type used to feed piglets.

The prisoners—including many teachers and society people—surrounded Renia, examined her carefully, and peppered her with questions. Where was she from? Why had she been arrested? How long was she in for? Hearing that she was caught only two weeks ago, they asked about the outside world. Renia felt like a stranger among these women, a mixed group: nice and evil, young and old, accused of both severe and petty crimes. One of them, probably insane, started dancing for her and sang nonsense.

Mean women taunted her. "You just arrived from freedom and already look awful. How will you manage? The hunger is so bad it whistles in your gut. Do you have a slice of bread? Give it to me."

Renia was taken by one young girl, maybe ten or fifteen, who had a pleasant face. Before they even spoke, she'd developed a fondness for her. This girl stood on the side and stared at Renia. Only later, she found the courage to approach and ask questions. "Are there any Jews left in Będzin and Sosnowiec?" Mirka was Jewish. She'd been deported from Sosnowiec but, with her sister, jumped off the train. Her sister was badly wounded but lived. Mirka, not knowing what to do, went to the nearby police station. They handed her over to the Gestapo. Her sister was apparently transported to a hospital, but she'd had no word from her; she was probably shot on the spot. Mirka was brought to Mysłowice and had been there for three weeks.

"I have such a passion for life," said little Mirka, even though she walked around like a zombie. "Maybe the war will end soon. Every night I dream about the prison gate opening and becoming free again."

Renia comforted her: "The war will end soon. You'll see, you'll be free one day."

"When you're released, madam, please send me help, anything, even a little food package."

Mirka eased Renia into prison life, teaching her how to behave, making sure Renia always got a bowl of food and a straw pillow at night.

Then Renia started to leave her soup on the table and whisper to Mirka to take it. "What about you?" Mirka was concerned, but Renia told her not to worry. How she longed to tell her the truth, to prove her own existence.

The ward held sixty-five women. Each day, a few were sent out—for interrogations and beatings, to another prison, or to their deaths. Each day, new women arrived to replace them. A factory line of torture.

Renia's jail supervisor was vicious, a true sadist, waiting for any excuse to use her bundle of keys or whip. At any moment, she could spontaneously attack a prisoner, beating her badly. Not a day went by without her provoking an incident for absolutely no reason. *When the war ends, we'll tear her to pieces and throw her to the dogs*, the women fantasized, swallowing their anger, lumps in their throats. Everything was postponed until after the war. One prisoner told Renia that before the war, the cruel supervisor and her husband had owned a little shop for combs, mirrors and toys, selling their merchandise at markets and fairs. At the beginning of the occupation, the husband died of starvation, and the supervisor escaped her house, changed her identity, and became a *folksdeutsche*. Her status went from impoverished widow to "German lady" in charge of five hundred prisoners. "You are Polish pigs!" she would yell while hitting them. The Gestapo liked her style.

Renia's daily routine was both tedious and horrifying. She was woken up at six in the morning. The women went to the bathroom in groups of ten, where they bathed in the sink, in cold water, and hastily, since others were waiting. At seven, the sadistic supervisor arrived, and nobody dared be in the hallway. They all stood in formation, three to a row. The hall monitor counted them and reported the number of prisoners to her two Gestapo supervisors. Afterward, a fifty-gram slice of bread, sometimes a little jam, and a cup of black, bitter coffee. The cell doors were locked, and the prisoners sat idle and starving, the food only teasing their appetites; they counted the minutes until eleven, when they were allowed a half-hour walk in the yard. Here, they heard whip lashes and bestial screams. They saw men being taken to or from interrogation, living corpses, their eyes bloody and gouged out, their heads bandaged, hands and teeth broken, limbs twisted out of sockets, faces yellow as wax, covered with scars and wrinkles, and torn clothes showing off rotting flesh.

Sometimes Renia saw dead bodies being loaded onto the buses that were taking prisoners to Auschwitz. She would have preferred to stay inside.

In the cell, silence. No one dared utter a word. Guards patrolled the hallway. Renia's stomach ached from hunger. Each woman held a bowl. When they heard the clattering of pots, they knew it was noon. Food was served by two prisoners accused of petty crimes, accompanied by an armed guard. The others waited in a straight line. The supervisor stood at the door. Despite a hunger that made them tremble, no one pushed. "Order is first and foremost," was Renia's dry description of the Nazi prison system.

Her bowl was filled with watery broth and some cooked cabbage and cauliflower leaves. Insects floated on top. The women got rid of any worms they could see and ate the rest, including the leaves. "Even dogs don't eat this kind of soup," she wrote later. No one had spoons, so anything thicker than liquid was eaten with fingers. If a prisoner got more leaves than usual, she considered herself lucky, able to relieve her hunger for a little while. Some women got only liquid. Unfortunately, there was no one to complain to about the service, Renia remarked sarcastically. For hours after eating, she wanted to vomit up the bugs and the spoiled vegetables. Her stomach felt like a stuffed sack. And yet she was grossly unsatiated. She could feel her insides contracting. She remembered how she initially had refused the soup. But now, if only she could get more . . .

Afterward, the prisoners sat idly on benches along the wall. Waiting for supper took a lifetime. Once they were freed, the women dreamed, the first thing they'd do is to eat until they were sick. They did not fantasize about cakes or delicacies, just a loaf of bread, sausage, soup without worms. "But who among us will get to leave here alive?" Renia wondered, the knowledge that she would not sinking in.

At seven o'clock they stood in formation for supper: a hundred-gram slice of bread with margarine and black coffee. They devoured the bread and sipped coffee to feel full. At nine, bedtime. The pangs of hunger that ripped through Renia's insides made it hard to fall asleep.

Mysłowice was cleaner than Katowice. In 1942 a fatal typhoid epidemic had broken out there due to malnutrition and unsanitary conditions. Since then, the jail was strict and provided the prisoners with mattresses—but they didn't have enough straw filling, so the bed boards stuck into their flesh. Renia covered herself with blankets that were clean, if torn. The prisoners slept in their dresses in case the partisans attacked and they'd need to flee immediately. All night, armed gendarmes patrolled the hallway, alert to any noise. Women could never leave their cells after bedtime; Renia relieved herself in a pot.

From time to time, the women were jolted awake by gunshots. Probably someone in the men's ward tried to break out, Renia figured. Escape was impossible: the windows had metal screens, the doors were locked, the prison walls were dotted with lookout posts. Guards surrounded the building and changed every two hours, shooting three times at anything suspicious.

Some mornings, she heard that men had hung themselves during the night, or that a woman tried to flee from the bathroom and was beaten and locked in a dark cell.

Renia spent sleepless nights thinking of escaping. But *how*?

One day five Jewish women from Sosnowiec arrived. They'd bleached their hair in disguise but were caught at the Katowice station. A Polish kid suspected them and alerted the Gestapo. All their possessions had been confiscated. Renia spoke to them at night, but was careful to hide her own Jewish identity; would they recognize her from the area? At the same time, recognition of her identity was one of the things she craved most. No one in the world knew where she was; she needed to tell someone, in case she died, so they would know. So *someone* would know.

Every few days, more Jewish women arrived. One was caught during a routine paper inspection. Another was hiding in the house of a gendarme's friend; she didn't know who exposed her. The entire German family was arrested. An elderly mother and her two daughters were caught on the train with bad papers— one cried and confessed to being Jewish. Most of the women, Renia wrote, had been turned over to the Gestapo by Poles.

When a group of twenty Jewish women was assembled, they were sent to Auschwitz. Renia's heart heaved seeing them leave. These were her people, even though they didn't know. *They are being sent, and I stay behind.* They deluded themselves until the last second—maybe the war would end!—but as they left, they wept, knowing full well they were going to die. Everyone cried with them.

Names of women wanted for interrogation were announced without warning. Some women fainted when they heard theirs called and were brought into the examination room on stretchers. The next day, they'd return beaten to a pulp. Sometimes they came back dead.

Most of the prisoners were suspected of political activity. Among them were entire families. Mothers and daughters were with Renia; the husbands, in the men's ward. A woman might be told during an interrogation that her husband had been killed or sent to Auschwitz. Mothers received this type of notification about their sons and daughters all the time. They would lose their will to live; everyone was affected.

Renia learned that many Polish men and women were executed for helping Jews. They hanged one woman who was suspected of hiding her Jewish former employer. Just twenty-five, she left behind two young children, a husband, and parents. Some prisoners were women in mixed marriages, brought in as hostages because their Jewish husbands were hiding from the police. Some didn't even know why they were arrested. They'd been locked up for three years, without formal accusations or anyone looking into their cases. It was also common to be sentenced in absentia: the incarcerated person would not know why or when she'd be executed. Once, an entire village—several hundred people—came in together. Apparently, the villagers had been in contact with a partisan.

One day Renia was in the yard during a break, and four trucks full of children arrived. Partisan gangs operated in that area; the Germans took revenge by tormenting innocent people, stealing their kids. The children lived in a special cell under the care of an elderly prisoner. They were fed and interrogated just like the adults. Seeing the whip, children would confess to anything and everything. These forced confessions were good enough for the Nazis. The children were sent to schools in Germany, where they were "educated" to become "respectable Germans."

One Polish woman showed Renia her hands: no fingernails. They'd fallen out after hot pins had been stuck underneath them. Her heels were rotten from being beaten with burning metal rods. Her armpits showed the marks of chains. She'd been hung for half an hour and beaten; then they'd hung her upside down and continued. The top of her head was bald where her hair had been pulled out. And what did she do to deserve all this? In 1940 her son had disappeared. Rumor had it that he was leading a gang of partisans. They suspected that his relatives had contact with him. She was the last person alive from her entire family.

Renia's fellow prisoners included petty offenders: women arrested for selling goods on the black market, or turning on the light during a blackout, and other such "nonsense," as she called it. Those prisoners' lives were a bit easier. They were allowed to receive food and clothing packages. The Germans riffled through them and kept the good items for themselves.

Why, Renia kept wondering, was she still at Mysłowice? Why hadn't she been taken away? Why was she still alive? So many women died, so many brought in to replace them.

Then, one afternoon, her turn. A male supervisor entered the cell. He looked at Renia and asked what she was in for. She told him that she was arrested while crossing the border.

"Let's go."

What would it be? A bullet? Hanging? Medieval torture? Or Auschwitz?

She didn't know the method. But she did know the result:

This was her end. This.

Auschwitz, the crowning example of bestial brutality, was only a bus ride away from Mysłowice. But despite the notorious conditions, resistance brewed beneath the camp's seams. The underground at Auschwitz comprised (often disagreeing) groups from several countries and philosophies, including young Jews who were not immediately sent to be gassed but selected for slave labor. (For this reason, many Jewish women tried to make themselves look younger at camps—they used red dye from shoe tassels as blush and lipstick, and margarine to slick back their hair and hide grays.) The transport from Będzin, with comrades from the move-ments, had contributed several members to the under-ground and renewed its energy.

Anna Heilman first heard about the resistance from one of her block mates, a Jewish girl who'd been taken for a Pole and had contacts with the Home Army. Anna, just fourteen years old, had arrived at Auschwitz a year earlier with her older sister Esther. The two girls, from a highly assimilated and upper-middle-class Warsaw family, had grown up with nannies and visits to gour-met ice cream parlors. Now they lived in the women's camp in Birkenau, "working" at the Union Factory. The self-proclaimed "bicycle factory" was in reality a munitions plant in a large, single-storey, glass-roofed structure that fabricated detonators for artillery shells for the German army. Auschwitz had about fifty sub-camps, and like the labor camps, many were leased to private industry.

Anna was thrilled by the news of rebellion. She'd joined The Young Guard in the Warsaw ghetto; it had been her spiritual savior. (Because of her lack of Hebrew or even Yiddish, the movement gave her the name Hagar—she was from another tribe.) Every eve-ning, her group of Jewish friends and her sister sang songs, told stories, and thought about resistance. She'd seen the ghetto uprising; she craved more activity.

Now she heard that the Home Army was organizing a revolt in Warsaw and had made contact with the Auschwitz underground. They were planning to attack the camp from the outside; when the inmates heard a password, they would attack from the inside. Men and women began to prepare. Anna and her group collected materials—matches, gasoline, heavy objects—that they placed in agreed-upon spots. They obtained keys to the farm toolshed, from which they would nab rakes and hoes. About five women in each block participated, coordinated by one leader. Only the leaders maintained contact in this secret and organized operation.

On Anna's way to work each day, she'd pass a man who worked as a locksmith and was always smiling at her. One morning, she gutsily asked him for a pair of insulated wire-cutting shears (to break through the electrified barbed wires). He looked at her, stunned, and said nothing. For days, she worried she'd been careless and would be caught. Then one afternoon he put a box on her worktable. The factory girls cooed, "He's your lover!"—the term for male protector. Anna put the container under her table and peeked. A whole loaf of bread! She was excited, but also disappointed. Thankfully, there was no inspection that day, so she smuggled the bread back to camp, hidden in a little purse, under her clothes.

Lovers often brought girls gifts. All possessions were forbidden, so, if caught, a girl would say, "I found it." Huddled on her bed, Anna showed Esther the loaf. They noticed that the bread had been hollowed out. Inside: shears, beautiful shears, with red insulated handles. The sisters hid this treasure in their mattress and—in case they were out when the password was called—told their friends, including Ala Gertner, their elegant bunkmate from Będzin whose prewar portrait shows her posed coquettishly in a fashionable woman's fedora and collared top.

Days later, Ala passed on a message from a friend, twenty-three-year-old Young Guard comrade Roza Robota, who worked in the clothing *kommando*, sorting the personal belongings, clothes, and underwear of murdered Jews. Roza had a lover in the work unit known as the *sonderkommando*, made up of Jewish men who manned the crematoria and moved the corpses. He told her that his group would soon be killed. (The *sonderkommando* were periodically "retired"—that is, killed off.) The revolt, he said, was coming.

They had no weapons, but it dawned on Anna: they worked in a factory with gunpowder. Anna asked Esther, one of the few women stationed in the *Pulverraum* (powder room), to steal some. According to other accounts, it was the men who implored Roza to ask the women for the powder, and she agreed immediately.

Steal from the *Pulverraum*? The entire factory was open, transparent, constructed especially to make secrets impossible, the tables surrounded by surveillance paths. The men in charge sat in booths from where they could watch. Bathrooms, food, a pause in work—all was prohibited. Anything led to an accusation of sabotage. The *Pulverraum* was barely ten by six feet. "Impossible, ridiculous, forget it," Esther said. But she thought about it.

Despite endless surveillance, maddening thirst, sickening torture, and the threat of collective punishment, Jewish women in concentration camps revolted. When Franceska Mann, a famous Jewish ballerina and dancer at Warsaw's Melody Palace nightclub, was told to undress at Auschwitz, the young woman slung her shoe at an ogling Nazi, grabbed his gun, and shot two guards, killing one of them. A group of five hundred women who'd been given sticks and ordered to beat two girls who had stolen potato peels refused to move, despite being beaten themselves and forced to stand in the freezing cold all night without food. At Budy, a farm-based subcamp, a whole group of women attempted an organized escape. At Sobibor, women stole arms from the SS men for whom they worked and gave them to the underground.

At Auschwitz, a Belgian woman named Mala Zimetbaum, who spoke six languages, was chosen to serve as an interpreter for the SS—a job that granted her freedom of movement. She used her privileged status to help Jews: bringing medicine, connecting family members, fudging lists of incoming Jews, finding lighter work for the weak, warning hospital patients of upcoming selections, and dissuading the SS from carrying out collective punishments and even asking them to let prisoners wear socks. Mala dressed up as a male prisoner and escaped the camp on a feigned "work duty"—the first woman to flee—but was caught trying to leave Poland. As her sentence was being read, she slashed her wrists with a razor blade she'd hidden in her hair. When an SS man grabbed her, Mala slapped him across the face with her bloody hand and snarled, "I shall die a heroine, but you shall die like a dog!"

Bela Hazan was at Mala's execution. Bela continued to maintain her Polish disguise and went back to work as a nurse. After Lonka's death, she was devastated, but then one day the marching band played a song that reminded her of a comrade from Będzin. Bela began to cry. One of the musicians noticed. The two talked, and it turned out the musician, Hinda, had been part of a youth movement. Bela took the risk and came out to her as a Jew. To be known was to *be*. The two cried together, desperate to hug, and spoke of resistance. Hinda's group of Jewish girls who arrived on transports wanted to rebel, she told Bela. One obtained a tool to cut barbed wire. In the evenings, the guards were usually drunk. On a moonless night, they went to work, digging a tunnel to smuggle Jewish girls to safety. Two girls dug while four stood guard. Bela helped dig. The tunnel stretched under the barbed wire, starting where the trains arrived. Bela recalled that they once snuck in two fifteen-year-old girls from Germany. The girls were shocked when told to shut up and roll into a tunnel, but Bela was full of joy when they made it to the work camp. She tutored them on how to behave as illegals and dressed them in the clothes of dead patients. One Jewish girl who worked in the bathroom hid them there during roll calls. Bela stole potatoes and carrots to feed them. The young girls couldn't understand why a Pole would help them.

Bela continually used her position as a nurse to help sick Jews, serving them soup that contained just a little bit more cabbage, gently caressing their foreheads while giving them sips of water, and volunteering to work in the Jewish scabies section. (Everyone assumed she took on this last task for her "Communist reasons," or as she claimed, to prevent scabies from reaching the Poles and the Germans.) She warned patients before Dr. Mengele arrived for selections, and hid the sickest.

Bela knew that her kindness seemed not only strange to the Jewish prisoners but also suspicious. She, of course, understood their Yiddish mutterings about her possibly being a spy. Nevertheless, they were pleased when she granted the Jewish women who worked in the hospital permission to throw a Chanukah party. Privately, Bela was devastated that she could not attend but had to act more "Polish than the Pope." Instead, she decorated a Christmas tree with Santa Claus figurines.

One of Bela's supervisors, Arna Cook, was short, angry, and cruel. She insisted that Bela clean her room, deliver coffee, and shine her boots. One morning, Bela came in to perform her duties, and Arna did not hear her enter. Bela saw Arna lying on her bed with her legs splayed wide, having sex with her German shepherd. Bela shut the door and fled, fearing that if she'd been caught, she would have been killed.

Later, Arna beat Bela for not coming to work on time. She marched her back to Birkenau for slave labor and forced her to join a unit digging trenches—a horribly demanding task. No rest allowed, constant beatings; girls were shot if they collapsed. The others had to carry their bodies, to the tunes of the marching band.

Once, during work, SS men dragged one of the girls to the forest nearby. Bela heard her screaming. She never returned. It turned out, they'd forced her to have sex with a dog. She begged to be killed. The SS laughed. "This dog found a good subject for pleasure," Bela heard them say. This was not the only time this happened. Another Auschwitz survivor related that the Nazis forced her to undress her young daughter and watch as she was raped by dogs.

Bela and her fellow inmates became terrified of going out to work. They decided that if it happened again, the entire *kommando* would rise up. After the third incident of dog rape, when they began to drag out yet another girl, the entire unit of twenty girls screamed. The SS put them in confinement in a basement, where they were forced to stand for days and nights on end, fed only once in ninety-six hours. They left solitary physically broken but comforted by the knowledge that they'd resisted. The women banded together and protected one another.

Women in many labor camps, including Auschwitz, rebelled by sabotaging the products they were being forced to make, marring productivity or quality. They weakened hemp threads in a spinning factory, mismeasured bomb parts, dropped a wire among ball bearings, and left windows open overnight so that pipes froze. Sabotaged munitions caused German weapons to backfire and explode. Fania Fainer, a Białystok native from a Bundist family, sometimes put sand instead of gunpowder in her product at Union.

When Fania was about to turn twenty, her friend Zlatka Pitluk decided that such a landmark needed to be celebrated. Zlatka, who loved crafts, risked her life to gather materials she found in the camp and used a mix of water and bread to glue them together and create a three-dimensional birthday card in the shape of a heart—similar to an autograph book, a popular item of the day. A small object with a purple fabric cover (ripped off Zlatka's secret underblouse), the card had an *F* on the cover, embroidered in orange thread. Zlatka then passed the booklet to eighteen other women prisoners, including Anna, who wrote their birthday messages. On eight carefully constructed origami-like pages, opening into a clover, are the prisoners' wishes, written in their diverse mother tongues: Polish, Hebrew, German, French.

"Freedom, Freedom, Freedom, Wishing on the day of your birthday," wrote a woman named Mania, at the risk of being murdered.

"Not dying will be our victory," wrote another.

One woman quoted a Polish poem: "Laugh among people. . . . Be light when you dance. . . . When you're old, put on glasses, and remember what we once went through."

Camaraderie, a defiance that was intimate and even illegal, gave women hope and helped them persevere.

In the end, Esther agreed to steal the gunpowder.

Anna's sister worked twelve-hour shifts in front a machine that pressed the powder—slate gray, the consistency of coarse salt—into a checker-like piece. This part ignited the bomb.

Anna walked down the acrid-smelling, dust-filled hall, past several supervisors, and headed to the *Pulverraum*, as if she were on trash collection duty. Esther's spot was near the door; she passed Anna a small metal box, the kind used for refuse. Esther had hidden bits of gunpowder, wrapped in knotted cloth, in the garbage. (Cloth came from ripping a shirt or trading bread for a kerchief.) Anna brought the box to her table, took out the cloth packets, and slid them under her dress. She met Ala in the bathroom, where they divided the packets and hid them in their clothes. At the end of the day, Esther transferred some to her own body before marching back to camp, in wooden shoes, nearly a mile in rain, snow, or sweltering sun. If ever there was an inspection, the girls tugged open the cloth and dumped the powder on the ground, rubbing it in with their feet. Ala gave the collected powder to Roza.

It wasn't just them. A network of about thirty Jewish women aged eighteen to twenty-two stole good powder and instead used waste powder in their products. They smuggled explosives in matchboxes, and in their bosoms, between their breasts. They wrapped miniature 250-gram caches in paper and slipped them into the pockets of their coarse blue dresses. In one day, three girls could collect two teaspoons. Marta Bindiger, one of Anna's close friends and a collector, held on to stashes for several days until there was a "pickup." Four-level chains of girls, unknown to one another were involved. All of it landed with Roza, who liaised between different resistance factions.

Roza gave the powder to the men. The *sonderkommando*, who were allowed in the women's camp to remove corpses, transported the explosives in a soup bowl that had a double bottom, in apron seams, and in a wagon used for removing the bodies of Jews who had died during the night. The gunpowder parcels were hidden under their corpses, then concealed in the crematoria. A Russian prisoner made the dynamite into bombs, using empty sardine or shoe polish cans as casings. Nearby, a teenager named Kitty Felix was forced to sort murdered male prisoners' jackets and search them for valuables. She stole diamonds and gold and concealed them behind a toilet hut; they were traded for explosives.

The girls lived in fear and excitement. Then, one day, commotion. No warning, no password. The uprising, arranged meticulously over months could not go ahead as scheduled because the sonderkommando found out that they would be gassed to death immediately. It was now or never.

On October 7, 1944, the Jewish underground attacked an SS man with hammers, axes, and stones, and blew up a crematorium, where they'd placed rags soaked in oil and alcohol. They dug out hidden weapons and killed a handful of SS guards, injuring others; they threw a particularly sadistic Nazi into the oven alive. They cut through the barbed wire and ran.

But not fast enough. The Nazis shot all three hundred of them, then held a formal roll call for the dead bodies, laying each corpse out in formation. Several hundred prisoners fled during the mayhem; they too were shot and killed.

Afterward, the Nazis found the handmade grenades: tin cans filled with gunpowder that was traced to the *Pulverraum*. An intensive investigation ensued. People were taken, tortured, and there are many conflicting accounts of squealing and betrayals. According to Anna's memoirs, their barrack mate Klara was caught with bread and traded her punishment for snitching on Ala. In turn, Ala, tortured, divulged that Roza and Esther were involved. In one version, the Nazis had an undercover agent, a Czech who was half Jewish, seduce Ala with chocolates, cigarettes, and affection until she revealed names.

Esther was taken to a punishment cell. Anna was horrified and despondent. One day, she, too, was brought in for questioning and beaten as a warning. They wiped the blood off her face. The "good cop" asked, in a fatherly tone: "Who stole the gunpowder? Why? Where? What did your sister tell you?"

Anna looked at him, dumb, silent.

"Esther confessed everything," he said, "so you may as well tell us."

"How can Esther confess to anything?" Anna asked. "She is innocent, and she is not a liar." They released her and, thankfully, sent Esther back to her barrack. She was black and blue. The skin on her back was ripped into stripes. She couldn't move or talk. Marta and Anna cared for her, and she was improving.

A few days later, however, the Nazis came back for Ala, Esther, Roza, and Będziner Regina, the *Pulverraum* supervisor.

The girls were sentenced to hanging. Anna went mad; Marta admitted her to the *revier* to stop her from suiciding. She tried to make contact with her sister, tried to see her, but never managed to.

A male underground member from Roza's hometown used vodka to convince the guard of the torture bunker to let him see Roza. "I entered Roza's cell," Noah Zabludowicz recalled. "On the cold cement lay a figure like a heap of rags. At the sound of the door opening, she turned her face to me. . . . Then she spoke her last words. She told me that she had not betrayed [anyone]. She wished to tell her comrades that they had nothing to fear. We must carry on." She was not regretful, not sorry, but wanted to die knowing that the movement's actions would continue. She handed him a note for the remaining comrades. It was signed with the exhortation "*Chazak V'Amatz.*" Be strong and courageous.

Esther wrote a last letter to Anna and one to Marta, asking her to "take care of my sister so that I may die easier."

"Camp sisters" were family.

On the day of the execution, the four women were hanged, rare public ceremonies intended to terrorize the female prisoners and dissuade them from further sabotage and rebellion. Two were executed during the day shift, two during the night shift. All Jewish women prisoners were forced to watch; they were beaten if their eyes strayed for a second. Anna's friends hid her and held her down so she wouldn't have to see. But she heard. "A thud of drums," she later described the scene, "a groan from thousands of throats, and the rest was mist." Bela Hazan was there too, as the Polish nurse assigned to carry out the corpses.

In her last breath, before the noose tightened, Roza cried out in Polish: "Sisters, revenge!"

Chapter 27
The Light of Days

Renia
October 1943

Now, outside the cell at Mysłowice, a gendarme was waiting for Renia.

"You," he said.

She had lingered for so long, grasping on to the last shed of hope. She was ready. Ready to die.

"Any day now," he said slowly, deliberately. "Any day, someone is going to take you out for a new task. You'll be working in the police kitchen."

What?

Renia said nothing but shook in relief. Miraculously,

not Auschwitz after all. Not even an interrogation, but a promotion.

One month into her incarceration, Renia left Mysłowice for the first time. On the street, the normal street, headed to the police station, she searched madly for someone she might know. Anyone familiar, anyone she could tell about her imprisonment. But they were all strangers.

Renia's shift ran from four in the morning until four in the afternoon. She left her cell in a darkness that lightened into dawn, then bled into daylight. The cook, she recalled, was a gluttonous German woman, but she gave Renia good food, and Renia regained her strength. Due to daily inspections, she couldn't bring food back to her cell, but satiated from work, she gave her prison dinners to women hungrier than she was, mostly Jewish women. Others eyed her angrily.

One of the gendarmes who accompanied Renia to work treated her graciously, giving her cigarettes, apples, and buttered bread. He told her that he had lived in Poland for many years but was originally from Berlin. He became *folksdeutsch*. He was forced to divorce his Polish wife; she took their baby and fled to her parents.

"I can't tell why I believed him and trusted him,"

Renia later wrote. "I genuinely felt that he was honest and that his friendship could benefit me."

One evening, when the prisoners were asleep, Renia wrote a letter. She had to take a chance. She asked the friendly gendarme to mail it to Warsaw for her, "to my parents." She explained that since she'd been arrested, no one knew her whereabouts. He promised he'd attach a stamp and send it. Then he waved a finger at Renia, warning her not to mention this to anyone.

But from that moment, Renia could not sleep. What had she done? What if the gendarme gave it to the Gestapo? That would make her situation much more difficult. The letter, albeit coded, contained information and a few addresses; items needed to be removed from those locations. Most important, she wanted the comrades to know where she was. But with each day, as she sunk further into the vortex of the Nazi prison compound, it seemed less and less likely that anyone would find her.

Late one night, four women and a baby were brought into the cell. They were all Jewish, except for one woman, Tatiana Kuprienko, a Russian, born in Poland. Renia befriended Tatiana. Speaking in a Polish-Russian mélange, Tatiana explained that she had been hiding these Jewish women who had helped her before the war. She sheltered and fed six adults and a baby in her attic, assuming nobody knew. She hired a counterfeiter and arranged for them to get wildly expensive Polish papers, hoping they could find work in Germany. Most of the women were hesitant to part from their husbands, whose features were too Jewish, but one woman left for Germany and had written to say that she'd found a job.

"Two and half months later, the police arrived at my house with a seventeen-year-old Polish boy," Tatiana continued. "Before I could say a word, the boy told the police that I was hiding Jews. We were all arrested. My two brothers and the counterfeiter too. I still don't know how they knew about the attic, the fake papers, the woman in Germany, even the counterfeiter's fee. Before taking my testimony, they read aloud what they knew; everything was true." At the police station, Tatiana was beaten. The Gestapo told her she was lucky to be Russian; otherwise, she'd have been hanged. They kept threatening to kill her or lock her up for life.

Two days later, the Jewish women and their husbands were transported to Auschwitz. Two days after that, the Jewish woman who had left for Germany was brought in, in a state of utter despair. Sure that she'd survive by spending the rest of the war working for a peasant near Berlin, she'd suddenly been arrested.

After interrogation, she was carried back to the cell on a stretcher, disfigured to the point that Renia hardly recognized her. Large pieces of flesh were torn off her body. The Nazis had gagged her mouth, then pounded her feet with metal rods, and pierced her skin with a hot iron. Despite this torture, the Jewish woman didn't disclose the name of the counterfeiter or that she knew Tatiana. The Nazis used similar methods to abuse Tatiana.

One day, when she was in better spirits, Tatiana told Renia, "After all I've been through, I have a feeling I'll be freed one day. I must live to take care of my mother. I have a wealthy brother-in-law in Warsaw; maybe he'll bail me out."

Renia smiled, assuming she had gone insane from all the beating.

A few days later, Tatiana's name was called. She went pale—another interrogation. It would be her end. She exited the cell and was taken by the Gestapo.

But a few minutes later, Renia heard maniacal laughter. Tatiana returned, kissed every one of them, and told them she'd been freed. She was going home!

When she came over to kiss Renia, she whispered in her ear that, indeed, her brother-in-law had paid a half kilogram of gold for her.

Renia's eyes lit up. If it was possible to bribe the Gestapo, even here at Mysłowice, maybe there was hope.

One afternoon a taxi arrived at the camp gate. Two men in civilian clothes got out, presented papers that said they were undercover Gestapo men, and headed to the men's ward, to the most terrible of cells, where living shadows were chained to their beds. The plainclothed Gestapo called out the names of two young men who'd been convicted of leading a partisan gang. They unchained them and hauled them to a waiting car that quickly disappeared. The guards saw the Gestapo carrying the prisoners, which was never done, became suspicious, and just after the taxi left, notified the Gestapo in Katowice. It turned out that the two "plainclothed Gestapo" were partisans who'd used fake papers. All four men had disappeared. Free.

Renia was simply elated. "That incident awoke my passion for life and my faith in freedom," she recalled. "Who knows, maybe a miracle could happen to me, too."

The prison overlords, however, were furious. The guards were imprisoned. Discipline was tightened, cases reopened. Suddenly one morning, Renia was told she was not going to work. Instead, she was hit and locked in a dark cell, allegedly as punishment for her lie that she'd simply stolen across the border. Now they suspected her of espionage. The beating left a permanent scar etched on her forehead.

Renia was moved to a cell for female political prisoners. No one here went out to work. Every few days, a Gestapo committee arrived to examine them, like cattle in the market. There was no hope of getting out.

By chance, Renia learned from a woman from Katowice that Ilza had confessed to being Jewish and was hanged. Her heart broke into a million pieces, but she didn't twitch a muscle. "Even if I was stabbed with a knife, I could not break."

Day and night, Renia contemplated the fate of her comrades. She felt like her memory was fading, as if she were going mad. She couldn't concentrate. She couldn't remember her testimony. She wasn't sure she could trust herself if they decided to interrogate her again. She had a constant headache. She was very weak, could barely stand. It was forbidden for the prisoners to lie on their beds during the day, but the key keeper pitied her and allowed her to perch on her cot. She jumped up whenever she heard the supervisor's jangle, so no one could see her, sitting idle, haunted by Ilza's young face.

She had been so close to freedom.

Chapter 28
The Great Escape

Renia and Gusta
November 1943

"This is for you," a woman whispered, handing Renia a note. "It was given to me while working in the field." Renia, on her way to the toilet, was startled. "The woman is coming tomorrow to get an answer and deliver a food package."

Renia's hands shook as she took the paper. Could it be? She clutched it the entire day.

Finally, at night, when everyone around her was asleep, Renia opened her treasure, devouring each word. Was it for real? The handwriting did look like Sarah's.

Her sister wrote that everyone was still alive. The comrades had found places to hide in Poles' homes. She had learned of Renia's fate from the letter that Zivia received in Warsaw. The gendarme had really sent it! Now Sarah wanted to know how they could help. The comrades would do anything to get her out. "Don't be discouraged," she counseled.

Renia reread the note dozens of times.

Thinking, planning, scheming.

Renia checked that everyone was still asleep. It was past midnight.

She snuck out of bed and padded over to the monitor's desk. As quietly as possible, she fumbled in the dark for a pencil. And found one!

Sarah, always prepared, had included a piece of paper for her reply.

Renia tiptoed back to her bed and wrote:

"First, you must pay the woman who carried the note generously, since she risked her life. Second, would it be possible to pay her to trade places with me, so I could go out to the field? Then we can meet and decide what to do."

In the morning, in the bathroom, Renia slipped the page to the woman, Belitkova, and arranged to meet her there again that night.

All day, whenever she could, Renia kept rereading Sarah's letter: "We will do anything to get you out of there. Zivia sent a person with money." Her friends were safe.

That very evening, another note arrived:

"Everything will be ok. After much persuasion, Belitkova agreed to let you go to the field in her place. She'll be paid with valuables and plenty of money. I'll send the goods to her house today. She's poor and happy for cash."

The next day, Renia quickly changed into Belitkova's dress and moved to her cell; Belitkova would attend roll call in Renia's place. It was a cold November morning, and Renia wrapped her face in all the rags she could find. Luckily, none of the guards knew her.

She arrived at the square with Belitkova's work group, meeting Russian, French, and Italian prisoners—so many people. They all got to work, carrying bricks onto a train car. Despite the relative ease of the task, Renia was still too weak to do it. Each brick she lifted fell to the ground, attracting stares. She was so impatient. When will Sarah arrive? Every second was an eternity.

Then, from a distance, Renia made out two well-dressed, elegant ladies—one of them with Sarah's assured gait. She saw her sister examining the surrounds. *She probably doesn't even recognize me.* Renia started to walk over. The women prisoners watched, puzzled: Who was this Warsaw girl, with no local relations, heading to talk to?

"They're acquaintances of a cell mate," Renia lied, attempting nonchalance, and made her way to the gate.

The chief guard walked right behind Renia. He didn't know her and, thankfully, did not know of her political prisoner history. Renia approached the wall, and despite the guard on her heels, the sisters could not hold back their tears. It was really her. Sarah handed the guard pastries, while Renia talked to the other girl, Halina. Zivia had sent her from Warsaw, and Renia could tell why. "It doesn't matter if you fail," Halina said, her green eyes locked on to Renia's face. "You must try to get out. Your life is in danger anyways."

They arranged to meet at that same spot the following week. The girls would bring clothes for Renia to change into. She needed to prepare to escape.

Renia couldn't stand at the wall for long without looking suspicious. She was shaken by emotion as she watched her sister and Halina walk off and disappear, feeling a resolve that hadn't been stirred in a long time. She repeated Halina's words in her mind: *You must try.*

But as soon as Renia returned from work, she collapsed. Her skull throbbed. She could not stand up. Her meeting with Sarah had triggered something in her head, she wrote later. Medicine didn't help. Her fever spiked to 104 degrees for three days straight. In her haze, she began to babble, a real threat. What if she spoke Yiddish? What if she revealed her truth? A few cellmates pitied Renia and offered her their breakfast bread, but she couldn't swallow a bite. She would miss her chance. She would die.

When finally, her fever miraculously subsided, Renia's fellow prisoners held a special Sunday prayer to thank God for her recovery. Renia, truly grateful, got up to join them, kneeling and praying intently, as she'd learned to do.

But in the midst of recitation, a hot flash. Renia fainted. The door was locked, and the women could not get any water. They splashed her with the dirty liquid used to wash their bowls.

Renia revived but lay in bed for another two days. How could this happen?

She had to get up, she had to get well. She had to. *You must try.*

"November 12, 1943. A date etched in my memory," Renia wrote in her memoirs. After a sleepless night, she was the first to jump out of bed. Today was it.

"No," the cell monitor suddenly told her. "You can't go to the fields today."

What? "Why not? You let me go last week." Belitkova had agreed once again to swap places, for a large sum.

"It's too risky. What if the camp chief realizes you are from the political prisoner's cell? We'll all be in trouble."

"Please," Renia pleaded. That was all she had left. "Please, I beg you."

The cell monitor grunted and let her out. The small miracles were endless.

Dressed in Belitkova's clothes and covered in kerchiefs, Renia left. The supervisor didn't recognize her. She was held upright by women on her right and left so that she didn't collapse; it took so many women to help her live. At last, they arrived at the square. Fifteen women, five guards. Renia arranged the bricks and looked around, searching for Sarah and Halina. Nowhere.

Ten in the morning. They arrived! Renia scanned around her: everyone was engaged with her own bricks, her own burdens. All clear. She swiftly left the work site.

But before she reached the girls, the head guard was next to her, yelling. "How dare you leave work without my permission!"

Sarah tried to appease him, flirting, pleading.

"Come back at two with cigarettes and liquor," Renia murmured to Halina.

The workers were angry with Renia for disobeying the head guard—she was putting everyone at risk.

Renia went back to the bricks, calm for now. Then, just before lunch, a guard called her over. "So you're a political prisoner," he said, to her horror. "You're very young, and I feel sorry for you. Otherwise, I would have informed the camp commander.'"

He wagged his finger in Renia's face and told her not to even think about trying to escape. They would cut her into pieces.

"There's no chance I'd escape," Renia answered. "I'm smart enough to know that I'd be caught. I was arrested for stealing across the border; I'll probably be released soon. Why would I spoil my chances?"

Renia assumed that the women had told the head guard her secret. No wonder: if Renia escaped, they'd all suffer. Everyone was extracautious since the partisan jailbreak.

All this made escaping even more difficult. Everyone was watching her: the guards and her fellow prisoners.

But Renia also knew that her cover was up. They knew she was a "political." She was doomed either way.

Where were Sarah and Halina? Renia was not wearing a watch—of course, it had been taken—but it felt like hours since they'd left. What if something happened? What if they didn't return? Could she jet on her own?

Finally, two silhouettes in the distance.

This time Renia played aggressive. "Come with me, please," she asked the head guard. He followed.

Three Jewish girls and the Nazi stood behind the wall of a bombed building.

Halina passed the guard several bottles of whiskey. He gulped down an entire flask while they stuffed his pockets with cigarettes. Renia picked up a few small bottles of liquor and packs of cigarettes and wrapped them in her kerchief. She distributed them to the watchmen and asked them to stop the other women from going behind the wall. Her acquaintances had brought her hot soup, she told them, and she didn't want to share it. The watchmen weren't too concerned, as they knew the head guard had his eye on her.

By now, the head guard was completely intoxicated. Renia needed to figure out how to handle him. "Why don't you go see if any of the women are looking in our direction?" she suggested. He stumbled off.

Now was her time. Now or never.

Renia was not the only Jewish female operative to attempt a jailbreak.

After the Kraków bombings, Shimshon Draenger had gone missing; Gusta went to every police station until she found him, then refused to leave his side. For the second time, his wife adhered to their marital pact and handed herself in.

Gusta was incarcerated at Helzlow, the woman's section of Montelupich Prison. Perched in the center of the beautiful old town, Montelupich was another horrific Gestapo jail priding itself on its use of medieval torture. After beating Gusta badly, the Nazis brought her to her husband, hoping to use her wounds to get a confession out of him. Instead, Gusta told them, "We did it. We organized fighting groups. And if we get out of here, we'll organize even stronger ones."

Gusta was placed in the large, lightless "cell 15" with fifty women, including several Jewish underground operatives. She organized a daily routine for her fellow prisoners: as long as water was available, she made them wash and brush their hair and clean their table, all to maintain hygiene and humanity. She initiated regular discussions of philosophy, history, literature, and the Bible. They celebrated Oneg Shabbat. They recited poems and composed new ones. And when a group was taken out to be shot, those remaining shared their grief in song.

Gola Mire, caught by Nazis in the Polish resistance's printing office, was also brought into the cell, setting off a period of "spiritual elevation" and "sisterhood." Gola constantly wrote Yiddish and Hebrew poetry, often dedicating her work to her husband and dead child. Beaten brutally in frequent interrogations, her body was gray, her fingernails ripped off, her hair torn out, her eyes temporarily blinded. But upon returning to the cell, she'd pick up her pencil, then recite her poems to her cellmates.

Gusta, too, wrote her memoirs between beatings. She placed herself in a corner, surrounded by a group of Jewish women, hiding her activity from the other prisoners, some of whom were not entirely trustworthy criminals. On triangular pieces of toilet paper sewn together with thread from the girls' skirts, with pencils donated by Polish women who had secretly received them in food packages, and with fingers crushed in torture, Gusta composed the story of the Kraków resistance. Everyone was given a fake name for security, and she wrote about herself—"Justyna," her underground code name—in the third person.

Much of the material came from the perspectives of others, especially Shimshon's and her cellmates', all of whom contributed. For security, Gusta included only past events that were already known to the Gestapo. She wrote until she became too tired and pained, then passed on the pencil, dictating as cell mates took turns transcribing, all the while maintaining her unique literary and introspective tone, providing psychological portraits of the fighters, hiders, and even enemies. To cover up her voice, women would sing; others would watch for the guard. Gusta checked every page, revising at least ten times, insisting on accuracy. Enchanted by the fantasy that their story might one day be told, the women wrote four copies of the diary simultaneously. Three copies were hidden in the prison—in the stove, in door upholstery, and under the floorboards—and one was smuggled out by Jewish auto mechanics who worked for the Gestapo (and who also brought Gusta pencils and additional toilet paper). After the war, text scraps that had been hidden under the cell floor were found.

On April 29, 1943, Gusta and her comrades, who had been planning an escape, knew that they would be on the next transport to death and, like Renia, decided it was now or never. While they were being led outside to the transport truck, right on the crowded city street, Gusta, Gola, their comrade Genia Meltzer, and a few others suddenly halted and refused to move. The

Gestapo guards were confused. One took out his gun. Genia sprinted behind him and pushed his arm up into the air.

In that moment, the girls fled, making their way around a horse and buggy. The Gestapo shot at them in the crowded streets as they searched for cover.

Only Gusta and Genia survived. Genia hid behind a door; Gusta was wounded in the leg.

Unbeknownst to the women, Shimshon had also broken out of jail that day. He and Gusta met up in a small town outside Kraków where several Akiva members were hiding. They resumed forest fighting, organizing fighting groups, and writing and distributing underground bulletins. A few months later, around the time of Renia's imprisonment, Shimshon was captured again while arranging for them to be smuggled to Hungary; he told the Gestapo to go get his wife. The Nazis arrived at Gusta's hiding place with a note from him, and she gave herself up right away. Three times unlucky. Both were killed.

In a flash, the girls helped Renia put on a new dress, shawl, and shoes.

Sarah and Renia faced one direction, Halina the other.

If they were destined to fail, Renia did not want Halina to fail with them.

Then they ran, fast as ever, out of breath, panting.

The sisters came to a hill—Renia could not climb it. There was no way, no way.

But another miracle: an Italian prisoner passed them. "Here." He held out his hand and helped Renia ascend.

She barely made it over the barbed wire fence surrounding the square. The girls landed in the street, open air. This was the most dangerous part of the escape and the most crucial moment of her life. They didn't know the way; they went straight. Renia's dress was caked in mud from climbing, but she continued to run, drawing on an impossible energy. Faster, faster. Renia turned back to make sure that no one was after them. The wind cooled her sweaty body and face. She felt her mother and father's presence, as if they were right there, protecting her.

A car approached.

Sarah cupped her head in her hands. "They got us! We're doomed."

But the car drove on.

Sarah shouted, "Renia, faster! This is it. If we make it, we'll both stay alive."

With every passing minute, Renia became weaker. She tried and tried, but her legs were failing. She fell on the road. Sarah picked her up. She was in tears. "Renia," she pleaded. "Please keep going. If not, it will be the end for us both. Make the effort. I have no one but you. I can't lose you. Please."

Her tears landed on her sister's face, reviving her. Renia stood, paused. They moved on.

But Renia gasped for air. Her lips were dry. She couldn't feel her arms, as if she'd had a stroke. Her legs were gummy, buckling under her.

Every time they heard the sound of a passing bus, their hearts stalled. Passersby slowed down to look at them, probably thinking they were insane.

Another bus stopped on the road near them. Renia was sure this was it. How would they make it? The Gestapo could trap them so easily, at any moment. The sisters were wearing muddy rags, their shoes covered in dirt, so incredibly suspect.

The bus passed.

Sarah walked a hundred feet ahead, Renia dragged behind. How strange it felt to walk alone, unaccompanied by a guard. Slowly the two of them approached Katowice. They'd covered four miles.

Sarah wiped Renia's face with her saliva and kerchief, and removed the mud and debris from her jacket.

She was beaming with happiness. She knew a German woman who lived nearby. Nacha Schulman, Meir's wife, was disguised as a Catholic and worked for her as a seamstress. They couldn't take the tram, in case a gendarme recognized them, but it wasn't too far. Only another four miles to go.

Renia walked slowly, step by step, on the side of the road. Then: a group of gendarmes in the distance.

The uniforms. Renia shivered. It was too late for them to turn around.

The men approached, observed the girls . . . and moved on.

Renia forced herself forward. She needed to pause every two or three steps. Her breath was heavy, hot.

"There's not far left to go," Sarah encouraged. She would have carried Renia if she could have.

Renia wobbled like a drunk. Sarah pulled her forward. Their clothes were drenched with sweat.

Renia made the effort—for her sister.

At last, they approached the first buildings outside the town of Siemianowice. Renia could not go more than two steps without stopping to lean against a wall. She ignored passersby; her vision was so blurry, she could barely see them.

Renia stopped at a well in someone's yard, splashed water on her face. *Wake up.*

The sisters walked through the town, Renia using all her strength to stay upright, to be inconspicuous. They crossed from alley to alley until they reached a small street. Sarah pointed at a two-storey building. "This is it."

Sarah then bent down and picked up her tiny sister, carrying Renia up the stairs like a bride. "I don't know where she found the strength," Renia later wrote. The door opened, but before Renia could even see inside, she fainted.

When she came to, Renia took a pill, but her fever persisted. She peeled off her filthy rags and got into a clean bed—a pleasure she wasn't sure she'd ever have again. Her teeth chattered and her bones felt hollow even under the blankets; spasms of cold shook her.

Sarah and Nacha sat by her side, crying. Nacha hadn't recognized Renia at all. But Sarah comforted them both. "Forget everything. What's important is that you're free."

But where was Halina?

Sarah told the German lady of the house that Renia was a friend of hers who was ill and needed to rest. But Renia could not stay there. The usual refrain.

That night, somehow, Renia was back on her feet. Two and half miles to Michalkowice. At least the darkness would help conceal their limping and loping.

They reached the village at eleven o'clock and headed to the house of Polish peasants. Mr. and Mrs. Kobiletz greeted them warmly. They'd heard of Renia and were full of praise for Sarah's skills. They offered Renia food, but she couldn't stay in the main room for long—she was there to enter the bunker. She slipped through a window underneath the stairs to the basement. It was so small that even emaciated Renia could barely fit through. Then she climbed down the ladder. Twenty comrades greeted her with joy, "as if I was just born."

They wanted to know everything, right away.

She was too weak and had to lie down, but Sarah told them the tale of her escape. Her head was spinning, as was her heart. She was here, with her comrades, her sister, and, for a moment, safe.

Renia observed everyone in the bunker as they listened. She was still burning up with fever, still felt as if she were in prison, still felt like she was being chased. Would that feeling ever leave her?

A few hours later, Halina arrived and regaled them with her story:

"As I started walking away from you, I turned my jacket inside out and took off my kerchief. Ahead of me, I saw a railroad worker. I asked him if he cared to join me as we walked. He took one look at me and said, 'Happily.' I held his arm, and we strolled and chatted about this and that. He probably thought I was a prostitute. Within ten minutes, we came across two guards who were maniacally running toward the camp. They asked if we'd seen three women escaping and described our clothes. I took such joy seeing them scramble. I continued talking to the railroad worker, as if nothing had happened. The worker accompanied me to the tram. We said we'd get together tomorrow!"

The next morning, Halina, in good spirits, left for Warsaw. A week later, they received a letter from her. Her journey had been uneventful. She'd crossed the border by foot. She was happy to have taken part in Renia's escape. A touching letter came from Marek Folman's mother and another from Zivia, Antek and Rivka Moscovitch, who had healed and was working as a courier, smuggling weapons and bringing aid to those in hiding—the trio were so happy that she'd gotten out.

Marek, on the other hand, met a less fortunate end. After he left Będzin for Warsaw, crippled with guilt about the Socha setup, he was so distraught that Nazis noticed him when he switched trains at Częstochowa. He was shot on the spot.

Day in, day out, Renia sat in the Kobiletz bunker, which had been built by Meir Schulman. Meir had been friends with the Kobiletz's eldest son, Mitek, before the war. Mitek had worked for the Gestapo in Kraków but had been in contact with the ghetto Jews. When one of his friends got drunk and spilled his secret, Mitek jumped on his motorcycle and fled. Meir learned that Mitek had been paid to arrange for Jews to stay with his friends in the city of Bielsko. That's when Meir got the idea to ask him to let Meir build a bunker underneath his parents' house. At first, Mr. Kobiletz refused, but his son's pleas convinced him, especially when he told his father that he could use it to hide from the Gestapo himself.

A few Jews hid in their small attic until the bunker was built. Meir had to construct it at night so that the neighbors wouldn't notice. In Renia's memoirs, she wrote that Kobiletz was paid a fortune to hide them. "He said he did it out of pity, but in fact, he did it for profit." Other accounts suggest that though the Kobiletzes took payment, they were motivated by anti-German politics and compassion. The question of whether Poles who received payment for helping Jews should be considered "righteous" remains a heated one.

Renia was secure and free—relatively—but life in the Kobiletz bunker was not a permanent solution. The shelter had been built to house two or three people, but more ghetto escapees kept arriving. People slept together on a few beds. Food was purchased with counterfeit ration tickets collected every few days by one of the girls, who risked her life to travel to the village of Jablonka. Lunch was prepared by Mrs. Kobiletz. At first, the comrades used their own money from the ghetto to pay for all this, but later, Halina brought additional funds from Zivia.

Alongside the stuffiness, the people in the bunker lived in constant fear of the neighbors finding out. So did the Kobiletzes, who would also be executed if caught.

A few days after Renia arrived, she climbed back up the ladder at midnight and was transferred to a hiding place at the home of the Kobiletzes' daughter, Banasikova. The move was uplifting. She was now with Dror comrades Chawka, the medic, and Aliza, who'd cared for the orphans. The door was locked at all times, so the neighbors knew nothing. If anyone knocked, they hid in the closet. Banasikova took care of all their needs. Her husband was in the army and barely earned a living wage, so she appreciated the money and goods she received for hiding people.

There were still a few hundred people scattered in the Będzin liquidation camp and local ghettos, a population dwindling with each transport. Sarah, Chawka, Kasia, Dorka—all the girls with non-Jewish features—continued to sneak in and try to save as many as possible, even though it was nearly impossible to find hiding places. Renia, though, was still too weak to go outside.

They all knew that the only way out of their suffocating lives was via Slovakia, where, for the time being, Jews had relative freedom. But to transfer comrades there, they needed connections. It took many attempts until they received an address from The Hague. But how would they get there? After having been betrayed so cruelly by Socha, the group was particularly cautious. The Zionist Youth group, Renia wrote, would not divulge who its smugglers were. Mitek tried to arrange for smugglers, but as always, this was no easy task. The Kobiletzes were becoming increasingly afraid for their lives and, despite the payments, were urging the group to leave. Yet another ticking time bomb.

Renia and the group were in constant contact with Warsaw. Zivia and Antek also urged them to go to Slovakia, though they offered to bring Renia to Warsaw, where it might be safer. But Renia didn't want to separate from her comrades. "Their fate is mine."

At last, Mitek found legitimate smugglers. They would send one group first, and if they made it, the rest would follow.

That first group left in early December. They dressed up as Poles and carried fake travel documents and work papers. The smuggler took them by train from Katowice to Bielsko, and then Jelesnia, the border town. The others sat in their bunkers, thinking and talking obsessively about the mortal danger they faced.

A week later the smuggler returned.

It had been a success! Their friends were already in Slovakia. This time they did write to the group, telling them that the journey was less difficult than they'd anticipated. "Do not," they warned, "wait any longer."

December 20, 1943: Aliza and Renia waited all day for Chawka or Sarah to arrive and tell them who would leave with the second group. At midnight, a knock on the door. Everyone jolted awake. The police?

A few nerve-wracking moments later, Chawka entered.

She turned to Renia. "Get ready for the journey." Eight people would leave in the morning. Renia would be one of them.

Fight or flight.

Renia refused.

This was not for ideology, but for love. Sarah had been on missions helping the Atid children who'd been smuggled to Germany, and Renia hadn't seen her in two weeks. She didn't want to leave without her sister's knowledge—certainly not without saying good-bye. "She's my sister," she told Chawka. "She risked her life during my prison escape. I can't go without her consent."

But Chawka and Aliza tried to convince her. The Gestapo was after Renia: "Wanted" posters showing her face, calling her a spy, and offering a cash reward hung on the streets. She needed to leave right away. Sarah would understand, they told her, and would follow soon. Sarah and Aliza had to gather the Atid children who'd been dispersed among German peasants' houses. Aliza promised that she, Sarah, and the children would join the very next group to Slovakia.

After an entire night of persuasion, Renia relented.

The train from Katowice left at six in the morning. Renia put her hair up in a new style and wore fresh clothes, all so that she wouldn't be recognized by the Gestapo or the police. "Only my face is the same." She took nothing but the clothes on her back.

Banasikova said good-bye with great compassion, asking only to be remembered after the war. Parting from Aliza was painful. Who knew who would make it?

At five thirty on a cold December morning, Renia and Chawka felt their way through a pitch-black field. They spoke quietly in German so as not to catch the attention of passersby hurrying to work in the mines. At the Michałkowice station, they met Mitek, who was to accompany them to Bielsko, as well the other six people who would flee with them—including Chajka Klinger.

Chajka had escaped from the liquidation camp, where entrances and exits were not highly supervised and the guards were easily bribed. At first, she hid with Meir at the Novaks but claimed Mrs. Novak became too nervous and greedy. She then went into hiding at various Kobiletz family locations, where she wrote the bulk of her diaries. Other comrades around Będzin were placed in barns and dovecots, but because of Chajka's assignment to chronicle their story, she was given larger, more comfortable *melinas*.

Chajka had initially resisted her documentarian role, but with so many comrades dead, she accepted her calling. It was terrifically difficult for her to write, to revisit her pain continually, while her comrades got to focus on day-to-day living. She had not heard music for four years, and now the sounds of German songs emanating from a radio reminded her of everyone who had been killed—of all that had been taken from her. Chajka, who had not cried when Zvi died, nor while being beaten, now wailed. *David.* Had she done enough? Her guilt over not saving her own family was so overwhelming that she could not write about them.

A depression lodged itself in her bones.

Now Renia, Chajka, Chawka, and the group took the train from Michałkowice to Katowice, where, despite the early hour, they met heavy traffic. Renia walked confidently along the platform with Mitek. Every time they saw a police or Gestapo man, they stepped aside, blended into the crowd. Mitek joked, "How great it would be if we were caught together—me, a former political instructor for the Gestapo and fugitive, and you, a suspected spy who escaped from jail!"

Suddenly three Gestapo men approached. Renia recognized them from Mysłowice; they'd seen her while she stood in formation. *Think fast.* Renia lowered her hat and covered her face with her kerchief, pretending she had a toothache.

The men walked away.

Within a few minutes, the group was all aboard the train car, en route from Katowice to Bielsko. For Renia, who risked being recognized in this area, this was the most dangerous leg of the entire journey. But the ride was seamless. Nobody asked to see their papers; no one even inspected their bags.

In Bielsko, smugglers waited for them. They bought tickets to Jelesnia, the station closest to the Slovak border, where they arrived that evening. Mitek parted from them as if he were a close relative. "Please," he pleaded, "do not forget what I've done for you." Mitek promised to join them in Slovakia after helping the remaining comrades get out. He told the smugglers to take care of the Jews. The comrades quickly jotted messages to those staying behind. Renia composed a "Hurry up and meet me" letter to her sister and Aliza. Mitek took the pages, folded them up, and got back on the train.

The escapees spent a few hours resting at one of the smuggler's houses, preparing for their trek through the Tatra Mountains. The rest of the way was by foot.

Then it was time. They stealthily exited the small village: eight comrades, two smugglers, two guides. In the distance they saw snow-covered mountains rising to the sky. The border. The goal.

The first few miles were flat. Their world was all white, but the snow was shallow. "The night was so bright it felt like morning," Renia wrote.

She was wearing nothing but a dress—no jacket—but she didn't feel the cold.

Then they reached the mountains. Walking became more difficult. The group progressed single file, stepping as fast as they could. The snow was knee deep, and where it wasn't, they slipped and slid. Every moving branch startled them—could it be police?

The guides knew the route well. One of them led, the other and the smugglers helped the comrades. It was blustering, which was actually helpful, as the sound muffled the crunch of their footsteps. But the walking became harder and harder. Without coats or boots, they climbed toward the peak, 6,233 feet—more than a mile high. Once in a while, they stopped to catch their breath, lying on the snow as if on a bed of feathers. Despite the cold, their sweaty clothes clung to their skin.

The group entered a forest; they toppled over like toddlers learning to walk. They were amazed by little Muniosh from the Atid kibbutz: Brown hair, pale skin, pointy ears, he was all grit, leading the line, mocking the rest of them for their substandard hiking skills.

Suddenly, in the distance, they saw black spots against the snow: border patrol.

They lay down, covering themselves in snow, until the officers passed.

Renia, wet, barely dressed, was still so weak from prison. She could hardly breathe in this altitude. *I'm not going to make it.*

The smugglers helped, walking her along like a child. She remembered her escape from Mysłowice; if she could make it out of there alive, she could make it now too. *Push.*

Slowly, quietly, the group carefully passed the border patrol building and approached the summit. Exhausted, they had to pick up the pace. They stumbled on each step, sinking into the snow. But this was the last leg of the trek, and they managed to find a miraculous second wind. *Flight.*

After six hours of torturous hiking, they found themselves in Slovakia.

Their most incredible crossing yet.

Renia had left Poland.

Now, for the rest of the world.

Chapter 29

"Zag nit keyn mol az du geyst dem letstn veg"

Never say the final journey is at hand
Never say we will not meet the Promised Land,
The longed-for hour shall come, oh never fear.
Our tread drums forth the tidings—we are here!

—From *"The Partisan Song,"* by Hirsh Glick, written
in Yiddish in the Vilna ghetto

Renia
December 1943

Slovakia, a state newly formed on the eve of World War II, was no Jewish paradise. The country, whose ruler was an outspoken antisemite, was aligned with the Axis nations and became a Hitler satellite. The majority of Slovakia's Jews had been deported to death camps in Poland in 1942. After that, there was a pause in deportations that lasted until August 1944. In those two years, Jews lived in relative security, either protected by papers or pretending to be Christian, or because of political pressure and bribes.

This period of calm can be credited partly to resistance leader Gisi Fleischmann. Born to a bourgeois, orthodox Jewish family, she, like most Slovakian Jews, did not speak Slovak or fit in with the country's new national consciousness. Gisi joined the Zionists early on. In the capital Bratislava, she was president of the Women's International Zionist Organization (WIZO) before taking on several public leadership roles. (In the much larger Poland, even the left-wing groups had no women in public positions. Gisi was unique.) By 1938, she ran an agency that aided German Jewish refugees, then became head of Slovakia's JDC. International money was funneled from a Swiss account to her.

At the outbreak of war, Gisi, then in her late thirties, was in London trying to arrange for large-scale Jewish immigration to Palestine. Her efforts were not successful, and though colleagues encouraged her to stay in England, she insisted on returning home, feeling obligations to her sickly mother and husband, and her community. She sent her two teenage daughters to Palestine for safety.

In wartime, Gisi was a Jewish community leader, insisting on joining the Judenrat leadership (the rare woman to do so) in order to help her people; she maintained contact with numerous international leaders, telling them what was going on. Slovakia had promised to send its people to German work camps, but the Slovak government struck a deal with the Nazis, asking them to deport their Jews instead. Slovakia was the only European country that formally requested that the Nazis take their Jewish citizens.

At first, the Nazis wanted to take only twenty thousand Jews to help build Auschwitz, but Slovakia pleaded with them to take more. In fact, the Slovak government paid the Nazis 500 marks for each additional Jew—yet another way the Nazis made money off their Final Solution. Hoping that money could sway the Nazis further, Gisi really got to work, negotiating with Germans and the Slovak government, eventually collecting funds and offering bribes to the Nazis to reduce the number of Jewish deportees. She set up work camps for Jews in Slovakia to save them from being taken to Poland. When several of her interventions seemed to work—though it's possible the reduced deportations occurred for other political reasons—she promoted the Europa Plan, an attempt to bribe the Germans to curb Jewish transportations and murders all across Europe.

Always active, Gisi sent medication and money to Polish Jews via paid emissaries. She was also instrumental in collecting international funds to help smuggle in Jews, known as "hikers," on an underground railroad from Poland—like the one Renia had taken.

In this new country, Renia and her hiker comrades descended the mountain into a valley. In the distance, a bonfire. Goods traffickers on a break. The comrades stopped at the spot where they were supposed to meet their local guides and started their own fire.

Now they felt the cold.

Their feet were wet and in danger of freezing. They dried off their shoes and socks in the blaze. Then they heard heavy footsteps in the snow. But it was only the Slovak smugglers, bringing liquor to warm up everyone. The comrades rested for an hour, and their original guides parted from them caringly, returning to Bielsko to bring over more groups. The guides too, Renia wrote later, were paid a large sum of money per person. Mountain people were poor, and this was how they made a living.

The comrades could barely put on their shrunken shoes, but they had to continue.

They walked with the Slovaks, trying to make conversation. Passing mountains, hills, valleys, and forests, they approached a sleepy village. A dog's bark welcomed them. They were led into a stable with horses, cows, pigs, and chickens. The only light came from a small oil lamp, and the stench of manure was unbearable, but they couldn't enter the house, for fear the neighbors would see.

Despite the cold, it was hot inside. Fatigue set in. Everyone dropped onto bales of hay. Renia's legs were so weak, she was unable to straighten them. She curled up and fell into a deep sleep.

At noon, the landlady, dressed in traditional mountain garb—a kerchief and colorful dress with felt shoes connected to a garter by white laces—woke the comrades with lunch. It was Sunday. She told them to stay put, as the villagers were all on their way to church. They needed to be careful. These days, everyone was spying on their neighbors; everyone was suspect. Of course, for them, nothing new.

After eating, Renia slept some more, lying next to her comrades on the hay like packed sardines. Rays of sun entered through a small window. The Jews started talking and—for the first time—recounting the events of the past months and years. On the threshold of safety, they began to fully realize all that they had lost.

Their happiness at having crossed the border was muted by fear of the future. Their trek was not over; neither was the war. At night, a sleigh arrived. The comrades hopped on and rode to the next village via small side roads and empty fields, away from police. A few hours later, they reached a town and were placed in a single room in a peasant's home and told not to leave until their car arrived. There was plenty of food here, as long as one had the money to buy it, and, fortunately, the comrades each had a bit of cash. The household head—an honest, compassionate person, Renia felt, who spoke of the Germans with great hatred—went out to buy them provisions. It turned out that the first group had been there a few days earlier. After feasting, the comrades slept some more.

That night, a car waited for them on the outskirts of the village. The driver was a customs clerk—he'd been bribed. He asked them questions about the Jews in Poland.

Suddenly he stopped the car.

What now? Dark, the middle of nowhere. They were completely vulnerable.

The driver got out, went to the backseat. Everyone clenched.

"Don't worry, I won't hurt you," he said.

To Renia's surprise, he hugged little Muniosh.

Then he asked each of them about their relatives. He could not believe that they were the sole survivors of their families. He was incensed by their stories of German atrocities.

The driver took them through Slovak towns and villages. It was dark, but here and there, they saw a glimmer of light from a window that wasn't properly blacked out, as was the law. The driver told them that he was taking them to Mikuláš, a town with a Jewish community that would take care of them. Renia was in awe of how well planned the whole operation was, everything arranged to the smallest detail.

In Mikuláš, the car stopped at the community center. The driver fetched a Jewish person, who took them to an inn. There they met Max Fischer, looking all dark haired and dashing. Max relayed that the rest of the first group was already in Hungary, from where they hoped to make legal aliyah to Palestine. Suddenly Renia felt like a bird released from a cage, finally able to untuck her wings.

The Mikuláš Jews were happy about their escape, but no one offered to host them, for fear of police raids. The comrades were put in a school auditorium set up for refugees. As far as the police were concerned, the shelter housed only people who had been caught by border patrol and were waiting for the authorities to look into their cases; when a few found out about the additional refugees, they shook them down for bribes. Here, Renia learned quickly, you could get anything from the cops for the right amount of money. The large room had beds, a table, a long bench, and a heater. Food was available for purchase from a special kitchen set up by refugees themselves. The comrades were to wait here for a few days until the next group arrived; together they'd continue to Hungary. Would Sarah be there?

The next day, Benito, a local from The Young Guard arrived, asking about the surviving comrades. Benito was constantly busy, making arrangements for escapees. He warned Renia not to get too relaxed—a huge number of Slovakian Jews had been deported to Poland. Here, too, Jews were required to wear a patch to identify them. Who knew how much longer they'd be able to stay?

Each day in the shelter, Renia met Jews arriving from Kraków, Warsaw, Radom, Tarnów, Ljubljana, Lvov—a hodgepodge of tortured asylum seekers brought together by fate. Chatty and energized, young Jews were different people when not in constant, mortal danger. But out of habit, they still whispered. Some had been caught by border guards, most had been hidden on the Aryan side. Hardly anyone had relatives, but everyone wanted to live—for many, they were driven by dreams of revenge. Renia learned about communities across Poland, the ghettos and labor camps that still existed, the thousands of Jews hiding in each large city. Could any of them be her family? She tried not to kindle any hopes.

Meanwhile, Chajka had an entirely different awakening. She and Benito fell for each other instantly. From a middle-class and assimilated Slovak family, Benito was the same age and had been a longtime Young Guard leader. He had survived the Slovakian deportations by escaping to Hungary—that is, after he arranged for sixty of his comrades to escape too. Following several arrests in Hungary, he returned to Slovakia to help receive incoming Jewish refugees. He was connected with movement leaders in Europe and Palestine. Chajka had lived through the horrors he'd only heard of secondhand. She stayed up late, telling him her stories, warmed by the auditorium's large oven. "She found everything she'd lost in the Slovak activist," their son explained many years later. "Like her, he was willing to risk his life for friends, and he also believed in the ideals of the future." Benito instantly felt the need to protect Chajka. As he recalled: "An entire generation was screaming through her mouth. She talked for hours and hours, as if fearing that she would not have time to deliver all of the information. . . . And I was listening to her, occasionally holding her hand, to feel the person who is carrying all of this on their heart and soul."

From the other side of the room, Max Fischer and Chawka watched the two whispering to each other. Max winked at Chawka. "I see trouble . . ."

A few days into Renia's stay, the next group of eight arrived.

No Sarah.

The Jews all planned to head to the Hungarian border together, accompanied by a bribed policeman. Their cover story: the comrades were Hungarian nationals, and the policeman was taking them to the border to deport them. The convoy left, but Renia remained in Slovakia, along with Chajka, waiting for the next group—waiting for Sarah, waiting for Benito.

The following group arrived the next week. Still no Sarah.

This group was traumatized.

Back in Poland, there had been an incident at the Kobiletzes'. Banasikova's husband, Pavel, returned home on army leave and visited his in-laws' home. Meir hadn't expected him and ran into him outside the bunker. Pavel, intoxicated, called him over and disclosed that he'd heard about the hidden Jews from Mitek's friends who had helped Jews escape the ghetto. "Don't worry," he insisted, "I won't harm the Jews."

Pavel was curious about how the bunker was made and opened its secret door. He was so drunk he could barely stand. The five people who remained in the bunker were shocked. Meir entered behind him, holding his homemade pistol. Pavel asked to hold it. Meir let him.

"The people who told us the story still don't understand why Meir did that," Renia wrote.

Pavel examined the pistol, looking at each part. Then, he pulled the trigger . . . and shot himself.

He was conscious when the comrades dragged him out of the bunker. But the family needed to report the incident to the police. Meir begged him not to disclose the bunker, and Pavel reassured them that he wouldn't. He was, however, not in a good state. The police arrived, and he testified, showing them Meir's homemade pistol, claiming he had stolen it from partisans during his military work, and that he'd been cleaning it when it accidentally went off. An ambulance arrived and took him to the hospital in Katowice. Two days later, he died.

The Kobiletzes still did not insist that the comrades leave, but they were too scared to stay, and, at first chance, escaped to Slovakia.

Then Renia got a message. She and Chajka were to leave immediately: they had received papers to immigrate to Palestine. Their photos had been sent to Hungary, and the girls needed to stop in Budapest to pick up all the documents.

Their dream.

Renia wrote to Sarah and Aliza, explaining that it was possible to make aliyah; that they needed to hurry to Slovakia with the children.

On the very day she was leaving for Hungary, the group received a letter from a smuggler. The snow in the mountains was now hip deep and the Poland-Slovakia border, impassable. They would not be doing any more crossings. That was it.

Everything went black. Renia knew that Sarah would not be coming. She sensed that she would never see her sister again. She was the last remaining Kukielka.

Early January 1944: Renia could not afford to miss a single connection.

She traveled with Chajka, Benito, and Moshe from The Young Guard, who spoke fluent Hungarian. They took the train to the final station in Slovakia. They were going to cross the border in the locomotive of a freight train.

It was late and dark. An engineer climbed down from the locomotive and gestured for them to follow him. Renia, Chajka, and Moshe climbed aboard. Benito, however, stayed behind to help more Jewish refugees. They crouched inside—a few other escapees were there. The engineers, paid per person, crammed them into hidden corners, and the train began to move, everyone united in praying that it would not be searched at the border. The heat from the boiler was unbearable, and Renia could not catch a full breath. Each time the train stopped, they all hunched down to the floor. Fortunately, the ride was quick. She did not let herself think about Aliza, the children, Sarah.

At the first station inside Hungary, the engineer released a long wave of steam, creating a heavy cloud. "Go!" he told Renia. This cloud obscured the escapees as they scrambled to disembark the locomotive and dash for the station. The engineer bought them tickets and showed them where to catch a passenger train to Budapest.

The ride took a day and a half, through increasingly warmer climes, during which time the comrades did not utter one word, not wanting to raise anyone's suspicions. "The Hungarian language sounds foreign and strange," Renia wrote. "The Hungarians themselves have semitic features. It's hard to tell who's Jewish and who's Aryan." Most Jews spoke Hungarian, not Yiddish or Hebrew. The radar that she'd developed in Nazi-ruled territory was no longer as functional. Jews were not required to wear ribbons or stars on their sleeves. There were no document checks or inspections on the train; it was probably unimaginable that they were Jewish refugees from Poland.

Then, at last, Budapest. The grand train station was crowded and hectic. The police inspected passengers' bags. Renia passed through quickly and hurried to the address they'd been given. Moshe's Hungarian skills were indispensable.

They took the tram to the Palestine bureau, which was bustling, echoing with German, Polish, Yiddish, and Hungarian pleas. Everyone wanted papers, everyone laid a claim as to why he or she needed to leave right away. *They all deserve to make aliyah!* Renia thought. The British, however, maintained their quotas and limited Jewish immigration. First in line for visas were the Polish refugees who'd endured the most terrible tortures. That meant Renia.

Renia waited impatiently for her departure date, which kept being postponed. First, her photos had not been received. Then, when the passports were ready, the visas were delayed from Turkey. The closer she was, the more nerve wracking the wait. The uncertainty was constant. "We kept thinking that something would happen that would postpone our aliyah," Renia later reflected. "Was all the trouble we went through for nothing? The situation in Hungary is good for now, but it could change at any moment." She had learned that life offered no stability, that moments flew past, that chances were paper thin, that the clock ruled all. She knew.

Renia needed the correct papers not only to make aliyah but also just to exist in Hungary. She watched as people were regularly stopped in the streets for inspections; those not registered with the police were arrested. Hitler had not invaded yet, but Jews' rights had been curtailed. People who had long assumed that they were safe from the savagery that occurred in Poland now lived on edge.

Renia went to the Polish consulate to report herself as a refugee from Poland. The Polish captain lobbed endless questions: Was she a member of the PPR? (Communism was illegal.) No, of course she wasn't. On the other hand, every Pole was obligated to support the Sikorski movement. Yes, of course she did.

One of the clerks asked: "Is Madame really Catholic?"

Renia told him in full certainly that she was.

"Thank God," he said. "Until now, only Jews disguised as Poles have come to us."

Renia feigned indignation. "What? Jews disguised as Poles?"

"Yes, unfortunately," he answered. The performance was never ending. A photograph taken of Renia on a Budapest street in 1944 shows her coiffed and styled, wearing a tailored coat with fur-trimmed pockets, and carrying a leather handbag, the hint of a smile on her lips, entirely betraying the physical and emotional brutalities of her preceding months.

She received 24 pengő for room and board to last a few days, and a certificate that allowed her to walk around the city freely.

When she returned to the comrades, she learned that though they'd all registered as Christian Poles, the clerks had suspected that the others were Jews and did not give them money, only a certificate to show during inspections. The JDC, Renia explained, had paid the Polish consulate to turn a blind eye.

Renia never returned to that office, thinking she'd be gone in a few days. But a month later, she was still in Budapest, still waiting for her visa to Palestine.

During this month, Renia, still thin but growing strong, began to write her memoirs. She knew she needed to tell the world what had happened to her people, her family, her comrades, but how? With which words? She scribbled in Polish, using initials instead of names, likely for security, figuring out for herself what had happened, how five years had lasted several lifetimes, who she was, could be, would be.

In a photograph of the comrades in Hungary, her sticklike wrist is adorned with a brand-new watch. Renewed time.

None of the comrades had been to their spiritual homeland outside their imaginations. Still, they knew it would be warm, familiar. "They will receive us with open arms," Renia believed, "like a mother receiving her children." They yearned for this land where they would find remedy for all their suffering—the hope that had kept them alive. There, finally, they would be free of the constant threat.

But still, Renia worried. "Will our friends in Israel understand what we'd gone through?" she asked presciently. "Will we be able to live a normal, mundane life, a life like theirs?"

And then, at long last, Renia was at the station. Chajka too. The platform was crowded with people who'd met only a few days earlier, but already a camaraderie had formed; an indelible spiritual closeness. Renia was on her way.

Everyone envied her, she knew it, but despite all her longing, she could not find happiness. "The memory of the millions that were murdered, the memory of the comrades who dedicated their lives to Eretz Israel but have fallen before reaching their destination, doesn't let up." Out of nowhere, the image of Jews being shoved into a train car would flash through her mind, shivers shooting through her body. Her family, her sister—she could barely begin to think about any of it.

Renia watched as a German army train passed the station on the other track. They must have known they were a group of Jews, she thought. They looked at her, at all the Jews, with evil eyes. A few of them grinned. If they'd been able to, they would have come over and beaten her. But then, Renia thought, if I could, I'd beat them back. She felt a strong urge to provoke them, to show them that she had successfully escaped from the Gestapo and was traveling to Palestine. She had done it.

Melancholy and joy. Warm embraces, sad farewells. *Remember us, those left behind*, the hugs said. *Do whatever you can, wherever you end up, to help the few who survived.*

The train moved slowly. People ran alongside, not wanting to let go of their loved ones. Renia too was unable to let go—not of hands, but of feelings. She so wanted to feel joyful, to be enchanted by the glorious sun and the lush landscape, but her heart was heavy, inconsolable, as she thought obsessively about Sarah, Aliza, the orphans that remained in Poland, her brother Yankel, all the children.

Renia was traveling with a group of ten people. Most had photos in their passports, while a few used fake names. According to Renia's Palestine immigration papers, she was "also known as Irena Glick and sometimes known as Irene Neuman." Her file includes a signed statement that her marriage to Yitzhak Fiszman, aka Vilmos Neuman was not a true union—presumably, they pretended to be betrothed to ease immigration. (Yitzhak, who posed in a debonair suit with wide lapel alongside Renia in a photo of the Freedom group in Budapest, was actually married to Chana Gelbard, the Freedom courier in Warsaw.) Every faux couple was accompanied by orphaned children or children of adults who had not been able to leave. The children were ecstatic, excited for a new adventure.

Renia reached the border the following night. Would the inspections ever end? The guards searched their belongings without incident. In Romania, they learned that the Palestine bureau's employees had been arrested. Though nervous, they managed to cross to Bulgaria peacefully. Here the train tracks were blocked by a large boulder. Renia had to walk a half mile to embark another train. The Bulgarians—military, railroad workers, and civilians—helped Renia and the Jews willingly. Their kindness left a lasting impression on Renia as they meandered all the way to the Turkish border.

They were about to leave Europe.

Now, at last, sensing a future where she could look at people and not fear their stares, Renia began to feel a tingle of joy.

Benito was waiting for them at the Istanbul station, with another comrade whom Renia named only as V. Everyone was elated; they all stayed together at an inn. V barraged them with questions about people he knew. He happily bathed Muniosh, who'd arrived with the first group; he was constantly busy, trying to reach the handful of remaining Jews across Europe. He "cried like a baby" hearing their stories of loss. V was desperate to get Zivia out of Poland, but she would not budge. She still had so much work to do, her letters said. She needed to stay put.

Jews roamed freely through the streets of Istanbul. Nobody was after them, nobody pointed fingers. Renia spent a week marveling at how strange this was, to not be suspect, to not be hunted. Then, a boat ride across the Bosporus Strait, a train across Syria, stops in Aleppo and the Lebanese capital of Beirut.

On March 6, 1944, Renia Kukielka, a nineteen-year-old stenographer from Jędrzejów, arrived in Haifa, Palestine.

PART 4

The Emotional Legacy

Interviewer: How are you?
Renia: [Pause] Usually, I'm fine.

—*Yad Vashem testimony, 2002*

We had been liberated from the fear of death, but we were not free from the fear of life.

—*Hadassah Rosensaft, a Jewish dentist who stole food, clothing, and medication for patients at Auschwitz*

Chapter 30
Fear of Life

The one who survives will be like a leaf cast about
by a gale, a leaf that doesn't belong to anyone and
has lost its mother tree, which has died. . . . The
leaf will fly with the wind and won't find a place
for itself, neither finding the old leaves it used to
know, nor a patch of the old sky. It's impossible to
accrete to a new tree. And the poor leaf will wander,
recalling the old, though very sad, days, and ever
longing to return, but it won't find its place.
—*Chajka Klinger*, I Am Writing These Words to You

March 1944

Renia made it to the homeland, foggy, elated. She
had left Poland a fugitive, wanted by the Gestapo,

and was now in her dreamland. After a rehabilitating stay at Kibbutz Givat Brenner's sanatorium, where Renia continued writing her memoirs, she settled with comrade Chawka at the verdant Kibbutz Dafna, in the Galilee region. (The same kibbutz is described in Leon Uris's novel *Exodus*.) Here, at last, with her fellow six hundred kibbutzniks, she felt comfort, "as if I'd arrived at the home of my parents." Many Zionist movement survivors came to Israel, finally joining the kibbutzim for which they'd prepared. Even non-Zionist survivors were attracted to the kibbutzim, not for their ideology but for providing work, pride and, structure to their lives.

And yet. There were still differences, difficulties. As relieved as she was to end her wandering and be free to sing the songs she'd suppressed for years, Renia was still weighed down by torment and the memories of those lost. "We feel like we're smaller and weaker than the people around us," she wrote shortly after arriving. "Like we don't have the same right to life as they do."

Like many survivors, Renia did not always feel understood. She traveled through Palestine, giving talks about her experience in the war, speaking at venues ranging from the Haifa amphitheater to the dining rooms of local kibbutzim, telling the world about the extermination of Polish Jewry. In a testimony for the National Library of Israel given in the 1980s, Renia recalled that she'd once been asked to speak at Kibbutz Alonim. She began to tell her story in Polish and Yiddish, when her speech was interrupted by a commotion. The moment she stopped talking, the audience members moved the chairs and tables. What was going on? It turned out, they were preparing for a dance. The music blared. Renia felt so offended, she rushed out, not sure if they simply didn't understand her language or didn't care.

There are many reasons the stories of Jewish women in the resistance went underground. The majority of fighters and couriers were killed—Tosia, Frumka, Hantze, Rivka, Leah, Lonka—and did not live to tell their tales. But even for survivors, female narratives were silenced for both political and personal reasons, which differed across countries and communities.

The politics of Israel's earliest years, as it developed into a nation, influenced how Holocaust stories came to be known. When Holocaust survivors arrived to the Yishuv (the Jewish settlement in Palestine) in the mid and late 1940s, tales of ghetto fighters were compelling to the left-wing political parties. Not only was anti-Nazi activity more palatable than horrific torture, these fighting stories helped bolster the party image and the call to fight for a new country. Like Renia, several women ghetto fighters were given a platform to speak—and they did so prolifically—but, at times, their words were edited to toe party lines. Some survivors accused the Yishuv of being passive and not supporting the Jews in Poland. This is when Hannah Senesh was made a symbol. Though she never carried out her mission, aside from boosting morale, her story of leaving Palestine to fight in Hungary proved that the Yishuv took an active role in helping the European Jews.

Soon after, scholars explain, early Israeli politicians tried to create a dichotomy between European Jews and Israeli Jews. European Jews, the Israelis said, were physically weak, naïve, and passive. Some sabras, or native-born Israelis, referred to the new arrivals as "soaps," from the rumor that the Nazis made soap out of murdered Jewish bodies. Israeli Jews, on the other hand, saw themselves as the strong next wave. Israel was the future; Europe, for more than a thousand years a cradle of Jewish civilization, was the past. The memory of resistance fighters—the Jews of Europe who were anything but feeble—was erased in order to reinforce the negative stereotype.

The resistance tale fell into further oblivion. A decade after the war, people were ready to hear about concentration camps, and trauma became the public interest. In the 1970s, the political landscape shifted, and tales of individual rebels were replaced by stories of "everyday resistance." In the early 2000s, Warsaw ghetto fighter Pnina Grinshpan (Frimer) was invited to Poland to receive an award. She stood on the stage, pained, apathetic. "Why do I need to come to Poland to receive a prize?" she asked in a documentary, reflecting that she *escaped* from that country. "Here [in Israel] we are so tiny."

Controversies continue today. Mordechai Paldiel, the former director of the Righteous Gentiles Department at Yad Vashem, Israel's largest Holocaust memorial, was troubled that Jewish rescuers never received the same recognition as their Gentile counterparts. In 2017 he authored *Saving One's Own: Jewish Rescuers During the Holocaust*, a tome about Jews who organized large-scale rescue efforts across Europe. Some Jews are critical that the underground activity of the Revisionist youth (Betar's ZZW) has gone largely unappreciated. This could be because so few survived; others say it's because historians tend to be left wing and only commemorate their own kind. Still, others point out that Menachem Begin, the early leader of the Israeli right wing and the country's sixth prime minister, escaped to Russia and did not fight in the Warsaw ghetto; he downplayed the uprising altogether. The Bund (based mainly outside Israel), the Zionists, and the Revisionists continue to disagree on who was responsible for initiating the Warsaw ghetto uprising. Even among left-wing Zionists, Freedom, The Young Guard, and the Zionist Youth each has its own Holocaust-based archives, galleries, and publishing houses in Israel.

History is different in the United States. In popular conception, the story goes that American Jews did not discuss the Holocaust in the 1940s and 1950s—presumably out of fear, guilt, and because they were busy becoming suburban and wanted to fit in with their middle-class non-Jewish neighbors. But as Hasia Diner shows in her groundbreaking book *We Remember with Reverence and Love: American Jews and the Myth of Silence After the Holocaust, 1945–1962*, this narrative is unfounded. If anything, there was a proliferation of writing and discussion about the Holocaust in the postwar years. One Jewish leader worried that there was *too much* focus on the war, even citing Renia's book as an example. As Diner points out, American Jews—in their new identity as the main Jewish community in the world—struggled with *how* to talk about the genocide, not whether they should.

Over time, the stories changed. Nechama Tec, author of *Resistance: Jews and Christians Who Defied the Nazi Terror* and *Defiance: The Bielski Partisans* (later the film), claims that there was a trend in American academia in the early 1960s to espouse Jewish submissiveness and even blame the victim. This "myth of passivity," spurred in part by political philosopher Hannah Arendt, was biased, and not grounded in fact. Diner claims that by the late 1960s, the American Jewish community had become public and established; an explosion of later Holocaust publications drowned out earlier work, which perhaps is partly why Renia's book disappeared from our collective memory.

Even today there are ethical complications in presenting this material in the United States. Writing about fighters might give the impression that the Holocaust was "not that bad"—a risk in a context where the genocide is fading from memory. Many writers fear that glorifying resisters places too much focus on agency, implying that survival was more than luck, judging those who did not take up arms, and ultimately blaming the victim. Further, this is a story that grays the victim-aggressor trope and unveils nuanced complications, foregrounding the intense discord *within* the Jewish community about how to deal with Nazi occupation. This tale inevitably includes Jewish Nazi collaborators and Jewish rebels who stole money to buy weapons—shaky ethics at every turn. The rage and violent rhetoric in these Jewish women's memoirs are halting. So is the fact that many of these resisters were middle class and urban, more modern and sophisticated, more like "us," than is comfortable. All these factors dissuade discussion.

And then there is gender. Women are routinely dropped from stories in which they played key roles, their experiences blotted out of history. Here, too, women's stories were particularly silenced. According to Chajka's Klinger's son, the Holocaust scholar Avihu Ronen, this has partly to do with women's roles in the youth movement. Women were usually the ones directed to escape with "the mission to tell." They were the appointed documenters and firsthand historians. Many of the earliest chronicles of the resistance were written by women. As authors, Ronen argues, they reported on *others'* activities—usually the men's—rather than their own. Their personal experiences fell into the background.

Lenore Weitzman, a foundational scholar of women and the Holocaust, explains that soon after these women's works were published, the major histories were written by men, who focused on men, not on courier girls who themselves downplayed their own activity. She suggests that only physical combat—which was public and organized—was held in esteem, while other undercover tasks were considered trivial. (Even so, many Jewish women *did* fight in the uprisings and engaged in armed combat, and should not be dropped from that tale either.)

Even when women tried to tell their stories, they were often deliberately silenced. Some women's writings were censored to fit political motivations, some women faced blatant indifference, and others were treated with disbelief, accused of making it all up. After liberation, an American army reporter warned Bielski partisans Fruma and Motke Berger not to repeat their story, because people would think they were liars, or insane. Many women faced scorn—accused by relatives of having fled to fight instead of staying to look after their parents; others were charged with "sleeping their way to safety." Women felt judged according to a lingering belief that while the pure souls perished, the conniving ones survived. So often, when their vulnerable outpourings were not received with empathy or comprehension, women turned inward and repressed their experiences, pushing them deep under the surface.

Then there was coping. Women self-silenced. Many felt like it was their "sacred duty" of "cosmic significance" to grow a new generation of Jews, and kept their pasts to themselves out of a desperate desire to create a "normal" life for their children—and for themselves.

Many of these women were in their midtwenties when the war ended; they had everything ahead of them and had to find ways to move forward. They did not all want to be "professional survivors." Family members also hushed women, worried that facing their memories would be too difficult, that lancing old wounds would cause them to unravel entirely.

Many women suffered from an oppressive survivor's guilt. By the time Białystok courier Chasia felt ready to share her past of weapon stealing and sabotage, Jews were opening up about their experiences in concentration camps. Compared with what they went through, she'd "had it easy." Her narrative seemed too "selfish." Others have spoken about the hierarchy of suffering in the survivor community. Fruma Berger's son once felt shunned at a second-generation event because his parents had been partisans. Some fighters and their families felt estranged from close-knit survivor communities—and turned away.

And then there are the narrative tropes that have reigned for women over the decades. Hannah Senesh may have been a good role model because she showed the Yishuv's involvement. But scholars mention that Hannah became famous over her fellow parachutist Haviva Reich—who convinced an American pilot to blind-drop her in Slovakia, where she organized food and shelter for thousands of refugees, rescued Allied servicemen, and helped children escape—because Hannah was young, beautiful, single, wealthy, and a poet. Haviva was a thirtysomething, brown-haired divorcee with a checkered romantic past.

For North American Jews, this is all distant past, and, still, the stakes are high. In Poland, where people continue to reel from years of Soviet rule, the women's collaboration with the Red Army takes on a different meaning. Poland's senate recently passed a law (later revised) dictating that Poland could not be blamed for any crimes committed in the Holocaust. The memory of the Polish resistance is wildly popular in Poland today, its anchor symbol graffitied on buildings. One is held in esteem if there was a Home Army fighter in your family. The narrative remains under construction, the resistance and its role tenuous. How the war is presented—to ourselves and to the outside world—can explain who we are, why we act as we do.

It was not just the silencing of their life stories that was immediately difficult for survivors and fighters, but also freedom.

This cohort of young women were homeless twentysomething adults who had lost their childhoods, who had not had the chance to study or train for a career, who did not have normal family networks, and whose sexual development had often been skipped over, traumatized, or deeply intensified. Many of these women—especially those who did not ascribe to strong political philosophies—simply did not know where to go, what to do, who to be, how to love.

Faye Schulman, the partisan who spent years wandering the forest, blowing up trains, performing outdoor surgeries, and photographing soldiers, wrote that liberation was not the epitome of joy but "the lowest point in my life. . . . Never in my life had I felt so lonely, so sad; never had I felt such yearning for the parents, family, and friends whom I would never see again." After the brutal murders of her family members, and all her losses, the rigor, duty, and social cohesion of partisan life had kept her sane, focused, and with purpose: survival and revenge. Now she was absolutely alone in the world, with nothing, not even a nationality. While fellow partisans sat around the campfire contemplating the end of war, dreaming of reunions and celebrations, she felt otherwise:

When the war was over, would I have a place where I belonged? Who would wait at the station to meet me? Who would celebrate freedom with me? There would be no homecoming parades for me, no time to even mourn the dead. If I did survive, where would I return? My home and my town had been razed to the ground, its people killed. I was not in the same situation as the colleagues surrounding me. I was a Jew and a woman.

Faye received a medal from the Soviet government but had to return her weapons. Without a sense of protection or identity, she decided to enlist in the Soviet army and continue to fight in Yugoslavia. On her way to the military bureau, she met a Jewish-looking officer who convinced her to stop risking her life. Faye became a government photographer in Pinsk. She was able to track down her surviving brothers, her access to trains and officials made possible by showing her medal. Through one brother, she met Morris Schulman, a partisan commander whom she'd encountered once in the forest and who knew her family from before the war. Some surviving women idealized dead fathers and struggled to form intimate bonds, but Faye's and Morris's feelings for each other were immediate, and Faye refused many other proposals for him. "We felt an urgency to proceed quickly with whatever love was left in us," she reflected.

Though they were a relatively wealthy, successful Soviet couple, the *Judenrein* city of Pinsk was too depressing. In numerous difficult and dangerous trips, they crisscrossed Europe, one couple among millions of displaced people who roamed the Continent; they were forced into an awful refugee camp that reminded Faye of the ghetto. Soon after, they joined the Bricha, an underground organization that illegally smuggled Jews to Palestine, where immigration quotas remained enforced. But Faye had a baby and craved safety. She and Morris changed course and spent the rest of their lives in Toronto, growing careers and a family. Faye spoke publicly about her war experience for decades. "Sometimes [the] bygone world feels almost more real to me than the present," she wrote. A part of her always remained rooted in her lost universe.

Another lifelong issue for survivors was guilt.

In the summer of 1944, from the window of her hiding place in Warsaw, Zivia could see weary horses pulling farmers' carts full of Germans fleeing for their lives. The Polish underground, controlled mainly by the Home Army, decided it was time to fight—to push away the weakened Nazis and to defend Poland from the encroaching Soviets. Though Zivia, the ZOB, and the Communist Poles did not agree with all these politics, they decided to join in—any effort to destroy the Nazis was worthwhile. Zivia put out word through the Polish underground press that all Jews should fight, no matter what affiliation, for a "free, independent, strong, and just Poland." The uprising began on August 1. Jews, including women, from all political factions participated. During this revolt, Rivka Moscovitch was killed when a Nazi drove by and machine-gunned her on the street.

The Home Army would not fight alongside Jews, but the People's Army welcomed the ZOB's collaboration. Worried about Jewish casualties, they offered them behind-the-scenes roles, but Zivia and her group insisted on active combat. She defended an important and isolated post, nearly forgotten in action. The twenty-two Jews' roles were minor, but it meant everything to Zivia that the ZOB remained alive and kicking, and working alongside Poles. The Home Army had been prepared to fight for a few days, but the Soviets held out on their involvement, and the gruesome battle lasted for two months. The magnificent city of Warsaw was razed, turned into a heap of rubble three stories high; nearly 90 percent of its buildings had now been destroyed. Eventually the Poles surrendered. The Germans drove out everyone. But what were Jews—especially those who looked it—to do?

Once again, the fighters escaped via sewage canals. This time Zivia was exhausted and nearly drowned.

Antek carried her on his back while she slept.

Even with the Red Army drawing near, Zivia remained realistic, or pessimistic, warning her comrades not to get too excited. After struggling through a number of *melinas*, the hiding Jews' situation was dire. Six weeks of life-threatening Soviet bombardment, of scarce food and water, of smoking leaves they picked off trees, of near suffocation in the tiny cellar where they hid—they were doomed. Especially when the Germans began digging trenches on their street, and then, in their very building.

The Nazis were breaking down the walls right near Zivia's shelter. The Jews could hear every shovel scoop. But, as always, the Germans stopped for their routine lunch break at noon. Five minutes later, a rescue group from the Polish Red Cross arrived. Bundist couriers had contacted a leftist Polish doctor at a nearby hospital, and he'd sent a team to retrieve them under the auspices of collecting typhoid patients—which he knew would keep away the Germans. The two most Jewish looking had their faces bandaged and were carried out on stretchers. The others put on Red Cross armbands and feigned being rescuers. Zivia pretended to be an old peasant scrambling through houses. The group wandered through the demolished city and, despite several altercations, managed to escape—even convincing a

Nazi who had lost an eye "to those Jewish bandits" to pull them with his horse and carriage. From the hospital, Zivia went into hiding in the suburbs.

When the Russians liberated Warsaw in January 1945, thirty-year-old Zivia felt empty. She described the day when the Soviet tanks rolled in. "A mob of people exuberantly rushed out to greet them in the town marketplace," she wrote. "The people rejoiced and embraced their liberators. We stood by crushed and dejected, lone remnants of our people." This was the saddest day of Zivia's life: the world she'd known officially ceased to exist. Like many survivors who coped through hyperactivity, Zivia threw herself into helping others.

Approximately three hundred thousand Polish Jews remained alive: just 10 percent of the prewar population. These included survivors of camps, "passers," people in hiding, forest partisans, and—the majority—the two hundred thousand Jews who had lived out the war in Soviet territory, many incarcerated in Siberian Gulags. (The "Asians," they were called.) These Jews were returning to nothing—no family, no home. Postwar Poland was a "Wild West" with rampant antisemitism. In small towns, especially where people feared Jews would reclaim their property, Jews could be killed on the streets. Zivia worked to bring the Jews aid; she also planned escape routes. In Lublin, she connected with Abba Kovner, and though they set out to collaborate, they fell out. Zivia prioritized community building; Kovner, immediate exit from Poland—and revenge.

The movements tried harder than ever to renew their Polish base, even sending emissaries to train stations to convince "Asians" to join their ranks. Zivia returned to Warsaw to work with survivors, setting up safe communes and attracting Jews to Freedom. As always, she was the mother figure whom everyone looked up to, yet she kept her own feelings private.

Suffering from exhaustion, in 1945 Zivia finally requested to make aliyah. The socialist Zionist from Byten arrived in Palestine—her long-delayed dream. It was as if she'd been miraculously resurrected from the dead, especially after so many obituaries had been published, but life was not easy. She lived in a hut on a kibbutz from which the British carried out raids on Yishuv leaders—episodes that reminded her of ghetto Aktions. The kibbutzim, she felt, did not do enough to welcome survivors. Though her sister was there, she didn't have time to see family and friends due to movement work, and she missed Antek, apparently fearing that his flirtatious nature was embroiling him in affairs with other women. Her depression and guilt soared. *She was supposed to have been in Mila 18. She was supposed to have died.*

Zivia was immediately sent on a speaking tour—"a circus," she called it. She received invitations from countless groups and felt she could not turn down any; too many organizations wanted her support, craved the glow of her heroism.

In June 1946 six thousand people gathered at Kibbutz Yagur to hear Zivia deliver an eloquent, firm, eight-hour testimony in Hebrew, orating without notes, articulate thoughts streaming from her head and heart. Everyone was riveted, stunned. "She stood there like a queen," an audience member observed later, noting that she gave off a feeling of holiness. Her lectures were about the war, the movement, the ZOB, and never about her feelings or personal life. Zivia defended the Jewish masses in the ghettos and called for empathizing with survivors, but most listeners wanted to hear about the uprising. Her ghetto fighting history was used by some left-wing politicians to further their agendas; Zivia's fighter stance echoed the militant philosophies of the burgeoning state. As requested, apparently, she toned down her criticism of the Yishuv for not sending more support to Warsaw. Appealing to women, promoting the importance of weapons and heroism, she was adored and helped the party gain support, but this exposure and its politics exhausted her. Each speech ripped open wounds, re-awakening her suffering and guilt. She wanted to be alone, to breathe.

The following year, Zivia was selected for a major role at the Zionist Congress in Basel. She and Antek met up in Switzerland, where they were secretly married by a rabbi. She returned to Israel pregnant—in the same dress that she wore at Yagur, but now it was snug. Antek followed a few months later. However, despite the heroic reputation of this power couple—they were the last remaining Zionists of the Warsaw ghetto uprising command—they never achieved high political positions in Israel, possibly because the Yishuv politicians felt threatened by their mythic status. Antek worked in the fields; Zivia, in the chicken coop. She shunned the public eye. According to those close to her, she did not think of herself as special, just as someone who did what had to be done.

In Zivia's writings, she emphasizes that she'd been trained for this. Most Jews simply did not know what *to do*, but the Jewish youth was educated to make goals for themselves and carry them through. When Chasia's daughter was asked what factors led to her mother's wartime behavior, her immediate response was that Chasia got her tolerance from her father and her strength from The Young Guard. As Chasia herself reflected six decades later, "We knew how to share, to work together, to defer to one another, to surmount obstacles, to outdo ourselves. We did not realize then how badly we would need [these skills] in the years to come." The youth movements had emerged in a context of Jews feeling threatened. They taught participants to deal with existential problems as well as to live and work together, to collaborate at all levels.

Now, feeling the need for a community that understood them and to memorialize their past, Zivia and Antek decided to found their own kibbutz—no easy feat. The movement feared that this kibbutz would focus on the traumas of yesterday; the ghetto fighters had to continually prove that they wouldn't break down mentally. After some struggle, they successfully established the Ghetto Fighters' House kibbutz, composed mainly of survivors. Zivia relied on work and motherhood—a constant balancing act—to mute her past and forge forward. Like many survivors who lived with the sense that "catastrophe could hit with no notice," fearing thunder and lightning (which reminded them of bombings), people on the kibbutz suffered from post-traumatic stress and night terrors. Overall, however, they worked hard to become a productive entity. Later, Antek opened Israel's first Holocaust memorial museum and archive there, in an elegant brutalist building with curved high ceilings. Controversies arose surrounding the nature of the narrative they presented, even among the kibbutz members. Discords with The Young Guard and Yad Vashem have faded with time, but one can still sense them just under the surface.

Zivia remained principled, restrained, and driven by movement ideals. She was tight with money, fiercely against German reconciliation and reparations (except when her practical side set in), and had to be forced by Leon Uris to buy a new dress for an important event. She allowed her children to receive only books for gifts; they were the last ones on the kibbutz to get bicycles. (Antek, the romantic visionary and bon vivant, enjoyed more material things.) When she wanted a new front porch, Zivia collected rocks and hammers and built it. Quotidian actions, she always felt, were the mark of value. She did not dwell on issues but believed that a person had to make a decision and carry it through. "Give yourself a slap on the ass!" was her motto .

Zivia worked, traveled, managed kibbutz finances, avidly read new books, hosted guests, and mothered two children. Like a majority of Holocaust survivors, she and Antek were overprotective and nurturing. Many survivor parents kept their pasts from their children, desperately wanting their offspring's lives to be normal, but this inadvertently caused rifts. On kibbutzim all over Israel, children lived in separate communal quarters and spent only the afternoons with their parents, creating further distance and troubles with developing physical intimacy. At GFH, the children had particular issues with nightmares and bedwetting, and Zivia agreed to hire a psychologist—a lavish expense on outsider work she normally would not condone. She too was haunted by the fact that her son was crying, and she had to leave him screaming because parents' hours in the children's wing were over.

Zivia remained in the periphery of the public eye. In 1961 she testified at the trial of Nazi Adolf Eichmann, and on a few occasions, agreed reluctantly to be on the Labor ticket for the Israeli parliament. She wanted to support the party, and went along with it only because she knew she'd lose. She was assigned a political position in government, but resigned, wanting to work on the kibbutz, to be with her family. She preferred cooking and poultry farming to the tiresome charades of being a figurehead. When, in the 1970s, intellectuals focused on the everyday resistance rather than singling out heroic fighters, and due to Zivia's evasion of the limelight, her name faded from Israelis' consciousness.

Her book about the war was based on her lectures, and edited by Antek. Though she insisted her writings be published posthumously, they contain no personal revelations. "You can tell a lot about a person," she said, "by the amount of times they say 'I' in a sentence."

Even in heroic Zivia and Antek's home, the past was secret. As was common with children of survivors who sensed it was not safe to probe, Zivia's children made few inquiries into their parents' history. Her daughter, Yael, a psychologist, wondered, *How could I not have sat them down and asked them?* As a child, she'd wanted younger, Hebrew-speaking, sabra parents. Their son, Shimon, felt pressure being the child of legends, unable to live up to expectations: "What am I supposed to do, throw a Molotov cocktail, kill a German, what?"

Many children of survivors felt the opposite pressure: to achieve what their parents couldn't and to accomplish goals for their entire extended family, while also being constantly happy, justifying their parents' survival. Others felt pressured simply to be "normal"— and rebelled by not marrying. Still others felt pushed to pursue particular careers, such as medicine. ("A philosopher [is] useless in the forest," a surviving partisan told his Californian children.) Many became mental health and social workers.

Just before Zivia died, her daughter-in-law bore her

a granddaughter: Eyal, which happens to be the Hebrew name for the ZOB. Zivia held the baby and cried
in public, the first time since the forests of Poland. Eyal
speaks publically about her family history, attribut-
ing her chattiness to her grandfather, with whom she
was close as a child. Though she wishes she'd known
more about her grandmother's inner life, Eyal looks to
Zivia's book—the tale of a carer, a doer, someone who
put others first, who held extremely high standards for
everyone, including herself—as a source of strength.

Eyal also exhibits a frank self-criticism; a legacy of
the Freedom philosophy. In an Israeli documentary
about the family, she questions whether she would have
had the strength to fight as Zivia did. When others
criticizes the Poles who stood by, she remarks that she
too has sat in restaurants bordering war zones, enjoying herself.

While Eyal works in human resources, organizing
people just like her grandmother did, her sister Roni
followed in Zivia's fighting footsteps. Roni was the
first female fighter pilot in the Israeli army, standing
out in formation with a long braid dangling down her
back. Roni rarely speaks publicly—partly because of
her military status but largely because she inherited her
grandmother's reserve. With her own "hypermorality,"
she lives for her grandmother, whom she never met

but whose "quiet leadership" she finds beautiful. The Zuckerman way, the sisters joked, was to keep everything close to your chest; to answer any question with one word. Most of all: "Zuckermans don't cry." What she learned most from her grandparents, Eyal said, was that "you never have full control over circumstances, but you have control over how you respond. You need to trust yourself to get through life."

"All I did was try to die, but I survived," was Zivia's refrain. "Fate determined that I should survive, and I am left with no other way." Despite her victorious life, Zivia was plagued by guilt. She could have saved more, done more, done things earlier. The remorse that began in Warsaw—the sense of missed opportunity, the fighters she lost—never subsided, but instead grew with survival. *Why did I make it through?* was a constant presence.

Another constant for Zivia was her cigarette habit. In her sixties, her smoking and remorse eating away at her, she developed lung cancer, and despite all her attempts to keep on working as usual, she died in 1978 at the age of sixty-three. As per Antek's request, only her first name appears on her tombstone. "Zivia is an institution," her son explained. No further words were necessary.

Without her, the fragile existence that Antek had

rebuilt shattered. He did not want to live in a world without Zivia. Against doctor's orders, he drank. "He worked on dying," Eyal said. Despite his charm and happy nature, Antek was deeply haunted, unable to let go of the past, reproaching himself for not having saved his family, and plagued by decisions he'd made during wartime. He never stopped considering the murder of a potential informer. What if the man had been innocent? Antek's regret only sharpened with time, "like lava gushing out of the ground and sprouting up" he said, reflecting on how his past and present became entwined. To lead the Warsaw ghetto uprising and then pick fruit on a kibbutz was a difficult life course. Many fighters never truly found themselves after their traumatic and hyperdramatic twenties. Antek died three years after Zivia, in a taxi on the way to a ceremony in her honor.

"Zivia was the branch, and Antek was the stem," Yael said. "If the branch bends, the stem falls, no matter how strong it looks."

Israel was a hard environment, but it was not easy for Polish resistance fighters in postwar Poland, either, which was governed by the USSR for decades. In a climate of surveillance and fear, anyone who had shown allegiances to the Home Army during the war could have been considered a "Polish nationalist" and therefore a rebel against the Soviet regime—and in mortal danger. Many Poles who'd helped Jews hid their heroic actions for fear they'd be accused of being on the wrong side of the state. One Polish woman who had sheltered a family that moved to Israel had to ask them to stop sending thank-you gifts with Israeli flags because the presents made the neighbors suspicious.

Even some Jews in Poland repressed their pasts and cut off contact. "Halina," who helped save Renia from prison, was actually Irena Gelblum. After the war, she and Kazik, her boyfriend, went to Israel. But she soon left, studied medicine, worked as a journalist, and became a famous poet in Italy, where she changed her name to Irena Conti. Eventually she settled back in Poland, but constantly changed her identity and friends, her past a deeper and deeper secret.

Others lived their lives more openly. Irena Adamowicz, the Catholic Scout, worked at the Polish National Library. She never married but cared for her mother and spent her time with friends she made during the war. Irena kept up written correspondence with the Jewish women she had worked with and visited Israel in 1958—a highlight of her life. She lived with a terrific fear of dying alone, and yet, as she aged, became reclusive. One day in 1973 she suddenly expired on the street at age sixty-three. In 1985 she was named a Righteous Among the Nations at Yad Vashem.

For others, the suffering of survival was simply too unbearable. Chajka Klinger made it to Palestine, arriving on the same train as Renia, but with growing depression. She and Benito moved to The Young Guard's Kibbutz Gal On, where they attempted to integrate into the communal life. Chajka spoke at numerous assemblies and conferences. But conflict with the movement erupted. Excerpts from her diaries were published by The Young Guard—but they were heavily edited, omitting and even reversing her criticism of the Yishuv (which she accused of not doing enough) and deleting her doubts that the resistance would ever really work. Chajka hadn't been silenced, but censored. Her words and thoughts—for an intellectual like her, her identity—had been tampered with by the very movement for which she had given her life.

The morbid thoughts that had begun when she was in hiding would ebb and flow, but they never left her permanently. She and Benito moved to a new kibbutz, Ha'Ogen, with fewer friends from the past. They lived in a room made of orange crates, but Chajka focused on enjoying family life. She began editing her diaries into a book, and finally felt happy, even though she felt guilty about her happiness. It was hard for her to get a permanent job on the kibbutz—especially her preferred work in the children's home—since she had no seniority. After all she'd been through, she had to start from scratch. "She who led a movement during the war, who stood up to the Gestapo," her son Avihu wrote, "was now just Chajka R." (Benito's surname, which she had taken, was Ronen, formerly Rosenberg.) Then Chajka became pregnant. During this pregnancy, she woke up during the nights with delusions, and Benito began to understand that these episodes were "mental illness," the all-encompassing term that was then used. Neither PTSD nor collective trauma was yet understood. At Ha'Ogen, survivors were not treated any differently and did not discuss their pasts. The kibbutz rules, the member's role in the labor force, the present, were all that counted.

She named her son Zvi, after Zvi Brandes.

Chajka did not have a survivor community who understood her, with whom she could reminisce or even fantasize about revenge. She did not make many friends. (Most of her fellow kibbutzniks spoke Hungarian.) Plus, Benito's ex-girlfriend also lived there. Chajka was sent for training to work in the chicken coop, not to study for an advanced degree, as she'd wanted. The important jobs went to men. Her career goals—the goals of an unabashed intellect—became dashed dreams.

Chajka found out that one of her sisters was alive, which gave her some hope and stability. But then the head of The Young Guard decided that Benito, who still worked in refugee aid, would return to Europe. Chajka was asked to give up all the comforts she'd made for herself and go back to the blood-soaked continent from which she narrowly escaped.

She did not stay long and returned to Israel to give birth to her second son, Avihu, the scholar. She suffered from severe postpartum depression, unable to get out of bed for weeks, afraid of taking medicine for fear she was being poisoned. She was hospitalized against her will. Afterward, no one discussed her illness—it was taboo.

Back on the kibbutz, Chajka grew distant from Będzin friends, and found no outlet for her talents. Then, during her third pregnancy, her diaries were used without her permission in an article that critiqued The Young Guard's leadership, placing her at the center of a heated controversy that again forced her to grapple with the conflict between her own truth and her loyalty to the movement. Again she suffered from postpartum depression and was hospitalized. As part of Chajka's treatment she was made to talk about the Gestapo torture. Traumatized by this intervention, she refused further medical help.

Avihu recalled happy memories of his mother but also remembered episodes where she sat in silence with a towel wrapped over her head. She had survived and wanted to fulfill The Young Guard's role for her: to tell the people what she'd witnessed. But ultimately she felt she was "condemned to live." At last, after deeper depressive episodes, Chajka, aged forty-two, agreed to return to the hospital. One evening she arrived at the children's home wearing a long coat; she'd come to say good-bye.

The next morning, in April 1958, on the fifteenth anniversary of the Warsaw ghetto uprising, Chajka Klinger hung herself from a tree, not too far from the kibbutz nursery where her three sons played.

Not everyone survives surviving.

Chapter 31
Forgotten Strength

1945

Renia might not have had luck speaking to that particular group in the kibbutz, but her lecture rounds led to other revelations. One day some couriers in a displaced persons camp mentioned her name. In front of them, a man fainted.

He was Renia's brother.

Zvi Kukielka had escaped to Russia and joined the Red Army. Their younger brother Aaron was also alive, having survived the work camps because of his blond good looks, charm, and melodic voice, singing in a church choir. Now Zvi was detained in the squalid

DP camp on the island of Cyprus with survivor refugees. Both brothers eventually reached Palestine.

Despite her premonitions, Renia had harbored hopes about Sarah—one never knew for sure. But after she arrived in Palestine, she found out that her sister had been caught, in Bielsko, near the Slovakian border, along with a group of comrades and orphans. "Please take care of my sister Renia," was her last recorded request.

In 1945 Renia found an audience with her book. Encouraged by poet and politician Zalman Shazar, she completed her memoirs in Polish. Hakibbutz Hameuchad, an organization that published many survivor stories from the movement, had her work translated to Hebrew by Chaim Shalom Ben-Avram, a renowned Israeli translator. The Hebrew edition was well received; the early fighters of the Palmach, the elite brigade of the Yishuv's underground army, carried it with them in their backpacks.

Renia's story was excerpted and translated to Yiddish, printed in *Freuen in di Ghettos* by the Pioneer Women's Organization (now Na'amat). In 1947 the full book was published in English by Sharon Books, a publisher with the same downtown Manhattan address as Pioneer Women, and titled *Escape from the Pit*. The introduction was penned by author Ludwig

Lewisohn, a translator of important European works and a founder of Brandeis University.

Escape from the Pit was mentioned by essayists in the late 1940s: in one, about the (excessive) proliferation of Holocaust publications in America; in another, as suggested reading for students. The book was referred to in the testimony of at least one other survivor, who was critical that the story focused only on Freedom. Renia contributed to the Zaglembie memorial book published by survivors, as well as to an anthology about Frumka and Hantze. Writing was therapeutic. She channeled her torment into words. After this catharsis, Renia felt able to move on.

Her English book, however, faded with time. Perhaps flooded out by the deluge of American Holocaust publishing, or, as some suggest, the 1950s "trauma fatigue" experienced by many Jews, her tale fell out of fashion. The story may also have lost traction because Renia, unlike Hannah Senesh and Anne Frank, remained alive. It is harder to lionize the living. She did not promote it or become a spokesperson; if anything, the whole point of its publication was to put Poland behind her.

Renewal was so very important. "It happened, and it *passed*," was her motto. Renia stayed close to her brothers and comrades, in particular Chawka. But she also threw herself into the life of the kibbutz, doing manual labor, joining social activities, and, for the first time, learning Hebrew.

Then Renia was introduced to Akiva Herscovitch, a man from Jędrzejów who had made aliyah in 1939, before the war. Renia had been friendly with his sister and well-to-do father back in Poland. Akiva remembered Renia as a young, attractive teenager. They quickly fell in love. She was no longer alone, and in 1949 officially became Renia Herscovitch.

Akiva did not want to live on a kibbutz, and though Renia was sad to lose the social camaraderie and the Kibbutz Dafna community that she adored, she stuck with her love. They moved to Haifa, the country's principal port, a picturesque coastal city set on the slopes of Mount Carmel. She worked at the Jewish Agency, receiving immigrants from ships, until two days before her first child was born, in 1950. After all she'd been through, she was faced with another hurdle: Yakov, named for her little brother Yankeleh, who had been killed, was born partially paralyzed. Renia stopped working and dedicated herself to healing him—which she did.

Five years later, she birthed her daughter Leah, named for her mother, whose appearance and stern demeanor she shared; later on, Renia jokingly nick-

named her Klavta, Yiddish for "bitch." Renia had
prayed for a daughter, feeling that naming her child
after her mother was the only way she could ever honor
her memory. Many survivors' children speak of feeling like "replacements" for dead relatives, especially
grandparents they never knew. "Missing relations"
impacted survivor families. Often left without grandparents, aunts, uncles, or cousins, family members had
to take on unusual roles, shifting kinship structures for
generations.

Renia stayed home when her children were young.
She was funny and full of life, quick witted and a good
judge of character. Still charismatic, she also remained
sartorially inclined. She had dozens of skirt suits, each
to be worn with specific shoes, handbag, and accessories. When her hair turned white, she panicked,
even though she was seventy-two. (Of course, she had
not witnessed her own mother's aging.) According to
Yakov, the main fights he had with his mother when
growing up concerned his appearance. She felt he
looked too unkempt.

When Yakov and Leah were older, Renia went to
work as an assistant in a preschool, where the children
adored her. After that, she was an administrator at a
health care clinic. Self-taught, she remained active in
the left-wing Labor Party. Akiva was the manager of a

national marble company and then an electric company. A man of encyclopedic knowledge, he was also an artist who created mosaics and woodcuts that hung at local synagogues. Though he'd grown up in a religious family, Akiva no longer believed in God. Most of his large family had been murdered. He refused to speak a word of Polish, and used Yiddish only if he didn't want his children to understand what he was saying. The family spoke Hebrew at home.

Though Renia gave talks to students at Ghetto Fighters' House, stayed in touch with Freedom comrades, and spent hours analyzing the past with her sensitive brother Zvi, she rarely spoke about the Holocaust with her new family. She wanted to show her children joy, to encourage exploration. Their lives were filled with books, lectures, concerts, classical music, home-baked cookies, homemade gefilte fish (her mother Leah's recipe), travel, and optimism. She loved lipsticks and earrings. On Friday nights, their house was crowded with fifty people. Records played: tango, ballroom. Adolescent Yakov had joined The Young Guard and was not allowed to participate in the drinking and dancing parties that his mother threw. "Life is short," she said. "Enjoy everything, appreciate everything."

Despite their jovial home, Yakov and Leah always felt the darkness of the past. They sensed that they were absorbing Renia's history, even though they did not quite understand it. Leah read her mother's memoir when she was thirteen but didn't comprehend most of it. Yakov changed his last name from Herscovitch to the Israeli Harel in order to distance himself from the old land. A self-declared pessimist, he read his mother's book for the first time when he was forty.

"My father treated Renia like an *etrog*," Leah said, referring to the ceremonial Sukkot citrus fruit that is rare and expensive, and kept protected in a small box covered in soft, wispy cotton or horsehair. "She was strong but also fragile." Renia was asked to testify at the Eichmann trial, but Akiva didn't let her, worried the experience would be too stressful. Renia never requested financial compensation from Germany because she didn't want to *have* to tell her story. Why should she owe them anything, her time or her narrative? On Holocaust Remembrance Day, the family turned off the television. Everyone worried that Renia's memories would be too difficult for her to face; that she might crack. Or would they? "I was afraid her story would hurt me," Yakov revealed, frank like his mother.

Yakov, a retired engineer and a graduate of the Technion—Israel Institute of Technology, watched his first Remembrance Day programming only in 2018. Neither of Renia's children had read her memoir in years; the details were hazy. In her sixties, Renia read her own book in disbelief: How had she possibly done those things? All she recalled from that period was her confidence and her incredible desire for revenge. Her adult life was so different: happy, passionate, filled with beauty.

Renia turned a new leaf, a thousand new leaves, a whole tree.

Renia spoke to her brothers on the phone every single morning. The five survivors of the Białystok ring, including Chaika Grossman, who became a well-known liberal Israeli member of parliament, spoke every single night at ten o'clock. Fania stayed in touch with several women from the Union Factory who'd signed the handmade heart card, and visited their families across continents. Many of the Vilna partisans remained close over the years; their offspring still gather for annual commemorative events. Countless forest romances among Jews who risked their lives for one another lasted for decades. Today there are twenty-five thousand descendants of the Jews saved in the Bielski group, "Bielski babies." "Sisters" from camps, ghettos, and forests became surrogate families; the only people they had left from their early lives.

Yet not everyone shared such postwar camaraderie. Perhaps because she'd been alone, living a fake life for so much of the Holocaust, Bela Hazan's postwar experience was also solo, her memories mostly kept to herself as she created a new world. "I raised my children and immersed myself in daily life. I tried to contain my personal story," she wrote. "I didn't want my children to grow up in the shadow of the Holocaust." But, of course, her story remained "alive inside of me with the same strength."

Back on January 18, 1945, as the Russians neared Auschwitz, where she was working in the infirmary, Bela was sent on a death march to Germany. In rags, without shoes, she slogged through the snow for three days and nights with no food or drink. Anyone who marched out of tempo, who stood for a moment, who bent over to pick up snow to quench their blistering thirst, was shot on the spot. Thousands died en route. As a presumed non-Jew, Bela, terribly ill herself, was shipped to a subcamp of Ravensbruck, and then to a labor camp near Leipzig, where she volunteered to work as a nurse, and from which she escaped while carrying sick prisoners out to the American side. Her memoir, written nonstop in 1945, opens with the chapter "From Death March—to Life."

The Americans, who cried with her when they saw her emaciated body, helped Bela reach the Zionist office in Paris, where she finally discarded her Aryan identity as Bronislawa Limanowska, years of awful disguise at last undone. She met up with Jewish Brigade soldiers from Palestine, who took her to Italy. One of them, journalist Haim Zelshinki, interviewed her and wrote up her story. Bela spent three months in Italy working as a counselor, guiding and listening to the harrowing tales of forty-three girl survivors aged six to fourteen, mainly from the partisan family camps. The group was called "the Frumka Group," after Frumka Płotnicka, who was posthumously awarded a Polish Order of the Cross.

(Similarly, Białystok courier Chasia established a children's home in Łódź, where, without any formal training, she counseled a ragtag assembly of seventy-three traumatized Jewish orphans who had been hiding in convents, Polish homes, partisan bases, Soviet territory, death camps, cupboards, and forests. Years later, a number of child "reclaimers" questioned their earlier actions: Was it right for them to uproot these kids who had already been so traumatized, who craved stability, who wanted to be part of a family, not part of a people? But according to Chasia, at the time, they feared for the children's and their protectors' safety in

Poland, and it seemed morally unacceptable to allow the few remnants of Polish Jewry to assimilate into Christianity. Over a two-year journey, Chasia reached Palestine with her orphans, and she kept in touch with them all her life.)

In 1945, Bela, along with her group of girls, immigrated to Palestine, where she married Haim the journalist, changed their name to the more Israeli Yaari, and raised two children. Despite her Freedom background, she never felt connected with the underground fighters and sensed that Ghetto Fighters' House was a closed society. She kept her story to herself—but never forgot it.

One day Bela was contacted by Bronka Kilbanski, one of the Białystok couriers who went on to work at Yad Vashem. Back in the ghetto, Bronka had become romantically involved with Mordechai Tenenbaum, Tema's fiancé before she was killed. Bronka had hidden his archive of the Białystok ghetto; he'd also given her Tema's copy of the incriminating Gestapo Christmas party photograph of Bela, Lonka, and Tema for safekeeping. Now Bronka passed it on. Bela placed this heirloom next to her bed, where it stood for the rest of her life.

When Bela was approached by Ghetto Fighters' House in 1990 about publishing her forty-five-year-old memoir, she refused initially, afraid to face her horrific memories. But eventually she decided to do it, to tell her story for the sake of the innocent and brave who did not live. She did it because Lonka, on her deathbed, had asked her to. She did it for her children, who had nested safely, and her grandchildren, and generations to come.

Bela's son Yoel described her as deeply modest, never thinking of herself as a hero, never requesting reparations or recognition; she received a medal from a partisan organization in the 1990s only because Yoel applied on her behalf. If anything, Bela was plagued by guilt that she hadn't saved her family. As with many fighters for whom being a mensch and aiding the less fortunate was paramount, Bela dedicated her life to helping the poor and ill: she volunteered with blind people and in hospitals. (Anna Heilman became a social worker at the Children's Aid Society in Canada, where she lobbied the government about the humanitarian crisis in Darfur.) Whereas Bela's husband was intellectual, she was practical and social, with dozens of girlfriends. "Each time she got on a bus," her son joked, "she got off with a new phone number." Later in life, she preferred a senior living home to being alone. She became passionate about poetry and theater in her eighties. She was an optimist, hopeful, always resourceful.

After she died, Yoel, a neurobiologist, found her Auschwitz mug shot, that photo taken on that first wet horrific day. In it, Bela is smiling and beautiful, bold and strong. Like many children of survivors, his knowledge of her story was fragmented, and he felt himself grasping at hazy memories, at disjointed emotional anecdotes rather than a full history. He became obsessed with his mother's tale, haunted by the details he'd never asked for, and has spent several years researching and writing about her, passing on her noble legacy.

Days after liberation, in the outskirts of Vilna, Ruzka saw a mother carrying a small, skinny boy. The boy was crying and mumbled to his mother—in Yiddish. Ruzka had never cried in the ghetto, never in the forest. Now she burst into tears and sobbed. She'd been sure she'd never again hear the voice of a Jewish child.

Just as Vitka and Ruzka were together throughout the war, so they were for most of their lives afterward. That is, following a short separation. Immediately after liberation, Abba sent Vitka to Grodno to study the state of Jewish refugees, seek Zionists, and report back. Vitka had to jump off a train, fearing tightening patrols. Only people who came out of the concentration camps could cross the border freely, and so many non–camp survivors tattooed themselves.

Ruzka was sent to Kovno, Lithuania, and then to Bucharest, Romania, so that she could be an "ambassador" of the partisans, meet Yishuv officials, and convince them to bring over all the survivors. Her presence, her personality, Kovner knew, were right for the job—people would believe her. The journey was difficult. Postwar Poland was torn up and dangerous, and yet the freedom to walk on the streets without being immediately killed was confounding for her. Ruzka's story was so compelling to the Yishuv emissaries—the tale of a fighter rather than a tragedy—that the leader commanded her to go straight to Palestine and share her narrative.

She traveled on false papers as someone's wife. The ship journey was lonely, totally disorienting. Aliyah had been her dream, but now she felt untethered. She landed at Atlit, the camp for illegal Jewish immigrants, and was appalled by the terrible conditions. No one came to get her; she felt forgotten, stranded until word of her story got out. Suddenly leaders and their wives began to visit her in a stream; she felt like a "curiosity on display." Eventually one of the leaders got her forged medical papers, claiming she had tuberculosis, and she was released. She was sent on a speaking tour, telling her story, everyone taken by her style and tale: the horrors, but through the eyes of a fighter. Many recall that she was "the first messenger."

None of this was easy for Ruzka. She felt that many of the Yishuv leaders did not understand her and were instead obsessed with the new. David Ben-Gurion, then a leading Labor Zionist who would soon become Israel's first Prime Minister, once took to the stage after an emotional testimony and insulted her use of Yiddish as a "grating language." Ruzka joined a kibbutz and began writing her memoirs, but she was desperately lonely and wrote pleading letters to Vitka, who was still "in the war."

Vitka was angry about Ruzka's departure—part of her life had ended. She didn't know how to respond to the letters, so she didn't. She and Abba officially became a couple in Vilna. But Abba had to leave because the Russians were after him for being a Zionist. One day Vitka decided it was time to join him—she schmoozed her way onto a flight to Lublin, what she called a "town of drunkenness and murder." There, the Zionists stayed in an apartment, talking, sharing, crying, laughing all day and night. They established Bricha, and Vitka worked on the underground railroad, shepherding Jews to the border by foot.

Abba, however, was still entirely intent on revenge.

He and Vitka gathered Jewish fighters and became leaders of a new brigade of Avengers. Based out of Italy, obsessed with retribution and destruction, they deployed fighters across Europe and near camps where Nazis were being held under arrest. Zelda Treger, after being sent out to find survivors and to smuggle Jews out of the country, was recruited to work on the revenge mission, transferring funds, helping the activists, finding them safe houses. Abba traveled to Palestine to obtain poison for his plan, while Vitka visited the brigades, worried for their mental stability. Abba was captured on the way back and imprisoned in Cairo. He sent the poison to Vitka, who, with fake papers and numerous arrests, had made it to Paris. Abba's note told her to carry out plan B. She did, "the CEO of Vengeance." The bread for a camp near Nuremberg, where Americans were holding former Nazis, was successfully poisoned, causing thousands of Germans to fall ill. Abba decided that the Avengers should carry on their fight in Palestine. This caused much conflict; some returned to Europe on revenge missions, but ultimately Ruzka convinced many to stay in Palestine and defend the land.

Vitka arrived in Palestine in 1946 on the very last boat that the British allowed to dock; soon after, she settled on Kibbutz Ein Horesh in a house twenty yards from Ruzka's. Despite that brief postwar split, Ruzka and Vitka spent most of their adult lives entwined, their children growing up together. Ruzka, married to an Austrian who'd made aliyah before the war, was the first to know of Vitka's pregnancy. They had all stopped menstruating back in the forest and assumed they were barren. Their fertility came as an astonishing surprise.

Zelda and her husband, Sanka, a fighter from the forest, also came to Palestine. They decided not to settle on the kibbutz but in Netanya and then Tel Aviv. Zelda had two children, to whom she insisted on passing on Holocaust stories despite Sanka's desire to detach. Zelda returned to her prewar career and worked as a kindergarten teacher. She also opened up a delicatessen in downtown Tel Aviv. From Nazi fighter to sandwiches—not an uncommon trajectory for these survivors.

Ruzka and Vitka, however, both worked on the kibbutz—at first in the fields, a tremendously cathartic social activity. Ruzka later became an educator and kibbutz secretary. With time, they developed additional careers. Ruzka was not allowed to study, as the kibbutz wanted all survivors to be "reeducated" as a priority, but eventually she and Abba founded Moreshet, a Young Guard center for the study of the Holocaust and the resistance, intended to differ from

Freedom's Ghetto Fighters' House in its desire to consider the war from different perspectives, including a strong focus on women as well as on the complex and dynamic Jewish life in Poland before 1939. Ruzka was its head. An editor, writer, historian, and activist, she empathized, encouraged, and taught. Ruzka was ill for years, but kept her symptoms a secret, even from her family. In 1988, less than a year after Abba passed, Ruzka died of cancer. One of Ruzka's three children, Yonat, a high school teacher, began to work at Moreshet, carrying on "the family business."

Vitka, who became the quiet backdrop to her husband's very public life, took her passions elsewhere. Unlike Abba and Ruzka, she never talked about her past—certainly not about her early life in Poland. When her first child was three, Vitka developed tuberculosis. Her doctor told her she had four months to live; she told him, "I will live." She did. Vitka was put in isolation, not able to see her son up close for nearly two years. While recuperating, she enrolled in correspondence courses in history, English, and French. Though she was told she must never have another child, she gave birth to a daughter several years later. This, too, was fraught with difficulties: she was forced to maintain distance from her baby and not breast-feed for fear of infecting her.

Vitka didn't settle into the kibbutz women's life of the kitchen and sewing; instead, she helped with children's education. At age forty-five, she went to university and trained as a clinical psychologist, completing a bachelor of arts and advanced degrees. She was a disciple of Dr. George Stern, a fiery and unusual practitioner who specialized in using instinct—her forte—to work with young children. She devised a method whereby disturbed children expressed themselves through color, navigating their prelinguistic minds just as she'd done in the forest, without a map. She developed a successful and busy practice, and trained many therapists interested in her technique. She retired at eighty-five.

Vitka's daughter, Shlomit, with whom she had a complex bond, wrote poems about Vitka for a book about her published by Moreshet after her death. Her son, Michael, an artist in Jerusalem, has created graphic novels and texts about both his parents' lives. When asked about his mother's personality, his immediate response was: "She had a *goyish* temperament. Despite her very Jewish looks, she had a non-Jewish personality in that she was someone who went *toward* danger." He explained that Vitka was attracted to intimidating people, from Abba to Stern; she gravitated toward fire, dared to touch it, figuratively and literally. "She didn't care about the rules. She had true chutzpah."

Vladka Meed arrived in the United States on the second ship that brought survivors to America, and settled in New York with her husband, Benjamin, the man who had helped her make hidden compartments in her valises. Soon after landing, she was dispatched by the Jewish Labor Committee—which had sent funding to Warsaw—to lecture about her experiences. Both Vladka and Ben became deeply involved in establishing Holocaust survivor organizations, memorials, and museums, including the United States Holocaust Memorial Museum in Washington, DC. Vladka was formally recognized as one of the country's leaders in this area. She organized exhibits about the Warsaw ghetto uprising as well as initiated and directed international seminars about Holocaust pedagogy. Vladka stayed connected to her Bundist roots and became vice president of the JLC, for which she served as a weekly Yiddish-language commentator on WEVD, the New York Yiddish station. Their daughter and son both became physicians. She retired to Arizona, where she died in 2012, a few weeks short of her ninety-first birthday.

Renia was always petite and thin, physically feeble. Yet she never stopped being a force. "When she walked into a room," her son explained, "it was like a fire hit."

Her joyful demeanor and optimistic outlook eluded her own family. "How could someone have gone through what she went through and be so happy?" her eldest granddaughter, Merav, wondered. "Usually it's the pessimists who survive, but not in her case," Merav said while reminiscing about how much her *savta* loved the sea, walks on the beach, promenades through town. At age seventy-four, Renia even traveled to Alaska.

Her husband, Akiva, died in 1995, and until Renia's late eighties, she was constantly being wooed by new suitors. Her primped and polished appearance never waned. But it became apparent that she needed more day-to-day help. So Renia convinced *her friends* to move into a senior home, try it out, set it up, and then, when her social world was already established, she came too. She continued to be funny, quick, and center stage, hypnotizing people with her looks and energy. At eighty-seven, she frequently left her assisted living facility, not returning until midnight. Her children panicked every evening.

"What am I doing here with all these old people?" she asked them, exasperated, theatrical as always.

"Mom, they're the same age as you."

But they were old in body and soul, while Renia was still frisky and full of life.

Many of the female fighters were decisive, instinct

driven, goal oriented, and optimistic; many of those who survived were blessed with energy and longevity. Hela Schüpper, who also settled in Israel, died at ninety-six, leaving behind three children and ten grandchildren. Vladka passed at ninety, Chasia at ninety-one, and Vitka died at ninety-two. At the time of this writing, Fania Fainer, Faye Schulman, and several Vilna partisans were still alive, all ranging in age from ninety-five to ninety-nine.

Renia never accepted the advances of her would-be beaus. In her twenty years of widowhood, she did not have even one boyfriend. Her dedication to her husband was a model of loyalty for her children and grandchildren. "Family is the most important thing," she never stopped telling them, certainly a lesson from her painful losses. "Always stay together."

Renia's grandchildren (and great-grandchild) were her utmost treasures, but their births also reminded her of all that had vanished. She hosted Friday-night and holiday dinners with zeal, and attended their weddings dressed in glimmering frocks and oversized smiles. But she also told them her stories: tales of the war, of her siblings who were murdered, passing on as much of her heritage as she could. Many survivors formed easier connections with their grandchildren, who were not "substitute family" and with whom they had less fraught dynamics. They were less protective of their grandkids, and their own fears of intimacy—stemming from having lost close relatives—had diminished over the decades. Renia may not have taken her own children, but she took her grandchildren to the Ghetto Fighters' House on Holocaust Remembrance Day, recognizing how important it was to send her story into the future. Like many third-generation children, her grandkids—who had learned about the Holocaust in school and had an intellectual response to it, too—asked her many questions, which she gladly answered. This opened her up to talking with Leah about her past as well. Renia's adolescence may have been hidden away, but it never disappeared.

On Monday, August 4, 2014, nearly ninety years after she was born on that Sabbath eve in Jędrzejów, Renia passed on. She was buried at the Neve David Cemetery in Haifa among lush grass and trees, just by the sea, and next to Akiva, exactly where she wanted to be. She had outlived most of her friends, but her funeral was filled with seventy loving people from her old-age home and the health clinic where she once worked, as well as many of her children's decades-old friends upon whom she'd made a lifelong impression. But mostly, there stood the strong family unit she had cultivated from nothing, the new branches from a decapitated tree. Her grandson Liran gave a eulogy, reminiscing about her sparkling conversation and, in particular, her sense of humor. Gesturing at Renia's generations, he said: "You always fought like a real hero."

Epilogue: A Missing Jew

Spring 2018. More than a decade after I first found *Freuen* in the dimly lit British Library, I boarded a flight to Israel. Those women who'd lived in my head for years—well, now I was going to have coffees with their kids. I would sift through boxes of their photos and letters. I would see where they ended up, lived the next phase of their lives, died. I chewed two pieces of gum at a time, reeling with anxiety. I had become a fearful flyer in general and was nervous about being in Israel, which I hadn't visited in ten years, and never alone. That week was a particularly pungent one, even by Israeli standards: Syria bombings, Nakba Day protests in Gaza, conflict with Iran, the US embassy moving to Jerusalem, and a heat wave. I was a flee-er who was headed into the fire.

There were not many books about these warrior women, but I'd brought what I could find with me on the plane, cramming for my interviews as if for an exam. I kept reminding myself that my project was not about abstract characters anymore. I was meeting the comrades' children, the people whom these women had birthed and raised. Then I worried again about my own young children, who I was leaving behind in New York for ten days—the longest time and farthest distance I'd ever been away from them.

I'd been shocked by the silencing of this story of Jewish women in the resistance, but the truth was, I too had been silent. It would take me a full twelve years to finally complete this book, a whole birth-to-bat-mitzvah period. Some of this time span was due to the difficulty of the project. My Yiddish was rusty, to say the least, and translating *Freuen*'s 1940s prose rife with Germanic words (which differed from the Polish dialect I heard at home and the Canadian one I studied at school) was arduous. *Freuen* was a scrapbook of writings by and about a slew of characters with hard-to-pronounce names. There were no annotations, footnotes, or explanations; there was zero context, especially challenging for a reader in pre-smartphone days.

But the other reason for the long time delay was emotional. While I could handle a few hours of translation here and there, I was not ready or willing to dive exclusively into the Holocaust day and night for months and years on end—the commitment necessary to complete a book. I was thirty when I found *Freuen*, single, desperate for career recognition, restless in my then-dense bones. Even back then, I knew how hard this project would be emotionally, intellectually, ethically, politically. The idea of spending my days in 1943 felt as if I would be removing myself from the contemporary world, from being present in my own life.

Some of this certainly had to do with my family background. My *bubbe* had fled, was imprisoned in Siberian Gulags, and lived, but never quite survived surviving. She did not stay quiet but every afternoon howled her pain at her sisters' deaths, the youngest just eleven. She swore aloud at our German neighbor (and the fruit store workers who she felt were cheating her), she refused to take elevators because they were enclosed, and was eventually medicated for paranoia. My mother, born in 1945 on my "Asian" grandmother's route back to Poland—a refugee before knowing what home was—also suffered from extreme anxiety. Both my mother and grandmother were hoarders, filling their cracked cores with bargain basement dresses, stacks of newspapers, and old Danish pastry. There was no question that my family members loved one another, but this love was intense—almost too deep at times. Emotions were explosive. My home life was fraught and fragile; the heavy mood lifted only by bursts of laughter at *Three's Company* and *Yes Minister*, by comedy performance.

And so, I spent most of my early life trying to make walls, clean up, run away. I fled to different countries and continents, through careers as far as possible from the Holocaust. Comedy, art theory. *Curator* was the least Yiddish word I knew, and I wanted in.

Only once I was forty, with a mortgage, memoir (about this very issue of the generational transmission of trauma in my family), and motherhood under my belt (loosened for the middle-aged spread), did I feel stable enough to dive in. But this meant that I had to face the Holocaust from a new perspective. I was no longer even in the realm of the age of the fighters. I was the age of the people the fighters rebelled against: the people who would not have been sent left for work, but right, to death. I was stronger, but also, so much more mortal as a middle-aged mother, deeply aware of how impossible it is to judge responses to terror, of how "flight" was also resistance. Now I had to fill my life not only with gruesome accounts of the horrors of the Holocaust but also of the specific tortures placed on parents, unable to protect their starving children; stories of girls, seven years old, like my own daughter, whose families were shot dead in front of them, leaving them to roam through forests alone, eating wild berries and grass. It was not easy to read horrific tales of toddlers being torn from their mothers' arms while I was working at a coffee shop across the street from my younger daughter's synagogue preschool, especially as the nursery began increasing its security measures due to armed white supremacist attacks on US synagogues. I had to open myself nearly every day, alone, to these raw testimonies, still so painful, seventy-five years later. And now I was going across the globe, leaving my daughters, to get even closer.

Fortunately, the smooth landing at Tel Aviv Ben Gurion International Airport—yes, the same Ben-Gurion who had chastised Ruzka for her grating Yiddish—distracted me from my morose thoughts and launched me into Israel, so full of conflict, so full of life. Right away, the political and landscape changes struck me: the building development, the posters, the boutique hotels. I took a long walk down the salty Jaffa coast to help my jet lag (it didn't) and prepare myself for six o'clock the next morning, when I would begin to work.

The most nerve-wracking and exciting meeting was the one I had managed to schedule with Renia's son and potentially, her daughter too. After her "Renia K." name in *Freuen*, and the book's mention that she was living on Kibbutz Dafna (in 1946), I visited online archives and tracked down a Renia Kokelka whose details cohered with the excerpts. I found her immigration file at the Israel State Archives—with photos! I found her Hebrew memoir. I discovered a genealogical report, which included the mention of a son, and a link to a condolence note after her death—it was from the Egged bus company and addressed to a Yakov Harel. Could that be her child? Was Harel a last name or a first?

After trying a few Yakov Harels on Facebook (with hipster moustaches, they did not look to be the right age), I managed, via my wonderful Israeli fixer, to contact the bus company. It was indeed him! He agreed to meet at his home in Haifa. It seemed he might even have a sister, and she might be interested in joining. I was going to meet the children of this writer with whom I'd felt years of intimate connection. Not to mention, the person who had to carry my whole tale.

But before even meeting Renia's family, there were so many others. I trawled through the country, north to south. From upscale and sleek suburban cafés, to Tel Aviv's Bauhaus living rooms. From a Jerusalem restaurant that happened to be on the corner of Haviva Reich Street, to the Israel National Library, where the 1940s books of obituaries and literary essays that had been the source material for *Freuen* were on open access, available to me in rooms where I could converse. (Not quite the same vibe as the British Library.) From the wide-open, wood-paneled, and elegant Ghetto Fighters' House to the vast archives of Yad Vashem (its entrance blocked by a pile of machine guns from soldiers on a lunch break). From the basement of Moreshet, where a gallery that was unlocked and lit especially for me displayed extensive exhibitions on women in the resistance and prewar Polish Jewry, to the International Style basement of the Yad Mordechai Museum, designed by renowned architect Arieh Sharon. I met scholars, curators, archivists, and the children and grandchildren of Ruzka, Vitka, Chajka, Bela, Chasia, and Zivia.

I had already visited Holocaust museums and archives in North America, and had interviewed many children of partisan Bundists and Yiddishists from New York to California to Canada. But the Israeli families felt different. The language, the mannerisms, the etiquette—their world was more political, more livewire, with strong feelings and high stakes. I often met with the "Holocaust spokesperson" of the family, the relative who worked or hobbied passionately in the subject. I was grilled by one who worried that my interest was superficial; another was concerned I would steal the work her group had compiled; and another did not want to reveal much unless I agreed to write a movie with him. Yet another told me of legal battles over the portrayal of their family member in academic publications. Each archive—all Labor Zionist—reiterated its specialty and why its view made more sense than the others.

Of all the meetings that week, it was the one with Renia's children that made me most nervous, barely able to eat my gourmet schnitzel beforehand. I had staked my project on this woman, whom I felt for, with whom I had a writerly bond. What if her family disliked me, refused to tell me anything, were cold or difficult, or had their own agendas?

But when I entered her son's home, a condo on a hill above breezy, blue Haifa, I found the opposite. Kind, welcoming people who were not in the "professional survivor business," they were grateful for the things I knew about Renia that I could share with them. I sat on the sofa, Renia's daughter, Leah, on an armchair— Renia's armchair, she told me, which no one was throwing out. The face from the photographs of my heroine that I'd dug up on archival sites stared at me in different embodiments: the strong jawline, the intense eyes. It was like seeing a childhood friend in their own children, the genetics knocking me for a loop. We were all amazed that we'd found one another.

And then I was amazed by what they told me. Yes, of course, Renia was funny, sharp, sarcastic, theatrical.

But also a fashionista who traveled the world. A ball of fire and laughter. A social whirlwind. A force of joy.

As I listened to them speak of their mother, whom they clearly adored and mourned deeply, it dawned on me that in all my questing, I had not actually been looking for my kindred soul. I stared out at the hills and valleys, the golden sunset over Haifa, and knew that Renia was not the writerly companion on my same page, but the opposite. My hero was the surrogate ancestor I'd wished for: the "happy relative" who survived, thrived, and celebrated life.

A month later, I was flying from a research trip in London to Warsaw. Or at least, I thought I was headed to Warsaw. I hadn't realized that the delayed budget airline flight I'd chosen would deposit me in a former military airfield an hour north of the city. In the middle of the night. Alone. *Welcome back to Poland.*

I'd taken my first trip to Poland soon after I originally discovered *Freuen in di Ghettos,* back in 2007. Accompanied by my then fiancé, my brother, and a friend, I went on an autumn "roots" voyage where I crisscrossed the country in a week, visiting all four shtetls where each of my grandparents grew up, as well as Jewish historical sites in several larger cities. Back then, I had my pick of tour guides who were eager to show me around, to tell me their versions of stories. One night my phone rang at midnight: it was the deputy mayor of Łódź, who'd heard I was in town. Could we meet for coffee the following day? Could he arrange a tour for me? New Jewish organizations were sprouting up to preserve cemeteries and provide kosher lunches. A Jewish Community Center was about to open in Kraków. I met twenty- and thirty-somethings who'd recently found out they were Jewish; their grandparents had kept it hidden during the years under Soviet rule. One of my guides was exactly my age, had a grandfather from the same town as mine, and had grown up across the street from the Majdanek concentration camp. He'd become obsessed with the war and talked with me through the night. I had come to Poland searching for my missing roots but found a Poland that was searching for its missing Jew.

On the other hand, I'd had dinner at a "Jewish themed" restaurant in Kraków where musicians played "Fiddler on the Roof," the waiters served hamantaschen for dessert, and my fellow diners were busloads of clapping German tourists. I met distant relatives of mine who had stayed in Poland after the war because of their Communist beliefs, and who lived through Soviet rule and antisemitic attacks. One of them relayed how as a young boy, his parents had grabbed his hand, and the three of them fled from the ghetto into the forest; he survived the war in a partisan camp. He was livid about the "new Jew" culture in Poland, furious about the kosher lunches that he felt did not address the needs of the long-suffering Jewish community, and convinced that this was just a way for Poles to exploit American donations.

I did not know what to make of these two conflicting takes. Admittedly, I felt skeptical about the growth of a Jewish consciousness and philosemitism, in a country drenched in Jewish blood.

Now, returning to Poland by myself in the summer of 2018 to conduct research for this book about female fighters, I was still unsure. But whatever I'd experienced a decade earlier was no longer. On the one hand, Warsaw had become an urban megapolis; I stayed on the forty-first story of a hotel that looked out onto a futuristic cityscape that had once been the area of the ghetto and, before that, where all my grandparents lived. The hotel was filled with Israeli tourists; apparently, Warsaw is a popular shopping destination, and as young Israelis are priced out of their own real estate market, they've started investing in the old country. I walked down the city streets, passed monuments to the likes of Frumka Płotnicka and the sewage canal of Zivia's story, to POLIN, the new, impressive museum of the history of Polish Jews, with exhibits about the Holocaust but also the thousand years of rich Jewish life that preceded it, and the decades after.

Kraków, this time around, was packed with tour buses, gelato shops, and pickpocket warnings; I kept confusing it for Venice, except that its café culture seemed more hip. Tour guides were harder to secure, most of them booked for months. The Kraków JCC, now well established, had opened a nursery school for Jewish offspring. (The director, American Jonathan Ornstein, referred to the old Kraków Jew-themed restaurants as "Jew-rassic Park.") There were Jewish organizations in numerous cities catering to older populations and to young "new Jews."

I attended the twenty-eighth annual Jewish Culture Festival in Kraków, founded and curated by a man who was not Jewish himself. The festival was based in the stylish, artsy Kazimierz, the old Jewish area, with seven still-standing synagogues dating from as early as 1407. The festival drew Jews and non-Jews from around the globe. Alongside klezmer music and art, the festival presented lectures, tours, and seminars probing contemporary Polish-Jewish relations, and asking why Poland needs, wants, and misses its Jews.

I had lunch with a group of literary Poles my age who surprised me with their keen interest in my work; when they found out that all four of my grandparents were from Poland, they mocked me for being more Polish than any of them. Once, at a busy crosswalk, I stopped and stared: I looked just like everyone around me. I was given a discount on a tour ticket because, based on my appearance, it was assumed I was a local. Since my London days, I thought I looked obviously Jewish, but nowadays here it was hard to tell . . . perhaps because there are so few Jews in Poland.

On the one hand, I felt eerily at home. On the other hand, the government had just passed a law making it illegal to blame Poland for any crimes committed in the Holocaust, and that doing so could result in incarceration. After decades of Soviet repression and Nazi conquest before that, the Poles were in a new nationalist phase. Their own victim status in World War II was important. The Polish underground was hugely popular, its anchor symbol graffitied across Warsaw buildings. People wore T-shirts with sleeve decorations that mimicked the resistance armband. A Home Army family legacy held great cache. In Kraków, a longtime exhibit about Jewish resisters in the ghetto was replaced by a broader non-Jewish war story. The Poles wanted to feel their heroism against the grand enemies.

And here I was, writing about this very issue. I felt connection and a new level of alienation and fear. Once again, a Poland of two extremes, just like many of the women described in their memoirs.

It is deeply troubling to make laws about what historical narratives are allowed to be told—it shows a rulership interested in propaganda, not truth. But I also understood that the Poles felt misunderstood. Warsaw had been decimated. The Nazi regime enslaved, terrorized, bombed, and killed many Christian Poles—Renia, after all, was jailed and tortured as a Pole, not a Jew. To be held responsible for the Holocaust did seem unfair, especially when the Polish government did not collaborate with Nazis and attempted to run a resistance faction—albeit one that was only mildly Jew friendly. Certainly, this claim is unjust to those who risked their lives to help Jews—a number that could be greater than we know. Those Poles had been silent about it under Soviet rule, but historian Gunnar S. Paulsson has argued that in Warsaw alone, seventy to ninety thousand Poles helped conceal Jews; this is a ratio of 3 to 4 Poles per hidden Jew. Some scholars have noted that Jews felt particularly hurt and betrayed by their Polish neighbors, and so their reports of Pole's anti-Jewish behavior are emphasized in their testimonies. Then again, there were many Poles who did nothing, and, worse, many who turned on and turned in Jews, selling them to the Gestapo for pennies or a bit of sugar, blackmailing, profiteering, happily stealing property; many were antisemites and themselves perpetrators. I have tried to understand the Polish sentiment of victimhood without whitewashing the antisemitism, without playing a game of "who suffered more."

Inspired by these women fighters' memoirs, I began to see the importance of laying out stories that were multifaceted, telling tales that were not black and white, that ached in their ambivalence. History needs to account for complexities; we must all confront our pasts honestly, face the ways we are both victims and aggressors. Otherwise, no one will believe the storyteller, and we will write ourselves out of any real conversation. Understanding does not have to mean forgiving, but it is a necessary step for self-possession and growth.

"Carefulski!" I said to the driver, trying not to appear rude—not to mention, my Polish was slightly lacking—but it looked like the truck was headed straight for us. Fast.

In doing research for this book, I found myself on a tour de monde, in myriad unusual situations, as authors often do. Eating *burekas* with the daughters of ghetto fighters who were cross-examining me in the kitchen of their kibbutz workplace in the Galilee; New York City commemorative gatherings of Bundists who stood to sing "The Partisan Song" as if their anthem; poring over photos of forest *ziemlankas* at a French café in Montreal, making sure not to stain them with croissant-buttery hands; carrying my sleepy three-year-old down flights of stairs in a Kraków hotel during a five-in-the-morning fire alarm to the background of blaring Polish directives.

And now this: one of my last days, a pilgrimage to find Renia's birthplace. I was carsick in the backseat of a cigarette-smoke-filled, decades-old Skoda with no power windows, power steering, or AC, soaked from the morning traipse through a thunderstorming tour of the Kamionka ghetto, where I hiked into drenched weeds to stand right on the site of Frumka's fighter bunker. Afterward, we'd had a snack at a Będzin "Jewish café" filled with Judaica and serving what was allegedly *the* Jewish dessert of sweet cheese, orange rind, syrup, and raisins—one I'd never heard of. (The restaurant had a reputation as a good local date spot.) We also stopped to see a refurbished prewar private prayer house, with glistening golden walls adorned with frescoes of Jewish tribes, uncovered a few years ago, by accident, by playing children—for decades, the room had been used for coal storage. Now the driver stopped smack in the middle of the road. In the middle of nowhere. Hour five of driving that day, with many more to go as I traced the sites of Renia's story. My chauffeur was screaming in Polish into her phone; my guide, originally from Lithuania, was in the passenger seat, lighting the next cigarette for her before the last was done.

Fortunately, the truck's blaring, angry honk convinced my driver to pull over. She promptly shut the engine, and stepped outside, pacing, smoking, and yelling into her cell.

"It's a divorce thing," my guide turned to the backseat to explain to me. "Her daughter is with her ex, and she's very upset. Sorry about the delay."

A mother of daughters myself, I couldn't complain, especially since both the driver and the guide were charging me minimal fees for such an intense day of trekking—they were interested in Renia's and the female fighters' stories, too, and wanted to be part of this journey. I sat in that backseat drinking Diet Coke, hoping it would settle my nausea, and thinking about the issues faced by women researchers who were researching women. Being a mother had affected my own work countless times. I was offered a funded research residency that I had to turn down; I couldn't move my family for a few months to a different city. Instead, I took many small trips, all of which were administrative feats, organizing childcare and drop-offs and small gifts for my daughters so they could mark off each day I was gone. My fridge door was a mosaic of pickup, lunch-packing and photo-day schedules, set down to the minute. I even had to bring my kids to Poland for several days (hence the fire alarm scenario). On other days, I walked so many miles that the age-old sciatica from my pregnancies flared, and my evenings were spent in the hotel bathtub.

And then, of course, there was always the issue of security. The late nights of research when I wanted to get dinner in a new city, and each step was anxious, preceded by a look around as I scouted for danger. Caution was a relic of my Jewish past and a reality of my female present. I could not wander listening to music—my ears and eyes had to be open. And then there I was, in rural Poland, in a truck's way, barely traceable, no one knowing my precise location, a flimsy wireless connection. What had I done? At least I was with women, I consoled myself to the sounds of an upset chain-smoking mother who continued to pace.

Per chance, I'd hired a woman local guide, who, in turn, hired this woman driver.

Three working women in the middle of nowhere. I thought of women's histories, stories that also get stuck in the middle of nowhere, that get lost. At last, our driver hung up her phone, got in the car, and jerked us into action, and as usual for that day, all my research materials went flying onto the wet Skoda floor. "Sorry," she turned back to me to say, "I'm starving."

Though my fragile innards were not quite ready, I agreed to stop for an early dinner at the next restaurant— they warned me that eateries were few and far between on these country roads. There was no main highway in these parts, which is why the 150 miles took five hours; I kept imagining how long it took the couriers, in disguise, in 1943. The roadside café was in a glorious open field, shimmering orange and gold in the summer sun. Here in the middle of nothing but pastoral beauty, there had been Jews, and there had been a well-oiled ghetto-and-murder system to kill them. The Nazi assault was pervasive. There was nowhere to run.

Inside, I waited while my team smoked and reapplied lipstick. Then, while I picked at my plate heaped with dozens of mushroom pierogis (the only vegetarian item available), and they quickly ate their beef stews and fried pork chops, I asked about their friendship.

These two women, roughly my age, had met recently. They were both self-described feminists, a label that they wore proudly, defiantly. They had met at a feminist rally. "For what?" I asked.

"For everything."

The government wanted to criminalize all abortion and disallow in vitro fertilization because it produced "wasted seed." The all-powerful church ran Kraków's top hotels but paid no taxes, they told me. My two companions were outraged at the misogyny, incensed by their government's unjust treatment of women. I certainly understood.

"It sounds like the Poland I write about, of the nineteen thirties and forties, was more feminist than now," I said.

"In some ways, it was!" they agreed, pounding fists on the wooden table.

We finally arrived at my last stop on this journey, in Jędrzejów, at the address Leah had given me for Renia's childhood home—the house where she was born on that Friday back in 1924, the beginning of it all. Klasztorna Street was easy to find, but number 16 did not seem to exist. If we counted plots, demarcated by trees well over a hundred years old, however, we ended up at a small stone structure, gray, with a triangular roof. Several matching houses surrounded a green yard, where a dog barked. My guide went ahead of me and found one of the inhabitants. I didn't understand the rapid-fire Polish, but I did understand the negative nod of the woman's head. "She says the addresses changed," my guide told me. "Number sixteen must have been a wooden house that burnt down. She said she never heard of the family. She asked if they were Jews."

"Did you tell her?"

"I tried to avoid the question," my fixer said, trying to fix things. "They get scared here," she whispered, "worried that the Jews will return to take back their property."

I was not invited inside.

I took some photos of the outside, then we headed back into the Skoda to drive through the Kielce region at dusk, the bleeding sun, the fertile fields, this secret pocket of beauty between Warsaw and Kraków, still. Nothing like the gray-hued Poland of my imagination. Things go backward and forward, but here we were, three women from very different backgrounds—a Pole, a Lithuanian, and a Jew—brought together by Renia and the female fighters, all of us ready to reclaim, to fight, all of us feeling strong, agent, and, for a brief moment, safe.

Author's Note: On Research

Unsurprisingly, conducting research around the world, using sources that span decades, continents, and alphabets, led to various research challenges and conundrums.

The primary source material for this project comprised mainly memoirs and testimonies. Some were oral and recorded on video or audio, some were written—in Hebrew, Yiddish, English, Polish, Russian, German. Some were translated, some were translations of translations, some I translated myself. Some were composed privately, others, for an interviewer. Some were fact-checked, edited, even cowritten with scholars and published (generally by small and academic presses); others were diaries, raw testimony, filled with passion, writing fueled by fury. Some were written immediately after the war or even during the war while in hiding, and contain mistakes, contradictory details, and omissions—things were simply not known or altered for security reasons, or emotional ones. (Some survivors found it too difficult to write about certain people's deaths.) Some were written quickly, fingers burning, in a desperate attempt not to forget, a purging of experience composed with a fear of being caught. Renia often used initials instead of names (her byline was "Renia K."), which I believe was for safety—she was writing in wartime about covert underground operations that still held terrific danger. She was also writing at a time when she genuinely did not know how other people's stories turned out; she herself was awaiting news of whether her friends and relatives were alive. Like many early scribes, Renia wrote out of a desire to tell the world what happened *objectively*, trying to veer away from her personal stance. Characteristically, she uses the word "we," and at times it can be hard to discern whether she is referring to herself, her family, her community, or to the Jewish people at large.

Other testimonies were offered later, especially in the 1990s, and though they are often composed with the depth of insight gained over time, the memories may be altered by contemporary trends, others' memories they've heard over the years, and the survivor's current concerns and goals. Some people argue that those who were traumatized suppressed many memories and that the fighters who were not tortured in camps have stronger recollections—"a surplus of memory," according to Antek. Others argue that traumatic memories are some of the most pungent, accurate, and relentless. I also sifted through ephemeral primary documents (articles, letters, notebooks) and interviewed dozens of family members—each of whom had his or her own versions of stories, often contradicting one another's.

Memory twists and turns; memoirs are not "cold data." Many differences came up among these dozens and dozens of accounts: the details of events were often at odds, and dates, all over the place. Sometimes the same person provided personal testimonies on several occasions over the years, and her own tellings differed dramatically; at times I found inconsistencies within the same text. I found discrepancies between primary and secondary sources; for instance, academic biographers and historians shared accounts of these women that differed from the women's own stories. Sometimes the differences in primary sources were intriguing— they had to do with taking responsibility, with whom to blame. When this was relevant, I tried to highlight it, usually in the endnotes. I attempted to understand where these differences were coming from and to cross-reference stories with historical analyses. I aimed to present the versions that seemed most reasonable and rich. At times I merged details from many accounts to build a full picture, to present the most emotionally authentic and factually accurate story that I could. Ultimately, when in doubt, I deferred to the women's testimonies and truths.

I have relayed scenes as directly as possible from my sources. My reconstructions sometimes enhance feelings that were implied in the original text and take into account multiple perspectives of the same event, but all are nonfiction, based on research.

While the differences in accounts were intriguing, overall, I was more taken by the tremendous number of overlaps. Sources from different corners of time and place told the same obscure anecdotes, described similar situations and people. In addition to helping me establish veracity, it was touching and exciting. Each time I revisited the story from another lens, I learned more, dug deeper, felt that I was truly entering their universe. These young people and their passions were connected, figuratively and literally.

Another complex issue in this type of multilinguistic study is names, of both people and places. Many Polish towns sport numerous titles—Slavic, German, Yiddish—having been relabeled continually with fluctuating rulership. To use one name over another is often a political choice—not my explicit intention here. I have tended to use the contemporary place names as they are written in English.

As for personal names, the women in my story, like most Polish Jews, had Polish, Hebrew, and Yiddish names, and nicknames. Some had wartime aliases. Or several. Sometimes they used additional fake identities for emigration papers. (It was usually easier to leave Europe if a woman was faux married.) Then they changed their names to suit the languages of the countries where they ended up. (For instance: Vladka Meed began as Feigele Peltel. Vladka was her Polish undercover name; she married a Miedzyrzecka, which was changed to Meed when they moved to New York.) Further, I searched for these Slavic and Hebraic words in English search engines, based on combinations of Latin letters. I found Renia under Renia, Renya, Rania, Regina, Rivka, Renata, Renee, Irena, and Irene; Kukielka has infinite Anglo spellings as does its Yiddish Kukelkohn; and then there were her various false wartime document names: Wanda Widuchowska, Gluck, Neuman. (I spent at least a half day trying to determine if Astrit the courier was the same person as Astrid, Estherit, A., and Zosia Miller—I believe she was.) On top of this, there is an added layer that often complicates women's traceability: the married name. "Renia Kukielka Herscovitch" (or is it Herskovitch, or Herzcovitz . . .) has endless permutations—she could so easily have slipped through, be missed, become unarchivable, lost forever.

Perhaps the ultimate example of name complexity: the three surviving Kukielka siblings ended up in Israel as Renia Herscovitch; Zvi Zamir, which sounded Israeli (*Zamir* is "cuckoo bird" in Hebrew); and Aaron Kleinman—changed because he fought in Palestine in the 1940s and was wanted by the British. Even within an immediate family, discrepancies are endless.

A final word on words:

For ease, imitating Renia, I have used the term *Pole* to refer to a non-Jewish (Christian) Polish national; however, Jews were also Polish nationals, and I'm enhancing a division that I do not necessarily mean to inflate. Influenced by the scholars at the POLIN Museum of the History of Polish Jews, I have used *antisemitism* as one word; to use a hyphen implies that "Semitism" exists as a racial category. The women in my story refer to the Nazis as "Germans," which I have retained, since these were the Germans they were in contact with; of course, there were anti-Nazi Germans as well.

Several scholars have criticized the use of the term "courier girls." *Courier*, they argue, is demeaning. It sounds trivial, passive, like a postman delivering letters. These women were anything but. They were weapons obtainers and smugglers, intelligence scouts, and, as in their Hebrew appellation, *kasharyiot*, connectors. The very act of courrying (from the French *courir*, or run) in the Holocaust was as risky as engaging in armed battle. Every time a Jew was found outside a Jewish ghetto or camp, she was punished by death. And these women spent months, sometimes years, crisscrossing the country, escaping from ghetto after ghetto. I found one account of a courier who apparently undertook 240 trips—per week. I, however, continued to use the term, among others, to describe their work in order to accord with existing research on the subject.

The word *girls* is also considered to be belittling. These were young women, around age twenty, some of them married. Again, I did use the term, among many others, to describe Renia and her cohorts. I also used *boys* for the youthful men of the movement. For one, I wanted to stress their youth. I am also writing in a context in which *girls* has been reappropriated and is employed widely in discussions of women's empowerment.

Acknowledgments

This book would not exist without the gracious support of myriad people. I owe my deepest gratitude:

To Alia Hanna Habib for being the first to see the potential in this project, and to Rachel Kahan, for nurturing that potential with wisdom and generosity, patience and passion. I could not have dreamed of more intelligent and dedicated guides.

To the team at William Morrow, for their verve, creativity and compassion: Andrea Molitor and Pamela Barricklow, Sharyn Rosenblum and Kelly Rudolph, Kayleigh George and Benjamin Steinberg, Ploy Siripant, Alivia Lopez, and Philip Bashe. To Jaclyn Hodson, Sandra Leef, and Lauren Morocco at HarperCollins Canada.

To Rebecca Gardner and Anna Worrall for their boundless savvy and encouragement. To Will Roberts, Ellen Goodson Coughtrey, and the rest of the Gernert team. To Lennie Goodings, Michelle Weiner, Holly Barrio, Peter Sample, Susan Solomon-Shapiro, and Nicole Dewey for their generous support and enthusiasm.

To the Hadassah-Brandeis Institute, including Shulamit Reinharz, Joanna Michlic, and Debby Olins, for initially funding the translation of *Freuen in di Ghettos* and believing in the importance of this material from day one. To Antony Polonsky for introducing me to the HBI in the first place and for countless additional introductions.

To all the resistors' relatives who benevolently shared their memories and impressions, several of whom are experts on the subject: Rivka Augenfeld, Ralph Berger, Sandy Fainer, Yoram Kleinman, Michael Kovner, Jacob Harel, Elliott Palevsky, Yonat Rotbain, Avihu Ronen, Lilian Rosenthal, Elaine Shelub, Holly Starr, Leah Waldman, Merav Waldman, Yoel Yaari, Racheli Yahav, and Eyal Zuckerman.

To all the scholars who took the time to meet with me and share their knowledge: Havi Dreifuss, Barbara Harshav, Emil Kerenji, Agi Legutko, Daniela Ozaky-Stern, Katarzyna Person, Rochelle Saidel, David Silberklang, Anna Shternshis, and Michał Trębacz.

To Sharon Geva, Bella Gutterman, Samuel Kassow, Justyna Majewska, Dina Porat, Eddy Portnoy, and the many academics who replied to my emails, directing me toward resources and specialists.

To all the librarians, archivists, and photo archivists for their indispensible help. To Arielle Berger at the Azrieli foundation; Anat Bratman-Elhalel and her colleagues at the Ghetto Fighters' House Museum; Misha Mitsel and Michael Geller at the JDC Archive; Eddie Paul, Penny Fransblow, and their colleagues at the Montreal Jewish Public Library; Janice Rosen at the Alex Dworkin Canadian Jewish Archive. To the library and archive staffs at YIVO/Center for Jewish History, US Holocaust Memorial Museum, Yad Vashem, Jewish Partisan Education Foundation, Emmanuel Ringelblum Jewish Historical Institute, POLIN Museum, Kibbutz Dafna, Montreal Holocaust Museum, and so many other institutions. To Jonathan Ornstein at the JCC Krakow, and all the guides who helped me navigate Poland. To Naomi Firestone-Teeter at the Jewish Book Council.

To my research assistants, translators, and fixers. To Elisha Baskin, for her ardor and acumen, her vital ingenuity and grace. To Ewa Kern-Jedrychowska and Lana Dadu for going above and beyond. To Paulina Blaszczykiewicz, Kuba Wesołowski, Eyal Solomon, and Yishai Chamudot.

To Sara Batalion, Nicole Bokat, Amy Klein, and Leigh McMullan Abramson, for reading chapters with diligence and care.

To Eleanor John, Mignon Nixon, Susan Shapiro, and my many mentors, for training me to triple-check every detail, to construct novel women's histories, and to write without apology.

To my "colleagues" at The Wing, and to my children's carers, for making my every workday possible, and even pleasant.

To all those who shared their family stories, sent me links to resistance articles and partisan songs, and listened to me yammer on about Jewish women outsmarting the Gestapo for over a decade. To all those—and I'm sure there are many—whom I forgot to include here due to the vagaries of memory.

To Zelda and Billie, for offering inspiration and hope. To Bram, for arriving at exactly the right time.

To Jon, for everything.

Finally, to Chayele Palevsky, a Vilna partisan who Skyped with me in 2019, and implored me to pass on her message: "We must never let this happen again. Hate is our fiercest enemy. Be peaceful, be loving, and work to create a world of happiness."

Notes

Introduction: Battle-Axes

3 *Freuen in di Ghettos:* Leib Spizman, ed. *Women in the Ghettos* (New York: Pioneer Women's Organization, 1946). *Women in the Ghettos* is a compilation of recollections, letters, and poems by and about Jewish women resisters, mainly from the Polish Labor Zionist movement, and includes excerpts of longer works. The text is in Yiddish and is intended for American Jews, though much of its content was originally published in Hebrew. The editor, Leib Spizman, escaped occupied Poland for Japan and then New York, where he became a historian of Labor Zionism.

6 *what "counts" as an act of Jewish resistance:* For discussion on the definition of "resistance," see, for instance: Brana Gurewitsch, ed. *Mothers, Sisters, Resisters: Oral Histories of Women Who Survived the Holocaust* (Tuscaloosa: Uni-

versity of Alabama Press, 1998), 221–22; Yehudit Kol-
Inbar, " 'Not Even for Three Lines in History': Jewish
Women Underground Members and Partisans During the
Holocaust," in *A Companion to Women's Military History*,
ed. Barton Hacker and Margaret Vining (Leiden, Neth.:
Brill, 2012), 513–46; Yitchak Mais, "Jewish Life in the
Shadow of Destruction," and Eva Fogelman, "On Blaming
the Victim," in *Daring to Resist: Jewish Defiance in the
Holocaust*, ed. Yitzchak Mais (New York: Museum of
Jewish Heritage, 2007), exhibition catalogue, 18–25 and
134–37; Dalia Ofer and Lenore J. Weitzman, "Resistance
and Rescue," in *Women in the Holocaust*, ed. Dalia Ofer
and Lenore J. Weitzman (New Haven, CT: Yale University
Press, 1998), 171–74; Gunnar S. Paulsson, *Secret City: The
Hidden Jews of Warsaw 1940–1945* (New Haven, CT: Yale
University Press, 2003), 7–15; Joan Ringelheim, "Women
and the Holocaust: A Reconsideration of Research," in *Different Voices: Women and the Holocaust*, ed. Carol Rittner
and John K. Roth (St. Paul, MN: Paragon House, 1993),
383, 390; Nechama Tec, *Resistance: Jews and Christians
Who Defied the Nazi Terror* (New York: Oxford Univer-
sity Press, 2013), especially 12–13; Lenore J. Weitzman,
"Living on the Aryan Side in Poland: Gender, Passing, and
the Nature of Resistance," in *Women in the Holocaust*, ed.
Dalia Ofer and Lenore J. Weitzman (New Haven, CT: Yale
University Press, 1998), 187–222. Paulsson and Weitzman
stress that hiding should be considered a form of resistance;
Paulsson says the same for flight.

8 *rescue networks*: For discussion of Jewish rescuers, see Mordechai Paldiel, *Saving One's Own: Jewish Rescuers During the Holocaust* (Philadelphia: Jewish Publication Society, University of Nebraska Press, 2017). According to Paldiel, large-scale rescue was less prominent in Poland than in other countries.

8 *hugging barrack-mates to keep them warm*: Vera Slymovicz testimony, p. 27, Alex Dworkin Canadian Jewish Archives, Montreal.

9 *full memoir*: Renia Kukielka, *Underground Wanderings* (Ein Harod, Isr.: Hakibbutz Hameuchad, 1945).

9 *(some say the first)*: See, for instance, the description of Renia's book in https://images.shulcloud.com/1281/uploads /Documents/Narayever-News/news-jan-feb-2014.pdf.

9 *English version*: Renya Kulkielko, *Escape from the Pit* (New York: Sharon Books, 1947). Sharon Books shared the same address as the Pioneer Women's Organization. (In 2018 Renia's family had no idea that this English edition existed.)

10 *relatively miniscule victories . . . number of Jews saved*: Though stories of the Jewish resistance had not reached my Jewish cultural sphere, they are told in survivor communities and discussed in academic circles in Israel. Some have claimed that these efforts were so miniscule they do not deserve attention; others have stated that there was a "mass" of resistance activity.

It is worth mentioning that many statistics in this story are estimates and are often contested. Much Holocaust "data" is drawn from Nazi records, and in the case of resistance, these records were biased. On the Jewish end, despite a few successful attempts at creating and saving archives, so much information was lost, or had to be kept secret—it was not recorded at all or was recorded in code. Many numbers come from personal memories.

10 *Jewish armed underground groups . . . eastern European ghettos*: Mais, "Jewish Life in the Shadow of Destruction," 24. Other sources offer slightly different numbers. According to the USHMM Encyclopedia, https://encyclopedia .ushmm.org/content/en/article/jewish-uprisings-in -ghettos-and-camps-1941-44, approximately a hundred ghettos had underground movements. (It does not specify if they were armed.) According to Agnes Grunwald-Spier, *Women's Experiences in the Holocaust: In Their Own Words* (Stroud, UK: Amberley, 2018), 180–81, seventeen ghettos in Poland and Lithuania each had an organized resistance group, and an estimated sixty-five ghettos in the Belarus area had armed groups that later fought from the forest.

10 *Będzin, Vilna, Białystok and Tarnów*: Wall text, "Fighting to Survive: Jewish Resistance," Montreal Holocaust Museum, Montreal. Wall text, POLIN Museum of the History of Polish Jews, Warsaw, also includes: Będzin, Braslaw, Brzesc, Kobryn, Krzemieniec, Mir, Nieswiez, Tuczyn and Vilna. USHMM Encyclopedia, https://encyclopedia.ushmm .org/content/en/article/jewish-uprisings-in-ghettos-and

-camps-1941-44 also includes: Lachva, Kremenets, Nesvizh. Mark Bernard, "Problems Related to the Study of the Jewish Resistance Movement in the Second World War," *Yad Vashem Studies* 3 (1959): 45, mentions that Jewish resistance acts also took place in: Kazimierz, Biala Podlaska, Pulawy, Radzyn, Jaslo, Sandomierz; he mentions that partisan units were formed in ghettos in Lukow, Pulawy, Biala Podlaska, Minsk Mazowiecki, Brest, Lublin, and Pinsk; he also refers to an uprising in the Trawniki camp. According to Yad Vashem, https://www.yadvashem.org/odot_pdf/Microsoft%20Word%20-%206316.pdf, fighters in Grodno also attempted unsuccessfully to assassinate ghetto commandants.

10 *five major concentration and death camps . . . eighteen forced-labor camps*: Tec, *Resistance*, 148.

10 *Thirty thousand*: Jewish Partisan Educational Foundation, http://www.jewishpartisans.org.

10 *Jewish networks financially supported twelve thousand fellow Jews-in-hiding*: The number of Jews supported by these networks is contested. See endnotes in chapter 20.

11 *little focus on women*: Grunwald-Spier, *Women's Experiences in the Holocaust*, 228–29, notes that when Zivia's granddaughter became a fighter pilot, the UK *Daily Telegraph* wrote an article about her and how her grandfather was a fighter in Warsaw, not even mentioning Zivia. In Matthew Brzezinski's *Isaac's Army: A Story of Courage and Survival in Nazi-Occupied Poland* (New York: Ran-

dom House, 2012), women are listed under men in the cast of characters, and referred to as the "girlfriend of." Men are not described as "boyfriend of."

12 *"glam girl" and "hussy"*: Ziva Shalev, *Tossia Altman: Leader of Hashomer Hatzair Movement and of the Warsaw Ghetto Uprising* (Tel Aviv, Isr.: Moreshet, 1992), 32–33. For more on "hussies," see Anna Legierska, "The Hussies and Gentlemen of Interwar Poland," Culture.pl, https://culture.pl/en/article/the-hussies-and-gentlemen-of-prewar-poland, 16 Oct 2014.

12 *"the Jewish girls were the nerve-centers of the movement"*: Chaika Grossman, "For Us the War Has Not Ended," in *Women in the Ghettos*, 180–82.

12 *"Without a murmur . . . history of Jewry during the present war."*: From Emanuel Ringelblum's diary entry, May 1942. One translation can be found in: Emanuel Ringelblum, *Notes from the Warsaw Ghetto: The Journal of Emanuel Ringelblum*, ed. and trans. Jacob Sloan (New York: ibooks, 2006).

Many leaders sang similar praises at the time. Jan Karski, the famous Polish resistance leader, also honored the couriers, stressing that they were more exposed than organizers and executors and carried out the hardest work for the least reward. Cited in Vera Laska, ed., *Different Voices*, 255.

13 *"our nation's great treasures" and will form the core of Jewish folklore*: Ruzka Korczak, "Women in the Vilna Ghetto," in *Women in the Ghettos*, 126.

13 *"the book of eternal memory"*: Gusta Davidson Draenger, *Justyna's Narrative*, trans. Roslyn Hirsch and David H. Hirsch (Amherst: University of Massachusetts Press, 1996), 33. As she wrote: "From this prison cell that we will never leave alive, we young fighters who are about to die salute you. We offer our lives willingly for our holy cause, asking only that our deeds be inscribed in the book of eternal memory."

Prologue: Flash Forward—Defense or Rescue?

15 *Będzin was first erected*: Information about Będzin is from "Będzin," Virtual Shtetl, https://sztetl.org.pl/en/towns /b/406-bedzin/99-history/137057-history-of-community; Bella Gutterman, "The Holocaust in Będzin," in *Rutka's Notebook: January–April 1943* (Jerusalem: Yad Vashem, 2007); Aleksandra Namyslo, *Before the Holocaust Came: The Situation of the Jews in Zaglebie During the German Occupation* (Katowice: Public Education Office of the Institute of National Remembrance, with the Emanuel Ringelblum Jewish Historical Institute in Warsaw and Yad Vashem, 2014); Anna Piernikarczyk, "Bedzin," Polskie Dzieje, https://polskiedzieje.pl/dzieje-miast-polskich/bedzin .html; Avihu Ronen, "The Jews of Będzin," in *Before They Perished . . . Photographs Found in Auschwitz*, ed. Kersten Brandt et al. (Oświęcim, Pol.: Auschwitz-Birkenau State Museum, 2001), 16–27; Marcin Wodziński, "Będzin," The YIVO Encyclopedia of Jews in Eastern Europe, http://

www.yivoencyclopedia.org/article.aspx/Bedzin; Ruth Zariz, "Attempts at Rescue and Revolt; Attitude of Members of the Dror Youth Movement in Będzin to Foreign Passports as Means of Rescue," *Yad Vashem Studies* 20 (1990): 211–36.

16 *Nearly half*: "Będzin," The YIVO Encyclopedia of Jews in Eastern Europe, https://yivoencyclopedia.org/article.aspx/Bedzin. Other sources offer statistics ranging from 45 percent to 80 percent.

17 *murdered dozens of Jews*: Varying sources offer numbers ranging from forty to two hundred. According to The YIVO Encyclopedia of Jews in Eastern Europe, forty-four Jews were killed.

17 *Star of David armbands*: Jews in different regions were forced to wear different badges. In many areas of Poland, Jews had to wear white armbands with a blue star of David; in others, they had to wear yellow stars. See: "Holocaust Badges," Holocaust Memorial Center, https://www.holocaustcenter.org/visit/library-archive/holocaust-badges.

18 *"liquidated" . . . "Final Solution"*: The Nazis used euphemisms for their murderous plans. The "Final Solution" refers to their plan to annihilate all of Europe's Jews. "Liquidation" is code for eliminating a ghetto by deporting its population to a death camp or mass murder sites.

19 *decision day*: This scene is an elaboration, based on a mention in Renia's memoir. Kukielka, *Undergound Wanderings*, 74–75.

20 *"so much Jewish folk character in him:* Description of Hershel is from Chajka Klinger, *I Am Writing These Words to You: The Original Diaries, Będzin 1943*, trans. Anna Brzostowska and Jerzy Giebułtowski (Jerusalem: Yad Vashem and Moreshet, 2017), 69.

21 *"racial dumping ground"*: "Generalgouvernement," Yad Vashem Shoah Resource Center, http://www.yadvashem .org/odot_pdf/Microsoft%20Word%20-%206246.pdf.

21 *her face chiseled with sharp cheekbones and dark, penetrating eyes*: This is based on photos of Sarah held in the Ghetto Fighters' House Museum archive.

22 *passport schemes*: Zariz, "Attempts at Rescue and Revolt," 211–36. For discussion of additional passport schemes, see, for instance, Vladka Meed, *On Both Sides of the Wall*, trans. Steven Meed (Washington, DC: United States Holocaust Memorial Museum, 1993), 175–80; Paldiel, *Saving One's Own*, 361–62; Avihu Ronen, *Condemned to Life: The Diaries and Life of Chajka Klinger* (Haifa and Tel Aviv, Isr.: University of Haifa Press, Miskal-Yidioth Ahronoth and Chemed, 2011), 234–94.

Part 1: Ghetto Girls

25 *Lemberg*: Lemberg was the Yiddish name for Lvov (in Polish), a city which is currently called Lviv (in Ukranian).

25 *"[H]eroic girls . . . these girls are indefatigable"*: Ringelbaum, *Notes from the Warsaw Ghetto*, 273–74.

Chapter 1: Po-Lin

27 *October 10, 1924*: Renia's birth date varies on different documents, but this is the date recognized by Yad Vashem's catalogue and by her children.

27 *Sabbath eve*: I constructed this birth scene based on Renia's testimony in the Yad Vashem archives and historical context. All the information about Renia and her family in this chapter was taken from her Yad Vashem testimony unless indicated otherwise.

28 *Yiddish and Polish clatter*: According to Renia's testimony at Yad Vashem, the family spoke Yiddish at home, and she spoke Polish with her friends. According to her oral testimony at Ghetto Fighters' House, she spoke Polish at home. Her nephew claimed they spoke Yiddish and Polish at home; personal interview, Yoram Kleinman, Telephone, 11 February 2019.

28 Kukielka *resembles the Polish* Kukielo, *the surname of the local funeral home family established generations earlier*: As told to me by a Jędrzejów local, June 2018.

29 *relatives*: The *Jędrzejów Yizkor Book* (Tel Aviv, Isr.: Irgun Ole Yendzéyov be-Yiśra'el, 1965), lists five branches of the "Kokielka" family as having been killed by the Nazis.

29 *delicacies of the day*: "Food and Drink," The Yivo Encyclopedia of Jews in Eastern Europe, http://www.yivo encyclopedia.org/article.aspx/Food_and_Drink. See also: Magdalena Kasprzyk-Chevriaux, "How Jewish Culture

Influenced Polish Cuisine," Culture.pl, https://culture.
pl/en/article/how-jewish-culture-influenced-polish
-cuisine.

30 *Jędrzejów*: The information about Jędrzejów in this chapter is primarily from: "Jędrzejów," Virtual Shtetl, https://
sztetl.org.pl/en/towns/j/40-Jędrzejów/99-history
/137420-history-of-community#footnote23_xgdnzma;
"Jędrzejów," Beit Hatfutsot: My Jewish Story, The Open
Databases of the Museum of the Jewish People, https://dbs
.bh.org.il/place/Jędrzejów; "Jędrzejów," Holocaust Historical Society, https://www.holocausthistoricalsociety.org.uk
/contents/ghettosj-r/Jędrzejów.html; "Jędrzejów," Jewish-
Gen, https://www.jewishgen.org/yizkor/pinkas_poland
/pol7_00259.html—originally published in *Pinkas Hake-
hillot: Encyclopedia of Jewish Communities, Poland*, Volume VII (Jerusalem: Yad Vashem), 259–62.

30 *would soon add three more*: These birth dates are
estimates, but it appears that Aaron was born in 1925, Esther, in 1928, and Yaacov, in 1932.

31 *130 in Yiddish, 25 in Hebrew and 25 in Polish*: Wall text,
POLIN Museum of the History of Polish Jews, Warsaw.

32 *"The Struggle for a Jewish Palestine" (in May 1937)*:
"Jędrzejów," Virtual Shtetl.

32 *navy blue "sailor" suit, pleated skirt and knee-high socks*:
Anna Legierska, "The Hussies and Gentlemen of Interwar
Poland." This was the common dress of the day, and I ex-
trapolate to Renia.

32 *a lover of promenades*: Personal interview with Merav Waldman, Skype, October 23, 2018.

32 *long sleeves and stockings*: As cited in "Jędrzejów," Virtual Shtetl.

33 *attended Polish public school*: According to Renia's Yad Vashem testimony, she briefly attended the Beit Yakov school, but it was far from their house so she changed to a Polish public school.

33 *a lasting impression*: In her Yad Vashem testimony, Renia relays that one teacher insisted on calling her "Kukiel-chanka" because Kukielka sounded too Polish for a Jew.

33 *Poland was evolving*: The information in this chapter on the history of Poland and of Poland's Jews comes primarily from "Poland," The YIVO Encyclopedia of Jews in Eastern Europe, https://yivoencyclopedia.org/article.aspx /Poland; Samuel D. Kassow, "On the Jewish Street, 1918–1939," *POLIN, 1000 Year History of Polish Jews—Catalogue for the Core Exhibition,* ed. Barbara Kirshenblatt-Gimblett and Antony Polonsky (Warsaw: POLIN Museum of the History of Polish Jews, 2014), 227–85; Jerzy Lukowski and Hubert Zawadzki, *A Concise History of Poland* (Cambridge: Cambridge University Press, 2001).

34 *Early Poland was a republic*: Adriel Kasonata, "Poland: Europe's Forgotten Democratic Ancestor," *The National Interest,* May 5, 2016, https://nationalinterest.org/feature /poland-europes-forgotten-democratic-ancestor-16073.

36 *This party's entire platform was concerned with slandering*

Polish Jews and a new Polish identity that was specifically defined as "not the Jew": Paul Brykczynski lecture given at "In Dialogue: Polish Jewish Relations During the Interwar Period," November 15, 2018, at Fordham University, with Columbia, YIVO.

38 *Jędrzejów saw increasing antisemitism*: Accounts given in "Jędrzejów," Virtual Shtetl.

38 *Dzigan and Schumacher*: Shimen Dzigan and Yisroel Schumacher met as part of a comedy performance troupe in Łódź. By the 1930s, they were so popular, they founded their own cabaret company in Warsaw.

38 *"The Last Jew in Poland"*: Samuel D. Kassow alerted me to this sketch in his lecture given at "In Dialogue: Polish Jewish Relations During the Interwar Period." Discussion of the sketch can be found in Ruth R. Wisse, *No Joke: Making Jewish Humor* (Princeton, NJ: Princeton University Press, 2015), 145–46.

39 *With time, the largest party was the Bund*: The Bund became the largest party in 1938 because immigration to Palestine seemed impossible due to the British White Papers and the Polish government was not heeding the religious party's requests. Before that, the population was split fairly equally between all three parties.

39 *it's likely she accompanied her older sister Sarah to youth group activities*: Renia's children speak of how, while Moshe was Renia's intellectual influence, Sarah was her leadership influence. However, seeing as Sarah was older and lived at various *hachshara* kibbutzim, it's possible that

Renia also accompanied Bela. In her Yad Vashem testimony, Renia claims that before the war, when she was younger than fifteen, she was focused on her life at school and not all that interested in the youth movements.

40 *"one could see the entire shoe!"*: "She was wearing a very wide skirt made of navy wool, extremely short—as one could see the entire shoe from underneath it. . . . People are going to point their fingers at you!" As cited in Legierska, "The Hussies and Gentlemen of Interwar Poland."

40 *A photo of Sarah*: Photos of Sarah Kukielka are from the Ghetto Fighters' House Museum archive.

40 *collective depression*: The YIVO, the eminent Yiddish Institute in Vilna, noted this crisis and organized a memoir competition, asking young Jews to write about their lives in the hopes of better understanding them and helping to improve morale.

40 *affiliated with the different parties*: The Young Guard was not affiliated with any political party, but were socialist Zionists.

41 *In some photos*: Photos of the *hachshara* in Jędrzejów are from "Jędrzejów," Beit Hatfutsot: My Jewish Story.

41 *She belonged to Freedom*: "Dror" (Freedom) was based on a 1938 amalgamation of Hechalutz HaTsair (Young Pioneer) and Freiheit (Freedom, in Yiddish), which was a Yiddish-based group that attracted working class members. Freedom, then, was a Zionist group where Yiddish was spoken alongside Hebrew, and which included more working youth. It was affiliated with the Poalei Zion politi-

cal party, and is still active. Freedom comrades had the reputation for being older, less pretentious, and more down to earth than The Young Guards (Bella Gutterman, *Fighting for Her People: Zivia Lubetkin, 1914–1978*, trans. Ora Cummings [Jerusalem: Yad Vashem, 2014], 132).

42 *defined themselves based on their group*: For instance: "I myself was never really much of a movement person. I was stuck with the name Akiba, since everybody in the ZOB took the name of his movement as part of his own, as if it were another last name." Simha "Kazik" Rotem, *Memoirs of a Ghetto Fighter*, trans. Barbara Harshav (New Haven, CT: Yale University Press, 1994), 22. There were rivalries between groups, and some attacked others' headquarters.

42 *received the vote*: Women, however, were not allowed to vote for the Jewish community council.

43 *Jewish women*: For discussions of both Polish and Jewish women in interwar Poland, see, for instance, Gershon Bacon, "Poland: Interwar," The Encyclopedia of Jewish Women, https://jwa.org/encyclopedia/article/poland-interwar; Judith Taylor Baumel-Schwartz and Tova Cohen, eds. *Gender, Place and Memory in the Modern Jewish Experience: Re-Placing Ourselves* (London: Vallentine Mitchell, 2003); Anna Czocher, Dobrochna Kałwa, et al., *Is War Men's Business? Fates of Women in Occupied Kraków in Twelve Scenes.* trans. Tomasz Tesznar and Joanna Bełch-Rucińska. (Kraków: Historical Museum of the City of Kraków, 2011); Nameetha Matur, "'The New Sportswoman': Nationalism, Feminism and Women's Physical

Culture in Interwar Poland," *The Polish Review* 48 (2003), no. 4: 441–62; Jolanta Mickute, "Zionist Women in Interwar Poland," on *The Macmillan Report*, https://www.youtube.com/watch?v=TrYt4oI4Mq4; Lenore J. Weitzman and Dalia Ofer, "Introduction to Part 1," Paula E. Hyman "Gender and the Jewish Family in Modern Europe," Gershon Bacon, "The Missing 52 Percent: Research on Jewish Women in Interwar Poland and Its Implications for Holocaust Studies," and Daniel Blatman, "Women in the Jewish Labor Bund in Interwar Poland," all in *Women in the Holocaust*; Puah Rakovsky, *My Life as a Radical Jewish Woman: Memoirs of a Zionist Feminist in Poland*, trans. Barbara Harshav with Paula E. Hyman (Bloomington: Indiana University Press, 2001); Avihu Ronen, "Poland: Women Leaders in the Jewish Underground in the Holocaust," The Encyclopedia of Jewish Women, https://jwa.org/encyclopedia/article/poland-women-leaders-in-jewish-underground-during-holocaust; Jeffrey Shandler, ed., *Awakening Lives: Autobiographies of Jewish Youth in Poland Before the Holocaust* (New Haven, CT: Yale University Press, 2002); Anna Zarnowska, "Women's Political Participation in Inter-War Poland: Opportunities and Limitations," *Women's History Review* 13 (No. 1, 2004): 57-68.

43 *"feminist"*: Most Polish "feminists" at the time would have called themselves "radical" or "revolutionary."

44 *young women experienced a degree of parity*: Avihu Ronen, "Young Jewish Women Were Leaders in the Jewish

Underground During the Holocaust," Jewish Women's Archive: The Encyclopedia of Jewish Women, https://jwa
.org/encyclopedia/article/Poland-women-leaders-in
-jewish-underground-during-holocaust. On the other
hand, Kol-Inbar, "Three Lines in History," 514, claims
that women did not have a great role in the youth movements in Poland.

45 *in some accounts, she claimed, because of antisemitism, in
others, because she needed to earn money*: The first is from
Renia's prologue in *Escape from the Pit*; the second is from
Renia's Yad Vashem testimony.

45 *"doctors"*: See, for instance, the women's testimonies in the
Alex Dworkin Canadian Jewish Archives, Montreal.

Chapter 2: From the Fire, to the Fire

48 *all casualties of the Nazis' relentless air attacks*: Hitler's blitz-
krieg strategy involved extensive bombing to destroy the
enemy's means of transportation and communication lines,
followed by a massive-scale land invasion. The Polish army
was under-equipped and antiquated (they attempted to fight
the Germans head-on with horsed cavaliers) and was no
match for the mechanized, modern German military.

48 *"to the skies"*: Kukielka, *Underground Wanderings*, 4. This
chapter is based on material from Kukielka, *Underground
Wanderings*, 3–8, and her Yad Vashem testimony.

49 *"Everyone was trying to escape from the frying pan into
the fire"*: Kukielka, *Underground Wanderings*, 4.

50 *pulled up the ladder to the attic*: In Renia's Yad Vashem testimony, she says they hid in the basement.

51 *80 percent Jewish*: "Chmielnik," Beit Hatfutsot: My Jewish Story, The Open Databases of the Museum of the Jewish People, https://dbs.bh.org.il/place/chmielnik.

51 *night number one*: An alternate account of that first night with different details is offered in "Chmielnik," Virtual Shtetl.

51 *Bread—now a gray, hard, and bitter substance*: Naomi Izhar, *Chasia Bornstein-Bielicka, One of the Few: A Resistance Fighter and Educator, 1939–1947*, trans. Naftali Greenwood (Jerusalem: Yad Vashem, 2009), 133.

51 *"Renia used to dread this time of year"*: Renia's Yad Vashem testimony.

Chapter 3: Founding the Female Fight

53 *New Year's Eve*: All the scenes about Zivia in this chapter are based on Zivia Lubetkin, *In the Days of Destruction and Revolt*, trans. Ishai Tubbin and Debby Garber, ed. Yehiel Yanay (Tel Aviv, Isr.: Am Oved; Hakibbutz Hameuchad; Ghetto Fighters' House, 1981). Additional information is primarily from: Zvi Dror, *The Dream, the Revolt and the Vow: The Biography of Zivia Lubetkin-Zuckerman (1914–1978)*, trans. Bezalel Ianai (Tel Aviv, Isr.: General Federation of Labor [Histadrut] and Ghetto Fighters' House, 1983); Chana Gelbard, "In the Warsaw Ghetto," in *Women in the Ghettos*, 3–16; Gutterman,

Fighting for Her People; Yitzhak "Antek" Zuckerman, *A Surplus of Memory: Chronicle of the Warsaw Ghetto Uprising*, trans. Barbara Harshav (Berkeley: University of California Press, 1993).

54 *"trembling with fear at the prospect of being caught by Nazis"*: Lubetkin, *Days of Destruction*, 16.

57 *"If I, Zivia, ever decide . . . I shall call it From Byten to Geneva"*: Gutterman, *Fighting for Her People*, 9.

57 *female movement leaders*: These included Frumka Płotnicka, Hantze Płotnicka, Leah Pearlstein, and Tosia Altman.

58 *"Antek"*: According to *The Zuckerman Code*, directed by Ben Shani and Noa Shabtai, Israel, 2018, Antek was his "internal moniker." He used different names when facing the Germans and Poles.

58 *"[We] raced about . . . an attempt to contact lost and remote members of the movement"*: Lubetkin, *Days of Destruction*, 14.

59 *"[I]t was impossible . . . the pioneer-youth underground."*: Lubetkin, *Days of Destruction*, 14.

59 *insisting that she go to Warsaw*: According to Eyal Zuckerman, Tel Aviv, Isr., May 15, 2018, it is possible she went to Warsaw looking for Shmuel. Gutterman, *Fighting for Her People*, 107, on the other hand, suggests she postponed going to Warsaw because of Shmuel's capture.

60 *"We ate, drunk, and made merry . . ."* Zivia later wrote, "and between drinks discussed the Movement and its future course": Lubetkin, *Days of Destruction*, 13.

60 *That night, despite pleas from Antek*: Gutterman, *Fighting for Her People*, 110. According to Lubetkin, *Days of Destruction*, 14, it was "the following evening." Lubetkin does not mention Antek in her account.

60 *"While I was still preoccupied . . . people pushed their way into the cars"*: Lubetkin, *Days of Destruction*, 15.

61 *"I clenched my teeth and didn't move an inch"*: Lubetkin, *Days of Destruction*, 17.

62 *Great Synagogue*: "The History of the Great Synagogue," Jewish Historical Institute, http://www.jhi.pl/en/blog/2013 -03-04-the-history-of-the-great-synagogue.

63 *375,000 Jews . . . population*: "Warsaw," The YIVO Encyclopedia of Jews in Eastern Europe. Dalia Ofer, "Gender Issues in Diaries and Testimonies of the Ghetto: The Case of Warsaw," in *Women in the Holocaust*, 144–45, states a prewar population of 359,000 and includes a demographic breakdown.

63 *in 2020, Jews make up roughly 13 percent of New York City's population*: 1.1 million Jews out of 8.6 million total. Statistics are from 2016, as reported in Uriel Heilman, "7 Things to Know About the Jews of New York for Tuesday's Primary," *Jewish Telegraphic Agency*, April 18, 2016, https://www.jta.org/2016/04/18/politics/7-things-to -know-about-the-jews-of-new-york-for-tuesdays-primary.

64 *The roads were filled with elegant cars . . . ornate prams*: Footage of prewar Warsaw can be seen on: https://www .youtube.com/watch?v=igv038Pqr34; https://www.you

tube.com/watch?v=CQVQQQDKyoo; https://www.you
tube.com/watch?v=Zk_8lTLGLTE.

64 *"There was a pleasant feeling in the air, as if nothing had happened"*: Lubetkin, *Days of Destruction*, 19.

64 *"a different mettle"*: Lubetkin, *Days of Destruction*, 21.

67 *"In gray times, . . . motherly worry"*: Eliezer, "In the Movement," in *Women in the Ghettos*, 87–91.

67 *"Her heart . . . inside her"*: Lutke, "Frumka," in *Hantze and Frumka*, 169.

67 *"magical accent . . . turned into fire"*: Y. Perlis, "In the Hachshara and the Movement," in *Hantze and Frumka*, 155.

67 *A friend wrote a story*: Zruvevel, "Meeting and Separation," in *Women in the Ghettos*, 91–95.

68 *surprised family with her leadership role*: Eliyahu Plotnicki, "Childhood Home," in *Hantze and Frumka*, 10.

69 *and return to Nazi-occupied Warsaw*: Yudka, "Catastrophe," in *Women in the Ghettos*, 95–102. According to this account, it seems that her zeal may have been spurred by a false rumor that Hantze had been killed in occupied Poland.

70 *"the pioneers longed to live . . . no anger"*: Gelbard, "Warsaw Ghetto," 5–7.

70 *She always won*: Zuckerman, *Surplus of Memory*, 104. Leah Pearlstein was a resistance leader at a movement farm, in Łódź and in Warsaw. She likely died in the Warsaw Aktion of January 1943.

71 *often young lawyers and graduates*: Zuckerman, *Surplus of Memory*, 244.

71 *only the worst type of people*: Kukielka, *Underground Wanderings*, 12. At other times, Renia recognizes that some militiamen tried to use their position to help others.

72 *The Judenrats as an institution . . . members varied*: Bernard, "Problems Related to the Study," 61–62. According to Ronen, "The Jews of Bedzin," 21, the Zaglembie Judenrat had 500 officials. Documents from the JDC archives report that 2,000 Jewish police served in Warsaw.

72 *heterogeneous groups*: See, for instance, Tec, *Resistance*, 14, for a review of literature on the complexity of Judenrats. Other accounts of Judenrats that supported the resistance, as well as considered discussions of their role, can be found in, for instance, Izhar, *Chasia Bornstein-Bielicka*, 124–25, 140; Rotem, *Memoirs of a Ghetto Fighter*, 15; Don Levin and Zvie A. Brown, *The Story of an Underground: The Resistance of the Jews of Kovno (Lithuania) in the Second World War* (Jerusalem: Gefen, 2018); Mira Shelub and Fred Rosenbaum, *Never the Last Road: A Partisan's Life* (Berkeley, CA: Lehrhaus Judaica, 2015), 78. Similar discussions exist about the Jewish police. See Bernard Goldstein, *The Stars Bear Witness*, trans. Leonard Shatzkin (London: Victor Gollancz, 1950), 34–36, for a take on the development of the Judenrat and labor forces.

72 *Gestapo puppets*: Zivia wrote at length about her disdain for the Judenrat, Jewish police, and Jewish collaborators. Lubetkin, *Days of Destruction*, 39–42.

72 *"vexations dissolved in the rings of smoke that she blew"*: Chana Gelbard, "Life in the Ghetto," *The Pioneer Woman*, No. 97, April 1944, 11.

75 *"I was amazed . . . talking like a wife"*: Zuckerman, *Surplus of Memory*, 44–45.

75 *and fell in love*: Personal interview, Eyal Zuckerman, Tel Aviv, Isr., May 15, 2018.

75 *"Jewish nose" and "halting Polish"*: Naomi Shimshi, "Frumka Plotniczki," Jewish Women's Archive, The Encyclopedia of Jewish Women, https://jwa.org/encyclopedia /article/plotniczki-frumka.

76 *She had grown close to . . . directed at her best friend*: Zuckerman, *Surplus of Memory*, 130, mentions rumors about their love triangle. Gutterman, *Fighting for Her People*, 101, 127, 134, 135, speculates about it.

76 *"for the entire movement in Poland"*: Ibid., 132. According to Sharon Geva *The Zuckerman Code*, and *Blue Bird*, directed by Ayelet Heller, Isr., 1998, "Zivia" was a code word for all of Poland.

Chapter 4: To See Another Morning—Terror in the Ghetto

77 *court secretary*: According to Renia's Yad Vashem testimony, a neighbor offered her a job as a courtroom secretary, and she readily accepted it.

77 *Renia's life was turned inside out*: Unless otherwise indicated, the scenes in this chapter, as well as descriptions and

information offered, are based on Kukielka, *Underground Wanderings*, 9–36. Additional information about the Jędrzejów ghetto can be found in sources cited in chapter 1.

78 *Singer sewing machine . . . for safekeeping*: Renia Kukielka, Yad Vashem testimony. According to Renia, they never saw him or their valuables again.

79 *help protect them*: See, for instance, Izhar, *Chasia Bornstein-Bielicka*, 104, 133.

79 *Accounts tell of mothers*: See, for instance, Izhar, *Chasia Bornstein-Bielicka*, 104–15.

79 *gold bracelet . . . sleeve of a sweater*: Barbara Kuper, "Life Lines," in *Before All Memory Is Lost: Women's Voices from the Holocaust*, ed. Myrna Goldenberg (Toronto: Azrieli Foundation, 2017), 198.

79 *Money was baked into cookies*: Myrna Goldenberg, "Camps: Forward," in *Before All Memory Is Lost*, 272.

79 *on a sack of flour*: Renia Kukielka, Yad Vashem testimony.

79 *Fifty people could be crammed*: See, for instance, Faye Schulman, *A Partisan's Memoir: Woman of the Holocaust* (Toronto, Canada: Second Story Press, 1995), 77.

80 *disrupting normal social order*: Tec, *Resistance*, 52–54.

80 *dried on neighbors' roofs*: Izhar, *Chasia Bornstein-Bielicka*, 108–10.

80 *more than four hundred ghettos in Poland*: Tec, *Resistance*, 52.

81 *And yet . . .* : This scene about smuggling was based on a mention in a testimony Renia gave to the Israel National

Library in 1985, held in the library archive. It is not clear whether she smuggled before or after the ghetto was "closed." I constructed this scene based on the stories of many Jewish women smugglers; for instance, see the chapter "Women" in *Warsaw Ghetto: Everyday Life*, The Ringelblum Archive, Volume 1, ed. Katarzyna Person, trans. Anna Brzostowska et al. (Warsaw: Jewish Historical Institute, 2017), 232–55.

82 *nine o'clock*: In Renia's account she claims to have gone in the morning, but in most accounts, women smugglers left the ghettos at night.

82 *the foragers*: examples are from "Women," *Warsaw Ghetto: Everyday Life.*

83 *role reversals*: Lenore J. Weitzman, "Resistance in Everyday Life: Family Strategies, Role Reversals, and Role Sharing in the Holocaust," in *Jewish Families in Europe, 1939–Present: History, Representation and Memory*, ed. Joanna Beata Michlic (Waltham, MA: Brandeis University Press, 2017), 46–66.

83 *municipalities or private enterprise*: Tec, *Resistance*, 59. Large ghettos had both.

83 *to look older*: Schulman, *Partisan's Memoir*, 78.

84 *"No one says a word . . . nighttime homes"*: Izhar, *Chasia Bornstein-Bielicka*, 120–22.

85 *Bitter cornbread . . . potatoes*: Izhar, *Chasia Bornstein-Bielicka*, 111.

85 *black market goods*: Chasia Bielicka explains that they

came into the ghetto in many ways, sometimes through
hidden areas in waste trucks. Izhar, *Chasia Bornstein-
Bielicka*.

85 *"the worst kind of death"*: Kukielka, *Underground Wanderings*, 21.

86 *marital conflicts*: See discussions in: Ofer, "Gender Issues
in Diaries and Testimonies of the Ghetto," 143–67; Ringelheim, "Women and the Holocaust," 378–79; Tec, *Resistance*, 55–57; Michael Unger, "The Status and Plight of
Women in the Łódź Ghetto," in *Women in the Holocaust*,
123–42.

86 *first generation to enjoy love matches*: Dalia Ofer, "Parent-
hood in the Shadow of the Holocaust," in *Jewish Families
in Europe*, 3–25.

86 *Women, who had been trained in domestic skills . . . even
from starvation*: See, for instance, Brana Gurewitsch,
"Preface," *Mothers, Sisters, Resisters*, xi–xxi; Esther Katz
and Joan Miriam Ringelheim, eds., *Proceedings of the
Conference on Women Surviving the Holocaust* (New
York: Institute for Research in History, c1983), 17-19;
Ringelheim, "Women and the Holocaust," 373–418; Tec,
Resistance, 50, 55.

87 *In Kraków . . . to save their lives*: Agi Legutko, tour of the
Kraków ghetto, Jewish Culture Festival, Kraków, June
2018.

87 *lack of daily schedule*: Izhar, *Chasia Bornstein-Bielicka*,
111.

87 *Children played . . . without its papers*: Izhar, *Chasia*

Bornstein-Bielicka, 112, and Shelub and Rosenbaum, *Never the Last Road*, 80–81.

87 *The equivalent of $60 today*: *Who Will Write Our History*, directed by Roberta Grossman, USA, 2019. Similar amounts are recorded in JDC reports held in the JDC archive and *Warsaw Ghetto, Everyday Life* (Ringelblum archive), chapter on Women. According to this chapter, in Warsaw in 1940, female factory workers earned three złotys per day; skilled women workers earned six złotys a day. A bowl of soup cost one złoty. Prices were sky-high compared with earnings in this irregular wartime economy. According to a JDC report, in Warsaw in 1942, it cost sixty groszy to ride the Jewish bus, and eighteen groszy for a glass of water.

In general, 1 złoty in 1940 is equivalent to about US $3.30 in 2020. Rates are not exact because conversions cannot fully take into account the massive fluctuation of currency value during the war—which occurred for many reasons—as well as inflation rates in the United States. Also, different currency notes were used in different occupied areas of Poland, but it seems that they corresponded with the złoty rate, which was actually set by the Nazis against the reichsmark to bolster the Germany economy. Some ghettos used their own currencies.

88 *"change in her pocket"*: It is difficult to estimate the prices of smuggled goods in this part of Poland at that time. Renia may have bartered for goods rather than for money.

89 *Janowska camp*: "Janowska," USHMM Encyclopedia,

https://encyclopedia.ushmm.org/content/en/article/janowska. This camp was established in September 1941. It is not clear from Renia's account when Aaron was taken.

89 *more than forty thousand*: Goldenberg, "Camps: Forward," 267. "Nazi Camps," The USHMM Encyclopedia, states that the Nazis set up more than 40,000 camps and other incarceration sites (this includes ghettos). Zuckerman, *Surplus of Memory*, 340, says there were 8,000 camps in Poland. According to Dalia Ofer and Lenore J. Weitzman, "Labor Camps and Concentration Camps: Introduction to Part 4," in *Women in the Holocaust*, 267, the Nazis established at least 437 labor camps for Jews in occupied Poland.

89 *The SS leased some of the labor camps to private companies*: Goldenberg, "Camps: Forward," 266–67. The SS was the Nazi force responsible for the Final Solution.

89 *Women cost less . . . arduous "male" hard-labor*: Ofer and Weitzman, "Labor Camps and Concentration Camps," 268. According to Felicja Karay, "Women in the Forced Labor Camps," in *Women in the Holocaust*, 285, the Skarzysko-Kamienna labor camp paid the SS five złotys per day for each male and only four złotys for each woman.

89 *vetch . . . tasted like boiled pepper*: Dyna Perelmuter, "Mewa (Seagull)," in *Before All Memory Is Lost*, 179.

92 *the Kukielkas*: The way Renia writes about this in her memoir makes it difficult to discern whether her family was included; however, according to her Yad Vashem testimony, her family was moved to Wodizłow.

92 *"Now each person cared . . . of their brethren"*: Kukielka, *Underground Wanderings*, 18.

93 *"if you saw a dead body on the street, you took its shoes"*: Jon Avnet mentioned this "rule of the ghetto" in discussion of his film *Uprising* at the Directors Guild, New York City, April 22, 2018.

94 *"No one could breathe, cough, or cry without having an audience"*: Izhar, *Chasia Bornstein-Bielicka*, 112.

96 *"They leave as if into an abyss"*: Kukielka, *Underground Wanderings*, 28.

96 *murdered in retaliation*: Schulman, *Partisan's Memoir*, 79–80.

96 *"Ukrainian savages"*: A small percentage of Ukrainians collaborated with the Nazis; some of them were POWs who were commanded to carry out the Germans' "dirty work." This subject is beyond the scope of this book, but many of the women's memoirs describe Ukrainian collaboration. As with Poles, the women were likely deeply hurt by this betrayal by their neighbors.

96 *Nazis and their collaborators*: In her diaries, Gusta Davidson attempted to analyze the psychology of the violent: "The Schupo, who occupy the lowest rung, are the ones most often in contact with the prisoners. They are more likely than the others to show mercy and even compassion. But in the presence of their superiors, they become hangmen, the cruelest of prison guards. . . . It's not the German or Ukrainian who tortures the Jew or the Pole. It is the beast lodged in human form that wields the levers of power

inflicting pain on us. And yet not all of them are the same. Not in all has savagery taken root so deep that they cannot occasionally suspend it. There are S.D. people who, in spite of their ideological antisemitism or hatred of Poles, are unable to torture or inflict pain. . . ." Draenger, *Justyna's Narrative*, 20–21.

97 *"Ukrainian . . . cigarette"*: Kukielka, *Underground Wanderings*, 27.

Chapter 5: The Warsaw Ghetto—Education and the Word

98 *traveled to Warsaw from the farms for a conference*: Zuckerman, *Surplus of Memory*, 65.

98 *Frumka's younger sister Hantze*: All information about Hantze in this section comes from *Hantze and Frumka*.

98 *characteristic allure*: Lubetkin, *Days of Destruction*, 37, writes about how moved she was by Hantze's talk.

99 *"I've never had a more exciting . . . that was captivating"*: Rachel Katznelson-Shazar, "Meeting Hantze," in *Hantze and Frumka*, 153.

100 *her refined aesthetic taste and love of poetry*: Zuckerman, *Surplus of Memory*, 104. Antek describes her as a fragile and sophisticated "flower bud" who was born in the wrong time.

100 *"he promised to edit . . . I'm butchering his short stories"*: From a letter to Z-L, Łódź, June 1939, Ghetto Fighters' House Museum archive.

100 *"movement, people, life"*: Eliezer, "In the Movement," 87–91. He describes their relationship at length.

101 *"I will always remember . . . help of God"*: Yudka, "Catastrophe," 95–102.

102 *more than four hundred thousand*: Irene Zoberman, "The Forces of Endurance," in *Before All Memory Is Lost*, 221, states that 460,000 Jews were crowded into one square mile. This meant that eight to ten Jews had to share one room. The ghetto walls, which shifted as the population bloated and then was murdered, were composed of existing structures and ten-foot-high walls built specifically for the purpose of imprisonment.

102 *thirty performance venues on one street alone*: Chaya Ostrower, *It Kept Us Alive: Humor in the Holocaust*, trans. Sandy Bloom (Jerusalem: Yad Vashem, 2014), 237. Ostrower includes a chapter on cabarets and performances, 229–330. *Women in the Ghettos*, 160, mentions Miriam Eisenstat, the daughter of the director of the well-known Warsaw synagogue choir. In the Warsaw ghetto, in her late teens, she quickly became popular as the "nightingale of the ghetto." She sold out concerts at the thousand-seat Femina theater, located in the ghetto, on the ground floors of an apartment building, not far from the Great Synagogue.

102 *The Bund also hosted concerts*: For the Bund's social activity in the ghetto, see, for instance, Goldstein, *Stars Bear Witness*, 41–42, 45, 82–84, 102–3. According to Vladka Meed, there were 85 illegal schools in the Warsaw ghetto

(Katz and Ringelheim, *Proceedings of the Conference on Women*, 80).

102 *Given that political . . . rendezvous*: In some accounts, Jews were not allowed to gather for prayer, ostensibly to avoid spreading disease. In other accounts, all Jewish meetings were banned; for instance, in Gelbard, "Life in the Ghetto," 7: "It was strictly forbidden for anyone to hold meetings or gatherings." She goes on to explain that with time, gatherings resumed. In several accounts, when Jews got together to lecture and learn, they blacked out windows and guarded the doors. Some claim that although Jewish gatherings were banned in the Warsaw ghetto, the Nazis were much more concerned with illegal smuggling (they did not believe that Jews could meet to discuss resistance).

102 *education was a priority*: Freedom's educational and social programs are discussed in Gelbard, "Warsaw Ghetto," 3–16; Lubetkin, *Days of Destruction*, 58–72; Zuckerman, *Surplus of Memory*, 52–64, 114–25.

104 *breeding ground for underground fighters*: Rotem, *Memoirs of a Ghetto Fighter*, 21.

104 *"With all our strength . . . to their age"*: Gelbard, "Warsaw Ghetto," 3–16.

105 *To keep a diary . . . equally punishable*: *Who Will Write Our History*.

105 *their own imprint*: For more on their press, see Lubetkin, *Days of Destruction*, 66–67; Zuckerman, *Surplus of Memory*, 55–56.

106 *Later, its members put out*: The first in 1940; the latter, in 1942.

106 *"Political publications ... twice a month"*: Wall text, POLIN Museum of the History of Polish Jews, Warsaw.

106 *Overall ... multiple people*: Information on these publications is from Barbara Engelking and Jacek Leociak, *The Warsaw Ghetto: A Guide to the Perished City* (New Haven, CT: Yale University Press, 2009), 683–88.

107 *"If we're not allowed ... for all inhabitants"*: Gelbard, "Warsaw Ghetto," 3–16.

107 *developed secret domestic libraries*: Goldstein, *Stars Bear Witness*, 49–50, on how they saved a Bund library. Antek also saved and created libraries.

107 *Henia Reinhartz*: Henia Reinhartz, *Bits and Pieces* (Toronto: Azrieli Foundation, 2007), 24–30.

107 *Autobiographical writing ... individuality*: Analysis by Rachel Feldhay Brenner, *Writing as Resistance: Four Women Confronting the Holocaust* (University Park: Pennsylvania State University Press, 2003).

108 *In writing*: Visual artists also created work to defy dehumanization and maintain sanity, identity, and a reason to live. For instance, Warsaw-born painter Halina Olomucki painted her experiences in the Warsaw ghetto, smuggling her artworks to Polish acquaintances while she was being taken out for forced labor. Her artistic talent gave her special status in concentration camps; she was given better food and art supplies to paint barracks and camp

staff. She used these materials to make secret drawings of her barrack mates. Her striking drawing *Women of Birkenau Camp* is a haunting portrait of three emaciated women in striped uniform, their eyes dark with horror, exhaustion, despair. She used a soft pencil that she'd stolen. See: Rochelle G. Saidel and Batya Brudin, eds., *Violated!: Women in Holocaust and Genocide* (New York: Remember the Women Institute, 2018), exhibition catalogue.

108 *could not be the only history*: Mordechai Tenenbaum, a Freedom leader in Białystok, also created an archive, which was hidden and is now accessible. Antek attempted to compile a Freedom archive.

109 *"I do not ask for praise . . . Margolit Lichtensztajn"*: Wall text, Emanuel Ringelblum Jewish Historical Institute, Warsaw.

109 *"The great crowding . . . speaking their hearts"*: Gelbard, "Warsaw Ghetto," 3–16.

109 *the childrens' cries for bread, audible all night, unbearable*: Lubetkin, *Days of Destruction*, 38–39. Gelbard says that those Jews who could buy bread were allowed "an eighth of a kilo three times per week." In 1941 the food ration for Jews in the Warsaw ghetto was 184 calories per day. According to Tec, *Resistance*, 60, 20 percent of the ghetto population in Poland died of hunger.

110 *Countless Jewish women*: See Tec, *Resistance*, 62–65, on how the JDC and other organizations supported soup kitchens, many run by women. For more women, see:

Women in the Ghettos; Meilech Neustadt, ed., *Destruction and Rising;* Katarzyna Person, ed., *Warsaw Ghetto: Everyday Life,* "Women" chapter.

110 *Nearly two thousand public kitchens in the ghetto, all organized by women*: According to Vladka Meed, in Katz and Ringelheim, Proceedings of the Conference on Women, 34, 80.

110 *Oneg Shabbat member Rachel Auerbach*: See, for instance, "A Bit Stubborn: Rachela Auerbach," Jewish Historical Institute, http://www.jhi.pl/en/blog/2018-05-30-a-bit -stubborn-rachela-auerbach, and Ofer, "Gender Issues in Diaries and Testimonies of the Ghetto," 143–67.

110 *"Greek appearance and grand poise"*: Yakov Kenner, "Paula Elster," *Women in the Ghettos,* 148–50. She was a courier and died fighting in the Warsaw uprising in 1944.

110 *who'd been arrested for political work while in middle school*: During certain periods, youth movement activity—especially of a Communist leaning—was illegal in Poland. See Ido Bassok, "Youth Movements," trans. Anna Barber, The YIVO Encyclopedia of Jews in Eastern Europe, https://yivoencyclopedia.org/article.aspx/Youth_ Movements.

110 *Basia Berman, an impassioned educator*: Information from Paldiel, *Saving One's Own,* 32–42. Later in the war, she was deeply involved in rescue missions. Her memoir *City Within a City* was published in 2012.

110 *Bundists . . . medical attention*: Goldstein, *Stars Bear Witness,* 82.

110 *Shayndl Hechtkop*: Information is from *Women in the Ghettos*, 162–163.

111 *to save time*: Gutterman, *Fighting for Her People*, 150.

111 *to create a "five"*: Lubetkin, *Days of Destruction*, 57.

111 *Chana Gelbard was an early courier*: She married Yitzhak Fiszman. Chana and Renia became friends at Kibbutz Dafna, after the war. More about her in Zuckerman, *Surplus of Memory*, 47.

112 *"It was dangerous . . . Zivia's girls"*: Gelbard, "Warsaw Ghetto," 3–16. Literally, "Zivia's children."

112 *Were developing a role*: According to Goldstein, *Stars Bear Witness*, 47, the Bund also had a countrywide courier system that covered sixty towns.

Chapter 6: From Spirit to Blood— Becoming the ZOB

114 *Nazi occupation would not deter Tosia Altman*: Information about Tosia Altman in this chapter comes primarily from Shalev, *Tosia Altman*.

115 *"hussy"*: Anna Legierska, "The Hussies and Gentlemen of Interwar Poland."

116 *"iron softness"*: Shalev, *Tosia Altman*, 215.

117 *"a jolt of electric energy"*: Shalev, *Tosia Altman*, 163.

117 *"inexhaustible optimism"*: Izhar, *Chasia Bornstein-Bielicka*, 157.

117 *"the art of living"*: Chaika Grossman, *The Underground*

Army: Fighters of the Białystok Ghetto, trans. Shmuel Beeri (New York: Holocaust Library, 1987), 42.

117 *"If you were not . . . of love and light"*: Ruzka Korczak, "Men and Fathers," in *Women in the Ghettos*, 28–34.

118 *tables and unhinged doors*: Grossman, *Underground Army*, 42.

118 *"She opened up . . . filled with vigor"*: Korczak, "Men and Fathers," 28–34.

119 *One young Vilna woman*: According to Kovner in *Partisans of Vilna*, she was an eleven-year-old girl (she is not named). According to Rich Cohen, *The Avengers: A Jewish War Story* (New York: Knopf, 2000), 38, she was seventeen. There are several stories about Ponary survivors bringing back their tales to the ghettos where they were often not believed. This account is from Cohen, 43–45

119 *seventy-five thousand*: Roughly seventy-five thousand Jews and twenty-five thousand non-Jews were shot here over the course of three years.

120 *"Don't believe these . . . to the slaughter!"*: From the Yiddish leaflet Abba read at the meeting, as read in *Partisans of Vilna*.

120 *When Zivia heard the news*: The following two sections are based on Lubetkin, *Days of Destruction*, 83–99.

120 *Other Jews had escaped . . . in the ghettos*: Some of their writings were kept in the Ringelblum archive and are held in the Jewish Historical Institute archives.

121 *Numerous courier girls, including Frumka*: Gutterman, *Fighting for Her People*, 159, lists messengers. According to Shimshi, "Frumka Plotniczki," Frumka was "the first to bring word of the scope of the extermination of Polish Jewry in the eastern districts."

121 *not believed*: Lenore J. Weitzman, "Kashariyot (Couriers) in the Jewish Resistance During the Holocaust," in The Encyclopedia of Jewish Women, https://jwa.org/encyclopedia/article/kashariyot-couriers-in-jewish-resistance-during-holocaust. For additional reasons why Jews did not suspect or believe: Izhar, *Chasia Bornstein-Bielicka*, 114; Mais, "Jewish Life in the Shadow of Destruction," 18–25; Meed, *Both Sides of the Wall*, 31, 47; Zuckerman, *Surplus of Memory*, 68, 72.

122 *"Jews are dying . . . a wall with your head?"*: Ziva Shalev, "Tosia Altman," The Encyclopedia of Jewish Women, https://jwa.org/encyclopedia/article/altman-tosia.

123 *"[T]his train is taking you to the worst death camps. . . . Do not enter this train"*: Vera Slymovicz testimony, pp. 23–24, Alex Dworkin Canadian Jewish Archives, Montreal.

123 *"This is wholesale planned murder"*: Lubetkin, *Days of Destruction*, 88.

124 *"They reproached us . . . among the people"*: Lubetkin, *Days of Destruction*, 92–93 (JDC leaders on 108). See also Zuckerman, *Surplus of Memory*, 194. In Ronen, *Condemned to Life*, 186–207, others argued that armed resistance was forbidden by Jewish law.

124 *"frustration and helpless rage"*: Lubetkin, *Days of Destruction*, 93.

125 *"It is our duty to look at the truth as it is"*: Cited in Gutterman, *Fighting for Her People*, 163.

125 *"our greatest enemy was false hope"*: Lubetkin, *Days of Destruction*, 92.

125 *"none of us knew . . . we had only two revolvers"*: Cited in Gutterman, *Fighting for Her People*, 161. In some accounts, they had one single gun. It's not clear where these initial guns came from.

125 *Before the war, the Bund . . . not as snipers*: Bela Hazan and Ruzka Korczak write about taking self-defense classes where they were taught to use weapons as part of Freedom and The Young Guard respectively. Self-defense was part of training for life in Palestine. Ronen, however, in a personal interview, stressed that the Bund and the Revisionists were much better prepared. Prior to the war, the Bund had established "Tzufunkt Shturem" (Future Storm), a militia to protect the community from antisemitic attacks (POLIN holds their poster from 1929).

The Bund participated in a "cold armed" resistance effort early on in the war, using iron pipes and brass knuckles to strike back against a massive pogrom in which Nazis paid Poles four złotys per day to attack Jews. They were the only party who fought and the first to call for armed defense in the ghetto. They also set up a protection force that patrolled the Jewish streets during the chaos of people moving into the ghetto. See Marek Edelman, *The Ghetto*

Fights (New York: American Representation of the General Jewish Workers' Union of Poland, 1946), 3; Goldstein, *Stars Bear Witness*, 45–65.

126 *the Bund, however . . . had a few weapons*: Marek Edelman, *The Last Fighters*, directed by Ronen Zaretsky and Yael Kipper Zaretsky, Isr., 2006. According to other Bundists, they were not anti-Zionist; they simply didn't see a point in fighting without Polish backing. Zuckerman, *Surplus of Memory*, 166, 173, 221, 249, describes his frustration with the Bund.

126 *in a leadership role*: Zivia was a leader of a special aid cell along with Paula Alster. Gutterman, *Fighting for Her People*, 167.

127 *"Bloody Sabbath"*: This occurred on a Friday night. According to Gutterman, *Fighting for Her People*, 167, it was called "Bloody Saturday." Other sources refer to it as "Bloody Friday." To Zuckerman, *Surplus of Memory*, 178, it was "The Night of Blood." Shalev, 141, calls it "The Day of Blood."

127 *Frumka arrived with news about Sobibor*: Frumka's report of June 15, 1942, was on display at the Jewish Historical Institute, in Warsaw.

127 *July 1942 in the ghetto*: This section is based on Meed, *Both Sides of the Wall*, 9–67.

128 *"Fear of what awaited . . . saving ourselves"*: Meed, *Both Sides of the Wall*, 22.

129 *Women physically fought . . . jumped from trains*: Tec, *Resistance*, 68.

129 *they themselves would be taken*: Tec, *Resistance*, 67.

130 *"That's how the life of a Jew became worth a slice of bread"*: Klinger, "The Pioneers in Combat," in *Women in the Ghettos*, 23–28. A literal translation: "Later, the Nazis claimed that the price of a captured Jew was a half kilo of bread and a quarter kilo of marmalade. That's how the life of the Jew became cheap."

131 *a "snow" of down—the "disemboweled intestines of Jewish bedclothes"*: "The Liquidation of Jewish Warsaw," a report drawn up by the Oneg Shabbat group, November 1942, on display at the Jewish Historical Institute, Warsaw.

131 *"Don't worry . . . Mama"*: Meed, *Both Sides of the Wall*, 65.

132 *the Jewish Fighting Organization*: Also known in English as the Jewish Combat Organization. The Hebrew Eyal is the acronym for Irgun Yehudi Lochem.

133 *"It is better to be shot in the ghetto than to die in Treblinka!"*: The text of the poster is printed in Lubetkin, *Days of Destruction*, 112. There are several accounts of who reported on Treblinka first, including escapees (who drew maps of the site), a Bund messenger, and a Freedom courier.

134 *"Success! . . . for so long"*: Lubetkin, *Days of Destruction*, 115.

135 *but failed to kill him*: Meed, *Both Sides of the Wall*, 70; Tec, *Resistance*, 72–73. Lubetkin, *Days of Destruction*, 116, describes that after his first shot, the gun jammed, but he threatened to kill anyone who approached him. It was Kanal's first time firing a gun.

135 *into the ghetto*: For discussion on Jews bringing weapons into the Warsaw ghetto, see, for instance, Shalev, *Tosia Altman*, 155, 174–75.

136 *"you can imagine . . . could carry it in a basket"*: Zuckerman, *Surplus of Memory*, 213.

136 *"a stunning blow"*: Cited in Gutterman, *Fighting for Her People*, 183.

137 *Three hundred thousand . . . sixty thousand*: According to "Warsaw," United States Holocaust Memorial Museum: Holocaust Encyclopedia, https://encyclopedia.ushmm.org/content/eu/article/warsaw, there were four hundred thousand Jews in the Warsaw ghetto at its largest. Three hundred thousand were deported to death in summer 1942. Up to seventy thousand remained afterward.

138 *"I reject the proposal . . . start all over"*: This quotation merges accounts of the speech given in Gutterman, *Fighting for Her People*, 189; Lubetkin, *Days of Destruction*, 122; Zuckerman, *Surplus of Memory*, 214.

Chapter 7: The Days of Wandering—Homeless to Housekeeper

139 *"fighting, but then falling like a fly . . . I am invincible!"*: Kukielka, *Underground Wanderings*, 37. This chapter is based on Renia's memoir and her Yad Vashem testimony.

140 *"But these poor babies . . . the babies' lives"*: Kukielka, *Underground Wanderings*, 38.

143 *"Mother is surely looking... Where is Mother?"*: Kukielka, *Underground Wanderings*, 42.

143 *"The wise... Where can they go?"*: Ibid., 43.

144 *most Jews set off wandering with no guide or destination*: "Jędrzejów," Virtual Shtetl.

144 *police*: "Police" can refer to German or Polish police. The Nazis took over the Polish police force to create the "Blue Police." The German police were known as Orpo, or the "Green Police." The cities had more German officers, the rural areas, more Polish police. "Gendarme" seems to generally refer to a German police officer. The issue of Polish police collaboration with the Nazis is addressed in Jan Grabowski, "The Polish Police: Collaboration in the Holocaust," Lecture at USHMM, November 17, 2016, text accessed online.

145 *an operation to reverse a circumcision*: According to Grunwald-Spier, *Women's Experiences in the Holocaust*, 245, the cost was between 3,000 and 10,000 złotys. See also Zoberman, "Forces of Endurance," 248; Weitzman, "Living on the Aryan Side, 201–5.

146 *The tiny Association of Tartar-Muslims... circumcisions*: Paulsson, *Secret City*, 4.

146 *"Schmaltzovniks," or blackmailers*: See Zuckerman, *Surplus of Memory*, 482–83, for a discussion of types.

146 *two pounds of sugar or a bottle of whiskey*: Weitzman, "Living on the Aryan Side," 188.

148 *"No matter what happens... you will always stay Jewish"*: Kukielka, Yad Vashem testimony.

148 *Renia made it*: The following two sections, including dialogue, are culled from Renia's memoir, 45–47, and her Yad Vashem testimony; the details differ in each account.

148 *Sedziszow, thanks to her brother*: According to Kukielka, *Underground Wanderings*, 45, she met him at a camp in Sedziszow. I haven't found much information about this particular camp, but here is another personal account that mentions a labor camp on the outskirts of Sedziszow: https://njjewishnews.timesofisrael.com/dor-ldor-a-polish-town-remembers-its-holocaust-victims/. According to "Jędrzejów," Holocaust Historical Society, https://www.holocausthistoricalsociety.org.uk/contents/ghettosj-r/Jędrzejów.html, men from Jędrzejów were sent to a labor camp at the Sedziszow railway depot, so it is likely men from Wodisłow were also sent here.

According to records from the ITS archive (International Tracing Service), however, Aaron was at the Skarzysko-Kamienna labor camp from March 1942 to July 1943, the Czenstochau labor camp from July 1943 to April 1944, and Buchberg from April 1944 to May 1945. The Skarzysko-Kamienna camp, however, was very large and it does not seem to fit Renia's description. From Skarzysko, Renia would have had to walk for days to reach Charsznica, the town where she meets the railway acquaintances in a later scene. From Sedziszow, it was only thirty kilometers. The ITS archive records also show a debatable birth date for Aaron, so all in all, I am inclined to think he was at Sedziszow at this time and at Skarzysko-Kamienna later.

Renia includes a longer story about her brother and the work camps in her Yad Vashem testimony, where she mentions that he was sent to build train tracks; the Sedziszow camp was at a railway depot.

148 *pretending to be a Pole wandering the woods*: Renia describes his journey in her Yad Vashem testimony.

149 *But there was more*: This scene is based on a combination of Renia's slightly differing accounts in *Underground Wanderings* and her Yad Vashem testimony.

152 *"From that moment on, I was on my own"*: Kukielka, *Underground Wanderings*, 47.

152 *September 12 . . . I don't want to die*: Kukielka, *Underground Wanderings*, 47.

152 *she found a small village*: Renia's Yad Vashem testimony offers a different account.

153 *knocking on her acquaintance's door*: The story of Renia and her acquaintance, as well as the dialogue, are based on Renia's accounts in *Underground Wanderings*, 48–50, and her Yad Vashem testimony, which differ slightly from each other.

153 *"My face is flabby . . . but who cares?"*: Kukielka, *Underground Wanderings*, 48.

154 *in another account*: According to Kukielka, Yad Vashem testimony. Zuckerman, *Surplus of Memory*, 485–86, explains that patriotic priests collected the names and papers of the dead and gave them to the Polish underground, who sold some to Jews.

154 *Fake documents*: See Meed, *Both Sides of the Wall*,

226–27; Paldiel, *Saving One's Own*, 37, 218–19; Weitzman, "Living on the Aryan Side," 213–15; Zuckerman, *Surplus of Memory*, 485–86.

157 *The train jerked into motion, and suddenly Renia ran cold*: This section and dialogue is based on Kukielka, *Underground Wanderings*, 49–51.

160 *she met a Jewish militia member*: Renia gives a different account of how she met him in her Yad Vashem testimony

160 *in the home of a half-German family*: This scene and dialogue are based on Kukielka, *Underground Wanderings*, 52.

162 *"Everywhere I go . . . I must play a part"*: Kukielka, *Underground Wanderings*, 53.

162 *"I hadn't even known . . . and imitate"*: Ibid.

Chapter 8: To Turn to Stone

165 *October 1942*: Renia provides conflicting dates for this scene, even within *Underground Wanderings*. The main Sandomierz ghetto liquidation took place in October. It appears that this chapter took place in either late October or early November.

165 *Sarah had arranged everything*: This chapter, including quotations and dialogue, is based on Kukielka, *Underground Wanderings*, 56–62. In her Yad Vashem testimony, Renia tells a different story about how the smuggler came to the Hollanders.

168 *prewar glory*: Będzin's architecture was an idiosyncratic

mix of Beaux Arts, Art Nouveau, Polish Neoclassical, Art Deco, Italian Fascist (the train station) and Dutch revival styles, indicating that the city had wealth from the 1870s to the 1930s.

171 *final farewell*: According to Kukielka's Yad Vashem testimony, Leah and Moshe were forty-five and forty-eight, respectively, when they were killed.

172 *More than twenty-five thousand*: Skarzysko-Kamienna, Yad Vashem Shoah Resource Center, https://www .yadvashem.org/odot_pdf/Microsoft%20Word%20-%20 6028.pdf.

173 *their newfound freedom accompanied grief and guilt, but also energy*: Draenger, *Justyna's Narrative*, 111–12. Weitzman, "Living on the Aryan Side," 192–93, explains that youth were particularly motivated once their mothers were killed. According to one account in the film about Jewish women partisans on JPEF, "When my mother died, I got tough."

Chapter 9: The Black Ravens

174 *Short, brown hair*: According to her son, she hadn't wanted it to be too short, because that would seem American-Hollywood bourgeois. Personal interview, Avihu Ronen, Tel Aviv, Isr., May 16, 2018.

175 *Chajka Klinger*: This scene of Chajka distributing leaflets is based on a mention in her diaries where it is ambiguous as to who was carrying out this activity. The scenes in this

chapter are based on Klinger, *Writing These Words*, and adaptations "Girls in the Ghettos" and "Pioneers in Combat," in *Women in the Ghettos*. Additional information is primarily from Ronen, *Condemned to Life*, as well as testimony offered by Fela Katz (in JHI archives) and in Jerzy Diatłowicki, ed., *Jews in Battle, 1939–1945* (Warsaw: Association of Jewish Combatants and Victims of World War II and Jewish Historical Institute, 2009–2015). I have also drawn on the sources on Będzin mentioned above.

175 *an early host of many Zionist movements*: According to Ronen, *Condemned to Life*, 29–38, one of the first cells of The Young Guard was established in Będzin.

177 *"the eyes of a dreamer"*: Klinger, *Writing These Words*, 167.

177 *"young tree"*: Klinger, *Writing These Words*, 167.

178 *"live, grow and die with it"*: Ibid., 81.

178 *"Outside the windows . . . stinking room and sew"*: Rutka Laskier, *Rutka's Notebook: January–April 1943* (Jerusalem: Yad Vashem, 2007), 54.

178 *One notable example was Alfred Rossner*: See, for instance Ronen, *Condemned to Life*, 125–43. According to some accounts the Zonder pass was yellow; in others it was blue.

181 *"We shall not let . . . go our own way"*: Klinger, *Writing These Words*, 84. Ronen, *Condemned to Life*, 104–24, relays a similar celebration, but says it was for the holiday of Chanukah.

182 *Photographs shows youths*: Klinger, *Writing These Words*, photo insert.

182 *Images of Sarah Kukielka*: Photos from 1943 are in the Ghetto Fighters' House Museum archive.

182 *"Hundreds joined us . . . looking for a patch of green grass"*: Ronen, *Condemned to Life*, 104–24.

182 *"the pots on the wall sparkled as if in a festive way"*: Klinger, *Writing These Words*, 131–32.

182 *Then, one night, a roundup*: This section is based on Klinger, *Writing These Words*, 136–43, but the scenes appear in a different order. Parts appear in *Women in the Ghettos*.

184 *With Nacia, she collected*: In one account, this was Leah; in another, it was Nacia.

186 *Gutan-Bricke . . . Markshdadt . . . Klatandorf"*: These names are from Klinger, "Girls in the Ghettos," in *Women in the Ghettos*; it is not clear what they refer to. *Writing These Words*, 138, simply says "labor camp."

186 *Work was no longer the ultimate savior*: There was a time in Zaglembie where the Nazi leader of the forced labor operation was more influential than that of the killing operation (Operation Reinhard).

186 *Chajka too*: This section is based on Ronen, *Condemned to Life*, 162–85.

186 *Thousands walked over . . . deportation and death*: From the descriptions in Rutka Laskier, *Rutka's Notebook*, 36–39. Rutka was selected for forced labor but jumped from a window and ran.

188 *The women of The Young Guard . . . innocent face*: Slightly different details for this story are provided in

Klinger, *Writing These Words*, 139; Klinger, "Girls in the Ghettos," *Women in the Ghettos*; Ronen, *Condemned to Life*, 162–85.

189 *During this time, Irka Pejsachson . . . two thousand people were freed*: There are different versions of this story. This version is from Klinger, "Girls in the Ghettos," *Women in the Ghettos*, where it states that several hundred people were freed. In Ronen, *Condemned to Life*, 162–85, the person who led the attic escape was David. In Klinger, *Writing These Words*, 139–40, it just says a "passage was found," and states that two thousand people were freed.

189 *energized visits from Tosia*: Shalev, *Tosia Altman*, 134.

189 *"pride of the movement" . . . because he truly was brave"*: Klinger, *Writing These Words*, 98.

190 *two hundred comrades from various movements*: Klinger, *Writing These Words*, 15. According to Fela Katz's testimonies, there were two hundred to three hundred members.

191 *Surviving postcards . . . with secret codes*: These messages, and their explanations, are from *Women in the Ghettos*. Zuckerman, *Surplus of Memory*, 89, explains that they used different codes for correspondences with different areas. For some, they used first initials instead of words; other codes were based on the Bible. Letters to the east used a "capital letter code" in which the hidden message was conveyed through the use of uppercase letters.

191 *"No revolutionary movement . . . hagana (defense)."*: Klinger, *Writing These Words*, 98.

192 *"The avant-garde . . . people are dying"*: Klinger, *Writing These Words*, 7.

193 *"thick, sinewy, muscular arms"*: Klinger, *Writing These Words*, 177. His name is also spelled Cwi.

193 *They formed groups of "fives"*: According to Lubetkin, *Days of Destruction*, 83, these units were conceived when the Russians and Germans fought (in 1941) as five-person Jewish self-defense squads. The youth assumed that the Russians would win and these units were meant to protect them from Polish attacks during the chaotic days between regimes. They did not imagine that these squads would become the basis of their anti-Nazi militia.

193 *life in Będzin was "heaven" for Renia*: Unless indicated otherwise, the next sections are based on Kukielka, *Underground Wanderings*.

194 *it appears . . . Nazi uniforms*: Kukielka, Yad Vashem testimony.

194 *Hantze arrived*: Hantze actually left Grochów for Będzin in the summer of 1942. Renia, however, writes about her arrival as if she herself was there (Kukielka, "The Last Days," *Women in the Ghettos*). It is possible that Renia is writing about Hantze's arrival based on others' impressions, or, alternately, that Hantze left briefly on a mission and returned once Renia was in Będzin. In either case, Renia was taken by Hantze's positive spirit.

195 *"In Grochów . . . even they stayed alive"*: Kukielka, "Last Days," 102–6.

196 *"The ground takes everything in . . . the truth"*: Kukielka, *Underground Wanderings*, 65.

197 *"I remember how they both sat . . . everything that they'd been through"*: Kukielka, "Last Days," 102–6. This section is based on this essay.

197 *"There's no help . . . forsaken us"*: Kukielka, *Underground Wanderings*, 67.

199 *roughly 2,500 reichsmarks . . . partisan detachment*: Ronen, *Condemned to Life*, 186–207.

200 *Jewish Telegraphic Agency's report*: The JTA, established in 1917, is a worldwide news-gathering organization serving Jewish community papers. The report was published on January 8, 1943; the incident took place on October 4, 1942. The women's revolt is described in both the JTA report and in *Women in the Ghettos*, though with different details in each. Source: JTA.org.

Chapter 10: Three Lines in History— A Krakówian Christmas Surprise

201 *The Akiva Pledge*: Draenger, *Justyna's Narrative*, 141. (They use "Akiba.")

203 *October 1942*: Based on Gusta's writings, this was the fall of 1942; it may have been September.

203 *Gusta Davidson arrived in Kraków*: The scenes in this chapter are based primarily on Gusta Davidson Draenger's diary, *Justyna's Narrative*. Information about Gusta and the Kraków resistance also comes from: Anna Czocher, Dobrochna

Kałwa, et al., *Is War Men's Business? Fates of Women in Occupied Kraków in Twelve Scenes*, trans. Tomasz Tesznar and Joanna Bełch-Rucińska (Kraków: Historical Museum of the City of Kraków, 2011), exhibition catalogue; Sheryl Silver Ochayon, "Armed Resistance in the Kraków and Białystok Ghettos," Yad Vashem, https://www.yadvashem.org/articles /general/armed-resistance-in-Kraków-and-Białystok.html; Yael Margolin Peled, "Gusta Dawidson Draenger," The Encyclopedia of Jewish Women, https://jwa.org/encyclopedia /article/draenger-gusta-dawidson.

203 *sixty thousand Jews lived in Kraków, a quarter of the city's population*: Because the seat of the General Government was in Kraków, the Germans wanted to "cleanse" the city of its Jews and expelled most to the countryside. By the time the ghetto was closed on March 20, 1941, only twenty thousand Jews remained in the city.

203 *"wafting the hum . . . surrounding buildings"*: Draenger, *Justyna's Narrative*, 46.

204 *"older folks lacked . . . bruised, despairing souls"*: Draenger, *Justyna's Narrative*.

205 *"The stillness exhaled . . . single leaf quivered"*: Draenger, *Justyna's Narrative*, 33.

205 *"rolled slowly through the azure sky"*: Draenger, *Justyna's Narrative*, 50.

206 *"to move the youth . . . cling to life"*: Draenger, *Justyna's Narrative*, 37–38.

206 *"You can't try to preserve fighters by shielding them in a shelter"*: Draenger, *Justyna's Narrative*, 39.

206 *"hands, now caked with fertile loam, would soon be soaked in blood"*: Draenger, *Justyna's Narrative*, 43.

207 *"femme fatale"*: Draenger, *Justyna's Narrative*, 48.

207 *"I only have a moment to spare"*: Draenger, *Justyna's Narrative*.

207 *The Nazis apparently admired . . . heavily protected*: Wojciech Oleksiak, "How Kraków Made it Unscathed Through WWII," Culture.pl, May 22, 2015, https://culture.pl/en/article/how-Kraków-made-it-unscathed-through-wwii. It appears that the Nazis created the Saxon myth to justify making this strategic location the capital. The Nazis also invested in developing Kraków's urban infrastructure. See: http://www.krakowpost.com/8702/2015/02/looking-back-70-years-wawel-under-occupation

208 *"find a direction for her new life that would give it significance"*: Draenger, *Justyna's Narrative*, 59.

209 *"The group had become . . . last port of their innermost feelings"*: Draenger, *Justyna's Narrative*, 61.

209 *"Their displays of exuberance . . . and never would?"*: Draenger, *Justyna's Narrative*, 62.

209 *"technical bureau" . . . "floating office"*: Draenger, *Justyna's Narrative*, 64–67.

210 *"cozy nest" . . . "cut an intimidating figure"*: Draenger, *Justyna's Narrative*, 101.

211 *Issued every Friday . . . the Kraków region*: Desciption of Kraków underground publications is in the testimony of Kalman Hammer (collected in Budapest, Hungary, on

September 14, 1943) held in the Ghetto Fighters' House Museum archive.

211 *"sisterly love"*: Draenger, *Justyna's Narrative*, 103.

212 *Hela Schüpper*: Information about Hela is from Hella Rufeisen-Schüpper, *Farewell to Mila 18* (Tel Aviv, Isr.: Ghetto Fighters' House and Hakibbutz Hameuchad, 1990); Yael Margolin Peled, "Hela Rufeisen Schüpper," The Encyclopedia of Jewish Women, https://jwa.org/encyclopedia/article/schupper-hella-rufeisen; Tec, *Resistance*, 171–77.

212 *"voluptuous beauty"*: Draenger, *Justyna's Narrative*, 94–95.

213 *"No one had ever been greeted . . . ecstasy inspired by those weapons"*: Draenger, *Justyna's Narrative*, 71.

213 *"happy as a child"*: Ibid., 72.

214 *Gola Mire*: Information about Gola Mire (nee Miriem Golda Mire) who is also referred to as Mire Gola and Gola Mira, is primarily from Grunwald-Spier, *Women's Experiences in the Holocaust*, 207–11; Kol-Inbar, "Three Lines in History," 520–21, and Yael Margolin Peled, "Mire Gola," The Encyclopedia of Jewish Women, https://jwa.org/encyclopedia/article/gola-mire.

214 *"a fierce fighter with a genuinely female heart"*: Draenger, *Justyna's Narrative*, 84.

215 *many active leading females*: Draenger, *Justyna's Narrative*. A photo captioned "Leading members of Akiba 1941" shows six women and three men.

216 *"the leaves . . . benevolent rays"*: Ibid., 112.

217 *"Even a minor attack here . . . cog in the machine"*: Ibid.

217 *"donned a Polish police uniform"*: Renia wrote about male comrades who used disguises to save Jews who were trapped in the burning Warsaw ghetto. A couple of Jewish men donned German uniforms from dead soldiers, or ones they'd stolen from forced-labor workshops, and acting like Nazis, screamed at Jews to get on a bus. Nazis who saw this assumed they were following orders to send them out to be killed in the forest; really they were setting them free. In another such incident, a Nazi-disguised Jew yelled at hidden Jews to come out of a tunnel. Some Jews hadn't realized it was a ruse and refused to leave. The Jew in disguise physically dragged several people out—then he told them to run. Other Jewish men dressed up as gendarmes were able to get close to unsuspecting Nazis and shoot them dead.

According to "The Battle of the Warsaw Ghetto," *The Pioneer Woman*, 5, 500 Jews dressed up as Nazis and attacked Pawiak Prison.

217 *"promoted himself"* to a Nazi: Lubetkin, *Days of Destruction*, 138–39. Lubetkin and Zuckerman, *Surplus of Memory*, both write about the Kraków resistance in their books. (Zuckerman was in Kraków.)

218 *Sexual relations . . . life-affirming*: Katz and Ringelheim, *Proceedings of the Conference on Women*, 36–38.

218 *"arrange a liquidation"*: Draenger, *Justyna's Narrative*, 115.

218 *"dedicated her life and soul to kitchen management"*: Draenger, *Justyna's Narrative*, 117.

218 *it looked like she was walking the police*: Ibid., 125.

219 *"this is the last supper"*: Ibid., 126.

219 *"to fight for three lines in history"*: Kol-Inbar, "Three Lines in History," 520.

221 *at least seven Nazis, and wounded many more*: According to Ochayon, "Armed Resistance in Kraków and Białystok," seven to twelve Nazis were killed; Lubetkin, *Days of Destruction*, says that thirteen were killed and fifteen were badly wounded. Kol-Inbar, "Three Lines in History," 519, states that seven Nazis were killed and many were injured.

221 *Hela was on a train*: Story in Draenger, *Justyna's Narrative*, 6–7.

Chapter 11: 1943, a New Year—Warsaw's Minirebellion

223 *Zivia was awoken with news*: The sections in this chapter from Zivia's perspective are based on Lubetkin, *Days of Destruction*, 125–36 (preparation for uprising) and 145–59 (January uprising). Varying accounts of the January uprising are offered by Goldstein, *Stars Bear Witness*; Gutterman, *Fighting for Her People*; Meed, *Both Sides of the Wall*; Ronen, *Condemned to Life*; Zuckerman, *Surplus of Memory*.

223 *Himmler*: Nazi leader Heinrich Himmler was considered to be an architect of the Holocaust.

224 *the better-armed Revisionist group Betar*: Betar was the youth group affiliated with the Zionist Revisionist move-

ment. They believed in establishing a Jewish state in Palestine with a "steel wall" of military force between Jews and their enemies. Betar was not socialist, and instead, was organized based on military behavior and structure (titles, parades, ranks); in the late 1930s their graduates created military "battalions." They were affiliated with Polish military organizations. There were frequent disagreements between Betar and the leftist Zionist youth and, in Warsaw, this continued through the war.

In the ghetto, the youth groups could not manage to collaborate. (In *The Last Fighters*, Marek Edelman tells a story of going to talk to Betar and the leader shot at him.) The left and right could not agree on who should lead the resistance, and on how to recruit fighters. Betar wanted one of their people to command the fight because they actually had military training, but the Labor Zionists wouldn't accept that. (Betar felt that the leftists were making unreasonable demands.) Betar lost many people in the Aktions and had an open call for fighters, which the others found terrifying—what if collaborators showed up? It was important for Freedom and The Young Guard that they all knew and trusted each other. Betar kept their weapons out in the open, which Antek found stupid (he'd experienced Nazi checks), as well as "arrogant and exhibitionistic" (Zuckerman, *Surplus of Memory*, 226–27, 412). The Revisionists, Zivia sensed (134), were in disarray after losing so many people in deportations. Unable to agree on terms, Betar created their own fighting faction, the ZZW. Because of their history and connections with Polish fighting groups, Betar was better armed, and apparently the ZZW consisted of three hundred well-armed fighters. See Lubetkin, *Days of Destruction*, 128, 133–36, and Tec, *Resistance*, 72–77.

225 *a new alliance: The "Jewish National Committee"*: According to Tec, *Resistance*, 72, the Bund agreed to join when they realized that the Polish underground was not going to collaborate with them.

225 *The Polish underground*: Tec, *Resistance*, 42–45, 78–80. From the perspective of Zuckerman, *Surplus of Memory*, 219–20, 349, 360–63. Bernard, *Problems Related to the Study*, 52–59, stresses that the AK was "not a single concept" but a vast and diverse underground army.

226 *electric lightbulbs . . . sulfuric acid*: According to Zuckerman, *Surplus of Memory*, 252–55, before the January uprising, the ZOB had fewer than twenty pistols and no rifles or Molotovs. It had grenades and lightbulbs.

226 *The Bundists strengthened their fighting units*: This section about Vladka is based on Meed, *Both Sides of the Wall*, 68–85. Vladka's oral testimonies can be found in the USHMM and USC Shoah Foundation collections.

226 *toiled . . . as slave labor*: Most Jews who remained in the ghetto worked as slave labor.

228 *According to . . . January 22*: Edelman, *The Ghetto Fights*, 30.

228 *the lack of time . . . led them to act*: Zuckerman, *Surplus of Memory*, 230, 251.

229 *"The mass of deportees . . . feet, teeth, and elbows"*: Meed, *Both Sides of the Wall,* 120. In Zivia's account, most Jews were confused and did not fight back.

230 *"a kind of emotional stock taking at the final moments of my life"*: Gutterman's translation, *Fighting for Her People,* 199.

230 *"Our armed struggle will be an inspiration to future generations"*: Lubetkin, *Days of Destruction,* 151.

231 *"We were totally unprepared. We hadn't expected to remain alive"*: Lubetkin, *Days of Destruction,* 154.

232 *"the silence of death permeated the air"*: Lubetkin, *Days of Destruction,* 155.

233 *"At the same time . . . former fear having disappeared"*: Lubetkin, *Days of Destruction,* 57.

233 *"a shower of bullets greeted them on all sides"*: Lubetkin, *Days of Destruction,* 158.

234 *Schultz workshop, killing him. . . . Hallman's furniture shop*: Schultz (Tobbens and Schultz) and Hallman were two of the factories in the Warsaw ghetto where thousands of Jews were slave laborers.

235 *they bound the guards at gunpoint and destroyed their records*: Meed, *Both Sides of the Wall,* 120–21.

235 *One comrade . . . Germans' heads below*: Klinger, *Writing These Words,* 152.

235 *took the Nazis days*: According to Tec, *Resistance,* 79, they had originally sent two hundred German policemen but ended up sending in eight hundred. They thought the

operation would take a few hours, and it took a few days. According to Ronen, *Condemned to Life*, 208–33, forty Germans were killed (he cites Chajka), and only four thousand of the eight thousand quota of Jews were expelled.

235 *"Hunger was a constant . . . carved its graves"*: Kukielka, "Last Days," 102–6.

237 *Kamionka*: Most sources agree that there were no ghettos in the Będzin area until the fall of 1942. According to "Będzin," Virtual Shtetl, the Jews had been living in an open ghetto before that date.

238 *"In the summer . . . fields and flowers"*: Laskier, *Rutka's Notebook*, 34.

238 *In Będzin . . . the decision to rise up was complex*: Ronen, "The Jews of Będzin," 16–27.

239 *crowded refugee camp . . . unhygienic*: Gutterman, "Holocaust in Będzin," 63. The USHMM holds numerous photos of the Kamionka ghetto. See, for instance, photographs 20745 and 19631.

240 *The ghetto was closed, guarded by the militia*: Renia says it was fenced and shuttered, but other sources say it was not fenced, but guarded. See Gutterman, "Holocaust in Będzin," 63.

240 *"disgraceful site"*: Kukielka, *Underground Wanderings*, 73.

241 *for the rest of her life*: According to a personal interview with Jacob Harel and Leah Waldman, Haifa, Isr., May 14, 2018, Renia described seeing this happen to her brother.

Part 2: Devils or Goddesses

243 *"They were not human"* . . . *Stroop*: Said to his cell mate, after the war. Cited in Witold Bereś and Krzysztof Burnetko, *Marek Edelman: Being on the Right Side*, trans. William R. Brand (Kraków, Pol.: Bereś Media, 2016), 170. Tec, *Resistance*, 81, stresses that Stroop was particularly impressed with Jewish women who fought equally alongside the men.

Chapter 12: In Preparation

245 *Będzin was buzzing*: Descriptions of these preparations are culled from Renia's memoir, Fela Katz's testimonies, Chajka's diary, Ronen's *Condemned to Life*, and Namyslo's catalogue. Freedom, Gordonia, and The Young Guard, and later HaNoar HaTzioni and Hashomer HaDati, all collaborated. Gordonia's leadership also included women like Szloma Lerner and Hanka Bornstein, who was a leader of the ZOB. It is unclear what the joint command in Będzin was at the time; overall, the underground saw itself as a satellite of the Warsaw ZOB and under their command. In Zaglembie, the adult parties were not involved.

245 *"We gained the reputation . . . the time comes"*: Kukielka, *Underground Wanderings*, 76.

247 *"smart like engineers with diplomas"*: Kukielka, *Underground Wanderings*, 77.

247 *They dug escape tunnels with their bare hands*: Ahron Brandes, "In the Bunkers," trans. Lance Ackerfeld, from the Bedzin yizkor book, https://www.jewishgen.org /Yizkor/bedzin/bed363.html.

247 *looked like the inhabitants had left in a hurry*: Tec, *Resistance*, 90.

248 *an episode of resistance—within the Jewish community*: This episode is based on Kukielka, *Underground Wanderings*, 77–82. According to Ronen, *Condemned to Life*, 208–33, there were a few such incidences.

249 *stared at the clash*: Kukielko, *Escape from the Pit*, 78, suggests that Renia may have also been beaten.

A while back, in the Warsaw ghetto, Frumka had had a scuffle with the Jewish police. During an Aktion, she, Zivia, Antek and another leader were suddenly surrounded. Frumka insulted a policeman. He responded with obscenities. She slapped his face. A group of police threw her into a horse and cart, her nose bleeding profusely, while Antek kicked like a wild man. A crowd of passersby admonished the police for detaining Hechalutz leaders, and a comrade helped release them. Antek and Frumka spat in the militiaman's face. See Lubetkin, *Days of Destruction*, 41–44; Zuckerman, *Surplus of Memory*, 190–91.

251 *News trickled in from Warsaw*: Unless indicated otherwise, the rest of this chapter, including quotes and dialogue, is based on Kukielka, *Underground Wanderings*, 82–88.

253 *Irena Adamowicz*: Information about Irena is from: "Adamowicz Irena," POLIN Polish Righteous, https://sprawiedliwi.org.pl/en/stories-of-rescue/story-rescue-adamowicz-irena; Izhar, *Chasia Bornstein-Bielicka*, 155; Anka Grupińska, *Reading the List* (Wołowiec: Czarne, 2014), 21; Lubetkin, *Days of Destruction*, 131; Zuckerman, *Surplus of Memory*, 96, 146–47. Despite her life-risking work, Antek claimed that her efforts were ultimately for missionary reasons. See Zuckerman, *Surplus of Memory*, 421.

254 *Idzia Pejsachson*: Information about Idzia is culled from varying accounts, including Klinger, *Writing These Words*, 112–13, 140–41.

254 *"You can't be occupied . . . transport of weapons"*: Klinger, "Girls in the Ghettos," *Women in the Ghettos*, 17–23.

255 *various hypotheses about her demise*: These are all from Klinger, *Writing These Words*, 141. According to Fela Katz's testimony, Idzia was recognized because of her partner.

255 *Astrid took Idzia's place*: Information about Astrid is culled from varying accounts, including Klinger, *Writing These Words*, 112–13, 140–41; Kukielka, *Underground Wanderings*, 85; Aaron Brandes, "The Underground in Bedzin," in *Daring to Resist*, 27–28. It appears that Idzia went to Warsaw to find weapons, and though she never returned to Będzin, Astrid arrived with pistols and grenades.

256 *"Warsaw customs had to be introduced"*: Klinger, *Writing These Words*, 113.

257 *A courier*: This was Astrid.

Chapter 13: The Courier Girls

259 *human worth was calculated by physical appearance:* Draenger, *Justyna's Narrative*, 1–57.

260 *That very same day:* The following two sections are based on Kukielka, *Underground Wanderings*, 88–91, including dialogue and quotations. Scenes are enhanced by descriptions of Warsaw at the time.

264 *a more nuanced term which better describes the job:* "connector": Sheryl Silver Ochayon, "The Female Couriers During the Holocaust," https://www.yadvashem.org /articles/general/couriers.html. General information about the couriers comes from Lubetkin, *Days of Destruction*, 73–81; Ochayon, "Female Couriers During the Holocaust"; Weitzman, "Kashariyot (Couriers) in the Jewish Resistance."

265 *"carved out kingdoms":* Lubetkin, *Days of Destruction*, 73.

265 *"One didn't ask directions to a ghetto":* Izhar, *Chasia Bornstein-Bielicka*, 167.

266 *"human radios":* Weitzman, "Kashariyot (Couriers) in the Jewish Resistance."

266 *"blitzed like meteors":* Korczak, "Men and Fathers," *Women in the Ghettos*, 28–33.

266 *necking all night in train stations:* Zuckerman, *Surplus of Memory*, 153.

267 *Most "connectors" had to be female:* According to Kol-Inbar, "Three Lines in History," 517, about 70 percent of couriers were women; there were about a hundred in total. Their average age was twenty.

268 *Tosia once arrived . . . for cheap*: Shalev, *Tosia Altman*, 165.

268 *light hair and blue, green, or gray eyes*: Myrna Goldenberg, "Passing: Foreword," in *Before All Memory Is Lost*, 131–34.

268 *wrapped it in pieces of paper to create Aryan styles*: Aliza Vitis-Shomron, *Youth in Flames: A Teenager's Resistance and Her Fight for Survival in the Warsaw Ghetto* (Omaha: Tell the Story, 2015), 176.

268 *The joke at the time*: Personal interview, Havi Dreifuss, Tel Aviv, Isr., May 16, 2018.

268 *wearing a fur muff helped curtail . . . the Jewish-seeming habit of gesticulating while talking*: Weitzman, "Living on the Aryan Side in Poland," 213.

269 *Jews brushed their teeth . . . Poles did neither*: Weitzman, *Living on the Aryan Side in Poland*, 208.

269 *"Institut de Beaute" salon*: Diane Ackerman, *The Zookeeper's Wife: A War Story* (New York: Norton, 2007), 220.

270 *When Tosia visited Będzin*: Shalev, *Tosia Altman*, 134.

270 *patron saint's days*: Chasia, one courier, knew how to genuflect, but had no idea that Halina was the name of two saints—after which one was she named?

270 *empathetic, adaptable . . . strong intuition*: Bronka Klibanski, a Białystok courier, wrote, "In comparison to men, it seems to me that we women were more loyal to the cause, more sensitive to our surroundings, wiser—or perhaps

more generously endowed with intuition." Klibanski, "In the Ghetto and in the Resistance," in *Women in the Holocaust*, 186.

270 *self-awareness, independence, collective consciousness, and transcending temptations*: They were also driven. According to Vladka Meed (in Katz and Ringelheim, *Proceedings of the Conference on Women*, 82), some couriers were competitive, vying for more missions.

270 *Once, on a train*: Story from Shalev, *Tosia Altman*, 150.

271 *"it wasn't easy to feign lightheartedness . . . her endurance"*: Draenger, *Justyna's Narrative*, 99.

271 *"We couldn't cry for real. . . . Nonstop actresses"*: Izhar, *Chasia Bornstein-Bielicka*, 237.

272 *an offensive strategy*: Meed, *Both Sides of the Wall*, 90–92.

272 *"every step outside the barbed wire . . . cleared with a machete"*: Draenger, *Justyna's Narrative*, 56.

Chapter 14: Inside the Gestapo

273 *Bela Hazan*: This section, including dialogue and quotations, is based primarily on Bela's memoir *Bronislawa Was My Name* (Ghetto Fighters' House, 1991), 24–67. Additional sources include: Sara Bender, "Bela Ya'ari Hazan," The Encyclopedia of Jewish Women, https://jwa.org /encyclopedia/article/hazan-bela-yaari; M. Dvorshetzky, "From Ghetto to Ghetto," *Women in the Ghettos*; and personal interview with Yoel Yaari, Jerusalem, Israel, 17 May

2018. Bela's written testimonies can be found at the Ghetto Fighters' House Museum (2 documents) and Yad Vashem archives.

281 *"a high priest . . . halo around her head"*: Grunwald-Spier, *Women's Experiences in the Holocaust*, 251. Information about Lonka is primarily from: Diatłowicki, ed., *Jews in Battle, 1939–1945*; Itkeh, "Leah Kozibrodska," *Women in the Ghettos*, 129–31; Lubetkin, *Days of Destruction*, 76–78; Zuckerman, *Surplus of Memory*, 106–7, 121, 176–77, etc. She was Antek's first main courier.

283 *Tema*: Information about Tema Schneiderman is primarily from: Bronia Klibanski, "Tema Sznajderman," The Encyclopedia of Jewish Women, https://jwa.org/encyclopedia/article/sznajderman-tema. Tema Schneiderman, Leah Pearlstein, and Sarah Granatshtein were all killed in the Warsaw January liquidation.

284 *posing for a photograph*: The story of this photo (here and in later chapters) is from Yoel Yaari, "A Brave Connection," *Yedioth Ahronoth*, Passover Supplement, April 5, 2018, and personal interview, Yoel Yaari, Jerusalem, Israel, May 17, 2018. In her Yad Vashem testimony, Bela says she invited the Gestapo to her home for a Christmas party.

289 *messages were scratched into the concrete walls*: As I saw on my visit to the site.

290 *"Lonka threw a note from Pawiak when she was arrested"*: Zuckerman, *Surplus of Memory*, 242. He explains how Dzielna found out; I extrapolate that Irena told this to Renia.

290 *tall, slender . . . heavy shoes*: Izhar, *Chasia Bornstein-Bielicka*, 155.

Chapter 15: The Warsaw Ghetto Uprising

292 *Zivia was sitting*: The three sections in this chapter that are told from Zivia's perspective are based on Lubetkin, *Days of Destruction*, 160–89.

292 *phone call*: There were phones in the Warsaw ghetto—for instance, in the workshops—and people were able to ring outside and receive calls. As with letters, they communicated in code. Zuckerman, *Surplus of Memory*, 354, relays how he called the workshop from a restaurant and communicated in code. Page 368 refers to the nightly telephone reports during the uprising. (Tosia rang courier Frania Beatis.) Vladka used a phone to organize her gun smuggling. According to Paulsson, *Secret City*, 237, these phones were probably functioning only due to Nazi oversight.

292 *"We received a phone call . . . at six"*: Based on reported conversation, Lubetkin, *Days of Destruction*, 178.

293 *as a little gift*: Tec, *Resistance*, 79.

293 *the ghetto psychology shifted*: According to Kol-Inbar, "Three Lines in History," 522, the deportation was curbed for reasons other than the resistance, but the Jews believed in the association.

293 *sophisticated, well-camouflaged hideouts . . . to the Aryan side*: Tec, *Resistance*, 67.

293 *purchased their own weapons*: According to Vitis-Shomron, *Youth in Flames*, 174–75, she sold clothes to forced laborers (to sell outside the ghetto) and saved up to buy guns from a Polish smuggler. With private Jews' demands for guns, a black-market trade developed.

294 *a respected national struggle*: On the other hand, according to Marysia Warman's testimony in *Mothers, Sisters, Resisters*, she had no idea about the uprising which came as a total surprise to her—even though she was a Bund courier.

294 *fifty pistols, fifty hand grenades, and several kilograms of explosives*: Meed, *Both Sides of the Wall*, 123. According to Zuckerman, *Surplus of Memory*, 292, one pistol was pinched along the way, and only forty-nine arrived in the ghetto.

294 *a suit that was only slightly too small for him*: Zuckerman, *Surplus of Memory*, 344–45, states that he wore "three quarter-length trousers." (Apparently these were taken from a smaller man; he later found out that people recognized him for them.) Page 235 describes his appearance when he was in Kraków for the rebellion: "I looked like a rural Polish nobleman. I wore a three-quarter-length coat, a hat, jodphurs stuffed into boots, a moustache."

294 *"munitions factory"*: Meed, *Both Sides of the Wall*, 135–38.

295 *The ZOB made . . . cement and beams*: Information about weapons is primarily from Zuckerman, *Surplus of Memory*, 292–95. According to Tec, *Resistance*, 80, in total, the

ZOB had two thousand Molotov cocktails, ten rifles, a couple of machine guns stolen from Germans, and a lot of ammunition.

295 *"the government"... ghetto casino*: Lubetkin, *Days of Destruction*, 166. Numerous small rebellions occurred in the ghetto during this period.

295 *Bakers helped*: According to *Blue Bird* and Zuckerman, *Surplus of Memory*, 318, the ZOB forced the bakers to help (though some did on their own accord).

295 *cobblers... hold their guns)*: Zuckerman, *Surplus of Memory*, 318.

295 *the JDC contributed significant funds*: David M. Schizer, "The Unsung, Unfinished Legacy of Isaac Giterman," *Tablet*, January 18, 2018, https://www.tabletmag.com /scroll/253442/the-unsung-unfinished-legacy-of-isaac -giterman.

296 *Zivia was appointed to colead the Finance Committee*: Gutterman, *Fighting for Her People*, 196.

296 *"One fine day... from the bank"*: Lubetkin, *Days of Destruction*, 166–67.

296 *They wrote notes... search their homes*: Rotem, *Memoirs of a Ghetto Fighter*, 25–30.

296 *They amassed millions*: Zuckerman, *Surplus of Memory*, 378, claims that they had jewelry and millions of złotys, dollars, and British pounds.

296 *Young Guard leader Miriam Heinsdorf*: Information about Miriam Heinsdorf is from Grupińska, 70; Zuckerman, *Surplus of Memory*, 78, 229, 259, etc. She was frequently

remembered for her singing. She was older than the others, about thirty.

297 *both women . . . adult parties*: Accounts differ about the women's position in the organizations. In some, Zivia was an elected ZOB leader; others suggest she stepped down voluntarily because she knew her limitations.

297 *her opinion carried weight*: Zuckerman, *Surplus of Memory*, 228–29.

297 *Zivia's reflections*: Culled from Gutterman, *Fighting for Her People*, 205–15, and Lubetkin, *Days of Destruction*, 170–77.

297 *Surprising the Nazis was their best bet*: As Gusta observed, 80–81: "The partisan's effectiveness depends not so much on sheer strength as on the element of surprise . . . [on] his ability to keep the enemy off balance."

297 *aged twenty to twenty-five*: Many Freedom members were from outside Warsaw and slightly older.

297 *Twenty-two fighting groups . . . were organized according to youth movement*: According to Lubetkin, *Days of Destruction*, 176–77, there were four Young Guard groups, one Gordonia, one Akiva, one Hanoar Hatzioni, five Freedom, one Poalei-Zion ZS, one Left Poalei Zion, four Bund, and four Communist. The ZZW also had a large and strong unit.

Most sources agree with Zivia that there were approximately 500 ZOB fighters and 250 ZZW fighters. However, some (like *The Last Fighters*) claim that there were only about 220 ZOB members. Grupińska, *Reading the List*, lists 233 fighters in total based largely on the list compiled by ZOB leaders in 1943, but they recognized it was not complete.

Not everyone was accepted into the ZOB; some rejects formed their own "feral" groups who also fought. Other unaffiliated fighters joined the ZZW.

297 *One third were women*: Kol-Inbar, "Three Lines in History," 522.

298 *first aid classes*: Rufeisen-Schüpper, *Farewell to Mila 18*, 99.

298 *marking up cardboard targets, nightly, until late*: Rotem, *Memoirs of a Ghetto Fighter*, 22.

298 *within seconds*: Zuckerman, *Surplus of Memory*, 304.

298 *"morning marked the beginning of the end"*: Lubetkin, *Days of Destruction*, 178.

299 *Each fighter . . . and a weapon*: Culled from Gutterman, *Fighting for Her People*, 215, and Zuckerman, *Surplus of Memory*, 313. According to *Blue Bird*, each fighter had a handgun and a grenade; each group had two rifles and a few homemade explosives.

300 *"pulverized bloody hulk of dismembered bodies"*: Lubetkin, *Days of Destruction*, 181.

300 *"This time they shall pay!"*: Lubetkin, *Days of Destruction*, 181.

300 *"rolling in their own blood"*: Lubetkin, *Days of Destruction*, 182.

301 *"We ourselves couldn't understand how it had happened"*: Cited in Gutterman, *Fighting for Her People*, 218.

301 *That night*: Description of that first night based on Gutterman, *Fighting for Her People*.

301 *acted on her own initiative, doing recon missions and night tours*: Gutterman, *Fighting for Her People*, 216.

301 *"For hours . . . pleasant stroke of my gun"*: Cited in Gutterman, *Fighting for Her People*, 220.

303 *"ripped to bits . . . flew in all directions"*: Goldstein, *Stars Bear Witness*, 190, offers detailed descriptions of this uprising from his Bundist perspective.

303 *"crushed bodies . . . complete chaos"*: Rotem, *Memoirs of a Ghetto Fighter*, 34.

303 *Zippora Lerer*: Lubetkin, *Days of Destruction*, 34–35, 187.

303 *Bundist Masha Futermilch*: Gleitman was her maiden name. In *The Last Fighter*, she describes an additional element of her attack: "I went out to the balcony and saw a German, and I didn't have ammunition anymore, and we were making chulent. So I decided that I will throw the pot, and it hit him. And in the pot was kishke, and the pot opened up and the kishke fell on his head, and he began fighting to untangle himself."

303 *She shook in terror . . . her entire life*: Masha Futermilch in *Pillar of Fire* (Hebrew version, probably episode 13), viewed at Yad Mordechai Museum, directed by Asher Tlalim, Israel, 1981.

304 *Hantze prepared to leave Warsaw, as had been the plan*: This section, including quotations, is from Kukielka, "Last

Days," 102–6. In other accounts, the movement sent Hantze back to Będzin.

305 *"a friendly woman"*: From the Yiddish version, *Women in the Ghettos.*

305 *Every street*: This description of the burning ghetto as seen from the Aryan side is culled from Kukielka, *Underground Wanderings*, 92–94; Mahut, 144; Meed, *Both Sides of the Wall*, 140–46; Vitis-Shomron, *Youth in Flames*, 191.

306 *"It seemed not merely . . . were at battle"*: Kukielka, *Underground Wanderings*, 92.

308 *Mostly Jews . . . Germans too*: Some reports claim that three hundred Nazis were killed; the Nazi reports claim a much smaller number, but they would, especially as General Stroop was desperate to show off his accomplishments. According to Ackerman, *Zookeeper's Wife*, 211–13, sixteen Nazis were killed and eighty-five wounded.

308 *A photograph shows*: In Meed, *Both Sides of the Wall*, insert.

308 *"There is no God . . . stay silent"*: Kukielka, *Underground Wanderings*, 94.

309 *"something of a happiness . . . the Germans"*: Kukielka, *Underground Wanderings*, 94.

309 *"the Jews picked . . . die like people"*: Kukielka, *Underground Wanderings*, 94.

310 *"Poles must be fighting . . . heroic battle"*: Kukielka, *Underground Wanderings*, 94. For similar accounts, see Kuper, "Life Lines," 201–2, and Meed, *Both Sides of the Wall*, 141.

Chapter 16: Bandits in Braids

311 *Zivia was blinded by the glare*: Unless indicated otherwise, this chapter is based primarily on Lubetkin, *Days of Destruction*, 190–259.

312 *"Pillars of flames . . . last throes of death"*: Lubetkin, *Days of Destruction*, 199–200.

313 *"rampage of flames" . . . She wrote: "we were burning alive"*: Ibid., 200–201.

313 *"it was not the Germans we had to fight, but the fire"*: Cited in Gutterman, *Fighting for Her People*, 222.

313 *and a hairdresser who helped people prepare to go to the Aryan side*: Tec, *Resistance*, 174–76.

314 *"Our hands have a knack for locks"*: Lubetkin, *Days of Destruction* 190–92.

314 *it was impossible to light a candle, for lack of air*: Cited in Meed, *Both Sides of the Wall*, 155.

315 *"even if it was the air . . . pierced the darkness"*: Lubetkin, *Days of Destruction*, 206–7.

315 *"even in the midst of burning desolation"*: Lubetkin, *Days of Destruction*, 205–8, includes discussion of those days in the burning ghetto.

315 *"Then, with the rising of the sun . . . last Jews?"*: Ibid., 209.

316 *a seventeen-year-old boy named Kazik*: "Kazik" was the nom de guerre of Simcha Rotem (born Simcha Rathajzer).

316 *The ZZW . . . were caught*: Lubetkin, *Days of Destruction*, 239–40; Zuckerman, *Surplus of Memory*, 412.

316 *"There is hardly anything left to fight with or anyone*

against whom to have a war": Cited in Gutterman, *Fighting for Her People*, 230.

317 *Warsaw's extensive sewer system*: Geography was important. Warsaw had a sewer system, which could be used for smuggling and escape. In the East, the proximity of the forest enabled partisan camps. Łódź, however, was isolated, with no sewer system

318 *"scorched skeletons of houses"*: Lubetkin, *Days of Destruction*, 220–24.

319 *Hela . . . the sole survivor*: Hela's escape story is based on Rufeisen-Schüpper, *Farewell to Mila 18*, 113.

319 *"Limping and bruised, I continue to walk"*: Lubetkin, *Days of Destruction*, 229.

320 *"Tosia and Zivia, heads of the pioneer underground in Poland, fell in Warsaw in defense of the Jewish people's dignity," read Davar*: Shalev, *Tosia Altman*, 208–11. A clipping of the article from *Davar*, June 1, 1943, is held at the Ghetto Fighters' House Museum archive.

320 *"Zivia is always near Mavetsky (death). Tosia is with Zivia."*: Dror, *The Dream, the Revolt*, 3.

320 *"Jeanne d'Arcs of the underground"*: Shalev, *Tosia Altman*, 208.

320 *Movement instructors . . . the United Kingdom, and Iraq*: Gutterman, *Fighting for Her People*, 244.

321 *"We raced about like madmen . . . retrieve their weapons"*: Lubetkin, *Days of Destruction*, 233.

322 *"a convoy of lifeless bodies among the shadows, like ghosts"*: Lubetkin, *Days of Destruction*, 234.

322 *"Responsibility for others ... everything"*: Lubetkin, *Days of Destruction*, 236.

323 *"yan"*: This story is from Pnina Grinshpan Frimer in *The Last Fighters*.

324 *"I now felt ... keep on walking!"*: Lubetkin, *Days of Destruction*, 244.

325 *Tosia was demoralized ... ultimately managed*: Shalev, *Tosia Altman*, 189.

325 *"gnawed cruelly at my heart"*: Lubetkin, *Days of Destruction*, 247.

326 *the rescue*: The details of this rescue operation differ across sources, with details that vary from Zivia's account. See, for instance, Gutterman, *Fighting for Her People*, 244–57; Rotem, *Memoirs of a Ghetto Fighter*, 48–58; Shalev, *Tosia Altman*, 189.

326 *"Let's go back and bring the others!"*: Lubetkin, *Days of Destruction*, 247.

326 *A group of fighters went off to a secondary location*: This is a controversial moment. Kazik claims he told everyone to stay close to the manhole, implying that Zivia should not have let them stray. (Rotem, *Memoirs of a Ghetto Fighter*, 53.)

328 *one account says nearly thirty minutes*: Rotem, 55.

328 *"We were filthy ... we were alive"*: Lubetkin, *Days of Destruction*, 252.

328 *a "famous fight" between Zivia and Kazik, though Zivia never wrote about it*: Kazik, however, did write about it, in *Memoirs of a Ghetto Fighter*, 53–56. Gutterman, *Fighting*

for *Her People*, 251–53, provides a few accounts of this incident, parimarily from Kazik's perspective; here she explains that Zivia threatened to shoot Kazik while they were on the truck. In Kazik's *Memoirs* he relays that Zivia threatened to shoot him once they were in the forest.

329 *"I understand . . . but with Zivia?!"*: Personal interview, Barbara Harshav, New York; March 9 and April 13, 2018.

329 *"The truck . . . in the heart of Nazi-occupied Warsaw"*: Lubetkin, *Days of Destruction*, 252.

330 *over one hundred Jewish women*: A number of these women's obituaries can be found in: Grupińska, *Reading the List*; Spizman, *Women in the Ghettos*; Neustadt, ed., *Destruction and Rising*.

330 *fought up to the bitter end*: Kol-Inbar, "Three Lines in History," 522.

330 *"with weapons in their hands"*: This description is reiterated throughout *Women in the Ghettos*.

330 *"Up to her throat in water . . . through the canals"*: *Women in the Ghettos*, 164.

330 *Courier Frania Batus . . . age seventeen*: Lubetkin, *Days of Destruction*, 81.

330 *"dreamed of forests and the fragrance of flowers"*: Rotem, *Memoirs of a Ghetto Fighter*, 26. For more on Dvora Baran, see Lubetkin, *Days of Destruction*, 214–15.

331 *Niuta Teitelbaum*: Information from: Grupińska, *Reading the List*, 132–33; Vera Laska, *Different Voices*, 258; Jack Porter, "Jewish Women in the Resistance," *Jewish Combatants of World War 2* 2, no. 3 (1981); Katrina Shawver,

"Niuta Teitelbaum, Heroine of Warsaw," https://katrina shawver.com/2016/02/niuta-teitelbaum-aka-little-wanda -with-the-braids.html.

333 *"pale and starving faces . . . appearance irrevocably"*: Gutterman, *Fighting for Her People*, 258.

334 *"Was there anything left to do that we had not done?"*: Lubetkin, *Days of Destruction*, 256.

334 *In the forest . . . and was there*: Gutterman, *Fighting for Her People*, 260–61. This is not mentioned in Lubetkin, *Days of Destruction*.

335 *despite his endless meetings*: He took meetings even while swimming laps; he walked everywhere to avoid trams. Zuckerman, *Surplus of Memory*, 352, 377.

335 *Vladka's attempts were also fruitless*: Meed, *Both Sides of the Wall*, 156–62.

335 *"[I]f anyone blames me for taking care of my wife, so be it"*: Zuckerman, *Surplus of Memory*, 390. Who got which hiding spot was a controversial issue.

336 *In another version*: There are several conflicting accounts about the factory fire and Tosia's death, a number of which can be found in Shalev, *Tosia Altman*, 194, 206. See also Lubetkin, *Days of Destruction*, 257, and Zuckerman, *Surplus of Memory*, 394–96.

Chapter 17: Arms, Arms, Arms

337 *Arms . . . to become free people*: Ruzka Korczak, "The Revenge Munitions," in *Women in the Ghettos*, 81.

338 *Renia repeated for the umpteenth time*: This section, including quotations and dialogue, is based on Kukielka, "Last Days," 102–6.

338 *Chajka pegged Frumka . . . realities of wartime*: Klinger, *Writing These Words*, 129.

340 *Renia would now become one of those* kashariyot: The rest of this section, including dialogue and direct quotes, is based on Kukielka, *Underground Wanderings*, 96–98.

340 *Ina Gelbart of The Young Guard*: From Sosnowiec's Young Guard, born 1923. Information based on Fela Katz's testimonies; Ronen, *Condemned to Life*, 311.

340 *Tarlow, a Jew who lived*: Renia has various names for him. He is called "Tarlow" in Ronen, *Condemned to Life*, 256–76, and Brandeis, "The Underground in Bedzin," 128.

340 *"and got paid dearly"*: Kukielka, *Underground Wanderings*, 97.

341 *Other women's accounts*: See, for instance, Chaya Palevsky, "I Had a Gun," in *Daring to Resist*, 120–21; Riezl (Ruz'ka) Korczak, *Flames in Ash* (Israel: Sifriyat Po'alim, Hakibbutz Ha'artzi Hashomer Hatzair, 1946), 109; Tec, *Resistance*, 92.

341 *After losing Stalingrad . . . more expensive*: Zuckerman, *Surplus of Memory*, 252–55, 292, for weapons acquisitions.

341 *Renia and Ina to a cemetery*: It's not clear which cemetery this was, but in general, the Jewish cemetery was an important site for the resistance. According to Lubetkin, *Days of Destruction*, 160, the Landau brothers, Jews who'd aided many Young Guard members during the deportations, owned a woodcraft factory. They asked the Nazis for a vegetable plot near the Jewish cemetery, the most peaceful part of Warsaw, Zivia felt, because Nazis rarely went there. With its remaining greenery, the cemetery was ironically the most alive place in the ghetto. The Jewish workers carried hoes and pitchforks and marched out of the ghetto to this plot of land, which was where they connected with their members on the Aryan side and worked on finding weapons. Antek used renowned Yiddish author I. L. Peretz's grave as a meeting site, sending letters in and out of the ghetto through gravediggers and corpse carriers. More in Zuckerman, *Surplus of Memory*, 260, 356.

342 *with barely any arms*: Weitzman, "Kashariyot (Couriers) in the Jewish Resistance." This section draws from this article as well as Ochayon, "Female Couriers During the Holocaust."

342 *they shared . . . reuse the bullets*: Cohen, *The Avengers*, 59.

343 *Hela Schüpper*: Hela's stories are based on Rufeisen-Schüpper, *Farewell to Mila 18*.

344 *A photo*: Hela poses with Shoshana Langer, dated June 1943. From the Ghetto Fighters' House Museum archive.

344 *"Anyone who observed . . . go on vacation"*: Draenger, *Justyna's Narrative*, 70.

344 *Vladka Meed began*: Vladka's weapons smuggling is based on Meed, *Both Sides of the Wall*, 9–109, 123–32.

345 *paid Polish guards . . . grab the package*: Shalev, *Tosia Altman*, 174.

345 *courthouse . . . and Aryan sides*: Zuckerman, *Surplus of Memory*, 125–26, 153.

In Vilna, they used fake traffic signs to divert cars to a street with a sewer opening, and transported long guns into the sewer in toolboxes.

Paulsson, *Secret City*, 61–65, explains the different ways that goods were transported in and out of the ghetto, all having started with food smuggling. These methods include: sewers and tunnels; vehicles (trams, trucks, garbage trucks, hearses, ambulances); work parties; legal passes; municipal offices and a pharmacy (in Warsaw); *metas*, rooftops or drain pipes in buildings that bordered the wall; scaling the wall; Gesia Street Market (in Warsaw); using the gate with bribes or eliciting a guard's sympathy.

346 *Havka Folman*: One of Antek's main couriers, she ended up in Auschwitz and survived the war. Her memoir, *They Are Still with Me*, was published in 2001.

346 *smuggled grenades . . . in their underwear*: There are a few different versions of this story. See, for instance, Havka Folman testimony in Diatlowicki, ed., *Jews in Battle, 1939–1945*; Lubetkin, *Days of Destruction*, 80; Ochayon, "Female Couriers During the Holocaust"; Yaari, "A Brave Connection." According to wall text at the Ghetto Fighters' House Museum, Nazi general Stroop reported that the Jewish women "repeatedly concealed the pistols in their underwear."

346 *Chasia Bielicka did not work alone*: Information about

Chasia and the Białystok couriers comes primarily from Izhar, *Chasia Bornstein-Bielicka*, as well as Liza Chapnik, "The Grodno Ghetto and its Underground," in *Women in the Holocaust*, 109–19; Chaika Grossman, *Underground Army*; Klibanski, "In the Ghetto and in the Resistance," 175–86.

347 *Her roommate, Chaika Grossman*: Chaika Grossman ("Halina Woranowicz") was blonde, blue-eyed and from a wealthy family of factory owners. In 1938 she postponed her studies at Hebrew University for The Young Guard. When Hitler attacked, she was rushed to Warsaw for Leadership B. She then ran the Vilna movement alongside Kovner in her measured, unsentimental stance. She lived on the Aryan side and traveled with information about Ponary to Warsaw and other ghettos, then returned to her native Białystok to organize the underground, basing herself inside the ghetto. She and her boyfriend Edek Borks worked to unify the youth movements into one fighting unit—eventually commanded by Mordechai Tenenbaum. Chaika always insisted on fighting from inside the ghetto rather than fleeing to the partisans. Close with the head of the Judenrat, she made many appeals for him to support resistance efforts. "The madness of the brave moves the world forward," is what she taught her young comrades. She fought in the Białystok resistance and then fled from the deportation by running against the crowd, sneaking into a factory and pretending to work there.

348 *Leah Hammerstein*: Leah's story is based on Tec, *Resistance*, 159–71. Her testimony is in the USHMM archive.

349 *Renia*: This section is culled from Renia's testimony for the Israel National Library, her Yad Vashem testimony, and *Underground Wanderings*, 98. According to Gelbard, "Life in the Warsaw Ghetto," 11, it cost them 7000 marks per weapon.

349 *"It cost an ocean of money ... during the delay?"*: Kukielka, *Underground Wanderings*, 98.

350 *she used the same tactic ... let her go*: Later in *Underground Wanderings*, Renia explains that she used this tactic.

350 *Some couriers ... would be in hand*: Izhar, *Chasia Bornstein-Bielicka*, 206–7. Faye always had an extra grenade attached to her belt to blow herself up in case she was captured alive. As another female partisan explained, "One for the enemy, and one for myself."

350 *"You had to be strong ... iron will"*: Kukielka, *Underground Wanderings*, 97.

Chapter 18: Gallows

351 *June 1943*: In *Underground Wanderings*, Renia writes that this occurs at the beginning of May 1943, but it doesn't quite make sense that she saw the Warsaw ghetto burn and completed weapons smuggling trips, and that it is still early May. There was a deportation in Będzin on June 22, 1943, and I think she might be referring to this. There are several

date conflicts within her book, and this appears to be one of them.

351 *Back in Będzin*: This chapter, including quotations and dialogue, is based on Kukielka, *Underground Wanderings*, 98–107.

352 *No time to implement any zealous plans*: According to Ronen, *Condemned to Life*, the group did not have it in them to take initiative. They were waiting for orders from Warsaw.

353 *Max Fischer, who'd cared for the Atid orphans*: His testimony at Ghetto Fighters' House suggests that he was involved with establishing Atid.

353 *Ilza Hansdorf*: Sometimes referred to as Aliza Hoysdorf.

356 *with a knife*: Ronen, *Condemned to Life*, 277–94, quoting Max Fischer.

357 *Even in this barbarism . . . over their lives*: Though it hardly seemed like a time for laughter, joking was its own form of resistance. Humor existed, and was even prevalent, in the ghettos and camps. Many women engaged in a particular type of humor centered on bodies, appearance, food, and cooking. An extended discussion is in Ostrower, *It Kept Us Alive*.

357 *the Nazis took eight thousand*: This is Renia's figure. According to "Będzin, Poland," Encyclopedia Judaica, Jewish Virtual Library, https://www.jewishvirtuallibrary.org/Będzin, on June 22, 1943, four thousand Jews were taken from Będzin.

Chapter 19: Freedom in the Forests—
The Partisans

361 *blond-haired, blue-eyed Marek Folman*: Fela Katz describes him as good-looking. Along with Aliza Zitenfeld, he taught and cared for the orphaned children. Folman had organized the Freedom school in the Warsaw ghetto.

363 *They read the list*: There are discrepancies in accounts regarding who was included in which group. Renia claims that Irka and Leah Pejsachson went out with a group, but according to Klinger, *Writing These Words*, 122–23, they were killed in other ways. According to Ronen, *Condemned to Life*, 295–312, David, who'd become The Young Guard commander, went with the first group; Chajka was upset because only men were allowed to go. Fela Katz, in her testimony, said that David was in the first group, which had a few guns; the group was all men, and each had a knife and some bullets. Both Ronen, *Condemned to Life*, 295–312, and Katz agree that only two women went out the second time, along with ten men.

363 *"In high boots . . . a woman"*: Klinger, "Girls in the Ghettos," 17–23.

363 *The remaining comrades . . . in celebration*: Fela Katz testimony.

364 *It was extremely difficult . . . a Jewish woman*: Information about the partisans is based primarily on the Jewish Partisan Education Foundation, http://www.jewish

partisans.org; Kol-Inbar, "Three Lines in History," 513–46; Nechama Tec, "Women Among the Forest Partisans," in *Women in the Holocaust*; Tec, *Resistance*, 84–121; Tamara Vershitskaya, "Jewish Women Partisans in Belarus," *Journal of Ecumenical Studies* 46, no. 4 (Fall 2011): 567–72. I also drew on personal accounts, including: Shelub and Rosenbaum, *Never the Last Road*; Schulman, *Partisan's Memoir;* and the sources listed below for the Vilna fighters.

364 *many types of partisan groups*: Soviet soldiers and POWs who did not want to fall into Nazi hands, Lithuanian units comprising dissenters and Communists, Belorussians dodging conscription to German forced labor camps, Poles backed by the Polish underground, and so forth.

364 *Thirty thousand . . . 10 percent*: From Jewish Partisan Education Foundation, http://www.jewishpartisans.org. These numbers include all partisan brigades, Jewish and non. Offering a variety of different statistics are Schulman, *Partisan's Memoir*; Tec, *Resistance*; Vershitskaya, "Jewish Women Partisans."

365 *Many women were raped*: Sex was forbidden for partisans, punishable by death. Regardless, some partisan men went to local villages to find girls. Rumor has it that the Nazis knew this and injected women with venereal disease, which they then passed on to the partisans. Tec, *Resistance*, 107.

365 *The great majority*: Tec, "Women Among the Forest Partisans," 223, states 77 percent.

366 *"in order to obtain some relative peace . . . a 'lack of peace'*

during the night": Fanny Solomian-Lutz, cited in Kol-Inbar, "Three Lines in History," 527.

366 *One Jewish woman . . . "select an officer"*: From the documentary video *Everyday the Impossible: Jewish Women in the Partisans*, Jewish Partisan Education Foundation, http://www.jewishpartisans.org/content/jewish-women-partisans.

366 *A female partisan . . . started shooting*: Vitka Kempner, interviewed in Yigal Wilfand, ed., *Vitka Fights for Life* (Givat Haviva, Isr.: Moreshet, 2013), 49.

366 *just so* other *men would stop harassing her*: Shelub and Rosenbaum, *Never the Last Road*, 111–14.

366 *only the strong man with a gun had real status*: As stressed by Kol-Inbar, "Three Lines in History," 526, the partisans may have been antiauthoritarian, but when it came to women they adopted the most conservative model of traditional society.

367 *performed several successful abortions with quinine, while others resulted in death on the operating table*: Fanny Solomian-Lutz, *A Girl Facing the Gallows* (Tel Aviv, Isr.: Moreshet and Sifryat Hapoalim, 1971), 113–14.

367 *skin peeling off with the clothes*: Personal interview, Holly Starr, telephone, November 13, 2018 regarding her mother Sara Rosnow. Vilna Partisan Liba Marshak Augenfeld was a cook and tailor, making boots out of leather that partisans brought her.

368 *Faye Schulman*: Née Faye Lazebnik. Faye's story is based on Schulman, *Partisan's Memoir* and *Daring to Resist*:

Three Women Face the Holocaust, directed by Barbara Attie and Martha Goell Lubell. USA, 1999.

368 *"The Nazis had covered . . . from the trenches"*: Schulman, *Partisan's Memoir,* 17.

369 *"I had lost . . . or be happy"*: Schulman, *Partisan's Memoir,* 149.

370 *others served as armed guards*: For instance, Fruma Berger (with the Bielski detachment); Mira and Sara Rosnow.

370 *Vilna comrades*: I have based my story of the Vilna resistance on accounts including: *Partisans of Vilna: The Untold Story of Jewish Resistance During World War II,* directed by Josh Waletsky, USA, 1986; Neima Barzel, "Rozka Korczak-Marla" and "Vitka Kempner-Kovner," The Encyclopedia of Jewish Women; Cohen, *Avengers*; Grossman, *Underground Army*; Moshe Kalchheim, ed., *With Proud Bearing 1939–1945: Chapters in the History of Jewish Fighting in the Narotch Forests* (Tel Aviv, Isr.: Organisation of Partisans, Underground Fighters and Ghetto Rebels in Israel, 1992); Michael Kovner, www.michalkovner.com; Korczak, *Flames in Ash*; Roszka Korczak, Yehuda Tubin, and Yosef Rab, eds., *Zelda the Partisan* (Tel Aviv, Isr.: Moreshet and Sifriyat Po'alim, 1989); Ruzka Korczak, "In the Ghettos and in the Forests," "The Revenge Munitions" and "Women in the Vilna Ghetto," in *Women in the Ghettos*; Dina Porat, *The Fall of a Sparrow: The Life and Times of Abba Kovner* (Stanford, CA: Stanford University Press, 2010); Ziva Shalev, "Zelda Nisanilevich Treger," The Encyclopedia of Jewish Women; Yehuda Tubin, Levi Deror, et al., eds., *Ruzka*

Korchak-Marle: The Personality and Philosophy of Life of a Fighter (Tel Aviv, Isr.: Moreshet and Sifriyat Po'alim, 1988); Wilfand, *Vitka Fights for Life.* I have also drawn from personal interviews with: Rivka Augenfeld, Montreal, August 10 and 17, 2018; Michael Kovner, Jerusalem, May 17, 2018; Daniela Ozacky-Stern and Yonat Rotbain, Givat Haviva, Isr., May 14, 2018; Chayele Palevsky, Skype, November 20, 2018.

371 *One morning*: The story of how Ruzka and Vitka met is based on Cohen, *Avengers*, 18–19. Throughout this chapter, I have used the exact dialogue presented by Cohen in case he was drawing on direct quotes. Their personal backgrounds are taken from many sources, including ibid., 13–23.

372 *No one dared . . . to say hi*: Michael Kovner, "In Memory of My Mother," https://www.michaelkovner.com/said04 eng. Cohen, *Avengers*, 19, also mentions this meeting.

373 *"Are you crazy? Are you trying to get killed?"*: Cohen, *Avengers*, 27. The story of Vitka's return to Vilna is from ibid., 26–27.

373 *once pretending to be officers' wives*: Tubin, Deror, et al., eds., *Ruzka Korchak-Marle*, 22.

373 *They paid a Jewish barber to do it with peroxide*: Cohen, *Avengers*, 38.

373 *"even the color . . . Jewish expression"*: Korczak, "Women in the Vilna Ghetto," 113–27.

373 *"Germans believe what they are told"*: Cohen, *Avengers*, 37.

373 *stuck on a yellow leaf instead*: Cohen, *Avengers*, 38.

373 *"I sleep in the middle"*: Ibid., 49. On p. 7, Cohen describes how others have speculated about their love triangle. Vitka addresses their romance in Tubin, Deror, et al., eds., *Ruzka Korchak-Marle*, 63.

374 *"For the sex!"*: As told to me by a Dror youth group member in the United Kingdom, 2018.

374 *his declaration of love*: According to Cohen, *Avengers*, 61, in European undergrounds, the commander sent "his girl" to lead the toughest assignments, reflecting his strength.

374 *Vitka's assignment*: This assignment, her preparation, and her near captures, are based on Cohen, *Avengers*, 62–64; Korczak, "Women in the Vilna Ghetto," 113–27; Wilfand, *Vitka Fights for Life*, 29–31. The details differ slightly in each account.

375 *approached a Nazi in tears*: Chasia was once caught delivering weapons to the forest outside Białystok. She cried and claimed she was lost. The Nazi gave her directions and warned her to be careful, telling her she could have been killed by the partisans! Izhar, *Chasia Bornstein-Bielicka*, 251.

375 *"icy calm" . . . extricate her safely*: Cohen, *Avengers*, 62.

375 *Under her jacket, a bomb built by Abba, made from a pipe*: According to Vitka in *Partisans of Vilna*, the bomb was primitive and enormous. An FPO comrade who held a position with the Jewish police snuck it out of the ghetto under his coat.

375 *Ruzka was part of the Paper Brigade*: Accounts about Ruzka and the Finnish bomb book vary. See, for instance,

David E. Fishman, *The Book Smugglers: Partisans, Poets, and the Race to Save Jewish Treasures from the Nazis* (Lebanon, NH: ForEdge, 2017), and Wilfand, *Vitka Fights for Life,* 29–31.

376 *"This is not something I felt guilty about . . . to forget who is who"*: Cohen, *Avengers,* 64.

377 *"The Germans . . . allowed to leave"*: Korczak, "Women in the Vilna Ghetto," 113–27.

377 *"She had just walked off . . . No one stopped her"*: Cohen, *Avengers,* 88.

377 commanded her own scouting troupe: Wilfand, *Vitka Fights for Life,* 46; Ruzka in Tubin, Deror, et al., eds., *Ruzka Korchak-Marle,* 42: "Fact: Vitka Kovner Kempner was the head commander in the forest. Not only did she partake in all of the patrolling, she was the commander!"

378 *Vitka recalled . . . in the carrying*: Wilfand, *Vitka Fights for Life,* 41. Vitka also discusses this in the film *Everyday the Impossible: Jewish Women in the Partisans.* According to Ruzka (Katz and Ringelheim, *Proceedings of the Conference on Women,* 93), women participated in almost every supply gathering, sabotage, ambush and combat mission.

379 *"You will have to . . . from this mission"*: Cohen, *Avengers,* 123. The story is on pp. 122–25.

379 *"I remember our first ambush . . . celebrated"*: Korczak, "In the Ghettos and in the Forests," *Women in the Ghettos,* 74–81. This likely refers to a different incident.

379 patrol unit commander: Tubin, Deror, et al., eds., *Ruzka Korchak-Marle,* 67.

379 *Ruzka was also the "quartermaster"*: Yehuda Tubin ed., *Ruzka Korchak-Marle*, 42.

379 *some comprised a whole village of underground huts . . . stolen from peasants, often at gunpoint*: From various accounts, including Aida Brydbord, *Women of Valor*, 16.

380 *They filled containers . . . from camp*: Izhar, *Chasia Bornstein-Bielicka*, 247.

380 *"putrid and nauseating"*: As Fruma later wrote in a poem, "Hidden in the earth, a deep hole / Today became my home." Ralph S. Berger and Albert S. Berger, eds., *With Courage Shall We Fight: The Memoirs and Poetry of Holocaust Resistance Fighters Frances "Fruma" Gulkowich Berger and Murray "Motke" Berger* (Margate: ComteQ, 2010), 82–83.

380 *Vitka once lent . . . transfer to the animal*: Wilfand, *Vitka Fights for Life*, 46.

381 *Zelda Treger was a major kasharit*: The information and scenes about Zelda, as well as dialogue, are primarily based on Korczak, Tubin, and Rab, *Zelda the Partisan*.

384 *"to borrow a few Jewish girls"*: Cohen, *Avengers*, 125. The story of this mission is related in ibid., 125–28; Korczak, "Women in the Vilna Ghetto," 113–27; Wilfand, *Vitka Fights for Life*, 42. According to Abba in *Partisans of Vilna*, it was his idea to carry out sabotage in Vilna to show the Germans that an underground operated there. He hoped to combine this mission with rescuing Jews and bringing them into the forest.

386 *"We made it . . . stronger than the men"*: Cited in Cohen, *Avengers*, 128.

386 *"[W]omen had more stamina"*: Wilfand, *Vitka Fights for Life*, 48.

386 *Years later . . . No great tragedy!*: Vitka Kempner in *Partisans of Vilna: The Untold Story of Jewish Resistance During World War II*, directed by Josh Waletsky, USA, 1986.

387 *"She didn't know . . . and initiative"*: Korczak, "Women in the Vilna Ghetto," 113–27.

387 *In 1944 . . . the ice between them*: Cohen, *Avengers*, 129–30.

387 *One April morning . . . "Where am I going?" Vitka asked*: Cohen, *Avengers*, 139. The following story is based on ibid., 139–42, and Tubin, Deror, et al., eds., 73. There are various versions of this story. According to Korczak, "Women in the Vilna Ghetto," 113–27, Vitka waited for a moment when her captors were distracted, broke free, and ran. According to Vitka in Wilfand, *Vitka Fights for Life*, 42, this incident is combined with her mission to blow up Vilna's electric supply. On the way back, she was trapped on a bridge by Nazis on motorbikes. She convinced her captors to let her go and told them she would testify in their favor after the war; she took Ponary escapees with her.

389 *"It is a miracle . . . depend on miracles?"*: Cited in Cohen, *Avengers*, 142.

389 *Isaac from The Young Guard*: According to Fela Katz's testimony, the leaders hid him in a bunker so that his reap-

pearance didn't cause panic. Fela has slightly different details in her account.

389 *"We left the ghetto . . . my spot and ran"*: Quote is culled from Kulielka, *Underground Wanderings*, 110–11 and Ronen, *Condemned to Life*, 295–312.

Chapter 20: *Melinas*, Money, and Rescue

392 *Renia knew what that meant*: Unless indicated otherwise, this section is based on Kukielka, *Underground Wanderings*, 112–13.

393 *"a slap in the face that stunned us"*: Klinger, *Writing These Words*, 119–20.

394 *"spiritually exhausted . . . was too great"*: Klinger, *Writing These Words*, 120–21.

394 *a main role of the courier girls . . . or in physical hiding*: Information in this section is primarily from Meed, *Both Sides of the Wall*; Ochayon, "Female Couriers During the Holocaust"; Weitzman, "Kashariyot (Couriers) in the Jewish Resistance."

394 *(melinas)*: Ackerman, *Zookeeper's Wife*, 173, refers to a "den of thieves."

394 *but not too often*: Rotem, *Memoirs of a Ghetto Fighter*, 96–98, describes the challenges and strategies of the couriers.

395 *particularly brutal with children*: According to Schulman, *Partisan's Memoir*, 89, the Nazis didn't waste bullets on children, burying them alive.

396 *In a testimony... London in 2008*: This is an oral testimony held in the Wiener Holocaust Library archives.

397 *killing those who helped any Jews*: Lubetkin, *Days of Destruction*, 260, for discussion of how the Germans tortured the Poles.

397 *Several Jewish relief organizations... were established*: See Paulsson, *Secret City*, 3–4, 201–210 for details about different organizations.

397 *"Żegota" (Council for Aid to the Jews)*: Paldiel, *Saving One's Own*, 32–42.

397 *an outspoken antisemite before the war*: Paldiel, *Saving One's Own*, 25.

397 *Though, apparently... leave Poland for good*: Samuel D. Kassow, lecture, at "In Dialogue: Polish Jewish Relations During the Interwar Period."

398 *JDC*: Information on JDC is from sources including: "American Jewish Joint Distribution Committee and Refugee Aid," USHMM Holocaust Encyclopedia, https://encyclopedia.ushmm.org/content/en/article/american-jewish-joint-distribution-committee-and-refugee-aid; Yehuda Bauer, "Joint Distribution Committee," in *Encyclopedia of the Holocaust*, ed. Israel Guttman (New York: Macmillan, 1990), 752–56.

398 *Most of the capital... private Polish market*: Nathan Eck, "The Legend of the Joint in the Ghetto," unpublished report, JDC archives.

398 *Memoirs tell... skimming off exchange rates*: Antek accused Polish underground groups of withholding sums.

Rotem, *Memoirs of a Ghetto Fighter*, 98–99; Zuckerman, *Surplus of Memory*, 419.

398 *more than $78 million*: Bauer, "Joint Distribution Committee," 752–56; Zuckerman, *Surplus of Memory*, 43n15.

398 *300,000*: Michael Beizer, "American Jewish Joint Distribution Committee," trans. I. Michael Aronson, The YIVO Encyclopedia of Jews in Eastern Europe, https://yivo encyclopedia.org/article.aspx/American_Jewish_Joint_ Distribution_Committee.

398 *Rescue groups . . . as well as abortions*: Paldiel, *Saving One's Own*, 32–42.

399 *a "factory" to forge fake documents*: Paldiel, *Saving One's Own*, 33. See also Lubetkin, *Days of Destruction*, 263; Meed, *Both Sides of the Wall*, 226–29; Zuckerman, *Surplus of Memory*, 486–87.

399 *Twelve thousand Jews in the Warsaw area*: There are no comprehensive records, and these figures are estimates; different sources offer different numbers. Lubetkin, *Days of Destruction*, 262, claims there were twenty thousand Jews passing or hiding in the Warsaw area, and twelve thousand came to her organization for help. Zuckerman, *Surplus of Memory*, 449, agrees and claims that three thousand names (in code) were in his card file. According to Kol-Inbar, "Three Lines in History," 531, Żegota saved four thousand Jews (and four thousand children). To Paldiel, *Saving One's Own*, 34, the rescue groups in total helped about eleven thousand to twelve thousand Jews. Paldiel, 26, says that of the estimated fifteen thousand to

twenty thousand Jews who hid in the Warsaw area, about half received help from Żegota and the Jewish organizations. Paulsson, *Secret City*, 3–4, 207, 229–30, figures that about 9000 Jews were helped by these organizations.

399 *without keeping any written records of Polish names or current addresses*: Zuckerman, *Surplus of Memory*, 435, 496, explains that in written records, they used only Jewish names that would not be recognizable. A Żegota receipt on display at POLIN museum shows 1/100 the sum that was given, and was backdated ten years to mask the operation. Paulsson, *Secret City*, 232–33, provides a discussion of all these records and receipts.

399 *twenty thousand to thirty thousand*: Sources offer varying numbers—some even go up to forty thousand. According to Paldiel, *Saving One's Own*, 26, an estimated fifteen thousand to twenty thousand Jews hid in the Warsaw area. According to Paulsson's study, about 28,000 Jews hid in Warsaw at some point (see *Secret City*, 2–5, for a summation).

400 *scribbled appeals*: Zuckerman, *Surplus of Memory*, 496.

400 *when the cost of living was about 2000*: According to wall text at POLIN, this amount barely covered food; the donation was most helpful in offering hope and connection.

402 *Emanuel Ringelblum*: The story of his bunker is in Meed, *Both Sides of the Wall*, 200.

402 *20,000 złotys per person*: Goldstein, *Stars Bear Witness*, 229.

404 *Marysia . . . offered her a choice*: Warman, *Mothers, Sisters, Resisters*, 285–86.

406 *Chasia had a "suitor" visit her*: Izhar, *Chasia Bornstein-Bielicka*, 230.

406 *roughly thirty thousand*: Weitzman, "Living on the Aryan Side," 189, suggests that 10 percent of Jews who survived did so by passing.

406 *Jews survived by "passing"*: This discussion of passing is from Weitzman, *Living on the Aryan Side*.

407 *"city within a city . . . documents of embassies"*: Cited in Paldiel, *Saving One's Own*, 35.

408 *neighbors assumed . . . of men*: For more accounts of and details about these *melinas*, see Rotem, *Memoirs of a Ghetto Fighter*, 86; Zuckerman, *Surplus of Memory*, 474; Warman, "Marysia Warman."

408 *To be in hiding . . . panicking to a shelter*: Rotem, *Memoirs of a Ghetto Fighter*, 76–77. In Zivia's case, the people she hid with were mainly Bundists who were nearly a decade younger than she.

408 *detective novels to help her pass the time*: Zuckerman, *Surplus of Memory*, 501.

Chapter 21: Blood Flower

410 *several trips together*: Ronen, *Condemned to Life*, 256–76.

411 *She was taking Rivka Moscovitch*: Information on Rivka is from Grupińska, 96, and Neustadt, ed., *Destruction and Rising*.

412 *"bestial joy"*: Draenger, *Justyna's Narrative*, 54.

412 *Zaglembie*: He actually refers to "Silesia," which is a bordering region with many cultural and historical similarities.

414 *backup plan*: Rotem, *Memoirs of a Ghetto Fighter*, 69, explains how the underground usually had backup plans in case a contact did not show up. For instance, they were instructed to return to same spot the next day.

414 *Then she had an idea*: In one version of Renia's story, she ran into this woman by chance; in her Ghetto Fighters' House testimony, she claims Antek gave her this address.

Overall, Renia describes her missions to Warsaw quite differently in her different testimonies (GFH, INL, YV, *Underground Wanderings*). In her Israel National Library testimony, she claims that she brought money for Zivia and Antek. She mentions meeting Kazik in her Ghetto Fighters' House testimony (which she claimed happened before she saw the ghetto burn), but he is not mentioned in the others. Here she states that she does not recall how she found Antek and that she received guns from a Pole. Her meeting with Antek is described differently in each testimony. The chronological order of her missions differs in each account as well. In some accounts, she states having gone on six or seven missions; in others, four. Throughout part 2, I have culled her varying (and sometimes contradictory) tales to construct narrative that seems most accurate.

415 *Renia returned . . . money on their rooms*: In oral and written testimonies in the Ghetto Fighters' House archive,

Renia relays that there was a scare at the hotel and authorities were searching for Jews so she was forced to wander the streets for several hours.

415 *Rosalie also helped the ZOB—a true fighter family*: Grunwald-Spier, *Women's Experiences in the Holocaust*, 254–55; Zuckerman, *Surplus of Memory*, 97, 242 (the mother was in her fifties). In the Ghetto Fighters' House Museum archive she is listed as "Shoshana-Rozalia."

416 *"[He] was a true Antek . . . rich lord"*: Kukielka, *Underground Wanderings*, 115.

418 *"seeming nobleman with a confident gait"*: Kukielka, *Underground Wanderings*, 115. As Havi Dreifuss articulates in *The Zuckerman Code*: "You needed endless courage and street smarts, and in those things, Antek was the master. Part of it was his appearance, but it was also his ability to behave like a Polish brat, so if anyone said anything to him, Antek knew how to shut him down."

421 *to save this object of joy*: Saving a harmonica was an act of resistance in a regime where Nazis controlled Jews' possessions. Nazis enforced countless laws about what Jews were or were not allowed to own. For instance, at the onset of war, Jews had to give the Nazis all of their gold, fur and weapons. Food was rationed. Possessing extra fare could result in execution. When Nazis were transporting Jews between locations, they told them exactly how much they were allowed to bring with them. But many Jews defied the laws, and saved objects—family jewelry hidden inside the wall of a barrack, currency and a diamond brooch stuffed

inside a shoe brush, an ornate grandmother's matza cover. Objects provided a sense of security and hope.

422 *a battle in the ghetto*: The story of the Częstochowa ghetto uprising is from Kukielka, *Underground Wandering*, 117–18; Brandeis, "Rebellion in the Ghettos," in *Daring to Resist*, 128–29; Binyamin Orenstayn, "Częstochowa Jews in the Nazi Era," *Czenstochov; A New Supplement to the Book "Czenstochover Yidn,"* trans. Mark Fromimowitz (New York: 1958), https://www.jewishgen.org/yizkor/Częstochowa/cze039.html.

422 *Rivka Glanz . . . a unit*: Brandeis, "Rebellion in the Ghettos," in *Daring to Resist*, 128–29.

422 *"How my heart cried . . . Częstochowa"*: Kukielka, *Underground Wanderings*, 118.

423 *Ina had been caught*: This account of Ina's capture is culled from Fela Katz's testimonies and Ronen, *Condemned to Life*, 311.

Chapter 22: Zaglembie's Jerusalem Is Burning

424 *August 1, 1943*: Unless indicated otherwise, this chapter, including dialogue and quotations, is based on Kukielka, *Underground Wandering*, 118–22.

427 *Renia Kukielka . . . Freedom courier*: Ronen, *Condemned to Life*, 349.

430 *Sexual violence was extant . . . outright rape*: See Rochelle G. Saidel and Batya Brudin, eds. *Violated! Women in Holocaust and Genocide* (New York: Remember the Women

Institute, 2018), exhibition catalogue; Rochelle G. Saidel and Sonja M. Hedgepeth, eds., *Sexual Violence Against Jewish Women During the Holocaust* (Waltham, MA: Brandeis University Press, 2010). Additional sources for this section are Karay, "Women in the Forced Labor Camps" and Laska, *Different Voices*, 261–67; Ostrower, *It Kept Us Alive*, 139–46; Gurewitsch, *Mothers, Sisters, Resisters.*

431 *One Nazi in Warsaw . . . less attractive*: Ringelheim, "Women and the Holocaust," 376–77.

431 *In the village of Ejszyszki . . . slaughtered*: See *Women of Valor: Partisans and Resistance Fighters*, Center for Holocaust Studies Newsletter 3, no. 6 (New York: Center for Holocaust Studies, 1990), 8.

432 *At a labor camp . . . a rod twenty-five times*: Grunwald-Spier, *Women's Experiences in the Holocaust*, 174.

432 *sex was a commodity to be traded for bread*: Ringelheim, "Women and the Holocaust," 376–77.

433 *"I only try to imagine the terror . . . the couple in motion"*: Izhar, *Chasia Bornstein-Bielicka*, 147–48.

433 *forced gynecological exams . . . in their vaginas*: Babey Widutschinsky Trepman, "Living Every Minute," in *Before All Memory Is Lost*, 383.

434 *Rivka Glanz . . . attempted to harass them too*: Zuckerman, *Surplus of Memory*, 108, on Rivka; Reinhartz, *Bits and Pieces*, 33, for a sense of his personality.

434 *Anka Fischer . . . arrested*: Draenger, *Justyna's Narrative*, 98–99.

434 *Mina Fischer*: The survivor asked that I use a pseudonymn. I found her unpublished testimony in the collection of the Azrieli Foundation.

Part 3: "No Border Will Stand in Their Way"

437 *"They are ready for anything, and no border will stand in their way"*: Chaika Grossman, "For Us the War Has Not Ended," *Women in the Ghettos*, 180–82.

Chapter 23: The Bunker and Beyond

439 *"One merely . . . from Będzin"*: Kukielka, *Underground Wanderings*, 123. This section is based on Renia's memoir, 123–24.

441 *Meir Schulman and his wife, Nacha*: Additional information from Ronen, *Condemned to Life*, 256–76.

441 *Chajka had her own version of the story*: The following sections about Chajka are all based on Klinger, "The Final Deportation," in *Writing These Words to You*, 33–79; the direct quotations are also taken from these pages. Chajka's account is similar to the account offered in Renia's memoir, told to her by Meir Schulman, 124–28. Fela Katz, a Sosnowiec Young Guard member, also presents a similar story in her testimonies (held in the Jewish Historical Institute archive and published in Jerzy Diatłowicki, ed. *Jews in Battle, 1939–1945*, though her story includes mention of several large shoot-outs. The details differ slightly in each version.

444 *People make love here*: Kazik, the male Warsaw ghetto fighter, wrote about his romance with Dvora Baran, with whom he fought in the Warsaw ghetto uprising before she was killed. They tried to keep their canoodling a secret, for fear of offending their fellow fighters who adhered to movement purity codes. "It was hard to tell who were couples: the leaders of the *halutz* movement were loyal to 'sexual purity,' and affairs were mostly platonic," he wrote later, referring to his fighting unit. "Couples talked a lot, exchanged feelings, dreamed." Kazik's unit commander, however, was upset that he hadn't told him of his romance with Dvora—he wanted to celebrate it. Exceptions were made by many in these fatal times. Sex and death were too inevitable a combination.

One night, in the bunker, on their own layer of a bunk-bed, the couple decided not to restrain themselves. "Do you have a condom?" Dvora asked, as if life were normal. *That* supply, Kazik did not have. So they lay together and chatted all night instead. After Dvora was killed, and Kazik lost his virginity to a Polish girl, he fell in love with courier Irena Gelblum "with all the fire of my youth." While living on the Aryan side, they used to make out in the park so as not to offend the movement leaders.

446 *no guns except the two they'd brought with them*: Chajka writes that the kibbutz bunker had no guns, and implies that their arms were the two guns The Young Guard group had brought with them According to Meir's account, they had several guns which they hid.

446 *Chawka Lenczner*: Information about Chawka is from her testimony in the Yad Vashem archives and Ronen, *Condemned to Life*, 91–103. Chawka came to Będzin as part of an emigration scheme that fell apart. In the ghetto, she was a medic and helped rescue orphans. She spoke fluent Polish and looked "good."

446 *Renia's sister Sarah*: Sarah's presence in the bunker is recorded in David Liwer, *Town of the Dead: The Extermination of the Jews in the Zaglembie Region* (Tel Aviv, Isr., 1946).

449 *Chajka had not known about the deal*: Ronen, *Condemned to Life*, and Meir (in his account in Renia's memoir) relay slightly different versions of this deal. According to Ronen, the comrade who went out was Max Fischer; to Meir, it was Moshe Marcus.

450 *so much money*: In her testimony at the Jewish Historical Institute, Fela Katz claims that at one point, The Young Guard, Freedom, and Gordonia shared about 70,000 reichsmarks (this may have been to resettle comrades with the partisans). Hershl Springer had a safe in the bunker.

451 *"We were going to help you, and you were going to kill us"*: This is from Meir's account in Kukielka, *Underground Wanderings*, 126.

461 *"We have a little . . . runs out?"*: Kukielka, *Underground Wanderings*, 127. This scene is based on ibid., 127–28.

461 *the tale of a different bunker*: The story of the fighters bunker is culled from Kukielka, *Underground Wander-*

ings. (relayed by Ilza), 128–30; Klinger, *Writing These Words*, 159–65 (she partly fictionalized her account to imagine what happened to her comrades in their last moments); and the testimony of Jewish policeman Abram Potasz which is published in Klinger, *Writing These Words*, 181–84. In several additional accounts, this bunker is referred to as the "laundry bunker."

462 *"an unusual sparkle . . . honorable death"*: Kukielka, *Underground Wanderings*, 129.

463 *"The house stood . . . An ocean of flames"*: Kukielka, *Underground Wanderings.*

464 *An inhuman moan . . . prostrate* chalutzim: Klinger, *Writing These Words*, 182–83.

464 *"with perfect stoic, sadistic calm"*: Klinger, *Writing These Words*, 183.

465 *"pounced on them . . . smashed pieces of humans"*: Klinger, *Writing These Words*, 164.

465 *Chajka was alive . . . camp kitchen*: This section from the liquidation camp is based on Klinger, *Writing These Words*, 71–79, including direct quotations.

Chapter 24: The Gestapo Net

468 *Desperate, wired, Renia*: Unless indicated otherwise, this chapter, including dialogue and quotations, is based on Kukielka, *Underground Wanderings*, 130–52.

468 *Hanoar Hatzioni*: A Labor Zionist youth group which was less political and more concerned with Jewish plurality and

unity, open to debate and to anyone who considered themselves Jewish. They promoted rescue.

469 *she did everything she could to get what she wanted*: From Renia's Yad Vashem testimony. "I'm also very stubborn in life. I do everything I can to get what I want in life."

471 *wake them . . . entire fictional lineages*: Rotem, *Memoirs of a Ghetto Fighter*, 63.

472 *so bloody angry*: According to Ronen, *Condemned to Life*, 357–70, Bolk did keep his word and helped them. According to Namyslo, *Before the Holocaust Came*, 25, his name was Boleslaw Kozuch.

473 *their comrades get out*: According to Liwer, *Town of the Dead*, 18, after this rescue, Sarah reported that there were twenty-three members and two children in hiding in various places on the Aryan side.

476 *"It was my first time . . . right now"*: Renia tells a different version of this story in her Yad Vashem testimony: a shoe seller hid cash in her shoe, and she cannot recall the address of this shoe store. In this account, Renia told the Gestapo she was from Warsaw because she knew that couriers had been caught around Białystok and Vilna.

480 *And do not say a word about me*: In Renia's Yad Vashem testimony, she claims to have threatened to strangle Ilza if she told anyone that Renia was Jewish.

481 *one of the most brutal*: For a prisoner's account of the brutality he faced, see "Escape from a Polish Prisoner of War Camp," WW2 People's War, https://www.bbc.co.uk/history/ww2peopleswar/stories/63/a3822563.shtml.

489 *"plucking feathers,"* or rather, removing the hard quills from the down: Grunwald-Spier, *Women's Experiences in the Holocaust*, 173–74.

Chapter 25: The Cuckoo

491 *Bela Hazan*: This section, including all dialogue and quotations, is based on Ya'ari-Hazan, *Bronislawa Was My Name*, 68–93. I have also drawn on Bela's testimony "From Ghetto to Ghetto," *Women in the Ghettos*, 134–39.

494 *"I feel like they're watching us"*: Cited in "From Ghetto to Ghetto," *Women in the Ghettos*, 134–39.

495 *Shoshana Gjedna*: In Bela's accounts, Shoshana was imprisoned as a Jew; according to *Women in the Ghettos*, she was killed. But Lubetkin, *Days of Destruction*, 305, and Zuckerman, *Surplus of Memory*, 472, say that she was mistaken for a Pole, survived several camps, and made aliyah. They list her married name as Klinger. GFH holds several photos of her from the 1940s.

496 *hanged from lampposts throughout Warsaw*: Bela does not indicate "from lampposts" but Zuckerman, *Surplus of Memory*, 429, mentions that this was a common method of hanging Pawiak prisoners.

497 *Auschwitz-Birkenau was established originally*: Paldiel, *Saving One's Own*, 382–84; Tec, *Resistance*, 124.

500 *marching band*: "Official Camp Orchestras in Auschwitz," Music and the Holocaust, http://holocaustmusic.ort.org /places/camps/death-camps/auschwitz/camp-orchestras.

500 *"community center" or "coffeehouse"*: Ostrower, 149.

504 *Mengele*: Josef Mengele conducted inhumane medical experiments on prisoners and sent many to the gas chambers.

504 *"I have pulled the thread of life . . . you will survive"*: This quote is an amalgamation of different versions in Bela's testimonies in *Women in the Ghettos* and *Bronislawa Was My Name*.

505 *She said a silent Kaddish*: Yaari, "A Brave Connection."

506 *Renia looked at Ilza*: This section, including dialogue and quotations, is based on Kukielka, *Underground Wanderings*, 152–60.

Chapter 26: Sisters, Revenge!

515 *September 1943*: Estimated date based on Renia's story.

515 *Mysłowice. They entered a large courtyard*: Unless indicated otherwise, this chapter, including dialogue and quotations, is based on Kukielka, *Underground Wanderings*, 160–73.

518 *teachers and society people*: Kukielka, Yad Vashem testimony.

519 *Mirka was Jewish*: Description of Mirka is also from Renia's Yad Vashem testimony.

525 *so someone would know*: In her Yad Vashem testimony, Renia offers a different story: At one point, she says, she came out to Mirka as a Jew and told her her real name, just in case she was killed and someone came looking for her. Mirka could not believe that a woman who prayed so flu-

ently with the Christians was a Jew. Renia could not show that she was developing a friendship with a Jew and warned Mirka never to approach her.

Years later, in Israel, Renia was heading to her brother's wedding in Jaffa with the wedding band. While rushing to the ceremony, she spotted a disheveled Mirka in the street, holding a child. Renia was elated and stunned, but couldn't stay and chat. Mirka told her she lived nearby with her husband and child—she pointed to the building—and said to come find her. Renia spent much time trying to track her down, going door to door, talking to neighbors. She even put out a call for her on an Israeli radio show that tracked survivors. She never found her.

528 *red dye from shoe tassels . . . slick back their hair and hide grays*: Goldenberg, "Camps: Foreword," 273; Rebekah Schmerler-Katz, "If the World Had Only Acted Sooner," in *Before All Memory Is Lost*, 332.

529 *the underground*: Brandeis, "Rebellion in the Ghettos," in *Daring to Resist*, 127. See Tec, *Resistance*, 124–27, for background on the Auschwitz underground.

529 *Anna Heilman*: Born Hannah (Hanka) Wajcblum. Her story is based on her memoir: Anna Heilman, *Never Far Away: The Auschwitz Chronicles of Anna Heilman* (Calgary: University of Calgary Press, 2001), as well as her testimony in *Mothers, Sisters, Resisters*, 295–98. Her oral testimony is in the USC Shoah Foundation collection.

Though I have told this story largely from Anna's point of view, other sources offer different versions with conflicting details about who was involved, who initiated the powder smuggling, how the smuggling worked, how they were caught, how the revolt transpired, and who survived. I have integrated information from several sources in my telling, including: from the oral history of Noach Zabludovits, "Death Camp Uprisings," in *Daring to Resist*, 133; *In Honor of Ala Gertner, Róza Robota, Regina Safirztajn, Ester Wajcblum: Martyred Heroines of the Jewish Resistance in Auschwitz Executed on January 5, 1945* (Unknown publisher, 1991?); "Prisoner Revolt at Auschwitz-Birkenau," USHMM, https://www.ushmm .org/learn/timeline-of-events/1942-1945/auschwitz -revolt; "Revolt of the 12th Sonderkommando in Auschwitz," Jewish Partisan Educational Foundation, http:// jewishpartisans.blogspot.com/search/label/Roza%20 Robota; Ronen Harran, "The Jewish Women at the Union Factory, Auschwitz 1944: Resistance, Courage and Tragedy," *Dapim: Studies in the Holocaust* 31, no. 1 (2017): 45–67; Kol-Inbar, *Three Lines in History*, 538–39; Rose Meth, "Rose Meth," in *Mothers, Sisters, Resisters*, 299–305; Paldiel, *Saving One's Own*, 384; Tec, *Resistance*, 124–44. Page 136 of *Resistance* discusses the lack of precise details and figures for this story.

529 *in a large, single-storeyed, glass-roofed*: According to footage in *The Heart of Auschwitz*, directed by Carl Leblanc, Canada, 2010. According to Harran, *Jewish Women at the Union Factory*, 47, Union was originally a bicycle parts company but in 1940 it set up a subsidiary that made weapons.

530 *male protector*: According to Anna's memoir, some "lovers" did have sexual relationships, some did not. These men, who had passes to enter the women's camp, brought women items such as food.

531 *Roza Robota*: In addition to the sources listed above regarding the resistance at Auschwitz, information about Roza is from: Jack Porter, "Jewish Women in the Resistance," *Jewish Combatants of World War 2*, No. 3 (1981); Na'ama Shik, "Roza Robota," The Encyclopedia of Jewish Women, https://jwa.org/encyclopedia/article/robota -roza.

531 *According to other accounts*: Most accounts concur that the men initiated this. Many state that they asked Roza to retrieve the gunpowder from her fellow female prisoners. Roza is often presented as the female leader of this operation.

532 *Francesca Mann, the famous Melody Palace ballerina*: There are many accounts of Francesca Mann; at times she is referred to as Katerina Horowicz. In some accounts, she purposely performed a tantalizing striptease, in others, she noted she was being ogled by Nazi guards. In some, she threw clothes; in others, a shoe. In some, other women joined her in attacking the Nazis. See, for instance: *Women of Valor*, 44; Grunwald-Spier, *Women's Experiences in the Holocaust*, 266–71; Kol-Inbar, *Three Lines of History*, 538. According to Vitis-Shomron, *Youth in Flames*, 200, she was a Nazi collaborator.

532 *five hundred women*: Reinhartz, *Bits and Pieces*, 42.

532 *At Budy, a farm-based subcamp*: Goldenberg, "Camps: Foreword," 269.

532 *At Sobibor*: In the Sobibor revolt, Jews killed eleven SS guards and police auxilaries and set the camp on fire. About three hundred Jews escaped through cut barbed wire; nearly two hundred made it out without being captured. In order to conceal his underground work, the leader of the Sobibor resistance pretended that he was having a romantic affair with a woman, "Lyuka" (Gertrude Poppert-Schonborn). As their cover, she overheard all the planning and gave the leader a good luck shirt on the eve of his breakout. See "Jewish Uprisings in Ghettos and in Camps," USHMM Encyclopedia, https://encyclopedia.ushmm.org/content/en/article/jewish-uprisings-in-ghettos-and-camps-1941-44; Paldiel, *Saving One's Own*, 371–82; Tec, *Resistance*, 153–57.

532 *women stole arms*: Tec, *Resistance*, 155.

533 *Mala Zimetbaum, who spoke six languages*: Information on Mala is culled from several accounts, each with different details about her background, escape, and murder. See Grunwald-Spier, *Women's Experiences in the Holocaust*, 271–75; Jack Porter, "Jewish Women in the Resistance"; Na'ama Shik, "Mala Zimetbaum," The Encyclopedia of Jewish Women, https://jwa.org/encyclopedia/article/zimetbaum-mala; Ya'ari-Hazan, *Bronislawa Was My Name*, 109–13.

534 *two fifteen-year-old girls from Germany*: In Bela's account in *Women in the Ghettos*, 134–39, it states that they smuggled fourteen girls from Łódź and Theresienstadt into the camp.

536 *Another Auschwitz survivor related*: Olga Lengyel, "The Arrival," *Different Voices*, 129.

536 *They weakened hemp threads . . . so pipes froze*: See, for instance, Karay, "Women in the Forced Labor Camps," 293–94, and Laska, "Vera Laska," *Different Voices*, 254; Suzanne Reich, "Sometimes I Can Dream Again," in *Before All Memory Is Lost*, 315.

537 *Fania Fainer*: Née Fania Landau. Originally from Białystok, Fania was deported to a forced labor camp, and then to Auschwitz, where she worked at the Union.

537 *Zlatka Pitluk*: Née Snajderhauz. This story about the heart card is from *The Heart of Auschwitz*, directed by Carl Leblanc, Canada, 2010; Personal interview, Sandy Fainer, telephone, November 27, 2018; wall text, Montreal Holocaust Museum, Montreal.

537 *eighteen other women prisoners, including Anna*: These are: Hanka, Mania, Mazal, Hanka W, Berta, Fela, Mala, Ruth, Lena, Rachela, Eva Pany, Bronia, Cesia, Irena, Mina, Tonia, Gusia, and Liza. In *The Heart of Auschwitz*, Anna claims that she did not sign this card and that "Hanka W." was not her.

537 *When Fania was about to turn twenty . . . once went through*: The heart was left on Fania's worktable, on her birthday, December 12, 1944. She hid the precious present

in a bit of straw in the ceiling of her barrack. On a death march in January 1945, Fania stashed the heart in her armpit, carrying it for the entire journey. Fania survived, as did the heart, the only relic from the first twenty years of her life, which she hid in her underwear drawer until her daughter found it many decades later.

In *The Heart of Auschwitz*, one woman who was at Union claims that this story is impossible, and there is no way that women could have smuggled the materials, or that Fania could have held on to it during a death march where people were being shot for stepping one inch to the side. Others mention that it was unheard of to celebrate a birthday at Auschwitz.

539 *Thirty Jewish women*: According to Harran, *Jewish Women at the Union Factory*, 51–52, more than thirty women were involved; most of them were Polish Jews. Five were from Warsaw and five from Bedzin; a number were Young Guard members. He lists additional names: Haya Kroin, Mala Weinstein, Helen Schwartz, Genia Langer. Other women involved include: Faige Segal, Mala Weinstein, Hadassah Zlotnicka, Rose Meth, Rachel Baum, Ada Halpern, Hadassah Tolman-Zlotnicki and Luisa Ferstenberg.

539 *in apron seams*: See Tec, *Resistance*, 139–41, for story about Roza transporting aprons with concealed layers.

539 *(Kitty Felix was forced to sort)*: Now goes by Kitty Hart Moxon. Grunwald-Spier, *Women's Experiences in the Holocaust*, 275–77.

540 *a crematorium*: In some accounts, it was crematorium number three; in others, number four.

540 *gunpowder that was traced to the* Pulverraum: In some accounts, the Union gunpowder was not actually linked to this explosion, while others claim that all the gunpowder came from Union and that women were integral to this unique case of armed resistance at Auschwitz.

541 *In one version*: Harran, *Jewish Women at the Union Factory*, 53–56, and Tec, *Resistance*, 138.

542 *The girls were sentenced to hanging*: According to Harran, *Jewish Women at the Union Factory*, 60–64, they were actually sentenced for product sabotage and not for their resistance efforts. The Nazis were upset by the widespread sabotage in their slave factories. The public hangings of these four Jewish girls were intended to deter others from sabotage and to prove to authorities in Berlin that they were taking control of the sabotage problem.

Chapter 27: The Light of Days

544 *a gendarme was waiting for Renia*: Unless indicated otherwise this chapter is based on Kukielka, *Underground Wanderings*, 173–79, including direct quotations.

545 *One of the gendarmes*: Renia describes him and their relationship slightly differently in her Yad Vashem testimony.

550 *"Even if I was stabbed with a knife, I could not break"*: Kukielka, Yad Vashem testimony.

Chapter 28: The Great Escape

557 *cigarettes and liquor*: In Renia's Yad Vashem testimony, she says it was sausage and vodka.

559 *Montelupich's woman's prison*: This section is based on: "Montelupich Prison," Shoah Resource Center, https:// www.yadvashem.org/odot_pdf/Microsoft%20Word%20 -%206466.pdf; Draenger, *Justyna's Narrative*, 9–15, 27–29; Grunwald-Spier, *Women's Experiences in the Holocaust*, 209–10; Kol-Inbar, *Three Lines of History*, 520–21; Margolin Peled, "Gusta Dawidson Draenger," Margolin Peled, "Mike Gola."

559 *"We did it . . . even stronger ones"*: Draenger, *Justyna's Narrative*, 29.

560 *"spiritual elevation" and "sisterhood"*: Quoted in Kol-Inbar, *Three Lines of History*, 521.

561 *who had been planning an escape*: Slightly different versions of their escape story are offered in: Draenger, *Justyna's Narrative*, 18–19; Grunwald-Spier, *Women's Experiences in the Holocaust*, 209–10; Peled, "Gusta Dawidson Draenger," and Peled, "More Gola" both in the *Encyclopedia of Jewish Women*.

562 *new dress, shawl, and shoes*: In another version, Halina gave Renia her very recognizable leather coat.

568 *Marek, however, had had less fortune*: Zuckerman, *Surplus of Memory*, 406.

569 *Day in, day out, Renia*: The rest of this chapter is based on

Kukielka, *Underground Wanderings*, 191–200, including direct quotations.

569 *Other accounts*: Ronen, *Condemned to Life*, 357–70.

569 *The question of whether . . . remains a heated one*: Yad Vashem's "Righteous Among the Nations" includes rescuers who accepted payment if the amount wasn't extortionate and so long as Jews were not mistreated or exploited by them. See Paulsson, *Secret City*, 129.

573 *in two weeks*: Paulsson, *Secret City*, 382–83.

573 *"Wanted" posters . . . on the streets*: Kukielka, Yad Vashem testimony.

574 *Chajka had escaped . . . write about them*: Ronen, *Condemned to Life*, 341–70.

577 *Muniosh from the Atid kibbutz—brown hair, pale skin, pointy ears*: From a photo of the group in Budapest held in the Ghetto Fighters' House Museum archive.

Chapter 29: "Zag nit keyn mol az du geyst dem letstn veg"

579 *The Partisan Song*: This Yiddish song was written by Hirsh Glick in the Vilna ghetto, and is one of the most well-known Jewish resistance songs. This English translation is by Miriam Schlesinger.

580 *Gisi Fleischmann*: Information about Gisi as well as Slovakia is primarily from: "Slovakia," Shoah Resource Center, http://www.yadvashem.org/odot_pdf/Microsoft%20Word%20-%206104.pdf; Yehuda Bauer, "Gisi

Fleischmann," *Women in the Holocaust*, 253–64; Gila Fatran, "Gisi Fleischmann," The Encyclopedia of Jewish Women, https://jwa.org/encyclopedia/article/fleischmann -gisi; Paldiel, *Saving One's Own*, 100–136.

581 *twenty thousand Jews . . . 500 marks per Jew*: Paldiel, *Saving One's Own*, 101–2.

583 *After eating, Renia*: The rest of this chapter based on Kukielka, *Underground Wanderings*, 147–218, including direct quotations.

585 *dark haired and dashing*: From a photo in the Ghetto Fighters' House Museum archive.

587 *Chajka had an entirely different awakening*: The story of Chajka and Benito, including direct quotations, is from Ronen, *Condemned to Life*, 384–402.

590 *They would not be doing any more crossings*: According to Ronen, *Condemned to Life*, 384–402, the smuggling operation ended when the smuggler betrayed the group and the refugees were captured and sent to Auschwitz.

590 *the last remaining Kukielka*: Renia's writing about Sarah is vague. My sense is that she did not know for sure that she would never see her again, but she had an inkling.

591 *"The Hungarians themselves . . . Aryan"*: Kukielka, *Underground Wanderings*, 211.

594 *photograph of Renia on a Budapest street*: Rotem, *Memoirs of a Ghetto Fighter*, 90, mentions that there were street photographers in Warsaw who would take your photo and send you a note when it was ready. You'd come pick it up and pay them. This might be how the street shots of Vladka,

Hela and Shoshana, and Renia were taken. (See photo insert.)

594 *The JDC had paid the Polish consulate to turn a blind eye*: This is according to Renia. The JDC Archive did not confirm this.

594 *began to write her memoirs*: According to Zariz, "Attempts at Rescue and Revolt," 23, Renia started writing her diary in Budapest.

595 *photograph of the comrades in Hungary*: Photo is from the Ghetto Fighters' House Museum archive.

599 *sixth of March*: Renia's Palestine immigration papers note that her arrival date was March 7. Two weeks later, Hitler invaded Hungary.

Part 4: The Emotional Legacy

601 *Interviewer . . . I'm fine.*: Video testimony, Yad Vashem archive #4288059, June 20, 2002.

601 *"We had been liberated . . . fear of life"*: Cited in Paldiel, *Saving One's Own*, 394.

Chapter 30: Fear of Life

603 *"the one . . . find its place"*: Klinger, *Writing These Words*, 49.

604 *"as if I'd arrived at the home of my parents"*: Renia's testimony, Israel National Library.

604 *Even non-Zionist survivors were attracted to the kibbut-*

zim: Avinoam Patt, "A Zionist Home: Jewish Youths and the Kibbutz Family After the Holocaust," in *Jewish Families in Europe*, 131–52.

604 *"We feel like . . . same right to life as they do"*: Kukielka, *Underground Wanderings*, 218.

605 *The politics of Israel's earliest years . . . came to be known*: This discussion about the Holocaust narrative in Israel is based on: Gutterman, *Fighting for Her People*, 12–19, 352–79, 455–67; Paldiel, *Saving One's Own*, xvii–xxi; Sharon Geva, *To the Unknown Sisters: Holocaust Heroines in Israeli Society* (Tel Aviv, Isr.: Hakibbutz Hameuchad, 2010). In *The Last Fighters*, Marek Edelman claims that Israel is antisemitic when it comes to European Jews. In Klinger, *Writing These Words*, 21, Ronen suggests that Chajka's diaries were never popular because they did not fit either the victim or armed-fighter narratives.

605 *Not only was anti-Nazi activity more palatable than horrific torture*: Kol-Inbar, *Three Lines of History*, 523–24, on how Zivia's heroic narrative was popular in Israel in 1946 as it was more palatable than victim stories.

607 *"Why do I need . . . we are so tiny"*: *The Last Fighters*.

607 *gone largely unappreciated*: See, for instance, Gutterman, *Fighting for Her People*, 473–74.

607 *Menachem Begin . . . downplayed the uprising altogether*: Personal interview, Eyal Zuckerman, Tel Aviv, Isr., May 15, 2018.

608 *not whether they should*: Diner also points out that the Warsaw Ghetto Uprising occurred on Passover; the theme

of liberation tied in with the seder. American Jews hosted many commemorative events around this time of year. But these were mourning events, while the uprising itself was never a central issue.

608 *trend in American academia . . . even blame the victim*: Tec, *Resistance*, 1–15.

609 *"myth of passivity"*: Schulman, *Partisan's Memoir*, 10. See Eva Fogelman, "On Blaming the Victim," in *Daring to Resist*, 134–37.

609 *"not that bad"*: Ostrower, *It Kept Us Alive*, 14, 20, 64, 231, acknowledges that certain lines of inquiry might unintentionally misrepresent the gravity and brutality of the Holocaust.

609 *a context where the genocide is fading from memory*: According to a 2018 study conducted by the Conference on Jewish Material Claims Against Germany, two-thirds of American millennials surveyed in a recent poll cannot identify what Auschwitz is.

609 *Many writers fear . . . ultimately blaming the victim*: One of the mottos of these fighters was "We will not be led like sheep to the slaughter," which was a formidable source of strength for them but later became viewed as an attack on victims. Most fighters—even those who shot Nazis in the face—died; out of 3.3 million Jews in Poland, only 300,000 lived. A multitude of factors determined how a person chose and was able to respond to the torture of the Holocaust, not to mention there were many ways of resisting. The greatest armies in the world could not defeat Hitler, so

it makes sense that starving Jews did not enter combat. In *The Last Fighters*, Marek Edelman stresses that the Jews who went to the gas chambers were the heroes: "It was easier to hold a weapon than to walk naked to your death."

610 *All these factors*: Additional factors include an embarrassment of failure as well as the worry that resistance efforts may have been counterproductive and even hastened more killing. According to Gutterman, "Holocaust in Będzin," 63, some historians say that the Warsaw ghetto uprising caused the Nazis to accelerate their plan to kill all Jews.

For the point of view that the resistance was ineffectual and even detrimental, see Eli Gat, "The Warsaw Ghetto Myth" and "Myth of the Warsaw Ghetto Bunker: How It Began," in *Ha'aretz*, December 19, 2013, and January 13, 2014, https://www.haaretz.com/jewish/.premium-fiction -of-warsaw-ghetto-bunkers-1.5310568 and https://www .haaretz.com/jewish/.premium-warsaw-ghetto-myths -1.5302604.

According to Mark, 41–65, the assumption that Jews do not fight back is so engrained in our minds that Jewish resistance is often considered "a miracle," rather than the common occurrence that it was. He points out that Jews devalue the resistance saying that a small fraction of the population does not count as a national struggle; but the actual combat in any national struggle is always only carried out by a few fighters.

610 *women's stories were particularly silenced*: The introduction of "women and the Holocaust" as a field of inquiry was

a controversial move, taking years to be institutionalized as
a legitimate area of study, due to discomfort that suffering
was being used in service of a political point. Even self-
declared feminist Holocaust scholars had problems focusing on women when that focus lent itself to uncritical
celebrations of friendship and domestics. Even some recently launched exhibitions and online resources specifically about women and the Holocaust still include the
"disclaimer" that all Jews suffered equally.

610 *As authors . . . into the background*: Ronen, "Women Leaders in the Jewish Underground During the Holocaust."

610 *Lenore Weitzman . . . considered trivial*: Weitzman, "Living
on the Aryan Side," 217–19. Weitzman claims that: armed
combat (by men) was noticeable, whereas rescue activities
(by women) were secret; women were generally not affiliated with an organization but engaged in private acts of resistance; women's roles were defined as auxiliary even
though they were more dangerous; women's acts (particularly rescuing children) were devalued; women did not
record their activities or seek public recognition after the
war. Her discussion of why the *kashariyot* were lost to history is in "Kashariyot (Couriers) in the Resistance During
the Holocaust."

611 *people would think they were liars, or insane*: Berger and
Berger, eds., *With Courage Shall We Fight*, 45. Several of
these factors pertained to male survivors too.

611 *accused by relatives . . . look after their parents*: In a personal interview, Anna Shternshis, New York, April 9, 2018,

told a story about a partisan whose sister never forgave her for abandoning their mother, even though all survived.

611 *"sacred duty" of "cosmic significance"*: Helen Epstein, *Children of the Holocaust: Conversations with Sons and Daughters of Survivors* (New York: Penguin, 1979), 23.

612 *"professional survivors"*: Personal interview, Rivka Augenfeld, Montreal, August 10, 2018.

612 *an oppressive survivors' guilt*: Liba Marshak Augenfeld's mother had given her daughter the blessing to run from the ghetto and join the partisans, and so Liba had made some degree of peace with her decision to leave her family. But so many others had not received this blessing and were overcome by guilt. Augenfeld interview.

612 *Her narrative seemed too selfish*: Izhar, *Chasia Bornstein-Bielicka*, on Chasia's silencing: 294, 309, 310, 313. Chasia did not talk much of her wartime experience, partly because she didn't feel that she'd had it that bad compared with other survivors, and partly for the sake of her children. Later in her life, when her grown daughters asked her about her past, she told them her incredible story. Only then did they learn that their mother had never once slept through the night.

613 *because Hannah was young, beautiful . . . a checkered romantic past*: For instance, personal interviews, Daniela Ozacky-Stern and Yonat Rotbain, Givat Haviva, Isr., May 14, 2018.

614 *Faye Lazebnik, the partisan who spent years*: This section is based on Schulman, *Partisan's Memoir*.

614 *"the lowest point in my life . . . I would never see again"*: Schulman, *Partisan's Memoir*, 192–93.

614 *When the war was over . . . and a woman*: Ibid., 188–89.

615 *Some surviving women . . . intimate bonds*: Starr interview.

615 *"We felt an urgency to proceed quickly with whatever love was left in us"*: Schulman, *Partisan's Memoir*, 206.

616 *"Sometimes [the] bygone . . . than the present"*: Schulman, *Partisan's Memoir*, 224.

616 *Zivia could see weary horses*: This section about Zivia and the Warsaw uprising is based on Gutterman, *Fighting for Her People*, 280–90; Lubetkin, *Days of Destruction*, 260–74; Zuckerman, *Surplus of Memory*, 526–29, 548–49, 550–56.

617 *Jews—including women—from all political factions participated*: For instance, Irene Zoberman was asked to distribute leaflets. Helen Mahut taught in underground Polish schools and joined the AK, for whom she stood at bus depots and memorized insignias on German army trucks, as well as translated Radio London to Polish. Mina Aspler, or "Mad Maria," tended to wounded soldiers and was a courier, sending messages between groups. Zofia Goldfarb-Stypułkowska was a sergeant in the Polish underground.

617 *Rivka Moscovitch was killed . . . on the street*: Grupińska, *Reading the List*, 96.

617 *nearly 90 percent of its buildings had now been destroyed*: Statistics differ based on the types of edifices considered. See Micholaj Glinski, "How Warsaw Came Close to Never Being Rebuilt," Culture.pl, February 3, 2015, https://

culture.pl/en/article/how-warsaw-came-close-to-never
-being-rebuilt.

618 *Zivia's shelter*: This rescue story has many versions. See, for instance, Gutterman, *Fighting for Her People*, 291–99; Lubetkin, *Days of Destruction*, 272–74; Warman, in *Mothers, Sisters, Resisters*, 288–94; Zuckerman, *Surplus of Memory*, 552–56.

619 *"The people rejoiced . . . lone remnants of our people"*: Lubetkin, *Days of Destruction*, 274. Zuckerman, *Surplus of Memory*, 558, 565, also describes liberation as depressing.

619 *This was the saddest day of Zivia's life: the world she'd known officially ceased to exist*: Zuckerman interview.

619 *Jews could be killed on the streets*: In 1946 more than forty Jews were killed by Polish soldiers, officers, and civilians in a pogrom in Kielce.

620 *Zivia worked to bring the Jews aid*: This paragraph is based on Gutterman, *Fighting for Her People*, 303–45.

620 *episodes that reminded her of ghetto Aktions*: Gutterman, *Fighting for Her People*, 381. This section about Zivia in Palestine is based on ibid., 349–487.

620 *fearing his flirtatious . . . affairs with other women*: Gutterman, *Fighting for Her People*, 386, 389. It is unclear from where Gutterman got this personal information.

620 *She could not stop asking: "why have I remained alive?"*: Zuckerman interview.

621 *"a circus," she called it*: Gutterman, *Fighting for Her People*, 361.

621 *"She stood there like a queen"*: *Blue Bird*.

622 *She returned to Israel pregnant . . . now snug*: Zuckerman interview.

622 *she got her tolerance from her father*: As mentioned in the story, Renia and Bela both took strength from their parents. Faye too felt that her mother's competence and her father's loving nature endowed her with independence and personal strength. "We felt very much loved by our parents," Faye later wrote. "I believe it was this love that gave me the security and the resources that served me well later in life."

623 *"catastrophe could hit with no notice"*: Shelub and Rosenbaum, *Never the Last Road*, 174. Liba Marshak Augenfeld and her husband always took separate flights. Fruma Berger was terrified of thunder which reminded her of a military attack.

624 *Controversies arose*: Discussed in Gutterman, *Fighting for Her People*, 418–23.

624 *had to be forced by Leon Uris . . . event*: Gutterman, *Fighting for Her People*, 452.

624 *"Give yourself a slap on the ass!"*: Zuckerman interview.

624 *hosted guests, and mothered two children*: According to *The Zuckerman Code*, some people referred to their home as an "ongoing shiva." Epstein, *Children of the Holocaust*, 176, writes about survivors who cope by working constantly; this gives them financial security and no time to think.

625 *but only went along with it because she knew she'd lose*: Zuckerman interview.

626 *"You can tell a lot . . . 'I' in a sentence"*: Zuckerman interview. Zuckerman, *Surplus of Memory*, ix, also mentions this motto.

626 *"How could I not have sat them down and asked them?"*: *The Zuckerman Code.*

626 *"What am I supposed to do, . . . what?"*: *The Zuckerman Code.*

626 *Many children of survivors felt . . . justifying their parents' survival*: Epstein, *Children of the Holocaust*, 170–71, 195–96, 207–10.

626 *"A philosopher [is] useless in the forest"*: Shelub and Rosenbaum, *Never the Last Road*, 186.

626 *Eyal, the Hebrew name for the ZOB*: According to *The Zuckerman Code*, this was just a coincidence, and she was not named for the ZOB.

627 *Though she wishes . . . a source of strength*: Zuckerman interview.

627 *She questions . . . enjoying herself*: *The Zuckerman Code.*

627 *"hypermorality"*: Eyal Zuckerman in *The Zuckerman Code.*

627 *With her own "hypermorality"*: In *The Zuckerman Code*, Roni refuses to enjoy herself in Warsaw. Epstein, *Children of the Holocaust*, 201, 230, gives examples of children of survivors who put themselves in dangerous situations just to prove that they can survive them.

628 *"Zuckermans don't cry"*: The Zuckerman Code.

628 *"you never have . . . get through life"*: The Zuckerman Code.

628 *"Fate determined . . . no other way"*: Lubetkin, *Days of Destruction*, 275.

628 *Zivia was debilitated by guilt*: Zuckerman interview.

628 *As per Antek's request . . . words were necessary*: Blue Bird.

628 *Without her, the fragile world . . . Eyal said*: Zuckerman interview.

629 *"like lava gushing out of the ground and sprouting up"*: Zuckerman, *Surplus of Memory*, 677.

629 *never truly found themselves after their traumatic and hyperdramatic twenties*: Personal interview, Barbara Harshav, New York, March 9 and April 23, 2018. Harshav stressed that many leaders of the Jewish defense in the Warsaw ghetto became "nobodies" in Israel; several had trouble finding themselves. (But not all—she did mention that Kazik became a happy owner of a supermarket chain.)

629 *"Zivia was the branch and Antek was the stem . . . no matter how strong it looks"*: Cited in Zuckerman interview.

629 *allegiances to the Polish underground . . . mortal danger*: Tec, *Resistance*, 31, includes a story about a Polish man who wouldn't admit his role in the resistance until the late 1970s. Some claim that Betar's ZZW was never mentioned in Poland because of its connection to the Polish nationalist underground faction.

630 *One Polish woman . . . suspicious*: Agi Legutko, tour of the

Kraków ghetto, Jewish Culture Festival, Kraków, June 2018.

630 *Irena Gelblum*: In several accounts, Renia refers to this woman as "Halina." She even states that she was frustrated that was never able to track her down after the war. But according to a footnote in Regina Kukelka, "In the Gestapo Net," *Memorial Book of Zaglembie*, ed. J. Rapaport (Tel Aviv, Isr., 1972), 436, "Halina" was Irena Gelblum.

Irena was romantically involved with Kazik, and was a daring Warsaw operative. She had been sent to Zaglembie, presumably by Zivia, to look for missing couriers and Jews hiding in Będzin and to give them money to join the partisans. According to one account, while she was there, she happened to find out about Renia and talked Sarah into going with her to Mysłowice. After the war, Irena moved to Italy, changed her name to Irena Conti and became a poet, distancing herself from her past. She is mentioned in Zuckerman, *Surplus of Memory*, 389, and referred to as "Irka." See: Joanna Szczesna, "Irena Conti," *Wysokie Obcasy*, 21 April 2014.

630 *Irena Adamowicz, the Catholic scout*: Grupińska, *Reading the List*, 21.

631 *Chajka Klinger made it to Palestine*: The rest of her story is based on Ronen, *Condemned to Life*, 403–79.

634 *Not everyone survives surviving*: Harshav interview. In a personal interview with Avihu Ronen, Tel Aviv, Isr., May 16, 2018, he discussed Chajka's legacy, saying she was always someone who went "against the current," and her

grandchildren—several of whom are refusniks—have carried that on. Avihu considers himself to be an academic outlier.

Chapter 31: Forgotten Strength

635 *Renia's brother*: I found conflicting accounts of Renia's brothers; it is possible that it was Aaron who found out about her in the DP camp or that he was in Cyprus. It seems that the brother originally thought that it was Sarah who had survived. See Renia's testimony at the Israel National Library and personal interview, Yoram Kleinman, telephone, February 11, 2019.

636 *Both brothers eventually reached Palestine*: While Renia lived a secular life, her brothers stayed religious throughout their lives in Israel. Aaron lived in Haifa, in Renia's neighborhood. He was an investigator for the customs authority and a cantor who performed internationally. According to his son Yoram, Aaron was like Renia: "ego driven, dominant, tough, and cared about respect." He changed his surname to Kleinman because, as a fighter for the Irgun, he'd been wanted by the British. Zvi was the soft, calm one. He settled in Jerusalem, was observant, and worked as a legal clerk for the Ministry of Justice. Renia and Zvi spent many hours analyzing their past and discussing the war and their family. He changed his name to Zamir, a Hebrew version for Kukielka, a cuckoo bird.

636 *Sarah had been caught . . . comrades and orphans*: Accord-

ing to a footnote in Kukelka, "In the Gestapo Net," 436. According to her Yad Vashem testimony, Renia found out about this from the Zuckermans after they arrived in Israel, perhaps in 1946.

636 *"Please take care of my sister Renia"*: Liwer, *Town of the Dead*, 23.

636 *Encouraged by poet and politician Zalman Shazar*: Renia's family related that Zalman Shazar was the one who told her to write her memoirs; other sources mentioned above indicate that she began writing in Hungary. Personal interview, Jacob Harel and Leah Waldman, Haifa, Isr., May 14, 2018.

636 *translated to Hebrew by Chaim Shalom Ben-Avram, a renowned Israeli translator*: According to her son, Renia took issue with elements of the translation. Harel and Waldman interview. I have not been able to locate the original Polish manuscript, though I have searched the following archives and organizations: Lavon, Yad Tabenkin, Kibbutz Dafna, Jewish Historical Institute, Hakibbutz Hameuchad and Naamat USA.

636 *carried it with them in their backpacks*: Geva, *To the Unknown Sisters*, 275.

637 *in one . . . reading for students*: Hasia R. Diner, *We Remember with Reverence and Love: American Jews and the Myth of Silence After the Holocaust, 1945–1962* (New York: New York University Press, 2009), 96–109, 134.

637 *one other survivor testimony*: Fredka Mazia, USHMM testimony, 1991, https://collections.ushmm.org/search/catalog

/irn502790. Fredka (Oxenhandler) Mazia was a leader of Hanoar Hatzioni, a group which Renia criticizes in her telling.

637 *contributed to the Zaglembie memorial book*: Her contribution was an edited and annotated translation of an excerpt from *Underground Wanderings*.

Memorial (Yizkor) books, written primarily in Yiddish and/or Hebrew by survivors, document Jewish communities destroyed in the Holocaust. More than two thousand memorial books were published.

637 *After this catharsis, Renia felt able to move on*: Harel and Waldman interview.

637 *fell out of fashion*: Personal interviews, Anna Shternshis, New York, April 9, 2018, and Avihu Ronen, Tel Aviv, Isr., May 16, 2018.

637 *Renewal was so very important*: The rest of this section is based on personal interviews with Renia's family.

639 *"replacements" for dead relatives*: Uta Larkey, "Transcending Memory in Holocaust Survivors' Families," in *Jewish Families in Europe*, 216.

639 *"Missing relations" . . . shifting kinship structures for generations*: See, for instance, Michlic, ed., *Jewish Families in Europe*, and Epstein, *Children of the Holocaust*.

639 *full of life*: According to her nephew Yoram Kleinman, she was "sarcastic, direct, and you could talk to her about anything." Kleinman interview

639 *not witnessed her own mother's aging*: Nor did they care for elderly parents. Rivka Augenfeld, daughter of Vilna

partisans, spoke about how her generation had to figure out how to do so for themselves. Personal interview, Rivka Augenfeld, Montreal, August 10 and 17, 2018.

640 *Freedom comrades*: Chawka Lenczner, Chana Gelbard, and Yitzhak Fiszman.

640 *They sensed . . . did not quite understand it*: See Larkey, "Transcending Memory in Holocaust Survivors' Families," 209–32.

641 *but also fragile*: Epstein, *Children of the Holocaust*, 168–69, 178, 251, tells stories of how survivor parents were seen as "fragile"; their children had to protect them.

642 *well-known liberal Israeli member of Parliament*: Chaika Grossman dedicated her life to public service, from helping Polish survivors, to being elected MP in the Israeli Knesset, where she was outspoken in advocating for youth, the elderly, and equality for women and the Arab population.

642 *spoke every single night at ten o'clock*: Izhar, *Chasia Bornstein-Bielicka*, 272.

642 *Fania stayed in touch . . . across continents*: Personal interview, Sandy Fainer, Telephone, November 27, 2018.

642 *Twenty-five thousand descendants*: Vershitskaya, 572.

642 *"Sisters" . . . from their early lives*: Gurewitsch, "Preface," *Mothers, Sisters, Resisters*, xi–xxi.

643 *"I raised my children . . . alive inside of me with the same strength"*: Ya'ari Hazan, *Bronislawa Was My Name*. This section is based on *Bronislawa Was My Name* and my personal interview with Yoel Yaari, Jerusalem, May 17, 2018. In an email correspondence on 23 December 2019,

Yoel informed me that the liberation story in *Bronislawa Was My Name* was incorrect and he provided updated details.

644 *"The Frumka Group"*: Yoseph Baratz, "The Frumka Group," *Women in the Ghettos*, 182–84, says the group comprised Bela and thirty girls aged eighteen to twenty-two.

644 *Order of the Cross*: Documentation about this award (the Grunwald Cross Third Class) is held in the Ghetto Fighters' House Museum archive in the form of a letter from Isaac Schwarzbart in London to Moshe Klinger in Mandate Palestine, April 26, 1945. (The HeHalutz archive in England.) There is some confusion as to whether the award went to Frumka or Hantze. Rivka Glanz also received a Polish military honor. Faye, Chasia, and the Białystok couriers all received medals from the Soviet government.

644 *she counseled a ragtag assembly of seventy-three traumatized Jewish orphans*: With no formal psychology training, Chasia, aged twenty-five, devised her own system for running this traumatized group. She created "family roles" for all of them, appointing herself as the "older sister." Izhar, *Chasia Bornstein-Bielicka*, 319–20.

645 *Now Bronia gave . . . the rest of her life*: Yaari, "A Brave Connection."

646 *her son Yoel described*: The rest of this section is from my personal interview with Yoel Yaari, Jerusalem, May 17, 2018.

646 *Anna Heilman . . . about Darfur*: "About Anna Heilman," http://www.annaheilman.net/About%20Anna%20 Heilman.htm.

According to her family, Chasia was quick witted but quiet, considered and giving, a humanist. In a recent political debate about refugees, the family had to decide how to vote. "What would Chasia have said?" they asked themselves. The answer was clear: always "think of the weak link in the chain," no matter the situation. Her family voted to help the refugees—Chasia's legacy of empathy.

Vilna partisan Liba Marshak Augenfeld always welcomed people into her home; the family seders were filled with guests who were "refugees from their families." Rivka credits her parents with passing on a legacy of "how to be an ultimate mentsch." Personal interview, Rivka Augenfeld, add details.

646 *"Each time . . . phone number"*: Personal interview, Yoel Yaari, Jerusalem, May 17, 2018.

647 *grasping at hazy memories . . . rather than a full history*: Epstein, *Children of the Holocaust*, 179 for instance, provides examples of children of survivors for whom the story was hard to piece together, the narrative disjointed and emotional rather than chronological.

647 *Days after liberation . . . voice of a Jewish child*: Cohen, *Avengers*, 148–49. Ruzka relays a slightly different version in *Partisans of Vilna* in which she was also sure that she herself would never cry or laugh again. This section is based on

Neima Barzel, "Rozka Korczak-Marla" and "Vitka Kempner-Kovner," The Encyclopedia of Jewish Women; Cohen, Avengers; Michael Kovner, www.michalkovner.com; Korczak, Flames in Ash; Korczak, Tubin, and Rab, Zelda the Partisan; Ziva Shalev, "Zelda Nisanilevich Treger," The Encyclopedia of Jewish Women; Yehuda Tubin, Levi Deror et al., eds., Ruzka Korchak-Marle: The Personality and Philosophy of Life of a Fighter; Wilfand, Vitka Fights for Life; and personal interviews with Michael Kovner, Jerusalem, May 17, 2018, and Daniela Ozacky-Stern and Yonat Rotbain, Givat Haviva, Isr., May 14, 2018.

647 insulted her use of Yiddish as a "grating language": Personal interview, Daniela Ozacky-Stern and Yonat Rotbain, Givat Haviva, Isr., May 14, 2018.

649 "town of drunkenness and murder": Cited in Cohen, Avengers, 172.

650 "the CEO of Vengeance": Personal interview, Michael Kovner, Jerusalem, May 17, 2018

651 she insisted on passing on Holocaust stories despite Sanka's desire to detach: Korczak, Tubin, and Rab, Zelda the Partisan, 150.

651 a delicatessen in downtown Tel Aviv: From an article written by Ruth Meged for Haaretz, April 19, 1971, reprinted in Zelda the Partisan, 136.

651 Moreshet . . . life in Poland before 1939: Ozacky-Stern and Rotbain interview.

652 she never talked . . . to her grandchildren: Kovner interview.

652 *"I will live"*: Personal interview, Kovner interview.

653 *age forty-five*: Some sources say age forty.

653 *She was a disciple of Dr. George Stern*: For more on Stern, see "Color Psychotherapy," http://www.colorpsy .co.il/colorPsyEng.aspx. For Vitka's psychotherapy work, see Michael Kovner, "In Memory of My Mother," https:// www.michaelkovner.com/said04eng.

653 *with whom she had a complex bond*: Ibid.

653 *Vitka was attracted to . . . She had true chutzpah."* Personal interview, Michael Kovner, Jerusalem, May 17, 2018.

654 *Vladka Meed arrived in the United States*: Leisah Woldoff, "Daughter of Survivors Continues Parents' Legacy," *Jewish News*, April 23, 2014, http://www.jewishaz.com /community/valley_view/daughter-of-survivors-continues -parents-legacy/article_7249bb6e-cafb-11e3-8208-0017a 43b2370.html.

654 *"When she walked . . . like a fire hit"*: Personal interview, Jacob Harel and Leah Waldman, Haifa, Isr., May 14, 2018. This section is based on personal interviews with Renia's family.

655 *"How could someone?" . . . promenades through town*: Personal interview, Merav Waldman, Skype, October 23, 2018.

655 *even traveled to Alaska*: In her Yad Vashem testimony, Renia stresses that she traveled the entire world—but she never returned to Poland.

656 *Vitka died at ninety-two*: Vitka's birth date is inconsistent across sources, but most agree that she died at ninety-two.

656 *were still alive, all ranging in age from ninety-five to ninety-nine*: Partisan Mira Rosnow was still alive at the time of this writing, aged ninety-nine. Her sister, Sara, a partisan fighter, died at ninety-two. Chayele Porus Palevsky, a Vilna partisan, was still alive. Liba Marshak Augenfeld, a Vilna partisan, died at ninety-five.

656 *"The most important thing . . . stay together"*: Epstein, *Children of the Holocaust*, 182, 310, mentions that family loyalty is an overwhelming value among survivors.

656 *glimmering frocks and oversized smiles*: Photo from the collection of Merav Waldman.

657 *Like many third-generation children . . . gladly answered*: See discussion of 3G in Uta Larkey, "Transcending Memory in Holocaust Survivors'." As Dina Wardi explains, 2G and 3G women are often the family's "memorial candles." As Irit Felsen explained at a talk about intergenerational trauma at The Wing, New York, 27 January 2020, 2Gs felt anger and shame about their parents' background, whereas 3Gs were proud of their survivor heritage. (The second generation had a "double wall" with their parents, each generation wanting to protect the other and so never discussing the war.)

Epilogue

670 *Restaurants and shop as "Jew-rassic Park"*: Personal interview, Jonathan Ornstein, Kraków, Pol., June 25, 2018.

672 *historian Gunnar S. Paulsson . . .* 3 to 4 Poles per hidden

Jew: Paulsson, *Secret City*, 5, 129–130. Paulsson mentions another estimate, in which 160,000 Poles helped hide Jews. On page 247 he explains that help is not the same as recue, highlighting that there were many ways in which Poles aided Jews.

672 *Several scholars . . . in their testimonies*: Paulsson, *Secret City*, 21–25, also stresses that people usually record the unexpected in their memoirs, and not necessarily the norm. He suggests that most Poles did not betray the Jews they hid, but the ones that did left a greater impression and so were written about.

673 *"who suffered more"*: I am indebted to Samuel J. Kassow (lecture given at "In Dialogue: Polish Jewish Relations During the Interwar Period" for inspiring the ideas in this paragraph, and in particular the final sentiment regarding not "whitewashing" antisemitism and not playing games of who suffered more.

675 *by playing children*: A different explanation: Marisa Fox-Bevilacqua, "The Lost Shul of Będzin: Uncovering Poland's Once-vibrant Jewish Community," *Haaretz*, 7 Sept 2014, https://www.haaretz.com/jewish/.premium-the-lost-shul-of-Będzin-1.5263609.

Author's Note: On Research

681 *memoirs and testimonies*: For discussion on using memoirs and testimonies as sources, see for instance: Michlic, ed., *Jewish Families in Europe*; Mervin Butovksy and Kurt

Jonassohn, "An Exploratory Study of Unpublished Memoirs by Canadian Holocaust Survivors,'" in Paula J. Draper and Richard Menkis, eds., *New Perspectives on Canada, the Holocaust and Survivors: Canadian Jewish Studies*, Special Issue (Montreal: Association for Canadian Jewish Studies, 1997), 147–61; Frumi Shchori, "Voyage and Burden: Women Members of the Fighting Underground in the Ghettos of Poland as Reflected in Their Memoirs (1945–1998)," thesis, Tel Aviv University, 2006.

682 *Some were written quickly . . . composed with a fear of being caught*: Ronen, *Condemned to Life*, 52–63, explains the conditions in which Chajka wrote her diary: quickly, afraid of forgetting her emotions, afraid of being caught.

682 *Characteristically, she uses the word "we"*: The chronicler's use of the collective "we" in an attempt to be subjective is addressed in Rita Horvath, "Memory Imprints: Testimony as Historical Sources," in *Jewish Families in Europe*, 173–95.

683 *"a surplus of memory"*: Zuckerman, *Surplus of Memory*, viii.

683 *not "cold data"*: According to Zuckerman, *Surplus of Memory*, 371, the ZOB's documents were not always precise. They weren't writing for a historical archive; they were often writing to arouse sympathy in the hope of receiving some help.

685 *As for personal names . . . and nicknames*: In this book, I have tended to use the form of the name under which the woman published or became known. I have tried to use

spellings that are simpler for English readers. I often included additional versions of names in the endnotes.

686 *I have used antisemitism . . . a hyphen implies that "semitism" exists*: See introduction to Kirshenblatt-Gimblett, Barbara and Antony Polonsky, eds., *POLIN, 1000 Year History of Polish Jews—Catalogue for the Core Exhibition* (Warsaw: POLIN Museum of the History of Polish Jews, 2014). Paulsson, *Secret City*, ix–xv, considers the complexities of terminology in this field.

687 *240 trips—per week*: Cited in Laska, *Different Voices*, 255.

Bibliography

This is a select bibliography that includes my most significant sources. Additional sources appear in the endnotes. I have used proper names as they are used by the source itself; the spelling does not always accord with my spelling throughout this book.

Archival Sources

Alex Dworkin Canadian Jewish Archives, Montreal, Canada.

Emanuel Ringelblum Jewish Historical Institute, Warsaw, Poland.

Ghetto Fighters' House Museum, Israel.

- An important source of written and oral testimonies, contemporary and historic news articles, photographs, correspondences, lecture transcripts, eulogies, and other unpublished documents related to most characters in this book including several testimonies by Renia Kukielka.

Israel National Archives, Jerusalem, Israel.

- Renia Kukielka immigration papers.

Israel National Library, Jerusalem, Israel.

- Renia Kukielka written testimony.

JDC Archives, New York, USA.
Kibbutz Dafna, Israel.
Massuah International Institute for Holocaust Studies, Tel Yitzhak, Israel.
Moreshet Mordechai Anielevich Memorial Holocaust Study and Research Center, Givat Haviva, Israel.
Ringelblum Archive. (Accessed in various locations and formats.)
United States Holocaust Memorial Museum, Washington, DC.

- Registries of survivors, rare books, pamphlets, oral history and conference transcripts, digitized archive of the Białystok ghetto, digitized version of the Ringelblum Archive, ephemera, photographs, video and written testimonies.

Yad Vashem, Jerusalem, Israel.

- An important source of written and oral testimonies including Renia Kukielka, Bela Hazan, Chawka Lenczner.

YIVO, New York, USA.
The Wiener Holocaust Library, London, UK.

Online Sources

Below are frequently used online sources; I have included the home page but not each individual article.

Arolsen Archives—International Center on Nazi Persecution: Online Archive; https://arolsen-archives.org/en/search-explore/search-online-archive.

"Before They Perished" Exhibition; https://artsandculture.google.com/exhibit/QRNJBGMI.

Beit Hatfutsot: My Jewish Story, The Open Databases of the Museum of the Jewish People; https://dbs.bh.org.il.

Brama Cuckermana Foundation; http://www.bramacuckermana.com.

Centropa; centropa.org.

Culture.pl; https://culture.pl/en.

Emanuel Ringelblum Jewish Historical Institute; http://www.jhi.pl/en.

Geni; https://www.geni.com/family-tree/html/start.

Historic Films Stock Footage Archive, YouTube channel; https://www.youtube.com/channel/UCPbqb1jQ7cgk UqX2m33d6uw.

The Hebrew University of Jerusalem: Holocaust Oral History Collection; http://multimedia.huji.ac.il/oral history/eng/index-en.html.

Holocaust Historical Society; https://www.holocaust historicalsociety.org.uk.

JewishGen; https://www.jewishgen.org/new.

Jewish Partisan Education Foundation; http://www .jewishpartisans.org.

Jewish Records Indexing—Poland; http://jri-poland.org.

Jewish Virtual Library; https://www.jewishvirtual library.org.

Jewish Women's Archive: The Encyclopedia of Jewish Women; https://jwa.org/encyclopedia.

Michael Kovner; https://www.michaelkovner.com.

Modern Hebrew Literature—a Bio-Bibliographical Lex-icon; https://library.osu.edu/projects/hebrew-lexicon /index.htm.

Museum of the History of Polish Jews POLIN: Virtual Shtetl; https://sztetl.org.pl/en.

Museum of the History of Polish Jews POLIN: Polish Righteous; https://sprawiedliwi.org.pl/en.

Narodowe Archiwum Cyfrow (National Digital Ar-chive); https://audiovis.nac.gov.pl.

The New York Public Library: Yizkor Book Collection; https://digitalcollections.nypl.org/collections/yizkor -book-collection#/?tab=navigation.

Organization of Partisans, Underground Fighters and Ghetto Rebels in Israel; http://eng.thepartisan .org/ and http://archive.c3.ort.org.il/Apps/WW/page .aspx?ws=496fe4b2-4d9a-4c28-a845-510b28b1e 44b&page=8bb2c216-624a-41d6-b396-7c7c161e78ce.

Polish Center for Holocaust Research: Warsaw Ghetto Database; http://warszawa.getto.pl.

Sarah and Chaim Neuberger Holocaust Education Center: In Their Own Words; http://www.intheirown words.net.

Sharon Geva; http://sharon-geva.blogspot.com/p/english .html.

Silesiaheritage YouTube channel; https://www.youtube .com/user/silesiaheritage/featured.

United States Holocaust Memorial Museum: Holocaust Encyclopedia; https://encyclopedia.ushmm.org.

USC Shoah Foundation: Visual History Archive; https:// sfi.usc.edu/vha.

Warsaw Before WW2, YouTube Channel; https:// www.youtube.com/channel/UC_7UzhH0KCna70a5 ubpoOhg.

The World Society of Częstochowa Jews and Their Descendants; https://www.czestochowajews.org.

Yad Vashem: Articles; https://www.yadvashem.org/articles/general.html.

Yad Vashem: Exhibitions; https://www.yadvashem.org/exhibitions.html.

Yad Vashem: Shoah Resource Center; www.yadvashem.org.

Yiddish Book Center: Oral Histories; http://www.jhi.pl/en.

YIVO Digital Archive on Jewish Life in Poland; http://polishjews.yivoarchives.org.

The YIVO Encyclopedia of Jews in Eastern Europe; https://yivoencyclopedia.org.

Zaglembie World Organization; zaglembie.org.

Exhibitions and Monuments

Faces of Resistance: Women in the Holocaust, Moreshet, Givat Haviva, Israel.

The Paper Brigade: Smuggling Rare Books and Documents in Nazi-Occupied Vilna, October 11, 2017–December 14, 2018, YIVO, New York.

Memorials, Mila 18, Warsaw, Poland.

Memorial, Prosta Street Sewer, Warsaw, Poland.

Permanent Exhibition, Emanuel Ringelblum Jewish Historical Institute, Warsaw, Poland.

Permanent Exhibition, Galicia Jewish Museum, Kraków, Poland.

Permanent Exhibition, Ghetto Fighters' House Museum, Ghetto Fighters' House, Israel.

Permanent Exhibition, Mizrachi House of Prayer, Museum of Zagłębie, Będzin, Poland.

Permanent Exhibition, Montreal Holocaust Museum, Montreal, Canada.

Permanent Exhibition, Moreshet, Givat Haviva, Israel.

Permanent Exhibition, Mausoleum of Struggle and Martyrdom, Warsaw, Poland.

Permanent Exhibition, Museum of Warsaw, Warsaw, Poland.

Permanent Exhibition, Museum of Pawiak Prison, Warsaw, Poland.

Permanent Exhibition, Oskar Schindler's Enamel Factory, Museum of Kraków, Kraków, Poland.

Permanent Exhibition, POLIN Museum of the History of Polish Jews, Warsaw, Poland.

Permanent Exhibition, United States Holocaust Memorial Museum, Washington, DC.

Permanent Exhibition, Warsaw Rising Museum, Warsaw, Poland.

Permanent Exhibition, Yad Mordechai Museum, Hof Ashkelon, Israel.

Permanent Exhibition, Yad Vashem, Jerusalem, Israel.

Permanent Exhibition, Zabinski Villa, Warsaw Zoological Garden, Warsaw, Poland.

Violated, Ronald Feldman Gallery, April 12 to May 12, 2018, New York.

Selected Events

"Hitler Hanging on a Tree: Soviet Jewish Humor During WW2." Lecture by Anna Shternshis. April 2018. New York. YIVO.

"In Dialogue: Polish Jewish Relations During the Interwar Period." Lectures by Samuel D. Kassow and Paul Brykczynski, November 15, 2018. New York. Fordham University, Columbia, YIVO.

"Kraków Ghetto: A Walking Tour." Agi Legutko. June 2018. Kraków, Poland, Jewish Culture Festival.

"Memorial for Warsaw Ghetto, Warsaw Ghetto Uprising Commemoration, 75th Anniversary." April 19, 2018. New York. The Congress for Jewish Culture with Friends of the Bund, the Jewish Labor Committee, the Workmen's Circle, and YIVO.

Nusakh Vilna Memorial Lecture and Concert. September 16, 2018, and September 22, 2019. New York. YIVO.

Uprising. Screening and Talk. April 22, 2018. New York City. Jewish Partisan Education Foundation, Directors Guild.

Personal Interviews

Rivka Augenfeld, Montreal, Canada, August 10 and 17, 2018.

Ralph Berger, New York, April 10, 2018.

Havi Dreifuss, Tel Aviv, Israel; May 16, 2018.

Sandy Fainer, telephone, November 27, 2018.

Yoram Kleinman, telephone, February 11, 2019 (interview conducted by Elisha Baskin).

Michael Kovner, Jerusalem, Israel, May 17, 2018.

Jacob Harel and Leah Waldman, Haifa, Israel; May 14, 2018.

Barbara Harshav, New York, March 9 and April 23, 2018.

Emil Kerenji, Washington, DC, April 27, 2018.

Agi Legutko, New York, May 2, 2018.

Jonathan Ornstein, Kraków, Poland, June 25, 2018.

Daniela Ozacky-Stern and Yonat Rotbain, Givat Haviva, Israel, May 14, 2018.

Chayele Palevsky, Skype, November 20, 2018.

Katarzyna Person, Warsaw, Poland, June 21, 2018.

Avihu Ronen, Tel Aviv, Israel, May 16, 2018.

Lilian Rosenthal, telephone, November 12, 2018.

Rochelle Saidel, New York, June 8, 2018.

Elaine Shelub, telephone, November 6, 2018.

Anna Shternshis, New York, April 9, 2018.

David Silberklang, Jerusalem, Israel, May 17, 2018.

Holly Starr, telephone, November 13, 2018.

Michał Trębacz, Warsaw, Poland, June 22, 2018.

Merav Waldman, Skype, October 23, 2018.

Yoel Yaari, Jerusalem, Israel, May 17, 2018.

Racheli Yahav, Tzora, Israel, May 17, 2018.

Eyal Zuckerman, Tel Aviv, Israel, May 15, 2018.

Additional Selected Unpublished Materials

Grabowski, Jan. "The Polish Police: Collaboration in the Holocaust." Lecture at USHMM, November 17, 2016. Text accessed online.

Jewish Telegraphic Agency Newswire. January 8, 1943. Vol. 10. Number 6. New York.

Kaslow, Maria Wizmur. "Mania: A Gestapo Love Story" and "Vanished." Family collection.

Kukielka, Renia. Photographs, letter, husband testimony, eulogy. Family collection.

Shchori, Frumi. "Voyage and Burden: Women Members of the Fighting Underground in the Ghettos of Poland as Reflected in their Memoirs (1945–1998)." Thesis, Tel Aviv University, 2006 (Hebrew).

Starr, Holly. Eulogy for Sara Rosnow, 2017.

Unpublished testimony, Azrieli Foundation.

Selected Books

I did not include individual chapters or articles. Many of these books appear in various editions and languages; I have provided relevant information when available.

Hantze and Frumka: Letters and Reminiscences. Tel Aviv, Israel: Hakibbutz Hameuchad, 1945 (Hebrew).

In Honor of Ala Gertner, Róza Robota, Regina Safirztajn, Ester Wajcblum: Martyred Heroines of the Jewish Resistance in Auschwitz Executed on January 5, 1945. N.p.: n.p., c. 1991 (English, Yiddish, Polish, German, French).

In the Face of Annihilation: Work and Resistance in the Ghettos 1941–1944. Berlin, Germany: Touro College, 2017. Exhibition catalogue.

Portraits of the Fighters: Biographies and Writings of Young Leaders of the Jewish Resistance During the Holocaust. American Friends of the Ghetto Fighters' Museum.

Voice of the Woman Survivor 9, no. 2. New York: WAGRO Women Auxiliary to the Community of Survivors, Holocaust Resource Centers and Libraries. Spring 1992.

Women of Valor: Partisans and Resistance Fighters. Center for Holocaust Studies Newsletter 3, no. 6. New York: Center for Holocaust Studies, 1990.

Ackerman, Diane. *The Zookeeper's Wife: A War Story.* New York: Norton, 2007.

Baumel-Schwartz, Judith Taylor, and Tova Cohen, eds. *Gender, Place and Memory in the Modern Jewish Experience: Re-Placing Ourselves.* London, UK: Vallentine Mitchell, 2003.

Berés Witold and Krzysztof Burnetko. *Marek Edelman: Being on the Right Side.* Translated by William R. Brand. Kraków, Poland: Berés Media, 2016.

Berger, Ralph S., and Albert S. Berger, eds. *With Courage Shall We Fight: The Memoirs and Poetry of Holocaust Resistance Fighters Frances "Fruma" Gulkowich Berger and Murray "Motke" Berger.* Margate, UK: ComteQ, 2010.

Blady-Szwajger, Adina. *I Remember Nothing More: The Warsaw Children's Hospital and the Jewish Resistance.* New York: Pantheon, 1990.

Brzezinski, Matthew. *Isaac's Army: A Story of Courage and Survival in Nazi-Occupied Poland.* New York: Random House, 2012.

Burstein, Dror. *Without a Single Case of Death: Stories from Kibbutz Lohamei Haghetaot.* Tel Aviv, Israel: Ghetto Fighters' House/Babel, 2007.

Cain, Larissa. *Ghettos in Revolt: Poland, 1943.* Paris, France: Autrement, 2003 (French).

Cohen, Rich. *The Avengers: A Jewish War Story.* New York: Knopf, 2000.

Czocher, Anna, Dobrochna Kałwa, et al. *Is War Men's Business? Fates of Women in Occupied Kraków in Twelve Scenes.* Translated by Tomasz Tesznar and Joanna Bełch-Rucińska. Kraków, Poland: Historical Museum of the City of Kraków, 2011. Exhibition catalogue.

Diatłowicki, Jerzy, ed. *Jews in Battle, 1939–1945.* 4 vols. Warsaw, Poland: Association of Jewish Combatants and Victims of World War II and Jewish Historical Institute, 2009–2015 (Polish).

Diner, Hasia R. *We Remember with Reverence and Love: American Jews and the Myth of Silence After the Holocaust, 1945–1962.* New York: New York University Press, 2009.

Draenger, Gusta Davidson. *Justyna's Narrative.* Translated by Roslyn Hirsch and David H. Hirsch. Amherst, MA: University of Massachusetts Press, 1996.

Draper, Paula J., and Richard Menkis, eds. *New Perspectives on Canada, the Holocaust and Survivors. Canadian Jewish Studies,* Special Issue. Montreal, Canada: Association for Canadian Jewish Studies, 1997.

Dror, Zvi. *The Dream, the Revolt and the Vow: The Biography of Zivia Lubetkin-Zuckerman (1914–1978).*

Translated by Bezalel Ianai. Tel Aviv, Israel: General Federation of Labor (Histadrut) and Ghetto Fighters' House, 1983.

Edelman, Marek. *The Ghetto Fights*. New York: American Representation of the General Jewish Workers Union of Poland, 1946.

Engel, David, Yitzchak Mais et al. *Daring to Resist: Jewish Defiance in the Holocaust*. New York: Museum of Jewish Heritage, 2007. Exhibition catalogue.

Engelking, Barbara, and Jacek Leociak. *The Warsaw Ghetto: A Guide to the Perished City*. New Haven, CT: Yale University Press, 2009.

Epstein, Helen. *Children of the Holocaust: Conversations with Sons and Daughters of Survivors*. New York: Penguin, 1979.

Feldhay Brenner, Rachel. *Writing as Resistance: Four Women Confronting the Holocaust*. University Park, Pennsylvania: Penn State University Press, 2003.

Fishman, David E. *The Book Smugglers: Partisans, Poets, and the Race to Save Jewish Treasures from the Nazis*. Lebanon, NH: ForEdge, 2017.

Freeze, ChaeRan, Paula Hyman et al., eds. *Polin: Studies in Polish Jewry* , vol. 18, *Jewish Women in Eastern Europe*. Liverpool, UK: Littman Library of Jewish Civilization, 2005.

Gabis, Rita. *A Guest at the Shooters' Banquet: My*

Grandfather's SS Past, My Jewish Family, A Search for the Truth. New York: Bloomsbury, 2015.

Geva, Sharon. *To the Unknown Sister: Holocaust Heroines in Israeli Society.* Tel Aviv, Israel: Hakibbutz Hameuchad, 2010 (Hebrew).

Goldenberg, Myrna, ed. *Before All Memory Is Lost: Women's Voices from the Holocaust.* Toronto, Canada: Azrieli Foundation, 2017.

Goldstein, Bernard. *The Stars Bear Witness.* Translated by Leonard Shatzkin. London, UK: Victor Gollancz, 1950.

Grossman, Chaika. *The Underground Army: Fighters of the Białystok Ghetto.* Translated by Shmuel Beeri. New York: Holocaust Library, 1987.

Grove, Kimberley Sherman, and Judy Geller. *Stories Inked.* Brighton, Canada: Reflections on the Past, 2012.

Grunwald-Spier, Agnes. *Women's Experiences in the Holocaust: In Their Own Words.* Stroud, UK: Amberley, 2018.

Grupińska, Anka. *Reading the List.* Wołowiec, Poland: Czarne, 2014 (Polish).

Gurewitsch, Brana, ed. *Mothers, Sisters, Resisters: Oral Histories of Women Who Survived the Holocaust.* Tuscaloosa, AL: University of Alabama Press, 1998.

Gutterman, Bella. *Fighting for Her People: Zivia Lubet-*

kin, *1914–1978.* Translated by Ora Cummings. Jerusalem, Israel: Yad Vashem, 2014.

Heilman, Anna. *Never Far Away: The Auschwitz Chronicles of Anna Heilman.* Calgary, Canada: University of Calgary Press, 2001.

Izhar, Naomi. *Chasia Bornstein-Bielicka, One of the Few: A Resistance Fighter and Educator, 1939–1947.* Translated by Naftali Greenwood. Jerusalem, Israel: Yad Vashem, 2009.

Kalchheim, Moshe, ed. *With Proud Bearing 1939–1945: Chapters in the History of Jewish Fighting in the Narotch Forests.* Tel Aviv, Israel: Organisation of Partisans, Underground Fighters and Ghetto Rebels in Israel, 1992 (Yiddish).

Katz, Esther, and Joan Miriam Ringelheim, eds. *Proceedings of the Conference on Women Surviving the Holocaust.* New York: Institute for Research in History, c1983.

Kirshenblatt-Gimblett, Barbara, and Antony Polonsky, eds. *POLIN, 1000 Year History of Polish Jews—Catalogue for the Core Exhibition.* Warsaw, Poland: POLIN Museum of the History of Polish Jews, 2014. Exhibition catalogue.

Klinger, Chajka. *I am Writing These Words to You: The Original Diaries, Będzin 1943.* Translated by Anna Brzostowska and Jerzy Giebułtowski. Jerusalem, Israel: Yad Vashem and Moreshet, 2017. (Original work published in Hebrew in 2016.)

Kloizner, Israel, and Moshe Perger. *Holocaust Commentary: Documents of Jewish Suffering Under Nazi Rule.* Jerusalem, Israel: Jewish Agency of Israel and the Rescue Committee for the Jews of Occupied Europe, 1945–1947.

Korczak, Riezl (Ruz'ka). *Flames in Ash.* Israel: Sifriyat Po'alim, Hakibbutz Ha'artzi Hashomer Hatzair, 1946 (Hebrew).

Korczak, Roszka, Yehuda Tubin, and Yosef Rab, eds. *Zelda the Partisan.* Tel Aviv, Israel: Moreshet and Sifriyat Po'alim, 1989 (Hebrew).

Kukielka, Renia. *Underground Wanderings.* Ein Harod, Israel: Hakibbutz Hameuchad, 1945 (Hebrew).

Kulkielko, Renya. *Escape from the Pit.* New York: Sharon Books, 1947.

Laska, Vera, ed. *Women in the Resistance and in the Holocaust: The Voices of Eyewitnesses.* Westport, CT: Praeger, 1983.

Laskier, Rutka. *Rutka's Notebook: January–April 1943.* Jerusalem, Israel: Yad Vashem, 2007.

Liwer, Dawid. *Town of the Dead: The Extermination of the Jews in the Zaglembie Region.* Tel Aviv, Israel, 1946 (Hebrew).

Lubetkin, Zivia. *In the Days of Destruction and Revolt.*

Translated by Ishai Tubbin and Debby Garber. Edited by Yehiel Yanay, biographical index by Yitzhak Zuckerman. Tel Aviv, Israel: Am Oved; Hakibbutz Hameuchad; Ghetto Fighters' House, 1981. (Original work published in Hebrew in 1979.)

Lukowski, Jerzy, and Hubert Zawadzki. *A Concise History of Poland.* Cambridge, UK: Cambridge University Press, 2001.

Meed, Vladka. *On Both Sides of the Wall.* Translated by Steven Meed. Washington, DC: United States Holocaust Memorial Museum, 1993. (Original work published in Yiddish in 1948.)

Michlic, Joanna Beata, ed. *Jewish Families in Europe, 1939–Present: History, Representation and Memory.* Waltham, MA: Brandeis University Press, 2017.

Milgrom, Frida. *Mulheres na resistência: heroínas esquecidas que se arriscaram para salvar judeus ao longo da história.* Sao Paolo, Brazil: Ipsis, 2016.

Namyslo, Aleksandra. *Before the Holocaust Came: The Situation of the Jews in Zaglebie during the German Occupation.* Katowice, Poland: Public Education Office of the Institute of National Remembrance, with the Emanuel Ringelblum Jewish Historical Institute in Warsaw and Yad Vashem, 2014. Exhibition catalogue.

Neustadt, Meilech, ed. *Destruction and Rising, The Epic of the Jews in Warsaw: A Collection of Reports and Biographical Sketches of the Fallen.* 2nd ed. Tel Aviv, Israel: Executive Committee of the General Federation of Jewish Labor in Israel, 1947.

Ofer, Dalia, and Lenore J. Weitzman, eds. *Women in the Holocaust.* New Haven, CT: Yale University Press, 1998.

Ostrower, Chaya. *It Kept Us Alive: Humor in the Holocaust.* Translated by Sandy Bloom. Jerusalem, Israel: Yad Vashem, 2014.

Paldiel, Mordechai. *Saving One's Own: Jewish Rescuers During the Holocaust.* Philadelphia, PA: The Jewish Publication Society; Lincoln: University of Nebraska Press, 2017.

Paulsson, Gunnar S. *Secret City: The Hidden Jews of Warsaw 1940–1945.* New Haven, CT: Yale University Press, 2003.

Person, Katarzyna, ed. *Warsaw Ghetto: Everyday Life.* The Ringelblum Archive, vol. 1. Translated by Anna Brzostowska et al. Warsaw, Poland: Jewish Historical Institute, 2017.

Porat, Dina. *The Fall of a Sparrow: The Life and Times of Abba Kovner.* Stanford, CA: Stanford University Press, 2010.

Prince, Robert M. *The Legacy of the Holocaust: Psychohistorical Themes in the Second Generation*. New York: Other Press, 1999. (Original work published in 1985.)

Rakovsky, Puah. *My Life as a Radical Jewish Woman: Memoirs of a Zionist Feminist in Poland*. Translated by Barbara Harshav with Paula E. Hyman. Bloomington, IN: Indiana University Press, 2001.

Rapaport, J. ed. *Memorial Book of Zaglembie*. Tel Aviv, Israel, n.p., 1972 (Yiddish, Hebrew, English).

Reinhartz, Henia. *Bits and Pieces*. Toronto, Canada: Azrieli Foundation, 2007.

Ringelblum, Emanuel. *Notes From the Warsaw Ghetto: The Journal of Emmanuel Ringelblum*. Translated by Jacob Sloan. New York: ibooks, 2006. (Original work published in 1958.)

Rittner, Carol, and John K. Roth, eds. *Different Voices: Women and the Holocaust*. St. Paul, MN: Paragon House, 1993.

Ronen, Avihu. *Condemned to Life: The Diaries and Life of Chajka Klinger*. Haifa and Tel Aviv, Israel: University of Haifa Press, Miskal-Yidioth Ahronoth and Chemed, 2011 (Hebrew).

Rosenberg-Amit, Zila (Cesia). *Not to Lose the Human Face*. Tel Aviv, Israel: Kibbutz Hameuchad, Moreshet, Ghetto Fighters' House, 1990 (Hebrew).

Rotem, Simha "Kazik." *Memoirs of a Ghetto Fighter.* Translated by Barbara Harshav. New Haven, CT: Yale University Press, 1994.

Rufeisen-Schüpper, Hella. *Farewell to Mila 18.* Tel Aviv, Israel: Ghetto Fighters' House and Hakibbutz Hameuchad, 1990 (Hebrew).

Saidel, Rochelle G., and Batya Brudin, eds. *Violated! Women in Holocaust and Genocide.* New York: Remember the Women Institute, 2018. Exhibition catalogue.

Saidel, Rochelle G., and Sonja M. Hedgepeth, eds. *Sexual Violence Against Jewish Women During the Holocaust.* Waltham, MA: Brandeis University Press, 2010.

Schulman, Faye. *A Partisan's Memoir: Woman of the Holocaust.* Toronto, Canada: Second Story Press, 1995.

Shalev, Ziva. *Tossia Altman: Leader of Hashomer Hatzair Movement and of the Warsaw Ghetto Uprising.* Tel Aviv, Israel: Moreshet, 1992 (Hebrew).

Shandler, Jeffrey, ed. *Awakening Lives: Autobiographies of Jewish Youth in Poland Before the Holocaust.* New Haven, CT: Yale University Press, 2002.

Shelub, Mira, and Fred Rosenbaum. *Never the Last Road: A Partisan's Life.* Berkeley, CA: Lehrhaus Judaica, 2015.

Solomian-Lutz, Fanny. *A Girl Facing the Gallows.* Tel

Aviv, Israel: Moreshet and Sifryat Hapoalim, 1971 (Hebrew).

Spizman, Leib, ed. *Women in the Ghettos.* New York: Pioneer Women's Organization, 1946 (Yiddish).

Tec, Nechama. *Resistance: Jews and Christians Who Defied the Nazi Terror.* New York: Oxford University Press, 2013.

Thon, Elsa. *If Only It Were Fiction.* Toronto, Canada: Azrieli Foundation, 2013.

Tubin, Yehuda, Levi Deror, et al., eds. *Ruzka Korchak-Marle: The Personality and Philosophy of Life of a Fighter.* Tel Aviv, Israel: Moreshet and Sifriyat Po'alim, 1988 (Hebrew).

Vitis-Shomron, Aliza. *Youth in Flames: A Teenager's Resistance and Her Fight for Survival in the Warsaw Ghetto.* Omaha, NE: Tell the Story, 2015.

Wilfand, Yigal, ed. *Vitka Fights for Life.* Givat Haviva, Israel: Moreshet, 2013 (Hebrew).

Ya'ari-Hazan, Bela. *Bronislawa Was My Name.* Tel Aviv, Israel: Hakibbutz Hameuchad, Ghetto Fighters' House, 1991 (Hebrew).

Yerushalmi, Shimshon Dov. *Jędrzejów Memorial Book.* Tel Aviv, Israel: Jędrzejów Community in Israel, 1965.

Zuckerman, Yitzhak "Antek." *A Surplus of Memory:*

Chronicle of the Warsaw Ghetto Uprising. Translated by Barbara Harshav. Berkeley, CA: University of California Press, 1993.

Selected Articles

This list includes a select few significant articles that do not appear in the books or online sources listed above.

Bernard, Mark. "Problems Related to the Study of the Jewish Resistance Movement in the Second World War." *Yad Vashem Studies* 3 (1959): 41–65.

Fox-Bevilacqua, Marisa. "The Lost, Shul of Będzin: Uncovering Poland's Once-vibrant Jewish Community," *Ha'aretz*, September 7, 2014, https://www.haaretz.com/jewish/.premium-the-lost-shul-of-Będzin-1.5263609.

Harran, Ronen. "The Jewish Women at the Union Factory, Auschwitz 1944: Resistance, Courage and Tragedy." *Dapim: Studies in the Holocaust* 31, no. 1 (2017): 45–67.

Kasonata, Adriel. "Poland: Europe's Forgotten Democratic Ancestor." *The National Interest.* May 5, 2016. https://nationalinterest.org/feature/poland-europes-forgotten-democratic-ancestor-16073.

Kol-Inbar, Yehudit. " 'Not Even for Three Lines in History': Jewish Women Underground Members and Partisans During the Holocaust." *A Companion to*

Women's Military History. Eds. Barton Hacker and Margaret Vining. Leiden, Netherlands: Brill, 2012.

Ofer, Dalia. "Condemned to Life? A Historical and Personal Biography of Chajka Klinger." Translated by Naftali Greenwood. *Yad Vashem Studies* 42, no. 1 (2014): 175–88.

The Pioneer Woman, no. 97, April 1944.

Porter, Jack. "Jewish Women in the Resistance." *Jewish Combatants of World War 2* 2, no. 3 (1981).

Ringelheim, Joan. "Women and the Holocaust: A Reconsideration of Research." *Signs* 10, no. 4 (Summer 1985): 741–61.

Ronen, Avihu. "The Cable That Vanished: Tabenkin and Ya'ari to the Last Surviving Ghetto Fighters." *Yad Vashem Studies* 41, no. 2 (2013): 95–138.

———. "The Jews of Będzin." *Before They Perished . . . Photographs Found in Auschwitz*. Edited by Kersten Brandt, Hanno Loewy, et al. Oświęcim, Poland: Auschwitz-Birkenau State Museum, 2001, 16–27.

Szczęsna, Joanna. "Irena Conti." *Wysokie Obcasy*. April 21, 2014 (Polish).

Tzur, Eli. "A Cemetery of Letters and Words." *Ha'aretz*, August 1, 2003, https://www.haaretz.com/1.5354308.

Vershitskaya, Tamara. "Jewish Women Partisans in Belarus." *Journal of Ecumenical Studies* 46, no. 4 (Fall 2011): 567–72.

Yaari, Yoel. "A Brave Connection." *Yedioth Ahronoth*. Passover Supplement, April 5, 2018 (Hebrew).

Zariz, Ruth. "Attempts at Rescue and Revolt; Attitude of Members of the Dror Youth Movement in Będzin to Foreign Passports as Means of Rescue," *Yad Vashem Studies* 20 (1990): 211–36.

Zerofsky, Elisabeth. "Is Poland Retreating from Democracy?" *New Yorker*. July 23, 2018.

Films and Audio

Blue Bird. DVD. Directed by Ayelet Heller. Israel, 1998. (Hebrew)

Daring to Resist: Three Women Face the Holocaust. DVD. Directed by Barbara Attie and Martha Goell Lubell. USA, 1999.

The Heart of Auschwitz. DVD. Directed by Carl Leblanc. Canada, 2010.

The Last Fighters. DVD. Directed by Ronen Zaretsky and Yael Kipper Zaretsky. Israel, 2006. (Hebrew)

Partisans of Vilna: The Untold Story of Jewish Resistance During World War II. Directed by Josh Waletsky. USA, 1986.

Pillar of Fire (Hebrew version, probably episode 13). Viewed at Yad Mordechai Museum. Directed by Asher Tlalim. Israel, 1981. (Hebrew)

Uprising. DVD. Directed by Jon Avnet. USA, 2001.

Who Will Write Our History. Cinema screening. Directed by Roberta Grossman. USA, 2019.

Yiddish Glory: The Lost Songs of World War 2. CD. Six Degrees Records, 2018 (Yiddish).

The Zuckerman Code. Accessed online at https://www.mako.co.il/tv-ilana_dayan/2017/Article-bb85dba8ec3b261006.htm. Directed by Ben Shani and Noa Shabtai. Israel, 2018. (Hebrew)

About the Author

JUDY BATALION is the author of *White Walls: A Memoir About Motherhood, Daughterhood, and the Mess in Between.* Her essays have appeared in the *New York Times*, the *Washington Post*, the *Forward*, *Vogue*, and many other publications. Judy has a BA in the History of Science from Harvard, and a PhD in the History of Art from the Courtauld Institute, University of London, and has worked as a museum curator and university lecturer. Born in Montreal, where she grew up speaking English, French, Hebrew, and Yiddish, she now lives in New York with her husband and three children.

HARPER LARGE PRINT

We hope you enjoyed reading
our new, comfortable print size and found it
an experience you would like to repeat.

Well – you're in luck!

Harper Large Print offers the finest in
fiction and nonfiction books in this same larger
print size and paperback format. Light and easy to read,
Harper Large Print paperbacks are for the book lovers
who want to see what they are reading without strain.

For a full listing of titles and
new releases to come, please visit our website:
www.hc.com

HARPER LARGE PRINT

SEEING IS BELIEVING!